Control, Optimization, and Mathematical Modeling of Complex Systems

Control, Optimization, and Mathematical Modeling of Complex Systems

Editors

Mikhail Posypkin
Andrey Gorshenin
Vladimir Titarev

MDPI • Basel • Beijing • Wuhan • Barcelona • Belgrade • Manchester • Tokyo • Cluj • Tianjin

Editors

Mikhail Posypkin	Andrey Gorshenin	Vladimir Titarev
Federal Research Center	Federal Research Center	Federal Research Center
"Computer Science and	"Computer Science and	"Computer Science and
Control" of the Russian	Control" of the Russian	Control" of the Russian
Academy of Sciences	Academy of Sciences	Academy of Sciences
Moscow	Moscow	Moscow
Russia	Russia	Russia

Editorial Office
MDPI
St. Alban-Anlage 66
4052 Basel, Switzerland

This is a reprint of articles from the Special Issue published online in the open access journal *Mathematics* (ISSN 2227-7390) (available at: https://www.mdpi.com/si/mathematics/Control_Optimization_Mathematical_Modeling_Complex_Systems).

For citation purposes, cite each article independently as indicated on the article page online and as indicated below:

LastName, A.A.; LastName, B.B.; LastName, C.C. Article Title. *Journal Name* **Year**, *Volume Number*, Page Range.

ISBN 978-3-0365-7640-4 (Hbk)
ISBN 978-3-0365-7641-1 (PDF)

Contents

About the Editors

Mikhail Posypkin

Mikhail Posypkin, Ph.D., DSc, is Deputy Director at the Federal Research Center "Computer Science and Control" of the Russian Academy of Sciences (RAS), Russia, Professor of the Faculty of Computational Mathematics and Cybernetics at Lomonosov Moscow State University, Russia and Department Head for the Intelligent Technologies in System Analysis and Management: Joint Department with Federal Research Center of Computer Science and Control of Russian Academy of Sciences in the Faculty of Computer Science at the National Research University Higher School of Economics (HSE University) in Moscow, Russia. Professor Posypkin was awarded the Candidate of Sciences degree in 2004 and the Doctor of Sciences degree in 2015. In June 2022, he was elected Corresponding Member of RAS in 'Computational Methods and Artificial Intelligence Systems'. His main research interests are in the field of discrete optimization, global optimization, parallel programming, multi-objective optimization and complex system modeling.

Andrey Gorshenin

Andrey Gorshenin, Ph.D., DSc, is Principal Researcher and Head of the Department "Probabilistic Modeling and Statistical Analysis of Complex Systems" at the Federal Research Center "Computer Science and Control" of the Russian Academy of Sciences, Russia, as well as Associate Professor of the Faculty of Computational Mathematics and Cybernetics at Lomonosov Moscow State University, Russia. Professor Gorshenin was awarded the Candidate of Sciences degree in 2011 and the Doctor of Sciences degree in 2021. He is a Member of the Coordination Council for Youth Affairs of the Presidential Council for Science and Education, Russia. He is an Expert of the Russian Academy of Sciences and a Member of the Skolkovo Expert Panel. He is a top-1% Web of Science reviewer since 2022. He is an Author of 175 scientific papers and textbooks as well as 92 certificates of state registration of software issued by the Russian Federal Service for Intellectual Property. His research focuses on the development and analytical study of semiparametric methods for constructing and analyzing probabilistic-statistical models of heterogeneous data under lack or absence of a priori information about the physical nature of the processes and the applications of these models to improve the forecasting accuracy of machine learning algorithms.

Vladimir Titarev

Vladimir Titarev, Ph.D., DSc, is Principal Researcher at the Federal Research Center "Computer Science and Control"of the Russian Academy of Sciences and Professor at the Department of Computer Science and Computational Mathematics of the Moscow Institute of Physics and Technology. Professor Titarev obtained the Candidate of Sciences degree from Bauman Moscow State Technical University in 2003 and the Ph.D. degree from the University of Trento, Italy in 2005. In 2018, Professor Titarev presented his habilitation at Keldysh Institute of Applied Mathematics and was awarded the Doctor of Sciences degree. His research interests include the Boltzmann equation with model collision integrals, hyperbolic conservation laws and numerical methods, very high-order essentially non-oscillatory methods in particular, for partial differential equations with applications in gas dynamics, rarefied flows, reactive multiphase flows as well as non-linear elasticity. Before joining the Federal Research Center "Computer Science and Control" of the Russian Academy of Sciences in 2011, he worked at the University of Trento, Italy, and Cranfield University, UK.

 *mathematics*

Editorial

Preface to the Special Issue on "Control, Optimization, and Mathematical Modeling of Complex Systems"

Mikhail Posypkin *, Andrey Gorshenin * and Vladimir Titarev *

Federal Research Center "Computer Science and Control" of the Russian Academy of Sciences, 119333 Moscow, Russia
* Correspondence: mposypkin@frccsc.ru (M.P.); agorshenin@frccsc.ru (A.G.); vladimir.titarev@frccsc.ru (V.T.)

Citation: Posypkin, M.; Gorshenin, A.; Titarev, V. Preface to the Special Issue on "Control, Optimization, and Mathematical Modeling of Complex Systems". *Mathematics* **2022**, *13*, 2182. https://doi.org/10.3390/math10132182

Received: 16 June 2022
Accepted: 20 June 2022
Published: 23 June 2022

Publisher's Note: MDPI stays neutral with regard to jurisdictional claims in published maps and institutional affiliations.

1. Aims, Scope, and Statistics of the Special Issue

Complex systems have long been an integral part of modern life and can be encountered everywhere. A comprehensive study of such systems is a challenging problem, the solution of which is impossible without the use of contemporary mathematical modeling techniques. Mathematical models form the basis for optimal design and control of complex systems.

This Special Issue is focused on recent theoretical and computational studies of complex systems modeling, control, and optimization. Topics include, but are not limited to, the following themes:

- Numerical simulation in physical, social, and life sciences [1–4];
- Modeling and analysis of complex systems based on mathematical methods and AI/ML approaches [5,6];
- Control problems in robotics [3,7–12];
- Design optimization of complex systems [13];
- Modeling in economics and social sciences [4,14];
- Stochastic models in physics and engineering [1,15–18];
- Mathematical models in material science [19];
- High-performance computing for mathematical modeling [20].

Cross-border modeling and numerical simulation in Physics and Engineering are particularly welcome in this Special Issue.

In total, 31 manuscripts were submitted, and 20 papers by 49 authors were successfully published. Authors come from the following 11 countries:

- China [4,7,18];
- Czech Republic [8];
- Great Britain [11];
- Hungary [10];
- Pakistan [4];
- Russia [1,2,5,6,8,10,13,15–17,19];
- Saudi Arabia [4];
- Spain [3,9,12,20];
- Taiwan [4];
- Tunisia [20];
- Vietnam [8,14].

A rose diagram of the number of unique authors from different countries is shown in Figure 1.

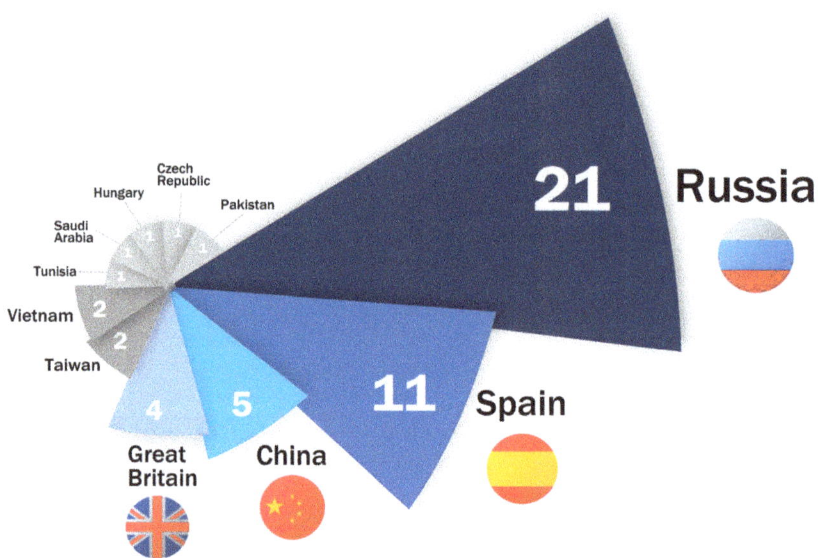

Figure 1. Authors and corresponding countries.

2. Papers of the Special Issue

Zeifman et al. [1] consider the computation of the (limiting) time-dependent performance characteristics of one-dimensional continuous-time Markov chains with discrete state space and time-varying intensities. Numerical solution techniques can benefit from methods providing ergodicity bounds because the latter can indicate how to choose the position and the length of the "distant time interval" (in the periodic case) on which the solution has to be computed. They can also be helpful whenever the state space truncation is required. In this paper, one such analytic method—the logarithmic norm method—is reviewed. Its applicability is shown within the context of the queuing theory with three examples: the classical time-varying M/M/2 queue; the time-varying single-server Markovian system with bulk arrivals, queue-skipping policy, and catastrophes; and the time-varying Markovian bulk-arrival and bulk-service system with state-dependent control. In each case, it is shown whether and how the bounds on the rate of convergence can be obtained. Numerical examples are provided.

Ilyin [2] considers the development of the two-dimensional discrete velocity Boltzmann model on a nine-velocity lattice. Compared with the conventional lattice Boltzmann approach for the present model, the collision rules for the interacting particles are formulated explicitly. The collisions are tailored in such a way that mass, momentum, and energy are conserved, and the H-theorem is fulfilled. By applying the Chapman–Enskog expansion, the author shows that the model recovers quasi-incompressible hydrodynamic equations for a small Mach number limit, and he then derives the closed expression for the viscosity, depending on the collision cross-sections. In addition, the numerical implementation of the model with the on-lattice streaming and local collision step is proposed. As test problems, the shear wave decay and Taylor–Green vortex are considered, and a comparison of the numerical simulations with the analytical solutions is presented.

Nagua et al. [3] design and simulate a soft joint to perform as a robotic joint with two degrees of freedom (DOF) (inclination and orientation). The joint actuation is based on a cable-driven parallel mechanism (CDPM). To study its performance in more detail, a test platform is developed using components that can be manufactured in a 3D printer using a flexible polymer. The mathematical model of the kinematics of the soft joint is developed, which includes a blocking mechanism and the morphology workspace. The model is validated using finite element analysis (FEA) software. Experimental tests are performed to validate the inverse kinematic model and to show the potential use of the prototype in robotic platforms such as manipulators and humanoid robots.

Masood et al. [4] analyze the designed fractional-order Stuxnet, the virus model, to investigate the spread of the virus in the regime of isolated industrial networks environment by bridging the air gap between the traditional and critical control network infrastructures. Removable storage devices are commonly used to exploit the vulnerability of individual nodes, as well as the associated networks, by transferring data and viruses in the isolated industrial control system. A mathematical model of an arbitrary order system is constructed and analyzed numerically to depict the control mechanism. Local and global stability analysis of the system is performed on the equilibrium points derived for the value of $\alpha = 1$. To understand the depth of fractional model behavior, numerical simulations are carried out for the distinct order of the fractional derivative system, and the results show that fractional-order models provide rich dynamics by means of fast transient and super-slow evolution of the model's steady-state behavior, which are seldom perceived in integer-order counterparts.

Gorshenin and Kuzmin [5] present a feature construction approach called statistical feature construction (SFC) for time-series prediction. The creation of new features is based on statistical characteristics of analyzed data series. First, the initial data are transformed into an array of short pseudo-stationary windows. For each window, a statistical model is created, and the characteristics of these models are later used as additional features for a single window or as time-dependent features for the entire time series. To demonstrate the effect of SFC, five plasma physics and six oceanographic time series are analyzed. For each window, unknown distribution parameters are estimated with the method of moving separation of finite normal mixtures. First, four statistical moments of these mixtures for initial data and increments are used as additional data features. Multilayer recurrent neural networks are trained to create short- and medium-term forecasts with a single window as input data; additional features are used to initialize the hidden state of recurrent layers. A hyperparameter grid search is performed to compare fully optimized neural networks for original and enriched data. A significant decrease in the RMSE metric is observed, with a median of 11.4%. There is no increase in the RMSE metric in any of the analyzed time series. The experimental results show that SFC can be a valuable method for forecasting accuracy improvement.

The paper by Diveev et al. [6] is devoted to an emerging trend in control—a machine learning control. Despite the popularity of the idea of machine learning, there are various interpretations of this concept, and there is an urgent need for its strict mathematical formalization. An attempt to formalize the concept of machine learning is presented in this paper. The concepts of an unknown function, work area, and training set are introduced, and a mathematical formulation of the machine learning problem is presented. Based on the presented formulation, the idea of machine learning control is considered. One of the problems of machine learning control is the general synthesis of control. It implies finding a control function that depends on the state of the object, which ensures the achievement of the control goal with the optimal value of the quality criterion from any initial state of some admissible region. Supervised and unsupervised approaches to solving a problem based on symbolic regression methods are considered. As a computational example, a problem of general synthesis of optimal control for a spacecraft landing on the surface of the Moon is considered as a supervised machine learning control, using a training set.

Li and Zhou [7] propose a novel control strategy to address the precise trajectory tracking control problem of a ship towing system. First, the kinematics and dynamics models of a ship towing system are established by introducing a passive steering angle and using its structure relationship. Then, by using the motion law derived from its nonholonomic constraints, the relative curvature of the target trajectory curve is used to design a dynamical tracking target. By applying the sliding mode control and inverse dynamic adaptive control methods, two appropriate robust torque controllers are designed via the dynamical tracking target, so that both the tugboat and the towed ship are able to track the desired path precisely. As the authors show, the proposed strategy provides an excellent agreement with the numerical simulation results.

Diveev et al. [8] present a numerical method based on the Pontryagin maximum principle for solving an optimal control problem with static and dynamic phase constraints for a group of objects. Dynamic phase constraints are introduced to avoid collisions between objects. Phase constraints are included in the functional in the form of smooth penalty functions. Additional parameters for special control modes and the terminal time of the control process are also introduced. The search for additional parameters and the initial conditions for the conjugate variables is carried out using the modified self-organizing migrating algorithm. An example of using this approach to solve the optimal control problem for the oncoming movement of two mobile robots is given. Simulation and comparison with the direct approach show that the problem is multimodal. The application of the evolutionary algorithm for its solution is presented.

Mena et al. [9] propose a modular robot with an origami structure. The idea is based on a self-scalable and modular link made of soft parts. The kinematics of single and multiple interconnected links is studied and validated. In addition, the link is prototyped, identified, and controlled in position. The experimental data show that the system meets the scalability requirements, and that its response is totally reliable and robust.

Diveev et al. [10] present a new formulation of the optimal control problem with uncertainty, in which an additive bounded function is considered as uncertainty. The purpose of the control is to ensure the achievement of terminal conditions with the optimal value of the quality functional, while the uncertainty has a limited impact on the change in the value of the functional. This article introduces the concept of feasibility of the mathematical model of the object, which is associated with the contraction property of mappings if we consider the model of the object as a one-parameter mapping. It is shown that this property is sufficient for the development of stable practical systems. To find a solution to the stated problem that would ensure the feasibility of the system, the synthesized optimal control method is proposed. This article formulates the theoretical foundations of the synthesized optimal control. The method consists of making the control object stable relative to some point in the state space and controlling the object by changing the position of the equilibrium points. The article provides evidence that this approach is insensitive to the uncertainties of the mathematical model of the object. An example of the application of this method for optimal control of a group of robots is given. A comparison of the synthesized optimal control method with the direct method on the model with and without disturbances is also presented.

Kuang et al. [11] investigate visual navigation, which is an essential part of planetary rover autonomy. Rock segmentation emerged as an important interdisciplinary topic in image processing, robotics, and mathematical modeling. It is a challenging topic for rover autonomy because of the high computational consumption, real-time requirement, and annotation difficulty. This research proposes a rock segmentation framework and a rock segmentation network (NI-U-Net++) to aid with the visual navigation of rovers. The framework consists of two stages: the pretraining process and the transfer-training process. The pretraining process applies the synthetic algorithm to generate the synthetic images; then, it uses the generated images to pretrain NI-U-Net++. The synthetic algorithm increases the size of the image dataset and provides pixel-level masks—both of which are challenges with machine learning tasks. The pretraining process accomplishes the state of the art, compared with the related studies, which achieved an accuracy, intersection over union (IoU), Dice score, and root-mean-squared error (RMSE) of 99.41%, 0.8991, 0.9459, and 0.0775, respectively. The transfer-training process fine-tunes the pretrained NI-U-Net++ using the real-life images, which achieved an accuracy, IoU, Dice score, and RMSE values of 99.58%, 0.7476, 0.8556, and 0.0557, respectively. Finally, the transfer-trained NI-U-Net++ is integrated into a planetary rover navigation vision and achieves a real-time performance of 32.57 frames per second (or the inference time is 0.0307 s per frame). The framework only manually annotates about 8% (183 images) of the 2250 images in the navigation vision, which is a labor-saving solution for rock segmentation tasks. The proposed rock segmentation framework and NI-U-Net++ improve the performance of the state-of-the-art models. The synthetic algorithm improves the process of creating valid data for the challenge of rock segmentation. All source codes, datasets, and trained models of this research are openly available in Cranfield Online Research Data (CORD).

The paper by Quevedo et al. [12] is devoted to soft robotics, which is becoming an emerging solution to many of the problems in robotics, such as weight, cost, and human interaction. In order to overcome such problems, bio-inspired designs have introduced new actuators, links, and architectures. However, the complexity of the required models for control has increased dramatically, and geometrical model approaches, widely used to model rigid dynamics, are not enough to model these new hardware types. In this paper, different linear and nonlinear models are used to model a soft neck consisting of a central soft link actuated by three motor-driven tendons. By combining the force on the different tendons, the neck is able to perform a motion similar to that of a human neck. In order to simplify the modeling, first a system input–output redefinition is proposed, considering the neck pitch and roll angles as outputs and the tendon lengths as inputs. Later, two identification strategies are selected and adapted to the case in hand: set membership, a data-driven, nonlinear, and nonparametric identification strategy that needs no input redefinition; and recursive least-squares (RLS), a widely recognized identification technique. The first method offers the possibility of modeling complex dynamics without specific knowledge of its mathematical representation. This method is selected considering its possible extension to more complex dynamics and the fact that its impact on soft robotics is yet to be studied according to the current literature. On the other hand, RLS shows the implication of using a parametric and linear identification in a nonlinear plant and also helps to evaluate the degree of nonlinearity of the system by comparing the different performances. In addition to these methods, neural network identification is used for comparison purposes. The obtained results validate the modeling approaches proposed.

Posypkin and Khamisov [13] investigate the problem of reliable bounding of a function's range, which is essential for deterministic global optimization, approximation, locating roots of nonlinear equations, and several other computational mathematics areas. Despite years of extensive research in this direction, there is still room for improvement. The traditional and compelling approach to this problem is interval analysis. They show that accounting convexity/concavity can significantly tighten the bounds computed by interval analysis. To make the approach applicable to a broad range of functions, the authors also develop techniques for handling nondifferentiable composite functions. Traditional ways to ensure convexity fail in such cases. Experimental evaluation shows the remarkable potential of the proposed methods.

Nguyen [14] investigates the logistics industry, which can be considered the economic lifeline of each country because of its role in connecting the production and business activities of enterprises and promoting socio-economic development between regions and countries. However, the COVID-19 pandemic, which began at the end of 2019, has seriously affected the global supply chain, causing heavy impacts on the logistics service sector. In this study, the authors use the Malmquist productivity index to assess the impact of the pandemic on logistics businesses in Vietnam. Moreover, the authors employ a super-slack-based model to find strategic alliance partners for enterprises. The authors also utilize the Grey forecasting model to forecast the business situation for enterprises during the period 2021–2024, in order to provide the leaders of these enterprises with a complete picture of their partners as a solid basis for making decisions to implement alliances that will help logistics enterprises in Vietnam to develop sustainably. The results show that the alliance between LO_7 and L_{10} is the most optimal, as this alliance can exploit freight in the opposite direction and reduce logistics costs, creating better competitiveness for businesses.

Popkov [15] has formulated the problem of randomized maximum entropy estimation for the probability density function of random model parameters with real data and measurement noises. This estimation procedure maximizes an information entropy functional on a set of integral equalities depending on the real dataset. The Gâteaux derivative technique is developed to solve this problem in analytical form. The probability density function estimates depend on Lagrange multipliers, which are obtained by balancing the model's output with real data. A global theorem for the implicit dependence of these Lagrange multipliers on the data sample's length is established using the rotation of homotopic vector fields. A theorem for the asymptotic efficiency of randomized maximum entropy estimate in terms of stationary Lagrange multipliers is formulated and proved. The proposed method is illustrated in the problem of forecasting the evolution of the thermokarst lake area in western Siberia.

Borisov [16] presents the guaranteeing estimation of parameters in uncertain stochastic nonlinear regression. The loss function is the conditional mean square of the estimation error given the available observations. The distribution of regression parameters is partially unknown, and the uncertainty is described by a subset of probability distributions with a known compact domain. The essential feature is the usage of some additional constraints describing the conformity of the uncertain distribution to the realized observation sample. The paper contains various examples of the conformity indices. The estimation task is formulated as the minimax optimization problem, which, in turn, is solved in terms of saddle points. The paper presents the characterization of both the optimal estimator and the set of least favorable distributions. The saddle points are found via the solution to a dual finite-dimensional optimization problem, which is simpler than the initial minimax problem. The paper proposes a numerical solution procedure to the dual optimization problem. The interconnection between the least favorable distributions under the conformity constraint, and their Pareto efficiency in the sense of a vector criterion is also indicated. The influence of various conformity constraints on the estimation performance is demonstrated by illustrative numerical examples.

Tsitsiashvili [17] develops a method for detecting synergistic effects of the interaction of elements in multielement stochastic systems of separate redundancy, multiserver queuing, and statistical estimates of nonlinear recurrent relations parameters. The detected effects are relatively strong and manifest themselves even with rough estimates. This allows their analysis with relatively simple mathematical methods and thereby helps expand the set of possible applications. The new methods are based on special techniques of the structural analysis of multielement stochastic models in combination with majorant asymptotic estimates of their performance indicators. They allow moving to more accurate and rather economical numerical calculations, as they indicate in which direction it is most convenient to perform these calculations.

A review of Ge [18] is devoted to the latest progress in the controllability of stochastic linear systems and some unsolved problems. Firstly, the exact controllability of stochastic linear systems in finite-dimensional spaces is discussed. Secondly, the exact, exact null, approximate, approximate null, and partial approximate controllability of stochastic linear systems in infinite-dimensional spaces are considered. Thirdly, the exact, exact null, and impulse controllability of stochastic singular linear systems in finite-dimensional spaces are investigated. Fourthly, the exact and approximate controllability of stochastic singular linear systems in infinite-dimensional spaces are studied. Lastly, the controllability and observability for a type of time-varying stochastic singular, linear system are studied using stochastic GE-evolution operator in the sense of mild solution in Banach spaces; some necessary and sufficient conditions are obtained, and the dual principle is proven to be true. An example is given to illustrate the validity of the theoretical results obtained in this part, and a problem to be solved is introduced. The main purpose of this paper is to facilitate readers to fully understand the latest research results concerning the controllability of stochastic linear systems and the problems that need to be further studied, thus prompting more scholars to engage in this research.

Morozov et al. [19] are concerned with the issues of modeling dynamic systems with interval parameters. In previous works, the authors proposed an adaptive interpolation algorithm for solving interval problems. The essence of the algorithm is the dynamic construction of a piecewise, polynomial function that interpolates the solution of the problem with a given accuracy. The main problem of applying the algorithm is related to the curse of dimension, i.e., exponential complexity relative to the number of interval uncertainties in parameters. The main objective of this work is to apply the previously proposed adaptive interpolation algorithm to dynamic systems with a large number of interval parameters. In order to reduce the computational complexity of the algorithm, the authors propose using adaptive sparse grids. This article introduces a novel approach to applying sparse grids to problems with interval uncertainties. The efficiency of the proposed approach has been demonstrated on representative interval problems of nonlinear dynamics and computational materials science.

Derbeli et al. [20] investigate a proton exchange membrane (PEM) fuel cell. This problem has recently gained widespread attention from many researchers due to its cleanliness, high efficiency, and soundless operation. The high-performance output characteristics are required to overcome the market restrictions of PEMFC technologies. Therefore, the main aim of this work is to maintain the system operating point at an adequate and efficient power stage with high-performance tracking. To this end, a model predictive control (MPC) based on a global minimum cost function for a two-step horizon is designed and implemented in a boost converter integrated with a fuel cell system. An experimental comparative study is carried out between the MPC and a PI controller to reveal the merits of the proposed technique. Comparative results indicate that a reduction of 15.65% and 86.9%, respectively, in the overshoot and response time can be achieved using the suggested control structure.

Author Contributions: Conceptualization, A.G.; formal analysis, A.G., V.T., M.P.; project administration, M.P.; supervision, M.P.; visualization, A.G., V.T.; writing—original draft, A.G., V.T., M.P.; writing—review and editing, A.G., V.T., M.P. All authors have read and agreed to the published version of the manuscript.

Funding: This research received no external funding.

Acknowledgments: The authors are grateful to Dinara Yambaeva (Moscow, Russia) for helping to create the rose diagram and https://icons8.com/ for their icons of the countries.

Conflicts of Interest: The authors declare no conflict of interest.

References

1. Zeifman, A.; Satin, Y.; Kovalev, I.; Razumchik, R.; Korolev, V. Facilitating Numerical Solutions of Inhomogeneous Continuous Time Markov Chains Using Ergodicity Bounds Obtained with Logarithmic Norm Method. *Mathematics* **2021**, *9*, 42. [CrossRef]
2. Ilyin, O. Discrete Velocity Boltzmann Model for Quasi-Incompressible Hydrodynamics. *Mathematics* **2021**, *9*, 993. [CrossRef]
3. Nagua, L.; Relaño, C.; Monje, C.; Balaguer, C. A New Approach of Soft Joint Based on a Cable-Driven Parallel Mechanism for Robotic Applications. *Mathematics* **2021**, *9*, 1468. [CrossRef]
4. Masood, Z.; Raja, M.; Chaudhary, N.; Cheema, K.; Milyani, A. Fractional Dynamics of Stuxnet Virus Propagation in Industrial Control Systems. *Mathematics* **2021**, *9*, 2160. [CrossRef]
5. Gorshenin, A.; Kuzmin, V. Statistical Feature Construction for Forecasting Accuracy Increase and Its Applications in Neural Network Based Analysis. *Mathematics* **2022**, *10*, 589. [CrossRef]
6. Diveev, A.; Konstantinov, S.; Shmalko, E.; Dong, G. Machine Learning Control Based on Approximation of Optimal Trajectories. *Mathematics* **2021**, *9*, 265. [CrossRef]
7. Li, O.; Zhou, Y. Precise Trajectory Tracking Control of Ship Towing Systems via a Dynamical Tracking Target. *Mathematics* **2021**, *9*, 974. [CrossRef]
8. Diveev, A.; Sofronova, E.; Zelinka, I. Optimal Control Problem Solution with Phase Constraints for Group of Robots by Pontryagin Maximum Principle and Evolutionary Algorithm. *Mathematics* **2020**, *8*, 2105. [CrossRef]
9. Mena, L.; Muñoz, J.; Monje, C.; Balaguer, C. Modular and Self-Scalable Origami Robot: A First Approach. *Mathematics* **2021**, *9*, 1324. [CrossRef]
10. Diveev, A.; Shmalko, E.; Serebrenny, V.; Zentay, P. Fundamentals of Synthesized Optimal Control. *Mathematics* **2021**, *9*, 21. [CrossRef]
11. Kuang, B.; Wisniewski, M.; Rana, Z.; Zhao, Y. Rock Segmentation in the Navigation Vision of the Planetary Rovers. *Mathematics* **2021**, *9*, 3048. [CrossRef]
12. Quevedo, F.; Muñoz, J.; Castano Pena, J.; Monje, C. 3D Model Identification of a Soft Robotic Neck. *Mathematics* **2021**, *9*, 1652. [CrossRef]

13. Posypkin, M.; Khamisov, O. Automatic Convexity Deduction for Efficient Function's Range Bounding. *Mathematics* **2021**, *9*, 134. [CrossRef]
14. Nguyen, H. Application of Mathematical Models to Assess the Impact of the COVID-19 Pandemic on Logistics Businesses and Recovery Solutions for Sustainable Development. *Mathematics* **2021**, *9*, 1977. [CrossRef]
15. Popkov, Y. Qualitative Properties of Randomized Maximum Entropy Estimates of Probability Density Functions. *Mathematics* **2021**, *9*, 548. [CrossRef]
16. Borisov, A. Minimax Estimation in Regression under Sample Conformity Constraints. *Mathematics* **2021**, *9*, [CrossRef]
17. Tsitsiashvili, G. Study of Synergistic Effects in Complex Stochastic Systems. *Mathematics* **2021**, *9*, 1396. [CrossRef]
18. Ge, Z. Review of the Latest Progress in Controllability of Stochastic Linear Systems and Stochastic GE-Evolution Operator. *Mathematics* **2021**, *9*, 3240. [CrossRef]
19. Morozov, A.; Zhuravlev, A.; Reviznikov, D. Sparse Grid Adaptive Interpolation in Problems of Modeling Dynamic Systems with Interval Parameters. *Mathematics* **2021**, *9*, 298. [CrossRef]
20. Derbeli, M.; Charaabi, A.; Barambones, O.; Napole, C. High-Performance Tracking for Proton Exchange Membrane Fuel Cell System PEMFC Using Model Predictive Control. *Mathematics* **2021**, *9*, 1158. [CrossRef]

 *mathematics*

Article

Facilitating Numerical Solutions of Inhomogeneous Continuous Time Markov Chains Using Ergodicity Bounds Obtained with Logarithmic Norm Method

Alexander Zeifman [1,2,3,*], Yacov Satin [2], Ivan Kovalev [2], Rostislav Razumchik [1,3], Victor Korolev [1,3,4]

[1] Institute of Informatics Problems, Federal Research Center "Computer Science and Control" of the Russian Academy of Sciences, Vavilova 44-2, 119333 Moscow, Russia; rrazumchik@ipiran.ru
[2] Department of Applied Mathematics, Vologda State University, Lenina 15, 160000 Vologda, Russia; yacovi@mail.ru (Y.S.); kovalev.iv96@yandex.ru (I.K.)
[3] Moscow Center for Fundamental and Applied Mathematics, Moscow State University, Leninskie Gory 1, 119991 Moscow, Russia; vkorolev@cs.msu.ru
[4] Faculty of Computational Mathematics and Cybernetics, Lomonosov Moscow State University, 119991 Moscow, Russia
* Correspondence: a_zeifman@mail.ru

Abstract: The problem considered is the computation of the (limiting) time-dependent performance characteristics of one-dimensional continuous-time Markov chains with discrete state space and time varying intensities. Numerical solution techniques can benefit from methods providing ergodicity bounds because the latter can indicate how to choose the position and the length of the "distant time interval" (in the periodic case) on which the solution has to be computed. They can also be helpful whenever the state space truncation is required. In this paper one such analytic method—the logarithmic norm method—is being reviewed. Its applicability is shown within the queueing theory context with three examples: the classical time-varying $M/M/2$ queue; the time-varying single-server Markovian system with bulk arrivals, queue skipping policy and catastrophes; and the time-varying Markovian bulk-arrival and bulk-service system with state-dependent control. In each case it is shown whether and how the bounds on the rate of convergence can be obtained. Numerical examples are provided.

Keywords: continuous-time Markov chains; ergodicity bounds; discrete state space; rate of convergence; logarithmic norm

Citation: Zeifman, A.; Satin, Y.; Kovalev, I.; Razumchik, R.; Korolev, V. Facilitating Numerical Solutions of Inhomogeneous Continuous Time Markov Chains Using Ergodicity Bounds Obtained with Logarithmic Norm Method. *Mathematics* **2021**, *9*, 42. https://dx.doi.org/10.3390/math9010042

Received: 28 November 2020
Accepted: 19 December 2020
Published: 27 December 2020

Publisher's Note: MDPI stays neutral with regard to jurisdictional claims in published maps and institutional affiliations.

1. Introduction

The topic of this paper concerns the analysis of (one-dimensional) inhomogeneous *continuous-time Markov chains* (CTMC) with discrete state space. The inhomogeneity property implies that (some or all) transition intensities are non-random functions of time and (may or may not) depend on the state of the chain. For such mathematical models many operations research applications are known (see, for example, [1–4] and [Section 5] in [5]), but the motivation of this paper is queueing. Thus all the examples considered in this paper are devoted to time varying queues. Substantial literature on the problem exists in which various aspects (like existence of processes, numerical algorithms, asymptotics, approximations and others) are analyzed. The attempt to give a systematic classification of the available approaches (based on the papers published up to 2016) is made in [5]; up-to-date point of view is given in [Sections 1 and 1.2] of [4] (see also [6]).

The specific question, being the topic of this paper, is the computation of the long-run (see, for example, in [Introduction] of [7]), (limiting) time-dependent performance characteristics of a CTMC with time varying intensities. This question can be considered from different point of views: computation time, accuracy, complexity, storage use etc. As a result, various solution techniques have been developed, but none of them is the ubiquitous tool. One of the ways to improve the efficiency of a solution technique is to supply it with a method for the limiting regime detection, (or, in other words, a method providing ergodicity bounds): once the limiting regime is reached, there is no need to continue the computation indefinitely. The main contribution of this paper is the review of one such method (see Section 2) and presentation of its applicability in two new use-cases, not considered before in the literature (see Sections 4 and 5). It is worth noting that methods, which provide ergodicity bounds, can be also helpful, whenever a truncation of the countable state space of the chain is required. The method presented in Section 2, whenever applicable, is helpful in this aspect as well (see also [8,9]).

The end of this section is devoted to the review (by no means exhaustive) of the popular solution techniques for the analysis of Markov chains in time varying queueing models. The attention is drawn to the ability of a technique to yield limiting time-dependent performance characteristics of a Markov chain with time varying intensities. For each technique mentioned, (computer simulation methods and numerical transform inversion algorithms are not discussed here), it is highlighted if any benefit can be gained when the technique is used along with a method providing ergodicity bounds.

In many applied settings the performance analysis is based on the procedure known as point-wise stationary approximation [10] and its ramifications. According to it the time-dependent probability vector $\mathbf{x}(t)$ at time t is approximated by the steady-state probability vector $\mathbf{y}(t)$ by solving $\mathbf{y}(t)H(t) = 0$ and $\mathbf{y}(t)\tilde{1} = 1$, where $H(t)$ is the time-dependent intensity matrix (throughout the paper the vectors denoted by bold letters are regarded as column vectors, $\mathbf{e}_k$ denotes the kth unit basis vector, $\mathbf{1}^T$—row vector of 1's with T denoting the matrix transpose). In its initial version, the approximation breaks down if the instantaneous system's load is allowed to exceed 1. In general its quality depends on the values of the transition rates, and for some models (like time-dependent birth-and-death processes) the approach is proved to be correct asymptotically in the limit (as transition intensities increase). Another fruitful set of techniques, which help one understand the performance of complex queueing systems, is the (conventional and many-server) heavy-traffic approximations, (another approximation technique, worth mentioning here especially because of its applicability to non-Markov time varying queues, is robust optimization. See [4], Section 2.). Since scaling is important in heavy-traffic limits, usually the technique is more justified whenever the state space of a chain is in some intuitive sense close to continuous (see e.g., [11,12] and no doubt others), and less (or even not at all) justified if the state space is essentially discrete, (for example, when formed by the number of customers in the system $M_t/M_t/1/N$ (for fixed N) at time t). Due to the nature of both class of techniques mentioned above they do not benefit from methods providing ergodicity bounds.

The very popular set of techniques to calculate performance measures, which stands apart from the two mentioned above, is comprised of numerical methods for systems of ordinary differential equations (ODEs)—Kolmogorov forward equations, (for an illustration the reader can refer to, for example, [13]). Due to the increasing computer power such methods keep gaining popularity. By introducing approximations these methods can be made more efficient. For example, when only moments of the Markov chain are of interest one can use closure approximations, (since the moment dynamics are (when available) close to the true dynamics of the original process, the benefits from the methods providing ergodicity bounds, when used alongside, are clear), (see e.g., [14–16]). Another method for the computation of transient distributions of Markov chains is uniformization (see [17]). It is numerically stable and, as reported, usually outperforms known differential equation solvers (see [Section 6] in [18]).

The methods based on uniformization suffer from slow convergence of a Markov chain: whenever it is slow, computations involve a large number of matrix-vector products. An ODE technique yields the numerical values of performance measures, but it is complicated by a number of facts, among which we highlight only those which are related to the topic of this paper. Firstly, there can be infinitely many ODEs in the system of equations. Traditionally this is circumvented by truncating the system, i.e., making the number of equations finite. But there is no general "rule of thumb" for choosing the truncation threshold. Secondly, (time-dependent) limiting characteristics of a CTMC are usually considered to be identical to the solution of the system on some distant time interval (see, for example, [17–23]). This procedure yields limiting characteristics with any desired accuracy, whenever the CTMC is ergodic. Yet, in general, it is not suitable for Markov chains with countable (or finite but large) state space. Moreover it is not clear, (convergence tests are usually required, which result in additional computations). how to choose the position and the length of the "distant time interval", on which the solution of the system must be found. Thus in practice without an understanding a priori about when the limiting regime is reached, significant computational efforts are required to make oneself sure that the obtained solution is the one required, (and, for example, the steady-state is not detected prematurely (see [24]). The authors in [20] propose the solution technique equipped with the steady-state detection. As is shown, it allows significant computational savings and simultaneously ensures strict error bounding. Yet the technique is only applicable, when the stationary solution of a Markov chain can be efficiently calculated in advance).

The approaches mentioned in the previous paragraph have straightforward benefit from the methods providing a priori determination of point of convergence. Although generally this task is not feasible, certain techniques exist, which provide ergodicity bounds for some classes of Markov chains. In the next section we review one such technique, being developed by the authors, which is based on the logarithmic norm of linear operators and special transformations of the intensity matrix, governing the behaviour of a CTMC. In the Sections 3–5 it is applied to three use-cases. Section 6 concludes the paper.

In what follows by $\|\cdot\|$ we denote the l_1-norm, i.e., if $\mathbf{x}$ is an $(l+1)$-dimensional column vector then $\|\mathbf{x}\| = \sum_{k=0}^{l} |x_k|$. If $\mathbf{x}$ is a probability vector, then $\|\mathbf{x}\| = 1$. The choice of operator norms will be the one induced by the l_1-norm on column vectors, i.e., $\|A\| = \sup_{0 \leq j \leq l} \sum_{i=0}^{l} |a_{ij}|$ for a linear operator (matrix) A.

2. Logarithmic Norm Method

Ergodic properties of Markov chains have been the subject of many research papers (see e.g., [25,26]). Yet obtaining practically useful general ergodicity bounds is difficult and remains, to large extent, an open problem. Below we describe one method, called the "logarithmic norm" method, which is applicable in the situations, when the discrete state space of the Markov chain cannot be replaced by the continuous one and the transition intensities are such that the chain is either null or weakly ergodic. The method is based on the notion of the logarithmic norm (see e.g., [27,28]) and utilizes the properties of linear systems of differential equations.

Consider an ODE system

$$\frac{d}{dt}\mathbf{y}(t) = H(t)\mathbf{y}(t), \; t \geq 0, \tag{1}$$

where the entries of the matrix $H(t) = (h_{ij}(t))_{i,j=0}^{\infty}$ are locally integrable on $[0, \infty)$ and $H(t)$ is bounded in the sense that $\|H(t)\|$ is finite for any fixed t. Then

$$\frac{d}{dt}\|\mathbf{y}(t)\| \leq -\beta(t)\|\mathbf{y}(t)\|, \tag{2}$$

where $-\beta(t)$ is the logarithmic norm of $H(t)$ i.e.

$$-\beta(t) = \sup_i \left\{ h_{ii}(t) + \sum_{j \neq i} |h_{ji}(t)| \right\}. \tag{3}$$

Thus the following upper bound holds:

$$\|\mathbf{y}(t)\| \leq e^{-\int_0^t \beta(u)\,du}\|\mathbf{y}(0)\|. \tag{4}$$

If $H(t)$ has non-negative non-diagonal elements (and arbitrary elements on the diagonal, (such a matrix in the literature is called sometimes essentially nonnegative).) and all of its column sums are identical, then there exist $\|\mathbf{y}(0)\|$ such that in (4) the equality holds.

The logarithmic norm method is put into an application in four consecutive steps. Firstly one has to determine whether the given Markov chain (further always denoted by $X(t)$) is null-ergodic or weakly ergodic,(a Markov chain is called null-ergodic, if for all its state probabilities $p_i(t) \to 0$ as $t \to \infty$ for any initial condition; a Markov chain is called weakly ergodic if $\|\mathbf{p}^*(t) - \mathbf{p}^{**}(t)\| \to 0$ as $t \to \infty$ for any initial condition $\mathbf{p}^*(0), \mathbf{p}^{**}(0)$, where the vector $\mathbf{p}(t)$ contains state probabilities). Secondly one excludes one "border state" from the Kolmogorov forward equations and thus obtains the new system with the matrix which, in general, may have negative off-diagonal terms. The third step is to perform (if possible) the similarity transformation (see (11) and (24)), i.e., to transform the new matrix in such a way that its off-diagonal terms are nonnegative and the column sums differ as little as possible. At the final, fourth step one uses the logarithmic norm to estimate the convergence rate. The key step is the third one. The transformation is made using a sequence of positive numbers (see the sequences $\{\delta_n, n \geq 0\}$ below), which usually has to be guessed, does not have any probabilistic meaning and can be considered as an analogue of Lyapunov functions.

3. Time-Varying $M/M/2$ System

We start with the well-known time-varying $M/M/2/\infty$ system with two servers and the infinite-capacity queue in which customers arrive one by one with the intensity $\lambda(t)$. The service intensity of each server does not depend on the total number of customers in the queue and is equal to $\mu(t)$. The functions $\lambda(t)$ and $\mu(t)$ are assumed to be nonrandom, nonnegative and locally integrable on $[0, \infty)$ continuous functions. Let the integer-valued time-dependent random variable $X(t)$ denote the total number of customers in the system at time $t \geq 0$. Then $X(t)$ is the CTMC with the state space $\{0, 1, 2\dots\}$. Its transposed time-dependent intensity matrix (generator) $A(t) = (a_{ij}(t))_{i,j=0}^{\infty}$ has the form

$$A(t) = \begin{pmatrix} -\lambda(t) & \mu(t) & 0 & 0 & \dots \\ \lambda(t) & -(\lambda(t)+\mu(t)) & 2\mu(t) & 0 & \dots \\ 0 & \lambda(t) & -(\lambda(t)+2\mu(t)) & 2\mu(t) & \dots \\ 0 & 0 & \lambda(t) & -(\lambda(t)+2\mu(t)) & \dots \\ \vdots & \vdots & \vdots & \vdots & \ddots \end{pmatrix}.$$

For all $t \geq 0$ we represent the distribution of $X(t)$ as a probability vector $\mathbf{p}(t)$, where $\mathbf{p}(t) = \sum_{k=0}^{\infty} P(X(t) = k)\mathbf{e}_k$ (as above, $\mathbf{e}_k$ denotes the kth unit basis vector). Given any proper initial condition $\mathbf{p}(0)$, the Kolmogorov forward equations for the distribution of $X(t)$ can be written as

$$\frac{d}{dt}\mathbf{p}(t) = A(t)\mathbf{p}(t). \tag{5}$$

Assume that $X(t)$ is null ergodic. The condition on the intensities $\lambda(t)$ and $\mu(t)$, which guarantees null ergodicity will be derived shortly below, (clearly, if the intensities are constants, i.e., $\lambda(t) = \lambda$ and $\mu(t) = \mu$, then the condition is simply $\lambda > 2\mu$. If both are periodic and the smallest common multiple of the periods is T, then the condition is $\int_0^T \lambda(u)\,du > 2\int_0^T \mu(u)\,du$). Fix a positive number $d > 1$ and define the sequence $\{\delta_n, n \geq 0\}$ by $\delta_n = d^{-n}$. It is the decreasing sequence of positive numbers. By multiplying (5) from the right with $\Lambda = diag(\delta_0, \delta_1, \dots)$, we get

$$\frac{d}{dt}\tilde{\mathbf{p}}(t) = \tilde{A}(t)\tilde{\mathbf{p}}(t), \tag{6}$$

where $\tilde{\mathbf{p}}(t) = \Lambda \mathbf{p}(t)$ and $\tilde{A}(t) = \Lambda A(t)\Lambda^{-1}$. Denote by $-\tilde{\alpha}_k(t)$ the sum of all elements in the kth column of $\tilde{A}(t)$. By direct inspection it can be checked that

$$
\begin{aligned}
\tilde{\alpha}_0(t) &= \left(1 - d^{-1}\right)\lambda(t), \\
\tilde{\alpha}_1(t) &= \left(1 - d^{-1}\right)(\lambda(t) - d\mu(t)), \\
\tilde{\alpha}_k(t) &= \underbrace{\left(1 - d^{-1}\right)(\lambda(t) - 2d\mu(t))}_{=\beta(t)}, \ k \geq 2.
\end{aligned}
$$

Since $\tilde{\alpha}_0(t) \geq \beta(t)$ and $\tilde{\alpha}_1(t) \geq \beta(t)$, the upper bound follows from (4) applied to (6):

$$
\sum_{k=0}^{\infty} d^{-k} p_k(t) \leq e^{-\int_0^t \beta(u)\,du} \sum_{k=0}^{\infty} d^{-k} p_k(0). \tag{7}
$$

If d is chosen such that $d > 1$ and $\int_0^{\infty}(\lambda(t) - 2d\mu(t))\,dt = +\infty$, then from (7) it follows that $p_k(t) \to 0$ as $t \to \infty$ for each $k \geq 0$ and thus $X(t)$ is null ergodic. In such a case it is possible to extract more information from (7). Note that for any fixed $n \geq 0$ it holds that

$$
d^{-n} \sum_{i=0}^{n} p_i(t) \leq \sum_{k=0}^{n} d^{-k} p_k(t) \leq \sum_{k=0}^{\infty} d^{-k} p_k(t).
$$

Thus, if $X(0) = N$, i.e., $p_N(0) = 1$ then for any $n \geq 0$ the following upper bound for the conditional probability $P(X(t) \leq n | X(0) = N)$, $N \geq 0$, holds:

$$
P(X(t) \leq n | X(0) = N) \leq d^{n-N} e^{-\int_0^t \beta(u)\,du}. \tag{8}
$$

Now assume that $X(t)$ is weakly ergodic (the corresponding condition on the intensities $\lambda(t)$ and $\mu(t)$ will be derived shortly below). Using the normalization condition $p_0(t) = 1 - \sum_{i \geq 1} p_i(t)$ it can be checked that the system (5) can be rewritten as follows:

$$
\frac{d}{dt}\mathbf{z}(t) = B(t)\mathbf{z}(t) + \mathbf{f}(t), \tag{9}
$$

where the matrix $B(t)$ with the elements $b_{ij}(t) = a_{ij}(t) - a_{i0}(t)$ has no probabilistic meaning and the vectors $\mathbf{f}(t)$ and $\mathbf{z}(t)$ are

$$
\mathbf{f}(t) = (\lambda(t), 0, , 0 \dots)^T, \quad \mathbf{z}(t) = (p_1(t), p_2(t), \dots)^T.
$$

Let $\mathbf{z}^*(t)$ and $\mathbf{z}^{**}(t)$ be the two solutions of (9) corresponding to two different initial conditions $\mathbf{z}^*(0)$ and $\mathbf{z}^{**}(0)$. Then for the vector $\mathbf{y}(t) = \mathbf{z}^*(t) - \mathbf{z}^{**}(t) = (y_1(t), y_2(t), \dots)^T$, with arbitrary elements we have the system

$$
\frac{d}{dt}\mathbf{y}(t) = B(t)\mathbf{y}(t). \tag{10}
$$

The matrix $B(t)$ in (10) may have negative off-diagonal elements. But it is straightforward to see, that the similarity transformation $TB(t)T^{-1} = B^*(t)$, where T is the upper triangular matrix of the form

$$
T = \begin{pmatrix}
1 & 1 & 1 & \cdots \\
0 & 1 & 1 & \cdots \\
0 & 0 & 1 & \cdots \\
\vdots & \vdots & \vdots & \ddots
\end{pmatrix},
$$

gives the matrix $B^*(t)$:

$$B^*(t) = \begin{pmatrix} -(\lambda(t)+\mu(t)) & \mu(t) & 0 & 0 & \cdots \\ \lambda(t) & -(\lambda(t)+2\mu(t)) & 2\mu(t) & 0 & \cdots \\ 0 & \lambda(t) & -(\lambda(t)+2\mu(t)) & 2\mu(t) & \cdots \\ \vdots & \vdots & \vdots & \vdots & \ddots \end{pmatrix}, \tag{11}$$

which off-diagonal elements are always nonnegative. Let $\mathbf{u}(t) = T\mathbf{y}(t) = (u_1(t), u_2(t), \dots)^T$. Then by multiplying both parts of (10) from the left by T, we get

$$\frac{d}{dt}\mathbf{u}(t) = B^*(t)\mathbf{u}(t). \tag{12}$$

Fix a positive number $d > 1$ and define the increasing sequence of positive numbers $\{\delta_n, n \geq 0\}$ by $\delta_n = d^{n-1}$. Let $D = diag(\delta_1, \delta_2, \dots)$. By putting $\mathbf{w}(t) = D\mathbf{u}(t)$ in (12), we obtain the system of equations

$$\frac{d}{dt}\mathbf{w}(t) = B^{**}(t)\mathbf{w}(t), \tag{13}$$

where the matrix $B^{**}(t) = DB^*(t)D^{-1}$ has nonnegative off-diagonal elements. Denote by $-\alpha_k(t)$ the sum of all elements in the kth column of $B^{**}(t)$ i.e.

$$\begin{aligned} \alpha_1(t) &= \mu(t) - (d-1)\lambda(t), \\ \alpha_2(t) &= \left(1 - d^{-1}\right)\mu(t) + \mu(t) - (d-1)\lambda(t), \\ \alpha_k(t) &= \underbrace{\left(1 - d^{-1}\right)(2\mu(t) - d\lambda(t))}_{=\beta(t)}, \quad k \geq 3. \end{aligned}$$

Note that if $1 < d \leq 2$ then $\alpha_1(t) \geq \beta(t)$ and $\alpha_2(t) \geq \beta(t)$. Now, remembering that $\mathbf{w}(t) = D\mathbf{u}(t) = DT\mathbf{y}(t)$, the upper bound for $\mathbf{y}(t) = \mathbf{z}^*(t) - \mathbf{z}^{**}(t)$ in the weighted norm due to (4) is (from (14) the purpose of the similarity transformation $DB^*(t)D^{-1}$ can be recognized: it is to make $\beta(t)$ in the exponent as large as possible).

$$\|DT\mathbf{y}(t)\| \leq e^{-\int_0^t \beta(u)\,du}\|DT\mathbf{y}(0)\|. \tag{14}$$

The upper bound for $\|\mathbf{p}^*(t) - \mathbf{p}^{**}(t)\|$ is obtained from (14). Firstly notice that $\|\mathbf{y}(t)\| \leq 2\|\mathbf{p}^*(t) - \mathbf{p}^{**}(t)\|$ since $\mathbf{y}(t)$ is the solution of (10)—the system with the excluded state (0). Secondly, it can be proved, (this is shown, for example, in [Equation (18)] of the [29]), that $\|\mathbf{x}\| \leq 2\|DT\mathbf{x}\|$ for any vector $\mathbf{x}$. Hence

$$\|\mathbf{p}^*(t) - \mathbf{p}^{**}(t)\| \leq 4e^{-\int_0^t \beta(u)\,du}\|DT\mathbf{y}(0)\|. \tag{15}$$

If d is chosen such that $d > 1$ and $\int_0^\infty (2\mu(t) - d\lambda(t))\,dt = +\infty$, then from (15) it follows that $\|\mathbf{p}^*(t) - \mathbf{p}^{**}(t)\| \to 0$ as $t \to \infty$ for any initial conditions $\mathbf{p}^*(0)$ and $\mathbf{p}^{**}(0)$, i.e., $X(t)$ is weakly ergodic. Note that it is sufficient to choose $d \in (1, 2]$: if the integral diverges for $d > 2$ it also diverges for $d = 2$ and this is sufficient for (14) to hold.

Sometimes it is also possible to obtain bounds similar to (15) for other characteristics of $X(t)$. For example, denote by $E(t, k)$ the conditional mean number of customers in the system at time t, given that initially there where k customers in the system, i.e., $E(t, k) = \sum_{n \geq 1} nP(X(t) = n | X(0) = k)$. Then using [Equation (22)] of [29] it can be shown, that

$$|E(t, k) - E(t, 0)| \leq \frac{4(1 - d^k)}{W(1 - d)}e^{-\int_0^t \beta(u)\,du}, \quad k \geq 1, \quad W = \inf_n \frac{d^n}{n+1}. \tag{16}$$

The results obtained above for both, null and weak ergodic, cases can be put together in the single theorem.

Theorem 1. *Let there exist a positive $d \neq 1$ such that $\int_0^\infty \left((1-d)\lambda(t) + 2(1-d^{-1})\mu(t) \right) dt = +\infty$. Then $X(t)$ is null (weakly) ergodic if $d < 1$ ($d > 1$) and the ergodicity bounds (7) and (15) hold.*

Whenever the intensities $\lambda(t)$ and $\mu(t)$ are constants or periodic functions stronger results can be obtained.

Corollary 1. *If in the Theorem 1 the intensities $\lambda(t)$ and $\mu(t)$ are constants or $1-$periodic, (i.e., $\lambda(t)$ and $\mu(t)$ are periodic functions and the length of their periods is equal to one), then $X(t)$ is exponentially null (weakly) ergodic if $d < 1$ ($d > 1$) and there exist $R > 0$ and $a > 0$ such that $e^{-\int_s^t \beta(u)\, du} \leq Re^{-a(t-s)}$ for $0 \leq s \leq t$.*

We now consider the numerical example. Let $\lambda(t) = 9(1 + \sin 2\pi t)$ and $\mu(t) = 8(1 + \cos 2\pi t)$. It is straightforward to check from the *Theorem 1* that if $d = \frac{4}{3}$ then $X(t)$ is weakly ergodic. Then the ergodicity bounds follow from (15) and (16):

$$\|\mathbf{p}^*(t) - \mathbf{p}^{**}(t)\| \leq 72e^{-t}\|DT(\mathbf{p}^*(0) - \mathbf{p}^{**}(0))\|, \tag{17}$$

$$|E(t,k) - E(t,0)| \leq 162\left(\frac{4}{3}\right)^k e^{-t}, \; k > 0. \tag{18}$$

Figure 1 shows the graph of the probability $p_0(t)$ as t increases. It can be seen that for any initial condition $\mathbf{p}(0)$ there exists one periodic function of t, say $\pi_0(t)$ (i.e., $\pi_0(t) = \pi_0(t + T)$, where $T = 1$ is the smallest common multiple of the periods of $\lambda(t)$ and $\mu(t)$), such that $\lim_{t\to\infty}(p_0(t) - \pi_0(t)) = 0$. Figure 2 shows the detailed behaviour of $\pi_0(t)$. Now consider (17). If $t \geq 37$ then the right part of (17) does not exceed 10^{-3} i.e., starting from the instant $t = 37 = t^*$ the system "forgets" its initial state and the distribution of $X(t)$ for $t > t^*$ can be regarded as limiting. The error (in l_1-norm), which is thus made, is not greater than 10^{-3}. Moreover, since the limiting distribution of $X(t)$ is periodic, it is sufficient to solve numerically the system of ODEs only in the interval $[0, t^* + T]$. The distribution of $X(t)$ in the interval $[t^*, t^* + T]$ is the limiting probability distribution of $X(t)$ (with error not greater than 10^{-3} in l_1-norm). Note that the system of ODEs contains infinite number of equations. Thus in order to solve it numerically one has to truncate it; this truncation was performed according to the method in [30]. The upper bound on the rate of convergence of the conditional mean $E(t,k)$ is given in (18). If $t \geq t^*$ then the right part does not exceed 10^{-2} i.e., starting from $t = t^*$ the system "forgets" its initial state and the value of $E(t,k)$ can be regarded as the limiting value of the conditional mean number of customers with the error not greater than 10^{-2}. The rate of convergence of $E(t,k)$ and the behaviour of its limiting value is shown in the Figures 3 and 4. Note that the obtained upper bounds are not tight: the system enters the periodic limiting regime before the instant $t = t^*$.

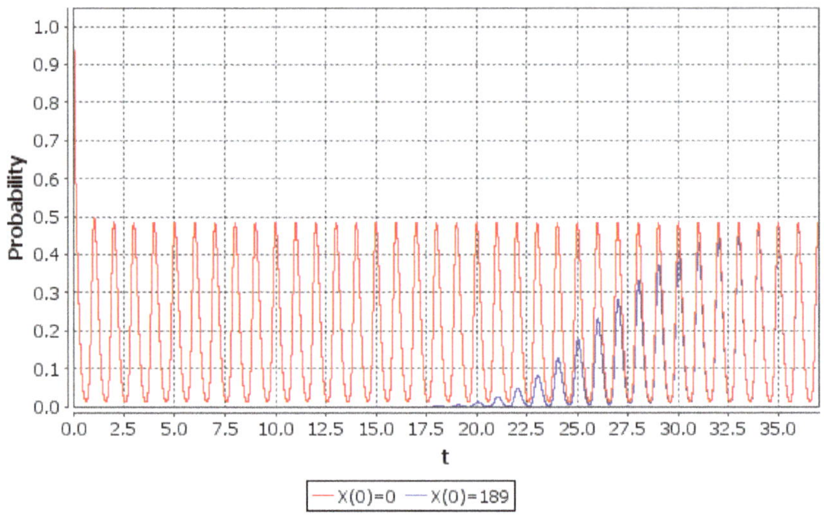

Figure 1. Rate of convergence of the empty system probability $p_0(t)$ in the interval $[0, 37]$ given two different initial conditions: $p_0(0) = 1$ (**red line**), $p_{189}(0) = 1$ (**blue line**).

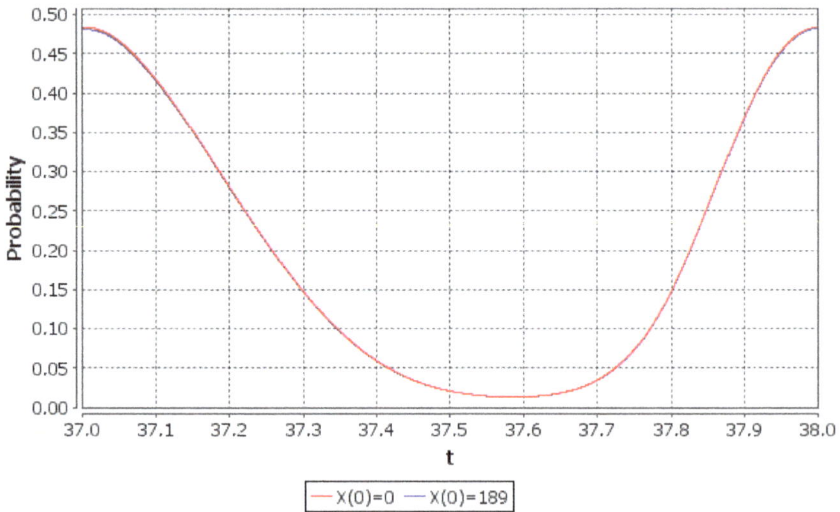

Figure 2. Limiting probability $p_0(t)$ of the empty queue given two different initial conditions: $p_0(0) = 1$ (**red line**), $p_{189}(0) = 1$ (**blue line**).

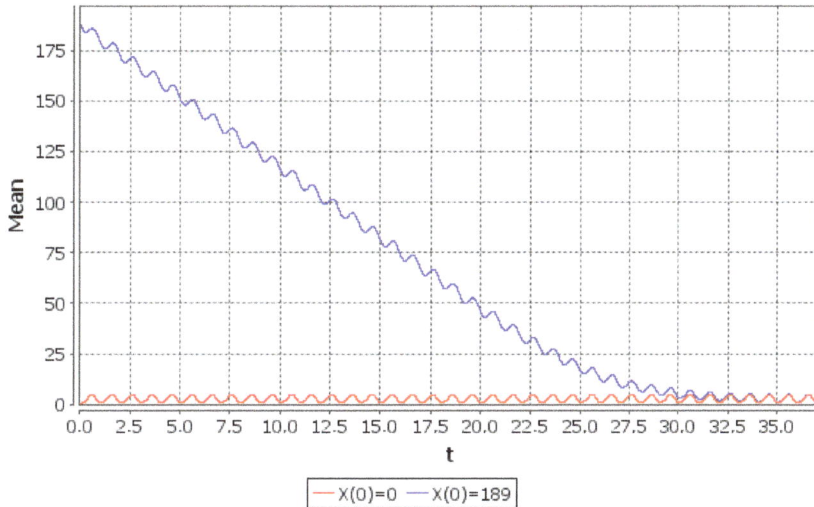

Figure 3. Rate of convergence of the conditional mean $E(t, k)$ number of customers in the system in the interval $[0, 37]$: $E(t, 0)$ **(red line)**, $E(t, 189)$ **(blue line)**.

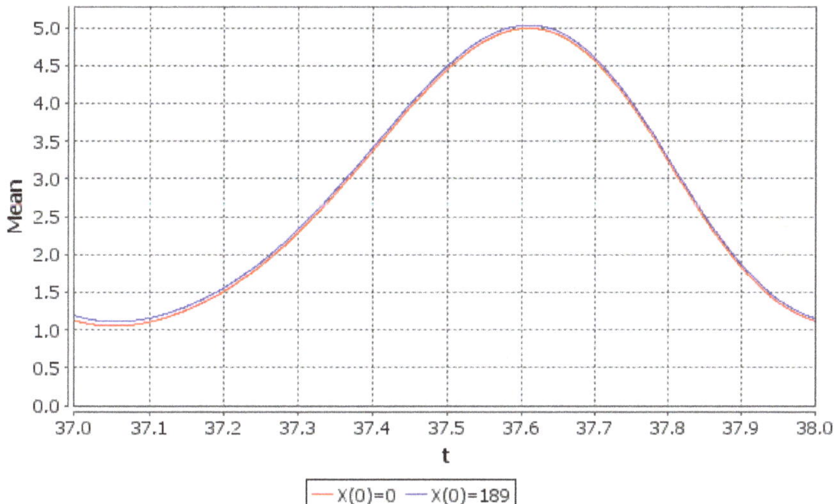

Figure 4. Limiting conditional mean $E(t, k)$ number of customers in the system: $E(t, 0)$ **(red line)**, $E(t, 189)$ **(blue line)**.

4. Time-Varying Single-Server Markovian System with Bulk Arrivals, Queue Skipping Policy and Catastrophes

Consider the time-varying $M/M/1$ system with the intensities being periodic functions of time and the queue skipping policy as in [31] (see also [32]). Customers arrive to the system in batches according to the inhomogeneous Poisson process with the intensity $\lambda(t)$. The size of an arriving batch becomes known upon its arrival to the system and is the random variable with the given probability distribution $\{b_n, n \geq 1\}$, having finite mean $\bar{b} = \sum_{k=1}^{\infty} B_k$, $B_k = \sum_{n=k}^{\infty} b_n$. The implemented queue skipping policy implies that whenever a batch arrives to the system its size, say $\widehat{B}$, is compared with the remaining total number of customers in the system, say $\widetilde{B}$. If $\widehat{B} > \widetilde{B}$, then all customers, that are currently in the system, are instantly removed from it, the whole batch $\widehat{B}$ is placed in the the queue and one customer from it enters server. If $\widehat{B} \leq \widetilde{B}$ the new batch leaves the system without having any effect on it. Whenever the server becomes free the first customer from the queue (if there is any) enters server and gets served according to the exponential distribution with the intensity $\mu(t)$. Finally the additional inhomogeneous Poisson flow of negative customers with the intensity $\gamma(t)$ arrives to the system. Each negative arrival results in the removal of all customers present in the system at the time of arrival. The negative customer itself leaves the system. Since $\gamma(t)$ depends on t it can happen that the effect of negative arrivals fades away too fast as $t \to \infty$ (for example, if $\gamma(t) = (1+t)^{-n}, n > 1$). Such cases are excluded from the consideration.

Let $X(t)$ be the total number of customers in the system at time t. From the system description it follows that $X(t)$ is the CTMC with state space $\{0, 1, 2, \ldots, b^*\}$, where b^* is the maximum possible batch size i.e., $b^* = \max_{n \geq 1}(b_n > 0)$. Thus if the batch size distribution has infinite support then the state space is countable, otherwise it is finite.

It is straightforward to see that the transposed time-dependent generator $A(t) = (a_{ij}(t))_{i,j=0}^{\infty}$ for $X(t)$ has the form

$$A(t) = \begin{pmatrix} -\lambda(t) & \mu(t)+\gamma(t) & \gamma(t) & \gamma(t) & \cdots \\ \lambda(t)b_1 & -(\lambda(t)B_2+\mu(t)+\gamma(t)) & \mu(t) & 0 & \cdots \\ \lambda(t)b_2 & \lambda(t)b_2 & -(\lambda(t)B_3+\mu(t)+\gamma(t)) & \mu(t) & \cdots \\ \lambda(t)b_3 & \lambda(t)b_3 & \lambda(t)b_3 & -(\lambda(t)B_4+\mu(t)+\gamma(t)) & \cdots \\ \vdots & \vdots & \vdots & \vdots & \ddots \end{pmatrix}.$$

We represent the distribution of $X(t)$ as a probability vector $\mathbf{p}(t)$, where $\mathbf{p}(t) = \sum_{k=0}^{b^*} P(X(t) = k)\mathbf{e}_k$ tor all $t \geq 0$. Given a proper $\mathbf{p}(0)$, the probabilistic dynamics of $X(t)$ is described by the Kolmogorov forward equations $\frac{d}{dt}\mathbf{p}(t) = A(t)\mathbf{p}(t)$, which can be rewritten in the form

$$\frac{d}{dt}\mathbf{p}(t) = A^*(t)\mathbf{p}(t) + \mathbf{g}(t), \quad t \geq 0, \tag{19}$$

where $\mathbf{g}(t) = (\gamma(t), 0, 0, \ldots)^T$ and $A^*(t)$ is the matrix with the terms $a_{ij}^*(t)$ equal to

$$a_{ij}^*(t) = \begin{cases} a_{0j}(t) - \gamma(t), & \text{if } i = 0, \\ a_{ij}(t), & \text{otherwise.} \end{cases} \tag{20}$$

Due to the restrictions imposed on $\gamma(t)$, we have that $\int_0^{\infty} \gamma(t)\, dt = \infty$. Thus $X(t)$ cannot be null ergodic irrespective of the values of $\lambda(t)$ and $\mu(t)$.

Theorem 2. *Assume that the catastrophe intensity $\gamma(t)$ is such that $\int_0^{\infty} \gamma(t)\, dt = \infty$. Then the Markov chain $X(t)$ is weakly ergodic and for any two initial conditions $\mathbf{p}^*(0)$ and $\mathbf{p}^{**}(0)$ it holds that*

$$\|\mathbf{p}^*(t) - \mathbf{p}^{**}(t)\| \leq e^{-\int_0^t \gamma(u)\, du} \|\mathbf{p}^*(0) - \mathbf{p}^{**}(0)\| \leq 2e^{-\int_0^t \gamma(u)\, du}, \quad t \geq 0. \tag{21}$$

Proof. It is straightforward to check, that the logarithmic norm (see (3)) of the operator $A^*(t)$ is equal to $-\gamma(t)$. Denote now by $U^*(t,s)$ the Cauchy operator of the Equation (19). Then the statement of the theorem follows from the inequalities $\|U^*(t,s)\| \leq e^{-\int_s^t \gamma(u)\, du}$ and

$$\|\mathbf{p}^*(t) - \mathbf{p}^{**}(t)\| \leq \|U^*(t,0)\|\|\mathbf{p}^*(0) - \mathbf{p}^{**}(0)\|.$$

$\square$

Even though (21) is the valid ergodicity bound for $X(t)$, it is of little help whenever the state space of $X(t)$ is countable and one needs to perform the numerical solution of (5). This is due to the fact that the bound (21) is in the uniform operator topology, which does not allow to use the analytic frameworks (for example, [29]) for finding proper truncations of an infinite ODE system. For the latter task ergodicity bounds for $X(t)$ in stronger (than l_1), weighted norms are required. It can be said that with such bounds we have a weight assigned to each initial state and thus a truncation procedure becomes sensitive to the number of states. Below (in the Theorem 3) we obtain such a bound under the additional assumption, (for the definition used see [33]; appropriate test for monotone functions can be found in [Proposition 1] of [34]. Although the Theorem 2 below holds for any distribution $\{b_n, n \geq 1\}$, this assumption is essential for the Theorem 3. For distributions with tails heavier than the geometric distribution we were unable to find the conditions, which guarantee the existence of the limiting regime of queue-size process even for periodic intensities). that the batch size distribution $\{b_n, n \geq 1\}$ is harmonic new better than used in expectation i.e., $\sum_{j=k}^{\infty} B_{j+1} \leq \bar{b}(1 - \bar{b}^{-1})^k$ for all $k \geq 0$.

Using the normalization condition $p_0(t) = 1 - \sum_{i \geq 1} p_i(t)$ the forward Kolmogorov system $\frac{d}{dt}\mathbf{p}(t) = A(t)\mathbf{p}(t)$ can be rewritten as

$$\frac{d}{dt}\mathbf{z}(t) = A^{**}(t)\mathbf{z}(t) + \mathbf{f}(t), \ t \geq 0, \tag{22}$$

where
$$\mathbf{f}(t) = (\lambda(t)b_1, \lambda(t)b_2, \lambda(t)b_3, \lambda(t)b_4, \dots)^T \text{ and}$$

$$A^{**}(t) = \begin{pmatrix} -(\lambda(t)+\mu(t)+\gamma(t)) & \mu(t)-\lambda(t)b_1 & -\lambda(t)b_1 & -\lambda(t)b_1 & \dots \\ 0 & -(\lambda(t)B_2+\mu(t)+\gamma(t)) & \mu(t)-\lambda(t)b_2 & -\lambda(t)b_2 & \dots \\ 0 & 0 & -(\lambda(t)B_3+\mu(t)+\gamma(t)) & \mu(t)-\lambda(t)b_3 & \dots \\ 0 & 0 & 0 & -(\lambda(t)B_4+\mu(t)+\gamma(t)) \dots \\ \vdots & \vdots & \vdots & \vdots & \ddots \end{pmatrix}. \tag{23}$$

Fix $d \subset (1,1 \mid (\bar{b}\ \ 1)^{-1}]$ and define the increasing sequence of positive numbers $\{\delta_n, n \geq 0\}$ by $\delta_n = d^{n-1}$. Then instead of the matrix $B^{**}(t)$ in (13) we have the matrix $\tilde{A}(t) = (\tilde{a}_{ij}(t))_{i,j=0}^{\infty}$ with the following structure:

$$\tilde{A}(t) = \begin{pmatrix} -(\lambda(t)+\mu(t)+\gamma(t)) & \frac{1}{d}\mu(t) & 0 & 0 & \dots \\ 0 & -(\lambda(t)B_2+\mu(t)+\gamma(t)) & \frac{1}{d}\mu(t) & 0 & \dots \\ 0 & 0 & -(\lambda(t)B_3+\mu(t)+\gamma(t)) & \frac{1}{d}\mu(t) & \dots \\ 0 & 0 & 0 & -(\lambda(t)B_4+\mu(t)+\gamma(t)) \dots \\ \vdots & \vdots & \vdots & \vdots & \ddots \end{pmatrix}. \tag{24}$$

Since the logarithmic norm (see (3)) of $\tilde{A}(t)$ is equal to

$$-\beta^*(t) = \sup_i \left\{ \tilde{a}_{ii}(t) + \sum_{j \neq i} \tilde{a}_{ji}(t) \right\} = -\inf_i \left\{ \gamma(t) + \left(1 - \frac{1}{d}\right)\mu(t) + \lambda(t)B_i \right\}$$

$$= -\gamma(t) - \left(1 - \frac{1}{d}\right)\mu(t),$$

then from (4) we get:

$$\|\mathbf{z}^*(t) - \mathbf{z}^{**}(t)\|_{1D} \leq e^{-\int_0^t \left(\gamma(u) + (1-d^{-1})\mu(u)\right) du} \|\mathbf{z}^*(0) - \mathbf{z}^{**}(0)\|_{1D}. \tag{25}$$

Arguments similar to those used to establish the *Theorem 1* lead to the following ergodicity bounds for $\|\mathbf{p}^*(t) - \mathbf{p}^{**}(t)\|$ and the conditional mean $E(t,k)$:

$$\|\mathbf{p}^*(t) - \mathbf{p}^{**}(t)\| \leq 4e^{-\int_0^t \left(\gamma(u) + \left(1 - d^{-1}\right)\mu(u)\right) du} \|\mathbf{z}^*(0) - \mathbf{z}^{**}(0)\|_{1D}, \tag{26}$$

$$|E(t,k) - E(t,0)| \leq \frac{1 + d^{k-1}}{W} e^{-\int_0^t \left(\gamma(u) + \left(1 - d^{-1}\right)\mu(u)\right) du}, \quad k \geq 1, \ W = \inf_n \frac{d^n}{n+1}. \tag{27}$$

These results can be put together in the single theorem.

Theorem 3. *Assume that the distribution $\{b_n, n \geq 1\}$ with finite mean $\bar{b}$ is harmonic new better than used in expectation. Then if $\int_0^\infty \left(\gamma(t) + (1 - d^{-1})\mu(t)\right) dt = +\infty$ for some $d \in (1, 1 + (\bar{b} - 1)^{-1}]$, then the Markov chain $X(t)$ is weakly ergodic and the ergodicity bound (26) holds.*

We close this section with the example, showing the dependence on t of the same two quantities — $p_0(t)$ and $E(t,k)$—considered in the Section 3. Assume here that $b_k = \frac{1}{3}\left(\frac{2}{3}\right)^{k-1}$, $\lambda(t) = 9(1 + \sin 2\pi t)$, $\mu(t) = 8(1 + \cos 2\pi t)$ and $\gamma(t) = 1$, i.e., the catastrophe intensity is constant and the mean size $\bar{b}$ of an arriving batch is equal to 3. It can be checked that $d = \frac{3}{2}$ satisfies the conditions of the *Theorem 3*. Then from (26) and (27) we get the upper bounds

$$\|\mathbf{p}^*(t) - \mathbf{p}^{**}(t)\| \leq 4e^{-\frac{5}{3}t} \|\mathbf{z}^*(0) - \mathbf{z}^{**}(0)\|_{1D}, \tag{28}$$

$$|E(t,k) - E(t,0)| \leq \frac{1 + \left(\frac{3}{2}\right)^{k-1}}{\frac{9}{8}} e^{-\frac{5}{3}t}, \ k \geq 0. \tag{29}$$

In Figure 5 it is depicted how $p_0(t)$ behaves as t increases and Figure 6 shows its limiting value. If $t \geq 60$ then the right part of (28) does not exceed $3 \cdot 10^{-2}$, i.e., starting from the instant $t = 60 = t^*$ the system "forgets" its initial state and the distribution of $X(t)$ for $t > t^*$ can be regarded as limiting. Moreover, since the limiting distribution of $X(t)$ is periodic, it is sufficient to solve (numerically, (it must be noticed that since $b_k > 0$ for all k, the system of ODEs contains infinite number of equations. Thus in order to solve it numerically one has to truncate it. We perform this truncation according to the method in [30])). the system of ODEs only in the interval $[0, t^* + T]$, where T is the smallest common multiple of the periods of $\lambda(t)$ and $\mu(t)$ i.e., $T = 1$. The probability distribution of $X(t)$ in the interval $[t^*, t^* + T]$ is the estimate (with error not greater than $3 \cdot 10^{-2}$ in l_1-norm) of the limiting probability distribution of $X(t)$. The upper bound on the rate of convergence of the conditional mean number of customers in the system $E(t,k)$ is given in (29). If $t \geq t^*$ then the right part does not exceed $0,3$, i.e., starting from the instant $t = t^*$ the system "forgets" its initial state and the value of $E(t,k)$ can be regarded as the limiting value of the mean number of customers with the error not greater than $0,3$. The rate of convergence of $E(t,k)$ and the behaviour of its limiting value can be seen in Figures 7 and 8. As in the previous numerical example, the obtained upper bounds are not tight: the system enters the periodic limiting regime before the instant $t = t^*$.

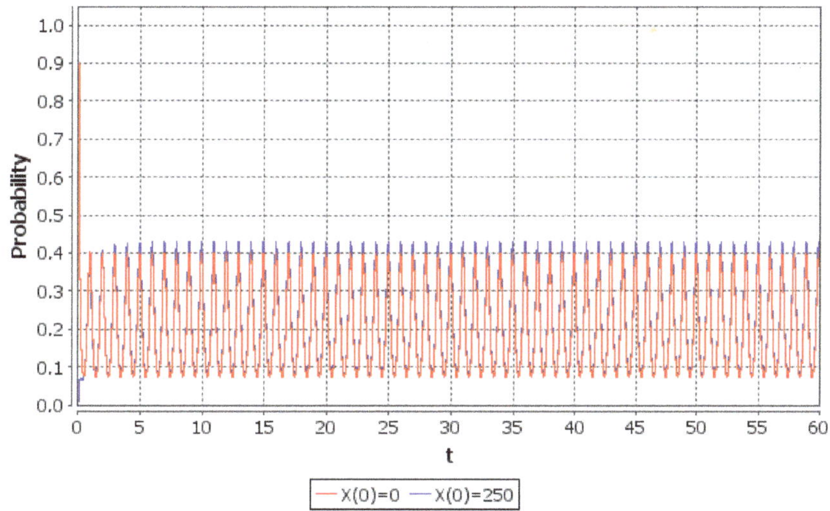

Figure 5. Rate of convergence of the empty system probability $p_0(t)$ in the interval $[0, 60]$ given two different initial conditions: $p_0(0) = 1$ (**red line**), $p_{250}(0) = 1$ (**blue line**).

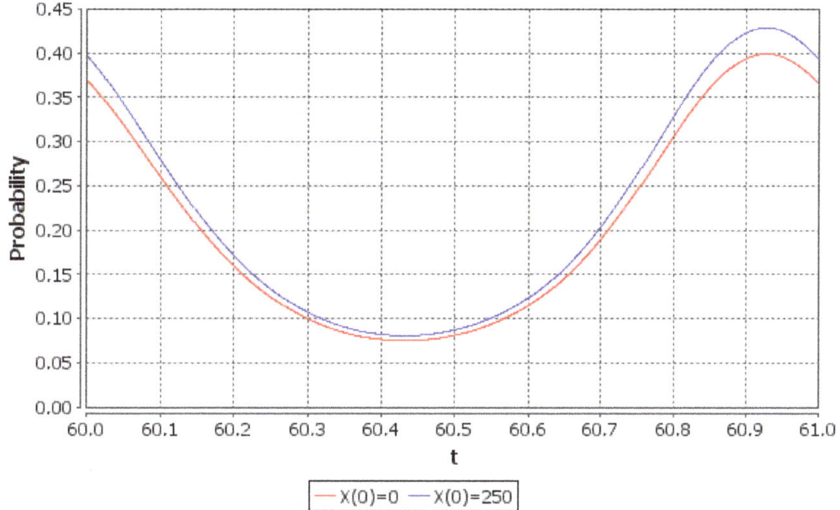

Figure 6. Limiting probability $p_0(t)$ of the empty queue given two different initial conditions: $p_0(0) = 1$ (**red line**), $p_{250}(0) = 1$ (**blue line**).

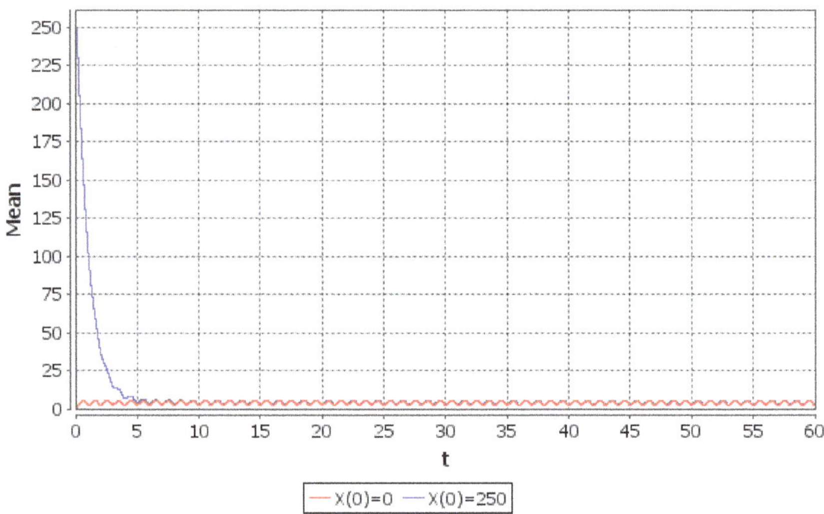

Figure 7. Rate of convergence of the conditional mean $E(t,k)$ number of customers in the system in the interval $[0,60]$: $E(t,0)$ (**red line**), $E(t,250)$ (**blue line**).

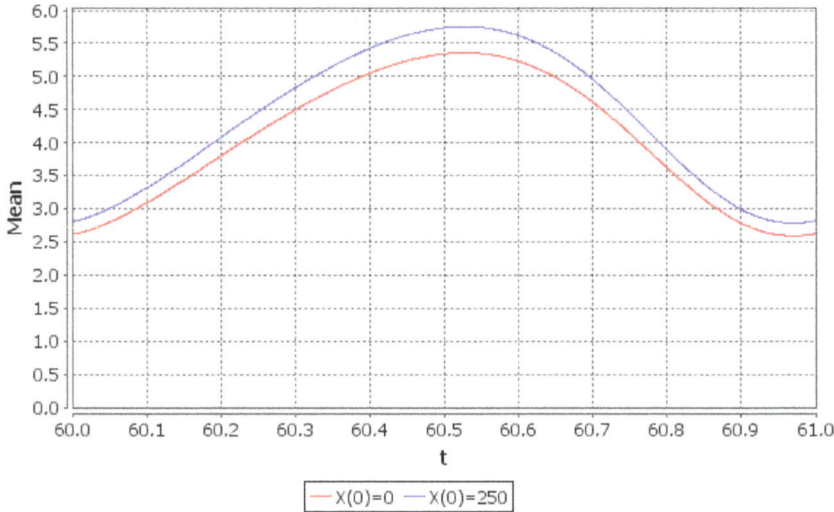

Figure 8. Limiting conditional mean $E(t,k)$ number of customers in the system: $E(t,0)$ (**red line**), $E(t,250)$ (**blue line**).

5. Time-Varying Markovian Bulk-Arrival and Bulk-Service System with State-Dependent Control

In the recent paper [35] the authors considered the Markovian bulk-arrival and bulk-service system with the general state-dependent control (see also [35–39]). The total number

$X(t)$ of customers at time t in that system constitutes CTMC with state space $\{0, 1, 2, \dots\}$. Its generator $Q(t) = (q_{ij}(t))_{i,j=0}^{\infty}$ has quite a specific structure:

$$
q_{ij} = \begin{cases} h_{ij}, & \text{if } 0 \le i \le k-1, \; j \ge 0, \\ b_{i-j+k}, & \text{if } i \ge k, \; j \ge i-k, \\ 0, & \text{otherwise,} \end{cases}
\tag{30}
$$

where $k \ge 1$ is the fixed integer. For further explanations and the motivation behind such structure of $Q(t)$ we refer the reader to [Section 1] in [35]. The purpose of this section is to show that for at least one particular case of this system, even when the intensities are time-dependent, one can obtain the upper bounds for the rate of convergence using the method based on the logarithmic norm. Specifically, we take the example, (in the example of [Section 7] in [35] the entries of the intensity matrix $Q(t)$ are: $h_{i,i-1} = \mu$, $h_{i,i+1} = \lambda$, $h_{i,i} = -(\lambda + \mu)$, $b_0 = a$, $b_{k+1} = b$, $b_k = -(a+b)$ and $k = 3$). from the Section 7 of [35], with the exception that all the transition intensities are time-dependent i.e., $b_i = \lambda(t)$ and $a_i = \mu(t)$ and are both nonnegative locally integrable on $[0, \infty)$. Then the transposed generator $A(t) = (a_{ij}(t))_{i,j=0}^{\infty} = Q^T(t)$ of $X(t)$ has the form

$$
A(t) = \begin{pmatrix}
-\lambda(t) & \mu(t) & 0 & \mu(t) & 0 & 0 & \cdots \\
\lambda(t) & -(\lambda(t)+\mu(t)) & \mu(t) & 0 & \mu(t) & 0 & \cdots \\
0 & \lambda(t) & -(\lambda(t)+\mu(t)) & 0 & 0 & \mu(t) & \cdots \\
0 & 0 & \lambda(t) & -(\lambda(t)+\mu(t)) & 0 & 0 & \cdots \\
0 & 0 & 0 & \lambda(t) & -(\lambda(t)+\mu(t)) & 0 & \cdots \\
0 & 0 & 0 & 0 & \lambda(t) & -(\lambda(t)+\mu(t)) & \cdots \\
\vdots & \vdots & \vdots & \vdots & \vdots & \vdots & \ddots
\end{pmatrix}
\tag{31}
$$

Denote the distribution of $X(t)$ by $\mathbf{p}(t)$ i.e., $\mathbf{p}(t) = (p_0(t), p_1(t), \dots)^{\mathrm{T}} = \sum_{k=0}^{\infty} \mathrm{P}(X(t) = k)\mathbf{e}_k$ (as above, $\mathbf{e}_k$ denotes the kth unit basis vector). The ergodicity bound for $X(t)$ in the null ergodic case is given below in the *Theorem 4*.

Theorem 4. *If* $\int_0^{\infty} \left(\lambda(t)(1-\sigma) + \mu(t)(1-\sigma^{-3})\right) dt = +\infty$ *for some* $\sigma \in (0,1)$, *then the Markov chain $X(t)$ is null ergodic,*

$$
\sum_{i=0}^{\infty} \sigma^i p_i(t) \le e^{-\int_0^t \left(\lambda(u)+\mu(u)-\sigma\lambda(u)-\sigma^{-3}\mu(u)\right) du} \sum_{i=0}^{\infty} \sigma^i p_i(0), \quad t \ge 0,
\tag{32}
$$

and for any $n \ge 0$ and $N \ge 0$ the following inequality holds:

$$
\mathrm{P}(X(t) > n \mid X(0) = N) \ge 1 - \sigma^{N-n} e^{-\int_0^t \left(\lambda(u)+\mu(u)-\sigma\lambda(u)-\sigma^{-3}\mu(u)\right) du}.
\tag{33}
$$

Proof. Fix $\sigma > 0$ and define the decreasing sequence of positive numbers $\{\delta_n, n \ge 0\}$ by $\delta_n = \sigma^n$. Put $\tilde{\mathbf{p}}(t) = \Lambda \mathbf{p}(t)$, where $\Lambda = diag(\delta_0, \delta_1, \dots)$. Then we have (6). Denote by $-\tilde{\alpha}_k(t)$ the sum of all elements in the kth column of $\tilde{A}(t)$ i.e.

$$
\begin{aligned}
\tilde{\alpha}_0(t) &= (1-\sigma)\lambda(t), \\
\tilde{\alpha}_k(t) &= (1-\sigma)\left(\lambda(t) + \mu(t) - \sigma^{-1}\mu(t)\right), \; k = 1, 2, \\
\tilde{\alpha}_k(t) &= \underbrace{\lambda(t) + \mu(t) - \sigma\lambda(t) - \sigma^{-3}\mu(t)}_{=\beta(t)}, \; k \ge 3.
\end{aligned}
$$

If $0 < \sigma < 1$ then $\tilde{\alpha}_0(t) \ge \beta(t)$, $\tilde{\alpha}_1(t) \ge \beta(t)$ and $\tilde{\alpha}_2(t) \ge \beta(t)$, and thus (32) and (33) follow from (4) and (8) respectively. $\square$

The ergodicity bound in the weakly ergodic case, state below in the Theorem 5, is obtained by analogy with the Theorem 1. Define an increasing sequence of positive numbers $\{\delta_n, n \geq 0\}$. Then the matrix $B^{**}(t)$ built from the matrix $A(t)$, in the same way as it is done in the Section 3, has the form:

$$
B^{**}(t) = \begin{pmatrix}
-(\lambda(t)+\mu(t)) & \mu(t)\frac{\delta_1}{\delta_2} & -\mu(t)\frac{\delta_1}{\delta_3} & \mu(t)\frac{\delta_1}{\delta_4} & 0 & 0 & \cdots \\
\lambda(t)\frac{\delta_2}{\delta_1} & -(\lambda(t)+\mu(t)) & 0 & 0 & \mu(t)\frac{\delta_2}{\delta_5} & 0 & \cdots \\
0 & \lambda(t)\frac{\delta_3}{\delta_2} & -(\lambda(t)+\mu(t)) & 0 & 0 & \mu(t)\frac{\delta_3}{\delta_6} & \cdots \\
0 & 0 & \lambda(t)\frac{\delta_4}{\delta_3} & -(\lambda(t)+\mu(t)) & 0 & 0 & \cdots \\
0 & 0 & 0 & \lambda(t)\frac{\delta_5}{\delta_4} & -(\lambda(t)+\mu(t)) & 0 & \cdots \\
0 & 0 & 0 & 0 & \lambda(t)\frac{\delta_6}{\delta_5} & -(\lambda(t)+\mu(t)) & \cdots \\
\vdots & \vdots & \vdots & \vdots & \vdots & \vdots & \ddots
\end{pmatrix}
\tag{34}
$$

Denote by $-\tilde{\alpha}_k(t)$ the sum of all elements in the kth column of $B^{**}(t)$ i.e.,

$$
\alpha_1(t) = \lambda(t) + \mu(t) - \lambda(t)\frac{\delta_2}{\delta_1},
$$

$$
\alpha_2(t) = \lambda(t) + \mu(t) - \lambda(t)\frac{\delta_3}{\delta_2} - \mu(t)\frac{\delta_1}{\delta_2},
$$

$$
\alpha_3(t) = \lambda(t) + \mu(t) - \lambda(t)\frac{\delta_4}{\delta_3} - \mu(t)\frac{\delta_1}{\delta_3},
$$

$$
\alpha_k(t) = \lambda(t) + \mu(t) - \lambda(t)\frac{\delta_{k+1}}{\delta_k} - \mu(t)\frac{\delta_{k-3}}{\delta_k}, \ k \geq 4.
$$

Since the logarithmic norm of $B^{**}(t)$ is equal to $-\beta(t) = -\min(\min_{1 \leq k \leq 3} \alpha_k(t), \inf_{k \geq 4} \alpha_k(t))$, we can apply (4) to (13) and (15) with $\delta_{k+1} = \sigma\delta_k, k \geq 5$.

Theorem 5. *If $\int_0^\infty \left(\lambda(t)(1-\sigma) + \mu(t)(1-\sigma^{-3})\right) dt = +\infty$ for some $\sigma > 0$, then the Markov chain $X(t)$ is weakly ergodic and the ergodicity bound (15) holds.*

As the numerical example we again consider the periodic case: $\lambda(t) = 3(1 + \sin \pi t)$ and $\mu(t) = 4(1 + \cos 2\pi t)$. By direct inspection it can be checked that the sequence $\{\delta_n, n \geq 1\}$, defined by $\delta_n = \frac{10}{9}^{n-1}$, leads to $\beta(t) = \alpha_2(t)$. Thus the conditions of the *Theorem 5* are fulfilled with $\sigma = \frac{10}{9}$. The pre-limiting and the limiting values of the same quantities as in the two previous examples—$p_0(t)$ and $E(t,k)$—are shown in Figures 9–12.

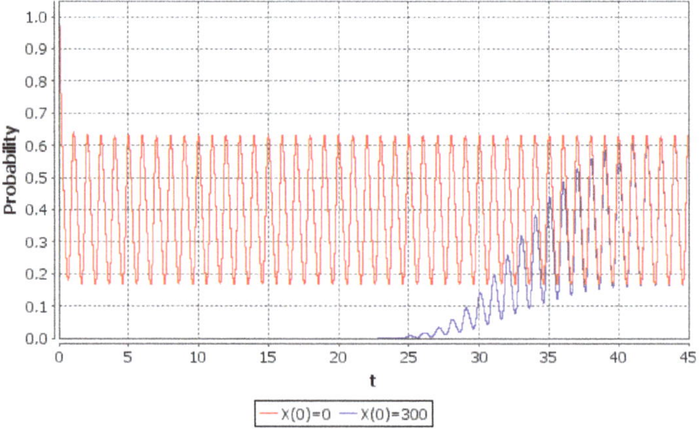

Figure 9. Rate of convergence of the empty system probability $p_0(t)$ in the interval $[0, 45]$ given two different initial conditions: $p_0(0) = 1$ (**red line**), $p_{250}(0) = 1$ (**blue line**).

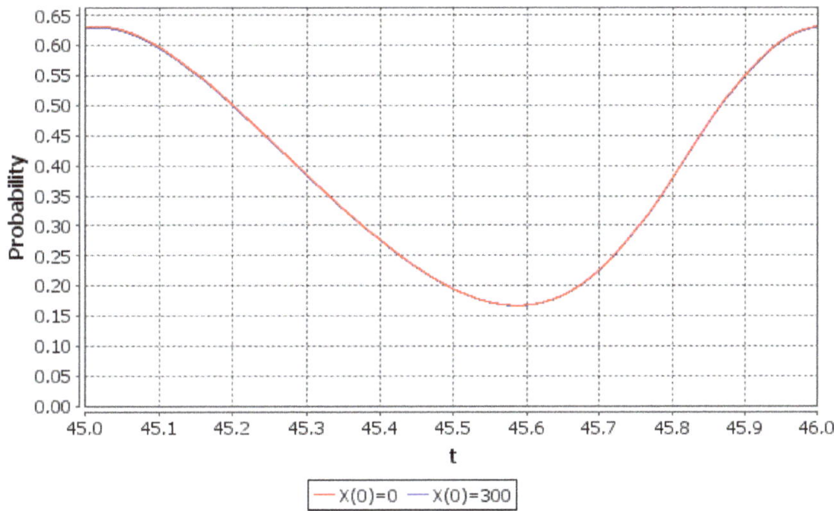

Figure 10. Limiting probability $p_0(t)$ of the empty queue given two different initial conditions: $p_0(0) = 1$ (**red line**), $p_{300}(0) = 1$ (*blue line*).

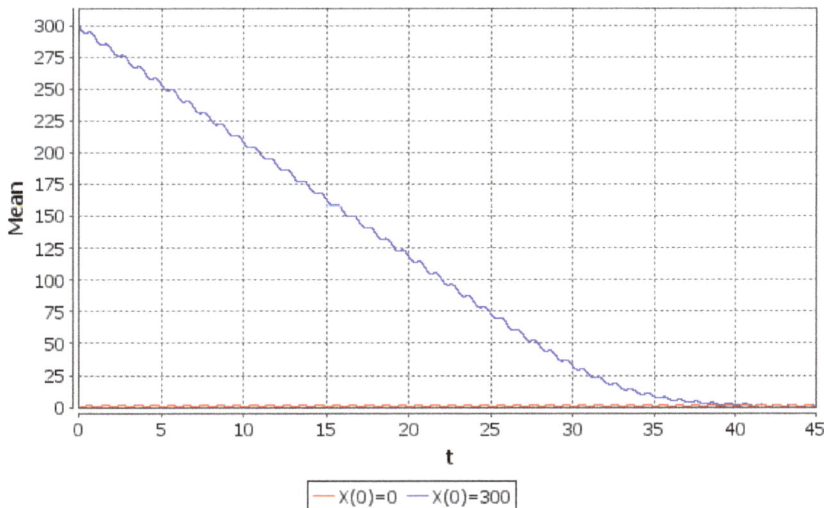

Figure 11. Rate of convergence of the conditional mean $E(t, k)$ number of customers in the system in the interval $[0, 45]$: $E(t, 0)$ (**red line**), $E(t, 300)$ (**blue line**).

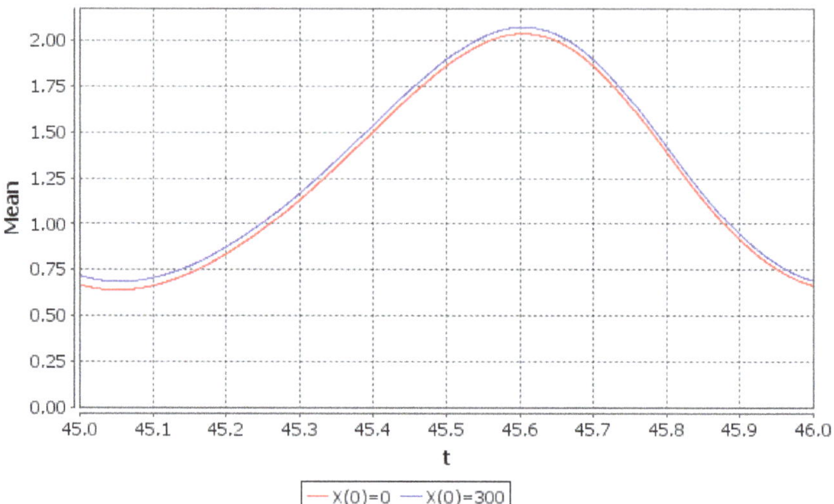

Figure 12. Limiting conditional mean $E(t,k)$ number of customers in the system: $E(t,0)$ (**red line**), $E(t,300)$ (**blue line**).

6. Conclusions

As can be seen from the last three sections, in order to obtain the ergodicity bounds the values of $\lambda(t)$ and $\mu(t)$ for each t may not be needed. Instead it may be sufficient to know only the time-average intensities $\overline{\lambda} = \frac{1}{t}\lim_{t\to\infty}\int_0^t \lambda(u)du$ and $\overline{\mu} = \frac{1}{t}\lim_{t\to\infty}\int_0^t \mu(u)du$. For periodic intensities with the smallest common multiple of the periods T, the values $\overline{\lambda}$ and $\overline{\mu}$ are exactly the average arrival and service intensity over one period.

The classes of CTMC to which the logarithmic norm method is applicable and gives meaningful results is not limited to those considered in this paper, (necessary and sufficient conditions for a CTMC "to fit" the logarithmic norm method are not known). For example, the same reasoning, which has led to the Theorem 1, can be used to obtain the upper bounds for the rate of convergence of the $M_t/M_t/S/\infty$ system with any (finite) number of servers. Moreover, whenever $X(t)$ is weakly ergodic, the analysis can be carried on beyond what is stated in the *Theorem 1*. For example, one can obtain the perturbation bounds (see e.g., [40]) and study different state space truncation options: one-sided or two sided (see e.g., [29,41,42]).

Author Contributions: Investigation, A.Z., R.R., Y.S., I.K. and V.K. All authors contributed equally to this work. All authors have read and agreed to the published version of the manuscript.

Funding: The research was supported by the Ministry of Science and Higher Education of the Russian Federation, project No. 075-15-2020-799.

Institutional Review Board Statement: Not applicable.

Informed Consent Statement: Not applicable.

Data Availability Statement: Data sharing is not applicable to this article.

Conflicts of Interest: The author declares no conflict of interest.

References

1. Liu, Y.; Whitt, W. Stabilizing performance in a service system with time-varying arrivals and customer feedback. *Eur. J. Oper. Res.* **2017**, *256*, 473–486. [CrossRef]
2. Liu, Y. Staffing to stabilize the tail probability of delay in service systems with time-varying demand. *Oper. Res.* **2018**, *66*, 514–534. [CrossRef]

3. Kwon, S.; Gautam, N. Guaranteeing performance based on time-stability for energy-efficient data centers. *IIE Trans.* **2016**, *48*, 812–825. [CrossRef]
4. Whitt, W.; You, W. *Time-Varying Robust Queueing*; Columbia University: New York, NY, USA, 2019.
5. Schwarz, J.A.; Selinka, G.; Stolletz, R. Performance analysis of time-dependent queueing systems: Survey and classification. *Omega* **2016**, *63*, 170–189. [CrossRef]
6. Whitt, W. Time-Varying Queues. Available online: http://www.columbia.edu/~ww2040/TVQ_082617.pdf (accessed on 28 October 2020).
7. Falin, G.I. Periodic queues in heavy traffic. *Adv. Appl. Probab.* **1989**, *21*, 485–487. [CrossRef]
8. Masuyama, H. Error bounds for augmented truncations of discrete-time block-monotone Markov chains under geometric drift conditions. *Adv. Appl. Probab.* **2015**, *47*, 83–105. [CrossRef]
9. Tweedie, R.L. Truncation approximations of invariant measures for Markov chains. *J. Appl. Probab.* **1998**, *35*, 517–536. [CrossRef]
10. Green, L.; Kolesar, P. The pointwise stationary approximation for queues with nonstationary arrivals. *Manag. Sci.* **1991**, *37*, 84–97. [CrossRef]
11. Di Crescenzo, A.; Nobile, A.G. Diffusion approximation to a queueing system with time-dependent arrival and service rates. *Queueing Syst.* **1995**, *19*, 41–62. [CrossRef]
12. Di Crescenzo, A.; Giorno, V.; Nobile, A.G.; Ricciardi, L.M. On the $M/M/1$ queue with catastrophes and its continuous approximation. *Queueing Syst.* **2003**, *43*, 329–347. [CrossRef]
13. Kolesar, P.J.; Rider, P.J.; Craybill, T.B.; Walker, W.E. A queueing linear-programming approach to scheduling police patrol cars. *Oper. Res.* **1975**, *23*, 1045–1062. [CrossRef]
14. Taaffe, M.R.; Ong, K.L. Approximating Nonstationary $Ph(t)/M(t)/s/c$ queueing systems. *Ann. Oper. Res.* **1987**, *8*, 103–116. [CrossRef]
15. Clark, G.M. Use of Polya distributions in approximate solutions to nonstationary $M/M/s$ queues. *Commun. ACM* **1981**, *24*, 206–217. [CrossRef]
16. Massey, W.; Pender, J. Gaussian skewness approximation for dynamic rate multiserver queues with abandonment. *Queueing Syst.* **2013**, *75*, 243–327. [CrossRef]
17. Van Dijk, N.M.; van Brummelen, S.P.J.; Boucherie, R.J. Uniformization: Basics, extensions and applications. *Perform. Eval.* **2018**, *118*, 8–32. [CrossRef]
18. Arns, M.; Buchholz, P.; Panchenko, A. On the numerical analysis of inhomogeneous continuous-time Markov chains. *Informs J. Comput.* **2010**, *22*, 416–432. [CrossRef]
19. Andreychenko, A.; Sandmann, W.; Wolf, V. Approximate adaptive uniformization of continuous-time Markov chains. *Appl. Math. Model.* **2018**, *61*, 561–576. [CrossRef]
20. Burak, M.R.; Korytkowski, P. Inhomogeneous CTMC Birth-and-Death Models Solved by Uniformization with Steady-State Detection. *ACM Trans. Model. Comput. Simul.* **2020**, *30*, 1–18. [CrossRef]
21. Burak, M.R. Efficiency Improvements to Uniformization for Markovian Birth-and-Death Models. In Proceedings of the 2018 23rd International Conference on Methods & Models in Automation & Robotics (MMAR), Miedzyzdroje, Poland, 27–30 August 2018; pp. 741–746.
22. Ingolfsson, A.; Akhmetshina, E.; Budge, S.; Li, Y.; Wu, X. A survey and experimental comparison of service-level-approximation methods for nonstationary M (t)/M/s (t) queueing systems with exhaustive discipline. *Informs J. Comput.* **2007**, *19*, 201–214. [CrossRef]
23. Li, Y.F.; Zio, E.; Lin, Y.H. Methods of solutions of inhomogeneous continuous time Markov chains for degradation process modeling. *Appl. Reliab. Eng. Risk Anal. Probab. Models Stat. Inference* **2013**, 3–16. [CrossRef]
24. Katoen, J.-P.; Zapreev, I.S. Safe on-the-fly steady-state detection for time-bounded reachability. In Proceedings of the 3rd International Conference on the Quantitative Evaluation of Systems, California, CA, USA, 11–14 September 2016.
25. Down, D.; Meyn, S.P.; Tweedie, R.L. Exponential and uniform ergodicity of Markov processes. *Ann. Probab.* **1995**, *23*, 1671–1691. [CrossRef]
26. Meyn, S.P.; Tweedie, R.L. *Markov Chains and Stochastic Stability*; Springer Science and Business Media: New York, NY, USA, 2012.
27. Zeifman, A.; Satin, Y.; Kiseleva, K.; Korolev, V. On the Rate of Convergence for a Characteristic of Multidimensional Birth-Death Process. *Mathematics* **2019**, *7*, 477. [CrossRef]
28. Zeifman, A.; Satin, Y.; Kryukova, A.; Razumchik, R.; Kiseleva, K.; Shilova, G. On Three Methods for Bounding the Rate of Convergence for Some Continuous-Time Markov Chains. *Int. J. Appl. Math. Comput. Sci.* **2020**, *30*, 251–266.
29. Zeifman, A.; Satin, Y.; Korolev, V.; Shorgin, S. On truncations for weakly ergodic inhomogeneous birth and death processes. *Int. J. Appl. Math. Comput. Sci.* **2014**, *24*, 503–518. [CrossRef]
30. Zeifman, A.I.; Korotysheva, A.; Satin, Y.; Kiseleva, K.; Korolev, V.; Shorgin, S. Bounds for Markovian Queues With Possible Catastrophes. In Proceedings of the 31st Conference on Modelling and Simulation, Budapest, Hungary, 23–26 May 2017; pp. 628–634.
31. Marin, A.; Rossi, S. A Queueing Model that Works Only on the Biggest Jobs. *Lect. Notes Comput. Sci. Book Ser.* **2020**, *12039*, 118–132.
32. Zeifman, A.; Razumchik, R.; Satin, Y.; Kovalev, I. Ergodicity Bounds for the Markovian Queue With Time-Varying Transition Intensities, Batch Arrivals and One Queue Skipping Policy. *arXiv* **2020**, arXiv:2007.15833.
33. Klefsjö, B. The hnbue and hnwue classes of life distributions. *Nav. Res. Logist.* **1982**, *29*, 331–344. [CrossRef]

34. Conti, P.L.J. An asymptotic test for a geometric process against a lattice distribution with monotone hazard. *Ital. Statist. Soc.* **1997**, *6*, 213–231. [CrossRef]
35. Chen, A.; Wu, X.; Zhang, J. Markovian bulk-arrival and bulk-service queues with general state-dependent control. *Queueing Syst.* **2020**, 1–48. [CrossRef]
36. Chen, A.; Renshaw, E. Markovian bulk-arriving queues with state-dependent control at idle time. *Adv. Appl. Probab.* **2004**, *36*, 499–524. [CrossRef]
37. Chen, A.; Pollett, P.; Li, J.; Zhang, H. Markovian bulk-arrival and bulk-service queues with state-dependent control. *Queueing Syst.* **2010**, *64*, 267–304. [CrossRef]
38. Chen, A.; Li, J.; Hou, Z.; Ng, K.W. Decay properties and quasi-stationary distributions for stopped Markovian bulk-arrival and bulk-service queues. *Queueing Syst.* **2010**, *66*, 275–311. [CrossRef]
39. Li, J.; Chen, A. Decay property of stopped Markovian bulk-arriving queues. *Adv. Appl. Probab.* **2008**, *40*, 95–121. [CrossRef]
40. Zeifman, A.; Korolev, V.; Satin, Y. Two approaches to the construction of perturbation bounds for continuous-time Markov chains. *Mathematics* **2020**, *8*, 253. [CrossRef]
41. Satin, Y.; Kiseleva, K.; Shorgin, S.; Korolev, V.; Zeifman, A. Two-Sided Truncations for The Mt/Mt/S Queueing Model. In Proceedings of the 31st European Conference on Modelling and Simulation, Budapest, Hungary, 23–26 May 2017; pp. 635–641.
42. Zeifman, A.; Leorato, S.; Orsingher, E.; Satin, Y.; Shilova, G. Some universal limits for nonhomogeneous birth and death processes.*Queueing Syst.* **2006**, *52*, 139–151. [CrossRef]

Article

Discrete Velocity Boltzmann Model for Quasi-Incompressible Hydrodynamics

Oleg Ilyin

Dorodnicyn Computing Center, Federal Research Center "Computer Science and Control" of Russian Academy of Sciences, Vavilova-40, 119333 Moscow, Russia; oilyin@gmail.com

Abstract: In this paper, we consider the development of the two-dimensional discrete velocity Boltzmann model on a nine-velocity lattice. Compared to the conventional lattice Boltzmann approach for the present model, the collision rules for the interacting particles are formulated explicitly. The collisions are tailored in such a way that mass, momentum and energy are conserved and the *H*-theorem is fulfilled. By applying the Chapman–Enskog expansion, we show that the model recovers quasi-incompressible hydrodynamic equations for small Mach number limit and we derive the closed expression for the viscosity, depending on the collision cross-sections. In addition, the numerical implementation of the model with the on-lattice streaming and local collision step is proposed. As test problems, the shear wave decay and Taylor–Green vortex are considered, and a comparison of the numerical simulations with the analytical solutions is presented.

Keywords: discrete velocity method; lattice Boltzmann method; computational fluid dynamics

Citation: Ilyin, O. Discrete Velocity Boltzmann Model for Quasi-Incompressible Hydrodynamics. *Mathematics* **2021**, *9*, 993. https://doi.org/10.3390/math9090993

Academic Editors: Mikhail Posypkin, Andrey Gorshenin, Vladimir Titarev and Janos Sztrik

Received: 27 March 2021
Accepted: 20 April 2021
Published: 28 April 2021

Publisher's Note: MDPI stays neutral with regard to jurisdictional claims in published maps and institutional affiliations.

1. Introduction

In the kinetic theory, the distribution function of a rarefied gaseous system is governed by the Boltzmann equation or its models [1]. In the applications, the discretization of these equations in the velocity (and physical) space is usually performed. One of the most popular discretization approaches is the Lattice–Boltzmann (LB) method [2–5] which was initially developed as an alternative to the continuum fluid methods like Navier–Stokes equations [6]; furthermore, the method has been extended to the rarefied flows modeling [7–19]. The conventional LB model has the following form

$$\frac{df_i}{dt} = \frac{1}{\tau}(f_i^{eq} - f_i), \quad i = 1\ldots N,$$

where $f_i(t, x)$ is the distribution function related to the particles with the velocity c_i, $i = 1\ldots N$, τ is the relaxation time, f_i^{eq} is the local equilibrium, N is the number of the discrete velocities, $\frac{d}{dt} = \frac{\partial}{\partial t} + c_i\frac{\partial}{\partial r}$, r is the spatial variable. In this approach, the collisions between the particles are described in a phenomenological way, i.e., it is postulated that, due to the collisions, the distribution function tends to the local equilibrium state at a rate proportional to $f_i^{eq} - f_i$. For LB models, the local equilibrium is usually taken as a finite-order polynomial on the bulk velocity, and the conservation laws for mass and momentum are satisfied by construction. On the other hand, for this form of the local equilibrium, the *H*-theorem does not exist [20–22]. To overcome this issue, models with non-polynomial equilibria have been proposed [23–26].

Another possible discretization technique is the discrete velocity (DV) Boltzmann method [27–30], the general DV Boltzmann model reads as

$$\frac{df_i}{dt} = \sum_{jkl}^{N} A_{kl}^{ij}(f_k f_l - f_i f_j) \equiv I_i[f_1, \ldots f_N], \quad i = 1\ldots N, \tag{1}$$

where $A_{kl}^{ij} = A_{ij}^{kl} \geq 0$ are the transition probabilities.

Compared to the LB method, the DV models have some attractive properties. Similarly to the Boltzmann equation, the binary collisions are described explicitly. Moreover, by construction, the H-theorem is valid for these models [28], i.e.,

$$\frac{dH}{dt} \leq 0, \quad H(t) = \int d\mathbf{r} \sum_{i}^{N} f_i \log(f_i).$$

Moreover, the local equilibrium for DV kinetic Boltzmann models can be obtained as an exponential function of the macroscopic variables. The DV Boltzmann approach attracted the attention of many researchers several decades ago, but, at present, is significantly less popular than the LB method. For instance, the well-known four velocity Broadwell equation in two dimensions has been investigated thoroughly [31–36], this model has correct collision invariants, but its discrete velocity set is too small and lacks isotropy [37]; therefore, the correct description of the hydrodynamics is impossible in the framework of this model. In addition, another subtle feature should be mentioned: for the discrete velocity models, the molecular chaos hypothesis can be violated, i.e., the particles can be correlated before the collision [38]. This is undesirable, but the influence of this effect on the flow properties in applications is not clear. Furthermore, one should construct the DV Boltzmann models in such a way that the only conserved variables are mass, momentum and energy. The equilibrium state is obtained as minimum of the H-function under the constraint that these variables are not changed by collisions. The presence of other conserved quantities (spurious invariants) changes the form of the local equilibrium state, this, in turn, leads to a distortion of the hydrodynamic equations. The construction of DV Boltzmann models without excessive invariants is a non-trivial procedure [39–42].

In this paper we consider a DV Boltzmann model on a nine velocity, two-dimensional lattice. As a starting point, we consider the local equilibrium for the general DV Boltzmann model and its expansion at the vicinity of the absolute Maxwell distribution. Next, the Chapman–Enskog expansion for the DV Boltzmann model is performed in order to derive the hydrodynamic equations. In addition, we show that the model does not have invariants without physical meaning. The considered model has four different possible transition probabilities. In terms of the LB theory, this model can be considered as a scheme with multiple relaxation times. For viscosity, we obtain a closed expression depending on the values of the transition probabilities. If the viscosity is fixed, we obtain a constraint on the transition probabilities, but three of them can be chosen as free parameters; for instance, they can be adjusted to improve stability properties. As benchmark problems, we consider the shear wave decay and Taylor–Green vortex. The numerical experiments show excellent agreement between the numerical simulation results and analytical solutions.

2. Equilibrium for DV Boltzmann Kinetic Model and the Euler Equations

The local equilibrium of the model (1) is obtained as a minimum of the H functional with the constraints corresponding to the conservation laws; it has the following form (Formula (5) in [43])

$$f_i^{eq} = \exp(a + \mathbf{b} \cdot \mathbf{c}_i + d c_i^2), \quad i = 1 \dots N, \tag{2}$$

where the coefficients $a_i, \mathbf{b}_i, d_i$ depend on the density, flow velocityand temperature $\rho, \mathbf{u}, \theta$ and "·" defines scalar product. In this paragraph, we consider the particle's dynamics in D spatial dimensions. We assume that the local equilibrium is close to the absolute equilibrium with the density $\rho_0 = 1$ flow velocity $u_0 = 0$ and the temperature θ_0; then, one can write down the absolute equilibrium denoted as w_i in the form

$$w_i = \exp(a^0 + d^0 c_i^2), \quad i = 1 \dots N,$$

where $a^0 = a^0(\rho_0, \theta_0), d^0 = d^0(\rho_0, \theta_0)$, we also term w_i as lattice weights. The conservation laws for mass, momentum, energy yield the following equations for the lattice velocities and the lattice weights

$$\sum_i w_i = 1, \quad \sum_i w_i \boldsymbol{c}_i = 0, \quad \sum_i w_i \boldsymbol{c}_i \boldsymbol{c}_i = \theta_0 \delta, \tag{3}$$

note that $\boldsymbol{c}_i \boldsymbol{c}_i$ is a tensor with elements $c_{i,\alpha} c_{i,\beta}, \alpha, \beta = 1 \dots D$, and that D is the number of spatial dimensions. For the coefficients, we have the expression

$$a_i = a_i^0 + \Delta a, \quad \boldsymbol{b}_i = \Delta \boldsymbol{b}, \quad d_i = d_i^0 + \Delta d,$$

where $\Delta a, \Delta \boldsymbol{b}, \Delta d$ are small quantities. Similarly to the previous studies [43] we expand the expression (2) on $\Delta a, \Delta \boldsymbol{b}, \Delta d$, and one has

$$f_i^{eq} = w_i \left(1 + \Delta a + \frac{1}{2} \Delta a^2 + o(\Delta a^2) \right) \times$$

$$\times \left(1 + \Delta \boldsymbol{b} \cdot \boldsymbol{c}_i + \frac{1}{2} \Delta \boldsymbol{b} \Delta \boldsymbol{b} : \boldsymbol{c}_i \boldsymbol{c}_i + o(\Delta b^2) \right) \left(1 + \Delta d c_i^2 + \frac{1}{2} \Delta d^2 c_i^4 + o(\Delta d^2) \right) =$$

$$= w_i \left(1 + \Delta a + \Delta \boldsymbol{b} \cdot \boldsymbol{c}_i + \Delta d c_i^2 + \right.$$

$$\left. + \frac{1}{2} \Delta a^2 + \Delta a \Delta \boldsymbol{b} \cdot \boldsymbol{c}_i + \Delta a \Delta d c_i^2 + \frac{1}{2} \Delta \boldsymbol{b} \Delta \boldsymbol{b} : \boldsymbol{c}_i \boldsymbol{c}_i + \Delta d \Delta \boldsymbol{b} \cdot \boldsymbol{c}_i c_i^2 + \frac{1}{2} \Delta d^2 c_i^4 \right) + o(\Delta^2) \tag{4}$$

where $o(\Delta^2)$ stands for $o(\Delta a^2), o(\Delta b^2), o(\Delta d^2)$, also the operator ":" is tensor convolution. Next, we assume that

$$\rho = 1 + \Delta \rho, \quad u = \Delta u, \quad \theta = \theta_0 + \Delta \theta,$$

where $\Delta \rho, \Delta u, \Delta \theta$ are small. Taking (4) into account, for the first local equilibrium moments, we derive the following equations

$$\sum_i f_i^{eq} = 1 + \Delta \rho = 1 + \Delta a + D\theta_0 \Delta d + \frac{1}{2} \Delta a^2 + D\theta_0 \Delta a \Delta d + \frac{\theta_0}{2} \Delta b^2 + \frac{m_4}{2} \Delta d^2, \tag{5}$$

$$\sum_i f_i^{eq} \boldsymbol{c}_i - \Delta u + \Delta \rho \Delta u = \theta_0 \Delta \boldsymbol{b} + \theta_0 \Delta a \Delta \boldsymbol{b} + D^{-1} m_4 \Delta d \Delta \boldsymbol{b}, \tag{6}$$

$$\sum_i f_i^{eq} c_i^2 = D\theta_0 + D\theta_0 \Delta \rho + D\Delta \theta + \Delta u^2 + D\Delta \rho \Delta \theta =$$

$$= D\theta_0 \left(1 + \Delta a + \frac{1}{2} \Delta a^2 \right) + m_4 \left(\Delta d + \Delta a \Delta d + \frac{1}{2D} \Delta b^2 \right) + \frac{m_6}{2} \Delta d^2, \tag{7}$$

and we omitted third-order terms and used the definitions

$$m_4 = \sum_i w_i c_i^4, \quad m_6 = \sum_i w_i c_i^6. \tag{8}$$

We assume that $\Delta \rho, \Delta u, \Delta \theta$ are of the same order of smallness, which we define as $O(\Delta)$. Then, we seek solutions to the Equations (5)–(7) in the form

$$\Delta a = \Delta a_{lin} + \Delta a_{nonl}, \quad \Delta \boldsymbol{b} = \Delta \boldsymbol{b}_{lin} + \Delta \boldsymbol{b}_{nonl}, \quad \Delta d = \Delta d_{lin} + \Delta d_{nonl},$$

where the terms $\Delta a_{lin}, \Delta \boldsymbol{b}_{lin}, \Delta d_{lin}$ are solutions to the linearized Equations (5)–(7) of order $O(\Delta)$ and $\Delta a_{nonl}, \Delta \boldsymbol{b}_{nonl}, \Delta d_{nonl}$ are nonlinear corrections of order $O(\Delta^2)$. First, from the linearized Equations (5)–(7), one has

$$\Delta \rho = \Delta a_{lin} + D\theta_0 \Delta d_{lin}, \quad \Delta u = \theta_0 \Delta \boldsymbol{b}_{lin}, \quad D\theta_0 \Delta \rho + D\Delta \theta = D\theta_0 \Delta a_{lin} + m_4 \Delta d_{lin},$$

these equations have the solutions

$$\Delta a_{lin} = \Delta \rho - \frac{D^2 \theta_0 \Delta \theta}{m_4 - D^2 \theta_0^2}, \quad \Delta \boldsymbol{b}_{lin} = \frac{\Delta u}{\theta_0}, \quad \Delta d_{lin} = \frac{D\Delta \theta}{m_4 - D^2 \theta_0^2}. \tag{9}$$

Next, we find the nonlinear corrections Δa_{nonl}, $\Delta \boldsymbol{b}_{nonl}$, Δd_{nonl} from the Equations (5)–(7). It would be convenient to start with the Equation (6), which can be rewritten as

$$\Delta \rho \Delta \boldsymbol{u} = \theta_0 \Delta a_{lin} \Delta \boldsymbol{b}_{lin} + D^{-1} m_4 \Delta d_{lin} \Delta \boldsymbol{b}_{lin} + \theta_0 \Delta \boldsymbol{b}_{nonl},$$

from the last equation, we immediately obtain

$$\Delta \boldsymbol{b}_{nonl} = -\frac{\Delta \theta \Delta \boldsymbol{u}}{\theta_0^2}. \tag{10}$$

Consideration of the Equations (5) and (7) yields

$$\Delta a_{nonl} + D\theta_0 \Delta d_{nonl} + \frac{1}{2}\Delta a_{lin}^2 + D\theta_0 \Delta a_{lin}\Delta d_{lin} + \frac{1}{2}\theta_0 \Delta \boldsymbol{b}_{lin}^2 + \frac{m_4}{2}\Delta d_{lin}^2 = 0,$$

$$D\theta_0 \Delta a_{nonl} + m_4 \Delta d_{nonl} + \frac{D\theta_0}{2}\Delta a_{lin}^2 + m_4 \Delta a_{lin}\Delta d_{lin} + \frac{m_4}{2D}\Delta \boldsymbol{b}_{lin}^2 + \frac{m_6}{2}\Delta d_{lin}^2 = \Delta \boldsymbol{u}^2 + D\Delta \rho \Delta \theta,$$

by applying (9) we get the solutions

$$\Delta a_{nonl} = -\frac{\Delta \rho^2}{2} - \frac{D\theta_0 \Delta \boldsymbol{u}^2}{(m_4 - D^2\theta_0^2)} - \frac{D^4\theta_0^2\Delta\theta^2}{2(m_4 - D^2\theta_0^2)^2} + \frac{(D\theta_0 m_6 - m_4^2)D^2\Delta\theta^2}{2(m_4 - D^2\theta_0^2)^3}, \tag{11}$$

$$\Delta d_{nonl} = -\frac{\Delta \boldsymbol{u}^2}{2D\theta_0^2} + \frac{\Delta \boldsymbol{u}^2}{(m_4 - D^2\theta_0^2)} + \frac{D^3\theta_0\Delta\theta^2}{(m_4 - D^2\theta_0^2)^2} - \frac{(m_6 - D\theta_0 m_4)D^2\Delta\theta^2}{2(m_4 - D^2\theta_0^2)^3}. \tag{12}$$

The combination of (9) and (10)–(12) leads to the following expression for f_i^{eq}

Proposition 1. *The DV local equilibrium f_i^{eq} in the form (2) can be expressed as*

$$f_i^{eq} = w_i(k_0 + \boldsymbol{k_1} \cdot \boldsymbol{c_i} + k_2 c_i^2 + \boldsymbol{k_3} : \boldsymbol{c_i c_i} + \boldsymbol{k_4} \cdot \boldsymbol{c_i} c_i^2 + k_5 c_i^4) + O(\Delta^3), \quad i = 1\ldots N, \tag{13}$$

where

$$k_0 = 1 + \Delta\rho - \frac{D\theta_0}{(m_4 - D^2\theta_0^2)}(D\Delta\theta + D\Delta\rho\Delta\theta + \Delta\boldsymbol{u}^2) + \frac{D\theta_0 m_6 - m_4^2}{2(m_4 - D^2\theta_0^2)^3}D^2\Delta\theta^2, \tag{14}$$

$$\boldsymbol{k_1} = \frac{\Delta\boldsymbol{u}}{\theta_0} + \frac{\Delta\rho\Delta\boldsymbol{u}}{\theta_0} - \frac{m_4}{\theta_0^2(m_4 - D^2\theta_0^2)}\Delta\theta\Delta\boldsymbol{u}, \tag{15}$$

$$k_2 = -\frac{\Delta\boldsymbol{u}^2}{2D\theta_0^2} + \frac{1}{(m_4 - D^2\theta_0^2)}(D\Delta\theta + D\Delta\rho\Delta\theta + \Delta\boldsymbol{u}^2) - \frac{m_6 - D\theta_0 m_4}{2(m_4 - D^2\theta_0^2)^3}D^2\Delta\theta^2, \tag{16}$$

$$\boldsymbol{k_3} = \frac{\Delta\boldsymbol{u}\Delta\boldsymbol{u}}{2\theta_0^2}, \tag{17}$$

$$\boldsymbol{k_4} = \frac{D\Delta\theta\Delta\boldsymbol{u}}{\theta_0(m_4 - D^2\theta_0^2)}, \tag{18}$$

$$k_5 = \frac{D^2\Delta\theta^2}{2(m_4 - D^2\theta_0^2)^2} \tag{19}$$

and $\Delta\rho$, $\Delta\boldsymbol{u}$ $\Delta\theta$ are small density, flow velocity and temperature variations of order $O(\Delta)$; moreover, the moments m_4 and m_6 are defined by (8), and the absolute equilibrium w_i satisfies the conditions

$$\sum_i w_i = 1, \quad \sum_i w_i \boldsymbol{c_i} = 0, \quad \sum_i w_i \boldsymbol{c_i c_i} = \theta_0 \delta,$$

where θ_0 is the reference temperature.

By applying (13)–(19), the pressure tensor P with the components $P_{\alpha\beta}, \alpha, \beta = 1 \dots D$ at the local equilibrium can be derived

$$P = \sum_i f_i^{eq}(c_i - \Delta u)(c_i - \Delta u) = \sum_i f_i^{eq}(c_i c_i - 2c_i \Delta u + \Delta u \Delta u) =$$

$$= (\theta_0 k_0 + D^{-1} m_4 k_2 + D^{-1} m_6 k_5)\delta + k_3 : R - \Delta u \Delta u + O(\Delta^3) =$$

$$= \rho \theta \delta + \frac{2D\theta_0^2 - m_4}{2D^2\theta_0^2}\Delta u^2 \delta + \frac{\Delta u \Delta u}{2\theta_0^2} : R - \Delta u \Delta u + O(\Delta^3),$$

where $\rho\theta = (1 + \Delta\rho)(\theta_0 + \Delta\theta)$ and

$$R = \sum_i w_i c_i c_i c_i c_i.$$

Now, let us assume that R is isotropic tensor; in such a case, its components can be written in the form (Formula (69) in [37])

$$R_{\alpha\beta\lambda\gamma} = \frac{m_4}{D(D+2)}(\delta_{\alpha\beta}\delta_{\lambda\gamma} + \delta_{\alpha\gamma}\delta_{\beta\lambda} + \delta_{\alpha\lambda}\delta_{\beta\gamma}), \tag{20}$$

one can see that the tensor P equalling $\rho\theta\delta + O(\Delta^3)$ is obtained, if

$$m_4 = D(D+2)\theta_0^2. \tag{21}$$

Compared to P for the local Maxwell distribution, in the DV approach, the error $O(\Delta^3)$ is observed; therefore, we can conclude that the hydrodynamics (mass and momentum equations) at the Euler level of accuracy is recovered with the errors of order $O(\Delta^3)$ if the conditions (3), (20) and (21) are satisfied.

Finally, we consider the heat flow q at the level of the Euler equations

$$2q = \sum_i f_i^{eq}(c_i - \Delta u)^2(c_i - \Delta u) = \sum_i f_i^{eq} c_i^2 c_i - 2\Delta u \cdot P - 2\rho E \Delta u + O(\Delta^3),$$

where $E = (\rho/2)(D\theta + \Delta u^2), \theta = \theta_0 + \Delta\theta, \rho = 1 + \Delta\rho$, applying (13)–(19) we obtain

$$2q = \frac{1}{D\theta_0}\left(m_4 + m_4\Delta\rho + \frac{D\theta_0 m_6 - m_4^2}{\theta_0(m_4 - D^2\theta_0^2)}\Delta\theta\right)\Delta u -$$

$$-2(\theta_0 + \Delta\theta + \theta_0\Delta\rho)\Delta u \cdot \delta - (D\theta_0 + D\theta_0\Delta\rho + D\Delta\theta)\Delta u + O(\Delta^3) =$$

$$= \frac{1}{D\theta_0}(m_4 - D(D+2)\theta_0^2)(\Delta u + \Delta\rho\Delta u) + \left(\frac{D\theta_0 m_6 - m_4^2}{D\theta_0^2(m_4 - D^2\theta_0^2)} - (D+2)\right)\Delta\theta\Delta u + O(\Delta^3),$$

one can see that the terms proportional $\Delta u, \Delta\rho\Delta u$ are eliminated if m_4 satisfies (21), in addition, the second term can be removed if $m_6 = D(D+2)(D+4)\theta_0^3$ or we are restricted by the isothermal flows $\Delta\theta = 0$; in such a case, the heat flow (which equals zero for the Euler equations) is only of order $O(\Delta^3)$. In the present study, we assume that the temperature variations are negligible, $\Delta\theta = 0$.

3. Navier–Stokes Equations

In order to obtain the Navier–Stokes equations, one needs to find the corrections to the pressure tensor corresponding to the viscous terms. This can be performed by applying the Chapman–Enskog expansion for DV Boltzmann model [29]. Then, following the previous results [29], we assume that the solution to (1) can be expressed in the form

$f_i = f_i^{eq} + f_i^{(1)} + O(Kn^2)$, where $f_i^{(1)}$ are of order $O(Kn)$ and Kn is the Knudsen number. At the limit of small Mach numbers, the equations for $f_i^{(1)}$ read as (Equation (19) in [43])

$$\frac{df_i^{eq}}{dt} = \sum_{jkl}^{N} A_{kl}^{ij}(w_k f_l^{(1)} + w_l f_k^{(1)} - w_i f_j^{(1)} - w_j f_i^{(1)}), \quad i = 1 \ldots N, \tag{22}$$

one can see from (22) that the solutions $f_i^{(1)}$ are determined by the concrete DV Boltzmann model, i.e., $f_i^{(1)}$ depend on A_{kl}^{ij}. The solution to the linear Equations (22) can be obtained as (Formula (22) in [43])

$$f_i^{(1)} = a_i Q_i : \frac{\partial}{\partial r} \Delta u + b_i div(\Delta u), \tag{23}$$

where Q_i is a second-order tensor whose exact form we will discuss further, and a_i, b_i are numerical coefficients.

4. Spurious Invariants

For a collision, in which the particles with the velocities c_i, c_j turn into the particles with the velocities c_k, c_l, we introduce the following **reaction vector** [40,41,44]

$$e = (\ldots, \overset{k}{1}, \ldots, \overset{i}{-1}, \ldots, \overset{l}{1}, \ldots, \overset{j}{-1}, \ldots) \in \mathbb{R}^N, \quad A_{kl}^{ij} > 0,$$

where the entries denoted by dots equal zero. Assume that we have p linearly independent reaction vectors $e_s, s = 1 \ldots p$. We denote a matrix consisting of all reaction row vectors e_s as the **collision matrix**

$$C = (e_1; e_2; \ldots; e_p) \in \mathbb{R}^p \times \mathbb{R}^N.$$

Note that the collision invariants $\varphi(c_1, \ldots c_N) \in R^N$ are defined by the relation [28]

$$\varphi_i + \varphi_j = \varphi_k + \varphi_l, \quad A_{kl}^{ij} > 0,$$

this condition can also be rewritten in the following form [44,45]

$$\varphi \cdot e_s = 0, \quad s = 1 \ldots p, \tag{24}$$

i.e., the linear subspace spanned by the invariants is orthogonal to the subspace spanned by the reaction vectors. The condition (24) can be applied for the detection of spurious invariants:

Proposition 2. *Assume that, for some DV Boltzmann models, the number of linearly independent physical collision invariants equals q, then additional invariants do not exist if [40,41,44,45]*

$$rank(C) = N - q,$$

where N is the number of the discrete velocities.

5. Nine Velocity DV Boltzmann Model for *D2Q9* Lattice

We consider the DV Boltzmann model on a nine-velocity lattice (Figure 1). This lattice is popular in LB theory [3], since the corresponding LB model recovers hydrodynamics at small Mach numbers limit and, in addition, its numerical implementation is very simple. For this model, we have three types of discrete velocities: zero velocity $c_0 = (0,0)$ with the weight $w_0 = 16/36$; four velocities, parallel to x, y axes, i.e., $c_{\pm 1} = (\pm 1, 0)c, c_{\pm 2} = (0, \pm 1)c$ with the weight $w_0 = 4/36$; four diagonal velocities $c_{\pm 3} = (\pm 1, \pm 1)c, c_{\pm 4} = (\pm 1, \mp 1)c$ with the weight $w_0 = 1/36$—here, c is the positive constant. The lattice velocity magnitudes for these three groups are $0, c, \sqrt{2}c$. Moreover, $\theta_0 = \sum_i w_i c_i^2 = c^2/3$.

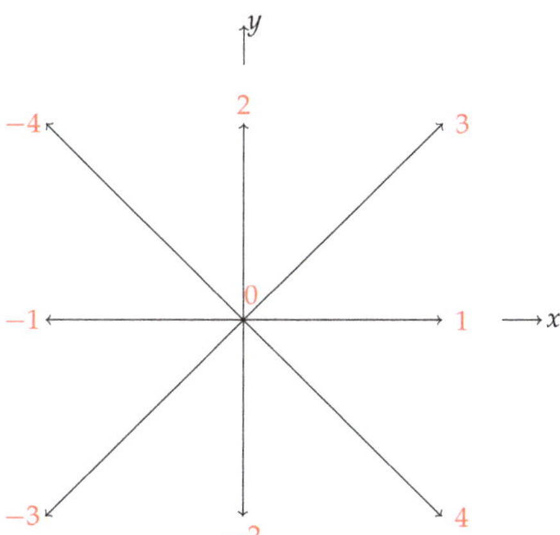

Figure 1. Two-dimensional nine-velocity lattice (*D2Q9*). Lattice velocities are labeled by red color.

It is well-known that these lattice velocities and weights satisfy the conditions (3), (20) and (21); therefore, if it is possible to construct the collisions in such a way that the mass and momentum are conserved then the Euler equations are satisfied. We mention that the lattices and collision rules for DV Boltzmann models, which can potentially recover the hydrodynamics, have been considered previously [46,47]—for instance, the model with single-relaxation time describing Navier–Stokes equations has been proposed [46,47]. In here we consider only the collisions for the nine-bit lattice in a more detailed way; the considered model is of the multiple-relaxation-time type:

a. **Broadwell type collision** is the reaction between the particles 1 and -1, which turn into the particles 2 and -2 (Figure 1); schematically, we can denote this reaction as $(1, -1) \longrightarrow (2, -2)$. The contribution of this collision to right side of (1) denoted as J_0 is as follows

$$J_0 = f_{-2}f_2 - f_{-1}f_1; \tag{25}$$

b. **the collisions linking all three different energy states**, they define transitions between the particle's states with different kinetic energies, and evidently can not be excluded. We have four different reactions $(1, 2) \longrightarrow (0, 3)$, $(1, -2) \longrightarrow (0, 4)$, $(-1, -2) \longrightarrow (0, -3)$, $(-1, 2) \longrightarrow (0, -4)$. The corresponding contributions to the collision kernel are

$$J_1 = f_0 f_3 - f_1 f_2, \quad J_2 = f_0 f_4 - f_1 f_{-2},$$
$$J_3 = f_0 f_{-4} - f_{-1}f_2, \quad J_4 = f_0 f_{-3} - f_{-1}f_{-2}; \tag{26}$$

c. **Broadwell type collision between the particles with the velocity magnitudes $\sqrt{2}c$** is defined by the reaction $(3, -3) \longrightarrow (4, -4)$, the contributions to the collision kernel are

$$J_5 = f_{-4}f_4 - f_{-3}f_3; \tag{27}$$

d. **the collisions between the particles with the velocity magnitudes $\sqrt{2}c$ and c**, we have four different reactions $(-4, 1) \longrightarrow (-1, 3)$, $(-3, 1) \longrightarrow (-1, 4)$, $(-3, 2) \longrightarrow (-4, -2)$, $(4, 2) \longrightarrow (-2, 3)$, the contributions to the collision kernel are

$$J_6 = f_3 f_{-1} - f_{-4}f_1, \quad J_7 = f_{-1}f_4 - f_{-3}f_1,$$
$$J_8 = f_{-4}f_{-2} - f_{-3}f_2, \quad J_9 = f_3 f_{-2} - f_4 f_2. \tag{28}$$

The collisions (25)–(28) conserve mass, momentum and energy; the corresponding D2Q9 DV Boltzmann model reads as

$$\frac{\partial f_1}{\partial t} + c\frac{\partial f_1}{\partial x} = \alpha J_0 + \beta(J_1 + J_2) + \lambda(J_6 + J_7), \tag{29}$$

$$\frac{\partial f_{-1}}{\partial t} - c\frac{\partial f_{-1}}{\partial x} = \alpha J_0 + \beta(J_3 + J_4) - \lambda(J_6 + J_7), \tag{30}$$

$$\frac{\partial f_2}{\partial t} + c\frac{\partial f_2}{\partial y} = -\alpha J_0 + \beta(J_1 + J_3) + \lambda(J_8 + J_9), \tag{31}$$

$$\frac{\partial f_{-2}}{\partial t} - c\frac{\partial f_{-2}}{\partial y} = -\alpha J_0 + \beta(J_2 + J_4) - \lambda(J_8 + J_9), \tag{32}$$

$$\frac{\partial f_3}{\partial t} + c\frac{\partial f_3}{\partial x} + c\frac{\partial f_3}{\partial y} = \gamma J_5 - \beta J_1 - \lambda(J_6 + J_9), \tag{33}$$

$$\frac{\partial f_{-3}}{\partial t} - c\frac{\partial f_{-3}}{\partial x} - c\frac{\partial f_{-3}}{\partial y} = \gamma J_5 - \beta J_4 + \lambda(J_7 + J_8), \tag{34}$$

$$\frac{\partial f_4}{\partial t} + c\frac{\partial f_4}{\partial x} - c\frac{\partial f_4}{\partial y} = -\gamma J_5 - \beta J_2 + \lambda(-J_7 + J_9), \tag{35}$$

$$\frac{\partial f_{-4}}{\partial t} - c\frac{\partial f_{-4}}{\partial x} + c\frac{\partial f_{-4}}{\partial y} = -\gamma J_5 - \beta J_3 + \lambda(J_6 - J_8), \tag{36}$$

$$\frac{\partial f_0}{\partial t} = -\beta(J_1 + J_2 + J_3 + J_4), \tag{37}$$

where $\alpha, \beta, \lambda, \gamma$ in (29)–(37) are positive transition probabilities. Now, we can consider the analogs of the Navier–Stokes equations for the model (29)–(37).

Proposition 3. *The Equations (29)–(37) lead to Navier–Stokes equations for nearly incompressible flows with errors of order $O(\Delta^3)$ if*

$$4\alpha = \gamma + 4\beta + 4\lambda, \tag{38}$$

the shear viscosity ν equals

$$\nu = \frac{3}{4\alpha}. \tag{39}$$

Proof. From (22), one can deduce that the corrections to the DV distribution function $f_i^{(1)}$ corresponding to the viscous terms can be represented as a linear combination of $\frac{df_i^{eq}}{dt}$ terms. In the case of nearly incompressible flow, these terms can be represented as (Formula (2.12) in [2])

$$\frac{df_i^{eq}}{dt} = w_i \frac{c_i c_i}{\theta_0} : \frac{\partial}{\partial r}\Delta u, \tag{40}$$

where $\frac{\partial}{\partial r} = (\frac{\partial}{\partial x}, \frac{\partial}{\partial y})$. According (23) we can try add the terms proportional $div(\Delta u)$, but they equal zero for the incompressible limit; then, we seek the solution in the form

$$f_i^{(1)} = a_i Q_i, \quad Q_i = w_i \frac{c_i c_i}{\theta_0} : \frac{\partial}{\partial r}\Delta u, \tag{41}$$

where the coefficients a_i are equal for the indexes i corresponding to the discrete velocities c_i with the same kinetic energy. The substitution of (41) into (29)–(37) leads to three algebraic equations for the coefficients a_i, (29)–(32) yield the first equation

$$3w_1\frac{\partial}{\partial x}\Delta u_x = 2\alpha w_1 a_1\left(\frac{\partial}{\partial y}\Delta u_y - \frac{\partial}{\partial x}\Delta u_x\right) =$$

$$= 2\alpha w_1 a_1\left(\frac{\partial}{\partial y}\Delta u_y - \frac{\partial}{\partial x}\Delta u_x - div(\Delta u)\right) = -4\alpha w_1 a_1\frac{\partial}{\partial x}\Delta u_x,$$

from which we obtain

$$a_1 = -\frac{3}{4\alpha},$$

(33)–(36) yield the second equation

$$3w_2\left(\frac{\partial}{\partial x}\Delta u_y + \frac{\partial}{\partial y}\Delta u_x\right) = -(4\gamma w_2 + \beta w_0 + 4\lambda w_1)a_2\left(\frac{\partial}{\partial x}\Delta u_y + \frac{\partial}{\partial y}\Delta u_x\right),$$

then

$$a_2 = -\frac{3w_2}{4\gamma w_2 + \beta w_0 + 4\lambda w_1}.$$

The third equation, which can be obtained from (37) is satisfied automatically. Now, with the exact expressions for a_1, a_2, we can evaluate $f_i^{(1)}$ and the viscous corrections to the pressure tensor $\boldsymbol{P}^{(1)} = \sum_i f_i^{(1)} \boldsymbol{c}_i \boldsymbol{c}_i$. Then, the Navier–Stokes viscous terms can be evaluated as

$$-\sum_\sigma \frac{\partial}{\partial r_\sigma}P_{\eta\sigma}^{(1)} = -\sum_\sigma \frac{\partial}{\partial r_\sigma}\left(\sum_i f_i^{(1)} c_{i,\eta}c_{i,\sigma}\right),$$

where σ, η equal x or y. For instance,

$$-\frac{\partial}{\partial x}P_{xx}^{(1)} - \frac{\partial}{\partial y}P_{xy}^{(1)} = \frac{3}{2\alpha}\frac{\partial^2}{\partial x^2}\Delta u_x + \frac{12w_2}{4\gamma w_2 + \beta w_0 + 4\lambda w_1}\left(\frac{\partial^2}{\partial x\partial y}\Delta u_y + \frac{\partial^2}{\partial y^2}\Delta u_x\right)$$

we require $4\alpha = \gamma + 4\beta + 4\lambda$, then by applying $div(\Delta\boldsymbol{u}) = 0$ we finally obtain

$$-\frac{\partial}{\partial x}P_{xx}^{(1)} - \frac{\partial}{\partial y}P_{xy}^{(1)} = \frac{3}{4\alpha}\left(\frac{\partial^2}{\partial x^2} + \frac{\partial^2}{\partial y^2}\right)\Delta u_x,$$

therefore $\nu = 3/4\alpha$. $\quad\square$

For the model (29)–(37), there are ten collisions. If we consider all reaction vectors and the corresponding collision matrix, one can convince that $rank(C) = 5$, the number of the discrete velocities $N = 9$. This means that we do not have any collision invariants except mass, momentum, energy (Proposition 2). We can exclude up to five reactions from the model; for instance, we can keep only the Broadwell collisions (type a.) and the collisions of type b., i.e., we set $\gamma = \lambda = 0$. On the other side, the numerical simulations show that the addition of the collisions from the group c. or d. enhances the stability properties.

Finally, we emphasize that, for the model (29)–(37), all the collisions conserve energy (elastic). Generally speaking, this is not necessary because we are focused on the correct reproduction of the mass and momentum equations. For instance, it is possible to construct the model of DV Boltzmann type in one spatial dimension with inelastic collisions [26] (quasi-chemical model with three discrete velocities) which leads to the correct Navier–Stokes equation at small Mach limit.

6. Numerical Implementation and Test Problems

The model is implemented similarly to the conventional LB *D2Q9* model [3]. Firstly, we perform the collision step, then post-collision distribution functions are streamed at appropriate directions. It is well-known from the LB theory that the discretization of space–time affects the viscosity. The DV Boltzmann model discretized in a similar form as LB model reads as

$$f_i(t + \delta t, \boldsymbol{r} + \boldsymbol{c}_i\delta t) - f_i(t, \boldsymbol{r}) = I_i[f_1, \dots f_N](t, \boldsymbol{r})\delta t, \tag{42}$$

by applying the Taylor expansion this equation can be rewritten as

$$\left(\frac{\partial}{\partial t} + c_i \frac{\partial}{\partial r}\right) f_i(t, r)\delta t + \frac{1}{2}\left(\frac{\partial}{\partial t} + c_i \frac{\partial}{\partial r}\right)^2 f_i(t, r)\delta t^2 + O(\delta t^3) = I_i[f_1, \dots f_N](t, r)\delta t,$$

then

$$\left(\frac{\partial}{\partial t} + c_i \frac{\partial}{\partial r}\right) f_i(t, r) = I_i[f_1, \dots f_N](t, r) - \frac{1}{2}\left(\frac{\partial}{\partial t} + c_i \frac{\partial}{\partial r}\right)^2 f_i(t, r)\delta t + O(\delta t^2),$$

therefore, we can conclude that the scheme (42) led to the hydrodynamic equations in which the contributions from $-\frac{1}{2}\left(\frac{\partial}{\partial t} + c_i \frac{\partial}{\partial r}\right)^2 f_i(t, r)\delta t + O(\delta t^2) = -\frac{\delta t}{2}\frac{d^2}{dt^2}f_i + O(\delta t^2)$ are present. The additional terms for the Navier–Stokes equations can be obtained with the application of the Chapman–Enskog expansion [3]. Note that the terms $O(\delta t^2)$ do not affect the Navier–Stokes equations, since they contain third order derivatives, which, in the Chapman–Enskog multiple-scale expansion, enter the equations for the moments at the Burnett level. For the Navier–Stokes equation, the additional viscosity terms result from $-\frac{\delta t}{2}\frac{d^2}{dt^2}f_i^{eq}$, its contribution to $\frac{\partial}{\partial r} \cdot P^{(1)}$ is $\frac{\delta t}{2}\sum_i c_i c_i \cdot \frac{d}{dr}\frac{d}{dt}f_i^{eq}$, remembering that $\frac{d}{dt}f_i^{eq}$ can be expressed by (40), we eventually obtain $\frac{\delta t}{6}\left(\frac{\partial^2}{\partial x^2} + \frac{\partial^2}{\partial y^2}\right)u$.

Then, for the DV $D2Q9$ Boltzmann model in the form (42), the viscosity is given by

$$\nu = \frac{3}{4\alpha} - \frac{\delta t}{6}.$$

In the simulations, the parameters are taken as follows

$$\alpha = \frac{3}{4(\nu + \frac{\delta t}{6})}, \quad \beta = 0.25\alpha, \quad \gamma = 4\alpha - 4\beta = 3\alpha, \quad \lambda = 0, \tag{43}$$

i.e., we have six different collisions.

To validate the second-order convergence of the presented scheme, we estimate the simulation error defined as

$$error = \frac{\sqrt{\sum_z (u_m(z) - u_{bench}(z))^2}}{\sqrt{\sum_z u_{bench}(z)^2}}, \tag{44}$$

where z denotes the spatial variable, u_m, u_{bench} are the modeled variable (velocity) and the benchmark solution, respectively. The convergence rate is evaluated by fitting the values of $\log(error)$ for the various $\log(h) = \log(\frac{1}{N})$ (N is the number of the lattice nodes, h is proportional to the lattice spacing) using the linear regression, the second-order convergence is achieved if the regression slope coefficient is close to 2.

Compared to LB $D2Q9$ model, the scheme (29)–(37) differs only in the collision term and the expression for the viscosity. This means that the computation time for (29)–(37) implemented in the form (42) is approximately the same as for LB $D2Q9$ model.

6.1. Shear Wave Decay

We consider the dynamics in terms of the time of the sinusoidal velocity wave in a square domain. The initial flow velocity in x direction is dependent on y coordinate and is given by

$$u_x(x, y, t = 0) = U_0 \sin(ky), \quad k = \frac{2\pi}{L},$$

where L is the length of the domain equals N lattice nodes and $U_0 = 0.01$. The periodic boundary conditions are applied for the present problem. This problem has the following analytical solution

$$u_x(x, y, t) = U_0 \sin(ky)e^{-\nu k^2 t}.$$

In the present case, we consider $\nu = 0.001$ and $N = 101$, the time step $\delta t = 1$. We compare the analytical solutions with the velocity profiles obtained by the application of the model (29)–(37) (implemented in the form (42)). The peak velocity time history and the velocity profiles for the different moments of time are plotted, Figure 2. One can see that the simulation results are very similar to the analytical profiles.

It is worth mentioning that it is possible to shorten the model and take $\gamma = \lambda = 0$, in this case $\alpha = \beta$, and we have only five different collisions. The numerical experiments show that this model becomes unstable for $\nu < 0.1$, while the setting (43) allows to model the flow with small viscosity and no instabilities are observed.

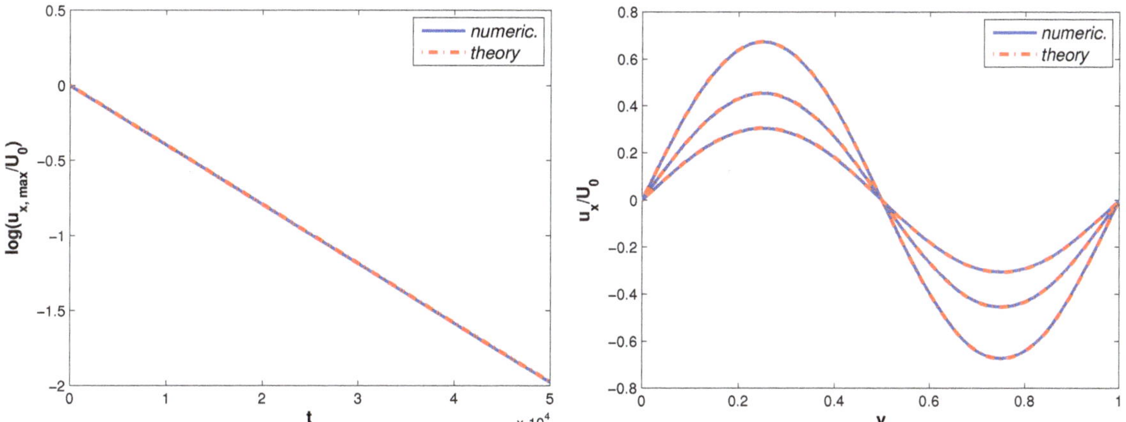

Figure 2. Shear wave decay. The logarithm of the peak velocity time histories obtained numerically and analytically are presented (**first slide**); velocity profiles at different moments of time ($t = 10^5$, $t = 2 \times 10^5$, $t = 3 \times 10^5$) obtained numerically and analytically are presented (**second slide**), the spatial variable y is normalized on the domain length L.

6.2. Taylor-Green Vortex

Similarly to the previous problem, we consider a square domain, and the initial velocity field is given by the formula

$$u_x(x, y, t = 0) = -U_0 \cos(kx) \sin(ky), \quad u_y(x, y, t = 0) = U_0 \sin(kx) \cos(ky),$$

where the size of the domain is $L \times L$ (or $N \times N$ in lattice units, where N is the number of the lattice nodes) and $k = \frac{2\pi}{L}$. The periodic boundary conditions are applied. For the present problem we set $U_0 = 0.01$, $\nu = 0.001$, $N = 51$, the time step $\delta t = 1$. The analytical solution to the problem is as follows

$$u_x(x, y, t) = -U_0 \cos(kx) \sin(ky)e^{-2\nu k^2 t}, \quad u_y(x, y, t) = U_0 \sin(kx) \cos(ky)e^{-2\nu k^2 t},$$

one can see that the initial structure of the velocity field persists in time, and only uniform decay of the velocity amplitudes is observed. The numerical simulations for the model (29)–(37) (implemented in the form (42)) show that the form of the velocity field does not change. We also present the behavior of the velocity $u_x(x, y = L/2, t)$ over time, obtained analytically and numerically for three different moments of time; obviously, both approaches give very similar profiles (Figure 3).

Finally, we consider the convergence rates of the numerical simulation results to the benchmark solutions. This can be performed by considering the logarithms of the simulation errors (44) for the different values of $\log(h) = \log(1/N)$. In the present case, we take $N = 25, 49, 73, 101$. In Figure 4, the logarithms of the errors of the velocities are presented for DV and the conventional LB $D2Q9$ models; the results are very similar for both models. One can see that the estimated slope values are close to 2; this indicates that the proposed scheme is accurate in the second-order.

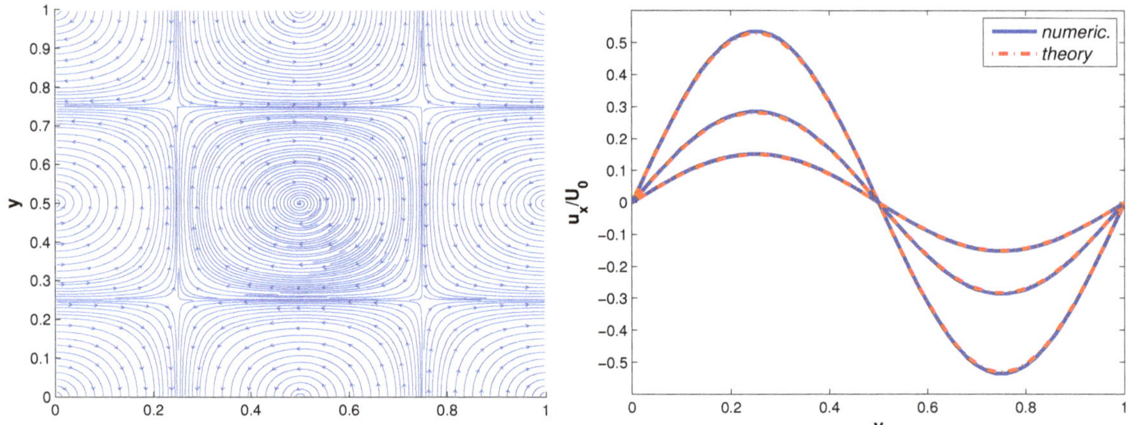

Figure 3. Taylor–Green vortex. The velocity streamlines are presented in the (**first slide**). The velocity profiles $u_x(x, y = L/2, t)$ for three different moments of time $t = 2 \times 10^4, t = 4 \times 10^4, t = 6 \times 10^4$ obtained analytically and numerically are presented (**second slide**), and the spatial variables x, y are normalized on the domain length L.

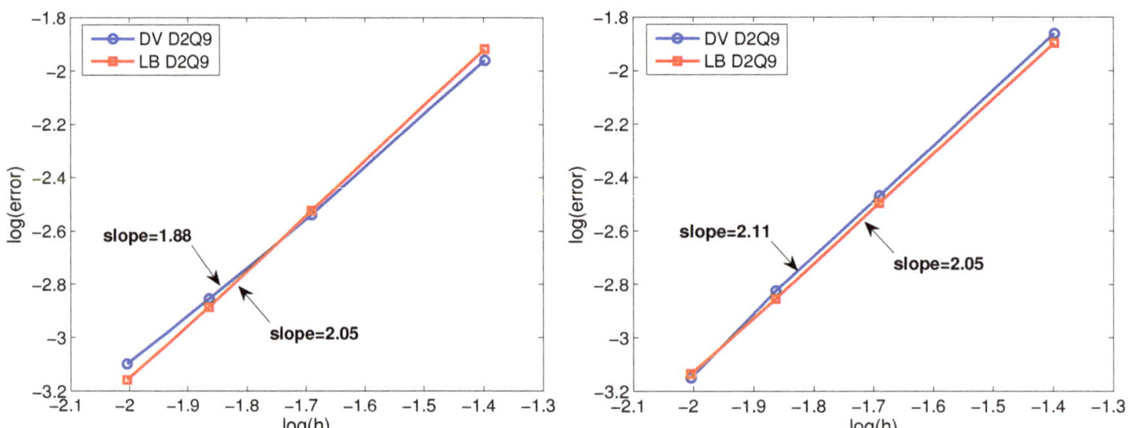

Figure 4. Convergence rates for the shear wave decay and Taylor–Green vortex problems are shown. The results are obtained by applying DV and the conventional LB *D2Q9* models. In the (**first slide**) (shear wave decay), the logarithms of the errors (44) for the velocity $u_x(y, t)$ computed at the moment of time $t = 1/(\nu k^2)$ are presented; in the (**second slide**) (Taylor–Green vortex), the logarithms of the errors of the velocity $u_x(x, y = L/2, t)$ computed at the moment of time $t = 1/(2\nu k^2)$ are presented, where the variable h is proportional to the lattice spacing. The slope estimates are obtained by fitting the values of $\log(error)$ using the linear regression.

7. Results and Discussion

In this paper, we have considered the DV Boltzmann model applicable to the modeling of viscous quasi-incompressible flows at a small Mach number limit. The presented model has the same discrete velocity structure and absolute equilibrium as LB *D2Q9*, but the collision rules for the particles are postulated exactly. There are four types of collision and ten possible different collisions; the unique transition probability corresponds to all possible reactions in the group. Moreover, these collisions conserve only mass, momentum and energy (spurious invariants do not exist). In terms of LB theory, this model can be considered as a scheme with multiple relaxation times. Note that the H-theorem is valid for the model by construction (at least for the continuous space–time variables).

We have demonstrated that DV Boltzmann equations can be a viable tool in modeling of hydrodynamic flows. The shear wave decay and Taylor–Green vortex have been considered as benchmark problems. The comparison of the simulation results with the analytical solutions has shown good accuracy.

One of the most intriguing problems is the evaluation of the stability properties of the presented DV Boltzmann system and the optimal choice of transition probabilities. One can expect that the DV Boltzmann model for $D2Q9$ lattice has a better stability than the conventional LB $D2Q9$ model, since the H-theorem is satisfied. In order to elucidate this issue, one can consider additional problems like Sod shock tube, double shear layer and lid-driven cavity. These problems are left for future study.

Funding: This research was supported by the Ministry of Science and Higher Education of the Russian Federation, project No 075-15-2020-799.

Institutional Review Board Statement: Not applicable.

Informed Consent Statement: Not applicable.

Data Availability Statement: The simulation code that supports the findings of this study is available from the author upon reasonable request.

Conflicts of Interest: The author declares no conflict of interest.

Abbreviations

The following abbreviations are used in this manuscript:

DV   discrete velocity
LB   lattice Boltzmann

References

1. Kogan, M. *Rarefied Gas Dynamics*; Plenum Press: New York, NY, USA, 1969.
2. Guo, Z.; Shu, C. *Lattice Boltzmann Method and Its Applications in Engineering*; World Scientific Publishing Company: Singapore, 2013.
3. Krüger, T.; Kusumaatmaja, H.; Kuzmin, A.; Shardt, O.; Silva, G.; Viggen, E. *The Lattice Boltzmann Method. Principles and Practice*; Springer: Berlin/Heidelberg, Germany, 2017.
4. Succi, S. *The Lattice Boltzmann Equation: For Complex States of Flowing Matter*; OUP: Oxford, UK, 2018.
5. Lallemand, P.; Luo, L.S.; Krafczyk, M.; Yong, W.A. The lattice Boltzmann method for nearly incompressible flows. *J. Comput. Phys.* **2020**, *431*, 109713. [CrossRef]
6. Qian, Y.H.; d'Humières, D.; Lallemand, P. Lattice BGK models for Navier-Stokes equation. *Europhys. Lett.* **1992**, *17*, 479–484. [CrossRef]
7. Toschi, F.; Succi, S. Lattice Boltzmann method at finite Knudsen numbers. *Europhys. Lett.* **2005**, *69*, 549. [CrossRef]
8. Ansumali, S.; Karlin, I. Consistent Lattice Boltzmann Method. *Phys. Rev. Lett.* **2005**, *95*, 260605. [CrossRef]
9. Shan, X.; Yuan, X.; Chen, H. Kinetic theory representation of hydrodynamics: A way beyond the Navier–Stokes equation. *J. Fluid Mech.* **2006**, *550*, 413–441. [CrossRef]
10. Zhang, R.; Shan, X.; Chen, H. Efficient kinetic method for fluid simulation beyond the Navier-Stokes equation. *Phys. Rev. E* **2006**, *74*, 046703. [CrossRef]
11. Ansumali, S.; Karlin, I.; Arcidiacono, S.; Abbas, A.; Prasianakis, N. Hydrodynamics beyond Navier-Stokes: Exact Solution to the Lattice Boltzmann Hierarchy. *Phys. Rev. Lett.* **2007**, *98*, 124502. [CrossRef]
12. Niu, X.; Hyodo, S.; Munekata, T.; Suga, K. Kinetic lattice Boltzmann method for microscale gas flows: Issues on boundary condition, relaxation time, and regularization. *Phys. Rev. E* **2007**, *76*, 036711. [CrossRef]
13. Kim, S.; Pitsch, H.; Boyd, I. Accuracy of higher-order lattice Boltzmann methods for microscale flows with finite Knudsen numbers. *J. Comput. Phys.* **2008**, *227*, 8655. [CrossRef]
14. Tang, G.; Zhang, Y.; Emerson, D. Lattice Boltzmann models for nonequilibrium gas flows. *Phys. Rev. E* **2008**, *77*, 046701. [CrossRef]
15. Meng, J.; Zhang, Y. Gauss-Hermite quadratures and accuracy of lattice Boltzmann models for non-equilibrium gas flows. *Phys. Rev. E* **2011**, *83*, 036704. [CrossRef]

16. Suga, K. Lattice Boltzmann methods for complex micro-flows: Applicability and limitations for practical applications. *Fluid Dyn. Res.* **2013**, *45*, 034501. [CrossRef]
17. Feuchter, C.; Schleifenbaum, W. High-order lattice Boltzmann models for wall-bounded flows at finite Knudsen numbers. *Phys. Rev. E* **2016**, *94*, 013304. [CrossRef]
18. Ambruş, V.; Sofonea, V. Lattice Boltzmann models based on half-range Gauss–Hermite quadratures. *J. Comp. Phys.* **2016**, *316*, 760–788. [CrossRef]
19. Ilyin, O. Gaussian Lattice Boltzmann method and its applications to rarefied flows. *Phys. Fluids* **2020**, *32*, 012007. [CrossRef]
20. Wagner, A. An H-theorem for the lattice Boltzmann approach to hydrodynamics. *Europhys. Lett.* **1998**, *44*, 144–149. [CrossRef]
21. Yong, W.A.; Luo, L.S. Nonexistence of H theorems for the athermal lattice Boltzmann models with polynomial equilibria. *Phys. Rev. E* **2003**, *67*, 051105. [CrossRef]
22. Yong, W.A.; Luo, L.S. Nonexistence of H Theorem for some Lattice Boltzmann models. *J. Stat. Phys.* **2005**, *121*, 91–103. [CrossRef]
23. Karlin, I.; Ferrante, A.; Öttinger, H. Perfect entropy functions of the Lattice Boltzmann method. *Europhys. Lett.* **1999**, *47*, 182–188. [CrossRef]
24. Ansumali, S.; Karlin, I.; Öttinger, H. Minimal entropic kinetic models for hydrodynamics. *Europhys. Lett.* **2003**, *63*, 798–804. [CrossRef]
25. Karlin, I.; Ansumali, S.; Frouzakis, C.; Chikatamarla, S. Elements of the Lattice Boltzmann Method I: Linear Advection Equation. *Commun. Comput. Phys.* **2006**, *1*, 616–655.
26. Karlin, I.; Chikatamarla, S.; Ansumali, S. Elements of the lattice Boltzmann method II: Kinetics and hydrodynamics in one dimension. *Commun. Comput. Phys.* **2007**, *2*, 196–238.
27. Broadwell, J. Shock structure in a simple discrete velocity gas. *Phys. Fluids* **1964**, *7*, 1243–1247. [CrossRef]
28. Godunov, S.; Sultangazin, U. On discrete models of the kinetic Boltzmann equation. *Russ. Math. Surv.* **1971**, *26*, 1–56. [CrossRef]
29. Gatignol, R. The hydrodynamical description for a discrete velocity model of gas. *Complex Syst.* **1987**, *1*, 709–725.
30. Platkowski, T.; Illner, R. Discrete velocity models of the Boltzmann equation: A survey on the mathematical aspects of the theory. *SIAM Rev.* **1988**, *30*, 213–255. [CrossRef]
31. Bobylev, A.; Spiga, G. On a class of exact two-dimensional stationary solutions for the Broadwell model of the Boltzmann equation. *J. Phys. A Math. Gen.* **1994**, *27*, 7451–7459. [CrossRef]
32. Bobylev, A. Exact solutions of discrete kinetic models and stationary problems for the plane Broadwell model. *Math. Methods Appl. Sci.* **1996**, *19*, 825–845. [CrossRef]
33. Bobylev, A.; Toscani, G. Two dimensional half-space problems for the Broadwell discrete velocity model. *Contin. Mech. Termodyn.* **1996**, *8*, 257–274. [CrossRef]
34. Bobylev, A.; Caraffini, G.; Spiga, G. Non-stationary two-dimensional potential flows by the Broadwell model equations. *Eur. J. Mech. B Fluids* **2000**, *19*, 303–315. [CrossRef]
35. Ilyin, O. The analytical solutions of 2D stationary Broadwell kinetic model. *J. Stat. Phys.* **2012**, *146*, 67–72. [CrossRef]
36. Ilyin, O. Symmetries, the current function, and exact solutions for Broadwell's two-dimensional stationary kinetic model. *Theor. Math. Phys.* **2014**, *179*, 679–688. [CrossRef]
37. Chen, H.; Goldhirsch, I.; Orszag, S. Discrete rotational symmetry, moment isotropy, and higher order lattice Boltzmann models. *J. Sci. Comput.* **2008**, *34*, 87–112. [CrossRef]
38. Uchiyama, K. On the Boltzmann-Grad limit for the Broadwell model of the Boltzmann equation. *J. Stat. Phys.* **1988**, *52*, 331–355. [CrossRef]
39. Bobylev, A.; Cercignani, C. Discrete velocity models without nonphysical invariants. *J. Stat. Phys.* **1999**, *97*, 677–686. [CrossRef]
40. Bobylev, A.; Vinerean, M. Construction of discrete kinetic models with given invariants. *J. Stat. Phys.* **2008**, *132*, 153–170. [CrossRef]
41. Vinerean, M.; Windfäll, Å.; Bobylev, A. Construction of normal discrete velocity models of the Boltzmann equation. *Nuovo Cim.* **2010**, *33*, 257–264.
42. Bernhoff, N.; Vinerean, M. Discrete velocity models for mixtures without nonphysical collision invariants. *J. Stat. Phys.* **2016**, *165*, 434–453. [CrossRef]
43. Chauvat, P.; Gatignol, R. Euler and Navier-Stokes description for a class of discrete models of gases with different moduli. *Transp. Theory Stat. Phys.* **1992**, *21*, 417–435. [CrossRef]
44. Vedenyapin, V.; Orlov, Y. Conservation laws for polynomial Hamiltonians and for discrete models of the Boltzmann equation. *Theor. Math. Phys.* **1999**, *121*, 1516–1523. [CrossRef]
45. Vedenyapin, V. Velocity inductive construction for mixtures. *Transp. Theor. Stat. Phys.* **1999**, *28*, 727–742. [CrossRef]
46. Babovsky, H. "Small" kinetic models for transitional flow simulations. *AIP Conf. Proc.* **2012**, *1501*, 272–278.
47. Babovsky, H. Discrete kinetic models in the fluid dynamic limit. *Comput. Math. with Appl.* **2014**, *67*, 256–271. [CrossRef]

Article

A New Approach of Soft Joint Based on a Cable-Driven Parallel Mechanism for Robotic Applications

Luis Nagua *,†, Carlos Relaño †, Concepción A. Monje and Carlos Balaguer

Robotics Lab of the Carlos III University of Madrid, Avda de la Universidad 30, Leganés, 28911 Madrid, Spain; crelgib@gmail.com (C.R.); cmonje@ing.uc3m.es (C.A.M.); balaguer@ing.uc3m.es (C.B.)
* Correspondence: lnagua@ing.uc3m.es; Tel.: +34-674859239
† These authors contributed equally to this work.

Abstract: A soft joint has been designed and modeled to perform as a robotic joint with 2 Degrees of Freedom (DOF) (inclination and orientation). The joint actuation is based on a Cable-Driven Parallel Mechanism (CDPM). To study its performance in more detail, a test platform has been developed using components that can be manufactured in a 3D printer using a flexible polymer. The mathematical model of the kinematics of the soft joint is developed, which includes a blocking mechanism and the morphology workspace. The model is validated using Finite Element Analysis (FEA) (CAD software). Experimental tests are performed to validate the inverse kinematic model and to show the potential use of the prototype in robotic platforms such as manipulators and humanoid robots.

Keywords: soft robotics; continuum mechanisms; modeling of complex systems; kinematic model of soft robots

Citation: Nagua, L.; Relaño, C.; Monje, C.A.; Balaguer, C. A New Approach of Soft Joint Based on a Cable-Driven Parallel Mechanism for Robotic Applications. *Mathematics* **2021**, *9*, 1468. https://doi.org/10.3390/math9131468

Academic Editors: Mikhail Posypkin, Andrey Gorshenin and Vladimir Titarev

Received: 10 May 2021
Accepted: 18 June 2021
Published: 23 June 2021

1. Introduction

Soft robotics is a growing research area that has shown advantages over conventional robotics. In this area highly adaptive robots have been developed for soft interactions, providing greater security such as safe human-machine interaction. Compliance and adaptability of the soft structures are used for better efficiency and ability to interact with the environment [1]. Soft robotics is a new solution that covers the unmet need to perform tasks in unstructured and poorly defined environments, where conventional rigid robotics mainly seeks to be fast and accurate.

The advantages of soft robots allow for a wide variety of applications. However, this requires a paradigm shift in the methods of modeling, operation, control, materials and new designs to develop soft robots. The deformation property of soft robots is a restrictive element when using many of the most common conventional rigid sensors or other conventional control techniques [2].

Soft robotics is a subdomain of what is known as continuum robotics, it is defined by [3] as those robots with an elastic, continuously flexing structure and an infinite degree of freedom (DOF); and which are related to (but distinct from) hyperredundant robots, consisting of a finite number of many short, rigid links [4,5]. These models are usually more complex than traditional robot models, which have a small number of rigid links.

The incorporation of soft robotics into robotic systems comes mainly with two types of approaches [6]. One approach involves the use of compliant joints between different rigid links of the robot, while in another approach continuous soft robots are used, such as those mentioned above. This article explores this last type of design. Continuum soft robotic arms show features of soft robotics such as adaptability, high dexterity, and conformability to the external environment. However, they often cannot achieve the high rigidity and robustness required to handle objects or higher loads. Therefore, it is necessary to find a solution capable of providing the robustness of rigid arms and the versatility of soft arms [7], which is one of the points addressed in this paper. From now own the term robustness will refer to the ability to cope with the action of external disturbances or loads that cause unwanted deformations in soft bodies, while providing sufficient stiffness.

Robots made of soft materials can generate complex behavior with simpler actuation by partially outsourcing control to their morphological properties and materials. That improves the active coupling of control, body and environment. Soft robots can be actuated in different ways, but the most common actuators are variable length tendons in the form of tension cables or shape memory alloys (SMA) [8,9], fluidic actuators such as pneumatic or hydraulic ones, and electro-active polymers (EAP) [2]. Other kinds of actuations focus on the morphological structure of the soft robot itself, as in [10], where the topological architecture of low-density soft robots is presented; Ref. [11], where a three-dimensional-printed soft origami rotary actuator is studied; or [12], which presents a soft origami tendon-driven actuator. For continuum robotic arms, pneumatic actuators are most used as they can continuously change their shape with a few DOF actuated [13]. However, arms with pneumatic actuators are usually less precise and difficult to control; less portable, since they rely on an external energy source such as a pneumatic compressor; and more expensive to maintain.

Many works have been carried out on the design and control of soft robots in recent years [14,15], but the state of the art shows that there are few approaches to soft robotic arms, either for integration into a manipulator robot or for use as a stand-alone manipulator. Some designs are based on soft silicone tentacles, as in [16] or [17]. Generally, this type of joint performs an instinctive gripping function that is actuated pneumatically or by cables, and its morphology does not allow its use in handling tasks that require greater precision and robustness. Nevertheless, other works such as [18–20] present soft robotic joint designs that combine a light weight and a high load-weight ratio. Others such as [21,22] present joints with an inflatable structure that can move through highly restricted environments by changing their three-dimensional structure.

Within the framework of soft servo-mechanical actuation, there are several examples, such as a cable-driven soft robot for cardiothoracic endoscopic surgery [23] or a practical 3D-printed soft robotic prosthetic hand [24]. In addition, servomechanically actuated soft limbs, which are closer to the proposal presented in this document, have been developed. An example is the neck developed by the DLR [25] and the soft robotic manipulator applying an adaptive algorithm [26] which includes a continuous silicone-based and tendon actuated mechanism. The RoboticsLab at the University Carlos III of Madrid has also developed a soft robotic neck [27,28] within the Humasoft project, with orientation and inclination capacity in the three-dimensional space and a large load capacity (with only 14 gr of weight, it can support up to 1 kg loads). Work has also been carried out on model identification of this robotic neck using different methods such as neural networks [29].

However, the use of those soft neck link designs cannot be generalized for soft robotic joints, as they do not meet the necessary robustness criteria. When working with different joint positions and orientations in 3D space, gravity comes into play depending on the orientation, and handling large loads can cause the joint to bend or break. Similarly, high stresses exerted on the tendons may seriously compromise the integrity of the actuation system.

These problems have motivated the approach presented in this paper, which is inspired by the soft robotic neck previously design by the authors [27,28]. Differently from that design, this new solution consists of a novel three-dimensional soft joint morphology based on asymmetric links. The joint is composed of a soft material that is flexible but robust. This material allows deformation to achieve bending movements, but prevents too complex deformations and undesired gravity effects. When the designed soft joint is bending, from a certain inclination angle and at certain orientation angles given by model measurements, a natural protection is provided by its own morphology, which limits maximum bending. Therefore, sufficient robustness is achieved to support different loads throughout its positioning range in 3D space, while maintaining the advantages of its soft nature.

Furthermore, the proposed joint is scalable and adaptable to operational requirements in a modular and simple way. Therefore, joint properties, such as maximum bending angle or blocking bending, can be configured by modifying the morphological design and number of the links in the joint, or the distance between them, as well as increasing the number of DOF by concatenating joints.

Finally, this proposal is a low-cost construction, primarily designed by 3D printing and actuated by three motors that vary the length of tendons. Tendons are integrated within the morphology itself, which favors constant curvature and simplification of the model. Electromechanical action is proposed for the articulation, as opposed to other energy sources such as pneumatics or hydraulics. This feature allows the portability of the prototype and a greater integrability in any system (a robot, a humanoid, etc.), as well as more precise control and easier maintenance.

The rest of the paper is organized as follows: Section 2 introduces the soft joint design and prototype. It also shows its geometric design and includes the analysis of its characteristics and configurations. The section also shows the performance and assembly of the prototype and examines the properties of the material chosen for the joint morphology. Section 3 introduces the description of the mathematical model developed for the soft link, considering its workspace and the tendon length ratio that enables performance. The experimental tests carried out with the platform are described in Section 4, where the behavior of the soft joint is analyzed against different inputs and movements using two different tests. The discussion of the experimental results is presented in Section 5, and Section 6 concludes by highlighting the main achievements. This work is under a licensing process and the patent details are given in Section 7.

2. Design and Prototype of the Soft Joint

This section presents in detail the design and prototype of the soft joint.

2.1. Geometry

The soft joint has an asymmetrical morphology that allows its end tip to be positioned in the three-dimensional environment, robustly supporting high loads during its performance. Its design provides greater flexibility and a wider range of movement than a rigid joint. It consists of a series of links with asymmetrical prism morphology and circular section pitch. A triangular morphology is represented in Figure 1.

The small section and soft nature of the central axis of action, allow a greater bending capacity in all directions. The asymmetrical prismatic section provides the property of blocking and a natural protection, as well as the routing of the tendons for their action.

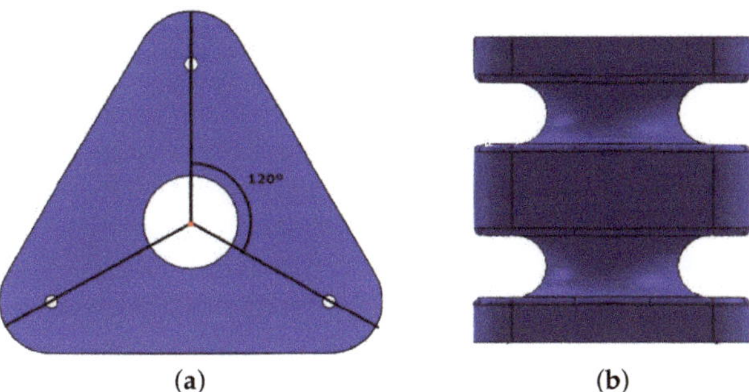

(a)   (b)

Figure 1. *Cont.*

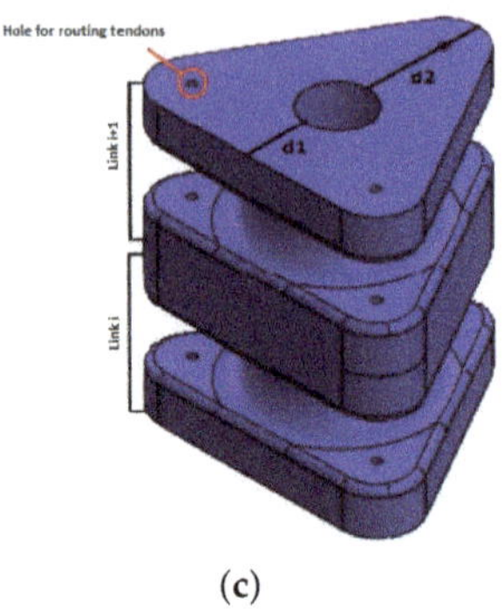

(**c**)

Figure 1. Triangular asymmetric geometry of the soft joint with two links in different views. (**a**) Top view showing the 120° angle relationship between the different tendon routing points. (**b**) Front view. (**c**) Perspective view, showing d1 and d2 distances defining asymmetry and holes for routing tendons.

The design performance is achieved by tendons that are routed through the asymmetric prismatic sections, as shown in Figure 2. It is possible to change the morphology of the prism and route the tendons through different points of these sections. This change would cause the variation of the forces and moments the joint is subjected to, therefore obtaining different kinematics and dynamics. By acting on the tendons, the joint can flex and orientate with two DOF.

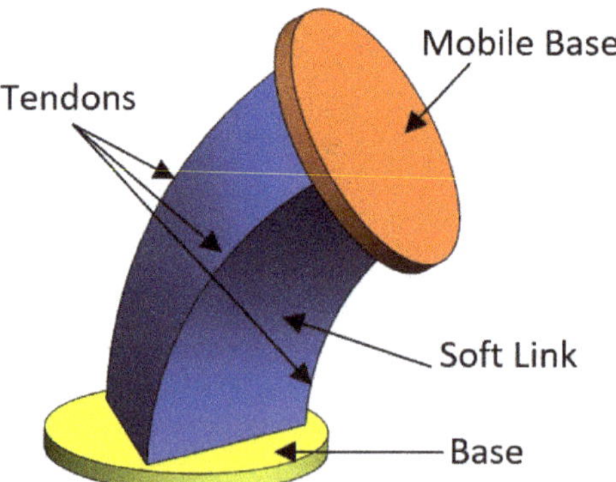

Figure 2. Conceptual design of the joint with its components: base, continuous soft axis, tendons for performance and tip (mobile base) of the soft joint.

One of the novel characteristics of this design is the natural morphological protection of the joint against large loads provided by the proposed asymmetrical morphology. An example of the triangular morphology are the two different configurations of extreme load:

- Configuration 1: Flexion towards one of the vertices of the triangle.
- Configuration 2: Flexion towards one of the edges of the triangle.

In configuration 1, protection when turning in the direction of one of the vertices is the most restrictive, as shown in Figure 3a. In the case of excessive bending, caused by high loads at the end of the joint or by control failures, the vertices contact each other. This produces a blocking curve of the structure that protects the joint from possible breakage due to wear or due to exceeding its elastic limit. This protection allows the joint to act with robustness and safety, especially in the regions of maximum flexion. In this configuration, the action is achieved by a single tendon, which is routed through the vertices that form the bending curve.

Configuration 2 allows larger flexion of the joint, compared to Configuration 1, while also maintaining the natural protection of the joint. When the flexion is towards one of the edges of the triangle, the blocking curve has a smaller radius, as shown in Figure 3b. This is because the edges are closer to the central axis of rotation, as can be seen from the distance ratio $d1 < d2$ in Figure 1c. A larger bending occurs due to the fact that a larger bending angle is necessary before these edges contact each other and lock the joint structure. In this configuration, performance is achieved by the action of the two tendons that form the edge of the triangle where bending occurs.

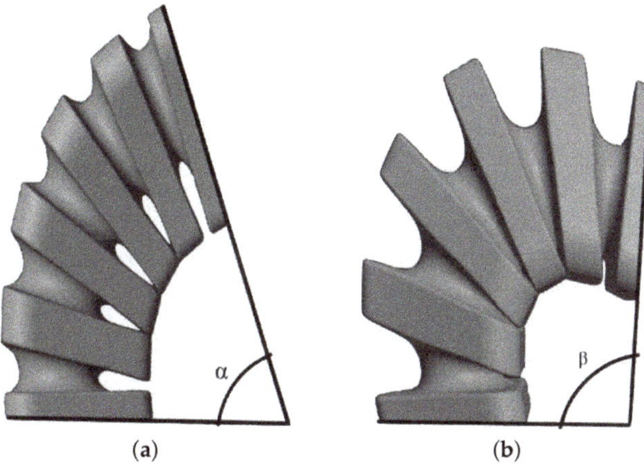

(a)   (b)

Figure 3. Different bending configurations. Relationship between bending angles: $\alpha < \beta$. (**a**) Flexion in configuration 1 has the lowest maximum bending angle. (**b**) Flexion in configuration 2 has the higher maximum bending angle.

2.2. Actuation

As mentioned above, there are several ways to operate soft robots. This paper focuses on operation by tendons of variable length using a winch coupled to a motor shaft. Tendon lengths must be translated into motor angular positions. $L_o = 0.2$ m is the length of the tendons when the joint is at rest position, and L_i is the target tendon length. The linear displacement is transformed into an angular displacement by the length of the arc formed by the circumference of the winch for a certain angle (Figure 4), following the equation below:

$$\Omega = \frac{(L_o - L_i)}{R} \tag{1}$$

R is the radius of the winch where the tendon is wound or unwound, in this case 9.3 mm, and Ω is the angle that provides that displacement.

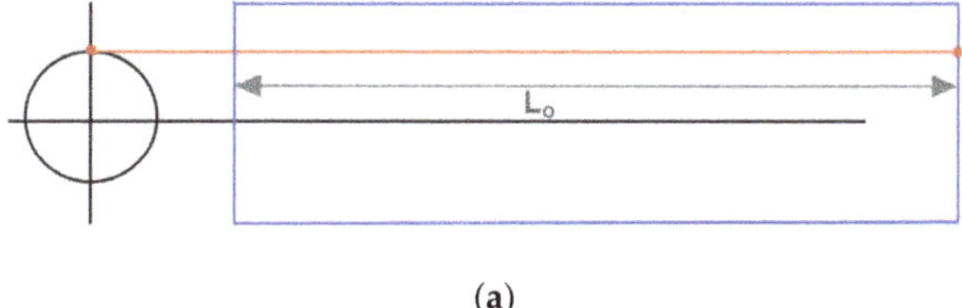

(a)

Figure 4. *Cont.*

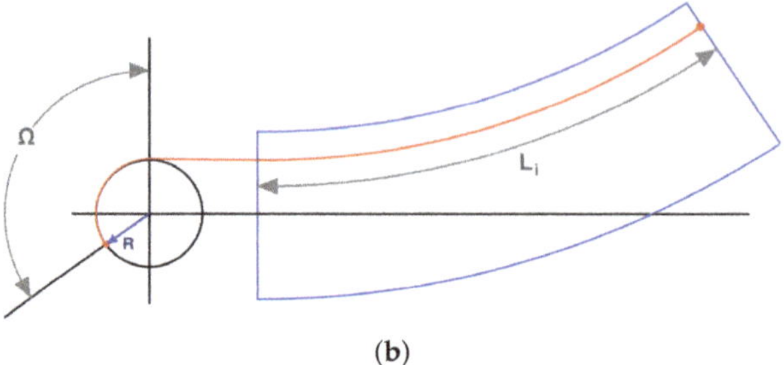

Figure 4. Diagram depicting winch winding based on radius and angle. $L_o - L_i$ is the distance for tendon winding, and Ω and R are the angle and the radius, respectively. (**a**) Tendon and soft joint prior winch actuation. (**b**) Tendon and soft joint when the winch is operating, with the radius R, and the angle Ω.

2.3. Prototype

To choose the soft joint operation, a test platform was designed. The goal is that the rest position of the joint is horizontal. Three motors will be used to operate the joint by tendons, each of which will wind the three tendons (Figure 5).

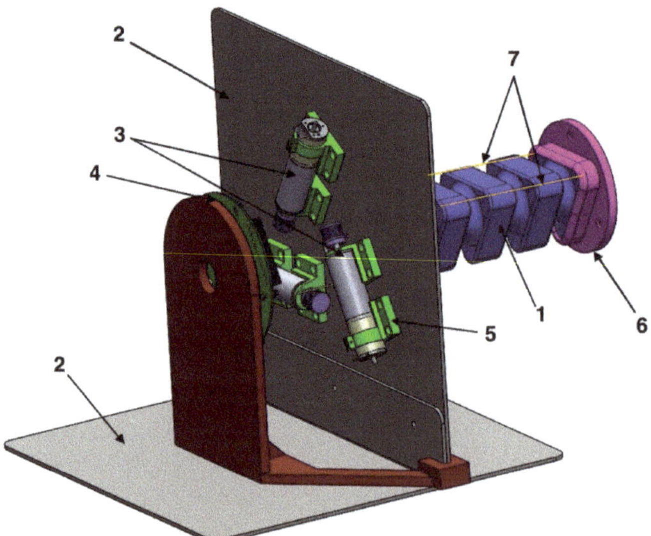

Figure 5. The elements of the platform are the soft joint (**1**), a metal base (**2**), motors (**3**), electronic elements to feed and control the motors (**4**) and other connective elements such as motor supports (**5**), joint bases (**6**) and tendons (**7**).

The fixing base is made up of two 3 mm thick metal plates, to be strong enough to support the test loads. The motors used for the drive are Maxon EC-max 22. The motors are controlled by Technosoft's Intelligent Drives iPOS 4808 MX, which communicate with the PC via busCAN.

Connecting elements have been printed on a 3D printer Creatbot600 pro and Zmorph from PLA (Polylactic acid) material. They are two bases for fastening the soft joint with the metal base, a platform for fastening the electronic elements, three motor fasteners with the metal platform and three winches that are attached to the motor shaft and the tendons, made of polyester thread, for the activation of the joint. The designed soft joint has been built by 3D printing from NinjaFlex using a Creatbot600 pro printer (Figure 6).

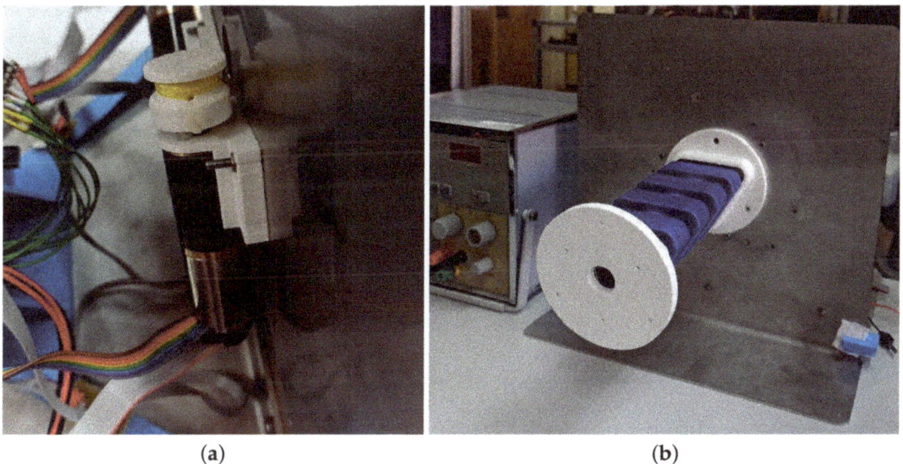

(a)   (b)

Figure 6. (**a**) Motor connected to the winch to wind the tendons for joint actuation. (**b**) Soft joint on the test platform.

2.4. Material Properties and Tests

One of the most important features when prototyping a soft robotic joint is the choice of material. This design uses NinjaFlex® 3D Printing Filament, a flexible polyurethane material for Fused Deposition Modeling (FDM) printers. This 3D printing manufacturing method and this material were chosen for their ease to use and for allowing variations in percentage or filling patterns of the soft joint body.

The mechanical properties of this material make it a good choice for the purpose of the prototype (Table 1). Its flexibility allows the joint to bend but, at the same time, it is rigid enough to prevent big deformations and resist loads.

Table 1. Mechanical properties of NinjaFlex®.

Mechanical Properties	Value
Young's modulus	12 MPa
Hardness	85 Shore A
Poisson Ratio	0.48
Density	1040 Kg/m^3

The soft joint design was analyzed in SolidWorks software, which applies a non-linear finite element study on the material. The prototype was modeled as a simple cantilever beam (one of its ends is fixed and a force is applied to its free end). This allows an efficient testing of the design under stresses and strains.

To simplify the simulation, the joint was assumed to be a completely filled solid except for the inner channel, and to simulate the assembly of the real prototype, the soft joint model was assembled including its two support pieces, one at each end.

After the design phase, the prototype was 3D printed using NinjaFlex material with 30% infill. The experiments were performed with this specific prototype.

The model in SolidWorks was tested under different conditions. First, a no-load test was performed on the soft joint, by only simulating gravity and fixing one of the ends, as shown in Figure 7, with the red arrow representing the orientation of the gravity action in the simulation.

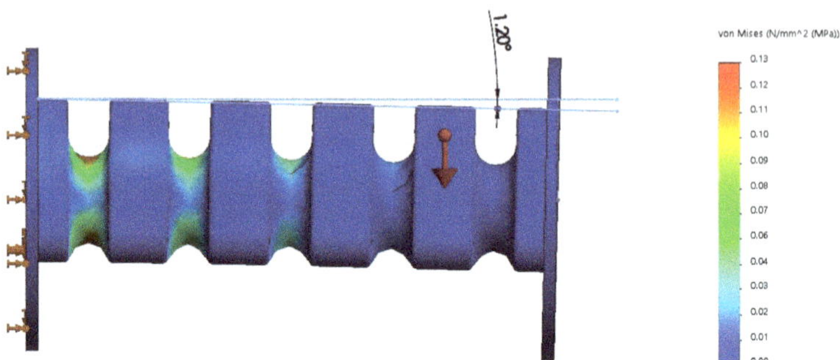

Figure 7. No-load simulation of soft joint.

One intended use of this soft joint is as a manipulator able to support different loads. Therefore, a second simulation was carried out with a rectangular prism with a fixed mass of 500 gr, homogeneously distributed. This prism represents the weight of the robot gripper in the simulation, Figure 8. In addition, a 10 Newtons downward force is applied to the end effector, simulating an external weight of 1 kg and causing a higher end torque. The simulation shows a deflection of 7.38° and a maximum deformation of 0.75 MPa.

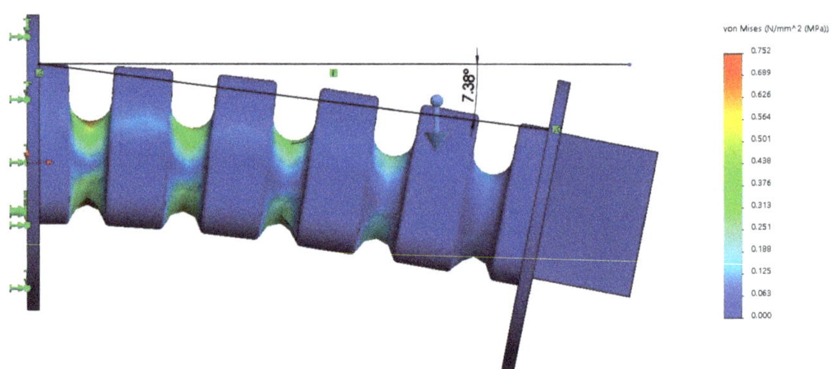

Figure 8. Simulation of soft joint with a 500 g prism and a 10 N downward force at the free end.

Additionally, another stress study was carried out to check if the yield strength of Ninjaflex is not exceeded. It was noted that when applying 60 N force at the end of the soft joint, as shown in Figure 9, a bending angle of 60° was reached and the maximum deformation was 2.9 MPa. Therefore, a no permanent deformation is confirmed when the soft link reaches an inclination angle of 60°.

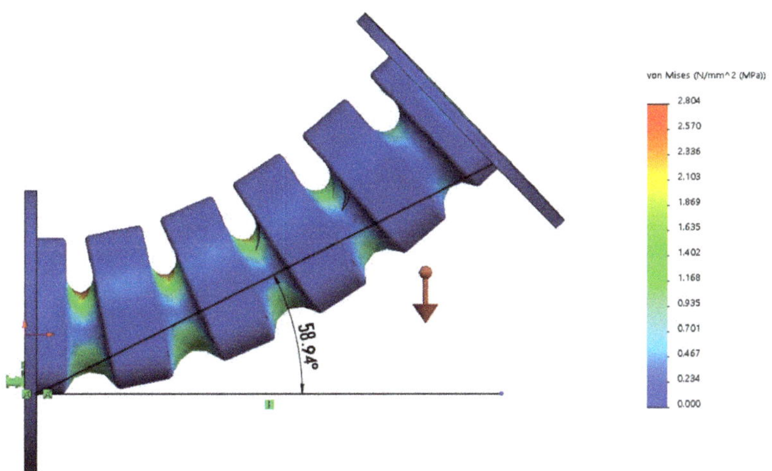

Figure 9. Simulation of soft joint with a 60 N upward force applied on the free end.

3. Mathematical Model of the Soft Link

The position of the soft joint is defined as the combination of orientation and inclination, where inclination is the curvature angle of the joint, and orientation is the angle of the plane perpendicular to the base that contains that curvature. It achieves two DOF of flexion from the three tendons, thus the position depends on the distance of the tendons and their combination. Therefore, a mathematical model of the joint has been created to obtain the theoretical distances of the tendons required for a specific position of the end of the joint. This angle is assumed to be zero when it coincides with the Y axis, and the actuators are named counterclockwise as this angle increases, Figure 10a.

3.1. Calculation of Tendon Lengths

The robot inputs are one inclination value, θ, and one orientation value, ψ, and the outputs will be tendons lengths:

$$L_i = [L_1 \; L_2 \; L_3]' \tag{2}$$

Inverse kinematics was used to calculate tendon lengths for the target end position. It is important to point out that unlike works such as [27] or [25], this design does not have the tendons in the open air, but the performance of the tendons is embedded within the morphology of the soft joint itself. This makes the length of the tendons not straight, but rather the tendons project the curvature of the soft joint, thus having a curvature similar to that of the joint. Therefore, L_i, the lengths of the tendons form an arc between both ends of the joint, Figure 10b.

Thus, tendons and joint are considered robots shaped by continuously bending actuators, such as those described by [30,31], where a pneumatic actuation is usually used, considering joint curvature and tendon curvature as a continuous curvature. The equations shown in [3] are adapted to this specific morphology case.

An angular-curved approach is used, with the inclination and orientation parameters. The lengths of the tendons L_i depend on both inclination and orientation angles. The length of the joint, L, remains constant in its central fiber at all times, regardless of the curvature; and the distance, a, of the tendons from the center of the joint section, remains constant, too (Figure 10b). For this morphology, a measures 0.035 m, L measures 0.2 m. The actuator for tendon 1 is placed at $v_1 = \frac{\pi}{2}$ radians, tendon 2 is placed at $v_2 = \frac{7 \cdot \pi}{6}$ radians and tendon 3 is placed at $v_3 = \frac{10 \cdot \pi}{6}$ radians.

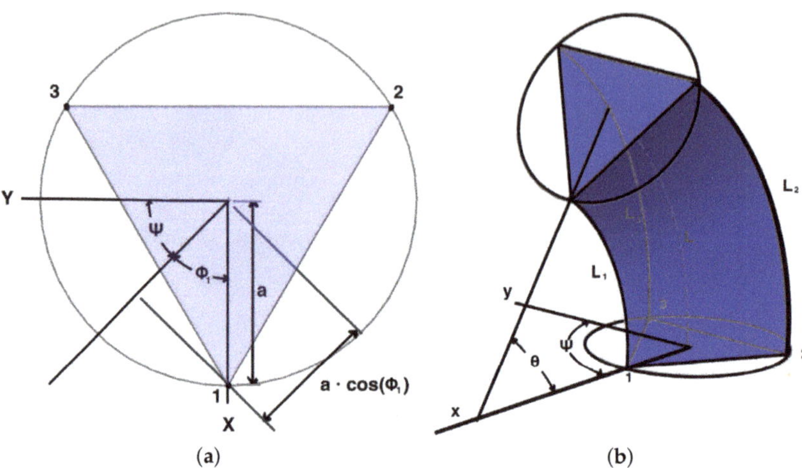

Figure 10. (**a**) Base projection of the soft joint, $\psi = 45°$, for the representation of orientation, distances and numbering of tendons. (**b**) Three-dimensional representation of the joint with $\theta = 45°$ orientation and $\psi = 90°$ inclination. Note the different curvatures for the soft joint and for each tendon L_i.

As previously discussed, it can be determined that L, the central fiber length of the soft joint, is constant independently of the inclination angle. Tendon lengths are calculated through the arc equations, due to the assumption of constant curvature. The radius r of the curvature L is determined as $L = r \cdot \theta$, where θ has a value in radians. As the central fiber and tendons move, they move in the direction given by the angle of orientation, and by projecting the arcs and radii, the representation in Figure 11 is obtained. Therefore, L_i can be determined as $L_i = r_i \cdot \theta$, where $r_i = r - a \cdot cos(v_i - \psi)$, resulting in the following equations:

$$L_1 = L - \theta \cdot a \cdot cos(v_1 - \psi) \tag{3}$$

$$L_2 = L - \theta \cdot a \cdot cos(v_2 - \psi) \tag{4}$$

$$L_3 = L - \theta \cdot a \cdot cos(v_3 - \psi) \tag{5}$$

Hence, ϕ_i is the angle between orientation, which is the plane containing the curvature, and the plane of tendon location, i. This angle ϕ_i depends on the configuration of the orientation and the number of actuators. The relationship of each tendon with the orientation is as follows:

$$\phi_1 = v_1 - \psi \tag{6}$$

$$\phi_2 = v_2 - \psi \tag{7}$$

$$\phi_3 = v_3 - \psi \tag{8}$$

A generic equation is obtained for lengths:

$$L_i = L - \theta \cdot a \cdot cos(\phi_i) \tag{9}$$

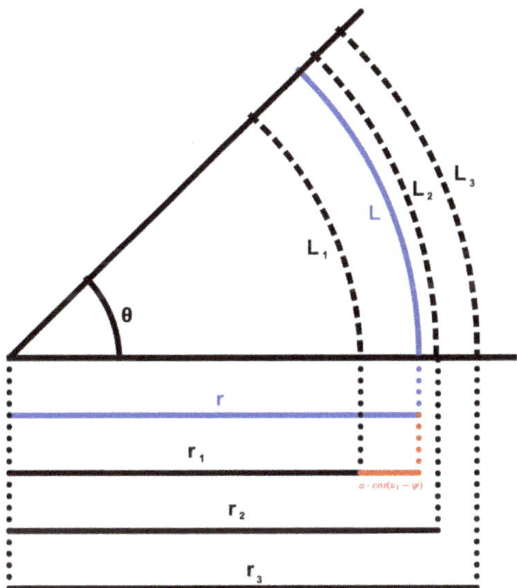

Figure 11. Representation in the perpendicular view of the orientation plane formed by the orientation angle ψ and an inclination angle θ. It can be seen that the projection of the radii of the constant curvature of the soft joint. The central fiber curvature L and its corresponding radius r are represented in blue. The arcs of tendons L_i are represented by dashed black lines, and their corresponding radii r_i by continuous black lines. The difference between r and r_i is represented by a red line whose distance for each tendon is given by equation $a \cdot cos(v_i - \psi)$.

3.2. Calculation of the Blocking Angle

The proposed morphology is designed with a blocking mechanism that protects or strengthens it at certain angles of inclination and orientation, and that must be parameterized in the kinematics. The angle of inclination at which the blocking occurs depends on the space between the triangular sections, where H_s is the height of the point of contact with the bending center of the link, and D_s is the distance from the point of contact with the bending center of the link, as shown in Figure 12. However, this distance D_s is not a constant parameter as it would be if the sections were circular. The blocking angle depends, in this asymmetric triangular design, on the distance D_s, which varies according to the orientation being a maximum value when the point of contact is the vertices of the triangle and a minimum value when the point of contact is the center of the edges of the triangle.

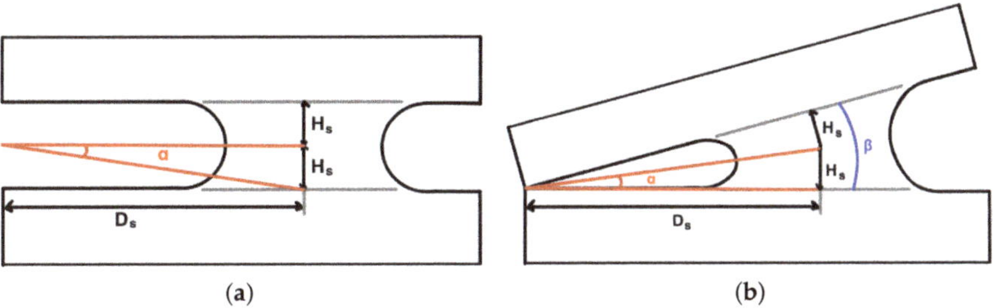

(a)   (b)

Figure 12. (**a**) Diagram showing the link bending with the joint at rest. (**b**) Bending of the beta link at the point where the morphology makes the blocking contact.

From the values H_s and D_s the angle α is obtained as:

$$\alpha = \arctan\left(\frac{H_s}{D_s}\right) \tag{10}$$

This angle is formed as the bisector of the blocking angle. The blocking angle of a link, β, is given as the double of alpha and it is obtained from the following equation:

$$\beta = 2 \cdot \alpha = 2 \cdot \arctan\left(\frac{H_s}{D_s}\right) \tag{11}$$

H_s has a fixed value (in our case, 8 mm) while D_s varies according to the orientation. To calculate D_s, we estimated the maximum, ϵ_{max}, and minimum, ϵ_{min}, possible distances with this morphology (40 mm and 25 mm, respectively), and the angles between them, $\psi_{dif} = 60°$. Knowing the orientation angles where the maximum and minimum occur, it can be parameterized according to a factor such that:

$$\frac{\epsilon_{max} - \epsilon_{min}}{\psi_{dif}} = 0.25 \tag{12}$$

Based on this factor, we know how the distance between the minimum and the maximum varies for each degree for D_s.

Once the theoretical blocking angle, β, is estimated for each link according to the orientation, we can calculate the final joint angle, Γ, when blocking occurs.

The final angle depends on the number of links within the joint, N, such that:

$$\Gamma = \beta \cdot N \tag{13}$$

3.3. Representation of the Workspace

Joint kinematics will block angles greater than the total blocking joint angle, creating an asymmetric workspace. X, Y and Z axes represent the soft joint final position in meters. The soft joint fixed base is at position $[0, 0, 0]$. Maximum Z value is 0.2 m when the joint is at rest. As the soft joint flexes, Z value decreases. X and Y values are the projection of the joint end position on the base plane. They are zero at resting position, and change with flexion. Therefore, the designed soft joint does not perform the same bending angle, both being performed in the same plane.

If this is done for different planes, we obtain a 3D mesh of '$*$' marks. The surface of a non-complete sphere is obtained, as seen in Figures 13 and 14. This allows knowledge of where the end will be and how the soft joint will move with respect to the fixed base.

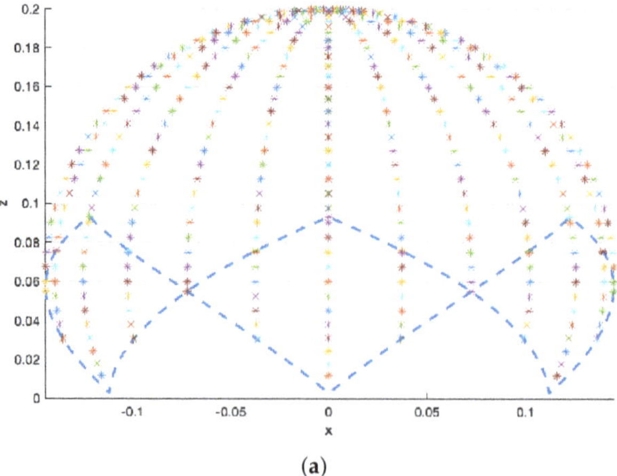

(a)

Figure 13. *Cont.*

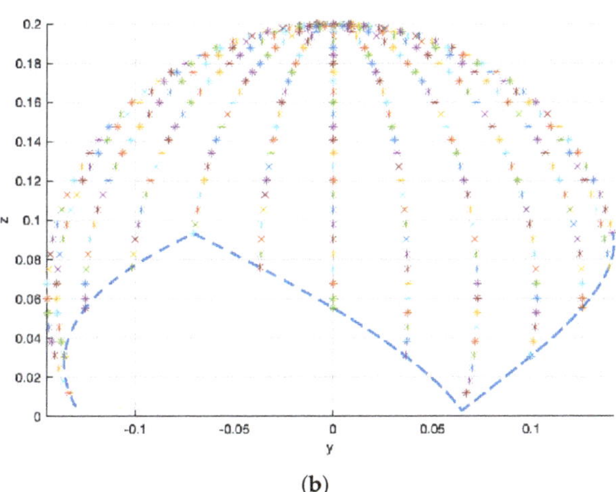

(b)

Figure 13. Diagram of soft joint end positions, represented by '∗' marks, at different orientation planes, every 15 degrees, and for every 5 inclination degrees. The dashed line indicates the flexion limits of the soft joint for each orientation. The soft joint cannot reach further positions due to blockages. (**a**) Front view. (**b**) Side view.

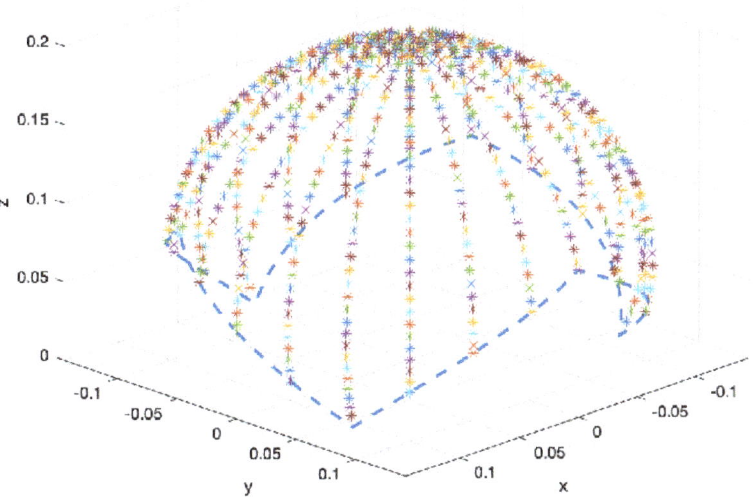

Figure 14. Perspective view of the soft link end positions represented by '∗' marks, at different orientation planes, every 15 degrees, and for every 5 inclination degrees. The dashed line indicates the flexion limits of the soft joint for each orientation. The soft joint cannot reach further positions due to blockages.

3.4. Representation of Variations in Tendon Lengths

Once tendon distances are adjusted to the joint kinematics, with the blocking angle restrictions, distance changes for each tendon can be represented as inclination and orientation input angles vary. Figure 15 shows tendon lengths according to inclination and orientation variations, the restrictions imposed by the design morphology, 0 to 359° orientation degrees and 0 to 170° inclination degrees, and the final length in meters.

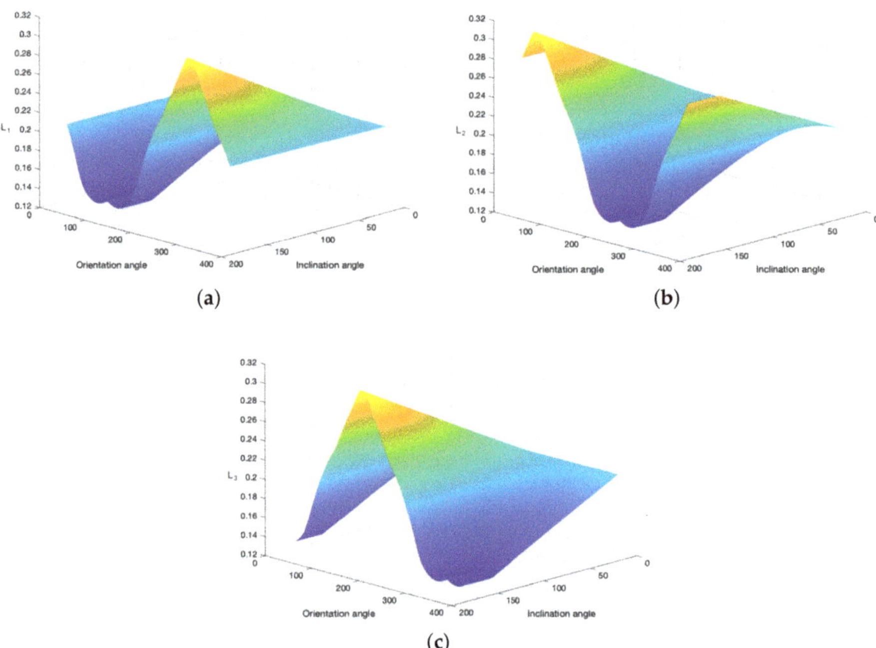

Figure 15. Representation of each tendon length variation for all possible values of inclination and orientation of the soft joint. The initial length of each tendon is 0.2 m (rest position). A color range from yellow to dark blue is used to show the variation from the highest tendon length value (yellow) to the lowest value (dark blue). (**a**) Length L_1 corresponding to tendon 1, (**b**) Length L_2 corresponding to tendon 2, (**c**) Length L_3 corresponding to tendon 3.

These graphs show how each tendon L_i varies according to inclination and orientation. The higher the inclination, the higher the variation of tendon length with changes of orientation. For a fixed inclination, when the orientation changes, as in a rotational movement, the tendon length increases and decreases in a sinusoidal shape, with the orientation corresponding to a maximum, a minimum or the initial length value. Due to the soft joint blockages, from certain degrees of inclination, the variation of tendon lengths is not sinusoidal, and, for certain orientation angle ranges, the length remains fixed.

3.5. Direct Kinematics

A direct kinematics is also provided through the works collected in [3]. This kinematics allows us to know the inclination and orientation for the input values L_1, L_2 and L_3. These equations assume that the curvature is constant throughout the flexible body.

$$\psi = \arctan\left(\frac{\sqrt{3}(l_2 + l_3 - 2l_1)}{3(l_2 - l_3)}\right) \tag{14}$$

$$\theta = \frac{2\sqrt{l_1^2 + l_2^2 + l_3^2 - l_2l_1 - l_2l_3 - l_1l_3}}{a(l_1 + l_2 + l_3)} \tag{15}$$

3.6. Simulation of the Model

Using the above equations, the mathematical model can be represented by simulation. From the inputs, inclination and orientation, the inverse kinematics is made, and the linear displacement of the tendons is calculated. Those values are turned into and angular displacement for each motor. The motor encoders can be used as sensors to measure the real angular motor position and close the control loop.

The motor models are represented as a function using the values from the motor datasheet. Following a general control diagram, where K is the motor speed constant in rpm/V, and τ is the mechanical time constant in seconds, we obtain the transfer function $G(s)$ [32], such that:

$$G(s) = \frac{K}{s(1 + \tau s)} = \frac{352}{s(1 + 0.00875s)} \tag{16}$$

For the simulation, a control loop is created in Simulink Matlab, in which the input values are entered interactively, Figure 16. The tendon lengths for these inputs are obtained through a Matlab function that has been designed from Equation (9), called "Inverse Kinematics", Algorithm 1.

Algorithm 1 Inverse kinematics.

1:    *input:* θ, ψ
2:    *internal constant:* N, L, a
3: **procedure**
4:     $\beta \leftarrow block\text{-}angle\text{-}equation(\psi)$
5:     **if** $\beta < \theta/N$ **then**
6:       $\theta = \beta \cdot N$
7:     $\phi_i \leftarrow phi\text{-}equation(\psi)$
8:     $L_i \leftarrow length\text{-}equation(L, a, \phi_i)$
9:     **return** L_i

The three values of L_i returned by the inverse kinematics block are used to obtain the target Ω (target angular position of the motors), using the "L_i to Omega" function block described by Equation (1), Algorithm 2.

Algorithm 2 L_i to Omega.

1:    *input:* L_i
2:    *internal constant:* L, r
3: **procedure**
4:     $\Omega \leftarrow Omega\text{-}equation(L_i, L, r)$
5:     **return** Ω

From these target Ω values, the motor control loops return the current Ω values. The direct kinematics is performed using the "Direct Kinematics and 3D representation" function block defined by Equations (14) and (15), Algorithm 3. The current inclination and orientation of the free end through the simulation are obtained. This function block also provides the position of the simulated soft joint represented in a 3D space, Figure 17.

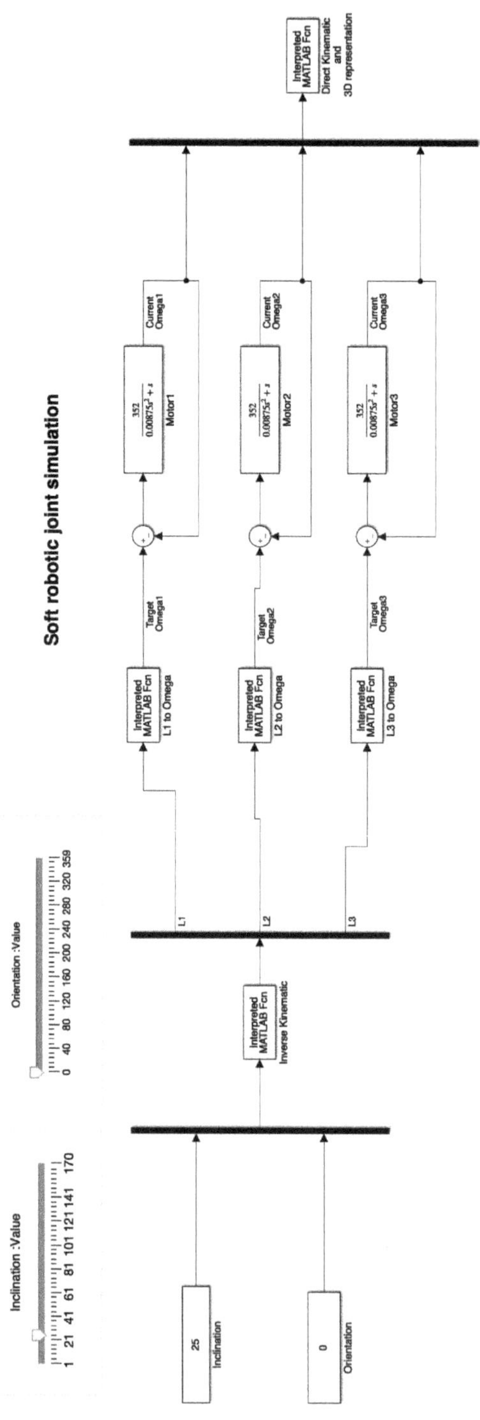

Figure 16. Simulink schematic for the soft joint model simulation.

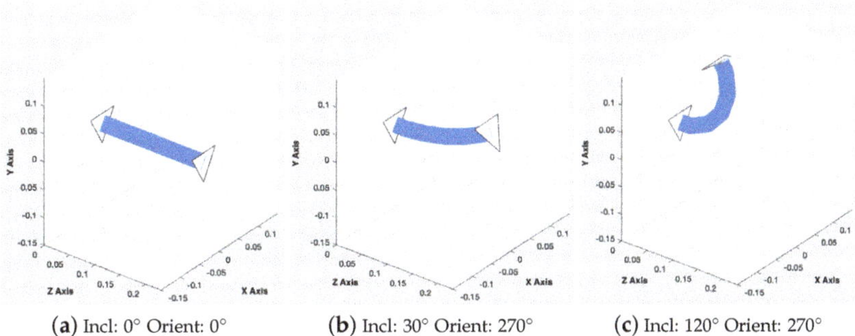

(**a**) Incl: 0° Orient: 0° (**b**) Incl: 30° Orient: 270° (**c**) Incl: 120° Orient: 270°

Figure 17. Three-dimensional representation of the simulation of the soft joint for different input values.

Algorithm 3 Direct Kinematics and 3D representation.

1: *input: ϕ_i*
2: *internal constant:* L, r, a
3: **procedure**
4:      $L_i \leftarrow Omega\text{-}equation\text{-}inverse(\phi_i, L, r)$
5:      $\theta_{Simu} \leftarrow Direct\text{-}Kinematics\text{-}\theta(L_i, a)$
6:      $\psi_{Simu} \leftarrow Direct\text{-}Kinematics\text{-}\psi(L_i)$
7:      $Draw\text{-}simulation(\theta_{Simu}, \psi_{Simu})$
8:      **return** $\theta_{Simu}, \psi_{Simu}$

---

4. Experimental Tests

The soft joint assessment is performed through two types of experimental tests. These tests allow us to evaluate motion performance and kinematics model accuracy, based on the error between the target end position and the real end position of the soft joint. A video showing these tests performance can be viewed at https://vimeo.com/537605947 (accessed on 10 May 2021).

Data were collected from the tests in two ways. Position data from motor encoders provided information on inclination and orientation through the direct kinematics. Data from the inertial sensor 3DM-GX5-10 IMU, the yaw, roll and pitch data, were transformed into inclination and orientation data for comparison with references.

4.1. Test 1

Test 1 consists of a bending movement towards a fixed inclination angle, in each of the four orientations: 0°, 90°, 180° and 270°. This test shows how the joint starts in a resting position, performs the action and then returns to the resting position before it bends at the next orientation. The resting position is 0 degrees of inclination and orientation. Tests were performed for 30°, 45° and 60° inclination and results are shown in Figure 18 for the encoder data and Figure 19 for the sensor data.

Test 1—Encoder data

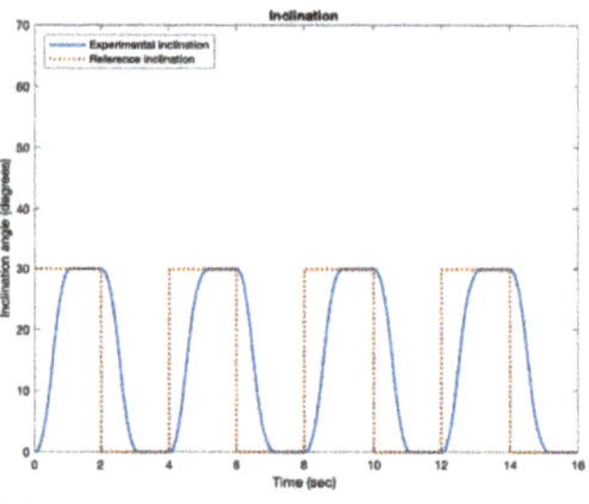

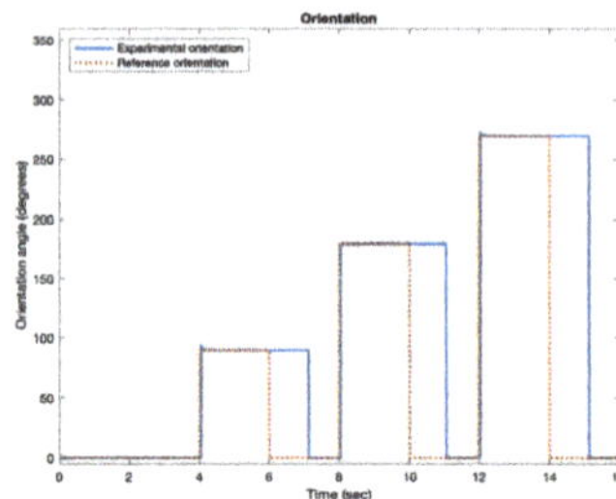

(**a**) Inclination versus time through encoder measurements for 30° inclination.

(**b**) Orientation versus time through encoder measurements for 30° inclination.

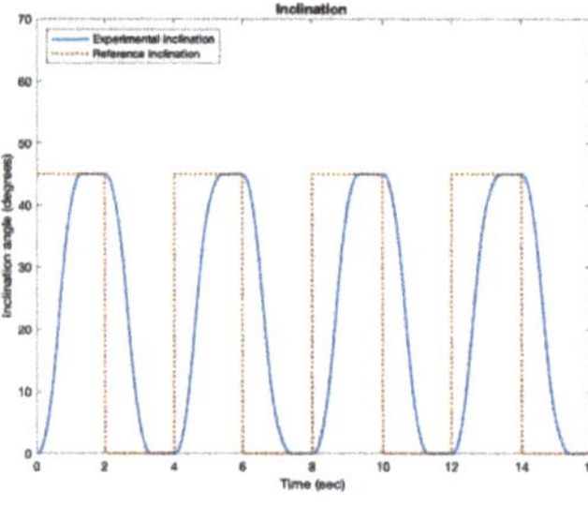

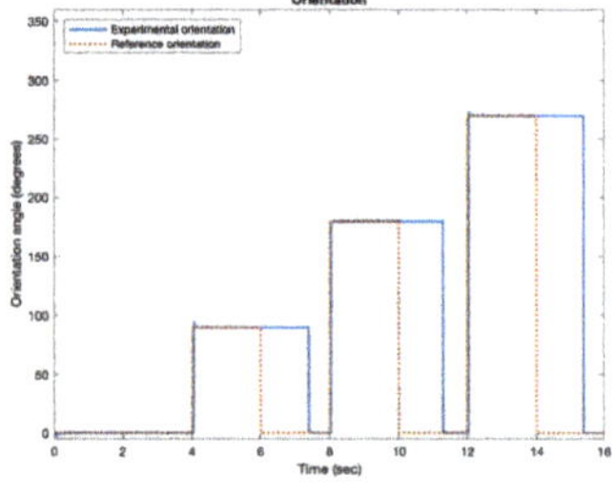

(**c**) Inclination versus time through encoder measurements for 45° inclination.

(**d**) Orientation versus time through encoder measurements for 45° inclination.

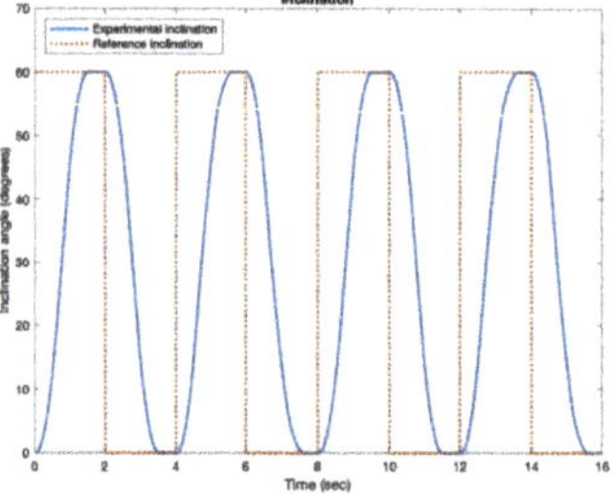

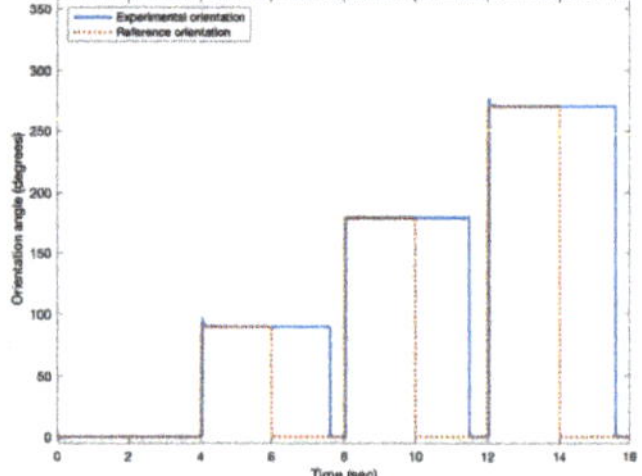

(**e**) Inclination versus time through encoder measurements for 60° inclination.

(**f**) Orientation versus time through encoder measurements for 60° inclination.

Figure 18. Test 1—Encoder data. Fixed 30°, 45° and 60° inclination for four orientations: 0°, 90°, 180° and 270°. The blue line is the experimental data obtained from the encoder and the orange dotted line is the reference.

Test 1—Sensor data

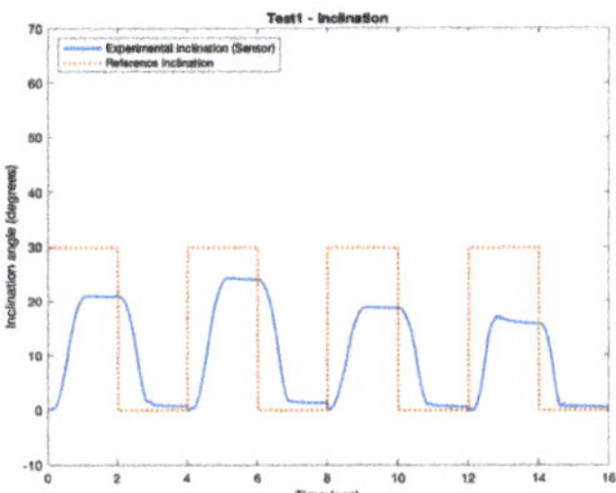

(a) Inclination versus time through inertial sensor measurements for 30° inclination.

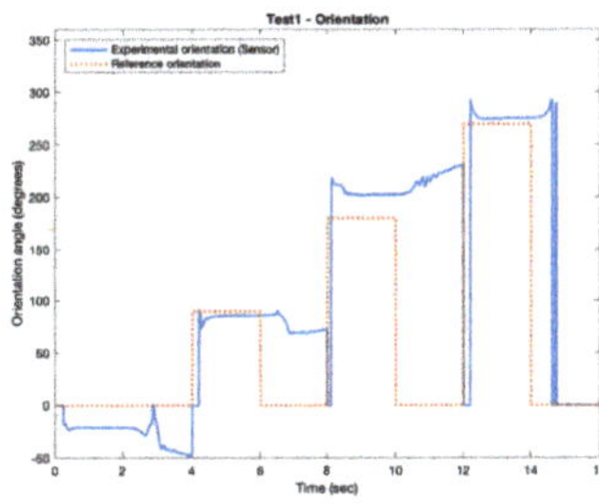

(b) Orientation versus time through inertial sensor measurements for 30° inclination.

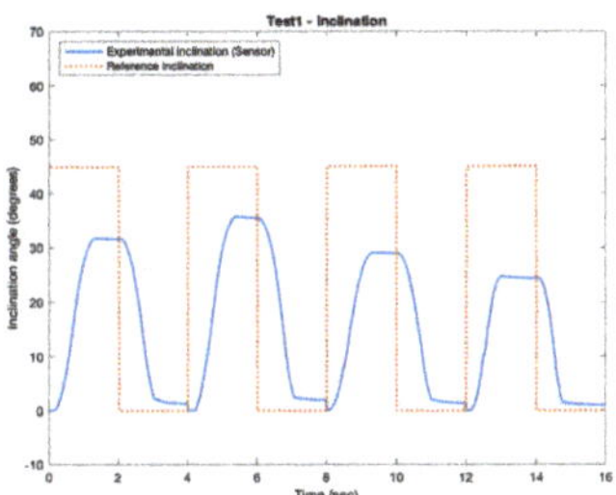

(c) Inclination versus time through inertial sensor measurements for 45° inclination.

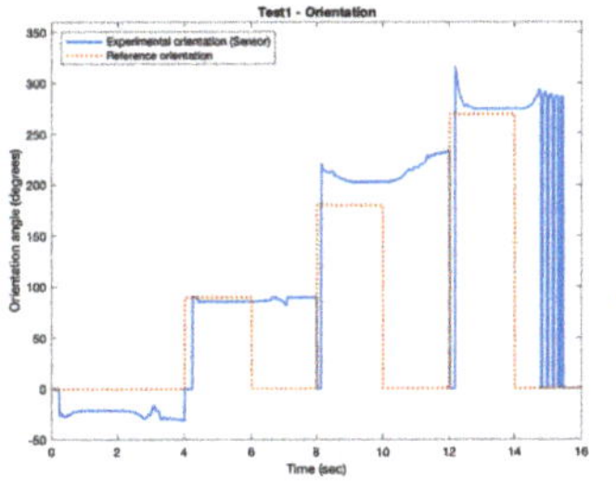

(d) Orientation versus time through inertial sensor measurements for 45° inclination.

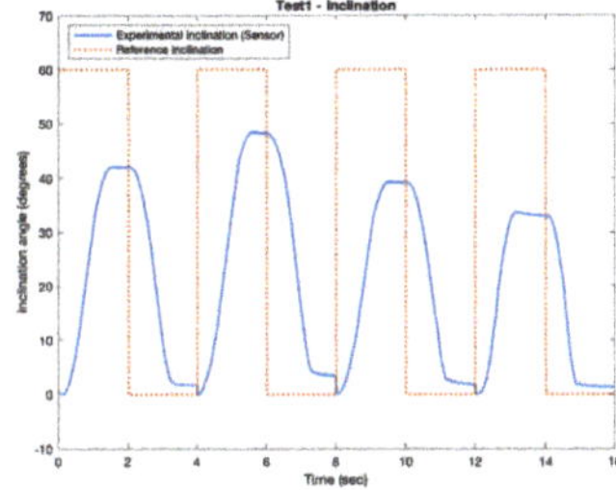

(e) Inclination versus time through inertial sensor measurements for 60° inclination.

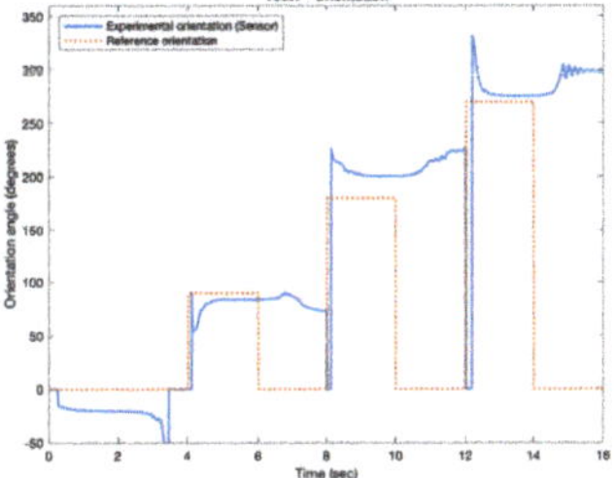

(f) Orientation versus time through inertial sensor measurements for 60° inclination.

Figure 19. Test 1—Sensor data. Fixed 30°, 45° and 60° inclination for four orientations: 0°, 90°, 180° and 270°. The blue line is the experimental data obtained from the encoder and the orange dotted line is the reference.

4.2. Test 2

Test 2 consists of a 360° rotation for a given inclination. This rotation starts in a resting position and is performed by increasing the orientation value by one degree every 0.1 s, starting from 0°. When the rotation is complete, it returns to the resting position. The test was performed for 30°, 45° and 60° inclination and results are shown in Figure 20 for the encoder data and Figure 21 for the sensor data.

Test 2—Encoder data

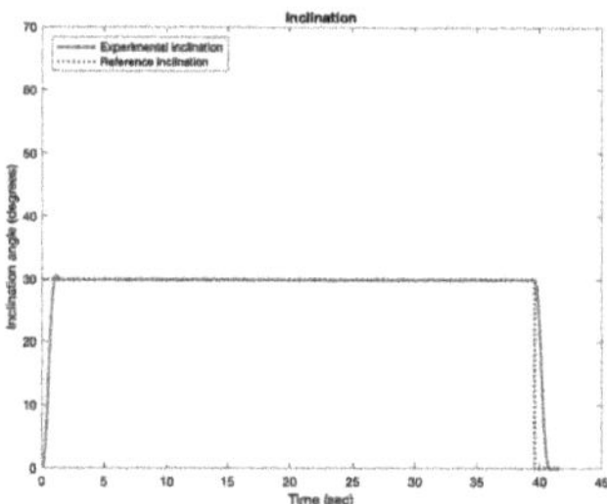

(**a**) Inclination versus time through encoder measurements for 30° inclination.

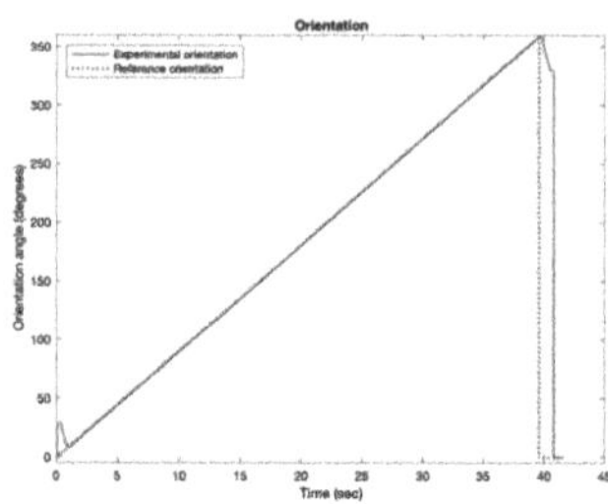

(**b**) Orientation versus time through encoder measurements for 30° inclination.

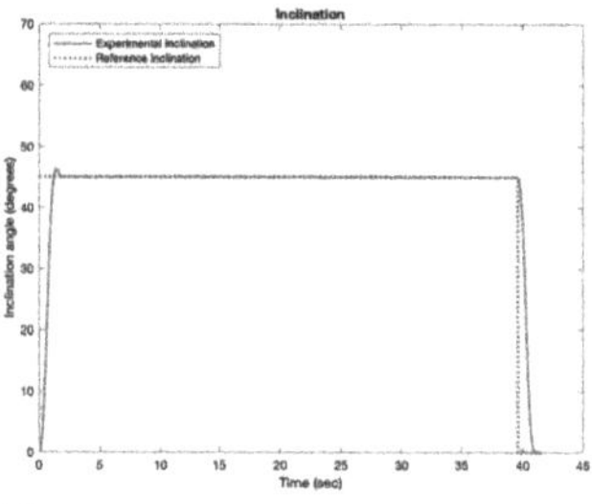

(**c**) Inclination versus time through encoder measurements for 45° inclination.

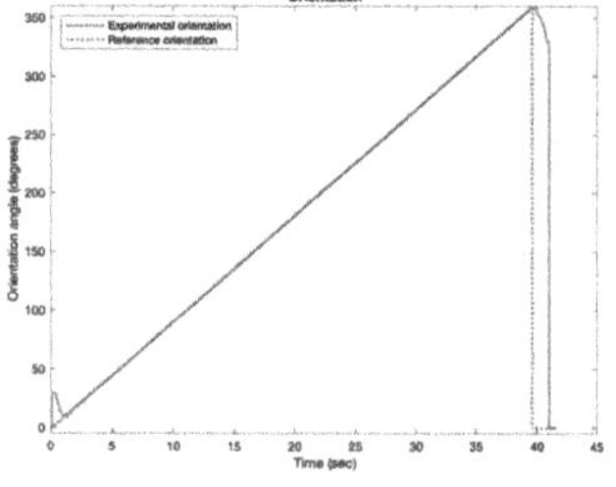

(**d**) Orientation versus time through encoder measurements for 45° inclination.

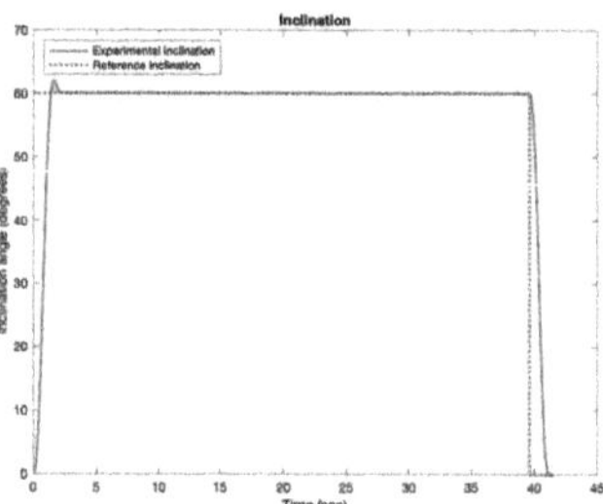

(**e**) Inclination versus time through encoder measurements for 60° inclination.

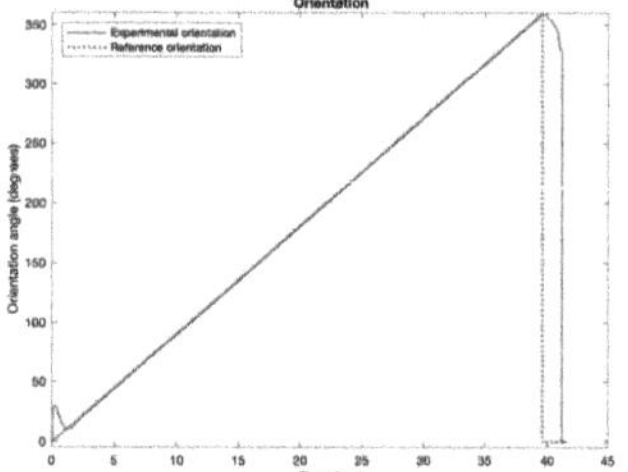

(**f**) Orientation versus time through encoder measurements for 60° inclination.

Figure 20. Test 2—Encoder data. Fixed 30°, 45° and 60° inclination for a 360° rotation. The blue line is the experimental data obtained from the encoder and the orange dotted line is the reference.

Test 2—Sensor data

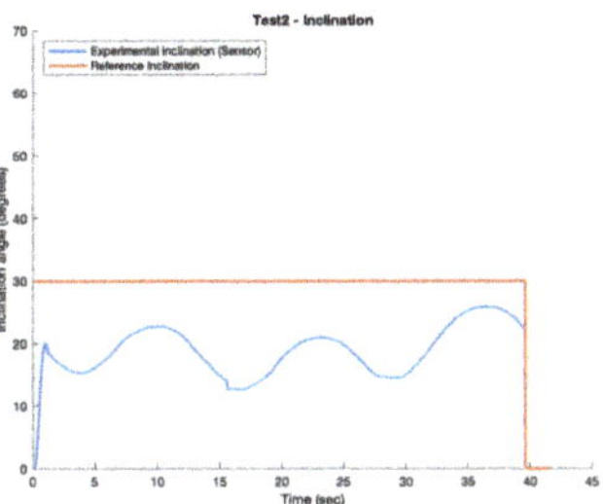

(**a**) Inclination versus time through inertial sensor measurements for 30° inclination.

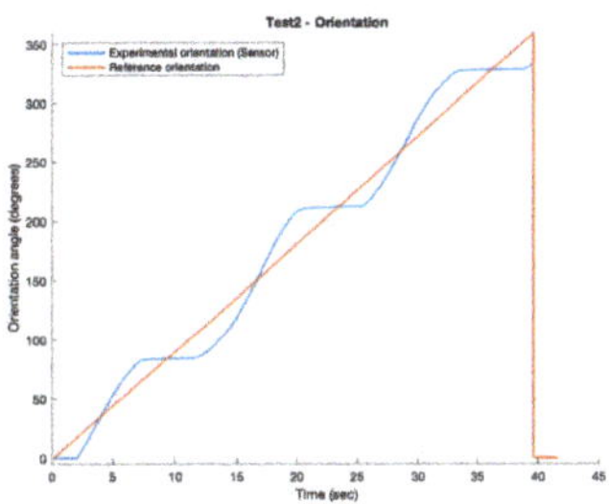

(**b**) Orientation versus time through inertial sensor measurements for 30° inclination.

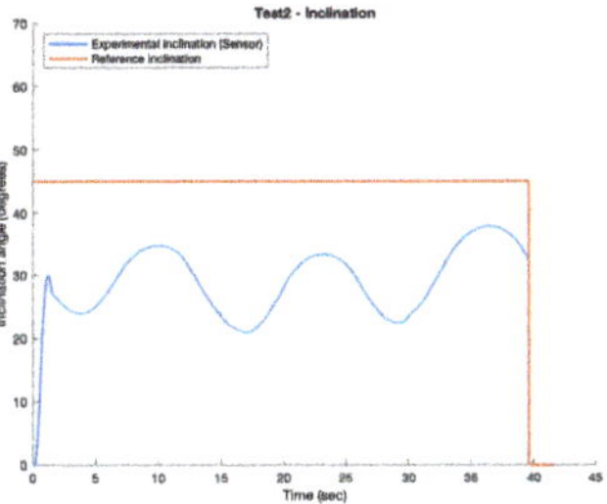

(**c**) Inclination versus time through inertial sensor measurements for 45° inclination.

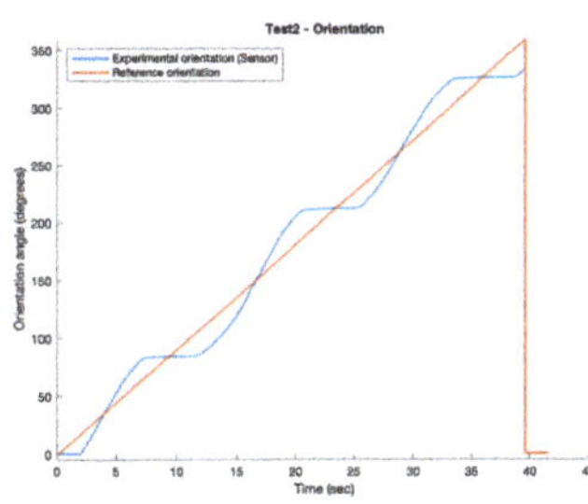

(**d**) Orientation versus time through inertial sensor measurements for 45° inclination.

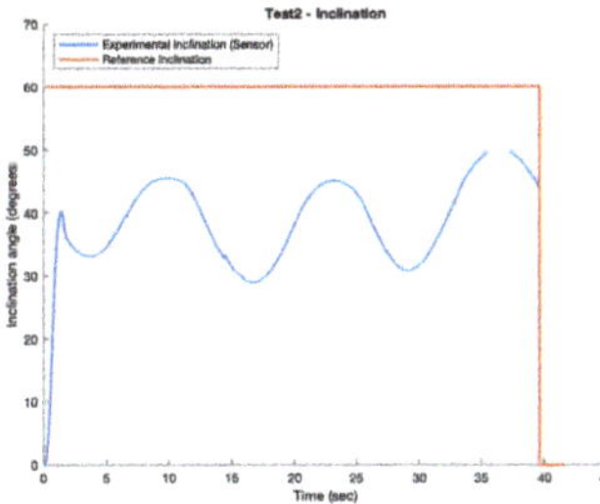

(**e**) Inclination versus time through inertial sensor measurements for 60° inclination.

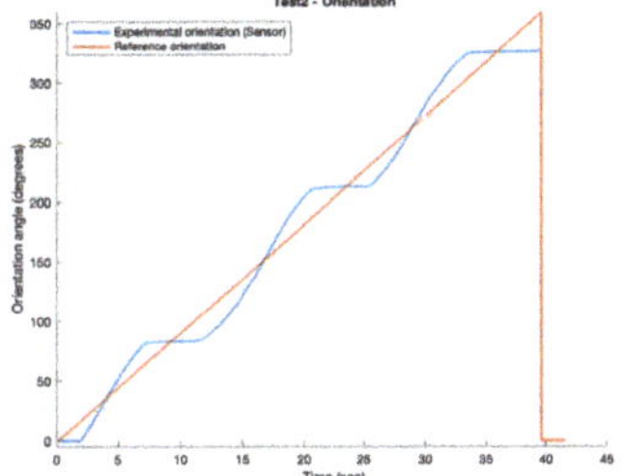

(**f**) Orientation versus time through inertial sensor measurements for 60° inclination.

Figure 21. Test 2—Sensor data. Fixed 30°, 45° and 60° inclination for a 360° rotation. The blue line is the experimental data obtained from the encoder and the orange dotted line is the reference.

5. Discussion

Simulation and experimental results have been performed to analyze and validate both the design and the proposed model for the cable-driven soft joint.

The simulation results allow the validation of the soft joint through a finite element study. The soft joint was simulated by applying a load of 60 N, which would be the maximum force expected for this prototype. It has made possible to validate the joint structure, ensuring that when maximum loads are applied, the structure does not exceed the elastic limit and does not lose its elasticity.

The experimental tests performed show the behavior of the soft joint system in different situations. Test 1 explores the behavior to reach a target position from a resting position and how the soft link behaves to return to the home position. It is a movement where the inclination changes with a fixed orientation that does not vary. Test 2 explores the ability to maintain a fixed inclination while gradually varying the orientation.

5.1. Results Using the Encoder Sensor

The inclination results, obtained from the encoder during Test 1, show that the experimental inclination reaches the reference inclination, and this is repeated for each of the four requested orientations. We also observed that the higher the requested reference, the longer it takes to reach it.

For the orientation results, the orientation reference is a set of four steps of different sizes. The first is a step of zero amplitude and the experimental orientation is quickly reached. This is because, from the zero-degree inclination position (fully extended joint), reaching any orientation is almost immediate. When the joint is requested to return to the resting position, the experimental orientation remains constant. Meanwhile, the inclination decreases and when it reaches zero, the orientation reaches zero, too. This is why, in this test, the orientation values change so quickly back to zero degrees and the time between the reference orientation and the experimental orientation reaching zero is longer.

5.2. Results Using the Inertial Sensor

The data obtained from the inertial sensor show more accurately the real behavior of the end of the soft joint.

The inclination results in Test 1 show that the position of the joint does not reach the reference inclination. The $90°$ orientation test (downwards, in the sense of gravity) is the one that presents lower errors when tracking the reference. The tests for $0°$ and $180°$ orientation angles show higher tracking errors, as shown in the attached video. The kinematics designed for these positions assumes that the length of tendon 1 (lower motor) should not change. These theoretical results, when taken to the experimental field, are not fulfilled because the tendons are not perfectly tensioned, and the two upper wires cause the position rise. This rise is reflected in the orientation that has a negative phase shift when the reference is $0°$ and a positive phase shift when the reference is $180°$.

We also observed that the orientation results do not reach the zero position when the reference is zero. This is because it is difficult to move the orientation to zero due to the fact that the inclination is not exactly zero when returning to the resting position, as the inclination graphs show. This causes a slight inclination while maintaining the same orientation. As discussed above for the encoder data, orientation is very sensitive to inclination.

For the sensor results in Test 2, the inclination graphs show how the experimental inclination does not reach the reference value. However, it should be noted that it has a sinusoidal behavior over time. As in the previous test, the reason for both is that the theoretical behavior of the joint is not the same as the real behavior, because the model assumes aspects such as a continuous curvature, and because there are also other influencing mechanical aspects, such as the precision in the tendon length or the tendon winding in the winches.

This undulatory behavior is observed again in the orientation graphs. However, it can be seen that for angles $90°$, $210°$ and $330°$ the orientation does not vary, which coincides with the vertices of the soft joint morphology. For these angles, the inclination is maximum. Moreover, when one of the vertices is passed, the opposite tendons cause the variation of orientation, and it takes a little time to change from unwinding to rewinding. This can be seen in the attached videos for this test.

6. Conclusions

This work presents a novel approach to soft robotics with the design of a flexible and compact soft joint. It is not only a low-cost prototype, assembled by 3D printing. It also has a morphology that allows better handling of external loads and gravity thanks to its blocking configuration. Actuated by tendons, the proposed design has a morphology with two main configurations of flexion, which provides more versatility and a flexion limit, unlike previous designs. These characteristics and configurations can be modified through the parameters of the joint morphology, to achieve different fields of work and functionality.

A mathematical model of the inverse kinematics of the soft joint is also presented to obtain the length of the tendons as a function of the morphology and the position (orientation and inclination) of the end of the joint. The modeling of the soft morphology is a complex task, but a simplified and sufficiently accurate kinematic model has been shown. For its validation, the soft link prototype has been built and simulation and experimental studies have been carried out.

According to the capabilities of the solution described and demonstrated throughout the paper, the soft joint proposed in this work shows an improvement over other designs and it could be used for many different applications requiring manipulation of loads. Our main application will be the use of this joint as an arm for the humanoid robot TEO so that the robot can perform manipulation tasks with the use of a gripper connected to the arm tip. There are several uncertainties and mismatches that affect the model of the prototype, especially when this is a low-cost 3D printed solution. For instance, the curvature of the real model is not constant, the tension and length of tendons are not exact, and small variations in the radius of the winches happen after several turns. Despite these facts, the proposed model is accurate enough to represent the kinematics of the system and will allow a later control of the soft joint in closed loop. Further research will lead to reducing these inaccuracies and prototyping effects and to closing the control loop and testing the platform with different loads during manipulation interactions.

7. Patents

The technology presented in this paper is under a patent licensing process. A patent entitled "Eslabón para articulación blanda y articulación blanda que comprende dicho eslabón" ("Link for soft articulation and soft articulation comprising such link") and reference number P202030726 (register number 5349) has been presented to the Oficina Española de Patentes y Marcas—OEPM (Spanish Patents Office) (5 July 2020).

Author Contributions: Conceptualization, L.N., C.R., C.A.M. and C.B.; methodology, L.N., C.R. and C.A.M.; software, L.N. and C.R.; validation, L.N., C.R. and C.A.M.; formal analysis, L.N. and C.R.; investigation, L.N., C.R., C.A.M. and C.B.; resources, C.A.M. and C.B.; data curation, L.N. and C.R.; writing—original draft preparation, L.N. and C.R.; writing—review and editing, L.N., C.R., C.A.M. and C.B.; visualization, L.N. and C.R.; supervision, C.A.M. and C.B.; project administration, C.A.M.; funding acquisition, C.A.M. and C.B. All authors have read and agreed to the published version of the manuscript.

Funding: The research leading to these results has received funding from the project Desarrollo de articulaciones blandas para aplicaciones robóticas, with reference IND2020/IND-1739, funded by the Comunidad Autónoma de Madrid (CAM) (Department of Education and Research), and from RoboCity2030-DIH-CM, Madrid Robotics Digital Innovation Hub (Robótica aplicada a la mejora de la calidad de vida de los ciudadanos, FaseIV; S2018/NMT-4331), funded by "Programas de Actividades I+D en la Comunidad de Madrid" and cofunded by Structural Funds of the EU.

Institutional Review Board Statement: Not applicable.

Informed Consent Statement: Not applicable.

Data Availability Statement: The data presented are available on request from the corresponding author.

Conflicts of Interest: The authors declare no conflict of interest.

Abbreviations

The following abbreviations are used in this manuscript:

CAD	Computer-aided Design
CDPM	Cable-Driven Parallel Mechanism
DLR	Germany's Research Centre for Aeronautics and Space
DOF	Degrees of Freedom
FDM	Fused Deposition Modeling
FEA	Finite Element Analysis
FEM	Finite Element Method
PC	Personal Computer
PLA	Polylactic Acid
SMA	Shape Memory Alloy

References

1. Hughes, J.; Culha, U.; Giardina, F.; Guenther, F.; Rosendo, A.; Iida, F. Soft manipulators and grippers: A review. *Front. Robot. AI* **2016**, *3*, 69. [CrossRef]
2. Lee, C.; Kim, M.; Kim, Y.J.; Hong, N.; Ryu, S.; Kim, H.J.; Kim, S. Soft robot review. *Int. J. Control Autom. Syst.* **2017**, *15*, 3–15. [CrossRef]
3. Webster, R.J., III; Jones, B.A. Design and kinematic modeling of constant curvature continuum robots: A review. *Int. J. Robot. Res.* **2010**, *29*, 1661–1683. [CrossRef]
4. Chirikjian, G.S.; Burdick, J.W. The kinematics of hyper-redundant robot locomotion. *IEEE Trans. Robot. Autom.* **1995**, *11*, 781–793. [CrossRef]
5. Wolf, A.; Brown, H.B.; Casciola, R.; Costa, A.; Schwerin, M.; Shamas, E.; Choset, H. A mobile hyper redundant mechanism for search and rescue tasks. In Proceedings of the Proceedings 2003 IEEE/RSJ International Conference on Intelligent Robots and Systems (IROS 2003) (Cat. No. 03CH37453), Las Vegas, NV, USA, 27–31 October 2003; Volume 3, pp. 2889–2895.
6. George Thuruthel, T.; Ansari, Y.; Falotico, E.; Laschi, C. Control strategies for soft robotic manipulators: A survey. *Soft Robot.* **2018**, *5*, 149–163. [CrossRef]
7. Mishra, A.K.; Mondini, A.; Del Dottore, E.; Sadeghi, A.; Tramacere, F.; Mazzolai, B. Modular continuum manipulator: Analysis and characterization of its basic module. *Biomimetics* **2018**, *3*, 3. [CrossRef]
8. Yang, H.; Xu, M.; Li, W.; Zhang, S. Design and implementation of a soft robotic arm driven by SMA coils. *IEEE Trans. Ind. Electron.* **2018**, *66*, 6108–6116. [CrossRef]
9. Copaci, D.; Muñoz, J.; González, I.; Monje, C.A.; Moreno, L. SMA-Driven Soft Robotic Neck: Design, Control and Validation. *IEEE Access* **2020**, *8*, 199492–199502. [CrossRef]
10. Goswami, D.; Liu, S.; Pal, A.; Silva, L.G.; Martinez, R.V. 3D-architected soft machines with topologically encoded motion. *Adv. Funct. Mater.* **2019**, *29*, 1808713. [CrossRef]
11. Yi, J.; Chen, X.; Song, C.; Zhou, J.; Liu, Y.; Liu, S.; Wang, Z. Customizable three-dimensional-printed origami soft robotic joint with effective behavior shaping for safe interactions. *IEEE Trans. Robot.* **2018**, *35*, 114–123. [CrossRef]
12. Mena, L.; Muñoz, J.; Monje, C.A.; Balaguer, C. Modular and Self-Scalable Origami Robot: A First Approach. *Mathematics* **2021**, *9*, 1324. [CrossRef]
13. Nazari, A.A.; Castro, D.; Godage, I.S. Forward and Inverse Kinematics of a Single Section Inextensible Continuum Arm. *arXiv* **2019**, arXiv:1907.06518.
14. Muñoz, J.; Piqué, F.; A. Monje, C.; Falotico, E. Robust Fractional-Order Control Using a Decoupled Pitch and Roll Actuation Strategy for the I-Support Soft Robot. *Mathematics* **2021**, *9*, 702. [CrossRef]
15. Slesarenko, V.; Engelkemier, S.; Galich, P.I.; Vladimirsky, D.; Klein, G.; Rudykh, S. Strategies to control performance of 3d-printed, cable-driven soft polymer actuators: From simple architectures to gripper prototype. *Polymers* **2018**, *10*, 846. [CrossRef]
16. Laschi, C.; Cianchetti, M.; Mazzolai, B.; Margheri, L.; Follador, M.; Dario, P. Soft robot arm inspired by the octopus. *Adv. Robot.* **2012**, *26*, 709–727. [CrossRef]
17. Calisti, M.; Giorelli, M.; Levy, G.; Mazzolai, B.; Hochner, B.; Laschi, C.; Dario, P. An octopus-bioinspired solution to movement and manipulation for soft robots. *Bioinspir. Biomim.* **2011**, *6*, 036002. [CrossRef]
18. Giannaccini, M.E.; Xiang, C.; Atyabi, A.; Theodoridis, T.; Nefti-Meziani, S.; Davis, S. Novel design of a soft lightweight pneumatic continuum robot arm with decoupled variable stiffness and positioning. *Soft Robot.* **2018**, *5*, 54–70. [CrossRef]
19. Walker, I.D.; Dawson, D.M.; Flash, T.; Grasso, F.W.; Hanlon, R.T.; Hochner, B.; Kier, W.M.; Pagano, C.C.; Rahn, C.D.; Zhang, Q.M. Continuum robot arms inspired by cephalopods. In *Unmanned Ground Vehicle Technology VII*; International Society for Optics and Photonics: Bellingham, WA, USA, 2005; Volume 5804, pp. 303–314.
20. Godage, I.S.; Medrano-Cerda, G.A.; Branson, D.T.; Guglielmino, E.; Caldwell, D.G. Dynamics for variable length multisection continuum arms. *Int. J. Robot. Res.* **2016**, *35*, 695–722. [CrossRef]
21. Hawkes, E.W.; Blumenschein, L.H.; Greer, J.D.; Okamura, A.M. A soft robot that navigates its environment through growth. *Sci. Robot.* **2017**, *2*. [CrossRef]

22. Best, C.M.; Gillespie, M.T.; Hyatt, P.; Rupert, L.; Sherrod, V.; Killpack, M.D. A new soft robot control method: Using model predictive control for a pneumatically actuated humanoid. *IEEE Robot. Autom. Mag.* **2016**, *23*, 75–84. [CrossRef]
23. Wang, H.; Zhang, R.; Chen, W.; Wang, X.; Pfeifer, R. A cable-driven soft robot surgical system for cardiothoracic endoscopic surgery: Preclinical tests in animals. *Surg. Endosc.* **2017**, *31*, 3152–3158. [CrossRef]
24. Mohammadi, A.; Lavranos, J.; Zhou, H.; Mutlu, R.; Alici, G.; Tan, Y.; Choong, P.; Oetomo, D. A practical 3D-printed soft robotic prosthetic hand with multi-articulating capabilities. *PLoS ONE* **2020**, *15*, e0232766. [CrossRef]
25. Reinecke, J.; Deutschmann, B.; Fehrenbach, D. A structurally flexible humanoid spine based on a tendon-driven elastic continuum. In Proceedings of the 2016 IEEE International Conference on Robotics and Automation (ICRA), Stockholm, Sweden, 16–21 May 2016; pp. 4714–4721.
26. Wang, H.; Chen, W.; Yu, X.; Deng, T.; Wang, X.; Pfeifer, R. Visual servo control of cable-driven soft robotic manipulator. In Proceedings of the 2013 IEEE/RSJ International Conference on Intelligent Robots and Systems, Tokyo, Japan, 3–7 November 2013; pp. 57–62.
27. Nagua, L.; Munoz, J.; Monje, C.A.; Balaguer, C. A first approach to a proposal of a soft robotic link acting as a neck. In Proceedings of the Actas de las XXXIX Jornadas de AutomÁTica, Badajoz, Spain, 5–7 September 2018. [CrossRef]
28. Mena, L.; Monje, C.A.; Nagua, L.; Muñoz, J.; Balaguer, C. Test Bench for Evaluation of a Soft Robotic Link. *Front. Robot. AI* **2020**, *7*, 27. [CrossRef]
29. Quevedo, F.; Yañez-Barnuevo, J.M.; Castano, J.A.; Monje, C.A.; Balaguer, C. Model Identification of a Soft Robotic Neck. In Proceedings of the 2020 IEEE/RSJ International Conference on Intelligent Robots and Systems (IROS), Las Vegas, NV, USA, 24 October 2020–24 January 2021; pp. 8640–8645.
30. Chen, G.; Thomann, G.; Pham, M.T.; Bétemps, M.; Redarce, T. Modeling and control of a colonoscopic tip under disturbance of the insertion of colonoscope. In Proceedings of the 2004 IEEE/RSJ International Conference on Intelligent Robots and Systems (IROS) (IEEE Cat. No. 04CH37566), Sendai, Japan, 28 September–2 October 2004; Volume 4, pp. 3315–3320.
31. Jones, B.A.; Walker, I.D. Practical kinematics for real-time implementation of continuum robots. *IEEE Trans. Robot.* **2006**, *22*, 1087–1099. [CrossRef]
32. Bhagat, N.A.; Bhaganagare, M.; Pandey, P. *DC Motor Speed Control Using PID Controllers*; Department of Electrical Engineering, IIT Bombay: Mumbai, India, 2009; pp. 1–18.

 *mathematics*

MDPI

Article

Fractional Dynamics of Stuxnet Virus Propagation in Industrial Control Systems

Zaheer Masood [1], Muhammad Asif Zahoor Raja [2,*], Naveed Ishtiaq Chaudhary [2], Khalid Mehmood Cheema [3] and Ahmad H. Milyani [4]

1   Department of Electrical and Electronics Engineering, Capital University of Science and Technology, Islamabad 44000, Pakistan; masood.zaheer@yahoo.com
2   Future Technology Research Center, National Yunlin University of Science and Technology, 123 University Road, Section 3, Douliou 64002, Taiwan; chaudni@yuntech.edu.tw
3   School of Electrical Engineering, Southeast University, Nanjing 210096, China; kmcheema@seu.edu.cn
4   Department of Electrical and Computer Engineering, King Abdulaziz University, Jeddah 21589, Saudi Arabia; ahmilyani@kau.edu.sa
*   Correspondence: rajamaz@yuntech.edu.tw

Abstract: The designed fractional order Stuxnet, the virus model, is analyzed to investigate the spread of the virus in the regime of isolated industrial networks environment by bridging the air-gap between the traditional and the critical control network infrastructures. Removable storage devices are commonly used to exploit the vulnerability of individual nodes, as well as the associated networks, by transferring data and viruses in the isolated industrial control system. A mathematical model of an arbitrary order system is constructed and analyzed numerically to depict the control mechanism. A local and global stability analysis of the system is performed on the equilibrium points derived for the value of $\alpha = 1$. To understand the depth of fractional model behavior, numerical simulations are carried out for the distinct order of the fractional derivative system, and the results show that fractional order models provide rich dynamics by means of fast transient and super-slow evolution of the model's steady-state behavior, which are seldom perceived in integer-order counterparts.

Keywords: fractional-order virus models; stuxnet virus; numerical computing; supervisory control and data acquisition systems; computer networks; lyapunov analysis

Citation: Masood, Z.; Raja, M.A.Z.; Chaudhary, N.I.; Cheema, K.M.; Milyani, A.H. Fractional Dynamics of Stuxnet Virus Propagation in Industrial Control Systems. *Mathematics* **2021**, *9*, 2160. https://doi.org/10.3390/math9172160

Academic Editors: Mikhail Posypkin, Andrey Gorshenin and Vladimir Titarev

Received: 20 June 2021
Accepted: 31 August 2021
Published: 4 September 2021

Publisher's Note: MDPI stays neutral with regard to jurisdictional claims in published maps and institutional affiliations.

1. Introduction

A small piece of software code or program in a computer system that works on a system without the consent of the user may cause damage or steal information for the exploitation of the desired targets. In strategic conflicting environments, as well as in the financial market, computer viruses can be used in a network operation as a digital weapon against the desired targets, e.g., a computer spyware program used as an information collection platform in the Syrian war [1], or Shamoon and Stuxnet viruses for cyber incidents [2]. The tools used for cyberwar vary from a tiny code that exhibits annoying messages on the console to a complicated routine that physically damages the system, such as Stuxnet [3]. Stuxnet was discovered at Natanz, Iran, a nuclear enrichment facility, in June 2010 [4]. The name of the Stuxnet virus was derived from two keywords in its source code, .stub and mrxnet.sys. The Stuxnet virus is a sophisticated piece of code that mainly targets the supervisory control and data acquisition systems (SCADA), exploits zero-day vulnerabilities/bugs to attack the targeted hosts, and uses advanced technology to hide from guard programs. The Stuxnet virus exploits different services, such as a print spooler (MS 10-061), the zero-day vulnerability of the windows system, network shares, file-sharing and server message block (SMB), etc. Stuxnet virus monitors the frequency of motors operating centrifuge machines before modification, which must be in the range of from 807 Hertz to 1210 Hertz. Stuxnet virus controls the running frequency of centrifuge machines for a short interval of time to 1410 Hertz and then decreases to 2 Hz and increases to 1064 Hertz. A change in the output frequency of the motors essentially sabotages the working of machines [5]. Due to the attack of the Stuxnet virus, approximately 1000 centrifuge machines were out of order, of a total of 5000 machines operating in the Iran nuclear facility at Natanz [6]. The purpose of the virus was not just to infect the computers, but to cause real-world physical damage.

A theoretical study of the Stuxnet's malicious code behavior was conducted through the strength of epidemic modeling of virus spread [7–9]. The control scheme of these malicious codes is very challenging because they often hide, and may exploit zero-day vulnerabilities, gain administrative rights and execute code as an authenticated program. The development in technologies creates new issues regarding the safety and security of the critical infrastructure of the countries in the presence of these vulnerabilities and smart viruses. The desire to manufacture an automated process immensely increases software dependencies, which ultimately require lengthy and complex routines.

These complex codes are challenging to screen out completely using software testing mechanisms, and leftover vulnerabilities in these codes can compromise the whole system [10]. Therefore, the comprehensive and dynamic study of these codes is a promising domain for research communities to investigate.

The spread of the virus in a computer network is closely related to the spread of biological viruses in the population. Mathematical and statistical models are often based on concepts and methods borrowed from physics. Models play an important role in infection control by quickly predicting and understanding disease outbreaks. In recent decades, new infectious diseases have been observed, together with the development of eliminated technologies.

The ability to quickly measure the unfolding of outbreaks, communications, and movements is key to capturing the spread of a virus. The inherent complexity of such methods limits the study of these processes. However, developments in technology are helping to lift these limitations [11]. Classical approaches and linear thinking are unable to effectively mitigate the problem due to the lack of equilibrium and non-linear nature of the problems. A complex system, its counter-intuitive behavior, and other macro-level changes can be addressed by applying complex sciences. The usual models did not provide an in-depth picture of real system dynamics because these systems neglect feedback scenarios, cascade effects, and instabilities. To predict the global-scale spread of disease dynamics, several factors, such as demographic disparity, mobility scenarios which include air-flow system, commuter movement in the area, disease-specific information, and control mechanisms, should be acccounted for. There has long been work on the development of mathematical models for use in the analysis of infectious disease behavior. The mathematical model of Daniel Bernoulli against smallpox disease was published in 1766. Mathematical models of these types were designed to elaborate the behavior of an epidemic over the course of time, in which every single population of the virus is assumed to interact with the individual of other populations. The ability to monitor hidden outbreaks, as well as contact and communication, are key to the portrayal of disease-spreading [12]. It is known that immunizing a large fraction of the population or a computer network, the epidemic that spreads upon contact between infected nodes or individuals can be stopped.

Some diseases require 80–90% immunization (measles requires 95%), and the same is true for the computer, where 100% immunization from the Internet may stop viruses in connected networks [13]. Mathematical modeling of infectious disease or viruses in biology or in computer systems gives us a thorough understanding of the problem and helps us to devise a reliable, viable, and robust control strategy [14]. It was observed that the state of the various biological organisms at a certain time depends on its past states and fractional derivatives that also contains those characteristics. Thus, a fractional derivative is a natural approach to the solution of these biological systems. Mathematical modeling is used in numerous disciplines of science and engineering problems [15,16]. Kermack and

McKendrick founded mathematical modeling at the beginning of twentieth century with a series of publications, and introduced a susceptible, infected and recovered epidemic model [17]. In this field, several other scientists, biologists, computer engineers and mathematicians have worked on epidemic modeling and published work in this area, such as time delay virus models [18], a fractional epidemiological model [19], antivirus strategy for computer virus model [20], modified susceptible, infected and susceptible models [21] and epidemic models with two control mechanisms, quarantine and immunity [22], and models that highlight the topological facets of the network [23]. Besides these, the role of fundamental concepts and underlying theories of fractional calculus was effectively applied in modeling complex systems in diversified fields with rich dynamics compared to its integer counterparts [24–27]. Considering these facts, the current study aims to exploit the rich heritage of fractional dynamics for the development of the fractional Stuxnet virus model by using the features of the Stuxnet model to illustrate the virus spread in SCADA systems [28]. In this study, a fractional-order mathematical model of the Stuxnet virus is presented to study the ultra-fast transient and slow evolutions of the virus spread dynamic and attack pattern on isolated critical infrastructures, managed by industrial control computers. The contribution of the proposed fractional Stuxnet virus model is briefly described as:

- A novel fractional-order Stuxnet virus model is proposed by exploiting the rich heritage of fractional calculus in an isolated and air-gapped network environment.
- Stability analysis of Stuxnet virus model for both local and global equilibrium points when disease-free, and endemic spread is performed.
- Correctness of the proposed Grunwald–Letnikov-based fractional numerical solver is ascertained, with close results to the state-of-the-art Runge–Kutta numerical solver for integer-order variants of the model.
- Numerical simulation with Grunwald–Letnikov-based fractional numerical solver for a distinct order of the fractional derivative terms in the system shows that fractional-order models offer rich characteristics by way of ultrafast transience and ultra-slow advancements of steady-state.

2. Fractional Calculus Fundamentals

2.1. Preliminaries

Fractional calculus is a branch of mathematics and a generalization of the calculus theory of integrals and derivatives of a real number or complex number power. The discussion of fractional calculus was started 300 years ago, and the idea of fractional calculus was first listed in the literature with a letter from Leibniz to L'Hostital in 1696. In this letter, a half-derivative term was introduced, i.e., the generalization of the derivative operator $D^\alpha f()$, where α, representing the order of a fractional derivative. The history of the fractional derivative is as long as the classical differential operators in calculus, but the inherent strength of the fractional operator is relatively less exploited in engineering domains until the early 1980s. The physical interpretation of the fractional derivative outcomes is still ambiguous, and remained an open debate for clarity in the research community. However, the fractional derivative is an inspiring operator to describe the physics of many modeling phenomena, which are difficult to realize through integer-order derivatives. Recently, the kernel function of a fractional derivative is referred to as a memory function, and fractional-order derivative is proposed as a memory index [29,30] with different types of kernel [31–36]. The theory development of fractional calculus belonged to the efforts of several scientists, such as Letnikov, Liouville, Euler, and Riemann [37,38]. Different definitions of fractional order derivatives have existed; the most-used definitions are those of Riemann–Liouville (RL), Caputo (CP), and Grunwald–Letnikov (GL) [39]. The GL definition of fractional derivative is as follows:

$$\,_a^{GL}D_t^\alpha f(t) = \lim_{h\to 0}\frac{1}{h^\alpha}\sum_{m=0}^{(t-a)/h}(-1)^m\binom{\alpha}{m}f(t-mh),\ t>a, a>0. \tag{1}$$

The definition of Caputos fractional derivatives can be written as:

$$
{}_{a}^{CP}D_t^\alpha f(t) = \frac{1}{\Gamma(n-\alpha)} \int_a^t \frac{f^n(x)}{(t-x)^{\alpha-n+1}}dx,
\tag{2}
$$

for $(n-1 < \alpha < n)$ and where $\Gamma(\cdot)$ is a gamma function.

The RL definition is given as:

$$
{}_{a}^{RL}D_t^\alpha f(t) = \frac{1}{\Gamma(n-\alpha)} \frac{d^n}{dt} \int_a^t \frac{f(x)}{(t-x)^{\alpha-n+1}}dx.
\tag{3}
$$

For $(n-1 < \alpha < n)$, while a and t are the bounds of the operation for $_aD_t^\alpha$, the Laplace transform method is normally used with CP, GL and-RL fractional derivatives under zero initial conditions, as: [40]

$$
\pounds\{_aD_t^{\pm\alpha}f(t);s\} = s^{\pm\alpha}F(s),
\tag{4}
$$

while the analytical expressions are represented by Mittag–Leffler (ML)-type functions [41] introduced by Agarwal and Humbert [42] and are given mathematically as:

$$
E_{\alpha,\beta}(z) = \sum_{k=0}^{\infty} \frac{z^k}{\Gamma(\beta+\alpha k)},
\tag{5}
$$

$$
\alpha,\beta,z \in C, \ \Re(\alpha) > 0, \Re(\beta) > 0,
$$

where C represents the set of complex numbers and $E_{\alpha,\beta}$ is a two-parameter-based ML function.

2.2. Grunwald–Letnikov-Based Numerical Solver for FDEs

Analytical solution to the fractional differential equations (FDEs) generally determined through the Laplace transform method (4), and these expressions are commonly represented by the ML function (5), while, for the numerical solutions, the most commonly used method is based on GL definition.

To introduce the numerical solver based on GL [43] for FDEs, let a general from of an FDE, along with its initial conditions, is given as follows:

$$
\begin{aligned}
&_aD_t^\alpha f(t) = f(y(t),t), \\
&y^{(k)}(0) = y_0^{(k)}, k = 0,1,2,\ldots n-1,
\end{aligned}
\tag{6}
$$

where $(n-1 < \alpha < n)$, using Equation (1), Ivo Petras [44] provided the final recursive expression of a GL-based solver is as follows:

$$
\frac{1}{h^\alpha} \sum_{j=0}^{[(t-a)/h]} (-1)^j \binom{\alpha}{k}y(t-jh) \approx f(y(t),t),
$$

simplifying above relation, we have

$$
y(t) + \sum_{j=1}^{[(t-a)/h]} (-1)^j \binom{\alpha}{k}y(t-jh) \approx h^{-\alpha}f(y(t),t).
$$

In case of discrete input grids between interval $t \in [0,T] = [0,h,2h,\ldots,Mh = T]$, where h represents the step size parameter, so $[0,T] = [t_0 = 0, t_1,\ldots,t_M = T]$ and any grid points in the interval are represented as $t_m = mh$ for $m = 0, 1, 2, \ldots, M$. Thus, in a discrete form, the above equation is written as:

$$y(t_m) + \sum_{j=1}^{m} (-1)^j \binom{\alpha}{j} y(t_m - jh) = h^{-\alpha} f(y(t_m), t_m), m = 0, 1, 2, \ldots, M.$$

In simple usage, the above term is written as:

$$y(t_m) + \sum_{j=1}^{m} c_j^\alpha y(t_m - jh) = h^{-\alpha} f(y(t_m), t_m), m = 0, 1, 2, \ldots, M,$$

where $c_j^{(\alpha)}$ is defined as:

$$c_j^\alpha = (-1)^j \binom{\alpha}{j}, \tag{7}$$

or equivalently with $c_0^\alpha = 1$,

$$c_j^\alpha = \left(1 - \frac{1+\alpha}{j} \right) c_{j-1}^\alpha, j = 0, 1, \ldots$$

GL numerical solver in the recursive form is written as:

$$y(t_m) = f(y(t_m), t_m) h^{-\alpha} - \sum_{j=1}^{k} c_j^\alpha y(t_{m-j}), m = 0, 1, 2, \ldots, M. \tag{8}$$

A further elaboration of the Grunwald–Letnikov (GL)-based numerical solver can be seen in [45].

3. Model Formulation of Fractional Order Stuxnet Virus

The formulation of a fractional-order Stuxnet virus model (FO-SVM) is presented here. A detailed workflow of the proposed FO-SVM is shown in Figure 1. The entire FO-SVM is segmented into five classes: three for computer population, i.e., susceptible $S(t)$, infected $I(t)$, and damaged $M(t)$, and two for removable storage media, i.e., susceptible storage media $U_s(t)$ and infected storage media $U_s(t)$. However, $N(t)$ represents the total population, i.e., $N(t) = S(t) + I(t) + M(t)$, and total removable devices $U(t)$, i.e., $U(t) = U_s(t) + U_I(t)$. In the rest of the article, the variables with respect to time t, $S(t)$, $I(t)$, $M(t)$, $U_s(t)$, $U_s(t)$, $N(t)$, and $U(t)$ are denoted by S, I, M, U_s, U_I, N, and U, respectively. Let A_1 and A_2 represent the arrival of new computing nodes and removable storage media, respectively, damage rate caused to PLC's due to virus infection is represented by ρ, β_1 is the infectious contact rate of susceptible nodes with infected nodes during the network scan, and β_2 denotes the contact rate of infectious-removable storage media with susceptible computer nodes, r_1 and r_2 represent the natural removal (death) of computer nodes and removable devices from the network, respectively. The number of nodes in Internet protocol version 4 (IPv4) is 2^{32}, and the probability of finding susceptible nodes in IPv4 scheme is $S/2^{32}$. Susceptible nodes can be infected at the rate $\beta_1 SI$ or at $\beta_2 SU_I/N$, while the removable storage media could be infected at a rate of $\beta_2 U_s I/N$. Removable storage media is a common source of virus spread in critical industrial air-gapped networks, which are isolated from normal networks. The removable storage devices facilitate the flow of information to and from the networks that make them as an easy prey for intruders [46]. In this study, fractional-order virus model is used to explain the spread of the virus, especially Stuxnet [47,48] in industrial networks through removable storage media. A proposed flow chart diagram of the Stuxnet virus model is shown in Figure 2, and the fundamental mathematical equations of the model are given as:

$$D^\alpha S = A_1 - \frac{\beta_1 SI}{2^{32}} - \frac{\beta_2 SU_I}{N} - r_1 S,$$

$$D^\alpha I = \frac{\beta_1 SI}{2^{32}} + \frac{\beta_2 SU_I}{N} - \rho I - r_1 I,$$

$$D^\alpha M = \rho I - r_1 M, \qquad (9)$$

$$D^\alpha U_s = A_2 - \frac{\beta_2 U_s I}{N} - r_2 U_s,$$

$$D^\alpha U_I = \frac{\beta_2 U_s I}{N} - r_2 U_I$$

where $\alpha \in [0,1]$ represents the order of the fractional derivative term $D^\alpha = d^\alpha / dt^\alpha$. For the value of $\alpha = 1$, the above-mentioned FO-SVM system provided in a set of Equation (9) will be converted into a first-order system. From the differential equations mentioned in (9), solving the equations by taking the value of $\alpha = 1$, we get

$$\frac{dN}{dt} = A_1 - r_1 N,$$
$$\frac{dU}{dt} = A_2 - r_2 U. \qquad (10)$$

The change in population is given by $c_1 = A_1 - r_1$ and $c_2 = A_2 - r_2$, and the values of these constants may be negative, positive or zero.

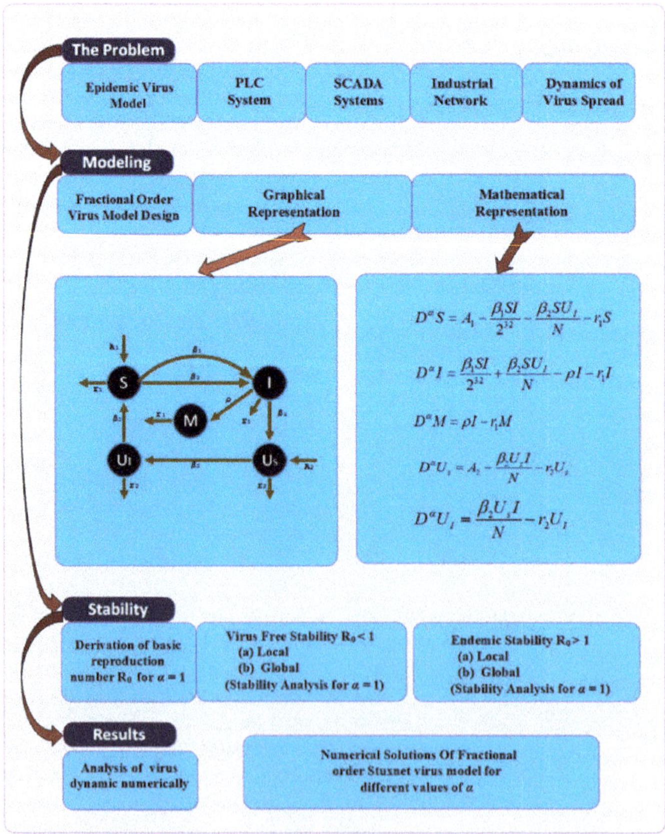

Figure 1. FO-SVM model proposed graphical overview.

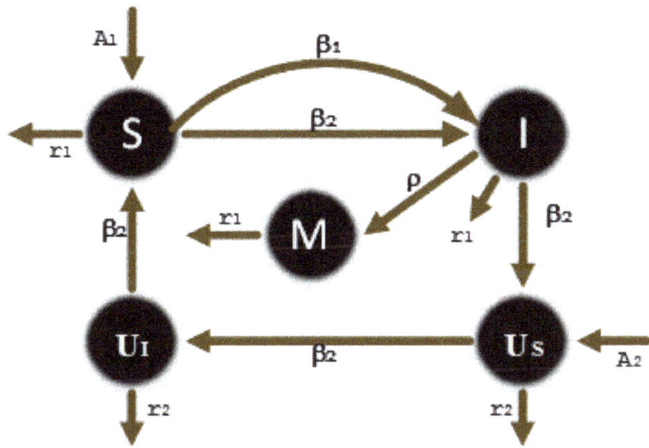

Figure 2. FO-SVM model schematic flow diagram.

Solving the set of Equation (10), we get

$$N(t) \to \frac{A_1}{r_1} \triangleq N^*, \, t \to \infty,$$

$$U(t) \to \frac{A_2}{r_2} \triangleq U^*, \, t \to \infty. \tag{11}$$

The system given in Equation (9) can be simplified by incorporating N and U variables, as in:

$$D^\alpha I = \frac{\beta_1 (N - I - M)I}{2^{32}} + \frac{\beta_2 (N - I - M)U_I}{N} - \rho I - r_1 I,$$

$$D^\alpha M = \rho I - r_1 M, \tag{12}$$

$$D^\alpha U_I = \frac{\beta_2 (U - U_I)I}{N} - r_2 U_I,$$

where

$$N(t) = N^* + (N(0) - N^*)e^{-r_1 t},$$

$$U(t) = U^* + (U(0) - U^*)e^{-r_2 t}. \tag{13}$$

Using Equation (11) in system (12), one may obtain a limit system (IMU_I), as in [49,50]:

$$D^\alpha I = \frac{\beta_1 (N^* - I - M)I}{2^{32}} + \frac{\beta_2 (N^* - I - M)U_I}{N^*} - \rho I - r_1 I,$$

$$D^\alpha M = \rho I - r_1 M, \tag{14}$$

$$D^\alpha U_I = \frac{\beta_2 (U^* - U_I)I}{N^*} - r_2 U_I.$$

The equations in system (14), are the reduced version of (9), and will be used in further investigations.

4. Model Analysis

In this unit, stability analysis of the model is performed through the derivation of basic reproduction number, R_0. The endemic and disease-free equilibrium points of the system are investigated for a local as well as global stability analysis.

4.1. Basic Reproduction Number (R_0)

In epidemiology modeling, a basic reproduction number is defined as the advent of a new infection in an entirely susceptible population due to an infected individual, and is usually represented by R_0. The value of R_0 determines the spread of infection; for $R_0 > 1$ infection will spread in the population, and for $R_0 < 1$ infection will soon end [51].

To simplify the derivation process, a reduced model (14) has been utilized for further investigation of R_0. The calculation of R_0 is based on the value of $\alpha = 1$. The necessary condition of a disease epidemic is based on the increase in the infected individuals, with the supposition that, initially, the entire population is susceptible.

For the case of $D^\alpha I > 0$, we have $D^\alpha U_I > 0$

$$\frac{\beta_1(N^* - I - M)I}{2^{32}} + \frac{\beta_2(N^* - I - M)U_I}{N^*} - \rho I - r_1 I > 0, \tag{15}$$

and, accordingly, in case of $D^\alpha U_I > 0$, we have

$$\frac{\beta_2(U^* - U_I)I}{N^*} - r_2 U_I > 0. \tag{16}$$

With the assumption that all the population is susceptible at the start, the above expressions may be written as:

$$\frac{\beta_1 N^* I}{2^{32}} + \frac{\beta_2 N^* U_I}{N^*} - \rho I - r_1 I > 0, \tag{17}$$

$$\frac{\beta_2 U^* I}{N^*} - r_2 U_I > 0. \tag{18}$$

Simplifying the above relations, we have

$$\frac{\beta_1 N^*}{(\rho + r_1)2^{32}} + \frac{\beta_2^2 U^*}{r_2 N^*(\rho + r_1)} > 1. \tag{19}$$

Accordingly,

$$R_0 = \frac{\beta_1 N^*}{2^{32}(\rho + r_1)} + \frac{\beta_2^2 U^*}{r_2 N^*(\rho + r_1)}. \tag{20}$$

Equation (20) represents the basic reproduction number derived for the model.

4.2. Equilibria Studies

In this subsection, we study the equilibrium points of FO-SVM model Equation (14). The FO-SVM model has virus-free equilibrium and endemic equilibrium points. In the endemic equilibrium point, the spread of infection is observed.

For equilibria studies, we have

$$D^\alpha I = 0, D^\alpha M = 0, D^\alpha U_I = 0,$$

equilibrium points of system (14) for virus-free and endemic are as: $K_0 = (I, M, U_I) = (0, 0, 0)$ and $K^* = (I^*, M^*, U_I^*)$ for $R_0 > 1$.

The analysis for the endemic equilibria of model (14) is written as:

$$\frac{\beta_1(N^* - I - M)I}{2^{32}} + \frac{\beta_2(N^* - I - M)U_I}{N^*} - \rho I - r_1 I = 0,$$

$$\rho I - r_1 M = 0, \tag{21}$$

$$\frac{\beta_2(U^* - U_I)I}{N^*} - r_2 U_I = 0.$$

Solving the equations in set (21), we obtain the expressions for the endemic equilibrium point (I^*, M^*, U_I^*) as:

$$I^* = \frac{\sqrt{b^2 - 4ac} - b}{2a}, \tag{22}$$

$$M^* = \frac{\rho}{r_1} I^*, \tag{23}$$

$$U_I^* = \frac{\beta_2 U^*}{\beta_2 I^* + r_2 N^*} I^*, \tag{24}$$

where

$$a = \frac{(\rho + r1)\beta_1\beta_2}{2^{32} r_1 N^*},$$

$$b = \frac{\beta_2(\rho + r_1)(1 - R_0)}{N^*} + \frac{\beta_2^3 U^*}{N^* r_2} + \frac{\beta_1(r_2)\beta_2^2 U^*}{2^{32} r_1}(\rho + r_1),$$

$$c = (\rho + r_1)(1 - R_0)r_2.$$

It is evident from Equation (22) that the possibility of infection spread, i.e., $I^* > 0$, is only verified for the value of $R_0 > 1$.

4.3. Disease Free Equilibrium

Theorem 1. *Disease-free equilibrium (DFE) point of a system is locally and asymptotically stable at K_0, if $R_0 < 1$.*

Proof. The DFE point of a system is locally asymptotically stable at $K_0 = (I, M, U_I) = (0, 0, 0)$. The Jacobian matrix of function $f : R^3 \to R^3$ with components:

$$D^\alpha I = \frac{\beta_1(N^* - I - M)I}{2^{32}} + \frac{\beta_2(N^* - I - M)U_I}{N^*} - \rho I - r_1 I,$$

$$D^\alpha M = \rho I - r_1 M, \tag{25}$$

$$D^\alpha U_I = \frac{\beta_2(U^* - U_I)I}{N^*} - r_2 U_I.$$

Thus, the Jacobian matrix at K_0, DFE point of integer-order model (14) is given as:

$$DFE(K_0) = \begin{pmatrix} \frac{\beta_1 N^*}{2^{32}} - \rho - r_1 & 0 & \beta_2 \\ \rho & -r_1 & 0 \\ \frac{\beta_2 U^*}{N^*} & 0 & -r_2. \end{pmatrix} \tag{26}$$

System (26) characteristic equation is

$$|\lambda I - DFE(K_0)| = \begin{vmatrix} \lambda - \frac{\beta_1 N^*}{2^{32}} + \rho + r_1 & 0 & -\beta_2 \\ -\rho & \lambda + r_1 & 0 \\ -\frac{\beta_2 U^*}{N^*} & 0 & \lambda + r_2 \end{vmatrix} = 0, \tag{27}$$

and simplify as:

$$(\lambda + r_1)\left[\left(\lambda - \frac{N^* \beta_1}{2^{32}} + \rho + r_1\right)(\lambda + r_2) - \frac{\beta_2^2 U^*}{N^*}\right] = 0. \tag{28}$$

The corresponding Eigen values of the above relation are

$$\lambda_1 = -r_1,$$
$$\left[\left(\lambda - \frac{N^* \beta_1}{2^{32}} + \rho + r_1\right)(\lambda + r_2) - \frac{\beta_2^2 U^*}{N^*}\right] = 0. \tag{29}$$

Simplifying the above expression to find the remaining Eigenvalues

$$r_1(\lambda + r_2) + \rho(\lambda + r_2) + \lambda(\lambda + r_2) - (\lambda + r_2)\frac{N^*\beta_1}{2^{32}} - \frac{\beta_2{}^2 U^*}{N^*} = 0,$$

$$\lambda^2 + \lambda\left(r_1 + r_2 + \rho - \frac{N^*\beta_1}{2^{32}}\right) + r_1 r_2 + \rho r_2 - r_2\frac{N^*\beta_1}{2^{32}} - \frac{\beta_2{}^2 U^*}{N^*} = 0,$$

$$\frac{\lambda^2}{r_2(\rho + r_1)} + \frac{\lambda\left(r_1 + r_2 + \rho - \frac{N^*\beta_1}{2^{32}}\right)}{r_2(\rho + r_1)} + \left(1 - \frac{N^*\beta_1}{2^{32}(\rho + r_1)} - \frac{\beta_2{}^2 U^*}{N^* r_2(\rho + r_1)}\right) = 0,$$

$$\frac{\lambda^2}{r_2(\rho + r_1)} + \frac{\lambda}{r_2}\left(\frac{r_2}{\rho + r_1} + \frac{r_1 + \rho}{\rho + r_1} - \frac{N^*\beta_1}{2^{32}(\rho + r_1)}\right) + (1 - R_0) = 0,$$

and rearranging the above expression

$$\frac{\lambda^2}{r_2(\rho + r_1)} + \frac{\lambda}{r_2}\left(\frac{r_2}{\rho + r_1} + 1 - \frac{N^*\beta_1}{2^{32}(\rho + r_1)}\right) + (1 - R_0) = 0, \tag{30}$$

and, for $R_0 < 1$, Equation (9) can be written as:

$$\frac{\lambda^2}{r_2(\rho + r_1)} + \frac{\lambda}{r_2}\left(\frac{r_2}{\rho + r_1} + 1 - \frac{N^*\beta_1}{2^{32}(\rho + r_1)}\right) + (1 - R_0) = 0. \tag{31}$$

Using the expression (31) in Section 4.3, make the coefficient positive for $R_0 < 1$, which shows that system Section 4.3 eigenvalues are in a stable region; this confirms that the system is asymptotically stable for point K_0 when $R_0 < 1$. If system is stable for the value of $\alpha = 1$, it will be stable for the value of $\alpha < 1$, as reported in [52]. This completes the proof. $\square$

Theorem 2. *If $R_0 < 1$, then point K_0 is globally asymptotically stable, and otherwise unstable.*

Proof. Considering the Lyapunov function mentioned below,

$$L(I, M, U_I) = I + \frac{\beta_1}{2^{33}\rho}M^2 + \frac{\beta_2}{r_2}U_I. \tag{32}$$

The function in R^3 is positive, for $R^3 = (I, M, UI)$ and $(I > 0, M > 0, UI > 0)$. For $\alpha = 1$, the derivative of Lyapunov function (32) is

$$D^\alpha L(I, M, U_I) = D^\alpha I + \frac{2\beta_1}{2^{33}\rho}MD^\alpha M + \frac{\beta_2}{r_2}D^\alpha U_I, \tag{33}$$

$$
\begin{aligned}
D^\alpha L(I, M, U_I) &= \frac{\beta_1(N^* - I - M)I}{2^{32}} + \frac{\beta_2(N^* - I - M)U_I}{N^*} - \rho I - r_1 I + \frac{\beta_1 MI}{2^{32}} + \frac{r_1\beta_1 M^2}{2^{32}\rho} \\
&\quad + \frac{\beta_2{}^2 U^* I}{N^* r_2} - \frac{\beta_2{}^2 U_I I}{N^* r_2} - \beta_2 U_I, \\
&= \left(\frac{\beta_1 N^*}{2^{32}} + \frac{\beta_2{}^2 U^*}{N^* r_2} - \rho - r_1\right)I - \frac{\beta_1 I^2}{2^{32}} - \frac{\beta_2(M + I)U_I}{N^*} - \frac{r_1\beta_1 M^2}{2^{32}\rho} \\
&\quad - \frac{\beta_2{}^2 M^2 U_I I}{N^* r_2}, \\
&= \left(\frac{(\rho + r_1)\left(\frac{\beta_1 N^*}{2^{32}(\rho+r_1)} + \frac{\beta_2{}^2 U^*}{N^* r_2(\rho+r_1)}\right)}{-\rho - r_1}\right)I - \frac{\beta_1 I^2}{2^{32}} - \frac{\beta_2(M + I)U_I}{N^*} - \frac{r_1\beta_1 M^2}{2^{32}\rho} \\
&\quad - \frac{\beta_2{}^2 M^2 U_I I}{N^* r_2}, \\
&= (\rho + r_1)(R_0 - 1)I - \frac{\beta_1 I^2}{2^{32}} - \frac{\beta_2(M + I)U_I}{N^*} - \frac{r_1\beta_1 M^2}{2^{32}\rho} - \frac{\beta_2{}^2 U_I I}{N^* r_2}.
\end{aligned}
\tag{34}
$$

For $R_0 < 1$, this implies that $D^\alpha L \leq 0$ and K_0 is the only invariant set of system (21). According to the LaSalle Invariance Principle, K_0 is proven to be globally asymptotically stable. Hence, equilibrium point K_0 is globally asymptotically stable for $R_0 < 1$. Additionally, if the system is stable for the value of $\alpha = 1$, then the system will be stable for $\alpha < 1$, as described in [52]. $\square$

4.4. Endemic Stability

The endemic stability of equilibrium point $K^* = (I^*, M^*, U_I^*)$ is investigated in this section for the values of $R_0 > 1$ and $I^* \geq 0$.

Theorem 3. *Endemic equilibrium point K^* is locally asymptotically stable, if $R_0 > 1$.*

Proof. Consider the function $f : R^3 \to R^3$ with components and the Jacobian matrix of the system (14) as:

$$D^\alpha I = f_1(I^*, M^*, U_I^*) = \frac{\beta_1(N^* - I^* - M^*)I^*}{2^{32}} + \frac{\beta_2(N^* - I^* - M^*)U_I^*}{N^*} - \rho I^* - r_1 I^*,$$

$$D^\alpha M = f_2(I^*, M^*, U_I^*) = \rho I^* - r_1 M^*,$$

$$D^\alpha U_I = f_3(I^*, M^*, U_I^*) = \frac{\beta_2(U^* - U_I^*)I^*}{2^{32}} - r_2 U_I^*,$$

$$J(I^*, M^*, U_I^*) = \begin{pmatrix} \frac{\partial f_1}{\partial I^*} & \frac{\partial f_1}{\partial M^*} & \frac{\partial f_1}{\partial U_I^*} \\ \frac{\partial f_2}{\partial I^*} & \frac{\partial f_2}{\partial M^*} & \frac{\partial f_2}{\partial U_I^*} \\ \frac{\partial f_3}{\partial I^*} & \frac{\partial f_3}{\partial M^*} & \frac{\partial f_3}{\partial U_I^*} \end{pmatrix}.$$

The endemic equilibrium of system (14) is $K^* = (I^*, M^*, U_I^*)$, for the value of $\alpha = 1$, the Jacobian matrix at endemic point is mentioned below.

$$J(K^*) = \begin{pmatrix} \Lambda & -\frac{\beta_1 I^*}{2^{32}} - \frac{\beta_2 U_I^*}{N^*} & \frac{\beta_2(N^* - I^* - M^*)}{N^*} \\ \rho & -r_1 & 0 \\ \frac{\beta_2(U^* - U_I^*)}{N^*} & 0 & \frac{\beta_2 I^*}{N^*} - r_2 \end{pmatrix}, \tag{35}$$

where $\Lambda = \frac{\beta_1(N^* - 2I^* - M^*)}{2^{32}} - \frac{\beta_2 U_I^*}{N^*} - \rho - r_1$.

The characteristic equation of (35) is

$$|\lambda I - J(K^*)| = 0,$$

$$\begin{vmatrix} \lambda - \Lambda & \frac{\beta_1 I^*}{2^{32}} + \frac{\beta_2 U_I^*}{N^*} & -\frac{\beta_2(N^* - I^* - M^*)}{N^*} \\ -\rho & \lambda + r_1 & 0 \\ -\frac{\beta_2(U^* - U_I^*)}{N^*} & 0 & \lambda + \frac{\beta_2 I^*}{N^*} + r_2 \end{vmatrix} = 0,$$

simplifies as:

$$\lambda^3 + (b_{11} + b_{22} + b_{33})\lambda^2 + (b_{11}b_{22} + b_{11}b_{33} + b_{22}b_{33} \tag{36}$$
$$- b_{12}b_{21} - b_{13}b_{31})\lambda + b_{11}b_{22}b_{33} - b_{12}b_{21}b_{33} - b_{13}b_{31}b_{22} = 0,$$

where

$$b_{11} = -\frac{\beta_1 N^*}{2^{32}} + \frac{\beta_1(2I^* + M^*)}{2^{32}} + \frac{\beta_2 U_I^*}{N^*} + \rho + r_1,$$
$$b_{12} = \frac{\beta_1 I^*}{2^{32}} + \frac{\beta_2 U_I^*}{N^*},$$
$$b_{21} = -\rho, b_{23} = 0, b_{22} = r_1, \quad b_{13} = -\frac{\beta_2(N^* - I^* - M^*)}{N^*},$$
$$b_{31} = -\frac{\beta_2(U^* - U_I^*)}{N^*}, \quad b_{33} = \frac{\beta_2 I^*}{N^*} + r_2, b_{32} = 0.$$

For stability analysis, Hurwitz criteria may be used, as reported in [53,54] for system (36). Equating the Equation (36) coefficient with the general characteristics equation, we have

$$b_0 = 1,$$
$$b_1 = b_{11} + b_{22} + b_{33},$$
$$b_2 = b_{11}b_{22} + b_{11}b_{33} + b_{22}b_{33} - b_{12}b_{21} - b_{13}b_{31},$$
$$b_3 = b_{11}b_{22}b_{33} - b_{12}b_{21}b_{33} - b_{13}b_{31}b_{22}.$$

Determinants (D_1, D_2 and D_3) of the Equation (36) are stated in Hurwitz as:

$$D_1 = b_1 = b_{11} + b_{22} + b_{33},$$
$$= -\frac{\beta_1 N^*}{232} + \frac{\beta_1(2I^* + M^*)}{232} + \frac{\beta_2 U_I^*}{N^*}$$
$$+ \rho + r_1 + r_1 + \frac{\beta_2 I^*}{N^*} + r_2,$$

using the value of Equation (20) for $R_0 > 1$ as:

$$\frac{\beta_1 N^*}{232} + \frac{\beta_2^2 U^*}{r_2 N^*} > \rho + r, \text{we have}$$

$$D_1 = -\frac{\beta_1 N^*}{232} + \frac{\beta_1(2I^* + M^*)}{232} + \frac{\beta_2 U_I^*}{N^*} + \frac{\beta_1 N^*}{232} + \frac{\beta_2^2 U^*}{r_2 N^*} + r_1 + \frac{\beta_2 I^*}{N^*} + r_2,$$

$$D_1 = \frac{\beta_1(2I^* + M^*)}{232} + \frac{\beta_2 U_I^*}{N^*} + \frac{\beta_2^2 U^*}{r_2 N^*} + r_1 + \frac{\beta_2 I^*}{N^*} + r_2,$$

$$D_1 > 0,$$

and

$$D_2 = b_1 b_2 - b_3 b_0,$$
$$D_2 = (b_{11} + b_{22} + b_{33})(b_{11}b_{22} + b_{11}b_{33} + b_{22}b_{33} - b_{12}b_{21}$$
$$- b_{13}b_{31}) - b_{11}b_{22}b_{33} + b_{12}b_{21}b_{33} + b_{13}b_{31}b_{22},$$
$$= b_{11}^2 b_{22} + b_{11}^2 b_{33} + b_{11}b_{22}b_{33} - b_{11}b_{12}b_{21} - b_{11}b_{13}b_{31}$$
$$+ b_{11}b_{22}^2 + b_{11}b_{22}b_{33} + b_{22}^2 b_{33} - b_{22}b_{12}b_{21}$$
$$- b_{22}b_{13}b_{31} + b_{11}b_{22}b_{33} + b_{11}b_{33}^2 + b_{22}b_{33}^2$$
$$- b_{33}b_{12}b_{21} - b_{33}b_{13}b_{31} - b_{11}b_{22}b_{33}$$
$$+ b_{33}b_{12}b_{21} + b_{22}b_{13}b_{31},$$
$$D_2 = b_{11}^2 b_{22} + b_{11}^2 b_{33} + b_{11}b_{22}^2 + b_{22}^2 b_{33} + b_{11}b_{33}^2 + b_{22}b_{33}^2$$
$$+ 2b_{11}b_{22}b_{33} - b_{11}b_{12}b_{21} - b_{11}b_{13}b_{31} - b_{22}b_{12}b_{21} - b_{33}b_{13}b_{31}.$$

The above expressions remain positive, except for $-b_{13}b_{31}(b_{11} + b_{33})$, D_2, which, if positive for $R_0 > 1$, is simply represented as:

$$D_2 = +\text{veterms} + (b_{11}b_{33} - b_{13}b_{31})(b_{11} + b_{33}),$$
$$D_2 = D_{2-1} + D_{2-2},$$

Here, D_{2-1} represent the positive terms in D_2, while, for the remaining terms, represented with D_{2-2}, we have

$$D_{2-2} = (b_{11}b_{33} - b_{13}b_{31})(b_{11} + b_{33})$$

$$= \left\{ \left(\frac{\beta_1(N^*-I^*-M^*)}{2^{32}} + \rho + r_1 \right) r_2 - \frac{\beta^2{}_2(N^*-I^*-M^*)(U^*-U_I{}^*)}{N^{*2}} \right\}(b_{11} + b_{33}),$$

$$= \left\{ \left(\frac{\frac{\beta_1(N^*-I^*-M^*)}{2^{32}} + \rho + r_1}{} - \frac{\beta^2{}_2(N^*-I^*-M^*)(U^*-U_I{}^*)}{r_2 N^{*2}} \right) r_2 \right\}(b_{11} + b_{33}),$$

$$= \left\{ \left(\frac{\beta_1(N^*-I^*-M^*)}{2^{32}} + \rho + r_1 - \frac{\beta^2{}_2(N^*-I^*-M^*)U^*}{r_2 N^{*2}} + \frac{\beta^2{}_2(N^*-I^*-M^*)U_I{}^*}{r_2 N^{*2}} \right) r_2 \right\}(b_{11} + b_{33}),$$

$$= \left\{ \left(\frac{\beta_1(N^*-I^*-M^*)}{2^{32}} + \rho + r_1 - \frac{\beta^2{}_2 U^*}{r_2 N^*} + \frac{\beta^2{}_2 I^* U^*}{r_2 N^{*2}} + \frac{\beta^2{}_2 M^* U^*}{r_2 N^{*2}} + \frac{\beta^2{}_2(N^*-I^*-M^*)U_I{}^*}{r_2 N^{*2}} \right) r_2 \right\}(b_{11} + b_{33}),$$

using the value of $R_0 > 1$, and after simplification, the above expression becomes

$$D_{2-2} > \left\{ \left(\frac{\beta_1(N^*-I^*-M^*)}{2^{32}} + \frac{\beta_1 N^*}{2^{32}} + \frac{\beta^2{}_2 U^*}{r_2 N^*} - \frac{\beta^2{}_2 U^*}{r_2 N^*} + \frac{\beta^2{}_2 I^* U^*}{r_2 N^{*2}} + \frac{\beta^2{}_2 M^* U^*}{r_2 N^{*2}} + \frac{\beta^2{}_2(N^*-I^*-M^*)U_I{}^*}{r_2 N^{*2}} \right) r_2 \right\}(b_{11} + b_{33}),$$

$$D_{2-2} > \left\{ \left(\frac{\beta_1(N^*-I^*-M^*)}{2^{32}} + \frac{\beta_1 N^*}{2^{32}} + \frac{\beta^2{}_2 I^* U^*}{r_2 N^{*2}} + \frac{\beta^2{}_2 M^* U^*}{r_2 N^{*2}} + \frac{\beta^2{}_2(N^*-I^*-M^*)U_I{}^*}{r_2 N^{*2}} \right) r_2 \right\}(b_{11} + b_{33}),$$

$$D_{2-2} > 0,$$

as a result

$$D_2 > 0.$$
$$D_3 = b_3(b_1 b_2 - b_0 b_3),$$
$$D_3 = b_3(D_2),$$
$$= (b_{11}b_{22}b_{33} - b_{12}b_{21}b_{33} - b_{13}b_{31}b_{22})((b_{11} + b_{22}$$
$$+ b_{33})(b_{11}b_{22} + b_{11}b_{33} + b_{22}b_{33} - b_{12}b_{21} - b_{13}b_{31})$$
$$- b_{11}b_{22}b_{33} + b_{12}b_{21}b_{33} + b_{13}b_{31}b_{22})$$
$$= (b_{11}b_{22}b_{33} - b_{12}b_{21}b_{33} - b_{13}b_{31}b_{22})D_2,$$
$$> (b_{11}b_{33} - b_{13}b_{31})b_{22}D_2,$$

The positivity of the expression $b_{11}b_{33} - b_{13}b_{31}$ for $R_0 > 1$ is already proved for the case D_2; therefore, $D_3 > 0$.

Thus, all the values of D_1, D_2 and D_3 are positive, so all the eigenvalues of the Equation (36) are negative, for $R_0 > 1$. This proves that the endemic equilibrium point K^* is locally asymptotically stable. The proof of theorem is completed. $\square$

5. Simulation and Results

In this section, the results of numerical simulations for FO-SVM are presented to understand the dynamics of virus spread in a critical network infrastructure in the presence of removable storage connectivity, which may compromise the air-gap between the networks. Numerical experimentation is conducted for the designed FO-SVM as given in Equation (9) for a different variation in parameters and initial start-up scenarios, as given in Tables 1 and 2, respectively. The dynamic behavior of the fractional order (FO) model is studied by varying the non-integer order derivative α. Most FO differential systems lack exact analytical solutions, so the numerical solver based on Grunwald–Letnikov (GL) procedure, as described in Section 2 is exploited for an approximate solution to the model. The security firms, including Symantec, tracked 100,000 infected computers as of 29 September 2010, in the world. Additionally, available real data are used to validate the accuracy and convergence of the model for the Stuxnet virus spread. The virus infects approximately 100,000 users from 155 different countries, and 63% were only in Iran. Due to this attack, the number of hosts that lost functionality (hardware connected to these hosts was damaged due to sudden increase in frequency of up to 1410 Hz, which then decreased to 2 Hz and increased to 1064 Hz in spite of the normal working range of from 807 Hz to 1210 Hz) due to virus attack. A virus operates the machines connected with the hosts at an extreme range of frequencies dictated by Stuxnet and caused physical damage to 1500 centrifuge machines (approximately 1200 in Iran only). Approximately 3280 unique samples and variants of the Stuxnet virus were recorded by Symantec and other security corporations [3,6,55].

Table 1. Values of parameters used in model simulation for different scenarios.

Parameter	Case 1	Case 2	Case 3	Case 4	Case 5	Case 6	Case 7	Case 8	Case 9
A_1	0.042	0.042	40	100	5600	5600	5600	412	5600
A_2	0.042	0.042	45.7	60	412	412	412	5600	412
β_1	0.6	0.4	0.385	0.4	0.4	0.4	0.745	0.4	0.4
β_2	0.6	0.8	0.795	0.635	0.745	0.745	0.4	0.745	0.004
ρ	0.00265	0.0051	0.001	0.009	0.021	0.8	0.021	0.021	0.021
r_1	0.1126	0.19	0.0804	0.1598	0.1276	0.0804	0.1276	0.1276	0.1276
r_2	0.0088	0.027	0.027	0.027	0.0131	0.0131	0.0131	0.0131	0.0131

Table 2. Starting values of variables used in the simulation of different scenarios.

Variables	S	I	M	U_S	U_I
Case 1	2.3×10^6	10,000	10	50,000	10,000
Case 2	2.3×10^6	30,000	10	50,000	10,000
Case 3	2.3×10^6	30,000	10	30,000	10,000
Case 4–9	2.3×10^6	30,000	10	30,000	5000

In order to establish the working accuracy of GL-based numerical solvers, the results of the scheme are compared with state-of-the-art numerical solvers based on the Runge–Kutta (RK) method for the value of $\alpha = 1$. The results are determined for nine cases of integer order models (9) by a GL-based computing technique for inputs $t \in [0, 60]$ with step size $h = 0.001$ (time t represents months). Numerical solutions to the model for the same inputs are also calculated by the RK method for each variation. Figure 3 highlights the comparison of model behavior with Stuxnet virus real-world data. FO-SVM model results shown in Figure 3 are calculated using the RK method to assume the value of fractional order $\alpha = 1$.

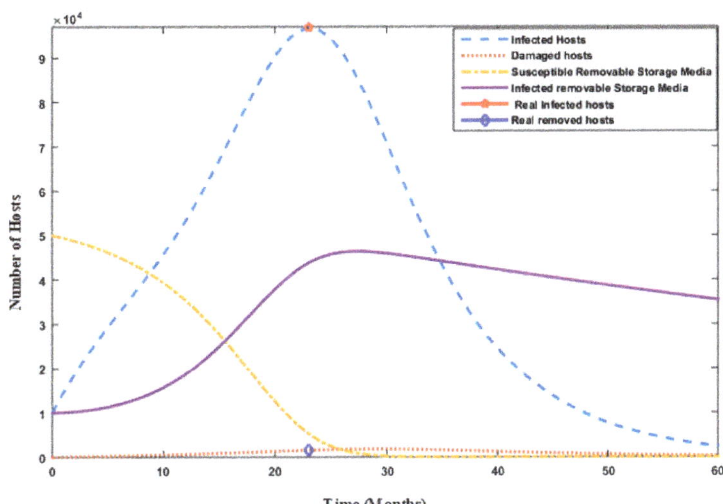

Figure 3. Simulation of Stuxnet virus spread with available data of parameters $A_1 = 0.042$, $A_2 = 0.042$, $\beta_1 = 0.366$, $\beta_2 = 0.6$, $\rho = 0.00265$, $r_1 = 0.1126$, $r_2 = 0.0088$, $S = 2.3 \times 10^6$, $I = 10{,}000$, $M = 10$, $U_s = 50{,}000$, $U_I = 10{,}000$.

In Figure 3, the number of hosts versus time in months is plotted, which shows the effect of the Stuxnet attack on the number of hosts as time passes. The number of infected hosts is 96,760 (real infected host number was 100,000), and the number of damaged hosts is 1500 (real damaged host number was 1500) in 23 months time, which shows the model accuracy for real-world virus data, as shown in Figure 3, with red and blue dots, respectively. In this case, removable media are considered to be 60,000, and, after increasing the number of removable-storage media, infection in the host nodes also increases (96,760 after 23 months).

The number of infected removable-storage devices is 43,740 in 23 months, and in 24 months, the time number of infected devices increases to 44,920. An increase in the number of damaged hosts is observed after the increase in infected hosts in 24 months' time. This highlights the role of removable-storage media in spreading the infection in isolated critical networks in the absence of any remedial strategy in the model. Stuxnet is an advanced, persistent threat (APT) type of malicious code that penetrates in the remote system in a quasi-autonomous fashion. Then, a 23-month decline in the number of infected hosts is observed due to the availability of remedial technique and other controlling mechanisms. However, the Stuxnet virus was carried by removable-storage media spreads in other·networks.

In Figure 4, the solutions to the RK method with GL solver is compared with an error analysis of susceptible hosts S: a and b for cases 2 to 4, c and d for cases 5 to 7, and e and f for cases 8 to 10. Comparisons of results from both the RK numerical solver and GL-based method (for fractional-order $\alpha = 1$) are presented for susceptible hosts S in nine cases. The error analysis, based on the absolute difference between the two approaches, is also plotted in Figure 4 to assess closeness. The results show a matching of both solutions of up to three decimal places of accuracy. The small errors in these plots show that the results of the GL method are in good agreement with the standard RK numerical technique, which establishes the working accuracy of the GL-based solver. In Figure 5, the solution of the RK method with the GL solver is compared in the case of infected hosts I and damaged hosts M: a and b for cases 1 to 3, c and d for cases 4 to 6, and e and f for cases 7 to 9. Figure 4 compares solutions for the RK method with GL solver in case of susceptible and infected removable-storage media: a and b for cases 1 to 3, c and d for cases 4 to 6, and e and f for cases 7 to 9. In Figures 5 and 6, the solution of the RK method with a GL solver are compared and presented for infected nodes I, damaged node M, susceptible removable-storage media U_s and infected removable-storage media U_I, respectively, for nine model cases.

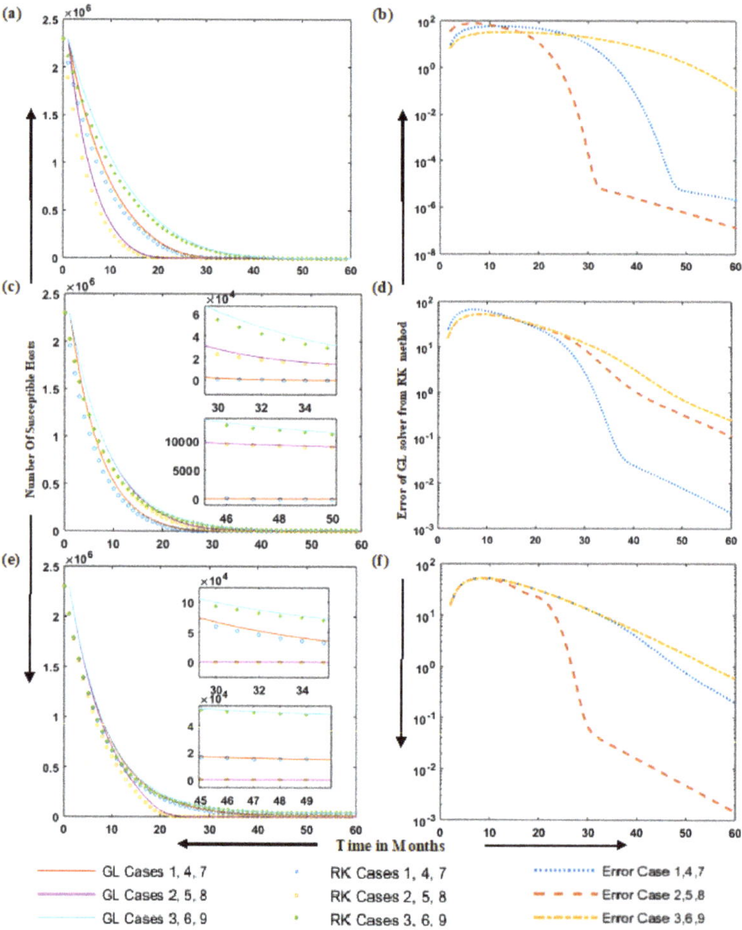

Figure 4. Solution comparison of the RK method with GL solver and error analysis with susceptible S hosts: a and b for cases 2 to 4, c and d for cases 5 to 7, and e and f for cases 8 to 10. (**a**) Solution comparison of the RK method with GL solver for cases 2 to 4, (**b**) error analysis for cases 2 to 4, (**c**) Solution comparison of the RK method with GL solver for cases 5 to 7, (**d**) error analysis for cases 5 to 7, (**e**) Solution comparison of the RK method with GL solver for cases 8 to 10, (**f**) error analysis for cases 8 to 10.

These nine cases also explain the virus spread behavior in different scenarios. Considering Figures 4–6, and the different cases simulated, we have the following comments.

The effect of changing the infectious contact rate β_1 from 36.6% to 60% is highlighted in case 1 of Equation (9) (value of β_1 in Figure 3 is 36.6%). It is observed that the number of infected hosts in 24 months is 96,760, as shown in Figure 5a (in Figure 3, the number of infected hosts in 24 months is 96,270), which shows a slight increase in infected hosts due to β_1. In case 2, the number of initially infected hosts is assumed to be 30,000. Increasing the contact rate of infectious removable media (in case 2) reduces the number of susceptible hosts rapidly as compared to case 1 (Figure 4a). However, the number of infected hosts is reduced (Figure 5a) due to an increase in the natural removal rate of hosts and removable storage r_1 and r_2 (hosts are removed to save them from the Stuxnet attack). In case 3, we reduce the damage rate and the quantity of initial susceptible removable-storage media, which reduces infected removable-storage media number (Figure 6b) and increases the infected hosts, as in Figure 5a). A decrease in damaged hosts is observed in case 3, despite the increase in the number of infected hosts.

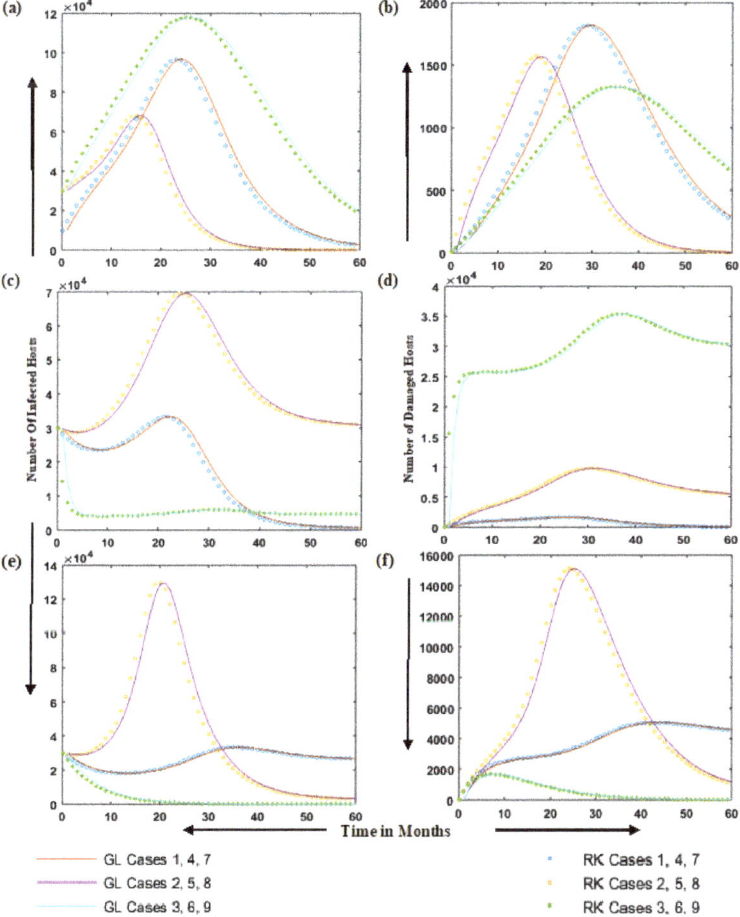

Figure 5. Solution comparison of RK method with GL solver for infected hosts I and damaged hosts M; a and b for cases 1 to 3, c and d for cases 4 to 6 while e and f for cases 7 to 9. (**a**) Comparison of RK method with GL solver for infected hosts in cases 1 to 3, (**b**) Comparison of RK method with GL solver for damaged hosts in cases 1 to 3, (**c**) Comparison of RK method with GL solver for infected hosts in cases 4 to 6, (**d**) Comparison of RK method with GL solver for damaged hosts in cases 4 to 6, (**e**) Comparison of RK method with GL solver for infected hosts in cases 7 to 9, (**f**) Comparison of RK method with GL solver for damaged hosts in cases 7 to 9.

In case 4, FO-SVM model dynamics are observed by increasing the arrival rate of new nodes and the arrival rate of new removable-storage devices, as mentioned in Tables 1 and 2. The results show that increasing the arrival rate of new hosts and arrival rate of new removable-storage media will not spread the infection faster without the presence of a sufficient number of infected removable-storage devices, as shown in Figure 5c. In cases 5 and 6, we further increase the values of the arrival rate of new nodes as well as removable-storage devices for an in-depth behavior analysis of the model. Both cases have similar parameters, except case 6, which represents a higher damage rate (especially for zero-day vulnerability or for a new virus attack) that increases the number of damaged computers and reduces the number of infected computers (removed due to high damage rate) in the networks as compared to case 5. Case 5 shows the high number of infected nodes (Figure 5c) because the Stuxnet virus only destroys the machines with specific hardware (Siemens specific PLCs) and remains dormant till it finds the target. In case 6 (Figure 5c,d), the number of infected hosts decreases; however an increase in the number of damaged hosts is observed due to an increase in damage rate ρ.

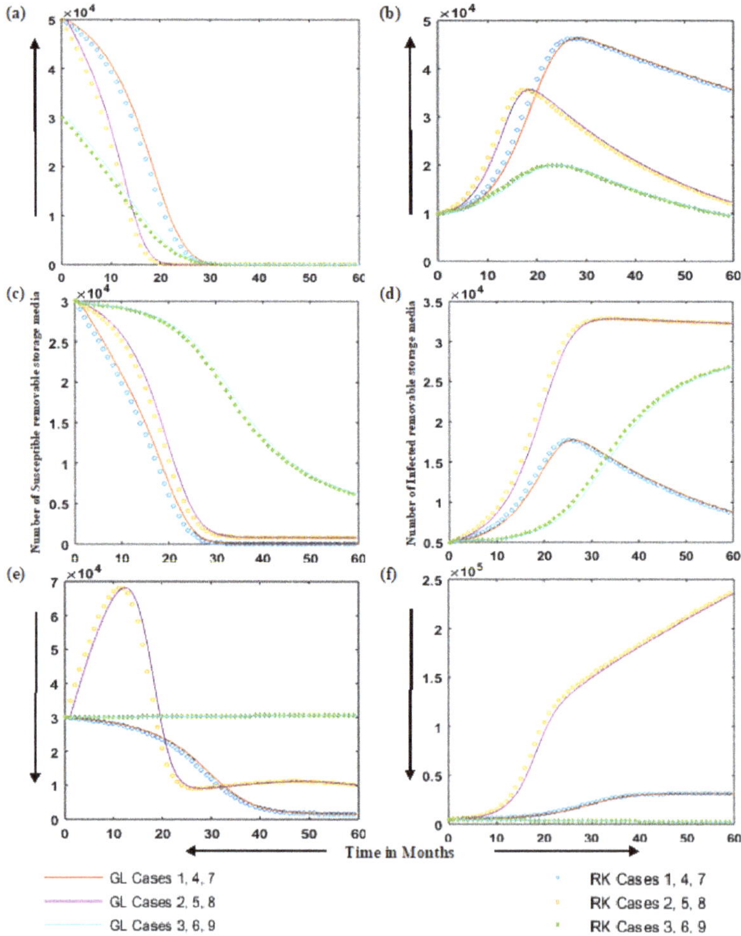

Figure 6. Solution comparison RK method with GL solver for susceptible and infected-removable-storage media: a and b for cases 1 to 3, c and d for cases 4 to 6, and e and f for cases 7 to 9. (**a**) Comparison of RK method with GL solver for susceptible removable storage media in cases 1 to 3, (**b**) Comparison of RK method with GL solver for infected removable storage media in cases 1 to 3, (**c**) Comparison of RK method with GL solver for susceptible removable storage media in cases 4 to 6, (**d**) Comparison of RK method with GL solver for infected removable storage media in cases 4 to 6, (**e**) Comparison of RK method with GL solver for susceptible removable storage media in cases 7 to 9, (**f**) Comparison of RK method with GL solver for infected removable storage media in cases 7 to 9.

In case 7, the values of β_1 and β_2 of case 6 are swapped to observe the behavior of the model. In case 7, the value of $\beta_1 = 0.745$, as compared to 0.4 in case 6, and the value of $\beta_2 = 0.4$, as compared to 0.745 in case 6. These swaps are carried out to observe the devastation effect of infected removable storage media as compared to the effect of infected nodes in the model, because infected removable media have a greater devastation effect. Simulation results show that the number of damaged nodes in case 6 is 35,000, whereas, in case 7, it is 5000, due to a decrease in the value of β_2 infectious contact rate of removable storage media (Figure 5e).

However, by increasing β_2 value (removable-storage media's infectious contact rate with susceptible computers) and A_2 (the arrival of removable-storage media) for case 8 will also increase the infection in the network. This outlines the importance of removable-storage media in spreading the virus in air-gapped networks (Figure 5e). In case 9, the contact rate of susceptible computer nodes with infectious removable-storage media β_2 is reduced, which results in a reduction in damaged nodes (Figure 5f) and infected nodes (Figure 5e), and an increase in the number of susceptible storage devices (Figure 6e). Case 9 further elaborates the scenario presented in case 8.

The derivative order $\alpha = 1$ is presented in Figures 4–6. The effect of change in fractional order α is presented in Figures 7–11. A detailed analysis of the FO-SVM model is conducted by changing the fractional order α in the system (9), such that one may observe fast-changing as well as super-slow growth in the model dynamics. The fractional order solution of the FO-SVM model for different values of the fractional order α is solved using a GL-based solver. The solutions are determined for nine cases of FO-SVM by a GL-based numerical procedure for different fractional orders, i.e., $\alpha = [0.5, 0.75, 0.8, 0.85, 0.9, 0.95, 1]$, for the inputs $t \in [0,\ 60]$ with step size $h = 0.001$. Results for the dynamics of the FO-SVM model in terms of susceptible S, infected I, and damaged M computers are plotted in Figures 7–9 for cases 1–3, 4–6, and 7–9, respectively. Susceptible removable-storage media U_s and infected-removable-storage media U_I are plotted in Figures 10 and 11 for cases 1–4 and 5–9, respectively, for different values of the fractional order α.

Figure 7 shows a simulation of fractional order, i.e., $\alpha = [0.5, 0.75, 0.8, 0.85, 0.9, 0.95, 1]$ for the FO-SVM model for different values of fractional order α for case 1–3 of susceptible S, infected I and damaged hosts M. In Figure 7, the number of susceptible, infected and damaged hosts is plotted versus time for cases 1–3 for different values of $\alpha = [0.5, 0.75, 0.8, 0.85, 0.9, 0.95, 1]$. A consistent pattern is observed in the evolution of curves with the value of α. The value of infected hosts in case 1 with $\alpha = 1$ is 96,760, and for $\alpha = 0.95$, the value of infected hosts is approximately 56,000 for $t = 24$ months, as shown in Figure 7b. In Figure 7c, the number of damaged hosts (hosts that were connected with specific models of Siemens PLCs) for the value of $\alpha = 0.95$ are 1000 for $t = 30$. Adjusting the value of α to 0.98 may adjust the number of damaged hosts to 1500, which matches the real published data of the Stuxnet virus. This illustrates the controllability feature of α for tuning the model. Despite the rapid spreadability of the Stuxnet virus, it causes little or no harm to the systems that do not have specific hardware.

Figure 8 shows the simulation of fractional order dynamics of the FO-SVM model for different values of fractional order α for cases 4–6, and Figure 9 depicts the simulation of fractional-order dynamics of the FO-SVM model for case 7–9. Figures 8 and 9 highlight the results for variation in fractional order α, which shows that variation in α gives smooth variations in the dynamics of the model. For $\alpha = 0.1$, we have the slowest evolution. Simulation of fractional order dynamics of FO-SVM model for different values of fractional order α for case 1–5 of susceptible removable-storage media U_s and infected-removable-storage media U_I are illustrated in Figure 10. Figure 11 shows the simulation of fractional order dynamics of FO-SVM model for different values of fractional order α, for cases 5–9 of susceptible removable-storage media U_s, and infected-removable-storage media U_I. In Figures 10 and 11, the number of susceptible storage media and infected storage media is plotted for case 1–9 against the time variation for different values of fractional order $\alpha = [0.5, 0.75, 0.8, 0.85, 0.9, 0.95, 1]$. It is observed that tuning the values of α tunes the dynamics of transients, as shown in Figure 10a. The value of susceptible storage media for $t = 1$ and $\alpha = 0.95$ is 35,000, which is effectively reduced to 10,000 by a slight change in fractional order α from 0.95 to 0.8. In contrast, a slow change is observed in the dynamics of the FO-SVM model for $\alpha = 0.1$. Increasing the fractional order α increases the rate of change of the variables. Fractional-order virus models provide extra tunable parameters in the form of α, which highlight more minute changes in the model dynamics.

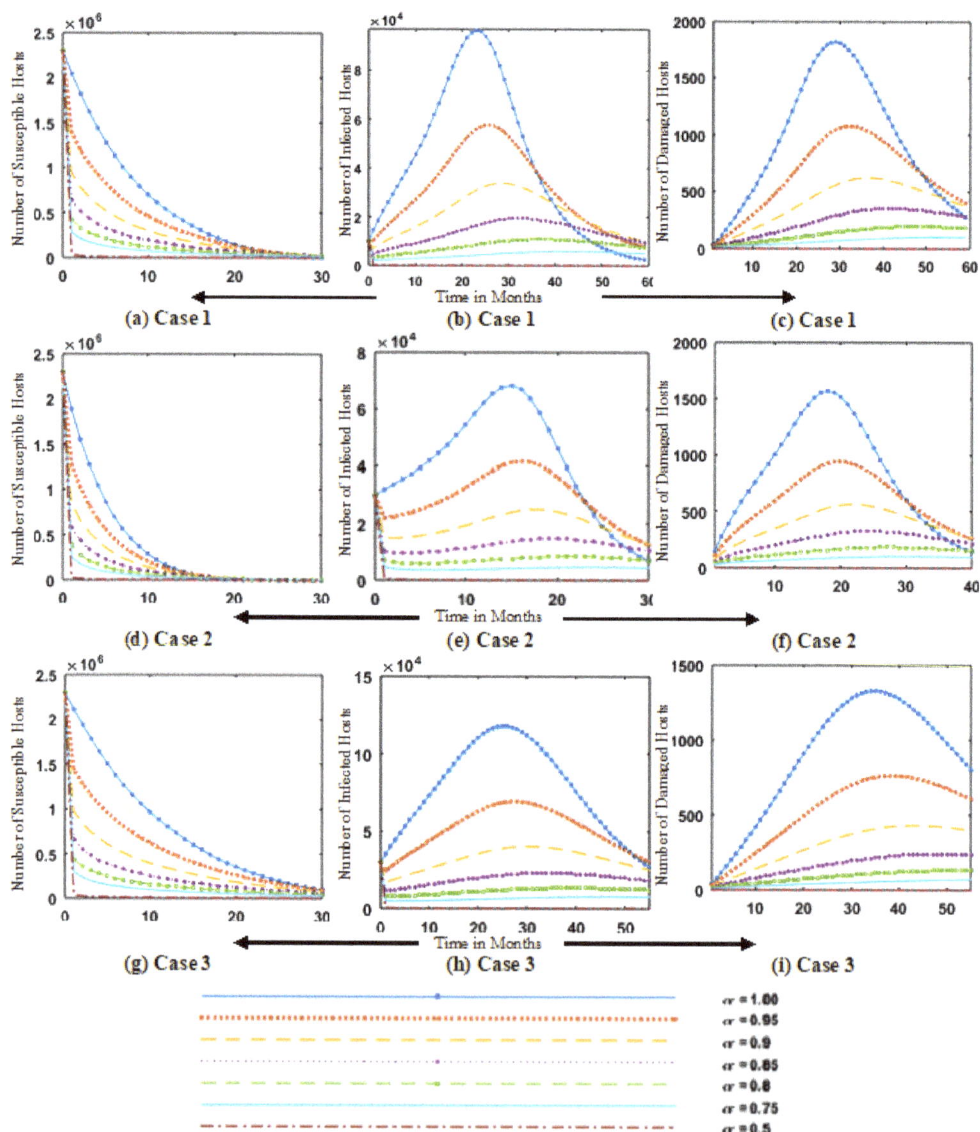

Figure 7. Simulation of fractional order dynamics of FO-SVM model for different values of fractional order α for cases 1 (**a–c**), 2 (**b–f**) and 3 (**g–i**) of susceptible S, infected I and damaged hosts M.

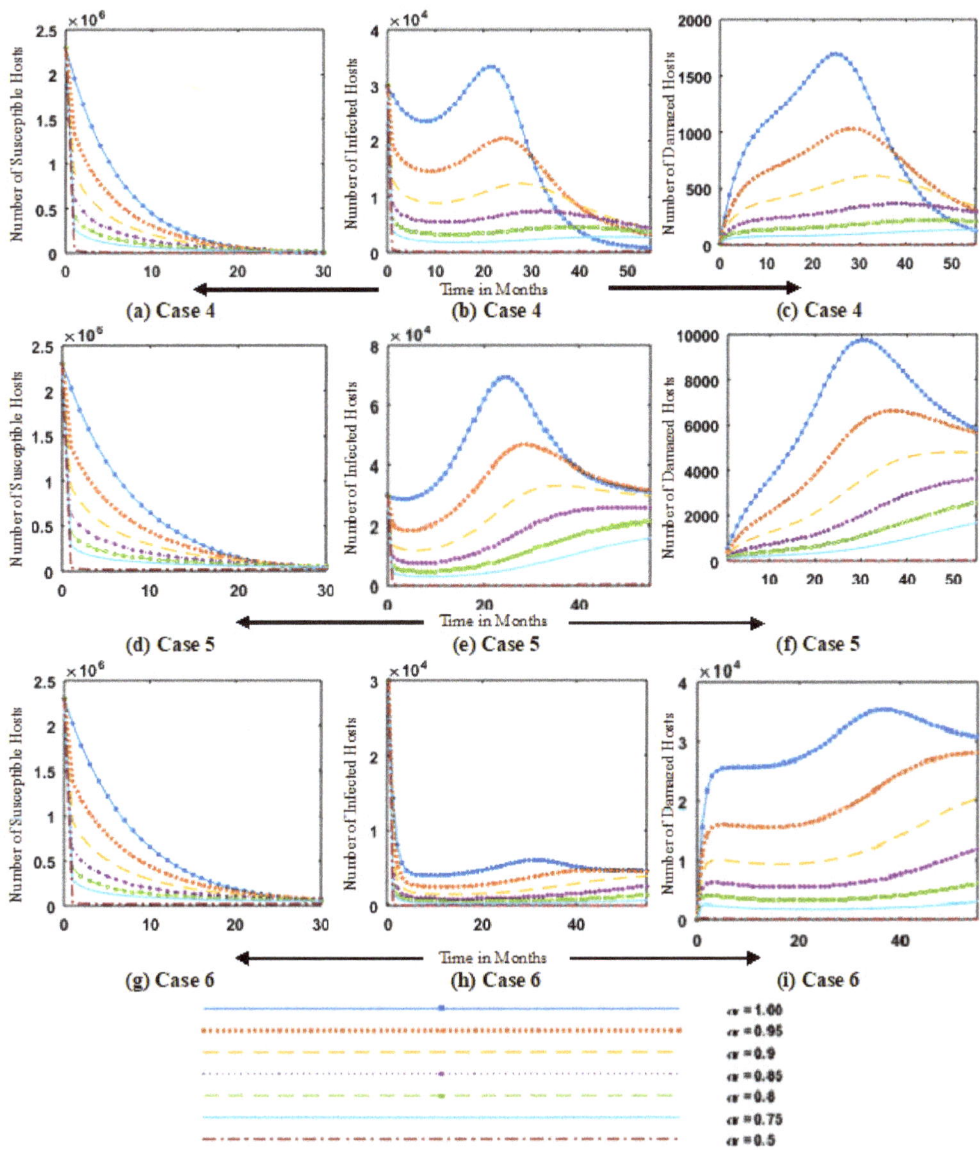

Figure 8. Simulation of fractional order dynamics of FO-SVM model for different values of fractional order α for cases 4 (**a**–**c**), 5 (**b**–**f**) and b (**g**–**i**) of susceptible S, infected I and damaged hosts M.

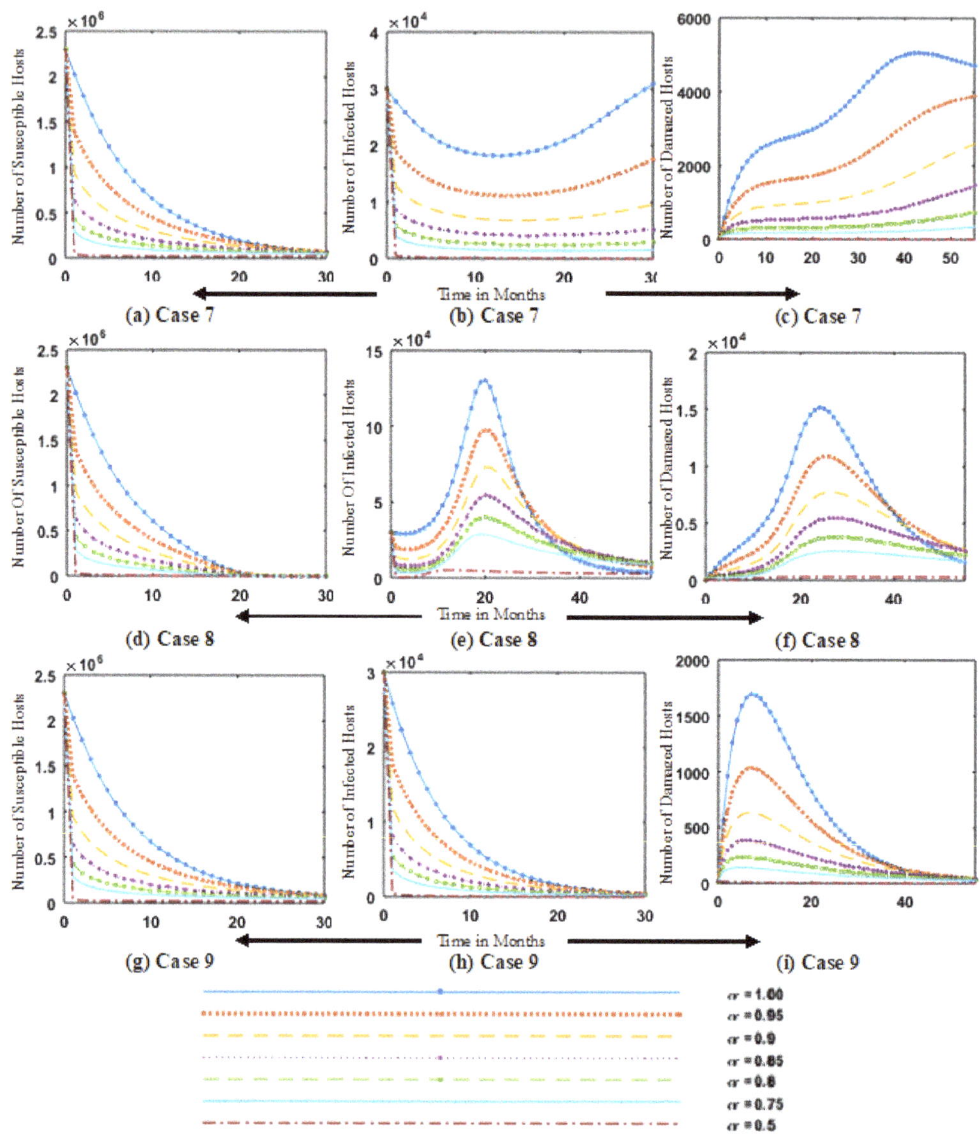

Figure 9. Simulation of fractional order dynamics of FO-SVM model for different values of fractional order α for cases 7 (**a–c**), 8 (**b–f**) and 9 (**g–i**) of susceptible S, infected I and damaged hosts M.

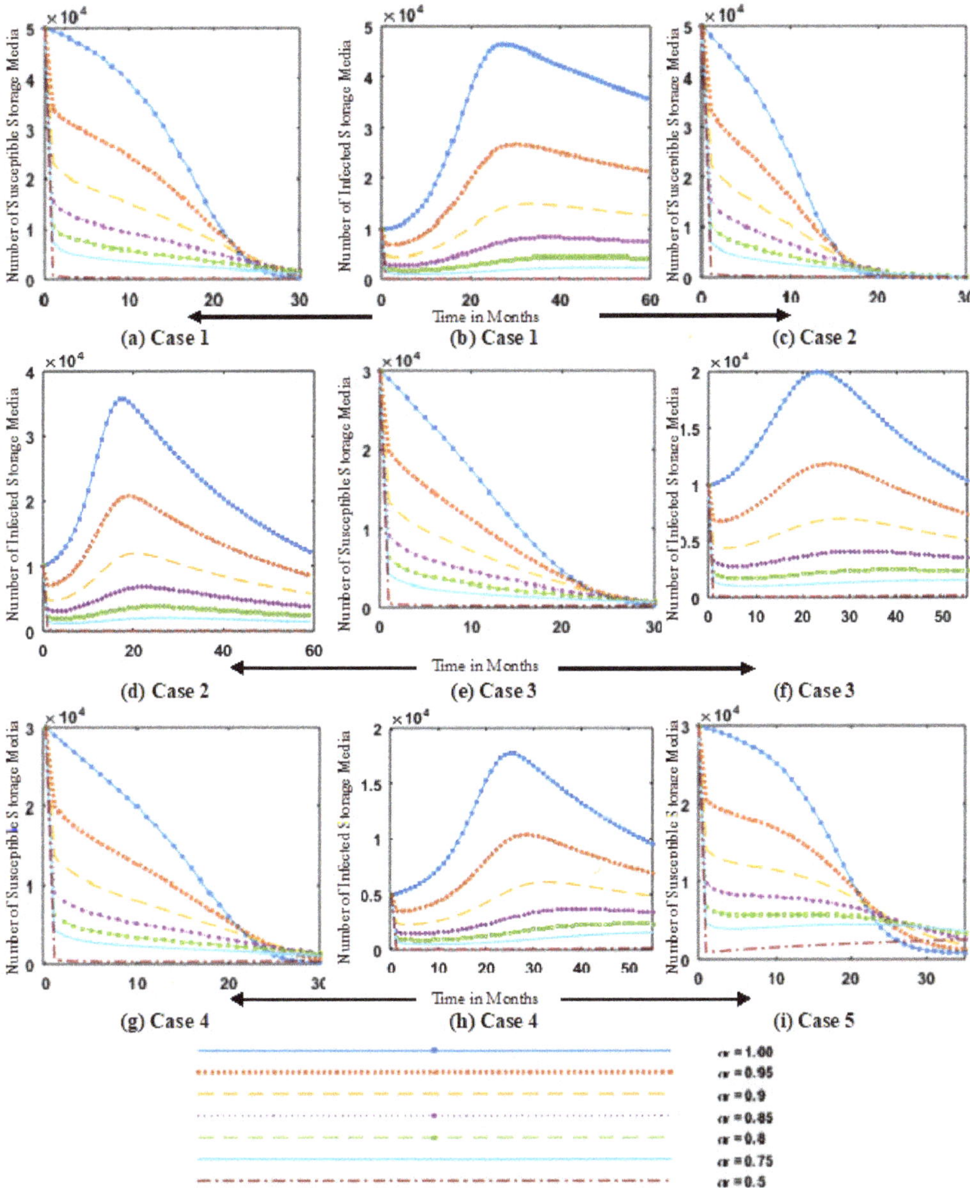

Figure 10. Simulation of fractional order dynamics of FO-SVM model for different values of fractional order α for cases 1 (**a**,**b**), 2 (**c**,**d**) and 3 (**e**,**f**), 4 (**g**,**h**) and 5 (**i**) of susceptible removable-storage media U_S and infected-removable-storage media U_I.

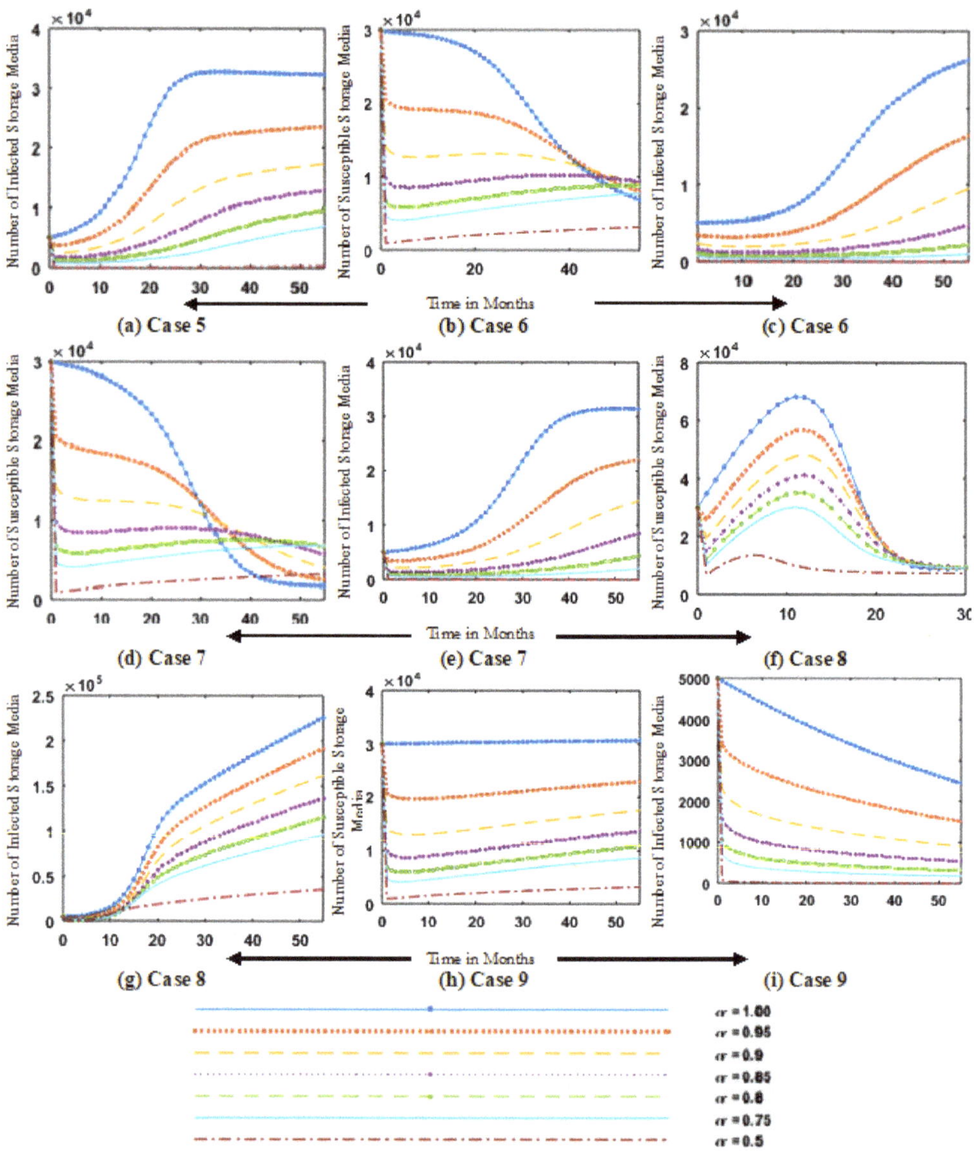

Figure 11. Simulation of fractional order dynamics of FO-SVM model for different values of fractional order α for cases 5 (**a**), 6 (**b,c**) and 7 (**d,e**), 8 (**f,g**) and 9 (**h,i**) of susceptible removable-storage media U_s and infected-removable-storage media U_I.

6. Conclusions

A detailed analysis of the novel design of the fractional order Stuxnet virus model is presented, with richer dynamics for the transmission of virus spread in an isolated critical network through removable-storage media. The fractional-order Stuxnet-virus-based mathematical models are found to be at least as stable as integer-order models. The fractional order value α of the proposed fractional Stuxnet virus model more effectively controls the solution reachability towards a steady state point. Additionally, the fractional order system of the Stuxnet virus model can tackle the different responses, including super-slow evolutions and very fast transients; these responses are found to have long memory characteristics in the system. Taking the value of $\alpha = 0.98$, one may adjust the number of damaged hosts to 1500 in case 1, which matches the damage caused by the Stuxnet virus. The transformation process of the classical model into a fractional model is very sensitive to the value of the order of differentiation α, and can be converted to a simple SIR model if we choose the values of the infectious contact rate $\beta_2 = 0$. A theoretical analysis of the model capturing the Stuxnet virus-spreading characteristics is determined by a mathematical derivation of the basic reproduction number R_0 for the value of $\alpha = 1$. Equilibrium points of the model are globally and asymptomatically stable for $R_0 < 1$ and $R_0 > 1$, respectively.

In the future, one may exploit the strength of stochastic numerical solvers [56–61] based on fractional evolutionary and swarming techniques [62–67] for a detailed analysis of the designed fractional-order Stuxnet virus model. Additionally, new definitions of the fractional operator, such as Yang–Machado [35] and Yang–Abdel–Aty–Cattani [36] fractional derivatives looks promising for the development of new computing solvers for the numerical solution of the fractional-order Stuxnet virus model and other fractional-order systems with better theoretical justifications, a better applicability domain, proof of the accuracy, convergence, stability, and robustness.

Author Contributions: Conceptualization, Z.M. and M.A.Z.R.; methodology, Z.M. and M.A.Z.R.; software, Z.M.; validation, M.A.Z.R.; formal analysis, N.I.C. and M.A.Z.R.; investigation, Z.M.; writing—original draft preparation, Z.M.; writing—review and editing, N.I.C. and M.A.Z.R.; visualization, N.I.C. and M.A.Z.R.; project administration, K.M.C. and A.H.M.; funding acquisition, K.M.C. and A.H.M. All authors have read and agreed to the published version of the manuscript.

Funding: This research received no external funding.

Institutional Review Board Statement: Not applicable.

Informed Consent Statement: Not applicable.

Data Availability Statement: Not applicable.

Conflicts of Interest: The authors declare no conflict of interest.

References

1. Rohde, M.; Aal, K.; Misaki, K.; Randall, D.; Weibert, A.; Wulf, V. Out of syria: Mobile media in use at the time of civil war. *Int. J. Hum.-Comput. Interact.* **2016**, *32*, 515–531. [CrossRef]
2. Bronk, C.; Tikk-Ringas, E. The cyber attack on saudi aramco. *Survival* **2013**, *55*, 81–96. [CrossRef]
3. Farwell, J.P.; Rohozinski, R. Stuxnet and the future of cyber war. *Survival* **2011**, *53*, 23–40. [CrossRef]
4. Albright, D.; Brannan, P.; Walrond, C. Stuxnet malware and natanz: Update of isis December 22, 2010 report. *Inst. Sci. Int. Secur.* **2011**, *15*, 739883.
5. Mueller, P.; Yadegari, B. The Stuxnet Worm. Département des Sciences de Linformatique, Université de lArizona. Available online: https://www2.cs.arizona.edu/~collberg/Teaching/466-566/2012/Resources/presentations/topic9-final/report.pdf (accessed on 12 December 2017).
6. Falliere, N.; Murchu, L.O.; Chien, E. W32. *Stuxnet Dossier*; White Paper; Symantec Corp., Security Response: Cupertino, CA, USA, 2011; Volume 5, p. 29.
7. Shahrear, P.; Chakraborty, A.K.; Islam, M.A.; Habiba, U. Analysis of computer virus propagation based on compartmental model. *Appl. Comput. Math.* **2018**, *7*, 12–21.
8. Khanh, N.H. Dynamical analysis and approximate iterative solutions of an antidotal computer virus model. *Int. J. Appl. Comput. Math.* **2017**, *3*, 829–841. [CrossRef]
9. Latha, V.P.; Rihan, F.A.; Rakkiyappan, R.; Velmurugan, G. A fractional order model for ebola virus infection with delayed immune response on heterogeneous complex networks. *J. Comput. Appl. Math.* **2018**, *339*, 134–146. [CrossRef]
10. Zhu, B.; Joseph, A.; Sastry, S. A taxonomy of cyber attacks on scada systems. In Proceedings of the 2011 IEEE International Conferences on Internet of Things, and Cyber, Physical and Social Computing, Dalian, China, 19–22 October 2011; pp. 380–388.
11. Wang, Z.; Bauch, C.T.; Bhattacharyya, S.; d'Onofrio, A.; Manfredi, P.; Perc, M.; Perra, N.; Salathe, M.; Zhao, D. Statistical physics of vaccination. *Phys. Rep.* **2016**, *664*, 1–113. [CrossRef]
12. Helbing, D.; Brockmann, D.; Chadefaux, T.; Donnay, K.; Blanke, U.; Woolley-Meza, O.; Moussaid, M.; Johansson, A.; Krause, J.; Schutte, S.; et al. Saving human lives: What complexity science and information systems can contribute. *J. Stat. Phys.* **2015**, *158*, 735–781. [CrossRef]

13. Cohen, R.; Havlin, S.; Ben-Avraham, D. Efficient immunization strategies for computer networks and populations. *Phys. Rev. Lett.* **2003**, *91*, 247901. [CrossRef]

14. Li, M.; Fu, C.; Liu, X.-Y.; Yang, J.; Zhu, T.; Han, L. Evolutionary virus immune strategy for temporal networks based on community vitality. *Future Gener. Comput. Syst.* **2017**, *74*, 276–290. [CrossRef]

15. Yang, X.-J. *General Fractional Derivatives: Theory, Methods and Applications*; Chapman and Hall/CRC: Boca Raton, FL, USA, 2019.

16. Duarte Ortigueira, M.; Tenreiro Machado, J. Fractional derivatives: The perspective of system theory. *Mathematics* **2019**, *7*, 150. [CrossRef]

17. Capasso, V.; Serio, G. A generalization of the kermack-mckendrick deterministic epidemic model. *Math. Biosci.* **1978**, *42*, 43–61. [CrossRef]

18. Mishra, B.K.; Saini, D.K. Seirs epidemic model with delay for transmission of malicious objects in computer network. *Appl. Math. Comput.* **2007**, *188*, 1476–1482. [CrossRef]

19. Kumar, S.; Ahmadian, A.; Kumar, R.; Kumar, D.; Singh, J.; Baleanu, D.; Salimi, M. An efficient numerical method for fractional SIR epidemic model of infectious disease by using Bernstein wavelets. *Mathematics* **2020**, *8*, 558. [CrossRef]

20. Dong, T.; Wang, A.; Liao, X. Impact of discontinuous antivirus strategy in a computer virus model with the point to group. *Appl. Math. Model.* **2016**, *40*, 3400–3409. [CrossRef]

21. Piqueira, J.R.C.; Araujo, V.O. A modified epidemiological model for computer viruses. *Appl. Math. Comput.* **2009**, *213*, 355–360. [CrossRef]

22. Masood, Z.; Majeed, K.; Samar, R.; Raja, M.A.Z. Design of epidemic computer virus model with effect of quarantine in the presence of immunity. *Fundam. Inform.* **2018**, *161*, 249–273. [CrossRef]

23. Calvert, K.L.; Doar, M.B.; Zegura, E.W. Modeling internet topology. *IEEE Commun. Mag.* **1997**, *35*, 160–163. [CrossRef]

24. Sabatier, J.; Agrawal, O.P.; Machado, J.T. *Advances in Fractional Calculus*; Springer: Dordrecht, The Netherlands, 2007; Volume 4.

25. Machado, J.T.; Silva, M.F.; Barbosa, R.S.; Jesus, I.S.; Reis, C.M.; Marcos, M.G.; Galhano, A.F. Some applications of fractional calculus in engineering. *Math. Probl. Eng.* **2010**, *2010*, 639801.

26. Tenreiro Machado, J.A.; Mata, M.E.; Lopes, A.M. Fractional dynamics and pseudo-phase space of country economic processes. *Mathematics* **2020**, *8*, 81. [CrossRef]

27. Masood, Z.; Samar, R.; Raja, M.A.Z. Design of fractional order epidemic model for future generation tiny hardware implants. *Future Gener. Comput. Syst.* **2020**, *106*, 43–54. [CrossRef]

28. Masood, Z.; Samar, R.; Raja, M.A.Z. Design of a mathematical model for the stuxnet virus in a network of critical control infrastructure. *Comput. Secur.* **2019**, *87*, 101565. [CrossRef]

29. Du, M.; Wang, Z.; Hu, H. Measuring memory with the order of fractional derivative. *Sci. Rep.* **2013**, *3*, 3431. [CrossRef]

30. Heymans, N.; Podlubny, I. Physical interpretation of initial conditions for fractional differential equations with riemann-liouville fractional derivatives. *Rheol. Acta* **2006**, *45*, 765–771. [CrossRef]

31. Yang, X.-J.; Feng, Y.-Y.; Cattani, C.; Inc, M. Fundamental solutions of anomalous diffusion equations with the decay exponential kernel. *Math. Methods Appl. Sci.* **2019**, *42*, 4054–4060. [CrossRef]

32. Yang, X.-J. New rheological problems involving general fractional derivatives with nonsingular power-law kernels. *Proc. Rom. Acad. Ser. A Math. Phys. Tech. Sci. Inf. Sci.* **2018**, *19*, 45.

33. Cao, Y.; Zhang, Y.; Wen, T.; Li, P. Research on dynamic nonlinear input prediction of fault diagnosis based on fractional differential operator equation in high-speed train control system. *Chaos Interdiscip. J. Nonlinear Sci.* **2019**, *29*, 013130. [CrossRef]

34. Yang, X.-J.; Srivastava, H.M.; Torres, D.F.; Debbouche, A. General fractional-order anomalous diffusion with non-singular power-law kernel. *Therm. Sci.* **2017**, *21*, 1–9. [CrossRef]

35. Yang, X.-J.; Machado, J.T. A new fractional operator of variable order: Application in the description of anomalous diffusion. *Phys. A Stat. Mech. Its Appl.* **2017**, *481*, 276–283. [CrossRef]

36. Yang, X.-J.; Abdel-Aty, M.; Cattani, C. A new general fractional order derivative with rabotnov fractional-exponential kernel applied to model the anomalous heat transfer. *Therm. Sci.* **2019**, *23*, 1677–1681. [CrossRef]

37. Miller, K.S.; Ross, B. *An Introduction to the Fractional Calculus and Fractional Differential Equations*; Wiley: New York, NY, USA, 1993.

38. Machado, J.T.; Galhano, A.M.; Trujillo, J.J. On development of fractional calculus during the last fifty years. *Scientometrics* **2014**, *98*, 577–582. [CrossRef]

39. Ortigueira, M.D.; Machado, J.T. What is a fractional derivative? *J. Comput. Phys.* **2015**, *293*, 4–13. [CrossRef]

40. Petráš, I. A note on the fractional-order chuas system. *Chaos Solitons Fractals* **2008**, *38*, 140–147. [CrossRef]

41. Haubold, H.J.; Mathai, A.M.; Saxena, R.K. Mittag-leffler functions and their applications. *J. Appl. Math.* **2011**, *2011*, 298628. [CrossRef]

42. Podlubny, I. The laplace transform method for linear differential equations of the fractional order. *arXiv* **1997**, arXiv:funct-an/9710005.

43. Cafagna, D. Fractional calculus: A mathematical tool from the past for present engineers [past and present]. *IEEE Ind. Electron. Mag.* **2007**, *1*, 35–40. [CrossRef]

44. Petráš, I. Fractional derivatives, fractional integrals, and fractional differential equations in matlab. In *Engineering Education and Research Using MATLAB*; InTech: London, UK, 2011.

45. Scherer, R.; Kalla, S.; Boyadjiev, L.; Al-Saqabi, B. Numerical treatment of fractional heat equations. *Appl. Numer. Math.* **2008**, *58*, 1212–1223. [CrossRef]

46. Yang, L.-X.; Yang, X. The spread of computer viruses under the influence of removable storage devices. *Appl. Math. Comput.* **2012**, *219*, 3914–3922. [CrossRef]
47. Langner, R. *To Kill a Centrifuge: A Technical Analysis of What Stuxnet's Creators Tried to Achieve*; The Langner Group: Dover, DE, USA, 2013.
48. Wueest, C. *Targeted Attacks against the Energy Sector*; Symantec Security Response: Mountain View, CA, USA, 2014
49. Markus, L. Ii. asymptotically autonomous differential systems. In *Contributions to the Theory of Nonlinear Oscillations (AM-36)*; Princeton University Press: Princeton, NJ, USA, 2016; Volume 3, p. 17.
50. Thieme, H.R. Asymptotically autonomous differential equations in the plane. *Rocky Mt. J. Math.* **1994**, *24*, 351–380. [CrossRef]
51. den Driessche, P.V.; Watmough, J. Reproduction numbers and subthreshold endemic equilibria for compartmental models of disease transmission. *Math. Biosci.* **2002**, *180*, 29–48. [CrossRef]
52. Petras, I. Stability of fractional-order systems with rational orders. *arXiv* **2008**, arXiv:0811.4102.
53. Gil, J.J.; Avello, A.; Rubio, A.; Florez, J. Stability analysis of a 1 dof haptic interface using the routh-hurwitz criterion. *IEEE Trans. Control. Syst. Technol.* **2004**, *12*, 583–588. [CrossRef]
54. Rohn, J. Positive definiteness and stability of interval matrices. *SIAM J. Matrix Anal. Appl.* **1994**, *15*, 175–184. [CrossRef]
55. Shakarian, P.; Shakarian, J.; Ruef, A. *Introduction to Cyber-Warfare: A Multidisciplinary Approach*; Newnes: Oxford, UK, 2013.
56. Pinto, C.M.; Carvalho, A.R. A latency fractional order model for hiv dynamics. *J. Comput. Appl. Math.* **2017**, *312*, 240–256. [CrossRef]
57. Chaharborj, S.S.; Chaharborj, S.; Mahmoudi, Y. Study of fractional order integro-differential equations by using chebyshev neural network. *J. Math. Stat.* **2017**, *13*, 1–13. [CrossRef]
58. Raja, M.A.Z.; Mehmood, A.; Rehman, A.u.; Khan, A.; Zameer, A. Bioinspired computational heuristics for sisko fluid flow and heat transfer models. *Appl. Soft Comput.* **2018**, *71*, 622–648. [CrossRef]
59. Raja, M.A.Z.; Shah, Z.; Manzar, M.A.; Ahmad, I.; Awais, M.; Baleanu, D. A new stochastic computing paradigm for nonlinear painlevé ii systems in applications of random matrix theory. *Eur. Phys. J. Plus* **2018**, *133*, 254. [CrossRef]
60. Ahmad, I.; Ahmad, S.; Awais, M.; Ahmad, S.U.I.; Raja, M.A.Z. Neuroevolutionary computing paradigm for painlevé equation-ii in nonlinear optics. *Eur. Phys. J. Plus* **2018**, *133*, 184. [CrossRef]
61. Raja, M.A.Z.; Manzar, M.A.; Samar, R. An efficient computational intelligence approach for solving fractional order riccati equations using ann and sqp. *Appl. Math. Model.* **2015**, *39*, 3075–3093. [CrossRef]
62. Akbar, S.; Zaman, F.; Asif, M.; Rehman, A.U.; Raja, M.A.Z. Novel application of fo-dpso for 2-d parameter estimation of electromagnetic plane waves. *Neural Comput. Appl.* **2019**, *31*, 3681–3690. [CrossRef]
63. Pires, E.S.; Machado, J.T.; Oliveira, P.d.; Cunha, J.B.; Mendes, L. Particle swarm optimization with fractional-order velocity. *Nonlinear Dyn.* **2010**, *61*, 295–301. [CrossRef]
64. Muhammad, Y.; Akhtar, R.; Khan, R.; Ullah, F.; Raja, M.A.Z.; Machado, J.T. Design of fractional evolutionary processing for reactive power planning with FACTS devices. *Sci. Rep.* **2021**, *11*, 593. [CrossRef] [PubMed]
65. Khan, M.W.; Muhammad, Y.; Raja, M.A.Z.; Ullah, F.; Chaudhary, N.I.; He, Y. A New Fractional Particle Swarm Optimization with Entropy Diversity Based Velocity for Reactive Power Planning. *Entropy* **2020**, *22*, 1112. [CrossRef] [PubMed]
66. Muhammad, Y.; Khan, R.; Raja, M.A.Z.; Ullah, F.; Chaudhary, N.I.; He, Y. Design of fractional swarm intelligent computing with entropy evolution for optimal power flow problems. *IEEE Access* **2020**, *8*, 111401–111419. [CrossRef]
67. Escalante-Martínez, J.E.; Gómez-Aguilar, J.F.; Calderón-Ramón, C.; Aguilar-Meléndez, A.; Padilla-Longoria, P. Synchronized bioluminescence behavior of a set of fireflies involving fractional operators of liouville–caputo type. *Int. J. Biomath.* **2018**, *11*, 1850041. [CrossRef]

Article

Statistical Feature Construction for Forecasting Accuracy Increase and Its Applications in Neural Network Based Analysis

Andrey Gorshenin [1,*] and Victor Kuzmin [1,2]

[1] Federal Research Center "Computer Science and Control", Russian Academy of Sciences, 119333 Moscow, Russia; shadesilent@yandex.ru
[2] Moscow Center for Fundamental and Applied Mathematics, Lomonosov Moscow State University, 119991 Moscow, Russia
* Correspondence: agorshenin@frccsc.ru

Abstract: This paper presents a feature construction approach called Statistical Feature Construction (SFC) for time series prediction. Creation of new features is based on statistical characteristics of analyzed data series. First, the initial data are transformed into an array of short pseudo-stationary windows. For each window, a statistical model is created and characteristics of these models are later used as additional features for a single window or as time-dependent features for the entire time series. To demonstrate the effect of SFC, five plasma physics and six oceanographic time series were analyzed. For each window, unknown distribution parameters were estimated with the method of moving separation of finite normal mixtures. First four statistical moments of these mixtures for initial data and increments were used as additional data features. Multi-layer recurrent neural networks were trained to create short- and medium-term forecasts with a single window as input data; additional features were used to initialize the hidden state of recurrent layers. A hyperparameter grid-search was performed to compare fully-optimized neural networks for original and enriched data. A significant decrease in RMSE metric was observed with a median of 11.4%. There was no increase in RMSE metric in any of the analyzed time series. The experimental results have shown that SFC can be a valuable method for forecasting accuracy improvement.

Keywords: feature selection; finite normal mixtures; moving separation of mixtures; deep LSTM; neural network architectures; deep learning; turbulent plasma; air–sea fluxes

MSC: 65C20; 62M45; 62P12; 62P35

Citation: Gorshenin, A.; Kuzmin, V. Statistical Feature Construction for Forecasting Accuracy Increase and Its Applications in Neural Network Based Analysis. *Mathematics* **2022**, *10*, 589. https://doi.org/10.3390/math10040589

Academic Editor: Shaul K. Bar-Lev

Received: 21 January 2022
Accepted: 7 February 2022
Published: 14 February 2022

Publisher's Note: MDPI stays neutral with regard to jurisdictional claims in published maps and institutional affiliations.

1. Introduction

Forecasting of real-world processes can be limited by the amount of information that can be reasonably collected. In many problems, data accumulation takes place under conditions of uncertainty caused by:

- the stochastic nature of the event flow intensity and interactions of a large number of random factors that cannot be exhaustively predicted;
- the heterogeneity or non-stationarity of data;
- the incompleteness of received and stored information that could arise both from resource limitations and from the stochastic nature of the external environment.

These stated conditions call for the need for research of probability mixture models for distributions of the observed processes [1]. A wide class of distributions with the form of $H(x) = \mathbb{E}_\mathbb{P}[F(x, \mathbf{y})]$ is usually chosen as the base family [2,3]. $\mathbb{E}_\mathbb{P}$ denotes the mathematical expectation with respect to some probability measure $\mathbb{P}$, which defines a mixing distribution. It is usually determined through the analysis of external factors behavior. $F(x, \mathbf{y})$ is a distribution function with a random vector of parameters $\mathbf{y}$ that is called a mixing (kernel) distribution.

There are two main problems:

- the analytical selection of the kernel type based on limit theorems of probability theory and mathematical statistics;
- methods of kernel parameter estimation which are random variables themselves.

The combination of parametric and non-parametric methods is the basis of a semi-parametric approach to the analysis of heterogeneous data. It was successfully applied to the complex tasks of the precipitation [4] and lunar regolith [5] analysis.

These principles are used as the basis for the method of moving separation of mixtures (MSM) [1]. MSM is used in this article as a tool for non-trivial extension of the feature space in neural network training problems. A significant relationship between EM algorithms and neural networks is well-known. First, backpropagation being the traditional method of training neural networks is also a specific case [6] of a generalized EM algorithm [7]. Secondly, finite normal mixtures and various modifications of the EM algorithm that are often used for estimating the parameters of probability mixture models [8–12] were successfully applied for solving clustering problems based on various deep neural networks [13,14].

Both short- and long-term data forecasts are essential to the decision-making, prediction of catastrophic events, and experiment planning. Machine learning algorithms, including neural networks, have proven to be effective forecasting tools for information flows [15] or weather prediction [16,17]. There are multiple ways to improve prediction accuracy, the majority of them being feature selection and construction [18–25]. Proper selection of features plays a critical role in the performance of many machine learning algorithms [26,27] and may result in better and/or faster trained models [28]. At the same time, in the analysis of one-dimensional time series, the process of feature construction becomes valuable as the collection of additional information for data enrichment and following feature selection may require additional time, resources, or be impossible in cases of historical data analysis.

Therefore, the idea of using probability mixture models characteristics as additional features for machine learning solutions of forecasting problems naturally arises. This allows us to take into account information derived from the mathematical model that is used to approximate data in a particular subject area. Additionally, a larger set of training data can be used without the direct increase of the initial observation volume.

In this paper, a new statistical approach to data enrichment and feature construction that is called Statistical Feature Construction (SFC) has been developed. SFC consists of two steps. In the first step, initial data are separated into pseudo-stationary sub-samples (windows). Then, for each of them, the MSM algorithm is used to evaluate parameters of a corresponding windows-based statistical model. The characteristics of such models are used to supply additional features to various machine learning methods. In the second step, moments of statistical models are used to enhance recurrent neural network forecasting performance.

This paper significantly expands and generalizes results obtained by the authors in the field of short- and medium-term neural networks based forecasting [29] including predictions of mixture moments themselves [30]. To demonstrate the effect of SFC, five plasma physics experimental datasets of stellarator L-2M [31] and six air–sea interactions time series were analyzed. New results are focused on the application of statistical characteristics to recurrent networks and comparison of the SFC performance with neural networks trained on non-enriched data.

The chosen data differ significantly. For example, there is no such phenomenon as seasonality in plasma while oceanographic data exhibit strong seasonal behavior. The possibility of significantly improving the accuracy of forecasts for both types of data will be demonstrated. This proves to be favorable for the generalized application of the proposed method for accuracy increase of neural network based forecasting.

Analyzed data are selected for the following reasons. First, for these types of observations, the possibility of qualitative approximation using finite normal mixtures has been demonstrated before [32,33]. Secondly, the application of moment characteristics allowed for obtaining significant results in the task of statistical analysis of experimental results in plasma physics [33]. Forecasting accuracy increase is the natural continuation of these studies. Additionally, neural networks were successfully applied in this area [34–38] including tasks of instability and destructive effect analysis [39,40] and in the interests of research on the international nuclear fusion ITER megaproject [41].

The paper is organized as follows: Section 2 outlines the MSM approach to the construction of statistical models. Section 3 summarizes the SFC methodology used. Feature construction and neural network architecture are described, and the question of computational complexity is addressed. Section 4 presents examples of the real data predictions in problems of plasma physics and oceanology. Forecasts and accuracy improvement levels achieved with SFC are shown. In Section 5, the results obtained and the directions for further research in this area are discussed. Appendix A contains simplified descriptions (pseudocodes) of the presented algorithms.

2. Finite Normal Mixtures and the MSM Method

The success of approximating distributions for heterogeneous data using arbitrary mixtures of normal distributions is based on the results for generalized Cox processes [1] and essentially uses the finiteness of variance of process increments. The main task in this area is related to the statistical estimation of mixing distribution random parameters.

It is well known that arbitrary continuous normal mixtures are not identifiable, while, for finite normal mixtures, identifiability holds [42,43]. Therefore, the original ill-posed problem of parameter estimation can be replaced with the solution closest to the true one in the space of finite normal mixtures. Such solution exists and is unique due to the aforementioned identifiability property.

However, the heterogeneity of data arising from the reasons mentioned at the beginning of Section 1 leads to the absence of a universal mixing distribution for a significantly long timescale. Therefore, the initial time series is divided into possibly intersecting subsamples called windows. Then, we can solve the problem of mixing distribution parameter estimation for each of these intervals while moving them along the time axis in the series. This procedure is the essence of the method of moving separation of mixtures.

It can be seen that the mixture itself will evolve during the time-movement of subsamples. This in turn allows us to observe the dynamics of the statistical patterns evolution in the behavior of the studied process.

Created statistical models can serve as qualitative approximations for the distributions of various processes. We propose to use the first four moments of the corresponding distributions as additional features for machine learning algorithms.

Let us consider a subsample (nth window) $\mathbf{X}$ with size $1 \times N$ and a cumulative distribution function (a finite normal mixture) of its elements:

$$F(x, k(n), \boldsymbol{\mu}_n, \boldsymbol{\sigma}_n, \mathbf{p}_n) = \sum_{i=1}^{k(n)} p_i \Phi\left(\frac{x - \mu_i(n)}{\sigma_i(n)}\right), \tag{1}$$

where $x \in \mathbb{R}$, $\Phi(x) = \int\limits_{-\infty}^{+\infty} e^{-x^2/2}\, dx$ and standard constraints on parameters

$$\mu_i(n) \in \mathbb{R}, \quad \sigma_i(n) \in \mathbb{R}, \quad \sigma_i(n) > 0, \quad \sum_{i=1}^{k(n)} p_i(n) = 1, \quad p_i(n) \geqslant 0,$$

hold for all $i = 1, \ldots, k(n)$.

Let a random value X_n have a cumulative distribution function (1). We will assume that it is an arbitrary element of the sample $\mathbf{X}$. We can assign a set of values to each vector $(\mathbb{E}_X^{(n)}, \mathbb{D}_X^{(n)}, \gamma_X^{(n)}, \kappa_X^{(n)})$. Those values are defined by the following formulas [44]:

- expectation:

$$\mathbb{E}_X^{(n)} = \mathbb{E}X_n = \sum_{i=1}^{k(n)} p_i(n)\mu_i(n);$$

(2)

- variance:

$$\mathbb{D}_X^{(n)} = \mathbb{D}X_n = \sum_{i=1}^{k(n)} p_i(n)\left(\mu_i(n) - \sum_{i=1}^{k(n)} p_i(n)\mu_i(n)\right)^2 + \sum_{i=1}^{k(n)} p_i(n)\sigma_i^2(n);$$

(3)

- skewness:

$$\gamma_X^{(n)} = \frac{\mathbb{E}X_n^3 - 3\mathbb{E}_X^{(n)} \cdot \mathbb{D}_X^{(n)} - \left(\mathbb{E}_X^{(n)}\right)^3}{\left(\mathbb{D}_X^{(n)}\right)^{3/2}} =$$

$$= \left[\sum_{i=1}^{k(n)} p_i(n)\left(\mu_i^3(n) + 3\mu_i(n)\sigma_i^2(n)\right) - \left(\sum_{i=1}^{k(n)} p_i(n)\mu_i(n)\right) \times \right.$$

$$\times \left(3\sum_{i=1}^{k(n)} p_i(n)\left(\mu_i(n) - \sum_{i=1}^{k(n)} p_i(n)\mu_i(n)\right)^2 + \right.$$

$$\left.\left. +3\sum_{i=1}^{k(n)} p_i(n)\sigma_i^2(n) - \left(\sum_{i=1}^{k(n)} p_i(n)\mu_i(n)\right)^2\right)\right] \times$$

$$\times \left[\sum_{i=1}^{k(n)} p_i(n)\left(\mu_i(n) - \sum_{i=1}^{k(n)} p_i(n)\mu_i(n)\right)^2 + \sum_{i=1}^{k(n)} p_i(n)\sigma_i^2(n)\right]^{-3/2};$$

(4)

- kurtosis:

$$\kappa_X^{(n)} = \frac{\mathbb{E}X_n^4 - 4\mathbb{E}_X^{(n)} \cdot \mathbb{E}X_n^3 + 6\left(\mathbb{E}_X^{(n)}\right)^2 \cdot \mathbb{E}X_n^2 - 3\left(\mathbb{E}_X^{(n)}\right)^4}{\left(\mathbb{D}_X^{(n)}\right)^2} - 3 =$$

$$= \left[\sum_{i=1}^{k(n)} p_i(n)\left(\mu_i^4(n) + 6\mu_i^2\sigma_i^2(n) + 3\sigma_i^4(n)\right) - 3\left(\sum_{i=1}^{k(n)} p_i(n)\mu_i(n)\right)^4 - \right.$$

$$-4\left(\sum_{i=1}^{k(n)} p_i(n)\mu_i(n)\right)\left(\sum_{i=1}^{k(n)} p_i(n)\left(\mu_i^3(n) + 3\mu_i(n)\sigma_i^2(n)\right)\right) +$$

$$\left. +6\left(\sum_{i=1}^{k(n)} p_i(n)\mu_i(n)\right)^2\left(\sum_{i=1}^{k(n)} p_i(n)\left(\mu_i^2(n) + \sigma_i^2(n)\right)\right)\right] \times$$

$$\times \left[\sum_{i=1}^{k(n)} p_i(n)\left(\mu_i(n) - \sum_{i=1}^{k(n)} p_i(n)\mu_i(n)\right)^2 + \sum_{i=1}^{k(n)} p_i(n)\sigma_i^2(n)\right]^{-2} - 3.$$

(5)

The argument n for each of these values (2)–(5) shows a strict dependence on the step number of the MSM method. That is, these moments are determined not for the entire time series, but only for a subsample of it. They are determined by observations that are separated from the first element $\mathbf{X}$—according to its location in the analyzed series—by the value L of the moving window of the MSM method.

It is well known that, for the initial moments of a random variable X with a normal distribution with parameters a and σ^2 (that is, $X \sim N(a, \sigma^2)$), the following equations hold:

$$\mathbb{E}X^m = \begin{cases} a^2 + \sigma^2, & m = 2; \\ a^3 + 3a\sigma^2, & m = 3; \\ a^4 + 6a^2\sigma^2 + 3\sigma^4, & m = 4. \end{cases} \tag{6}$$

For the initial moments of a random variable X_n with a cumulative distribution function $F(x, k(n), f_n, \sigma_n, \mathbf{p}_n)$ (1), we have ($m = 1, 2, \ldots$):

$$\mathbb{E}X_n^m = \sum_{i=1}^{k(n)} \frac{p_i(n)}{\sigma_i(n)\sqrt{2\pi}} \int_{-\infty}^{+\infty} z^m \exp\left\{ -\frac{(z - \mu_i(n))^2}{2\sigma_i^2(n)} \right\} dz = \sum_{i=1}^{k(n)} p_i(n) \mathbb{E}X_{[i]}^m,$$

where $X_{[i]} \sim N(\mu_i(n), \sigma_i^2(n))$. Thus, the analogues of the expressions (6) are as follows:

$$\mathbb{E}X_n^m = \begin{cases} \sum_{i=1}^{k(n)} p_i(n)\mu_i(n), & m = 1; \\ \sum_{i=1}^{k(n)} p_i(n)\left(\mu_i^2(n) + \sigma_i^2(n)\right), & m = 2; \\ \sum_{i=1}^{k(n)} p_i(n)\left(\mu_i^3(n) + 3\mu_i\sigma_i^2(n)\right), & m = 3; \\ \sum_{i=1}^{k(n)} p_i(n)\left(\mu_i^4(n) + 6\mu_i^2\sigma_i^2(n) + 3\sigma_i^4(n)\right), & m = 4. \end{cases} \tag{7}$$

Substituting these expressions into formulas for variance (3), skewness (4) and kurtosis (5) lead to formulae that depend only on the distribution parameters, namely the values $p_i(n)$, $\mu_i(n)$ and $\sigma_i(n)$.

Modern computing systems are optimized for performing matrix computations including parameter estimation problems that can be implemented with EM algorithms. Therefore, expressions (2)–(5) can be represented in an equivalent matrix form [30,45]:

- expectation:

$$\mathbb{E}X_n = \mathbf{p}_n \, \boldsymbol{\mu}_n^T; \tag{8}$$

- variance:

$$\mathbb{D}X_n = \mathbf{p}_n\left(D_{\mathbf{a}_n} \, \boldsymbol{\mu}_n^T + D_{\sigma_n} \, \sigma_n^T\right) - (\mathbf{p}_n \, \boldsymbol{\mu}_n^T)^2; \tag{9}$$

- skewness:

$$\gamma X_n = \frac{\mathbf{p}_n \, D_{\mathbf{a}_n}^2 \, \boldsymbol{\mu}_n^T + 3\,\mathbf{p}_n \, D_{\mathbf{a}_n} \, D_{\sigma_n} \, \sigma_n^T + 2\,(\mathbf{p}_n \, \boldsymbol{\mu}_n^T)^2}{(\mathbf{p}_n(D_{\mathbf{a}_n} \, \boldsymbol{\mu}_n^T + D_{\sigma_n} \, \sigma_n^T) - (\mathbf{p}_n \, \boldsymbol{\mu}_n^T)^2)^{3/2}} - 3 \cdot \frac{\mathbf{p}_n \, \boldsymbol{\mu}_n^T \, \mathbf{p}_n \, D_{\mathbf{a}_n} \, \boldsymbol{\mu}_n^T + \mathbf{p}_n \, \boldsymbol{\mu}_n^T \, \mathbf{p}_n \, D_{\sigma_n} \, \sigma_n^T}{(\mathbf{p}_n(D_{\mathbf{a}_n} \, \boldsymbol{\mu}_n^T + D_{\sigma_n} \, \sigma_n^T) - (\mathbf{p}_n \, \boldsymbol{\mu}_n^T)^2)^{3/2}}; \tag{10}$$

- kurtosis:

$$\kappa X_n = \frac{\mathbf{p}_n\left(D_{\mathbf{a}_n}^3 \, \boldsymbol{\mu}_n^T + 6\,D_{\sigma_n}^2 \, D_{\mathbf{a}_n} \, \boldsymbol{\mu}_n^T + 3\,D_{\sigma_n}^3 \, \sigma_n^T\right)}{(\mathbf{p}_n(D_{\mathbf{a}_n} \, \boldsymbol{\mu}_n^T + D_{\sigma_n} \, \sigma_n^T) - (\mathbf{p}_n \, \boldsymbol{\mu}_n^T)^2)^2} - \frac{4\,\mathbb{E}X_n \, \mathbf{p}_n \, D_{\mu_n}\left(D_{\mathbf{a}_n} \, \boldsymbol{\mu}_n^T + 3\,D_{\sigma_n} \, \sigma_n^T\right)}{(\mathbf{p}_n(D_{\mathbf{a}_n} \, \boldsymbol{\mu}_n^T + D_{\sigma_n} \, \sigma_n^T) - (\mathbf{p}_n \, \boldsymbol{\mu}_n^T)^2)^2} +$$

$$+ \frac{6\,(\mathbb{E}X_n)^2 \, \mathbf{p}_n\left(D_{\mathbf{a}_n} \, \boldsymbol{\mu}_n^T + D_{\sigma_n} \, \sigma_n^T\right) - 3\,(\mathbb{E}X_n)^4}{(\mathbf{p}_n(D_{\mathbf{a}_n} \, \boldsymbol{\mu}_n^T + D_{\sigma_n} \, \sigma_n^T) - (\mathbf{p}_n \, \boldsymbol{\mu}_n^T)^2)^2} - 3, \tag{11}$$

where

$$\mathbf{p}_n = \left(p_1, \ldots, p_{k(n)}\right), \quad \boldsymbol{\mu}_n = \left(\mu_1, \ldots, \mu_{k(n)}\right), \quad \boldsymbol{\sigma}_n = \left(\sigma_1, \ldots, \sigma_{k(n)}\right),$$

$$D_{\mathbf{a}_n} = diag\left\{\mu_1, \ldots, \mu_{k(n)}\right\}, \quad D_{\sigma_n} = diag\left\{\sigma_1, \ldots, \sigma_{k(n)}\right\},$$

and $diag\{\ldots\}$ denotes diagonal matrices with corresponding elements.

To obtain relations (8)–(11), it is enough to use the matrix representation of expressions (7):

$$\mathbb{E}X_n^m = \begin{cases} \mathbf{p}_n\,\boldsymbol{\mu}_n^T, & m = 1; \\ \mathbf{p}_n\left(D_{\mu_n} \cdot \mathbf{a}_n^T + D_{\sigma_n} \cdot \boldsymbol{\sigma}_n^T\right), & m = 2; \\ \mathbf{p}_n \cdot D_{\mu_n}\left(D_{\mu_n} \cdot \boldsymbol{\mu}_n^T + 3 \cdot D_{\sigma_n} \cdot \boldsymbol{\sigma}_n^T\right), & m = 3; \\ \mathbf{p}_n\left(D_{\mu_n}^3 \cdot \boldsymbol{\mu}_n^T + 6 \cdot D_{\sigma_n}^2 \cdot D_{\mu_n} \cdot \boldsymbol{\mu}_n^T + 3 \cdot D_{\sigma_n}^3 \cdot \boldsymbol{\sigma}_n^T\right), & m = 4. \end{cases}$$

To evaluate the parameters in expressions (2)–(5) and (8)–(11) for every position of moved window various modifications of the EM algorithm can be used [7]. For example, they may include grid modifications of the EM algorithm that were previously implemented by the authors in the form of a computing service [46]. In this article, we use modifications with a random selection of initial approximations [32].

3. Methodology of Statistical Feature Construction

3.1. Approach for Feature Construction

The Statistical Feature Construction method is a two step data enrichment algorithm. The first step of SFC is the creation of statistical models that is the estimation of the parameters of finite normal mixtures. It is worth noting that the time series of physical processes can often be non-stationary. Instead of creating one complex statistical model encompassing the whole time series, we implement the set of models. It consists of a sequence of models (1) that describes the evolution of the analyzed process.

Time series are split into shorter pseudo-stationary windows on which the models are constructed. The process of window separation is as follows. Initial data vector $V = \{V_1, V_2, \ldots, V_L\}$ of L observations serves as input data for the process. Let us choose some arbitrary window length N ($L \geqslant N \geqslant 1$) and divide V into shorter window vectors $X_1, X_2, X_3, \ldots$ where $X_i = \{V_i, V_{i+1}, \ldots V_{i+N-1}\}$ are sequences of N consecutive observations taken from V. We may notice that window vector X_i differs from window vector X_{i+1} only by two observations, namely the first observation in X_i and the last observation in X_{i+1}.

Once the collection of window vectors is obtained, new difference window vectors $Y_1, Y_2, Y_3, \ldots$ may be constructed, $Y_i^j = X_i^{j+1} - X_i^j$. Applying the same transformation to all window vectors, a collection of difference window vectors is built. Each vector has a length of $(N-1)$. Difference window vectors serve as input data for the MSM algorithm.

After window vector and difference vector sets are created, they can be used to estimate statistical parameters for data enrichment. Such process in the application to neural network forecasting was previously described and explored in [29].

Hyperparameters on the first step of SFC are the following:

- window length (N);
- kernel selection as described in Section 2;
- number of components (K);
- number (T) and composition of statistical features.

Exact choice of window length is open to debate. Window lengths that are too big lead to loss of stationarity across the window vector. Additionally, larger windows may contain observations that have little to no effect on the prediction introducing additional noise to the model. Smaller windows lead to lack of input data for both the machine learning part of the algorithm and to the construction of statistical models. A K-component mixture requires the evaluation of $3K - 1$ statistical parameters which can be hard to perform accurately on smaller windows.

Choice of the component number is also open to debate. Both empirical and classical statistical approaches based on information criteria (AIC [47], BIC [48]) can be used. For physical and oceanographic data, we analyzed cases of mixtures consisting of 3–5 components at each step.

The second step of SFC is the feature expansion; given a statistical model, its characteristics can be used for feature enrichment. As outlined in the previous section, the first four moments are used as additional features for the data enrichment process. The implementation of this approach will be discussed in the next section. We should notice that these moments do not contain information about how the series behaves after the last window observation, and therefore can be correctly used when making forecasts.

Algorithmic representation of SFC is presented in Appendix A, see Algorithms A1–A3. It can be implemented in computing services [49,50].

3.2. Neural Network Architectures with Additional Features

A deep recurrent neural network was created for forecasting. It consists of two recurrent neuron layers followed by several dense layers, see Figure 1.

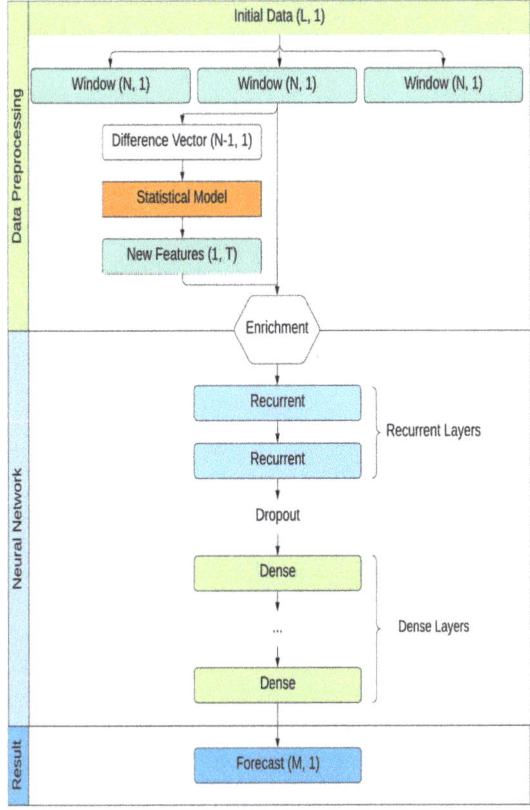

Figure 1. Architecture of SFC processing with a neural network.

While the general architecture of the network remained the same, the number of layers and number of neurons in each layer varied depending on the hyperparameter optimization process.

The hyperparameter optimization may improve the performance of neural networks and can be used to adapt commonly used architecture to specific domains [51–53]. In this research, the following hyperparameters are varied:

- type of recurrent layers: Long Short-Term Memory (LSTM) [54], recurrent neural network (RNN) [55,56] or Gated Recurrent Units (GRU) [57];
- exact number of dense layers;
- number of neurons in each layer;
- dropout rates [58];
- optimizers for the neural network.

Several recurrent layers were used in a neural network architecture. Deep recurrent neural networks allow for better flexibility compared to one-layer networks and serve as a powerful model for chaotic sequential data. Deep RNN were used for the task of forecasting and achieved better performance compared to shallow recurrent architectures [59,60]. Neural networks of similar architecture were applied to the analysis of indoor navigation [61], climate data [62], human activity classification [63], and health assessment [64]. Achieved results combined with the difference in analyzed data led to the choice of deep RNN architecture. Such combination of deep RNN and MSM algorithms were never used to process climate and physics data prior to this paper.

The enrichment process occurs in-between data processing and neural network construction. We should note that statistical model created on the window $\mathbf{X}$ is a characteristic of that entire window, not a time-dependent characteristic of any specific observation contained in the window. This also applies to the features based on that model.

There are several methods of passing features to the neural network. The simplest way to do so is to create a multi-input model by adding statistical features to the data flow after recurrent layers, see Figure 2a. Unfortunately, this also means that those layers would be trained without any information derived from SFC.

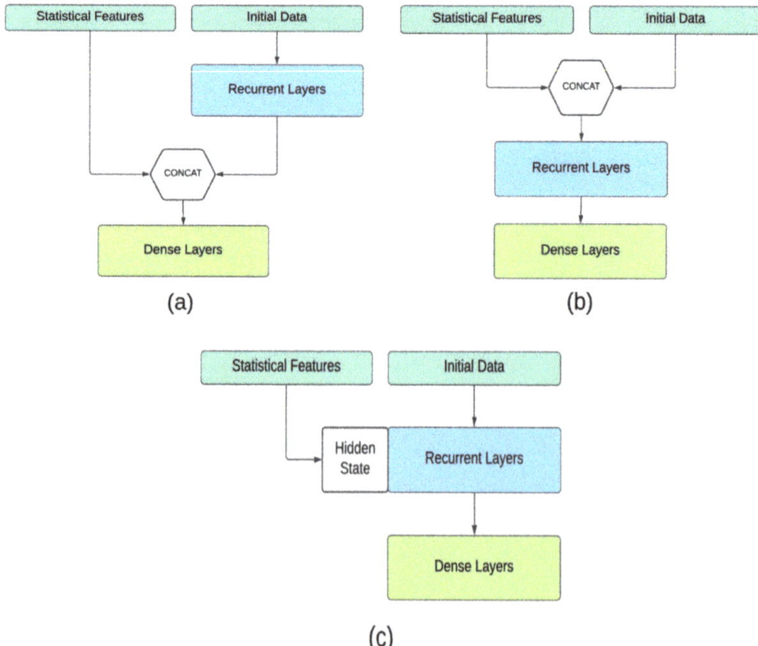

Figure 2. Methods of passing features to the neural network: (**a**) multi-input model; (**b**) adding features to window; (**c**) hidden state initialization.

In the second approach (see Figure 2b), additional data are added to the window itself. The input vector for neural network consists of original N window observations and additional K SFC features are applied to the end or to the beginning of the data vector. Adding time-independent data to a vector of time observations may create a harder learning task for the neural network. This approach was used but had proven to give worse accuracy compared to the hidden state initialization [65,66].

Finally, the approach presented in Figure 2c directly affects the hidden state of recurrent layers. Additional features for each training sample are transformed into a K-sized vector $\mathbf{v}$ defining the internal state of the recurrent layer:

$$\mathbf{v} = W\mathbf{x} + \mathbf{b},$$

where $\mathbf{x}$ is the vector of features, and W and $\mathbf{b}$ are trainable weights. Those weights can be obtained with an additional single dense layer placed before the recurrent layers of the neural network as a part of the enrichment process. For the first time step, the resulting tensor is added to the hidden state of the RNN. It allows both for conditioning of RNN on additional features and avoiding the problem of increasing the complexity of model training.

3.3. Computational Complexity

Compared to training on non-enriched data, SFC includes an additional step for model creation. We raise a question of computational complexity of the first SFC step compared to the overall complexity of the network training.

The total number of parameters in a LSTM layer can be calculated as follows [67]:

$$W = n_c^2 \times 4 + n_i \times n_c \times 4 + n_c \times n_o + n_o \times 3,$$

where n_c is the number of memory cells, n_i is the number of input units, and n_o is the number of output units. The computational complexity of training the LSTM model per weight and per time step with used optimizers is $O(1)$. This gives us the computational complexity of $O(W)$ per time step.

Given the window length N and relatively small prediction size, the computational complexity is dominated by the $n_c \times (n_c + N)$ factor. Finally, given the total time series length of L, the number of windows scales linearly with it. Assuming we have a constraint on maximum number of epochs, we may postulate that the computational complexity of training an LSTM model would be $O(L \times n_c \times (n_c + N))$. Calculations are similar for GRU and RNN layers.

At the same time, the computational complexity of the MSM algorithm, see Algorithm A1, on one window of length N is $O(K \times N)$, where K is the number of components. The main computational complexity lies in the updating of auxiliary matrix g of the algorithm. It gives us the complexity of $O(L \times K \times N)$ for the MSM analysis of the whole time series. This is comparable to the complexity of neural network training. The MSM algorithm can be tailored for operations with matrices leading to a performance improvement on GPU-assisted systems [68].

These results are confirmed by the practical application of SFC in GPU-assisted computing. MSM model construction required significantly less time than model training: the difference reached a factor of ten or even more. Additionally, SFC statistical models on different windows are independent from each other. It means that already computed models could be cached and would not be changed with the addition of new observations to series. This allows for application of SFC to a real-time tasks with continuous data flows.

4. Examples of Real Data Analysis

4.1. Test Data and Neural Networks' Configurations

Analyzed datasets consist of two distinct sets. The first set contains data obtained in physical experiments carried on the L-2M stellarator [31]. Time series consists of plasma density fluctuations after the medium had been agitated with an energy discharge. A total of five time series would be analyzed. Each series consists of 60,000 observations that correspond to a time interval from 48 to 60 ms of each experiment. The time gap between two consecutive observations is 0.2 microsecond (µs). Time series from this set had proven to be non-stationary, and the *p*-value of the Dickey–Fuller test [69] obtains up to 0.56. For model correctness, it is necessary to analyze not the entire series, but windows, subsamples for which the necessary assumptions are considered to be satisfied, that is, to use the MSM approach. The typical waveform as well as empirical distributions are presented in Figure 3.

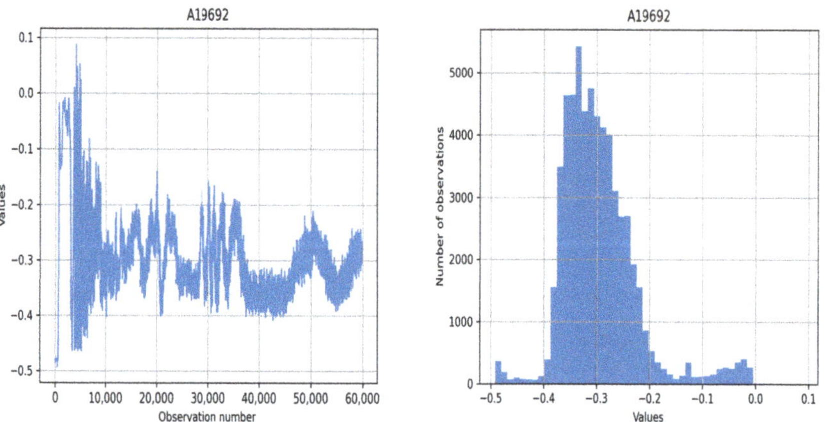

Figure 3. Physical time series A19692 (on the **left**) a corresponding histogram (on the **right**).

The experiment consists of three stages: the initiation stage when the impulse agitates the plasma, the main phase, and the relaxation phase. It is worth noting that the distribution of time series has a strongly non-Gaussian form. It can be seen that an excess of kurtosis and asymmetry exists. It would require complicated models to describe such data.

The second dataset consists of air–sea fluxes [70], see Figure 4.

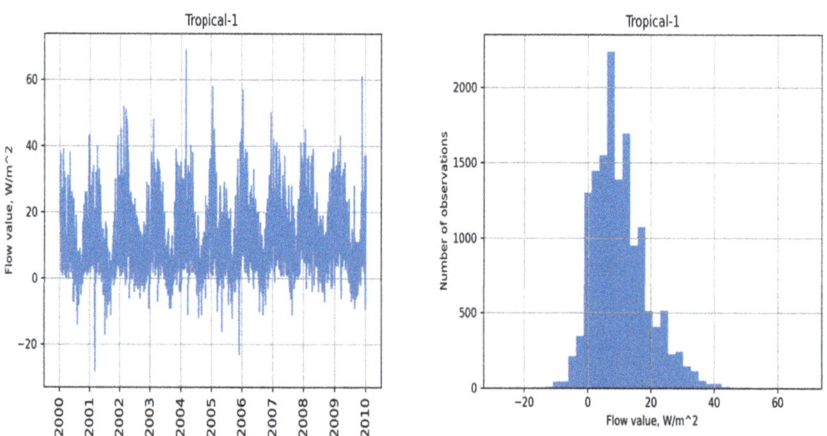

Figure 4. Tropical-1 time series (on the **left**) a corresponding histogram (on the **right**).

For each spot, two separate time series were collected for latent and hidden fluxes. Each time series consists of approximately 14, 600 observations, and the time gap between two consecutive observations is six hours. Tropical-1 time series and its distribution are shown in Figure 4. These data are highly seasonal in nature, and the distribution is non-Gaussian.

In order to measure the effect of statistical enrichment on the accuracy, two different predictions would be made for each set. Short-term prediction outputs $M = 12$ (see Figure 1) consecutive values given the 200 previous values. For oceanographic data, short-term prediction would be a prediction of data for three days after 50 days of observations.

Medium-term prediction outputs $M = 12$ consecutive values given the 200 previous values with a skip of 28 observations. Taking the oceanographic data as an example, medium-term prediction would be a prediction of three days on the next week after 50 days of observations.

For the purpose of this research, the size of window $N = 200$ (see Figure 1) was chosen to be the same as the size of input data for short- and medium-term predictions. This allows for a proper comparison of enriched and non-enriched accuracy values as no additional data are supplied to the enrichment process if compared to non-enriched data. The number of components $K = 3$ was selected for all time series as outlined in Section 3. Based on constructed models, four moments were used as additional statistical features for neural networks.

All data are normalized to the range of $[0, 1]$. Error decrease is measured with the root mean squared error metrics over the normalized data forecasts:

$$RMSE = \sqrt{\frac{1}{n} \sum_{i=1}^{n} (d_i - f_i)^2}.$$

Here, n denotes the number of data points, d_i is the predicted value of i-th data point, and f_i is the true value of the i-th data point. Such approach allows for comparison of the relative error decrease among all analyzed sets of data despite their different physical nature.

In order to demonstrate the efficiency of SFC, two neural network sets were constructed for each time series and prediction type. The original set accepts initial observations as input data. For the enriched network set, time series are supplemented by hidden state initialization with statistical moments. In both cases, the output consists of either a short- or medium-term prediction, in total four sets for each time series.

It is known that random search may provide for better results, but, in order to make a proper comparison of accuracy increase, a grid-search method was used for hyperparameter optimization [30]. Each set contains neural networks with all possible hyperparameter combinations, in total about 700 networks in a set. For each time series, error value is compared between best neural networks in original and enriched short-term sets and between best neural networks in original and enriched medium-term sets.

Input data were divided into training, validation, and test data sets in 60%/30%/10% proportion. The customized MSM algorithm and estimation of finite normal mixture parameters were implemented in MATLAB programming language. Neural networks were created, trained, and evaluated with TensorFlow/Keras Python libraries. Every network was ran several times, and the RMSE value was averaged among all runs.

The choice of optimizer varied among observed data sets, but mostly learning speed and accuracy were better with the Adam optimizer. No strong overfitting was observed in all constructed neural networks. A non-zero dropout rate affected learning rate negatively. In all observed cases, the choice of LSTM recurrent layers provided for better results than the use of GRU/RNN layers.

4.2. Results

The calculations were performed using a hybrid high-performance computing cluster (IBM Power 9, 1 TB RAM, 2 NVIDIA Tesla V100 (16 GB) with NVLink). Model training finished after a fixed cut out of 500 epochs or after the error metrics had not decreased for 10 epochs. In practice, training always finished before 500 epochs passed. It took about 20 h to perform a complete hyperparameter search for a single training set. Speed difference between enriched and non-enriched model training varied from 2% to 10% depending on the exact choice of hyperparameters.

Similar best-performing architectures for most analyzed series in both enriched and non-enriched cases were found. As in [16,29], neural networks with a smaller number of wide hidden layers made more accurate predictions than deep neural networks with stacked but narrower hidden layers. The difference in error metrics was significant and reached 35% in certain cases. The choice of optimizer varied among observed data sets. Accuracy and learning speed were mostly better with an Adam optimizer. The non-zero dropout rate affected the learning rate negatively. In all observed cases, the choice of LSTM recurrent layers provided for better results than the use of GRU/RNN layers. In general, the best performance was reached with two dense layers of 300 neurons each, two LSTM layers of 200 neurons each, the Adam optimizer, and no dropout.

Resulting predictions can be seen in Figures 5–8. Each graph denotes several windows and a forecast based on these windows.

The graph of a single forecast consists of three parts: input, designated by a thick blue line; optional skipped data part marked by a dotted line for medium-term forecasts (see Figures 6 and 8) and output designated by orange and green lines. The green line displays the true data, and the orange line is the constructed forecast for the data. Forecasting windows were chosen randomly from the test part of the window series.

It can be seen that the constructed forecasts are good at trend predictions and the direction of overall movement. Peaks are also predicted accurately. It should be noted that, in some cases, the model does not give the accurate forecast of the minimum and maximum values, but, in most observed cases, the minimum of the prediction would lie in a range of 1–2 observations from the true minimum of the forecasted data. The same is true for the maximum.

RMSE results for physical data analysis can be seen in Tables 1 and 2. A19692-2 is a clear outlier with almost no decrease of RMSE metric but overall satisfactory forecasts in both the enriched and non-enriched data set. A minor decrease in RMSE metrics is achieved for the short-term forecast, but, for the medium-term forecast, an RMSE decrease of 10% justifies the use of a more complex SFC approach.

Table 1. Physical RMSE results, short-term forecast.

Time Series	Non-Enriched	Enriched	Improvements
A19692	0.085	0.061	39%
A19692-1	0.086	0.061	41%
A19692-2	0.095	0.094	1%
A20229	0.091	0.084	9%
A20264	0.079	0.070	12%

Table 2. Physical RMSE results, medium-term forecast.

Time Series	Non-Enriched	Enriched	Improvements
A19692	0.068	0.057	19%
A19692-1	0.095	0.077	23%
A19692-2	0.096	0.088	10%
A20229	0.088	0.081	8%
A20264	0.078	0.071	9%

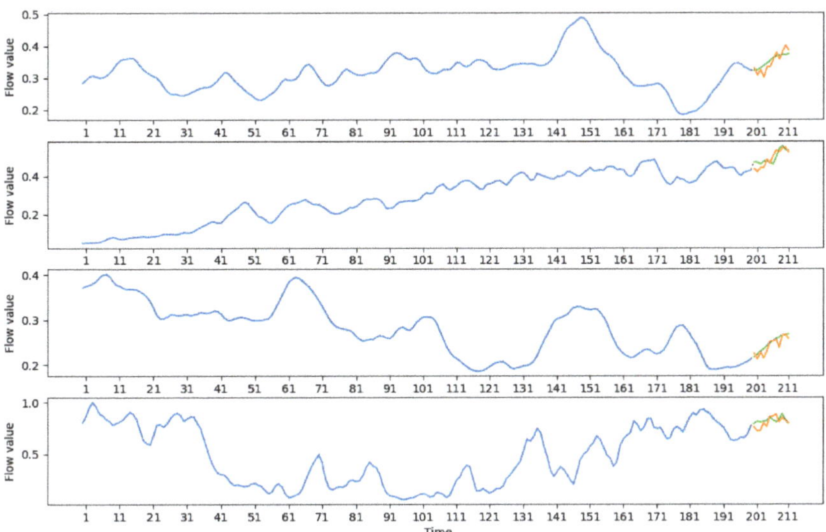

Figure 5. A19692 short-term forecasts.

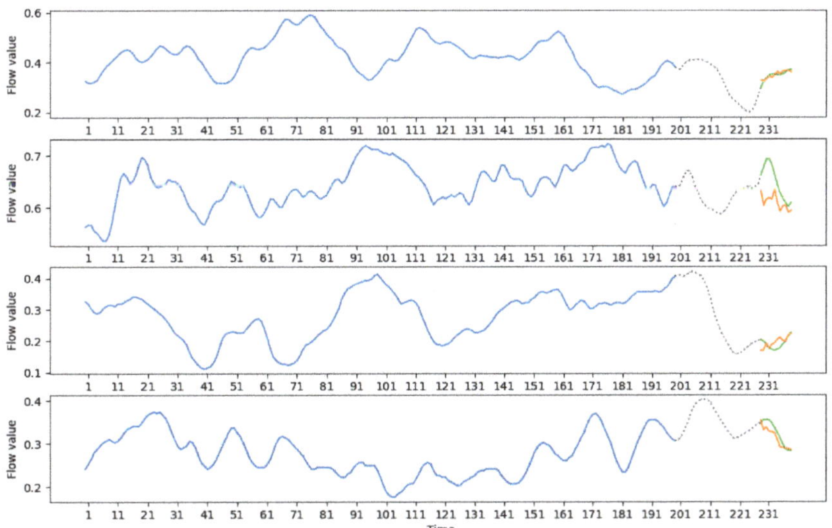

Figure 6. A19692-1 medium-term forecasts.

Analysis of oceanographic data leads to similar results. RMSE metrics and their improvement are presented in Tables 3 and 4.

The choice between enriched and non-enriched data greatly affected RMSE value for oceanographic data. SFC allowed for 2–21% decrease in RMSE with an average of 14% for short-term forecasts and 10% for medium-term forecasts. Effective decrease correlated with the analyzed time series. For both types of forecasts, enrichment performed best on Tropical-2 time series and worst on Tropical-1 time series.

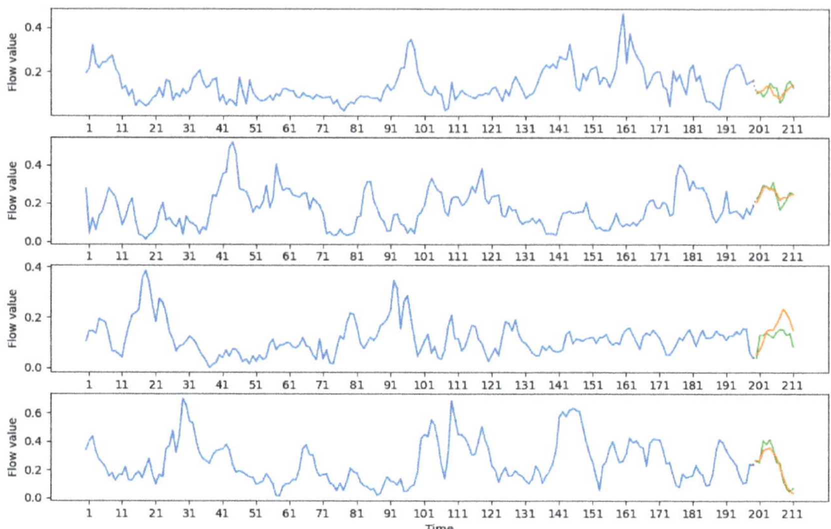

Figure 7. Gulfstream-1 short-term forecasts.

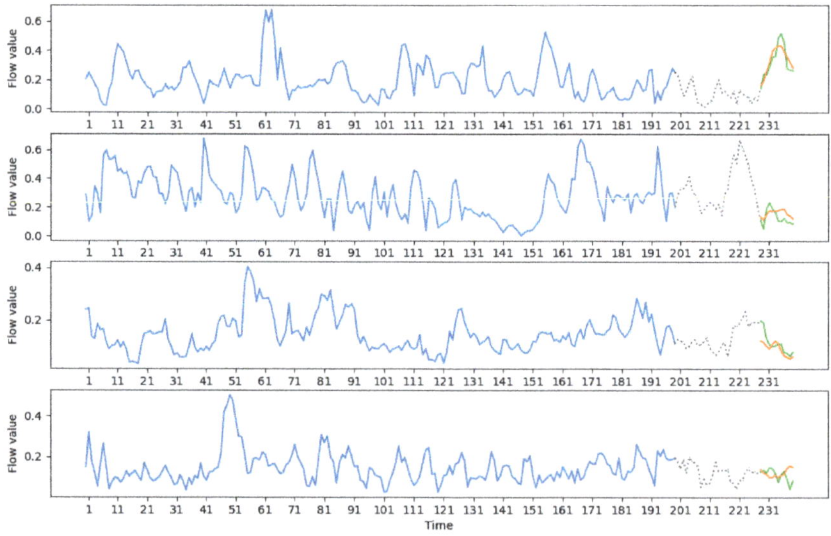

Figure 8. Gulfstream-1 medium-term forecasts.

This level of accuracy improvement according to the RMSE metric may be due to the fact that, for a specific set of Tropical-1, the basic neural network model already provides a complete description of the analyzed processes. Therefore, the feature space expansion provides only to a marginal decrease of learning error. In all other situations, the SFC based decrease is very noticeable, so such a series can be considered as an outlier for the proposed method. At the same time, it should be noted that there is still no error increase for Tropical-1. It means that the proposed method is effective in all situations, but the magnitude of its effect may vary.

Table 3. Oceanographic RMSE results, short-term forecast.

Time Series	Non-Enriched	Enriched	Improvements
Gulfstream-1	0.075	0.067	11%
Gulfstream-2	0.064	0.058	11%
Labrador-1	0.069	0.060	15%
Labrador-2	0.069	0.059	17%
Tropical-1	0.073	0.068	7%
Tropical-2	0.074	0.061	21%

Table 4. Oceanographic RMSE results, medium-term forecast.

Time Series	Non-Enriched	Enriched	Improvements
Gulfstream-1	0.081	0.075	8%
Gulfstream-2	0.072	0.066	9%
Labrador-1	0.068	0.061	11%
Labrador-2	0.075	0.066	14%
Tropical-1	0.073	0.072	2%
Tropical-2	0.074	0.063	17%

It should be noted that there was no increase of RMSE error observed among all enriched sets when compared to the original. For all sets, short-term and medium-term forecasts follow major data trends. At the same time, enriched sets produce forecasts that are better at adapting to quick shifts in data. Additionally enriched forecasts offer better prediction of peak values compared to non-enriched data.

5. Discussion and Conclusions

The paper presents a statistical approach to data modeling and feature construction with applications for two different sets of data. For six oceanographic datasets and five plasma physics datasets, multiple neural networks were constructed and trained in an enriched and non-enriched form. For all analyzed time series, a qualitative predictions were created for both methods with an average RMSE error of 0.068/0.078 for short-term forecasts and 0.071/0.079 for medium-term forecasts.

From the numerical perspective, statistical feature construction had shown a significant decrease in RMSE error metrics among all analyzed time series. The decrease ranged from 1% to 43% with the median of 11.4% and happened on all analyzed time series. It was also shown that SFC does not add significant computational complexity to the process of forecasting and can be used with continuous data flows and/or in real-time problems. This method can also be adjusted for GPU computing.

The significance of the work lies in the possibility of accuracy improvement with a relatively simple addition to preliminary data analysis. SFC does not require additional data collection and, as shown above, can be applied to a wide range of different problems where a stochastic external environment presents. The first step of SFC has relatively few hyperparameters for optimization, which leads to a smaller overhead on their optimization. Lastly, the increase of forecasting accuracy due to SFC application can serve as an indicator of correctness of the chosen statistical model.

For future research, it would be beneficial to apply another features from MSM models to forecast improvement. For example, in Figures 9 and 10, an evolution of MSM components [71] is demonstrated. These structural components do not correspond to the summands in formula (1) but are derived from them with the help of clustering algorithms. The colors signify the corresponding weight of the component in the mixture (1).

The MSM components based method allows us to determine significant changes in the stochastic structure of the forming processes. In particular, the detection of the time moment of an essential change in plasma parameters, which affects its confinement (the so-called transport transition), has been demonstrated, see Figure 9. Component number

5 with the maximum weight (red curve in the lower graphs in Figure 9) has the greatest contribution to the process. However, it breaks off at about 55 ms of the experiment and, after that, component number 3 dominates.

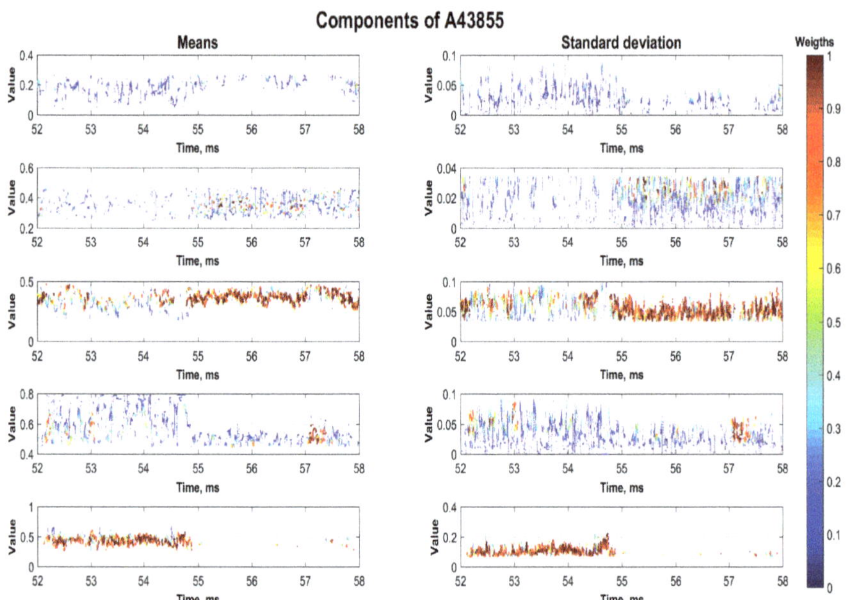

Figure 9. Example of MSM components for plasma time series.

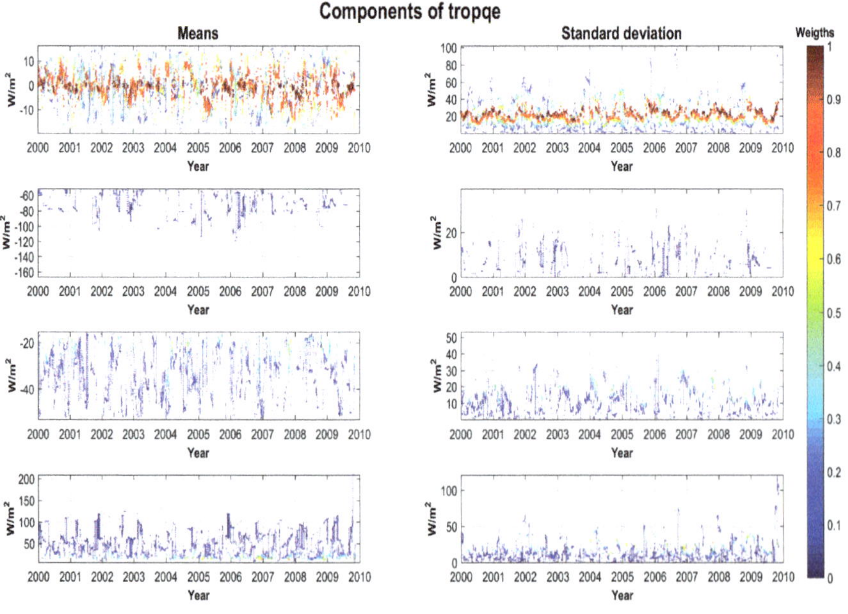

Figure 10. Example of MSM components for oceanographic time series.

A similar situation takes place for oceanographic time series, see Figure 10. Here, a smaller number of structural components are distinguished, and no abrupt disappearances or creation of new components are observed.

Other finite mixture models that have more features than a normal distribution could be employed. Those may include finite mixtures based on skew-normal or skew-t densities [12]. MSM components can be effectively used to process non-trivial trends in data, which would make it possible to better predict complex time series using neural networks. Surely, this will require sophisticated architectures such as ensembles of deep LSTM networks. However, such solutions are a natural development of the SFC approach proposed in this article.

Author Contributions: Conceptualization, A.G.; formal analysis, A.G., V.K.; funding acquisition, A.G.; investigation, A.G., V.K.; methodology, A.G.; project administration, A.G.; resources, A.G.; software, A.G., V.K.; supervision, A.G.; validation, A.G., V.K.; visualization, A.G., V.K.; writing— original draft, A.G., V.K.; writing—review and editing, A.G., V.K. All authors have read and agreed to the published version of the manuscript.

Funding: This research has been supported by the Ministry of Science and Higher Education of the Russian Federation, project No. 075-15-2020-799.

Data Availability Statement: Not applicable.

Acknowledgments: The authors are grateful to Victor Yu. Korolev for the joint research of the fundamental properties of the MSM method as well as for valuable discussions on the applications of mixture models to data analysis and MSM enrichment approaches. The authors also thank Corresponding Members of the Russian Academy of Sciences Sergey K. Gulev for providing data on air–sea fluxes and Nikolay K. Kharchev for access to the experimental turbulent plasma ensembles. The research was carried out using the infrastructure of the Shared Research Facilities "High Performance Computing and Big Data" (CKP "Informatics") of the Federal Research Center "Computer Science and Control" of the Russian Academy of Sciences. The authors would thank the reviewers for their detailed comments that helped to significantly improve the presentation of our results.

Conflicts of Interest: The authors declare no conflict of interest.

Appendix A. Algorithms

The section presents pseudocode of the MSM and SFC algorithms.

Algorithm A1. EM-based algorithm for estimating mixture parameters

---

```
 1: function CREATE_FINITE_MIXTURE(Data, K, EL, PreviousEstimation)
 2:     // Data: N-length window data vector
 3:     // K: Component number
 4:     // EL: Stop criteria level for MSM
 5:     err ← EL;                                    // Mixture parameter change during the step
 6:     // Vectors of expectation, variance and weights
 7:     if PreviousEstimation then
 8:         [E[K], D[K], W[K]] ← UPDATEPREVEST(Data, PreviousEstimation, K);
 9:     else
10:         [E[K], D[K], W[K]] ← RANDOMINITIALESTIMATION(Data, K);
11:     g[K][N] ← INITIALIZERANDOMPARAMMATRIX( );        // Matrix of cross-weights
12:     while err ⩾ EL do
13:         W2[K] ← UPDATEWEIGHTS(g, Data);
14:         E2[K] ← UPDATEE(g, Data);
15:         D2[K] ← UPDATED(g, E2, Data);
16:         // Calculating parameter change during the step
17:         err ← CALCULATEDISTANCE([E2, D2, W2], [E, D, W]);
18:         [E, D, W] ← [E2, D2, W2];
19:         g ← UPDATECROSSWEIGHTS(E, D, W, Data);
20:     return [E, D, W];
```

Procedure A1 is an implementation of the customized EM algorithm for estimating finite normal mixture parameters. Taking into consideration that consecutive windows differ only by two (first and last) observations, usage of previous estimations can be beneficial for increasing algorithm speed.

Algorithm A2. MSM moments

1: **function** MSM_MOMENTS(Mixture, T)
2:     // *Mixture: Parameters of finite normal mixture*
3:     // *T: Number of statistical features*
4:     Moments ← [];   // *Resulting array of moments*
5:     **for** i in (1, T) **do**
6:         // *Calculations of moments, see formulas* (2)–(5) *or* (8)–(11)
7:         Moment ← CALCULATEMOMENT(Mixture, i, Moments);
8:         MOMENTS.APPEND(Moment);
9:     **return** Moments;

An implementation of moment calculations, see line 7 of Algorithm A2, is described in Section 2. Analyzed realization of SFC uses all of first T moments, so the first two moments (expectation and variance) are used to greatly simplify calculations of the following statistical moments.

Algorithm A3. SFC algorithm

1: **function** SFC(Data, isManual)   // *see Figure* 1
2:     // ***Data***: *Initial Time Series*
3:     // ***isManual***: *Flag for manual input mode*
4:     **if** isManual **then**
5:         K ← INPUTDIALOG( );   // *Number of components*
6:         EL ← INPUTDIALOG( );   // *Stop criteria level*
7:         T ← INPUTDIALOG( );   // *Number of statistical features*
8:         N ← INPUTDIALOG( );   // *Window Length*
9:     **else**
10:         [K, EL, T, N] ← ANALYZEDATA(Data);
11:     // *Splitting data into windows and adding labels for learning*
12:     [Windows, Labels] ← SPLITANDNORMALIZEDATA(Data, N);
13:     Inputs[K-N+1] ← [];   // *Input array for machine learning*
14:     PreviousMixture ← [];   // *Previous statistical parameter estimation*
15:     **for** wnd in Windows **do**
16:         // *Calling function from Algorithm* A1
17:         CurrentMixture ← CREATE_FINITE_MIXTURE(Data, K, EL, PreviousMixture);
18:         StatisticalParams ← MSM_MOMENTS(CurrentMixture, T);
19:         AdditionalFeatures ← ENRICH(wnd, StatisticalParams);   // *see Figure* 2
20:         INPUTS.APPEND(AdditionalFeatures);
21:         PreviousMixture ← CurrentMixture;
22:     // *Neural Network based analysis*
23:     Model ← CREATEMODEL(Inputs);
24:     [Model, Evaluation] ← TRAINANDEVALUATEMODEL(Model, Inputs, Labels);
25:     **return** [Model, Evaluation];

Algorithm A3 is an outline of the SFC procedure. Initial data are divided into windows, and statistical models are constructed for each window and used to enrich input data vector with additional features. The output of SFC procedure is a trained neural network model and evaluation of its performance.

References

1. Korolev, V.Y. *Probabilistic and Statistical Methods of Decomposition of Volatility of Chaotic Processes*; Izd-vo Moskovskogo un-ta: Moscow, Russia, 2011.
2. Korolev, V.Y. Convergence of random sequences with independent random indexes I. *Theory Probab. Its Appl.* **1994**, *39*, 313–333. [CrossRef]
3. Korolev, V.Y. Convergence of random sequences with independent random indexes II. *Theory Probab. Appl.* **1995**, *40*, 770–772. [CrossRef]
4. Korolev, V.Y.; Gorshenin, A.K. Probability models and statistical tests for extreme precipitation based on generalized negative binomial distributions. *Mathematics* **2020**, *8*, 604. [CrossRef]
5. Gorshenin, A.K.; Korolev, V.Y.; Zeifman, A.I. Modeling particle size distribution in lunar regolith via a central limit theorem for random sums. *Mathematics* **2020**, *8*, 1409. [CrossRef]
6. Audhkhasi, K.; Osoba, O.; Kosko, B. Noise-enhanced convolutional neural networks. *Neural Netw.* **2016**, *78*, 15–23. [CrossRef] [PubMed]
7. McLachlan, G.; Peel, D. *Finite Mixture Models*; John Wiley & Sons: New York, NY, USA, 2000.
8. Gorshenin, A.; Korolev, V. Modelling of statistical fluctuations of information flows by mixtures of gamma distributions. In Proceedings of the 27th European Conference on Modelling and Simulation, Alesund, Norway, 27–30 May 2013; Digitaldruck Pirrot GmbHP: Dudweiler, Germany, 2013; pp. 569–572.
9. Liu, C.; Li, H.-C.; Fu, K.; Zhang, F.; Datcu, M.; Emery, W.J. A robust EM clustering algorithm for Gaussian mixture models. *Pattern Recognit.* **2019**, *87*, 269–284. [CrossRef]
10. Wu, D.; Ma, J. An effective EM algorithm for mixtures of Gaussian processes via the MCMC sampling and approximation. *Neurocomputing* **2019**, *331*, 366–374. [CrossRef]
11. Zeller, C.B.; Cabral, C.R.B.; Lachos, V.H.; Benites, L. Finite mixture of regression models for censored data based on scale mixtures of normal distributions. *Adv. Data Anal. Classif.* **2019**, *13*, 89–116. [CrossRef]
12. Abid, S.H.; Quaez, U.J.; Contreras-Reyes, J.E. An information-theoretic approach for multivariate skew-t distributions and applications. *Mathematics* **2021**, *9*, 146. [CrossRef]
13. Greff, K.; van Steenkiste, S.; Schmidhuber, J. Neural expectation maximization. In Proceedings of the 31st International Conference on Neural Information Processing Systems, Long Beach, CA, USA, 4–9 December 2017; MIT Press: Cambridge, MA, USA, 2017; pp. 6694–6704.
14. Viroli, C.; McLachlan, G.J. Deep Gaussian mixture models. *Stat. Comput.* **2019**, *29*, 43–51. [CrossRef]
15. Alawe, I.; Ksentini, A.; Hadjadj-Aoul, Y.; Bertin, P. Improving traffic forecasting for 5G core network scalability: A machine learning approach. *IEEE Netw.* **2018**, *32.6*, 42–49. [CrossRef]
16. Gorshenin, A.K.; Kuzmin, V.Y. Neural network forecasting of precipitation volumes using patterns. *Pattern Recognit. Image Anal. Adv. Math. Theory Appl.* **2018**, *28*, 450–461. [CrossRef]
17. Weyn, J.A.; Durran, D.R.; Caruana, R. Improving data-driven global weather prediction using deep convolutional neural networks on a cubed sphere. *J. Adv. Model. Earth Syst.* **2020**, *12*, e2020MS002109. [CrossRef]
18. Chandrashekar, G.; Sahin, F. A survey on feature selection methods. *Comput. Electr. Eng.* **2014**, *40. 1*, 16–28. [CrossRef]
19. Bennasar, M.; Hicks, Y.; Setchi, R. Feature selection using Joint Mutual Information Maximisation. *Expert Syst. Appl.* **2015**, *42*, 8520–8532. [CrossRef]
20. Jovic, A.; Brkic, K.; Bogunovic, N. A review of feature selection methods with applications. In Proceedings of the 38th International Convention on Information and Communication Technology, Electronics and Microelectronics (MIPRO), Opatija, Croatia, 25–29 May 2015; Biljanovic, P., Butkovic, Z., Skala, K., Mikac, B., Cicin-Sain, M., Sruk, V., Ribaric, S., Gros, S., Vrdoljak, B., Mauher, M., Eds.; IEEE: Manhattan, NY, USA, 2015; pp. 1200–1205.
21. Xue, B.; Zhang, M.J.; Browne, W.N.; Yao, X. A Survey on Evolutionary Computation Approaches to Feature Selection. *IEEE Trans. Evol. Comput.* **2016**, *20*, 606–626. [CrossRef]
22. Sheikhpour, R.; Sarram, M.A.; Gharaghani, S.; Chahooki, M.A.Z. A Survey on semi-supervised feature selection methods. *Pattern Recognit.* **2017**, *64*, 141–158. [CrossRef]
23. Abualigah, L.M.; Khader, A.T.; Hanandeh, E.S. A new feature selection method to improve the document clustering using particle swarm optimization algorithm. *J. Comput. Sci.* **2018**, *25*, 456–466. [CrossRef]
24. Cai, J.; Luo, J.W.; Wang, S.L.; Yang, S. Feature selection in machine learning: A new perspective. *Neurocomputing* **2018**, *300*, 70–79. [CrossRef]
25. Li, J.D.; Cheng, K.W.; Wang, S.H.; Morstatter, F.; Trevino, R.P.; Tang, J.L.; Liu, H. Feature Selection: A Data Perspective. *ACM Comput. Surv.* **2018**, *50*, 94. [CrossRef]
26. Gopika, N.; ME, A.M.K. Correlation based feature selection algorithm for machine learning. In Proceedings of the 3rd International Conference on Communication and Electronics Systems (ICCES), Coimbatore, Tamil Nadu, India, 15–16 October 2018; IEEE Computer Society Press: Piscataway, NJ, USA, 2018; pp. 692–695.
27. Lee, C.Y.; Shen, Y.X. Optimal feature selection for power-quality disturbances classification. *IEEE Trans. Power Deliv.* **2011**, *26*, 2342–2351. [CrossRef]
28. Wu, Y.; Xu, Y.; Li, J. Feature construction for fraudulent credit card cash-out detection. *Decis. Support Syst.* **2019**, *127*, 113155. [CrossRef]

29. Gorshenin, A.K.; Kuzmin, V.Y. Method for improving accuracy of neural network forecasts based on probability mixture models and its implementation as a digital service. *Inform. Primen.* **2021**, *15*, 63–74.

30. Gorshenin, A.K.; Kuzmin, V.Y. Improved architecture and configurations of feedforward neural networks to increase accuracy of predictions for moments of finite normal mixtures. *Pattern Recognit. Image Anal.* **2019**, *29*, 79–88. [CrossRef]

31. Batanov, G.M.; Berezhetskii, M.S.; Borzosekov, V.D.; Vasilkov, D.G.; Vafin, I.Y.; Grebenshchikov, S.E.; Grishina, I.A.; Kolik, L.V.; Konchekov, E.M.; Shchepetov, S.V.; et al. Reaction of turbulence at the edge and in the center of the plasma column to pulsed impurity injection caused by the sputtering of the wall coating in L-2M stellarator. *Plasma Phys. Rep.* **2017**, *43*, 818–823. [CrossRef]

32. Korolev, V.Y.; Gorshenin, A.K.; Gulev, S.K.; Belyaev, K.P. Statistical modeling of air–sea turbulent heat fluxes by finite mixtures of Gaussian distributions *ITMM'2015 Commun. Comput. Inf. Sci.* **2015**, *564*, 152–162.

33. Batanov, G.M.; Borzosekov, V.D.; Gorshenin, A.K.; Kharchev, N.K.; Korolev, V.Y.; Sarskyan, K.A. Evolution of statistical properties of microturbulence during transient process under electron cyclotron resonance heating of the L-2M stellarator plasma. *Plasma Phys. Control. Fusion* **2019**, *61*, 075006. [CrossRef]

34. Meneghini, O.; Luna, C.J.; Smith, S.P.; Lao, L.L. Modeling of transport phenomena in tokamak plasmas with neural networks. *Phys. Plasmas* **2014**, *21*, 060702. [CrossRef]

35. Raja, M.A.Z.; Shah, F.H.; Tariq, M.; Ahmad, I.; Ahmad, S.U. Design of artificial neural network models optimized with sequential quadratic programming to study the dynamics of nonlinear Troesch's problem arising in plasma physics. *Neural Comput. Appl.* **2018**, *29*, 83–109. [CrossRef]

36. Wei, Y.; Levesque, J.P.; Hansen, C.J.; Mauel, M.E.; Navratil, G.A. A dimensionality reduction algorithm for mapping tokamak operational regimes using a variational autoencoder (VAE) neural network. *Nucl. Fusion* **2021**, *61*, 126063. [CrossRef]

37. Mesbah, A.; Graves, D.B. Machine learning for modeling, diagnostics, and control of non-equilibrium plasmas. *J. Phys. Appl. Phys.* **2019**, *52*, 30LT02. [CrossRef]

38. Narita, E.; Honda, M.; Nakata, M.; Yoshida, M.; Hayashi, N.; Takenaga, H. Neural-network-based semi-empirical turbulent particle transport modelling founded on gyrokinetic analyses of JT-60U plasmas. *Nucl. Fusion* **2019**, *59*, 106018. [CrossRef]

39. Parsons, M.S. Interpretation of machine-learning-based disruption models for plasma control. *Plasma Phys. Control. Fusion* **2017**, *59*, 085001. [CrossRef]

40. Kates-Harbeck, J.; Svyatkovskiy, A.; Tang, W. Predicting disruptive instabilities in controlled fusion plasmas through deep learning. *Nature* **2019**, *568*, 526–531. [CrossRef] [PubMed]

41. Aymar, R.; Barabaschi, P.; Shimomura, Y. The ITER design. *Plasma Phys. Control. Fusion* **2002**, *44*, 519–565. [CrossRef]

42. Teicher, H. Identifiability of mixtures. *Ann. Math. Stat.* **1961**, *32*, 244–248. [CrossRef]

43. Teicher, H. Identifiability of Finite Mixtures. *Ann. Math. Stat.* **1963**, *34*, 1265–1269. [CrossRef]

44. Gorshenin, A.K. Concept of online service for stochastic modeling of real processes. *Inform. Primen.* **2016**, *10*, 72–81.

45. Gorshenin, A.K. On some mathematical and programming methods for construction of structural models of information flows. *Inform. Primen.* **2017**, *11*, 58–68.

46. Gorshenin, A.K.; Kuzmin, V.Y. Research support system for stochastic data processing. *Pattern Recognit. Image Anal.* **2017**, *27*, 518–524. [CrossRef]

47. Akaike, H. Information theory and an extension of the maximum likelihood principle. In Proceedings of the 2nd International Symposium on Information Theory, Tsahkadsor, Armenia, USSR, 2–8 September 1971; Petrov, B.N., Csáki, F., Eds.; Akadémiai Kiadó: Budapest, Hungary, 1973; pp. 267–281.

48. Schwarz, G.E. Estimating the dimension of a model. *Ann. Stat.* **1978**, *6*, 461–464. [CrossRef]

49. Gorshenin, A.; Kuzmin, V. Online system for the construction of structural models of information flows. In Proceedings of the 7th International Congress on Ultra Modern Telecommunications and Control Systems and Workshops (ICUMT), Brno, Czech Republic, 6–8 October 2015; IEEE Computer Society Press: Piscataway, NJ, USA, 2015; pp. 216–219.

50. Gorshenin, A.K.; Kuzmin, V.Y. On an interface of the online system for a stochastic analysis of the varied information flows. *AIP Conf. Proc.* **2016**, *1738*, 220009.

51. Kohavi, R.; John, G. Automatic Parameter Selection by Minimizing Estimated Error. In Proceedings of the Twelfth International Conference on Machine Learning, Tahoe City, CA, USA, 9–12 July 1995; Prieditis, A., Russell, S., Eds.; Morgan Kaufmann Publishers: Burlington, MA, USA, 1995; pp. 304–312.

52. Sanders, S.; Giraud-Carrier, C. Informing the Use of Hyperparameter Optimization Through Metalearning. In Proceedings of the 2017 IEEE International Conference on Big Data, Boston, MA, USA, 11–14 December 2017; Gottumukkala, R., Ning, X., Dong, G., Raghavan, V., Aluru, S., Karypis, G., Miele, L., Wu, X., Eds.; IEEE Computer Society Press: Piscataway, NJ, USA, 2017; pp. 1051–1056.

53. Bergstra, J.; Bengio, Y. Random Search for Hyper-Parameter Optimization. *J. Mach. Learn. Res.* **2012**, *13*, 281–305.

54. Greff, K.; Srivastava, R.K.; Koutnik, J.; Steunebrink, B.R.; Schmidhuber, J. LSTM: A Search Space Odyssey. *IEEE Trans. Neural Networks Learn. Syst.* **2017**, *28*, 2222–2232. [CrossRef]

55. Williams, J.; Hinton, E.; Rumelhart, E. Learning representations by back-propagating errors. *Nature* **1986**, *323*, 533–536. [CrossRef]

56. Buduma, N. *Fundamentals of Deep Learning: Designing Next-Generation Machine Intelligence Algorithms*; O'Reilly Media: Sebastopol, CA, USA, 2017.

57. Cho, K.; van Merrienboer, B.; Gulcehre, C.; Bahdanau, D.; Bougares, F.; Schwenk, H.; Bengio, Y. Learning Phrase Representations using RNN Encoder-Decoder for Statistical Machine Translation. In Proceedings of the 2014 Conference on Empirical Methods in Natural Language Processing, EMNLP, Doha, Qatar, 25–29 October 2014; Moschitti, A., Pang, B., Daelemans, W., Eds.; Association for Computational Linguistics: Stroudsburg, PA, USA, 2014; pp. 1724–1734.
58. Srivastava, N.; Hinton, G.; Krizhevsky, A.; Sutskever, I.; Salakhutdinov, R. Dropout: A Simple Way to Prevent Neural Networks from Overfitting. *J. Mach. Learn. Res.* **2014**, *15*, 1929–1958.
59. Sagheer, A.; Kotb, M. Time series forecasting of petroleum production using deep LSTM recurrent networks. *Neurocomputing* **2019**, *323*, 203–213. [CrossRef]
60. Sagheer, A.; Kotb, M. Unsupervised Pre-training of a Deep LSTM-based Stacked Autoencoder for Multivariate Time Series Forecasting Problems. *Sci. Rep.* **2019**, *9*, 19038. [CrossRef]
61. Chen, Z.; Zou, H.; Yang, J.; Jiang, H.; Xie, L. WiFi Fingerprinting Indoor Localization Using Local Feature-Based Deep LSTM. *IEEE Syst. J.* **2020**, *14*, 3001–3010. [CrossRef]
62. Majhi, B.; Naidu, D.; Mishra, A.P.; Satapathy, S.C. Improved prediction of daily pan evaporation using Deep-LSTM model. *Neural Comput. Appl.* **2020**, *32*, 7823–7838. [CrossRef]
63. Eyobu, O.S.; Han, D.S. Feature Representation and Data Augmentation for Human Activity Classification Based on Wearable IMU Sensor Data Using a Deep LSTM Neural Network. *Sensors* **2018**, *18*, 2892. [CrossRef]
64. Miao, H.; Li, B.; Sun, C.; Liu, J. Joint Learning of Degradation Assessment and RUL Prediction for Aeroengines via Dual-Task Deep LSTM Networks. *IEEE Trans. Ind. Inform.* **2019**, *15*, 5023–5032. [CrossRef]
65. Karpathy, A.; Joulin, A.; Fei-Fei, L. Deep fragment embeddings for bidirectional image sentence mapping. In Proceedings of the 27th International Conference on Neural Information Processing Systems, Montreal, QC, Canada, 8–13 December 2014; MIT Press: Cambridge, MA, USA, 2014; Volume 2, pp. 1889–1897.
66. Karpathy, A.; Fei-Fei, L. Deep visual-semantic alignments for generating image descriptions. In Proceedings of the IEEE Conference on Computer Vision and Pattern Recognition, Boston, MA, USA, 7–12 June 2015; IEEE Computer Society Press: Piscataway, NJ, USA; pp. 3128–3137.
67. Sak, H.; Senior, A.; Beaufays, F. Long short-term memory based recurrent neural network architectures for large vocabulary speech recognition. *arXiv* **2014**, arXiv:1402.1128.
68. Gorshenin, A.K. On Implementation of EM-type Algorithms in the Stochastic Models for a Matrix Computing on GPU. *AIP Conf. Proc.* **2015**, *1648*, 250008.
69. Dickey, D.A.; Fuller, W.A. Distribution of the Estimators for Autoregressive Time Series with a Unit Root. *J. Am. Stat. Assoc.* **1979**, *74*, 427–431.
70. Perry, A.H.; Walker, J.M. *The Ocean Atmosphere System*; Longman: New York, NY, USA, 1977.
71. Gorshenin, A.K.; Korolev, V.Y.; Shcherbinina, A.A. Statistical estimation of distributions of random coefficients in the Langevin stochastic differential equation. *Inform. Primen.* **2020**, *14*, 3–12.

Article

Machine Learning Control Based on Approximation of Optimal Trajectories

Askhat Diveev [1], Sergey Konstantinov [2], Elizaveta Shmalko [1,*] and Ge Dong [3]

1   Federal Research Center "Computer Science and Control" of the Russian Academy of Sciences, 119333 Moscow, Russia; aidiveev@mail.ru
2   Department of Mechanics and Mechatronics, RUDN University, 117198 Moscow, Russia; svkonstantinov@mail.ru
3   School of Aerospace Engineering, Tsinghua University, Beijing 100084, China; dongge@mail.tsinghua.edu.cn
*   Correspondence: e.shmalko@frccsc.ru

Abstract: The paper is devoted to an emerging trend in control—a machine learning control. Despite the popularity of the idea of machine learning, there are various interpretations of this concept, and there is an urgent need for its strict mathematical formalization. An attempt to formalize the concept of machine learning is presented in this paper. The concepts of an unknown function, work area, training set are introduced, and a mathematical formulation of the machine learning problem is presented. Based on the presented formulation, the concept of machine learning control is considered. One of the problems of machine learning control is the general synthesis of control. It implies finding a control function that depends on the state of the object, which ensures the achievement of the control goal with the optimal value of the quality criterion from any initial state of some admissible region. Supervised and unsupervised approaches to solving a problem based on symbolic regression methods are considered. As a computational example, a problem of general synthesis of optimal control for a spacecraft landing on the surface of the Moon is considered as supervised machine learning control with a training set.

Keywords: machine learning control; general synthesis problem; symbolic regression; optimal control; evolutionary algorithm

Citation: Diveev, A.; Konstantinov, S.; Shmalko, E.; Dong, G. Machine Learning Control Based on Approximation of Optimal Trajectories. *Mathematics* **2021**, *9*, 265. https://doi.org/10.3390/math9030265

Academic Editor: Mikhail Posypkin
Received: 30 December 2020
Accepted: 26 January 2021
Published: 29 January 2021

Publisher's Note: MDPI stays neutral with regard to jurisdictional claims in published maps and institutional affiliations.

1. Introduction

Complexity of the control synthesis problems for autonomous robots which must perform the assigned tasks and achieve the set goal, led to new ideas in the control theory. Now, to create a control system for an autonomous robot, this system needs to be trained [1,2], instead of obtaining it by solving some known optimization problems.

To formulate the real problem of mobile robot control, it is needed to describe a large number of different phase constraints. These can be walls, doors between the rooms, windows, columns and other obstacles. For example, a robot has to avoid a column, not to hit on a wall and to get in a door. Now, when control systems for mobile robots are being created, programmers imagine the problems that this robot must face and decide how it should overcome them. Quite a laborious process, but it is quite justified in conditions when control systems were developed on an individual basis for single technical objects, such as spacecraft. However, modern automation and robotization is reaching a broader level and becoming ubiquitous. This trend requires the development of new universal and even automatic approaches to the development of control systems.

Application of symbolic regression methods allows to automatically receive mathematical expressions for control functions. Such mathematical expressions describe how the robot should optimally reach the goal avoiding the obstacles.

Only symbolic regression methods can search structure and parameters of mathematical expression. Other methods, and even artificial neural networks, search only parameters.

The searching of control function structure in the control synthesis problem is called machine learning control [1]. This is a new technology in the development of control systems and it has not yet been proposed a rigorous mathematical formulation that defines this approach. In this paper, we propose some mathematical formalization of the machine learning problem (Section 2) and, on the basis of the proposed definitions, we single out a special area of machine learning—machine learning control (Section 3).

One of the main problems of machine learning control is the problem of control synthesis. The paper first presents the general mathematical formulation of the control synthesis problem, and then proposes its numerical formulation, since according to the methodology of machine learning control, the synthesis problem must be solved numerically using symbolic regression methods.

Further in the work in Section 4, we present our approach to solving the problem of machine learning control based on approximation of optimal trajectories. According to the technique of learning firstly it is necessary to create a training set in order to show to learning object what we want of it. For this purpose initially the optimal control problem is solved with the same quality criterion as for the synthesis problem from some different initial conditions. Obtained optimal trajectories are templates for learning. They show what forms of plots for variables must be obtained in the result of control synthesis problem solution and what values of functional must give these solutions. Then, obtained optimal trajectories for different initial conditions are approximated by a numerical method of symbolic regression. The proposed approach of machine learning based on approximation of optimal trajectories is demonstrated in the computational example of general synthesis of optimal control for a spacecraft landing on the surface of the Moon (Section 5).

2. Problem Statement of Machine Learning

Definition 1. *A set of computational procedures, that transforms a vector* $\mathbf{x}$ *from an input space* X *to a vector* $\mathbf{y}$ *from an output space* Y, *and there is not any algebraic equation* $\mathbf{y} = \mathbf{f}(\mathbf{x})$ *for them, is called an* **unknown function.**

For example, the system of ordinary differential equations $\dot{\mathbf{x}} = \mathbf{f}(\mathbf{x})$ is an unknown function for a vector of initial conditions $\mathbf{x}(0)$ and a vector of solutions as functions of time $\mathbf{x}(t, \mathbf{x}(0))$, if a general solution is unknown for this differential equation.

The unknown function between input vector $\mathbf{x}$ and output vector $\mathbf{y}$ is defined as

$$\mathbf{y} = \alpha(\mathbf{x}). \tag{1}$$

Then for differential equations without general solutions, an unknown function has a form

$$\mathbf{x}(t, \mathbf{x}^0) = \alpha(\mathbf{x}^0). \tag{2}$$

Definition 2. *A work area is a subset of input vector space, where the input vectors exist surely and that is used for solving the problem.*

The unknown function can be realized by a physical equipment or an experiment. Then unknown function will be called black box, but will be described as (1).

Let a set of input vectors be determined in the work area

$$\tilde{X} = \{\mathbf{x}^1, \ldots, \mathbf{x}^N\} \subseteq X. \tag{3}$$

For every input vector, output vector is determined by the unknown function (1)

$$\tilde{Y} = \{\mathbf{y}^1 = \alpha(\mathbf{x}^1), \ldots, \mathbf{y}^N = \alpha(\mathbf{x}^N)\} \subseteq Y. \tag{4}$$

Definition 3. *A pair of sets,*

$$(\tilde{X}, \tilde{Y}), \tag{5}$$

is called a training set.

It is known that there are supervised and unsupervised machine learning methods.

An **unsupervised machine learning problem** can be formulated as follows: for some unknown function (1) and a positive small value δ it is necessary to find a function

$$\mathbf{y} = \beta(\mathbf{x}, \mathbf{q}), \tag{6}$$

where $\mathbf{q}$ is a vector of parameters, $\mathbf{q} = [q_1 \ldots q_p]^T$, such that $\forall \mathbf{x} \in X$

$$\|\mathbf{y} - \beta(\mathbf{x}, \mathbf{q})\| \leq \delta. \tag{7}$$

A **supervised machine learning problem** consequently can be formulated as follows: for some unknown function (1) and a positive small value δ, it is necessary to determine a positive value ε, to build a training set (5) and to find a function (6) such that if the total error for the training sample is less than the given value ε

$$\sum_{i=1}^{N} \|\mathbf{y}^i - \beta(\mathbf{x}^i, \mathbf{q})\| \leq \varepsilon, \tag{8}$$

then for $\forall \mathbf{x}^*$ from work area, but not included in the training set $\mathbf{x}^* \in X$ and $\mathbf{x}^* \notin \tilde{X}$ the following inequation is performed

$$\|\mathbf{y}^* - \beta(\mathbf{x}^*, \mathbf{q})\| \leq \delta, \tag{9}$$

where $\mathbf{y}^* = \alpha(\mathbf{x}^*)$.

Here the function $\beta(\mathbf{x}, \mathbf{q})$ includes a parameter vector $\mathbf{q}$. In many approaches a structure of function is defined beforehand on the basis of experience or intuitively, and it is necessary to find only values of some parameters. For example, an artificial neural network [3–5], which is often used for solving of the machine learning problems, has a set structure and large number of unknown parameters. In contrast, symbolic regression methods [6–8] allow you to search for both function structure and parameters.

3. The Problem of General Control Synthesis as Machine Learning Control

In the field of control there are also problems that require machine learning. One of the main machine learning control problems is a search for a control function in the general control synthesis problem.

The problem of control general synthesis was formulated in the middle of the last century by Boltyanskii [9] after studying the Pontryagin's maximum principle for the optimal control problem.

The problem has the following description.

The mathematical model of the control object is given in the form of the system of ordinary differential equations

$$\dot{\mathbf{x}} = \mathbf{f}(\mathbf{x}, \mathbf{u}), \tag{10}$$

where $\mathbf{x}$ is a vector of state, $\mathbf{x} \in \mathbb{R}^n$, $\mathbf{u}$ is a vector of control, $\mathbf{u} \in U \subseteq \mathbb{R}^m$, U is a compact set, $m \leq n$.

The domain of initial conditions is given

$$X_0 \subseteq \mathbb{R}^n. \tag{11}$$

Existence of the initial condition domain is a main feature of the control general synthesis problem. Initially Boltyanskii defined the domain of initial conditions as a whole space of states $X_0 = \mathbb{R}^n$, because he tried to solve this problem analytically. In this case we assume to solve this problem numerically. Therefore the domain X_0 is a restricted set in the space of states.

The terminal condition is given

$$\mathbf{x}(t_f) = \mathbf{x}^f \in \mathbb{R}^n, \tag{12}$$

where t_f is unassigned time of getting from any initial condition $\mathbf{x}^0 \in X_0$ to the terminal state (12).

The finishing time is bounded

$$t_f \leq t^+, \tag{13}$$

where t^+ is a given positive value.

The phase constraints are given

$$\varphi_i(\mathbf{x}) \leq 0, \ i = 1, \ldots, r. \tag{14}$$

The quality criterion is given

$$J = \int_{X_0} \cdots \int \int_{t_0}^{t_f} f_0(\mathbf{x}(t, \mathbf{x}^0), \mathbf{u}(t)) dt \to \min_{\mathbf{u} \in U}, \tag{15}$$

where $\mathbf{x}(t, \mathbf{x}^0)$ is a partial solution of differential Equation (10) with control $\mathbf{u}(t) \in U$ from initial condition $\mathbf{x}^0 \in X_0$.

It is necessary to find a control function in the form

$$\mathbf{u} = \mathbf{h}(\mathbf{x}) \in U, \tag{16}$$

where $\mathbf{h}(\mathbf{x}) : \mathbb{R}^n \to \mathbb{R}^m$.

If one inserts the control function (16) in the right part of differential Equation (10), then the system of stationary differential equations is received

$$\dot{\mathbf{x}} = \mathbf{f}(\mathbf{x}, \mathbf{h}(\mathbf{x})), \tag{17}$$

which does not have a free control vector in the right part.

Any partial solution of the differential Equation (17) from initial conditions (11) achieves terminal condition (12), performing all conditions on phase constraints (14) with optimal value of the quality criterion (15).

Note, that the control function (16) can have simple discontinuities, therefore in many cases analytical methods could not be applied. The majority of analytical methods such as integrator backstepping [10,11] and analytical design of aggregated regulators [12,13] provides stability on Lyapunov by nonlinear smooth feedback control. The main drawback of all analytical methods of control synthesis solution is that they are bounded with the specific form of the mathematical model of control object. The control synthesis problem (10)–(17) under consideration is complicated by the arbitrary form of the mathematical model of the control object and sub-integral function of quality criterion, as well as the phase constraints and a wide class of control functions, which can have simple discontinuities.

In general case, this control general synthesis problem can be solved numerically by symbolic regression methods as machine learning control problem.

For application of the numerical methods it is necessary to reformulate the problem statement. The domain of initial conditions is changed onto finite set of initial state points

$$\tilde{X}_0 = \{\mathbf{x}^{0,1}, \ldots, \mathbf{x}^{0,K}\}. \tag{18}$$

The terminal condition (12) and the phase constraints are added into quality criterion (15), and the integral of the domain of initial conditions is changed onto sum of all initial state points.

$$J_1 = \sum_{i=1}^{K} \left(a_1 \|\mathbf{x}^f - \mathbf{x}(t_{f,i}, \mathbf{x}^{0,i})\| + \int_0^{t_{f,i}} \left(f_0(\mathbf{x}(t, \mathbf{x}^{0,i}), \mathbf{u}(t)) + \right. \right.$$

$$\left. \left. \vartheta(\varphi(\mathbf{x}(t, \mathbf{x}^{0,i}))) p(\mathbf{x}(t, \mathbf{x}^{0,i})) \right) dt \right) \to \min_{\mathbf{u} \in U}, \tag{19}$$

where a_1 is a weight coefficient, $\vartheta(A)$ is a Heaviside step function

$$\vartheta(A) = \begin{cases} 1, \text{ if } A > 0 \\ 0, \text{ otherwise} \end{cases}, \tag{20}$$

$p(B)$ is a penalty function, $t_{f,i}$ is a time of terminal state (12) achievement from initial condition $\mathbf{x}^{0,i}$,

$$t_{f,i} = \begin{cases} t, \text{ if } t \leq t^+ \text{and } \|\mathbf{x}^f - \mathbf{x}(t, \mathbf{x}^{0,i})\| \leq \varepsilon_0 \\ t^+, \text{ otherwise} \end{cases}, \; i = 1, \ldots, K, \tag{21}$$

ε_0 is a small positive value, that determines accuracy of terminal state achievement.

Within the framework of the formulation of the machine learning problem, the solution to the synthesis problem based on symbolic regression methods is machine learning control.

3.1. Control Synthesis as Unsupervised Machine Learning Control

The first approach is a direct search of the control function on basis of a quality criterion minimization. In this case we receive unsupervised machine learning control. The stated general control synthesis problem (10), (12), (18)–(21) can be solved in the concept of unsupervised machine learning control by different symbolic regression methods. Such approach is demonstrated by genetic programming [2], network operator method [14], variational genetic programming [15], variational analytic programming [16], multi-layer network operator [17], binary variational genetic programming [18], modified Cartesian genetic programming [19]. All mentioned symbolic regression methods search for mathematical expressions of control functions, that provide for the received solutions achievement of the terminal condition (12) from all the initial conditions (18) with optimal value of the quality criterion (19), describing the time and accuracy of terminal state hitting, and including phase constraints in the form of penalty functions.

Symbolic regression methods use evolutionary algorithms to search for functions and can achieve a certain level of accuracy when minimizing the functional, but it still remains unknown how the values of the criterion (19) for these solutions are far from real optimal values. To correct this problem it is possible to use a supervised machine learning with a training set received by the solution of the optimal control problem.

3.2. Control Synthesis as Supervised Machine Learning Control

The second approach is a learning with application of a training set. This is a supervised machine learning control. In this case firstly it is necessary to obtain the training set. For this purpose solutions of the optimal control problem can be used.

The statement of optimal control problem includes a mathematical model of control object (10), an initial condition given in one point

$$\mathbf{x}^0 \in \mathbb{R}^n, \tag{22}$$

terminal condition (12), (13) the phase constraints (14), and a quality criterion

$$J_2 = a_1 \|\mathbf{x}^f - \mathbf{x}(t_f)\| + \int_0^{t_f} (f_0(\mathbf{x}(t), \mathbf{u}(t)) + \vartheta(\varphi(\mathbf{x}(t))p(\mathbf{x}(t))))dt \to \min_{\mathbf{u} \in U}, \tag{23}$$

where

$$t_f = \begin{cases} t, & \text{if } t \le t^+ \text{and } \|\mathbf{x}^f - \mathbf{x}(t)\| \le \varepsilon_0 \\ t^+, & \text{otherwise} \end{cases}. \tag{24}$$

It is necessary to find a control in the form

$$\tilde{\mathbf{u}} = \mathbf{v}(t, \mathbf{x}^0) \in U. \tag{25}$$

When inserting the function (25) into the right part of the mathematical model of the control object (10), the following system of non-stationary differential equations is received

$$\dot{\mathbf{x}} = \mathbf{f}(\mathbf{x}, \mathbf{v}(t, \mathbf{x}^{0,i})). \tag{26}$$

To create a training set for the control synthesis problem it is necessary to solve the optimal control problem on criterion (23) for each particular initial condition from (18) and to receive sets of optimal controls

$$U_0 = \{\mathbf{v}(t, \mathbf{x}^{0,1}), \dots, \mathbf{v}(t, \mathbf{x}^{0,K})\} \tag{27}$$

and optimal trajectories

$$\tilde{X} = \{\tilde{\mathbf{x}}(t, \mathbf{x}^{0,1}), \dots, \tilde{\mathbf{x}}(t, \mathbf{x}^{0,K})\}. \tag{28}$$

Now we define the time interval *Deltat* and calculate the value of the state vector on each optimal trajectory at the interval boundaries. As a result, get a training set of optimal trajectories

$$\tilde{X} = \{\tilde{X}_1, \dots, \tilde{X}_K\}, \tag{29}$$

where

$$\tilde{X}_i = \{\tilde{\mathbf{x}}(0, \mathbf{x}^{0,i}) = \mathbf{x}^{0,i}, \tilde{\mathbf{x}}^i(t_1, \mathbf{x}^{0,i}), \dots, \tilde{\mathbf{x}}^i(t_{M_i}, \mathbf{x}^{0,i})\}, \ i = 1, \dots, K, \tag{30}$$

$t_j = t_{j-1} + \Delta t, j = 1, \dots, M_i, i = 1, \dots, K, \Delta t$ is a given time interval.

Now in order to solve the control synthesis problem (10), (12), (18)–(21), and to find the control function in the form (16) it is enough to approximate the training set (29) on a criterion

$$J_3 = \sum_{i=1}^{K} \sum_{j=0}^{M_i} \|\mathbf{x}(t_j, \mathbf{x}^{0,i}) - \tilde{\mathbf{x}}(t_j, \mathbf{x}^{0,i})\| \to \min_{\mathbf{h}(\mathbf{x}) \in U}, \tag{31}$$

where $t_0 = 0$, $\mathbf{x}(t, \mathbf{x}^{0,i})$ is a partial solution of the Equation (17) with the initial conditions $\mathbf{x}^{0,i}$, $\tilde{\mathbf{x}}(t, \mathbf{x}^{0,i})$ is a partial solution of the Equation (28), $i \in \{1, \dots, K\}$.

To ensure the fulfillment of phase constraints, both criteria (31) and (19) are applied. In result, the following combined criterion is used

$$J_4 = J_1 + \gamma J_3 \to \min_{\mathbf{h}(\mathbf{x}) \in U}, \tag{32}$$

where γ is a weight coefficient.

To solve the approximation problem, a symbolic regression is also used. The control synthesis on the base of optimal trajectories approximation allows to find a control function (16) that provides receiving optimal control with accuracy to approximation of the training set. The solution closest to the optimal one is determined by the accuracy of the optimal control problem.

4. Computational Algorithms

In order to solve the control synthesis problem as machine learning control on the base of optimal trajectories set approximation it is required to solve two complex problems, the optimal control problem in order to form a training set, and the approximation of optimal trajectories by some symbolic regression method. For both problems evolutionary computations are used.

4.1. Algorithms for the Optimal Control Problem

The optimal control problem with phase constraints is not uni-modal [20], therefore evolutionary algorithms are applied, which can solve a global optimization problem. Recently, it is popular to use hybrid evolutionary algorithms that combine different evolutionary algorithms. Studies of evolutionary algorithms for numerical solution of the optimal control problem show [21], that the most successful in solving this problem are genetic algorithm (GA) [22], Particle swarm optimization algorithm (PSO) [23] and Grey wolf optimizer algorithm (GWO) [24].

All evolutionary algorithms include evolution of possible solutions. It implies such changes in possible solutions that some of new possible solutions ensure obtaining the value of the goal functional not worse than the old possible solutions before the change. At evolution of possible solutions information about the values of the goal functional for other possible solutions is used.

PSO-algorithm uses the best current possible solution, and the best of solutions from some random selected ones as well as information about historical changes for this possible solution. An evolution is performed for each component of possible solution

$$\tilde{q}_j^i = q_j^i + \sigma v_j^i, \ j = 1, \ldots, p, \tag{33}$$

where $\tilde{q}_j^i$ is a new value of the component j of the possible solution i, $\tilde{\mathbf{q}}^i = [\tilde{q}_1 \ldots \tilde{q}_p]^T$, q_j^i is the component j of the old possible solution i, $\mathbf{q}^i = [q_1^i \ldots q_p^i]^T$, p is a dimension of the vector, v_j^i is the component j of a historical vector for possible solution i, $\mathbf{v}^i = [v_1^i \ldots v_p^i]$, this historical vector is changed one time in one cycle of generation

$$v_j^i \leftarrow \alpha v_j^i + \xi \beta (q_j^i(k) - q_j^i) + \xi \gamma (q_j^0 - q_j^i), j = 1, \ldots, p, \tag{34}$$

$\bar{q}_j^i$ is the component j of the best solution from k randomly selected ones, $\bar{\mathbf{q}}^i = [\bar{q}_1 \ldots \bar{q}_p]^T$, $q_j(0)$ is the component j of the best current possible solution, $\mathbf{q}(0) = [q_1(0) \ldots q_p(0)]^T$, ξ is a random value in the interval from 0 to 1, at each call this function gives a new random number, α, β, γ are constant parameters of the algorithm, vector $\mathbf{v}$ has zero initial value.

The GWO-algorithm performs the following changes of possible solution on the base of some best current solutions

$$\tilde{q}_j^i = \frac{1}{N} \sum_{k=0}^{N-1} (q_j(k) - r(2\xi - 1)|2\xi q_j(k) - q_j^i|), \ j = 1, \ldots, p, \tag{35}$$

where $q_j(0) \ldots q_j(N-1)$ are j components of N best possible solutions,

$$r = 2\left(1 - \frac{g}{G}\right), \tag{36}$$

r is calculated one time in a generation, g is a number of generation, G is a quantity of generations.

The GA considers vectors in the form of Grey code and performs evolution for two selected possible solutions as operations of crossover and mutation. For crossover two possible solutions are selected

$$\mathbf{z}^i = [z_1^i \ldots z_{c+d}^i]^T, \ \mathbf{z}^j = [z_1^j \ldots z_{c+d}^j]^T, \tag{37}$$

where $z_k^i, z_k^j \in \{0,1\}$, c is a number of bit for integer part, d is a number of bits for fractional part of Grey code.

Then the point of crossover s is determined. As a result two new possible solutions are received

$$\tilde{\mathbf{z}}^i = [z_1^i \ldots z_s^i \, z_{s+1}^j \ldots z_{c+d}^j]^T, \quad \tilde{\mathbf{z}}^j = [z_1^j \ldots z_s^j \, z_{s+1}^i \ldots z_{c+d}^i]^T. \tag{38}$$

In hybrid algorithms in each cycle of evolution for each possible solution one of three ways (33), (34) or (35), (36), or (37), (38) of obtaining new possible solutions is selected randomly. The algorithm stops calculation after all cycles of evolution are performed.

4.2. Numerical Methods of Symbolic Regression for the Control Synthesis Problem

For solution of the control synthesis problem numerical methods of symbolic regression are used. Now more than fourteen methods are know. The methods code a mathematical expression and search for optimal solution on the code space. All methods differ in the form of code.

For example, consider the following mathematical expression

$$y = \sin(x_1) + \exp(-q_1 x_1) \cos(q_2 x_2 + q_1). \tag{39}$$

To code this mathematical expression the following basic sets are used:
the set of arguments

$$F_0 = \{f_{0,1} = x_1, f_{0,2} = x_2, f_{0,3} = q_1, f_{0,4} = q_2\}, \tag{40}$$

the set of elementary functions

$$F = \{f_{1,1}(z) = z, f_{1,2}(z) = -z, f_{1,3}(z) = \sin(z), f_{1,4}(z) = \cos(z),$$

$$f_{1,5}(z) = \exp(z), f_{2,6}(z_1, z_2) = z_1 + z_2, f_{2,7}(z_1, z_2) = z_1 z_2\}, \tag{41}$$

where indexes of elements point the number of arguments and a function number, if the first index is equal to zero, then this is an argument of the mathematical expression.

The most popular and the earliest symbolic regression method is the genetic programming by J.Koza [6]. This method presents a mathematical expression in the form of computational tree. In the Figure 1 the computational tree for the mathematical expression (39) is presented.

In the Figure 1 the nodes of the tree contain numbers of functions, the leaves contain arguments of the mathematical expression.

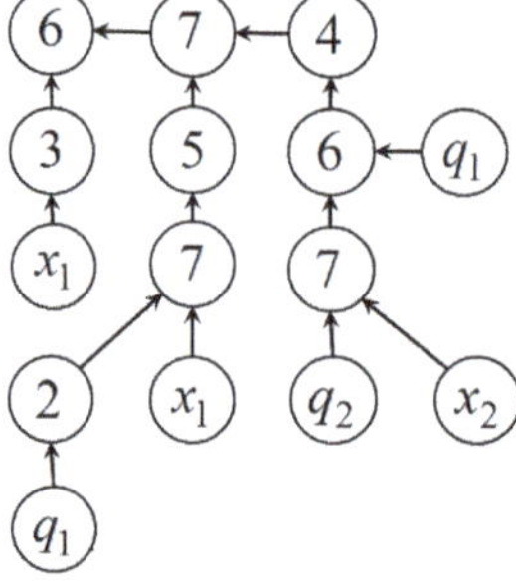

Figure 1. Computational tree of genetic programming.

A code of genetic programming for the mathematical expression (39) has the following form

$$\left(\begin{bmatrix} 2 \\ 6 \end{bmatrix}, \begin{bmatrix} 1 \\ 3 \end{bmatrix}, \begin{bmatrix} 0 \\ 1 \end{bmatrix}, \begin{bmatrix} 2 \\ 7 \end{bmatrix}, \begin{bmatrix} 1 \\ 5 \end{bmatrix}, \begin{bmatrix} 2 \\ 7 \end{bmatrix}, \begin{bmatrix} 1 \\ 2 \end{bmatrix}, \begin{bmatrix} 0 \\ 3 \end{bmatrix}, \begin{bmatrix} 0 \\ 1 \end{bmatrix},\right.$$

$$\left.\begin{bmatrix} 1 \\ 4 \end{bmatrix}, \begin{bmatrix} 2 \\ 6 \end{bmatrix}, \begin{bmatrix} 2 \\ 7 \end{bmatrix}, \begin{bmatrix} 0 \\ 2 \end{bmatrix}, \begin{bmatrix} 0 \\ 4 \end{bmatrix}, \begin{bmatrix} 0 \\ 3 \end{bmatrix}\right). \tag{42}$$

The code of genetic programming consists of indexes of elements of the computational tree on all branches from the top to the leaves. The code of genetic programming is used for presentation of the computational tree in the computer memory.

A code of genetic programming is not very comfortable, as codes of different mathematical expressions have different length that also changes after crossover operation. If in the mathematical expression one argument enters several times, then it has to be on leaves of the computational tree the same number of times.

Another method of symbolic regression—the network operator method [14]—codes mathematical expression in the form of oriented graph. In the Figure 2 the network operator graph for the mathematical expression (39) is presented.

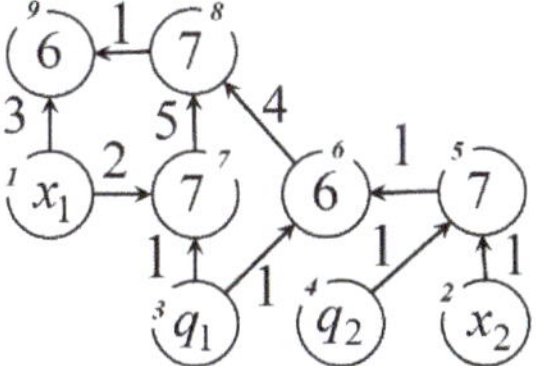

Figure 2. The network operator graph of the mathematical expression.

On the network operator graph the nodes contain the numbers of functions with two arguments, the source-nodes contain the arguments of the mathematical expression, the arcs are marked with the numbers of functions with one argument.

In the computer memory the network operator graph is presented as an integer matrix.

$$\Psi = \begin{bmatrix} 0 & 0 & 0 & 0 & 0 & 0 & 2 & 0 & 3 \\ 0 & 0 & 0 & 0 & 1 & 0 & 0 & 0 & 0 \\ 0 & 0 & 0 & 0 & 0 & 1 & 1 & 0 & 0 \\ 0 & 0 & 0 & 0 & 1 & 0 & 0 & 0 & 0 \\ 0 & 0 & 0 & 0 & 7 & 1 & 0 & 0 & 0 \\ 0 & 0 & 0 & 0 & 0 & 6 & 0 & 4 & 0 \\ 0 & 0 & 0 & 0 & 0 & 0 & 7 & 5 & 0 \\ 0 & 0 & 0 & 0 & 0 & 0 & 0 & 7 & 1 \\ 0 & 0 & 0 & 0 & 0 & 0 & 0 & 0 & 6 \end{bmatrix}. \tag{43}$$

Each row of the matrix corresponds to a graph node. The numbers of nodes are located at the top of the nodes (see Figure 2). The nodes are numbered in such a way that the number of the node from which the arc exits must be less than the number of the node where the arc enters. Then a network operator matrix has an upper triangular form. In the network operator matrix the numbers of functions with two arguments are located on the main diagonal. Zero element on the main diagonal shows that the row corresponds to a source-node. Other non-zero non-diagonal elements are the numbers of functions with one argument.

Consider one more symbolic regression method. In Cartesian genetic programming [25] the code of the mathematical expression (39) has the following form

$$\left(\begin{bmatrix} 7 \\ 1 \\ 3 \end{bmatrix}, \begin{bmatrix} 2 \\ 5 \\ 1 \end{bmatrix}, \begin{bmatrix} 5 \\ 6 \\ 2 \end{bmatrix}, \begin{bmatrix} 3 \\ 1 \\ 3 \end{bmatrix}, \begin{bmatrix} 7 \\ 2 \\ 4 \end{bmatrix}, \begin{bmatrix} 6 \\ 9 \\ 3 \end{bmatrix}, \begin{bmatrix} 4 \\ 10 \\ 1 \end{bmatrix}, \begin{bmatrix} 7 \\ 11 \\ 7 \end{bmatrix}, \begin{bmatrix} 6 \\ 8 \\ 12 \end{bmatrix}\right). \tag{44}$$

Here, every integer vector corresponds to one elementary function. The first element of vector is the function number, other elements are element numbers from the set of arguments (40). If a function has one argument, then the second argument is not used. The result of calculation according to each vector is added to the argument set, so a number of arguments increases in one every time after calculation of functions according to the vectors.

Due to redundancy, Cartesian genetic programming code has the same length for all mathematical expressions. A crossover operation for Cartesian genetic programming are performed by exchange of vectors after crossover point, so the length of codes does not change.

Studies of symbolic regression methods for the control synthesis problems show that it is effective to use in these methods the principle of small variations of the basic solution [26]. According to this principle only one basic solution is encoded by a method of symbolic regression. Other possible solutions are encoded by sets of variation vectors. Each variation vector makes one small change of basic solution code. After some generations the basic solution is changed on the best current found solution. This approach makes it possible to speed up the search process by narrowing the search space and avoiding additional checks for the correctness of the codes of possible solutions.

5. Computational Experiment

In a computational experiment a problem of general synthesis of optimal control for a spacecraft landing on the surface of the Moon is considered [27]. The differential equations of spacecraft state are the following

$$
\begin{aligned}
\dot{x}_1 &= \frac{g_E(P_c + u_2)\cos(u_1 - x_2)}{x_5} - g_{Mh}\cos(x_2), \\
\dot{x}_2 &= \frac{g_E(P_c + u_2)\sin(u_1 - x_2)}{x_5} + \frac{g_{Mh}\sin(x_2)}{x_1}, \\
\dot{x}_3 &= \frac{x_1\cos(x_2)}{1000}, \\
\dot{x}_4 &= \frac{x_1\sin(x_2)}{1000}, \\
\dot{x}_5 &= -\frac{P_c + u_2}{P_s},
\end{aligned}
\tag{45}
$$

where $\mathbf{x} = [x_1\ x_2\ x_3\ x_4\ x_5]^T$ is a state vector, namely x_1 is the current speed of the spacecraft (m/s), x_2 is a trajectory inclination angle (rad), x_3 is the current flight altitude relative to the lunar surface (km), x_4 is a flight distance (km), x_5 is the mass of spacecraft including fuel (kg). $\mathbf{u} = [u_1\ u_2]^T$ is a control vector, values of which are constrained

$$
-\frac{\pi}{2} \le u_1 \le \frac{\pi}{2}, \quad -80 \le u_2 \le 80.
\tag{46}
$$

Parameters of model have the following values: gravitational acceleration at the certain altitude above the lunar surface

$$
g_{Mh} = g_M\left(\frac{r_M}{r_M + x_3}\right)^2,
\tag{47}
$$

the Moon gravitational acceleration $g_M = 1.623$ m/s^2, the Earth gravitational acceleration $g_E = 9.80665$ m/s^2, the Moon radius $r_M = 1737$ km, nominal thrust of the spacecraft engine $P_c = 720$ kg, spacecraft engine thrust $P_s = 319$ s.

A domain of initial states is

$$
X_0 = \{x_{0,1} = 1689, \ -1.65 \le x_{0,2} \le -1.55, \ 17 \le x_{0,3} \le 20, \ x_{0,4} = 0, \ x_{0,5} = 1500\}.
\tag{48}
$$

A terminal state is

$$\mathbf{x}^f = \left[x_1^f = 10, \ x_3^f = 0.2\right]^T. \tag{49}$$

Phase constraints are determined by the mechanics of spacecraft flight. Obviously the speed x_1, altitude x_3 and fuel level x_5 cannot be negative, reaching a zero altitude x_3 or zero fuel level x_5 at a significant speed x_1 means that the spacecraft has crashed. Consider the following phase constraints

$$\begin{aligned} h_k(\mathbf{x}) &= -x_j \le 0, \ k = 1, 2, 3, \ j = 1, 3, 5, \\ h_k(\mathbf{x}) &= \vartheta(0.001 - x_j)(x_1 - V_{max}) \le 0, \ k = 4, 5, \ j = 3, 5, \end{aligned} \tag{50}$$

where V_{max} is the maximum landing speed, $V_{max} = 1$, $\vartheta(A)$ is the Heaviside function.

According to the proposed method at the first step the training set is to be formed. We determine the finite set of initial states within the domain (48) and solve the optimal control problem for each initial state from this set.

Let us replace the domain of initial states (48) with a set of $M = 21$ elements uniformly distributed on this domain

$$\tilde{X}_0 = \left\{\mathbf{x}^{0,j+7(i-1)} = [1689 \ -1.65 + 0.05(i-1) \ 17 + 0.5(j-1) \ 0 \ 1500]^T\right\}, \ i = \overline{1,3}, \ j = \overline{1,7}. \tag{51}$$

Quality criterion considers the proximity of reaching terminal state and the case of phase constraints violation

$$\begin{aligned} J_j = \alpha_1 \sqrt{\left(x_1\left(t_f(\mathbf{x}^{0,j})\right) - x_1^f\right)^2 + \left(x_3\left(t_f(\mathbf{x}^{0,j})\right) - x_3^f\right)^2} + \\ \alpha_2 \int_0^{t_f(\mathbf{x}^{0,j})} \left(\sum_{k=1}^K \vartheta\left(h_k(\mathbf{x}(t, \mathbf{x}^{0,j}))\right) h_k(\mathbf{x}(t, \mathbf{x}^{0,j}))\right) dt \to \min, \end{aligned} \tag{52}$$

where α_i, $i = 1, 2$ are given penalty factors, $K = 5$ is a number of phase constraints, $j = \overline{1, M}$.

To search for solution to the optimal control problem the direct approach was used. The original problem was reduced to a nonlinear programming problem by introducing the time interval Δt. The solution of each optimal control problem in form of control vector at discrete moments of time was searched independently by hybrid evolutionary algorithm combining modern Grey Wolf Optimizer (GWO), which does not require problem specific tuning of additional parameter, and well-known Particle swarm optimization (PSO). Separately these algorithms showed a high efficiency in solving optimal control problems. A hybrid realization is to increase their effectiveness.

In a computational experiment the size of the set of possible solutions was 100, number of search iterations was 5000. Modeling parameters were the following: maximum control time $t_{max} = 300$, discretization time interval $\Delta t = 30$, penalty factors $\alpha_1 = 10$, $\alpha_2 = 10$.

At the second step of proposed approach we use obtained optimal trajectories to synthesize a multidimensional control function of object state space. The search for a control function is conducted by a symbolic regression method that search for the most suitable expression that approximates provided optimal trajectories best.

We used the network operator method to synthesize a control function. NOP allows to search for the structure of mathematical expression simultaneously with the search for optimal values of parameter vector. In the computational experiment we used the following parameters of NOP: size of NOP matrix was 40, size of the set of input variables was 3, size of the set of input parameters was 12, number of outputs was 2, number of candidate solutions in the initial set was 256, maximum number of search iteration was 25,000.

As a result of computational experiment, a control function in the form of NOP matrix and a parameter vector was obtained. The mathematical expression for the found control function is as follows

$$u_1 = \begin{cases} \pi/2, & \text{if } \tilde{u}_1 > \pi/2 \\ -\pi/2, & \text{if } \tilde{u}_1 < -\pi/2 \\ \tilde{u}_1, & \text{otherwise} \end{cases}, \quad u_2 = \begin{cases} 80, & \text{if } \tilde{u}_2 > 80 \\ -80, & \text{if } \tilde{u}_2 < -80 \\ \tilde{u}_2, & \text{otherwise} \end{cases}, \tag{53}$$

where

$$\tilde{u}_1 = \chi_6(-z_{34}, \tanh(z_{35}), z_{37}),$$

$$\tilde{u}_2 = \text{sgn}(u_1)\sqrt{|u_1|} - z_{36} + \arctan(z_{35}) + \text{sgn}(z_{34})\sqrt{|z_{34}|} + \log(|z_{33}|) +$$

$$z_{32}^{-1} + z_{31} + z_{28} - z_{28}^3 + \log(|z_{26}|) - z_{25} + \arctan(z_{21}) + \text{sgn}((z_{17}))\sqrt{|z_{17}|} +$$

$$\exp(q_{12}) + \tanh(q_{10}) + q_9 + \log(q_5) + \tanh(q_1),$$

$$z_{37} = \min\{z_{36} - z_{36}^3, \log(|z_{35}|), z_{34} - z_{34}^3, z_{32}^{-1}, \text{sgn}(z_{28})\sqrt{|z_{28}|}, \tanh(z_{27}), \exp(z_{25}), z_{20}^{-1}, \sqrt[3]{x_2}\},$$

$$z_{36} = \min\{\exp(z_{29}), \tanh(z_{28}), \text{sgn}(z_{27})\sqrt{|z_{27}|}, \arctan(z_{26}), \sqrt[3]{z_{22}}, z_{20}^3, \tanh(q_6), \sqrt[3]{q_1}, x_3^3\},$$

$$z_{35} = \arctan(z_{23}) + \tanh(z_{22}) + \tanh(q_{12}) + \log(|x_3|),$$

$$z_{34} = \max\{\text{sgn}(z_{33})\sqrt{|z_{33}|}, \log(|z_{30}|), z_{29}^{-1}, z_{22}^{-1}, z_{20}^{-1}\},$$

$$z_{33} = \min\{z_{32}^{-1}, \arctan(z_{29}), \tanh(z_{24}), z_{22}^3, z_{19}, -z_{16}, z_{11}^{-1}, \tanh(q_3), \tanh(q_2), \exp(x_2)\},$$

$$z_{32} = \min\{z_{31}^3, z_{26}, \log(|z_{25}|), z_{18}^{-1}, \sqrt{q_{10}}, \arctan(q_6), \sqrt[3]{q_2}\},$$

$$z_{31} = \log(|z_{27}|) + z_{26}^2 + z_{24}^2 + \arctan(z_{22}) + \sqrt[3]{z_{21}} + \exp(z_{20}) + \exp(z_{17}) +$$

$$z_{16}^{-1} + q_{12}^3 - q_5 + \sqrt[3]{q_2} + \sqrt[3]{x_1},$$

$$z_{30} = \max\{z_{29}, -z_{26}, \tanh(z_{25}), \arctan(z_{18}), \text{sgn}(z_{16})\sqrt{|z_{16}|}, q_{11}\},$$

$$z_{29} = \chi_6(z_{28}, z_{27}^{-1}, z_{26}^3, \log(|z_{24}|), -z_{22}^3, -z_{20}, \sqrt[3]{z_{17}}, q_7, q_2^{-1}, \sqrt{q_1}),$$

$$z_{28} = \max\{z_{27}, z_{23}^{-1}, -z_{20}, \log(|z_{19}|), z_{18} - z_{18}^3, -z_{17}, \log(|z_{16}|), q_7, \log(q_5)\},$$

$$z_{27} = \chi_6(z_{24}, \arctan(z_{20}), \sqrt{q_{11}}, q_8 - q_8^3, q_6^3, -q_5, \log(q_4)),$$

$$z_{26} = \chi_5(\sqrt[3]{z_{23}}, -z_{20}, z_{19} - z_{19}^3, -z_{18}, \text{sgn}(z_{15})\sqrt{|z_{15}|}, q_{12}, \sqrt[3]{x_3}),$$

$$z_{25} = \max\{z_{23}^2, z_{22}, z_{21} - z_{21}^3, \arctan(z_{17}), q_{11}, q_9, \sqrt{q_5}\},$$

$$z_{24} = \max\{\tanh(z_{21}), z_{20} - z_{20}^3, z_{15}^3, q_{12} - q_{12}^3, q_{10}, q_8^3, \sqrt[3]{q_5}, q_4^3, \exp(x_2)\},$$

$$z_{23} = z_{20}z_{18}z_{16}q_9\sqrt{q_7}\,\text{sgn}(x_1)\sqrt{|x_1|},$$

$$z_{22} = \chi_6(z_{19}, z_{17}^{-1}, \exp(z_{16}), \sqrt[3]{q_{10}}, \arctan(q_9), q_8^{-1}, \sqrt{q_2}),$$

$$z_{21} = \max\{\tanh(z_{18}), q_8^2, q_7, -q_6, \sqrt{q_3}\},$$

$$z_{20} = \chi_6(-z_{19}, z_{17}, \arctan(z_{10}), q_6, -q_2, x_3^{-1}),$$

$$z_{19} = z_{16} + \arctan(q_{11}) + q_8^{-1} + q_5 + \arctan(x_3),$$

$$z_{18} = \chi_5(z_{15}, q_{12}^{-1}, q_7^{-1}, q_4, x_1 - x_1^3),$$

$$z_{17} = q_3 + x_3 - q_3x_3,$$

$$z_{16} = q_2x_2\tanh(q_5),$$

$$z_{15} = \text{sgn}(\sqrt{q_{10}} + q_5 - q_5^3 + q_3^{-1} + q_1 + x_1)\sqrt{q_{10} + (q_5 - q^3)^2 + q_3^{-2} + q_1^2 + x_1^2},$$

$$\chi_5(a_1, a_2) = a_1 + a_2 - a_1a_2,$$

$$\chi_5(a_1, \ldots, a_s) = \chi_5(\chi_5(a_1, \chi_5(\ldots, \chi_5(a_{s-1}, a_s)\ldots),$$

$$\chi_6(a_1,\ldots,a_s) = \mathrm{sgn}\left(\sum_{i=1}^{s} a_i\right)\sqrt{\sum_{i=1}^{s} a_i^2},$$

$$q_1 = 2.3474,\ q_2 = 10.5066,\ q_3 = 9.9106,\ q_4 = 13.1419,\ q_5 = 9.6631,\ q_6 = 4.4541,$$

$$q_7 = 2.1899,\ q_8 = 4.8552,\ q_9 = 3.1116,\ q_{10} = 6.6172,\ q_{11} = 12.6812,\ q_{12} = 15.6148.$$

Functions χ_5 and χ_6 are commutative, associative, and have a unit element, zero.

To check the solution we used the found control function to obtain optimal control and corresponding trajectories for various initial states from (48). Among considered initial states were both those that were present in the training set (51) and those that were not present.

Table 1 shows the values of quality criterion J^* obtained using the found control function (53) for 21 initial states from the finite set (51). The optimal trajectories known for these initial states were previously used as a training set. This test is to show the quality of approximation. The value of the quality criterion J_{ocp} obtained by solving the optimal control problem for the same initial state is showed in the table as a reference value. The average deviation of the quality criterion values from the reference ones is 0.0591, maximum deviation is 0.2514, the standard deviation is 0.0648.

Table 1. Results of the computational experiment using initial states from the training set.

Initial State x^0	J^*	J_{ocp}	Initial State x^0	J^*	J_{ocp}
$[1689 \ -1.65\ \ 17\ \ \ 0\ 1500]^T$	0.1777	0.0018	$[1689 \ -1.55\ \ 18.5\ 0\ 1500]^T$	0.2525	0.0011
$[1689 \ -1.6\ \ \ 17\ \ \ 0\ 1500]^T$	0.0295	0.0056	$[1689 \ -1.65\ \ 19\ \ \ 0\ 1500]^T$	0.0240	0.0012
$[1689 \ -1.55\ \ 17\ \ \ 0\ 1500]^T$	0.0049	0.0029	$[1689 \ -1.6\ \ \ 19\ \ \ 0\ 1500]^T$	0.0501	0.0024
$[1689 \ -1.65\ \ 17.5\ 0\ 1500]^T$	0.1433	0.0060	$[1689 \ -1.55\ \ 19\ \ \ 0\ 1500]^T$	0.0030	0.0009
$[1689 \ -1.6\ \ \ 17.5\ 0\ 1500]^T$	0.0264	0.0044	$[1689 \ -1.65\ \ 19.5\ 0\ 1500]^T$	0.1035	0.0036
$[1689 \ -1.55\ \ 17.5\ 0\ 1500]^T$	0.0127	0.0024	$[1689 \ -1.6\ \ \ 19.5\ 0\ 1500]^T$	0.0822	0.0027
$[1689 \ -1.65\ \ 18\ \ \ 0\ 1500]^T$	0.0780	0.0033	$[1689 \ -1.55\ \ 19.5\ 0\ 1500]^T$	0.0045	0.0045
$[1689 \ -1.6\ \ \ 18\ \ \ 0\ 1500]^T$	0.0439	0.0084	$[1689 \ -1.65\ \ 20\ \ \ 0\ 1500]^T$	0.0954	0.0036
$[1689 \ -1.55\ \ 18\ \ \ 0\ 1500]^T$	0.0061	0.0023	$[1689 \ -1.6\ \ \ 20\ \ \ 0\ 1500]^T$	0.0635	0.0052
$[1689 \ -1.65\ \ 18.5\ 0\ 1500]^T$	0.0703	0.0019	$[1689 \ -1.55\ \ 20\ \ \ 0\ 1500]^T$	0.0334	0.0099
$[1689 \ -1.6\ \ \ 18.5\ 0\ 1500]^T$	0.0111	0.0019			

Table 2 shows the values of quality criterion J^* obtained using the found control function (53) for 10 initial states generated randomly within the domain (48). This test is to show the suitability of the found control function for any initial state from the domain (48). The value of the quality criterion J_{ocp} obtained by solving the optimal control problem for the same initial state is showed in the table as a reference value. The average deviation of the quality criterion values from the reference ones is 0.0366, maximum deviation is 0.1122, the standard deviation is 0.0341.

Table 2. Results of the computational experiment for random initial states.

Initial State x^0	J^*	J_{ocp}	Initial State x^0	J^*	J_{ocp}
$[1689 \ -1.565\ 18.92\ 0\ 1500]^T$	0.0176	0.0034	$[1689 \ -1.628\ 18.2\ \ \ 0\ 1500]^T$	0.0398	0.0016
$[1689 \ -1.571\ 17.21\ 0\ 1500]^T$	0.0048	0.0018	$[1689 \ -1.614\ 19.24\ 0\ 1500]^T$	0.0508	0.0022
$[1689 \ -1.63\ \ 19.39\ 0\ 1500]^T$	0.1136	0.0014	$[1689 \ -1.644\ 18.57\ 0\ 1500]^T$	0.0613	0.0052
$[1689 \ -1.558\ 19.91\ 0\ 1500]^T$	0.0567	0.0083	$[1689 \ -1.563\ 18.33\ 0\ 1500]^T$	0.0032	0.0023
$[1689 \ -1.582\ 17.62\ 0\ 1500]^T$	0.0042	0.0016	$[1689 \ -1.589\ 18.9\ \ \ 0\ 1500]^T$	0.0464	0.0043

Figures 3 and 4 illustrate the results of computational experiment for initial state $x^0 = [1689\ -1.565\ 18.92\ 0\ 1500]^T$. Graphs of the trajectories obtained using the found control function are shown by black solid lines. For comparison the trajectories obtained by solving the optimal control problem are shown by grey dashed lines. Figure 5 shows the found control function values over time.

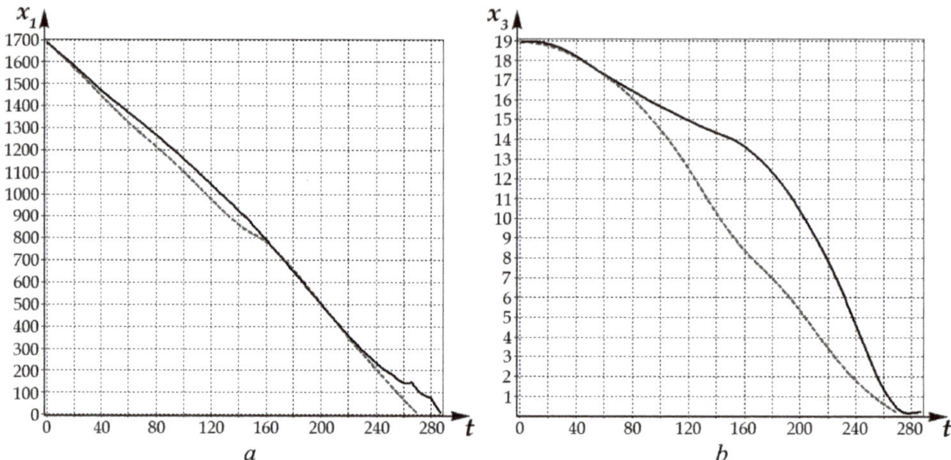

Figure 3. The graphs of trajectories: (**a**) spacecraft speed over time $x_1(t)$; (**b**) spacecraft altitude over time $x_3(t)$. Found solution—black solid line; reference solution—grey dashed line.

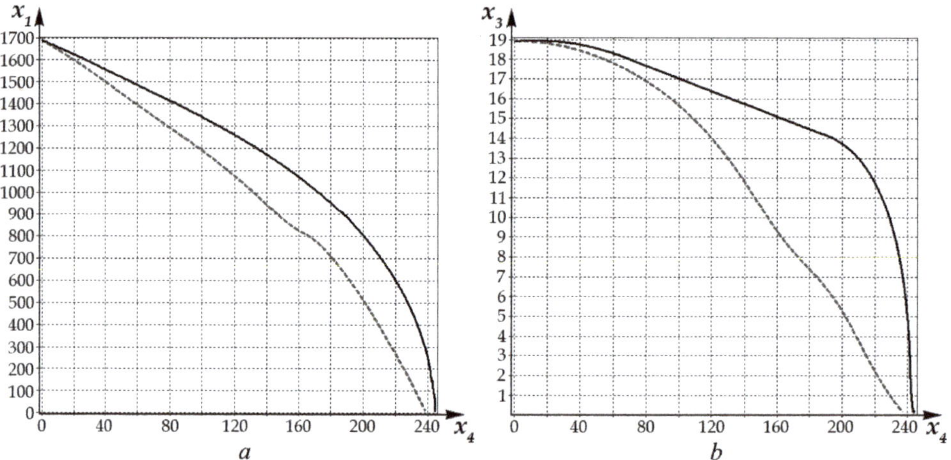

Figure 4. The graphs of trajectories: (**a**) spacecraft speed over distance $x_1(x_4)$; (**b**) spacecraft altitude over distance $x_3(x_4)$. Found solution—black solid line; reference solution—grey dashed line.

The computational experiment showed that the found multidimensional control function allows one to obtain a close to optimal solution for any initial states from the given domain (48) even for those initial states that were not in the training set (51).

According to the analysis of the standard deviation, the training set contained a sufficient number of optimal trajectories. A better value of the standard deviation for the experiment with randomly distributed in (48) initial states can be explained by the fact that the set (51) had a large number of initial states on the boundaries of the set (48).

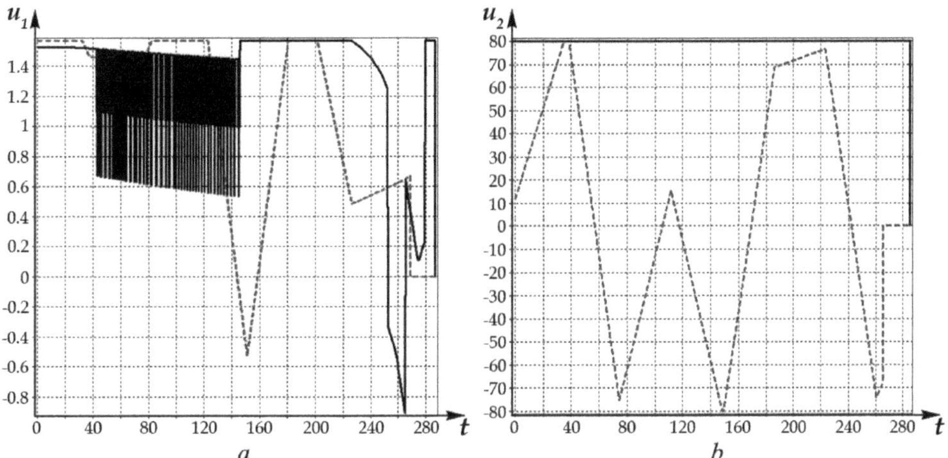

Figure 5. The graphs of control values over time: (**a**) control $u_1(t)$; (**b**) control $u_2(t)$. Found solution—black solid line; reference solution—grey dashed line.

6. Conclusions and Perspectives

The paper provides mathematical formulations of the machine learning problem, supervised and unsupervised, defines the basic concepts, such as the work area and the training set. Based on the presented formulations, it is shown that the main task of machine learning is to find a function that determines the correspondence between the input data and the resulting data. It is shown that today this problem can be solved numerically using symbolic regression methods. The problem of obtaining a mathematical expression arises in various situations—approximation of experimental data to determine a physical law or a trend model; efficiently analyze and predict variables or indicators based on previous observations; identification of a mathematical model of a process or a dynamic object; generalization of the control law based on the current state of the control object. The application of machine learning based on symbolic regression methods to control opens up the possibility of solving such a complex problem in control theory as the problem of general control synthesis. The paper presents a mathematical formulation of the control synthesis problem and provides methods for its solution using machine learning both directly and based on a training set. An important result of the article is the methodology for solving the problem of general control synthesis as machine learning control based on a training set. An approach to constructing a training sample based on multiple solutions to the optimal control problem is proposed. An example of solving a specific problem of synthesis of control of a complex technical object based on the approximation of optimal trajectories is given. It is shown that such a control, obtained on the basis of machine learning, gives good results not only for the input data from the training set, but also not from it.

The concept of machine learning is widely known, but very often limited by its association with neural network technology. We are expanding the concept of machine learning to include a description of an unknown function in its formulation. Thus, a function can be specified and training is aimed only at finding parameters, as in neural networks, but you can also search for the structure of the function and its parameters. This became possible with the advent of symbolic regression methods. The complexity of these methods lies in the need to organize search in a space in which there is no metric. This greatly complicates the solution of the problem of finding the required structure of the function. This complexity opens up a wide field of research. One of the ways to solve this problem is to use the principle of small variations of the basic solution indicated in the article. This approach allows you to concentrate the search for a solution around a basic solution based on the developer's experience or intuition. This approach also requires further study.

Author Contributions: Conceptualization, A.D. and E.S.; methodology, A.D., E.S. and S.K.; software, S.K.; validation, E.S. and G.D.; formal analysis, A.D., G.D.; investigation, S.K.; data curation, S.K.; writing—original draft preparation, A.D., E.S. and S.K.; writing—review and editing, E.S. All authors have read and agreed to the published version of the manuscript.

Funding: This research is supported by the Ministry of Science and Higher Education of the Russian Federation, project No. 075-15-2020-799.

Conflicts of Interest: The authors declare no conflict of interest.

References

1. Duriez, T.; Brunton, S.L.; Noack, B.R. *Machine Learning Control–Taming Nonlinear Dynamics and Turbulence*; Fluid Mechanics and Its Applications; Springer International Publishing Switzerland: Berlin/Heidelberg, Germany, 2017; Volume 116, 211p.
2. Alibekov, E.; Kubalík, J.; Babushka, R. Symbolic method for deriving policy in reinforcement learning. In Proceedings of the 55th IEEE Conference on Decision and Control (CDC), Las Vegas, NV, USA, 12–14 December 2016; pp. 2789–2795.
3. Levine, S.; Koltun, V. Learning complex neural network policies with trajectory optimization. In Proceedings of the International Conference on Machine Learning, Beijing, China, 21–26 June 2014; pp. 829–837.
4. Nagabandi, A.; Kahn, G.; Fearing, R.S.; Levine, S. Neural network dynamics for model-based deep reinforcement learning with model-free fine-tuning. In Proceedings of the 2018 IEEE International Conference on Robotics and Automation (ICRA), Brisbane, Australia, 21–25 May 2018; pp. 7559–7566
5. Gao, T.; Liu, Y.; Liu, L.; Li, D. Adaptive neural network-based control for a class of nonlinear pure-feedback systems with time-varying full state constraints. *IEEE/CAA J. Autom. Sin.* **2018**, *5*, 923–933. [CrossRef]
6. Koza, J.R. *Genetic Programming: On the Programming of Computers by Means of Natural Selection*; MIT Press: Cambridge, MA, USA; London, UK, 1992; 819p.
7. Dracopoulos, D.; Kent, S. Genetic Programming for Prediction and Control. *Neural Comput. Appl.* **1998**, *6*, 214–228. [CrossRef]
8. Dracopoulos, D. Genetic Algorithms and Genetic Programming for Control. In *Evolutionary Algorithms in Engineering Applications*; Springer: Berlin/Heidelberg, Germany, 1997; pp. 329–343.
9. Boltyanskii, V.G. *Mathematical Methods of Optimal Control*; Holt, Rinehart and Winston: New York, NY, USA, 1971; 272p.
10. Krstic, M.; Kanellakopoulos, I.; Kokotovic, P.V. *Nonlinear and Adaptive Control Design*; Wiley–Interscience: New York, NY, USA, 1995; 576p.
11. Khalil, H.K. *Nonlinear Control*; Pearson Education, Inc.: Prentice Hall, NJ, USA, 2015; 403p.
12. Kolesnikov, A.A. Introduction of synergetic control. In Proceedings of the American Control Conference ACC-2014, Portland, OR, USA, 4–6 June 2014; pp. 3013–3016.
13. Kolesnikov, A.; Veselov, G.; Kolesnikov, A.; Monti, A.; Ponci, F.; Santi, E.; Dougal, R. Synergetic synthesis of DC-DC boost converter controllers: Theory and experimental analysis. In Proceedings of the IEEE Applied Power Electronics Conference and Exposition—APEC, Dallas, TX, USA, 10–14 March 2002; pp. 409–415.
14. Diveev, A.I. A Numerical Method for Network Operator for Synthesis of a Control System with Uncertain Initial Values. *J. Comput. Syst. Sci. Int.* **2012**, *51*, 228–243. [CrossRef]
15. Diveev, A.I.; Ibadulla, S.I.; Konyrbaev, N.B.; Shmalko, E.Y. Variational Genetic Programming for Optimal Control System Synthesis of Mobile Robots. *IFAC-PapersOnLine* **2015**, *48*, 106–111. [CrossRef]
16. Diveev, A.I.; Ibadulla, S.I.; Konyrbaev, N.B.; Shmalko, E.Y. Variational Analytic Programming for Synthesis of Optimal Control for Flying Robot. *IFAC-PapersOnLine* **2015**, *48*, 75–80. [CrossRef]
17. Diveev, A.I.; Shmalko, E.Y. Optimal Motion Control for Multi-Robot System by Multilayer Network Operator. In Proceedings of the 11th IEEE Conference on Industrial Electronics and Applications (ICIEA 2016), Hefei, China, 5–7 June 2016; pp. 2168–2173.
18. Diveev, A.I.; Balandina, G.I.; Konstantinov, S.V. Binary Variational Genetic Programming for the Problem of Synthesis of Control System. In Proceedings of the 13th International Conference on Natural Computation, Fuzzy Systems and Knowledge Discovery (ICNC-FSKD 2017), Guilin, China, 29–31 July 2017; pp. 165–170.
19. Diveev, A.I. Cartesian Genetic Programming for Synthesis of Optimal Control System. In Proceedings of the Future Technologies Conference (FTC) 2020, Vancouver, BC, Canada, 5–6 November 2020; Springer Nature Switzerland AG: Cham, Switzerland, 2021; Volume 2, pp. 205–222.
20. Diveev, A.I.; Shmalko, E.Y.; Sofronova, E.A. Theoretical Fundamentals for Unimodality Estimation of an Objective Functional in the Optimal Control Problem. In Proceedings of the 2019 6th International Conference on Control, Decision and Information Technologies (CoDIT), Paris, France, 23–26 April 2019; pp. 767–772.
21. Diveev, A.I.; Konstantinov, S.V. Study of the Practical Convergence of Evolutionary Algorithms for the Optimal Program Control of a Wheeled Robot. *J. Comput. Syst. Sci. Int.* **2018**, *57*, 561–580. [CrossRef]
22. Goldberg, D.E. *Genetic Algorithms in Search, Optimization, and Machine Learning*; Addison–Wesley: Reading, MA, USA, 1989.

23. Kennedy, J.; Eberhart, R. Particle swarm optimization. In Proceedings of the ICNN'95-International Conference on Neural Networks, Perth, Australia, 27 November–1 December 1995; Volume 4, pp. 1942–1948.
24. Mirjalili, S.; Mirjalili, S.M.; Lewis, A. Grey Wolf Optimizer. *Adv. Eng. Softw.* **2014**, *69*, 46–61. [CrossRef]
25. Miller, J.; Thomson, P. Cartesian Genetic Programming. In *Proceedings EuroGP 2000R 3rd European Conf. Genetic Programming*; Poli, R., Banzhaf, W., Langdon, W.B., Miller, J.F., Nordin, P., Fogarty, T.C., Eds.; Springer: Edinburgh, UK; Berlin, Germany, 2000; Volume 1802, pp. 121–132.
26. Diveev, A.I. Small Variations of Basic Solution Method for Nonnumerical Optimization. *IFAC-PapersOnLine* **2015**, *48*, 28–33. [CrossRef]
27. Liu, X.L.; Duan, G.R.; Teo, K.L. Optimal Soft Landing Control for Moon Lander. *Automatica* **2008**, *44*, 1097–1103. [CrossRef]

Article

Precise Trajectory Tracking Control of Ship Towing Systems via a Dynamical Tracking Target

Ouxue Li and Yusheng Zhou *

School of Mathematics and Statistics, Guizhou University, Guiyang 550025, China; gs.oxli19@gzu.edu.cn
* Correspondence: yszhou@gzu.edu.cn

Abstract: This paper proposes a novel control strategy to address the precise trajectory tracking control problem of a ship towing system. At first, the kinematics and dynamics models of a ship towing system are established by introducing a passive steering angle and using its structure relationship. Then, by using the motion law derived from its nonholonomic constraints, the relative curvature of the target trajectory curve is applied to design a dynamical tracking target. By applying the sliding mode control and inverse dynamic adaptive control methods, two appropriate robust torque controllers are designed via the dynamical tracking target, so that both the tugboat and the towed ship are able to track the desired path precisely. As we show, the proposed strategy has excellent agreement with the numerical simulation results.

Keywords: dynamical tracking target; ship towing system; relative curvature; adaptive control

Citation: Li, O.; Zhou, Y. Precise Trajectory Tracking Control of Ship Towing Systems via a Dynamical Tracking Target. *Mathematics* **2021**, *9*, 974. https://doi.org/10.3390/math9090974

Academic Editors: Mikhail Posypkin, Andrey Gorshenin, Vladimir Titarev and Stevan Dubljevic

Received: 18 February 2021
Accepted: 24 April 2021
Published: 27 April 2021

Publisher's Note: MDPI stays neutral with regard to jurisdictional claims in published maps and institutional affiliations.

1. Introduction

A ship towing system (STS) consists of a tugboat, a towline, and a towed ship [1]. Owing to its powerful transportation ability, the STS plays an increasing role in the development of marine resources, such as oil, natural gas, mineral resource, etc. In the past, due to external environmental disturbances and inherent internal uncertainties, the motion control of the STS was mostly based on experimental works or numerical simulations, rather than theoretical analysis [2]. As a result, an improper control would cause the actual towing trajectory deviate from the target towing route. This may lead to collisions, capsizing, and other safety accidents. As a consequence, it is necessary to investigate the precise motion control of the STS for its safe navigation at sea.

For the STS, it is subject to non-holonomic constraints when the lateral drift motion is small enough to be neglected. In this case, the inter-coupling action generated by the relative motion among tugboat, towline, and towed ship makes the trajectory planning and motion control of the STS especially challenging [3]. In addition, the STS is affected by various factors and its dynamics model is extremely complex, thus imposing challenges to the model of STS. Accordingly, the related research studies mainly focus on the simplified models. For example, in References [4,5], based on the local linearization stability analysis method, the nonlinear dynamics model of the STS was approximated into a linearized model. In Reference [6], the nonlinear dynamics equation of the STS was transformed into a six-dimensional state space model, then the equation was approximated by Taylor series. However, these methods only solve the nonlinear problem of the STS locally. In addition, in Reference [7], the investigation showed that the nonholonomic constraints were destroyed when the hull occurred lateral drift motion. As a result, it is difficult to analyze the motion law of the STS clearly. To overcome this drawback, the relative width of the towed ship should be small. In this case, the STS is not prone to lateral drift so as to ensure the nonholonomic constraints of zero lateral velocity.

In general, STSs could be divided into two types. One is the towed ship without steering capacity, and the other is the towed ship with certain steering ability. To the former, its motion ability is completely depended on the traction of the tugboat, so it is fully passive.

To the latter, it has a certain steering ability to achieve steering motion. For the case of the towed ship without steering ability, the dynamics equation of the STS can be derived by conventional method since the nonholonomic constraint is relatively simple. However, the main drawback of such systems is that the towed ship cannot follow the same trajectory as the tugboat during turning movements. In this case, the STS is easy to collide with obstacles. To address this issue, it is necessary to equip the towed ship with a steering assembly, so that it has a certain steering ability. In general, active steering and passive steering are two main steering strategies in practical implementation. Active steering commonly depends on an active control input, and the corresponding nonholonomic constraints become complex. So, it imposes difficulty in deducing the dynamics model [8]. Thus, it is a challenge to design the model-based controllers. In practice applications, the active controller is usually designed by measuring numerous accurate datas, which leads to complicated calculation and expensive cost. In terms of the passive steering method, the rear beam of the towed ship steers passively through a passive steering mechanism, such as the following-up steering. This is helpful to the system lateral stability against rollover.

Since the STS is an underactuated, nonholonomic, and nonlinear system, its motion control is indeed a challenging problem in the control community. The challenge is even harder when the external disturbance or internal uncertainty influence the system. At present, there are mainly two kinds of relevant research methods for the motion control of the STS. On the one hand, extensively studies consider kinematic models only. Usually, advanced control methods, such as model predictive control [9,10], adaptive control [11,12], sliding mode control [13], back-stepping control [14], etc., are used to design speed controllers [15,16] for the STS. According to the kinematics model, the nonlinear adaptive tracking control and nonlinear feedback tracking control methods, together with the path tracking algorithm, are adopted to make the towed ship track the trajectory of the towing boats [17,18]. On the other hand, some studies consider both kinematic and dynamics models at the same time [19,20]. Howeever, the main drawback of these research studies is that they do not make full use of the motion laws, resulting in complex control and insufficient precision. In addition, the problem of inconsistent tracking path between the tugboat and the towed ship cannot be fundamentally solved by only depending on advanced control methods and measurement technologies, which is mainly due to the following two reasons. At first, the steering of the towed ship is not matched with the tugboat, so that the towed ship is easy to deviate from the trajectory of the tugboat. Second, the speed error of the STS at the initial moment is very large, and the accumulated position errors cannot be adjusted. This leads to increasing accumulated position errors, so that the towed ship deviates increasingly from the trajectory of the tugboat. Therefore, it is reasonable to design trajectory tracking controllers by combining the motion laws with its dynamics equation, so that both the tugboat and the towed ship are able to track the same motion path.

In this paper, motivated by the above observations, we aim to seek a novel control strategy to solve the precise tracking control of the STS with two robust torque controllers and a passive steering angle. The major contributions of this paper are summarized as follows.

- An appropriate passive steering angle is introduced to make the towed ship track well the trajectory of the tugboat.
- A dynamical tracking target, sliding mode control, and inverse dynamics adaptive control methods are introduced to design two robust torque controllers for the STS, so that the tugboat and the towed ship can move along the same target trajectory curve accurately under uncertainties.

The remainder of this paper is structured as follows. Section 2 describes the mathematical model of the ship towing system. Section 3 focuses on designing two robust trajectory tracking controllers. Simulation results are reported and discussed in Section 4. Finally, some conclusions are given in Section 5.

2. System Modeling

Consider a STS consisting of a tugboat, a towed ship, and a towline, as depicted in Figure 1. The tugboat is equipped with two motors, and the towed ship is connected passively with the tugboat. O_0 and O_1 represent the midpoints of the tugboat and the towed ship, respectively. Both the tugboat and the towed ship are connected with a rigid towline. That is, one end of the towline is flexibly connected to the towing hook of the tugboat at O_{p0}, and the other end is flexibly hinged to the joint of the towed ship at O_{p1}. The length of the towline $O_{p0}O_{p1}$ is defined as a. Then, definitions of symbols used in the text are presented in Table 1.

Table 1. Parameters and variables of the ship towing system.

Notation	Definition
T_v, T_ω	Torques provided by the propeller and rudder of the tugboat
φ_0, φ_1	Yaw angles of the tugboat and the towed ship
ω_0, ω_1	Yaw rotation speeds of the tugboat and the towed ship, and $\omega_i = \dot{\varphi}_i$, $i = 0,1$
x_0, y_0	The coordinates of the midpoint O_0 of the tugboat
x_1, y_1	The coordinates of the midpoint O_1 of the towed ship
θ	Angular difference of yaw angles between the tugboat and the towed ship, and $\theta = \varphi_0 - \varphi_1$
v_0, v_1	Forward speeds of the tugboat and the towed ship
v_{p0}	The forward speed of the stern midpoint O_{p0} of the tugboat
v_{p1}	The forward speed of the bow midpoint O_{p1} of the towed ship
Ψ	Steering angle of the towed ship, and $\Psi = \mu\theta$
μ	Steering coefficient of the steering angle
a	Length of the rigid towline
m_0, m_1	Masses of the tugboat and the towed ship
M_{x0}, M_{x1}	Additional lateral masses of the tugboat and the towed ship
I_{z0}, I_{z1}	Moment of inertia of the tugboat and the towed ship about Z-axis through the center point
J_{z0}, J_{z1}	Additional moments of inertia of the tugboat and the towed ship about Z-axis through the center point

The goal of the paper is to design two robust torque controllers for the tugboat, so that both the tugboat and the towed ship are able to follow the desired trajectory curve precisely. As such, we introduce a passive steering angle for the towed ship, so that it can follow the trajectory of the tugboat. The steering angle Ψ is defined as the angle between vector $\overrightarrow{O_{p0}O_{p1}}$ and $\overrightarrow{v_{p1}}$. For convenience, we further assume $\Psi = \mu(\varphi_0 - \varphi_1)$, where μ is an appropriate steering coefficient which makes the towed ship follow well the trajectory of the tugboat. In modeling of the STS, some assumptions are considered, as follows:

A1. The motion of the STS is in a horizontal plane. The ship roll, pitch, heave, and lateral drift motions are negligibly small.

A2. The motion of the towed ship is achieved by the system coupling action.

A3. The nonlinear force is ignored, since the STS commonly does not make large maneuvers.

A4. The rudder cannot be controlled directly, and the motion of the towed ship is controlled indirectly by the coupling action of nonholonomic constraints.

A5. The resistance force of the towline is ignored.

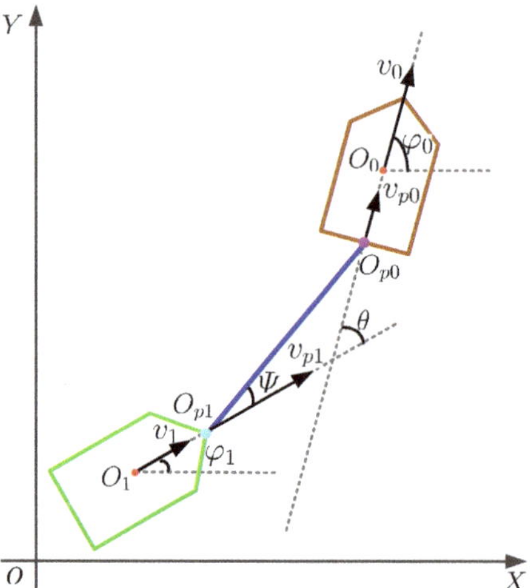

Figure 1. Model of a ship towing system.

2.1. Kinematics Modeling

The generalized coordinate of the STS is defined as $\mathbf{p} = (x_0, y_0, \varphi_0, \theta)^{\mathrm{T}}$, and the system state is described by $(\mathbf{p}, \dot{\mathbf{p}})$. Then, the motion states of other degrees of freedom can be deduced by its constraint equations.

For the STS, the motion of the tugboat and the towed ship is subject to the following nonholonomic constraints, respectively,

$$\begin{cases} -\dot{x}_0\sin\varphi_0 + \dot{y}_0\cos\varphi_0 = 0, \\ v_0 = \dot{x}_0\cos\varphi_0 + \dot{y}_0\sin\varphi_0, \end{cases} \tag{1}$$

and

$$\begin{cases} -\dot{x}_1\sin\varphi_1 + \dot{y}_1\cos\varphi_1 = 0, \\ v_1 = \dot{x}_1\cos\varphi_1 + \dot{y}_1\sin\varphi_1. \end{cases} \tag{2}$$

As shown in Figure 1, the speed relation between the tugboat and the towed ship is expressed as

$$\begin{cases} v_{p1}\cos\Psi = \cos(\theta - \Psi)v_{p0}, \\ v_{p0}\sin(\theta - \Psi) + v_{p1}\sin\Psi = a(\dot{\Psi} - \dot{\theta} + \dot{\varphi}_0). \end{cases} \tag{3}$$

Here, the first equation denotes that the velocity of joints O_{p0} and O_{p1} along the towline direction are equal. The second equation desribes the speed relation between the joints O_{p0} and O_{p1} in the vertical direction. Such speed relation causes coupling motion between the adjacent structures.

Substituting $\Psi = \mu\theta$ and the first equation of (3) into the second equation of (3), we obtain

$$\dot{\theta} = -\frac{\sin\theta}{a(1-\mu)\cos\Psi}v_{p0} + \frac{1}{1-\mu}\dot{\varphi}_0. \tag{4}$$

Define $\Omega = \frac{\sin\theta}{\cos\Psi}$, and then (4) can be rewritten as

$$\dot{\theta} = -\frac{\Omega}{a(1-\mu)}v_{p0} + \frac{1}{1-\mu}\dot{\varphi}_0. \tag{5}$$

Furthermore, according to the coordinates of point O_0 and O_1, we can get the positional coordinates of $O_{p0}(x_0 - \frac{L}{2}\cos\varphi_0, y_0 - \frac{L}{2}\sin\varphi_0)$ and $O_{p1}(x_1 + \frac{L}{2}\cos\varphi_1, y_1 + \frac{L}{2}\sin\varphi_1)$, where

L is the length of the tugboat, as shown in Figure 1. In this way, the speed relations of points O_{p0} and O_0, O_{p1} and O_1 are expressed as

$$\begin{cases} v_{p0}^2 = \dot{x}_0^2 + \dot{y}_0^2 + \frac{L^2}{4}\dot{\varphi}_0^2 + L\dot{\varphi}_0(\dot{x}_0\sin\varphi_0 - \dot{y}_0\cos\varphi_0), \\ v_{p1}^2 = \dot{x}_1^2 + \dot{y}_1^2 + \frac{L^2}{4}\dot{\varphi}_1^2 + L\dot{\varphi}_1(\dot{y}_1\cos\varphi_1 - \dot{x}_1\sin\varphi_1). \end{cases} \tag{6}$$

Squaring both sides of the two equations of (1) and adding the two square equations, we obtain $v_0^2 = \dot{x}_0^2 + \dot{y}_0^2$. Similarly, from (2), we have $v_1^2 = \dot{x}_1^2 + \dot{y}_1^2$. In this way, (6) becomes

$$\begin{cases} v_{p0}^2 = v_0^2 + \frac{L^2}{4}\dot{\varphi}_0^2, \\ v_{p1}^2 = v_1^2 + \frac{L^2}{4}\dot{\varphi}_1^2 = v_1^2 + \frac{L^2}{4}(\dot{\varphi}_0 - \dot{\theta})^2. \end{cases} \tag{7}$$

Substituting v_{p0} and v_{p1} of (7) into(3), one has

$$v_1 = \sqrt{\frac{\cos^2(\theta - \Psi)}{\cos^2\Psi}(v_0^2 + \frac{L^2}{4}\dot{\varphi}_0^2) - \frac{L^2}{4}(\dot{\varphi}_0 - \dot{\theta})^2}. \tag{8}$$

Then, substituting v_{p0} of (7) into (5) gives

$$\dot{\theta} = -\frac{\Omega}{a(1-\mu)}\sqrt{v_0^2 + \frac{L^2}{4}\dot{\varphi}_0^2} + \frac{1}{(1-\mu)}\dot{\varphi}_0. \tag{9}$$

With these preparations, all constraint equations of the STS are formulated by

$$\begin{cases} -\dot{x}_0\sin\varphi_0 + \dot{y}_0\cos\varphi_0 = 0, \\ v_0 = \dot{x}_0\cos\varphi_0 + \dot{y}_0\sin\varphi_0, \\ \dot{\varphi}_0 = \omega_0, \\ \dot{\theta} = -\frac{\Omega}{a(1-\mu)}\sqrt{v_0^2 + \frac{L^2}{4}\dot{\varphi}_0^2} + \frac{1}{(1-\mu)}\dot{\varphi}_0. \end{cases} \tag{10}$$

By using the motion laws derived from (10), the target trajectory curve can be transformed into a speed target of the tugboat [21], so that the dynamics equation of the STS can match the tracking target well. In fact, the towline is flexibly connected with the two ships. The angle between the rigid towline and the forward speed direction of the towed ship can be adjusted by a gear steering equipment. Then, according to the relationship of motion speed between the towed ship and the tugboat, the towed ship can move along the trajectory of the tugboat by choosing an appropriate steering angle coefficient μ.

2.2. Dynamics Modeling of a Single Ship

In order to establish the dynamics model of the STS, we should first clarify the dynamics equation of a single ship, taking the single tugboat for example. As shown in Figure 2, an earthbound coordinate frame $O - XYZ$ is used to describe the motion of the single ship in the horizontal plane. The body-fixed coordinate frame $O_0 - X_bY_bZ_b$ centered at midship point O_0 of the single ship is used for better force analysis.

On the one hand, according to the kinematics equation in Reference [22] and neglecting the drifting speed, the dynamics equation of the tugboat is given by

$$\begin{cases} x_b = m_0\dot{v}_0, \\ z_b = I_{z0}\dot{\omega}_0, \end{cases} \tag{11}$$

where x_b represents the component of the external force in the X_b direction, and z_b denotes the component of the external moment of inertia in the Z_b direction.

On the other hand, according to force analysis of the hull [23], one has

$$
\begin{cases}
x_b = -M_{x0}\dot{v}_0 - \frac{1}{2}\rho C_f S v_0^2 + X_p + X_r, \\
z_b = -J_{z0}\dot{\omega}_0 - \frac{1}{2}\rho L^2 dv_0\omega_0(0.45\lambda - \lambda^2)(1 + 0.3\tau) + N_p + N_r,
\end{cases}
\tag{12}
$$

where X_p denotes the component force acting on the propeller along the X_b-axis, and N_p represents the corresponding component of the inertia moment along the Z_b-axis. X_r represents the component force on the rudder along the X_b-axis and N_r is the corresponding component of the inertia moment along the Z_b-axis. ρ is the water density. d is the full load draft height of the tugboat. S is the hull wet area of the tugboat. λ is the aspect ratio of the rudder of the tugboat. τ is the trim value of the tugboat. And C_f is the coefficient of frictional resistance.

It follows from (11) and (12) that the desired dynamics equation of the single tugboat is expressed by

$$
\begin{cases}
(m_0 + M_{x0})\dot{v}_0 = -\frac{1}{2}\rho C_f S v_0^2 + X_p + X_r, \\
(I_{z0} + J_{z0})\dot{\omega}_0 = -\frac{1}{2}\rho L^2 dv_0\omega_0(0.45\lambda - \lambda^2)(1 + 0.3\tau) + N_p + N_r.
\end{cases}
\tag{13}
$$

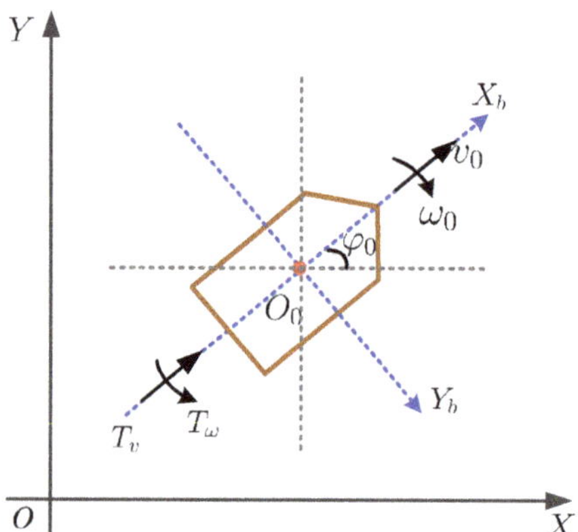

Figure 2. Force analysis of a single ship.

2.3. Dynamics Modeling

According to the dynamics Equation (13) of the single tugboat, the dynamics model of the STS can be presented by Reference [24]:

$$
\begin{cases}
(m_0 + M_{x0})\dot{v}_0 = -\frac{1}{2}\rho C_f S v_0^2 + X_p + X_r - T\cos(\theta - \Psi), \\
(I_{z0} + J_{z0})\dot{\omega}_0 = -\frac{1}{2}\rho L^2 dv_0\omega_0(0.45\lambda - \lambda^2)(1 + 0.3\tau) + N_p + N_r \\
\qquad\qquad - \frac{1}{2}TL\sin(\theta - \Psi).
\end{cases}
\tag{14}
$$

$$
\begin{cases}
(m_1 + M_{x1})\dot{v}_1 = -\frac{1}{2}\rho C_f S v_1^2 + T\cos\Psi, \\
(I_{z1} + J_{z1})\dot{\omega}_1 = -\frac{1}{2}\rho L^2 dv_1\omega_1(0.45\lambda - \lambda^2)(1 + 0.3\tau) + \frac{1}{2}TL\sin\Psi,
\end{cases}
\tag{15}
$$

where T is the towline tension. From (14), one has

$$
\begin{cases}
\dot{v}_0 = \dfrac{-\frac{1}{2}\rho C_f S v_0^2 + X_p + X_r - T\cos(\theta - \Psi)}{(m_0 + M_{x0})}, \\
\dot{\omega}_0 = \dfrac{-\frac{1}{2}\rho L^2 dv_0\omega_0(0.45\lambda - \lambda^2)(1 + 0.3\tau) + N_p + N_r - \frac{1}{2}TL\sin(\theta - \Psi)}{I_{z0} + J_{z0}}.
\end{cases}
\tag{16}
$$

According to (15), the towline tension T is expressed as

$$T^2 = [(m_1 + M_{x1})\dot{v}_1 + \frac{1}{2}\rho C_f S v_1^2]^2 + [\frac{2}{L}(I_{z1} + J_{z1})\dot{\omega}_1$$
$$+ \rho L d v_1 \omega_1 (0.45\lambda - \lambda^2)(1 + 0.3\tau)]^2, \tag{17}$$

where v_1, φ_1 can be obtained according to (8), (9), and $\omega_1 = \dot{\varphi}_1 = \dot{\varphi}_0 - \dot{\theta}$.

It follows from (16) and (17) that the dynamics equation of the STS is ultimately formulated as

$$\begin{cases} \dot{v}_0 = \frac{-\Delta_2 v_0^2 + u_1}{\Delta_1}, \\ \dot{\omega}_0 = \frac{-\Delta_4 v_0 \omega_0 + u_2}{\Delta_3}, \end{cases} \tag{18}$$

where $\Delta_1 = m_0 + M_{x0}$, $\Delta_2 = \frac{1}{2}\rho C_f S$, $\Delta_3 = I_{z0} + J_{z0}$, $\Delta_4 = \frac{1}{2}\rho L^2 d(0.45\lambda - \lambda^2)(1 + 0.3\tau)$, $u_1 = X_p + X_r - T\cos(\theta - \Psi)$, and $u_2 = N_p + N_r - \frac{1}{2}TL\sin(\theta - \Psi)$.

3. Trajectory Tracking Control of the Ship Towing System

In order to make the tugboat track a given target trajectory curve accurately, the target trajectory curve should be firstly converted into a speed target form so as to match the dynamics equation. As such, the original motion task is converted into a general trajectory tracking control problem of the tugboat. Then, two torque controllers can be designed from the forward and yaw speed subsystems, to achieve the given trajectory tracking task.

3.1. Dynamical Tracking Target

In this subsection, we will solve the problem of converting the target curve to an appropriate speed tracking target so as to match the dynamics Equation (18). For a target trajectory curve $\tilde{\mathbf{r}}(t) = (\tilde{x}(t), \tilde{y}(t))^T$, the speed form of the target trajectory curve is expressed as [21]

$$\begin{cases} \tilde{v}_0 = \sqrt{\dot{\tilde{x}}^2 + \dot{\tilde{y}}^2}, \\ \tilde{\omega}_0 = \dot{\tilde{\varphi}}_0 = \frac{\dot{\tilde{x}}\ddot{\tilde{y}} - \dot{\tilde{y}}\ddot{\tilde{x}}}{\dot{\tilde{x}}^2 + \dot{\tilde{y}}^2} = k(t)\tilde{v}_0, \end{cases} \tag{19}$$

where $k(t) = \frac{\dot{\tilde{x}}\ddot{\tilde{y}} - \dot{\tilde{y}}\ddot{\tilde{x}}}{(\dot{\tilde{x}}^2 + \dot{\tilde{y}}^2)^{\frac{3}{2}}}$ is the relative curvature of the target trajectory curve. We note that the relative curvature is the key point of the target trajectory curve. If the relative curvature is tracked very well, the tugboat can follow the target trajectory curve precisely. On this basis, the target trajectory curve $\tilde{\mathbf{r}}(t)$ can be further improved into a dynamical tracking target form as

$$\begin{cases} \tilde{v}_0 = \phi(t), \\ \tilde{\omega}_0 = \dot{\tilde{\varphi}}_0 = k(s(t))v_0, \end{cases} \tag{20}$$

where v_0 stands for the actual forward speed of the tugboat, and $\phi(t)$ represents an appropriate forward speed target which is given by

$$\dot{\phi}(t) = l\beta^2 t e^{-\beta t}. \tag{21}$$

In (21), l is the length of the target curve, β is an appropriate parameter according to actual needs [21].

It can be seen from (20) that the target trajectory curve can be converted into a speed target form with the relative curvature. Combined with the dynamics model, two torque controllers can be designed to implement the tracking task of the target trajectory curve. In fact, there are two main advantages by using the dynamical tracking target. First, by choosing an appropriate forward speed target, the initial speed error is equal to zero, which can significantly reduce the position error caused by the accumulated speeds errors. Second, the yaw rotation speed target depends on the actual forward speed, which can be adjusted from moment to moment. Moreover, no matter how large the actual forward speed error is, as long as the curvature tracking error is small enough, satisfactory tracking performance can still be achieved. As a consequence, the idea of dynamical tracking target can fundamentally solve the problem of accurate trajectory tracking.

3.2. Control Design

In this subsection, we will design two torque controllers (u_1, u_2) for the dynamics Equation (18) by using the dynamical tracking target (20). We see that the yaw rotation speed target $\tilde{\omega}$ in the second equation of (20) is the product of the actual forward speed v and the relative curvature $k(s(t))$. Therefore, the controller u_1 in the first equation of (18) should be firstly considered so as to obtain the actual forward speed.

3.2.1. Forward Speed Control Subsystem

At first, we consider the first equation of the dynamics model (18)

$$\dot{v}_0 = \frac{-\Delta_2 v_0^2 + u_1}{\Delta_1}. \tag{22}$$

Applying the feedback linearization method to (22) and letting

$$u_1 = \Delta_1 h_1 + \Delta_2 v_0^2, \tag{23}$$

a simple control system is obtained as

$$\dot{v}_0 = h_1(t).$$

Defining $\mathbf{X}_1 = (s_1, v_0)^\mathrm{T}$ and $s_1 = \int_0^t v_0(\zeta)\mathrm{d}\zeta$, the forward speed subsystem is rewritten in a matrix form as

$$\dot{\mathbf{X}}_1(t) = \mathbf{A}_1 \mathbf{X}_1(t) + \mathbf{B}_1 h_1(t), \tag{24}$$

where $\mathbf{A}_1 = \begin{bmatrix} 0 & 1 \\ 0 & 0 \end{bmatrix}$, and $\mathbf{B}_1 = \begin{bmatrix} 0 \\ 1 \end{bmatrix}$. In this way, (24) is transformed into an error system as

$$\dot{\mathbf{Y}} = \mathbf{A}_1 \mathbf{Y} + \mathbf{B}_1 h_1(t) + \boldsymbol{\eta}(t), \tag{25}$$

where $\tilde{\mathbf{X}}_1 = (\tilde{s}_1, \tilde{v}_0)^\mathrm{T}$, $\tilde{s}_1 = \int_0^t \tilde{v}_0(\tau)\mathrm{d}\tau$, $\mathbf{Y} = (y_1, y_2)^\mathrm{T} = \mathbf{X}_1 - \tilde{\mathbf{X}}_1$, and $\boldsymbol{\eta}(t) = \mathbf{A}_1 \tilde{\mathbf{X}}_1 - \dot{\tilde{\mathbf{X}}}_1$. It is obvious that the integral of (21) with respect to t from 0 to infinity is convergent. Thus, a linear quadratic performance index is introduced as

$$J = \frac{1}{2} \int_0^{+\infty} [\mathbf{Y}^\mathrm{T}(t)\mathbf{Q}_1 \mathbf{Y}(t) + h_1^\mathrm{T}(t)\mathbf{R}h_1(t)]\mathrm{d}t.$$

Here, matrix $\mathbf{Q}_1$ should be large weight of the forward speed error. In this way, the forward speed error is able to be small enough by using optimal control. According to the linear quadratic optimal control theory, the optimal control of forward speed error subsystem (25) is formulated as

$$h_1(t) = -\mathbf{R}^{-1}\mathbf{B}_1^\mathrm{T}[\mathbf{P}\mathbf{Y} + \mathbf{b}(t)]. \tag{26}$$

where $\mathbf{P} \in \mathbb{R}^{2\times 2}$ and $\mathbf{b}(t) \in \mathbb{R}^2$ satisfy the following equations, respectively,

$$\begin{cases} -\mathbf{P}\mathbf{A}_1 - \mathbf{A}_1^\mathrm{T}\mathbf{P} + \mathbf{P}\mathbf{B}_1\mathbf{R}^{-1}\mathbf{B}_1^\mathrm{T}\mathbf{P} - \mathbf{Q}_1 = 0, \\ \dot{\mathbf{b}} = -[\mathbf{A}_1 - \mathbf{B}_1\mathbf{R}^{-1}\mathbf{B}_1^\mathrm{T}\mathbf{P}]^\mathrm{T}\mathbf{b} - \mathbf{P}\boldsymbol{\eta}(t), \quad \mathbf{b}(+\infty) = 0. \end{cases}$$

Substituting (26) into (23), the controller u_1 is formulated by

$$u_1 = -\Delta_1 \mathbf{R}^{-1}\mathbf{B}_1^\mathrm{T}[\mathbf{P}\mathbf{Y} + \mathbf{b}(t)] + \Delta_2 v_0^2.$$

3.2.2. Yaw Rotation Speed Control Subsystem

Since the actual forward speed v is obtained, we now consider the yaw rotation speed subsystem in the second equation of (18). First, the state equation of the reference model is obtained as

$$\Delta_3\dot{\omega}_0 + \Delta_4 v_0\omega_0 = \mathbf{Y}_{21}\mathbf{D}_2\mathbf{Y}_{22} = u_2, \tag{27}$$

where $\mathbf{D}_2 = \mathrm{diag}(\Delta_3, \Delta_4)$, $\mathbf{Y}_{21} = (\dot{\omega}_0, 1)$, and $\mathbf{Y}_{22} = (1, \omega_0 v_0)^{\mathrm{T}}$. Since (27) is strongly nonlinear, it is unlikely to obtain an exact solution. Therefore, to seek an approximate solution, we introduce the adaptive control method based on its inverse dynamics. To this end, the basic part of controller u_2 is designed as

$$u_{20} = \hat{\Delta}_3 s_2 + \hat{\Delta}_4 v_0\omega_0, \tag{28}$$

which yields the adjusted system of (27) as follows:

$$\Delta_3\dot{\omega}_0 + \Delta_4 v_0\omega_0 = u_{20}. \tag{29}$$

Here, $s_2 = \dot{\omega}_0 - k_2(\omega_0 - \tilde{\omega}_0)$ is the adaptation law, $\tilde{\omega}_0$ is the ideal yaw rotation speed target of the tugboat, k_2 is an adjustable control parameter, $e_2 = \omega_0 - \tilde{\omega}_0$ is the yaw rotation speed error, and $\hat{\Delta}_3, \hat{\Delta}_4$ are the estimated values of Δ_3, Δ_4, respectively. Besides, $\hat{\mathbf{D}}_2 = \mathrm{diag}(\hat{\Delta}_3, \hat{\Delta}_4)$ is defined as the estimated value of $\mathbf{D}_2$. The adjustment gain coefficient k_2 can be obtained by using Lyapunov stability theory, thereby getting the adaptation law s_2. It can be seen from (28) and (29) that large errors between $\hat{\Delta}_3$ and Δ_3, $\hat{\Delta}_4$ and Δ_4 may deteriorate the tracking performance, which can be overcome by adjusting the adjustable control parameter k_2. Substituting (28) into (29), one has

$$\hat{\Delta}_3(\dot{\omega}_0 - k_2(\omega_0 - \tilde{\omega}_0)) + \hat{\Delta}_4 v_0\omega_0 = \Delta_3\dot{\omega}_0 + \Delta_4 v_0\omega_0,$$

which yields

$$-\hat{\Delta}_3(\dot{\omega}_0 - \dot{\tilde{\omega}}_0 + k_2(\omega_0 - \tilde{\omega}_0)) + (\hat{\Delta}_3 - \Delta_3)\dot{\omega}_0 + (\hat{\Delta}_4 - \Delta_4)v_0\omega_0 = 0. \tag{30}$$

It follows from (30) and $\dot{e}_2 = \dot{\omega}_0 - \dot{\tilde{\omega}}_0$ that

$$\hat{\Delta}_3(\dot{e}_2 + k_2 e_2) = \Delta_{3e}\dot{\omega}_0 + \Delta_{4e}v_0\omega_0, \tag{31}$$

where $\Delta_{3e} = \hat{\Delta}_3 - \Delta_3$, $\Delta_{4e} = \hat{\Delta}_4 - \Delta_4$, and $\mathbf{D}_{2e} = \hat{\mathbf{D}}_2 - \mathbf{D}_2$. Then, together with (27), one has

$$\Delta_{3e}\dot{\omega}_0 + \Delta_{4e}v_0\omega_0 = \mathbf{Y}_{21}\mathbf{D}_{2e}\mathbf{Y}_{22}. \tag{32}$$

Assume that $\hat{\Delta}_3$ is reversible, and then (31) can be written as

$$(\dot{e}_2 + k_2 e_2) = \hat{\Delta}_3^{-1}(\Delta_{3e}\dot{\omega}_0 + \Delta_{4e}v_0\omega_0).$$

Combining (32), one has

$$\dot{e}_2 + k_2 e_2 = \hat{\Delta}_3^{-1}\mathbf{Y}_{21}\mathbf{D}_{2e}\mathbf{Y}_{22}, \tag{33}$$

which is the error state equation of (27). Furthermore, (33) can be rewritten in a state equation form as

$$\dot{\mathbf{X}}_2 = \mathbf{A}_2\mathbf{X}_2 + \mathbf{B}_2\hat{\Delta}_3^{-1}\mathbf{Y}_{21}\mathbf{D}_{2e}\mathbf{Y}_{22}, \tag{34}$$

where $\mathbf{A}_2 = \begin{pmatrix} 0 & 1 \\ 0 & -k_2 \end{pmatrix}$, $\mathbf{B}_2 = \begin{pmatrix} 0 \\ 1 \end{pmatrix}$ and $\mathbf{X}_2 = \begin{pmatrix} \zeta_2 \\ e_2 \end{pmatrix}$ with $\zeta_2 = \int_0^t e_2(\tau)\mathrm{d}\tau$.

On the other hand, to improve the precision of the estimated matrix $\hat{\mathbf{D}}_2$, a symmetric matrix $\mathbf{Q}_2$ is chosen to satisfy the following Lyapunov equation:

$$\mathbf{A}_2^{\mathsf{T}}\mathbf{D}_2 + \mathbf{D}_2\mathbf{A}_2 + \mathbf{Q}_2 = 0, \tag{35}$$

which can be rewritten in a more detailed form as

$$
\begin{pmatrix} 0 & 0 \\ 1 & -k_2 \end{pmatrix} \begin{pmatrix} \Delta_3 & 0 \\ 0 & \Delta_4 \end{pmatrix} + \begin{pmatrix} \Delta_3 & 0 \\ 0 & \Delta_4 \end{pmatrix} \begin{pmatrix} 0 & 1 \\ 0 & -k_2 \end{pmatrix} = \begin{pmatrix} 0 & \Delta_3 \\ \Delta_3 & -2k_2\Delta_4 \end{pmatrix}
$$
$$
= \begin{pmatrix} -\mathbf{Q}_{11} & -\mathbf{Q}_{12} \\ -\mathbf{Q}_{21} & -\mathbf{Q}_{22} \end{pmatrix}, \tag{36}
$$

where $\mathbf{Q}_2 = \begin{pmatrix} \mathbf{Q}_{11} & \mathbf{Q}_{12} \\ \mathbf{Q}_{21} & \mathbf{Q}_{22} \end{pmatrix}$. It follows from (36) that

$$
\begin{cases} \mathbf{Q}_{11} = 0, \\ \mathbf{Q}_{12} = \mathbf{Q}_{21} = -\Delta_3, \\ \mathbf{Q}_{22} = 2k_2\Delta_4. \end{cases}
$$

Therefore, we can uniquely determine the positive definite matrix $\mathbf{D}_2$ by selecting an appropriate matrix $\mathbf{Q}_2$.

After that, apositive definite quadratic function is defined as

$$
V = \mathbf{X}_2^{\mathsf{T}} \mathbf{D}_2 \mathbf{X}_2 + \mathbf{Y}_{22}^{\mathsf{T}} \mathbf{D}_{2e}^{\mathsf{T}} \mathbf{\Gamma}_2 \mathbf{D}_{2e} \mathbf{Y}_{22}, \tag{37}
$$

where $\mathbf{D}_2$ is the unique positive definite solution of (34), and $\mathbf{\Gamma}_2$ is an appropriate positive definite symmetric matrix. Differentiating both sides of (35) with respect to t and combining (34) with (35), one has

$$
\begin{aligned}
\dot{V} =& \dot{\mathbf{X}}_2^{\mathsf{T}} \mathbf{D}_2 \mathbf{X}_2 + \mathbf{X}_2^{\mathsf{T}} \mathbf{D}_2 \dot{\mathbf{X}}_2 + \dot{\mathbf{Y}}_{22}^{\mathsf{T}} \mathbf{D}_{2e}^{\mathsf{T}} \mathbf{\Gamma}_2 \mathbf{D}_{2e} \mathbf{Y}_{22} + \mathbf{Y}_{22}^{\mathsf{T}} \dot{\mathbf{D}}_{2e}^{\mathsf{T}} \mathbf{\Gamma}_2 \mathbf{D}_{2e} \mathbf{Y}_{22} \\
& + \mathbf{Y}_{22}^{\mathsf{T}} \mathbf{D}_{2e}^{\mathsf{T}} \mathbf{\Gamma}_2 \dot{\mathbf{D}}_{2e} \mathbf{Y}_{22} + \mathbf{Y}_{22}^{\mathsf{T}} \mathbf{D}_{2e}^{\mathsf{T}} \mathbf{\Gamma}_2 \mathbf{D}_{2e} \dot{\mathbf{Y}}_{22} \\
=& (\mathbf{A}_2 \mathbf{X}_2 + \mathbf{B}_2 \hat{\mathbf{\Delta}}_3^{-1} \mathbf{Y}_{21} \mathbf{D}_{2e} \mathbf{Y}_{22})^{\mathsf{T}} \mathbf{D}_2 \mathbf{X}_2 + \mathbf{X}_2^{\mathsf{T}} \mathbf{D}_2 (\mathbf{A}_2 \mathbf{X}_2 + \mathbf{B}_2 \hat{\mathbf{\Delta}}_3^{-1} \mathbf{Y}_{21} \mathbf{D}_{2e} \mathbf{Y}_{22}) \\
& + \dot{\mathbf{Y}}_{22}^{\mathsf{T}} \mathbf{D}_{2e}^{\mathsf{T}} \mathbf{\Gamma}_2 \mathbf{D}_{2e} \mathbf{Y}_{22} + \mathbf{Y}_{22}^{\mathsf{T}} \dot{\mathbf{D}}_{2e}^{\mathsf{T}} \mathbf{\Gamma}_2 \mathbf{D}_{2e} \mathbf{Y}_{22} + \mathbf{Y}_{22}^{\mathsf{T}} \mathbf{D}_{2e}^{\mathsf{T}} \mathbf{\Gamma}_2 \dot{\mathbf{D}}_{2e} \mathbf{Y}_{22} + \mathbf{Y}_{22}^{\mathsf{T}} \mathbf{D}_{2e}^{\mathsf{T}} \mathbf{\Gamma}_2 \mathbf{D}_{2e} \dot{\mathbf{Y}}_{22} \\
=& \mathbf{X}_2^{\mathsf{T}} \mathbf{A}_2^{\mathsf{T}} \mathbf{D}_2 \mathbf{X}_2 + \hat{\mathbf{\Delta}}_3^{-1} \mathbf{Y}_{22}^{\mathsf{T}} \mathbf{D}_{2e}^{\mathsf{T}} \mathbf{Y}_{21}^{\mathsf{T}} \mathbf{B}_2^{\mathsf{T}} \mathbf{D}_2 \mathbf{X}_2 + \mathbf{X}_2^{\mathsf{T}} \mathbf{D}_2 (\mathbf{A}_2 \mathbf{X}_2 + \mathbf{B}_2 \hat{\mathbf{\Delta}}_3^{-1} \mathbf{Y}_{21} \mathbf{D}_{2e} \mathbf{Y}_{22}) \\
& + \dot{\mathbf{Y}}_{22}^{\mathsf{T}} \mathbf{D}_{2e}^{\mathsf{T}} \mathbf{\Gamma}_2 \mathbf{D}_{2e} \mathbf{Y}_{22} + \mathbf{Y}_{22}^{\mathsf{T}} \dot{\mathbf{D}}_{2e}^{\mathsf{T}} \mathbf{\Gamma}_2 \mathbf{D}_{2e} \mathbf{Y}_{22} + \mathbf{Y}_{22}^{\mathsf{T}} \mathbf{D}_{2e}^{\mathsf{T}} \mathbf{\Gamma}_2 \dot{\mathbf{D}}_{2e} \mathbf{Y}_{22} + \mathbf{Y}_{22}^{\mathsf{T}} \mathbf{D}_{2e}^{\mathsf{T}} \mathbf{\Gamma}_2 \mathbf{D}_{2e} \dot{\mathbf{Y}}_{22} \\
=& \mathbf{X}_2^{\mathsf{T}} (-\mathbf{Q}_2 - \mathbf{D}_2 \mathbf{A}_2) \mathbf{X}_2 + \hat{\mathbf{\Delta}}_3^{-1} \mathbf{Y}_{22}^{\mathsf{T}} \mathbf{D}_{2e}^{\mathsf{T}} \mathbf{Y}_{21}^{\mathsf{T}} \mathbf{B}_2^{\mathsf{T}} \mathbf{D}_2 \mathbf{X}_2 + \mathbf{X}_2^{\mathsf{T}} \mathbf{D}_2 (\mathbf{A}_2 \mathbf{X}_2 + \mathbf{B}_2 \hat{\mathbf{\Delta}}_3^{-1} \mathbf{Y}_{21} \mathbf{D}_{2e} \mathbf{Y}_{22}) \\
& + \dot{\mathbf{Y}}_{22}^{\mathsf{T}} \mathbf{D}_{2e}^{\mathsf{T}} \mathbf{\Gamma}_2 \mathbf{D}_{2e} \mathbf{Y}_{22} + \mathbf{Y}_{22}^{\mathsf{T}} \dot{\mathbf{D}}_{2e}^{\mathsf{T}} \mathbf{\Gamma}_2 \mathbf{D}_{2e} \mathbf{Y}_{22} + \mathbf{Y}_{22}^{\mathsf{T}} \mathbf{D}_{2e}^{\mathsf{T}} \mathbf{\Gamma}_2 \dot{\mathbf{D}}_{2e} \mathbf{Y}_{22} + \mathbf{Y}_{22}^{\mathsf{T}} \mathbf{D}_{2e}^{\mathsf{T}} \mathbf{\Gamma}_2 \mathbf{D}_{2e} \dot{\mathbf{Y}}_{22} \\
=& -\mathbf{X}_2^{\mathsf{T}} \mathbf{Q}_2 \mathbf{X}_2 + 2\mathbf{Y}_{22}^{\mathsf{T}} \mathbf{D}_{2e}^{\mathsf{T}} \mathbf{Y}_{21}^{\mathsf{T}} \hat{\mathbf{\Delta}}_3^{-1} \mathbf{B}_2^{\mathsf{T}} \mathbf{D}_2 \mathbf{X}_2 + 2\mathbf{Y}_{22}^{\mathsf{T}} \mathbf{D}_{2e}^{\mathsf{T}} \mathbf{\Gamma}_2 \dot{\mathbf{D}}_{2e} \mathbf{Y}_{22} + 2\mathbf{Y}_{22}^{\mathsf{T}} \mathbf{D}_{2e}^{\mathsf{T}} \mathbf{\Gamma}_2 \mathbf{D}_{2e} \dot{\mathbf{Y}}_{22} \\
=& -\mathbf{X}_2^{\mathsf{T}} \mathbf{Q}_2 \mathbf{X}_2 + 2\mathbf{Y}_{22}^{\mathsf{T}} \mathbf{D}_{2e}^{\mathsf{T}} [\mathbf{Y}_{21}^{\mathsf{T}} \hat{\mathbf{\Delta}}_3^{-1} \mathbf{B}_2^{\mathsf{T}} \mathbf{D}_2 \mathbf{X}_2 + \mathbf{\Gamma}_2 \dot{\mathbf{D}}_{2e} \mathbf{Y}_{22} + \mathbf{\Gamma}_2 \mathbf{D}_{2e} \dot{\mathbf{Y}}_{22}].
\end{aligned} \tag{38}
$$

Since $\dot{\mathbf{D}}_{2e} = \dot{\mathbf{D}}_2$, $\dot{\mathbf{D}}_2$ is assumed to

$$
\dot{\mathbf{D}}_2 = -\mathbf{\Gamma}_2^{-1} (\mathbf{Y}_{21}^{\mathsf{T}} \hat{\mathbf{\Delta}}_3^{-1} \mathbf{B}_2^{\mathsf{T}} \mathbf{D}_2 \mathbf{X}_2 + \mathbf{\Gamma}_2 \mathbf{D}_{2e} \dot{\mathbf{Y}}_{22}) \mathbf{Y}_{22}^{-1}. \tag{39}
$$

If follows from (38) and (39) that

$$
\dot{V} = -\mathbf{X}_2^{\mathsf{T}} \mathbf{Q}_2 \mathbf{X}_2 \leq 0. \tag{40}
$$

We have seen, from (37) and (40), that (33) is stablized. In this way, the adaptive control u_{20} can track the ideal yaw rotation speed $\tilde{\omega}_0$ well, which ensures that all signals of the control system are bounded. Thus, by choosing appropriate parameters, the tracking error of the yaw speed can be controlled in a small area.

In order to improve the robustness of the yaw rotation speed subsystem, we introduce an integral sliding mode control method. On the one hand, the basic part of controller u_2 is designed as (28). On the other hand, a sliding mode function $S(\omega(t))$ is defined as [25]

$$
S(\omega(t)) = G[\omega(t) - \omega_0(0)] - G \int_0^t \dot{\omega}_0(\eta) \mathrm{d}\eta,
$$

where G is an appropriate constant. Then, the switching control part is designed on the integral sliding mainifold which is defined as

$$S(\omega_0(t)) = 0.$$

Thus, the switching control part of controller u_2 is designed as

$$u_{21} = -(G^{-1}\gamma + \varepsilon \parallel e_2 \parallel)\mathrm{sgn}(S(\omega_0(t))). \tag{41}$$

where ε is the control parameter related to the uncertainties, and γ is the sliding mode control parameter. As a consequence, from (28) and (41), the controller is eventually designed as

$$u_2 = u_{20} + u_{21}.$$

4. Simulation Results

In this section, we present three simulation results to verify the effectiveness of the proposed method. First, we performed a comparison between using the dynamical target and the statical target. Then, we report the actual trajectories of the towed ship affected by different steering coefficients. Finally, we give an uncertain factor acted on the forward speed subsystem to validate the robustness of the proposed controller.

The target trajectory curve of the STS is assumed to be

$$\tilde{r}_0 = (\tilde{x}_0(t), \tilde{y}_0(t))^{\mathrm{T}} = (80\sin(\frac{t-\pi}{2}) + 40t - 40\pi, 80 - 80\cos(\frac{t-\pi}{2}))^{\mathrm{T}},$$

where $t \in [0, 2\pi], l = 80\sqrt{2}, \phi(t) = 80\sqrt{2}te^{-t}, k_0(s(t)) = \frac{1}{320\cos(\frac{t-\pi}{4})}$.

4.1. A Comparison between the Dynamical Target and Statical Target

On the one hand, the statical tracking target (19) is expressed by

$$\begin{cases} \tilde{v}_0 = \sqrt{\dot{x}^2 + \dot{y}^2} = 80\cos(\frac{t-\pi}{4}), \\ \tilde{\omega}_0 = \frac{\dot{x}\ddot{y} - \ddot{x}\dot{y}}{\dot{x}^2 + \dot{y}^2} = \frac{1}{4}. \end{cases} \tag{42}$$

If we use the statical tracking target (42) to design controller u_1 and u_2, the initial speed error is not zero, given by

$$\begin{cases} v_0(0) - \tilde{v}_0(0) = -80\cos(-\frac{\pi}{4}) = -40\sqrt{2}, \\ \omega_0(0) - \tilde{\omega}_0(0) = -\frac{1}{4}. \end{cases}$$

On the other hand, the dynamical tracking target (20) is expressed by

$$\begin{cases} \tilde{v}_0 = 80\sqrt{2}te^{-t}, \\ \tilde{\omega}_0 = k_0(s)v_0(t). \end{cases}$$

The relative parameters of the towing system are set as $\lambda = 1.3, L = 2.6$ m$, \tau = 0.25, S = 3.3$ m$^2, \rho = 1000$ kg/m$^3, d = 0.1$ m$, C_f = 0.063, m_0 + M_{x0} = 103$ kg$, m_1 + M_{x1} = 103$ kg$, I_{z0} + J_{z0} = 30$ kg$\cdot$m$^2, I_{z1} + J_{z1} = 30$ kg$\cdot$m$^2, Q_1 = \mathrm{diag}(10, 100), R = 1, k_2 = 204, G = 1, \varepsilon = 0.1, \gamma = 0.3$. Therefore, all the required quantities in the trajectory tracking controllers u_1 and u_2 are available in hand. Accordingly, the time histories of all state variables can be simulated.

As can be seen in Figure 3, by using the dynamical tracking target, both the initial forward speed and yaw rotation speed errors are smaller than the one using statical tracking target. Comparing Figure 4a with Figure 4b, we see that the actual motion trajectory of the tugboat deviates largely from the target curve by using the statical tracking target, whereas the actual motion trajectory of the tugboat coincides well the target curve via the dynamical tracking target. In other words, by using the dynamical tracking target, accurate trajectory tracking can be achieved as long as the curvature tracking error is controllable. Even though forward speed and yaw rotation speed errors are large, accurate tracking can be also maintained as long as the relative curvature is well tracked.

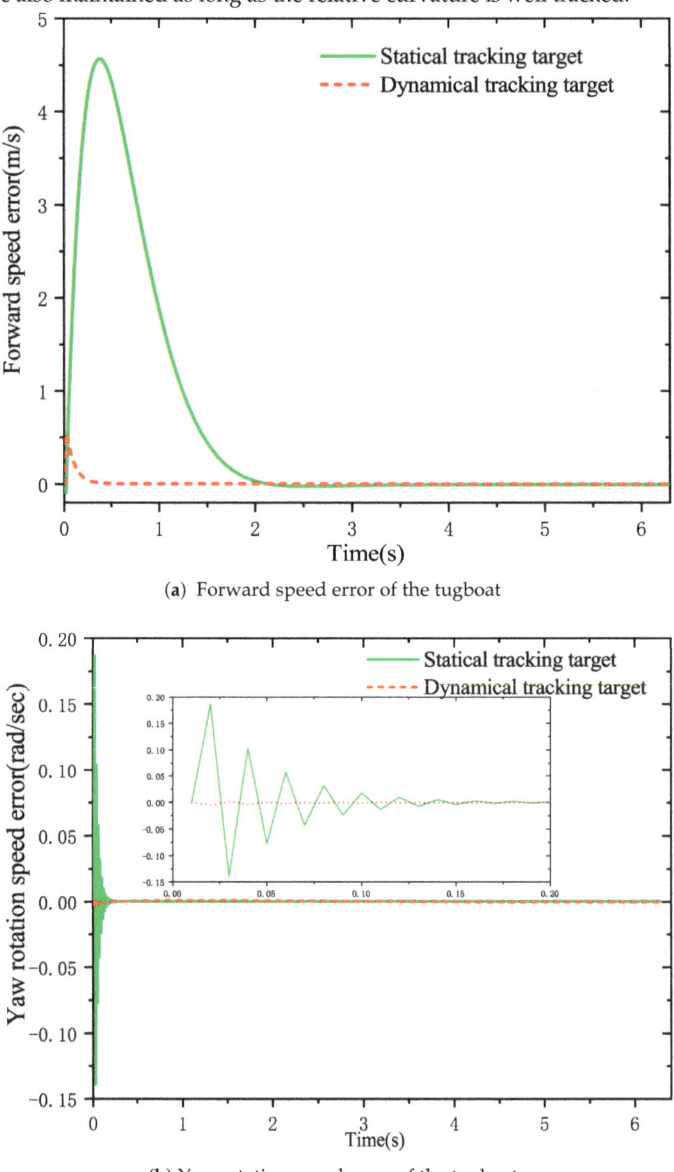

(**a**) Forward speed error of the tugboat

(**b**) Yaw rotation speed error of the tugboat

Figure 3. Actual speed error of the tugboat.

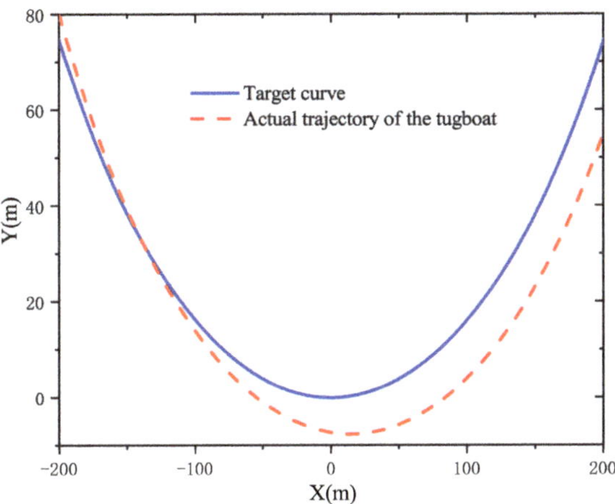

(**a**) Actual motion trajectory of the tugboat with statical target

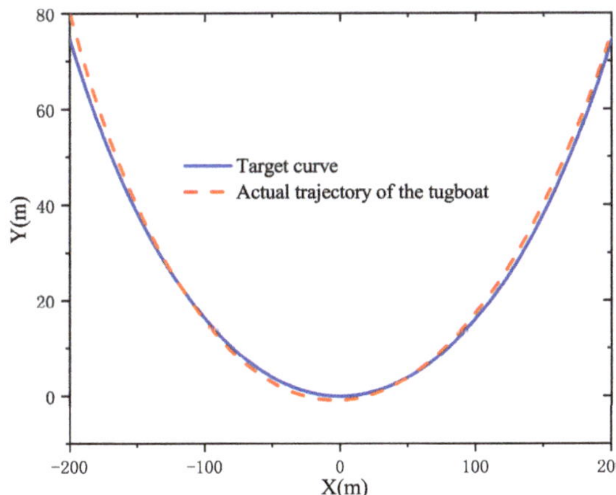

(**b**) Actual motion trajectory of the tugboat with dynamical target

Figure 4. Actual motion trajectory curve of the tugboat by using different speed targets.

4.2. Actual Trajectories of the Towed Ship with Different Steering Coefficients

In order to further investigate the influence of the steering coefficient on the actual trajectory of the towed ship, we choose different steering coefficients and lengths of towline for simulations.

When the length of towline is relatively small, such as $a = 20$ m, the actual motion trajectory of the towed ship deviates largely from the target curve, if the steering coefficient $\mu = -12$ is adopted, as depicted in Figure 5a. However, for the same length of the towline, the actual trajectory of the towed ship follows very well with the target curve by using the steering coefficient $\mu = -16$ in Figure 5b. When the length of the towline is relatively large, such as $a = 40$ m, we need a larger steering coefficient to obtain a satisfactory tracking performance, such as $\mu = -20$, as depicted in Figure 6. As a consequence, when the length of the towline is smaller, a satisfactory trajectory tracking performance can be obtained with smaller steering coefficient, whereas, when the length of the towline is large, a larger steering coefficient must be applied to keep the tracking error of the towed ship within a smaller range.

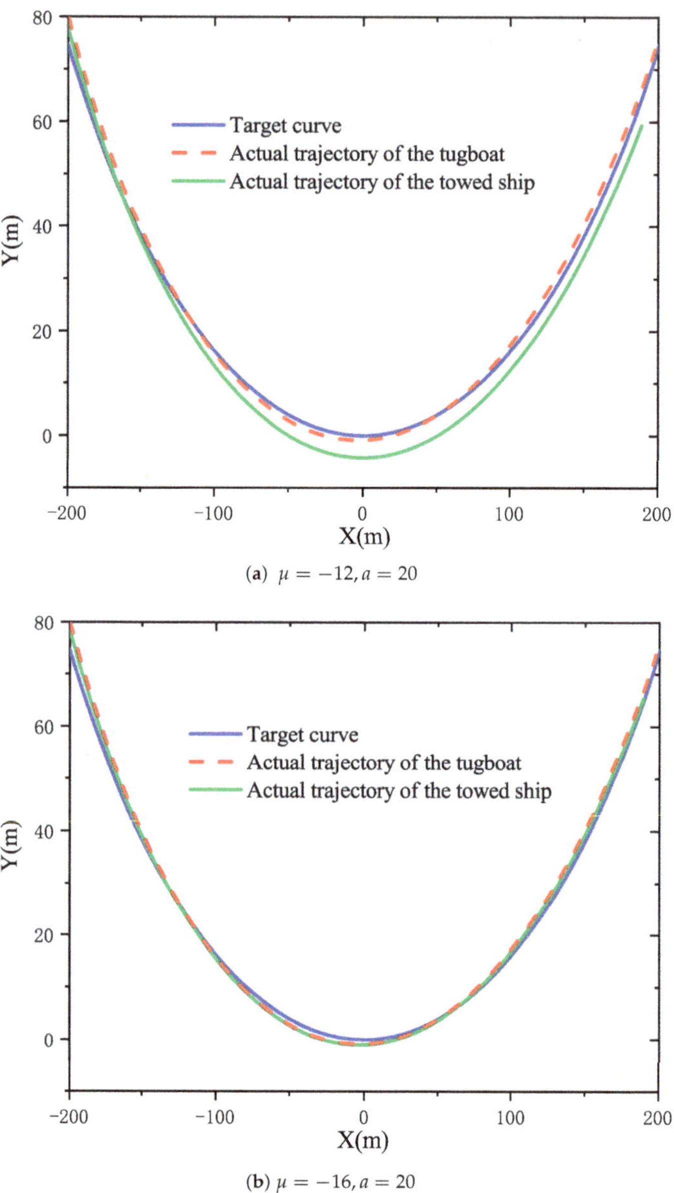

(**a**) $\mu = -12, a = 20$

(**b**) $\mu = -16, a = 20$

Figure 5. Comparison of actual motion trajectories of the towed ship between different steering coefficients.

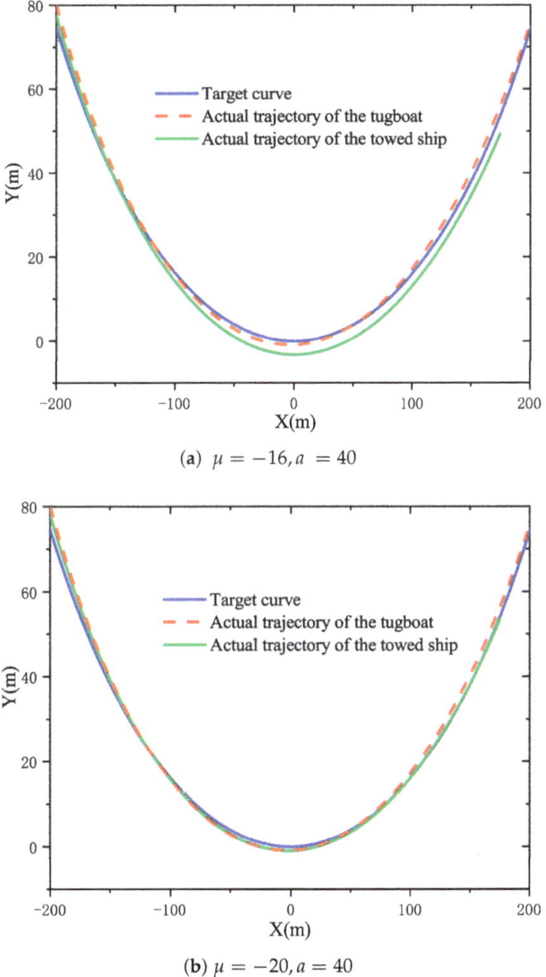

(**a**) $\mu = -16, a = 40$

(**b**) $\mu = -20, a = 40$

Figure 6. Comparison of actual motion trajectories of the towed ship between different steering coefficients.

4.3. Robustness of the Proposed Controller

Since the controllers are designed by considering the sliding mode control and inverse dynamics adaptive control methods simultaneously, it has highly robust. Moreover, by using the dynamical tracking target, even though the forward speed and yaw rotation speed error subsystems are unstable due to uncertain factors, the towed ship is also able to achieve satisfactory tracking performance.

Assume that the forward speed error subsystem is subject to an uncertain factor, which is given by

$$\dot{\mathbf{Y}} = \mathbf{A}_1 \mathbf{Y} + \mathbf{B}_1 u_1(t) + \boldsymbol{\eta}(t) + \boldsymbol{d}(t),$$

where $\boldsymbol{d}(t) = (10.2y_1, 10.2y_2)^{\mathrm{T}}$ is an uncertain factor.

As shown in Figures 7 and 8, although forward speed and yaw rotation speed errors are large and even divergent, the actual motion trajectory of the tugboat almost coincides with the target curve. The main reason is that the relative curvature error which is obtained by dividing the actual yaw rotation speed by the actual forward speed is small via the dynamical tracking target. Therefore, as long as the relative curvature error is small enough, the accurate tracking of the target trajectory curve can still be guaranteed. Moreover, the towed ship can also obtain satisfactory tracking performance by means of an appropriate steering coefficient, such as $\mu = -20$. Otherwise, there will be a large deviation from the target trajectory curve, such as $\mu = -16$, as depicted in Figure 8.

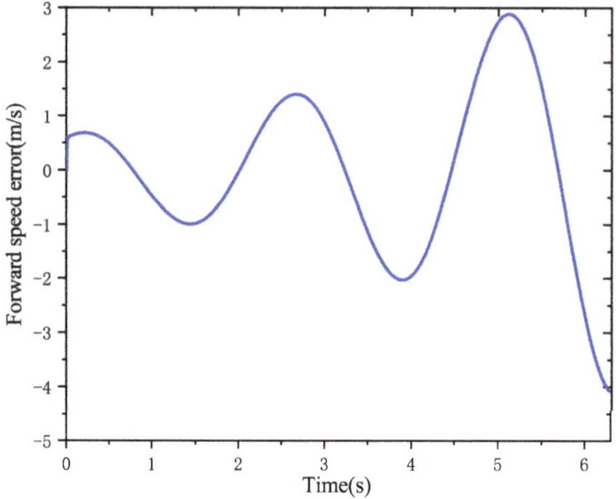

(**a**) Forward speed error of the tugboat

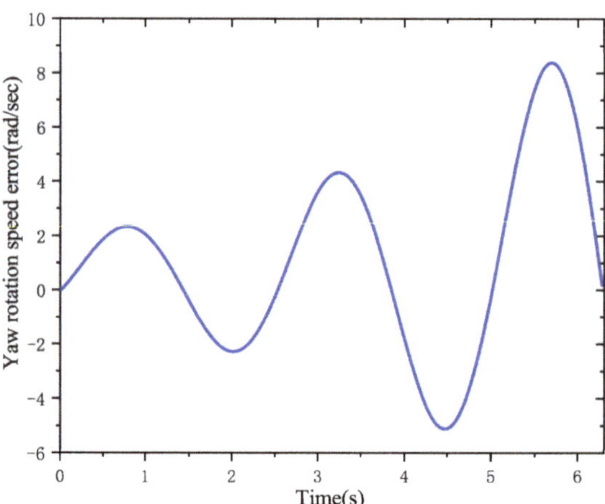

(**b**) Yaw rotation speed error of the tugboat

Figure 7. Actual motion speed error of the tugboat under the uncertain factor $d(t)$.

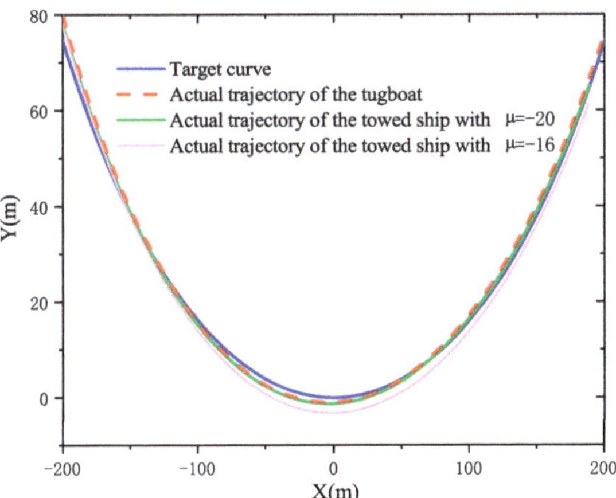

Figure 8. Actual motion trajectory curve under the uncertain factor $d(t)$.

5. Conclusions

A novel control strategy for the ship towing system is proposed, so that both the tugboat and the towed ship move along the given target trajectory curve accurately. Compared with the existing research studies, the proposed method has the following features.

- The towed ship is able to move along the trajectory of the tugboat by introducing an appropriate passive steering angle. Then, the original motion control problem is transformed into the tugboat tracking the target trajectory curve.
- The target trajectory curve is converted into a dynamical tracking target by using the relative curvature of the target curve, which can fundamentally solve the problem of accurate tracking for the ship towing system.
- By combining dynamical tracking target, sliding mode control and inverse dynamic adaptive control, the torque controller has strong robustness. Even if the error speed subsystem is unstable affected by an uncertain factor, all bodies can still track the target trajectory curve accurately.

The proposed method makes full use of the motion laws under the kinetics model and solves the accuracy problem of trajectory tracking by using the dynamical tracking method. In fact, the proposed method can be applied to the precise motion control design of general mechanical models.

Author Contributions: Conceptualization, O.L. and Y.Z.; methodology, O.L.; software, O.L.; validation, O.L.; formal analysis, O.L.; investigation, O.L.; resources, Y.Z.; data curation, O.L.; writing—original draft preparation, O.L.; writing—review and editing, O.L. and Y.Z.; visualization, O.L.; supervision, Y.Z.; project administration, Y.Z.; funding acquisition, Y.Z. All authors have read and agreed to the published version of the manuscript.

Funding: This work was supported by Research Foundation for Talents of Guizhou University ([2017]61), the Science and Technology Program of Guizhou Province ([2018]1047), the fund project of Key Laboratory of Advanced Manufacturing technology, Ministry of Education, Guizhou University (KY[2018]478) and the Foundation of Postgraduate of Guizhou Province (2019032).

Institutional Review Board Statement: Not applicable.

Informed Consent Statement: Not applicable.

Data Availability Statement: Not applicable.

Conflicts of Interest: The authors declare no conflict of interest. The funders had no role in the design of the study; in the collection, analyses, or interpretation of data; in the writing of the manuscript, or in the decision to publish the results.

References

1. Tao, J.; Du, L.; Dehmer, M.; Wen, Y.Q.; Xie, G.G.; Zhou, Q. Path following control for towing system of cylindrical drilling platform in presence of disturbances and uncertainties. *ISA Trans.* **2019**, *95*, 185–193. [CrossRef]
2. Kishimoto, T.; Kijima, K. The manoeuvring characteristics on tug-towed ship systems. *IFAC Proc. Vol.* **2001**, *34*, 173–178. [CrossRef]
3. Laumond, J.P.; Risler, J.J. Nonholonomic systems: Controllability and complexity. *Theor. Comput. Sci.* **1996**, *157*, 101–114. [CrossRef]
4. Tao, J.; Henn, R.; Sharma, S.D. Dynamic behavior of a tow system under an autopilot on the tug. *Int. Symp. Workshop Forces Act. Manoeuring Vessel* **1998**, *2*, 16–18.
5. Tao, J. Autonomous oscillations and bifurcations of a tug-tanker tow. *Ship Technol. Res.* **1997**, *44*, 4–12.
6. Lee, M.L. Dynamic stability of nonlinear barge-towing system. *Appl. Math. Model.* **1989**, *13*, 693–701. [CrossRef]
7. Wu, Y.Y.; Wu, Y.Q. Robust stabilization for nonholonomic systerms with state delay and nonline drifts. *J. Control Theory Appl.* **2011**, *9*, 256–260. [CrossRef]
8. Zhang, D.S. Optimization Design of Ship Rudder Steering Stability Optimization Control System. *Inst. Manag. Sci. Ind. Eng.* **2019**, *1*, 535–538.
9. Alessandretti, A.; Aguiar, A.P.; Jones, C.N. Trajectory-tracking and path-following controllers for constrained underactuated vehicles using Model Predictive Control. In Proceedings of the 2013 European Control Conference (ECC), Zurich, Switzerland, 17–19 July 2013; Volume 1, pp. 1371–1376.
10. Abdelaal, M.; Fränzle, M.; Hahn, A. Nonlinear model predictive control for tracking of underactuated vessels under input constraints. In Proceedings of the 2015 IEEE European Modelling Symposium (EMS), Madrid, Spain, 6–8 October 2015; Volume 1, pp. 6–8.
11. Xu, H.; Ioannou, P.A. Robust adaptive control for a class of MIMO nonlinear systems with guaranteed error bounds. *IEEE Trans. Autom. Control* **2003**, *48*, 728–742.
12. Jin, H.K.; Sung, J.Y. Adaptive Event-Triggered Control Strategy for Ensuring Predefined Three-Dimensional Tracking Performance of Uncertain Nonlinear Underactuated Underwater Vehicles. *Mathematics* **2021**, *9*, 137.
13. Ashrafiuon, H.; Muske, K.R.; McNinch, L.C.; Soltan, R.A. Sliding-mode tracking control of surface vessels. *IEEE Trans. Ind. Electron.* **2008**, *55*, 4004–4012. [CrossRef]
14. Lefeber, E.; Pettersen, K.Y.; Nijmeijer, H. Tracking control of an underactuated ship. *IEEE Trans. Control Syst. Technol.* **2003**, *11*, 52–61. [CrossRef]
15. Sun, L. Dynamic Modeling, Trajectory Generation and Tracking for Towed Cable Systems. Ph.D. Thesis, Brigham Young University, Provo, UT, USA, 2012; pp. 1–137.
16. Zhang, Q.; Ding, Z.; Zhang, M. Adaptive self-regulation PID control of course-keeping for ships. *Pol. Marit. Res.* **2020**, *27*, 39–45. [CrossRef]
17. Fossen, T.I.; Pettersen, K.Y.; Galeazzi, R. Line-of-sight path following for dubins paths with adaptive sideslip compensation of drift forces. *IEEE Trans. Control Syst. Technol.* **2015**, *23*, 820–827. [CrossRef]
18. Fossen, T.I.; Breivik, M.; Skjetne, R. Line-of-sight path following of underactuated marine craft. *IFAC Proc. Vol.* **2003**, *36*, 211–216. [CrossRef]
19. Paliotta, C.; Lefeber, E.; Pettersen, K.Y.; Pinto, J.; Costa, M. Trajectory tracking and path following for underactuated marine vehicles. *IEEE Trans. Control Syst. Technol.* **2018**, *27*, 1423–1437. [CrossRef]
20. Zhang, G.Q.; Zhang, X.K.; Zheng, Y.F. Adaptive neural path-following control for underactuated ships in fields of marine practice. *Ocean Eng.* **2015**, *104*, 558–567. [CrossRef]
21. Zhou, Y.S.; Wang, Z.H.; Chung, K.K. Turning motion control design of a two-wheeled inverted pendulum by using planar curve theory and dynamical tracking target. *J. Optim. Theory Appl.* **2019**, *181*, 634–652. [CrossRef]
22. Benedict, K.; Kirchhoff, M.; Fischer, S.; Gluch, M.; Klaes, S.; Baldauf, M. Application of Fast Time Simulation Technologies for enhanced Ship Manoeuvring Operation. *IFAC Proc. Vol.* **2010**, *43*, 79–84. [CrossRef]
23. Bernitsas, M.M.; Kekridis, N.S. Simulation and stability of ship towing. *Int. Shipbuild. Prog.* **1985**, *32*, 112–123. [CrossRef]
24. Bernitsas, M.M.; Kekridis, N.S. Nonlinear stability analysis of ship towed by elastic rope. *J. Ship Res.* **1986**, *30*, 136–146. [CrossRef]
25. Zhou, Y.S.; Wang, Z.H. Robust motion control of a two-wheeled inverted pendulum with an input delay based on optimal integral sliding mode manifold. *Nonlinear Dyn.* **2016**, *85*, 2065–2074. [CrossRef]

 *mathematics*

Article

Optimal Control Problem Solution with Phase Constraints for Group of Robots by Pontryagin Maximum Principle and Evolutionary Algorithm

Askhat Diveev [1], Elena Sofronova [1,*] and Ivan Zelinka [2,3]

[1] Department of Robotics Control, Federal Research Center "Computer Science and Control" of the Russian Academy of Sciences, 119333 Moscow, Russia; frccsc@frccsc.ru

[2] Faculty of Electrical and Electronics Engineering, Ton Duc Thang University, Ho Chi Minh City 758307, Vietnam; ivan.zelinka@tdt.edu.vn or ivan.zelinka@vsb.cz

[3] Department of Computer Science, FEI, VSB Technical University of Ostrava, 70800 Ostrava, Czech Republic

* Correspondence: sofronova_ea@mail.ru

Received: 29 October 2020; Accepted: 20 November 2020; Published: 25 November 2020

Abstract: A numerical method based on the Pontryagin maximum principle for solving an optimal control problem with static and dynamic phase constraints for a group of objects is considered. Dynamic phase constraints are introduced to avoid collisions between objects. Phase constraints are included in the functional in the form of smooth penalty functions. Additional parameters for special control modes and the terminal time of the control process were introduced. The search for additional parameters and the initial conditions for the conjugate variables was performed by the modified self-organizing migrating algorithm. An example of using this approach to solve the optimal control problem for the oncoming movement of two mobile robots is given. Simulation and comparison with direct approach showed that the problem is multimodal, and it approves application of the evolutionary algorithm for its solution.

Keywords: optimal control problem; evolutionary computation; robotics applications

---

1. Introduction

The optimal control belongs to complex computational problems for which there are no universal solution algorithms. The most well-known result in this area [1] transforms the optimization problem into a boundary-value problem, and the dimension of the problem doubles. The goal of solving the boundary-value problem is to find the initial conditions for conjugate variables such that the vector of state variables falls into a given terminal condition. In general, for this problem, there is no guarantee that the functional for the boundary-value problem is not unimodal and convex on the space of initial conditions of conjugate variables.

The optimal control problem with phase constraints is considered. Phase constraints are included in the functional, so they are included in the system of equations for conjugate variables. This greatly complicates the analysis of the problem on the convexity and unimodality of the target functional. The accurate solution of optimal control problem has to use additional functions and regularization of equations at the search of control [2,3]. An additional problem in solving a boundary-value problem is determination of time for checking the fulfillment of boundary conditions.

In this paper, for the numerical solution of the problem, it is proposed to use evolutionary algorithms that have shown efficiency in solving optimal control problems [4]. SOMA is a universal algorithm for various difficult optimization problems [5,6]. However, our attempt to apply SOMA to the optimal control problem of four robots with constraints has failed to find a good solution for any values of the algorithm parameters. We supposed that the modification of each possible solution in population in the process of evolution using the best current possible solution is not enough [7]. We expanded the modification of SOMA by introducing the best historical solution among randomly selected ones for each possible solution in the population.

The article consists of an introduction and eight sections. Statement of the optimal control problem with phase constraints is presented in Section 2. Section 3 contains Pontryagin maximum principle as one of main approaches for its numerical solution. Section 4 contains a description of one of the evolutionary algorithms, modified SOMA. An example is given in Section 5. The computational experiment and results are presented in Section 6. Section 7 describes the search of optimal control by direct method. Alternative non-deterministic control methods are observed in Section 8. Results and future research directions are discussed in Section 9.

2. Optimal Control Problem with Phase Constraints for Group of Robots

Consider the problem of optimal control for a group of robots with phase constraints. Given a mathematical model of control objects in the form of the system of ordinary differential equations

$$\dot{\mathbf{x}}^j = \mathbf{f}^j(\mathbf{x}^j, \mathbf{u}^j), \tag{1}$$

where $\mathbf{x}^j$ is a state space vector of control object j, $\mathbf{x}^j \in \mathbb{R}^{n_j}$, $\mathbf{u}^j$ is a control vector of object j, $\mathbf{u}^j \in \mathrm{U}^j \subseteq \mathbb{R}^{m_j}$, U^j is a compact limited set, $m_j \leqslant n_j$, $j = 1, \ldots, M$, M is a number of objects. For the system (1) initial conditions are given

$$\mathbf{x}^j(0) = \mathbf{x}^{j,0} \in \mathbb{R}^{n_j}, j = 1, \ldots, M. \tag{2}$$

Given terminal conditions

$$\mathbf{x}^j(t_{f,j}) = \mathbf{x}^{j,f} \in \mathbb{R}^{n_j}, \tag{3}$$

where $t_{f,j}$ is an unknown limited positive value, that corresponds to time when object j achieves its terminal position

$$t_{f,j} \leqslant t^+, \tag{4}$$

t^+ is a given time of achievement of terminal conditions (3),

$$t_{f,j} = \begin{cases} t, \text{ if } t < t^+ \text{ and } \|\mathbf{x}^j(t) - \mathbf{x}^{j,f}\| \leqslant \varepsilon_1 \\ t^+, \text{ otherwise} \end{cases}, \tag{5}$$

ε_1 is a small positive value, $j = 1, \ldots, M$. The phase constraints are given

$$\varphi_i(\mathbf{x}^j(t)) \leqslant 0, \ i = 1, \ldots, r, \ j = 1, \ldots, M. \tag{6}$$

The conditions of collision avoidance are described as

$$\chi(\mathbf{x}^j(t), \mathbf{x}^k(t)) \leqslant 0, \ j = 1, \ldots, M-1, \ k = j+1, \ldots, M. \tag{7}$$

The quality functional is given in general integral form

$$J_0 = \int_0^{t_f} f_0(\mathbf{x}^1(t), \dots, \mathbf{x}^M(t), \mathbf{u}^1(t), \dots, \mathbf{u}^M(t))dt \to \min, \tag{8}$$

where

$$t_f = \max\{t_{f,1}, \dots, t_{f,M}\}. \tag{9}$$

It is necessary to find control as a time function

$$\mathbf{u}^j = \mathbf{v}^j(t),\ j = 1, \dots, M, \tag{10}$$

in order to provide terminal conditions (3) with optimal value of functional (8) without violation of constraints (6) and with collision avoidance (7). For a numerical solution of the problem, let us insert phase constraints and terminal conditions in quality functional (8)

$$J_1 = \int_0^{t_f} f_0(\mathbf{x}^1(t), \dots, \mathbf{x}^M(t), \mathbf{u}^1(t), \dots, \mathbf{u}^M(t))dt + a \int_0^{t_f} \sum_{i=1}^{r} \sum_{j=1}^{M} \mu^2(\varphi_i(\mathbf{x}^j(t)))dt +$$

$$b \int_0^{t_f} \sum_{j=1}^{M-1} \sum_{k=j+1}^{M} \mu^2(\chi(\mathbf{x}^j(t), \mathbf{x}^k(t)))dt + c \sum_{j=1}^{M} ||\mathbf{x}^j(t_f) - \mathbf{x}^{j,f}|| \to \min, \tag{11}$$

where a, b, c are given positive weight coefficients, $\mu(A) = \max\{0, A\}$.

To solve the problem stated above, we use the Pontryagin maximum principle.

3. The Pontryagin Maximum Principle

The Pontryagin maximum principle allows one to transform the problem of optimization on infinite dimensional space to the boundary-value problem for the system of differential Equations (1). Let us construct Hamilton function for this problem on the base of the system (1) and the quality functional (2) without terminal conditions

$$H(\mathbf{x}^1, \dots, \mathbf{x}^M, \mathbf{u}^1, \dots, \mathbf{u}^M, \psi) = -f_0(\mathbf{x}^1, \dots, \mathbf{x}^M, \mathbf{u}^1, \dots, \mathbf{u}^M) -$$

$$a \sum_{i=1}^{r} \sum_{j=1}^{M} \mu^2(\varphi_i(\mathbf{x}^j)) - b \sum_{j=1}^{M-1} \sum_{k=j+1}^{M} \mu^2(\chi(\mathbf{x}^j, \mathbf{x}^k)) + \psi^T \mathbf{f}^j(\mathbf{x}^j, \mathbf{u}^j), \tag{12}$$

where $\psi = [\psi_1 \dots \psi_n]^T$ is a vector of conjugate variables, $n = n_1 + \dots + n_M$,

$$\dot{\psi} = -\frac{\partial H(\mathbf{x}^1, \dots, \mathbf{x}^M \mathbf{u}^1, \dots, \mathbf{u}^M, \psi)}{\partial \mathbf{x}^1, \dots, \partial \mathbf{x}^M}. \tag{13}$$

According to the Pontryagin maximum principle, a necessary condition for optimal control is the maximum of Hamilton function (12)

$$\max_{\mathbf{u}^1 \in U^1, \dots, \mathbf{u}^M \in U^M} H(\mathbf{x}^1, \dots, \mathbf{x}^M, \mathbf{u}^1, \dots, \mathbf{u}^M, \psi). \tag{14}$$

Pontryagin maximum principle allows one to transform the optimal control problem to a boundary-value problem. It is necessary to find the initial values of conjugate variables so that the state vector reaches terminal conditions (3). To solve the boundary-value problem, we have to solve a finite dimensional problem of nonlinear programming with the following functional

$$F(\mathbf{q}) = \sum_{j=1}^{M} \|\mathbf{x}^j(t_{f,j}) - \mathbf{x}^{j,f}\| \to \min_{\mathbf{q} \in Q}, \tag{15}$$

where $\mathbf{q} = [q_1 \ldots q_n]^T$, Q is a limited compact set, $q_i = \psi_i(0)$, $i = 1, \ldots, n$,

$$\sum_{i=1}^{n} q_i^2 = 1. \tag{16}$$

In a boundary-value problem, it is not known exactly when it is necessary to check the boundary conditions (15). The maximum principle does not provide equations for definition of terminal time $t_{f,j}$ of the control process, while a numerical search of some possible solutions may not reach the terminal condition. To avoid this problem, let us add parameter q_{n+1} for the time limit of reaching the terminal state. As a result, the goal functional for the boundary-value problem is the following

$$\tilde{F}(\mathbf{q}) = \sum_{j=1}^{M} \|\mathbf{x}^j(t^+ + q_{n+1}) - \mathbf{x}^{f,j}\| \to \min_{\tilde{\mathbf{q}} \in \tilde{Q}}, \tag{17}$$

where $\tilde{\mathbf{q}} = [q_1 \ldots q_{n+1}]^T$, $\tilde{Q} = Q \times [q_{n+1}^-; q_{n+1}^+]$, q_{n+1}^-, q_{n+1}^+ are low and up limitations of the parameter q_{n+1}. During the search process, we can decrease time t^+ according to sign of parameter q_{n+1}. If found parameter q_{n+1} is less than zero, then t^+ is decreased and the interval for values of parameter $[q_{n+1}^-; q_{n+1}^+]$ is also narrowed.

4. Evolutionary Algorithm

The boundary-value problem may have a nonconvex and nonunimodal objective functional (15) on the parameter space $\mathbf{q}$, therefore, to solve this problem, it is advisable to use an evolutionary algorithm.

Evolutionary algorithms differ in the form of changing possible solutions. The first evolutionary algorithms appeared at the end of the XX century and continue to appear. Currently, hundreds of evolutionary algorithms are known. Most of them are named after animals, although the connection between animal behavior and computational algorithms is not strictly proven anywhere and is determined only by the statement of the author of the algorithm. Common steps of evolutionary algorithms are: generation of a set of possible solutions, assessment of solutions by objective function to find one or more best solutions, modification of solutions in accordance with the value of its objective function and with information about the values of the objective functions of other solutions by evolutionary operators.

In this work, we investigate the application of the Pontryagin maximum principle to solve the optimal control problem for a group of robots with phase constraints, and do not compare evolutionary algorithms. We applied one of the effective evolutionary algorithms, self-organizing migrating algorithm (SOMA) [5,6], with modification [7] to find the parameters, i.e., initial conditions of conjugate variables and additional parameter q_{n+1} for terminal time. The modified SOMA includes the following steps.

Generate a population of H possible solutions, taking into account

$$\tilde{q}_i^j = \xi(q_i^+ - q_i^-) + q_i^-, \ i = 1, \ldots, n+1, \ j = 1, \ldots, H, \tag{18}$$

where $q_i^+ = 1$, $q_i^- = -1$, $i = 1, \ldots, n$, $q_{n+1}^+ = 0.2$, $q_{n+1}^- = -2.5$, H is a cardinal number of the population set, ζ is a random number from 0 to 1. Normalize the first n possible solutions according to (16)

$$q_i^j = \frac{\tilde{q}_i^j}{\sqrt{\sum_{k=1}^n (\tilde{q}_k^j)^2}}, \ i = 1, \ldots, n, \ j = 1, \ldots, H. \tag{19}$$

In the optimization problem, we have to find a vector of optimal parameters $\mathbf{q} = [q_1 \ldots q_{n+1}]^T$ in order to receive the minimal value of functional

$$J_1(\mathbf{q}) = \sum_{j=1}^M \|\mathbf{x}(t^+ + q_{n+1}) - \mathbf{x}^{f,j}\| \to \min. \tag{20}$$

For each vector of parameters, we set a historical vector. Initially, historical vectors contain zero elements

$$\tilde{q}_i^j = 0, \ i = 1, \ldots, n+1, \ j = 1, \ldots, H. \tag{21}$$

Calculate the values of functional for each possible solution

$$f_j = J_1(\mathbf{q}^j), \ j = 1, \ldots, H. \tag{22}$$

Find the best possible solution $\mathbf{q}^{j_0}$ on a stage of evolution

$$J_1(\mathbf{q}^{j_0}) = \min\{f_1, \ldots, f_H\}. \tag{23}$$

For each historical vector, find the best vector among the randomly selected ones $\tilde{\mathbf{q}}^j$ in current population

$$J_1(\mathbf{q}^{j*}) = \min\{f_{j_1}, \ldots, f_{j_K}\}, \tag{24}$$

where $j_i \in \{1, \ldots, H\}$, $i = 1, \ldots, K$. Transform each historical vector

$$\tilde{q}_i^j \leftarrow \alpha \tilde{q}_i^j + \beta(q_i^{j*} - q_i^j), \tag{25}$$

where $i = 1, \ldots, n+1, j = 1, \ldots, H$, α and β are parameters of the algorithm, positive numbers less than one. Let us set a step $t = \delta$. Calculate some new values for each possible solution

$$\hat{q}_i^j(t) = \begin{cases} q_i^j + \tilde{q}_j^i + t(q_i^{j_0} - q_i^j), & \text{if } \zeta < P_{rt} \\ q_i^j + \tilde{q}_j^i, & \text{otherwise} \end{cases}, \tag{26}$$

where $i = 1, \ldots, n+1$, P_{rt} is a parameter of the algorithm. Check each component of a new vector for restrictions

$$q_i^j(t) = \frac{\hat{q}_i^j(t)}{\sqrt{\sum_{k=1}^n (\hat{q}_k^j(t))^2}}, \ i = 1, \ldots, n, \tag{27}$$

$$q_{n+1}^j = \begin{cases} q_{n+1}^+, & \text{if } \hat{q}_{n+1}^j(t) > q_{n+1}^+ \\ q_{n+1}^-, & \text{if } \hat{q}_{n+1}^j(t) < q_{n+1}^- \\ \hat{q}_{n+1}^j(t), & \text{otherwise} \end{cases}. \tag{28}$$

Calculate the functional for a new vector

$$f_j(t) = J_1(\mathbf{q}^j(t)). \tag{29}$$

If $f_j(t) \leqslant f_j$, then we change possible solution $\mathbf{q}^j$ by a new vector

$$\mathbf{q}^j \leftarrow \mathbf{q}^j(t), \tag{30}$$

$$f_j \leftarrow f_j(t). \tag{31}$$

Increase t

$$t = t + \delta. \tag{32}$$

If $t < P_{length}$ then repeat calculations (25)–(32), P_{length} is a parameter of the algorithm. Repeat calculations (22)–(32) for all possible solutions in the population. Then again, find the best solution (23) and change historical vector (25). Repeat all stages R times. The last best vector is a solution of the optimization problem.

An applied algorithm with historical vector is called a modified SOMA. The value of parameter $\beta = 0$ transforms the algorithm from modified SOMA to classical SOMA. Pseudo code of the modified SOMA has the following form, see Algorithm 1.

Algorithm 1: Modified SOMA for Optimal Control Problem.

```
Procedure ModSOMA (H, R, P_length, P_rt, δ ; var q^j0)
  for (j = 1, ..., H)              //generation of initial population
    s = 0
    for (i = 1, ..., n)           //normalization of first n elements of each q^j
      q^j_i = 2 · Random − 1
      s = s + (q^j_i)^2
    end for
    for (i = 1, ..., n)
      q^j_i = q^j_i / √s
      q̃^j_i = 0                   //* setting of initial values of historical vector
    end for
    q^j_{n+1} = q^-_{n+1} + Random · (q^+_{n+1} − q^-_{n+1})
    q̃^j_{n+1} = 0                 //*
    f_j = J_1(q^j)                //estimation of each possible solution
  end for
  for (r = 1, ..., R)        ;                          //generations
    j0 = 1
    for j = 2, ..., H             //search for the best current solution
      if f_j < f_j0 then
        j0 = j
    end for
    for (j = 1, ..., H)           //evolution of all solutions
      j* = Random(H)       //*
      for (l = 1, ..., K)    //* search for the best solutions among randomly selected ones
        j_l = Random(H)     //*
```

Algorithm 1: *Cont.*

```
            if f_{j_l} < f_{j*} then
                j* = j_l         //*
            end if          ;                                    //*
        end for              //*
        for (i = 1,...,n + 1)    //* transformation of historical vectors
```
$$\tilde{q}_i^j = \alpha \tilde{q}_i^j + Random \cdot \beta(q_i^{j*} - q_i^j) \quad //*$$
```
        end for              //*
        t = δ
        while t < P_{length} do       //termination condition
            s = 0
            for (i = 1,...,n)    //calculation of new values of parameters
            if Random < P_{rt} then
```
$$\hat{q}_i^j(t) = q_i^j + \tilde{q}_i^j + t(q_i^{j_0} - q_i^j)$$
```
            else
```
$$\hat{q}_i^j = q_i^j + \tilde{q}_i^j$$
```
            end if
```
$$s = s + (\tilde{q}_i^j)^2$$
```
            end for
            for (i = 1,...,n)        //normalization
```
$$q_i^j(t) = \hat{q}_i^j(t) / \sqrt{s}$$
```
            end for
            if  Random < P_{rt} then
```
$$\hat{q}_{n+1}^j(t) = q_{n+1}^j + \tilde{q}_{n+1}^j + t(q_{n+1}^{j_0} - q_{n+1}^j)$$
```
            else
```
$$\hat{q}_{n+1}^j(t) = \hat{q}_{n+1}^j(t)$$
```
            end if
            if  \hat{q}_{n+1}^j > q_{n+1}^| then
```
$$q_{n+1}^j = q_{n+1}^+$$
```
            end if
            if  \hat{q}_{n+1}^j < q_{n+1}^- then
```
$$q_{n+1}^j = q_{n+1}^-$$
```
            end if
            f_j(t) = J_1(q^j(t))            //estimation of new vector of parameters
            if f_j(t) < f_j then
                f_j = f_j(t)
                for (i = 1,...,n + 1)
```
$$q_i^j = q_i^j(t) \quad //\text{transformation of vector of parameters}$$
```
                end for
            end if
            t = t + δ
        end while do
    end for (j = H)
end for (r = R)
```

In pseudo code, subroutine Random generates a random real number from 0 to 1, and subroutine *Random(A)* generates random integer number from 0 to $A - 1$. We used * in comments to highlight the modification of modified SOMA in comparison to original SOMA.

The effectiveness of modified SOMA, as with all evolutionary algorithms, depends on the parameters that influence the number of computational operations, i.e., number of elements in initial population (H), number of generations (R), number of evolutions (P). To evaluate one single solution, we need to simulate the whole system, thus, for the problem, we have to calculate the functional minimum $H + nRP$ times, where n depends on parameter of algorithm P_{length}.

As for all evolutionary algorithms, the convergence of modified SOMA is determined by probability. The more solutions are looked through, the more is the probability to find the optimal one. In evolutionary algorithms, the value of goal function depends on the number of generations as descending exponent. If the solution is not improved for some generations, then the search is stopped, and the best current solution is considered to be the solution to the problem. The optimal control problem with phase constraints is not unimodal, and the search algorithm is not deterministic, thus, to find the solution, the algorithm ran multiple times.

5. An Example

Consider a control problem for two similar mobile robots. Mathematical model of control objects has the following form

$$\dot{x}^j = 0.5(u_1^j + u_2^j)\cos\theta^j,$$
$$\dot{y}^j = 0.5(u_1^j + u_2^j)\sin\theta^j, \tag{33}$$
$$\dot{\theta}^j = 0.5(u_1^j - u_2^j),$$

where $j = 1, 2$.

The control is limited

$$u_i^- \leqslant u_i^j \leqslant u_i^+, \tag{34}$$

where $j = 1, 2$, u_i^-, u_i^+ are the given constraints, $i = 1, 2$. For the system (33), the initial conditions are

$$x^j(0) = x_0^j,\ y^j(0) = y_0^j,\ \theta^j(0) = \theta_0^j. \tag{35}$$

The terminal conditions are

$$x^j(t) = x_f^j,\ y^j(t) = y_f^j,\ \theta^j(t) = \theta_f^j. \tag{36}$$

The static phase constraints are

$$\varphi_i(x^j, y^j) = r_i^2 - (x_i^* - x^j)^2 - (y_i^* - y^j) \leqslant 0, \tag{37}$$

where $j = 1, 2$, r_i, x_i^*, y_i^* are the given parameters of constraints, $i = 1, \ldots, r$, r is a number of static phase constraints. For two robots, we have only one dynamic phase constraint

$$\chi(\mathbf{x}^1, \mathbf{x}^2) = d^2 - (x^1 - x^2)^2 - (y^1 - y^2)^2 \leqslant 0, \tag{38}$$

where d is a given minimal distance between robots.

A quality functional is

$$J = t_f + \sum_{j=1}^{2} \delta_j(t_f), \tag{39}$$

where

$$t_f = \begin{cases} t, \text{ if } t < t^+ \text{ and } \sum_{j=1}^{2} \delta_j(t) < \varepsilon \\ t^+ \text{ otherwise} \end{cases}, \tag{40}$$

$$\delta_j(t) = \sqrt{(\Delta_x^j)^2(t) + (\Delta_y^j)^2(t) + (\Delta_\theta^j)^2(t)},\tag{41}$$

$$\Delta_x^j(t) = x^j(t) - x_f^j,$$

$$\Delta_y^j(t) = y^j(t) - y_f^j,$$

$$\Delta_\theta^j(t) = \theta^j(t) - \theta_f^j,$$

$j = 1, 2$, ε is a small positive value.

To obtain equations for conjugate variables, all constraints are included in the quality criterion, and terminal conditions are excluded as follows

$$J = t_f + a \int_0^{t_f} \sum_{j=1}^{2} \mu^2(\varphi_i(x^j, y^j)) dt + b \int_0^{t_f} \mu^2(\chi(\mathbf{x}^1, \mathbf{x}^2)) dt.\tag{42}$$

Suggesting that the problem is not abnormal, let us write down the Hamilton function in the following form

$$H(\mathbf{x}, \mathbf{u}, \psi) = -1 - \sum_{j=1}^{2} \mu^2(\varphi_i(x^j, y^j)) - a\mu^2(\chi(\mathbf{x}^1, \mathbf{x}^2)) + 0.5 \sum_{j=1}^{2} \psi_{1+3(j-1)}(u_1^j + u_2^j)\cos\theta^j +$$

$$0.5 \sum_{j=1}^{2} \psi_{2+3(j-1)}(u_1^j + u_2^j)\sin\theta^j + 0.5 \sum_{j=1}^{2} \psi_{3j}(u_1^j - u_2^j).\tag{43}$$

As a result, the differential equations for conjugate variables are

$$\dot{\psi}_{1+3(j-1)} = -\frac{\partial H(\mathbf{x}, \mathbf{u}, \psi)}{\partial x^j} = 4\mu(r_1^2 - (x_1^* - x^j)^2 - (y_1^* - y^j))(x_1^* - x^j) +$$

$$4\mu(r_1^2 - (x_2^* - x^j)^2 - (y_2^* - y^j))(x_2^* - x^j) - 4\mu(d^2 - (x^1 - x^2)^2 - (y^1 - y^2))(x^1 - x^2),$$

$$\dot{\psi}_{2+3(j-1)} = -\frac{\partial H(\mathbf{x}, \mathbf{u}, \psi)}{\partial y^j} = 4\mu(r_1^2 - (x_1^* - x^j)^2 - (y_1^* - y^j))(y_1^* - y^j) +\tag{44}$$

$$4\mu(r_1^2 - (x_2^* - x^j)^2 - (y_2^* - y^j))(y_2^* - y^j) + 4\mu(d^2 - (x^1 - x^2)^2 - (y^1 - y^2))(y^1 - y^2),$$

$$\dot{\psi}_{3j} = -\frac{\partial H(\mathbf{x}, \mathbf{u}, \psi)}{\partial \theta^j} = 0.5\psi_{1+3(j-1)}(u_1^j + u_2^j)\sin\theta^j - 0.5\psi_{2+3(j-1)}(u_1^j + u_2^j)\cos\theta^j,$$

where $j = 1, 2$. Optimal control is calculated from equations

$$\tilde{u}_1^j = \begin{cases} u_1^{j+}, & \text{if } W_j + \psi_{3j} > 0 \\ u_1^{j-}, & \text{if } W_j + \psi_{3j} < 0 \\ \text{special control mode}, & \text{if } W_j + \psi_{3j} = 0 \end{cases},\tag{45}$$

$$\tilde{u}_2^j = \begin{cases} u_2^{j+}, & \text{if } W_j - \psi_{3j} > 0 \\ u_2^{j-}, & \text{if } W_j - \psi_{3j} < 0 \\ \text{special control mode}, & \text{if } W_j - \psi_{3j} = 0 \end{cases},\tag{46}$$

where

$$W_j = \psi_{1+3(j-1)} \sin\theta^j + \psi_{2+3(j-1)} \cos\theta^j,\tag{47}$$

$u_1^{j+}, u_2^{j+}, u_1^{j-}, u_2^{j-}$ are upper and lower values of control for robot j, $j = 1, 2$.

The nonlinear programming problem consists of finding initial conditions for conjugate variables

$$q_i = \psi_i(0), \ i = 1, \ldots, 6, \tag{48}$$

so that initial conditions have to allocate on a sphere with a unit radius

$$\sqrt{\sum_{i=1}^{6} q_i^2} = 1, \tag{49}$$

as well as terminal time

$$t_f = t^+ + q_7, \tag{50}$$

and special control modes

$$u_1^1 = q_8, \ \text{if} \ |W_1 + \psi_3| < \varepsilon_0, \tag{51}$$

$$u_2^1 = q_9, \ \text{if} \ |W_1 - \psi_3| < \varepsilon_0, \tag{52}$$

$$u_1^2 = q_{10}, \ \text{if} \ |W_2 + \psi_6| < \varepsilon_0, \tag{53}$$

$$u_2^2 = q_{11}, \ \text{if} \ |W_1 - \psi_6| < \varepsilon_0, \tag{54}$$

where ε_0 is a small positive value.

A goal function for the nonlinear programming has the following form

$$F = \sum_{j=1}^{2} \delta_j(t_f) + a \int_0^{t_f} \sum_{j=1}^{2} \mu^2(\varphi_i(x^j, y^j))dt + b \int_0^{t_f} \mu^2(\chi(x^1, x^2))dt. \tag{55}$$

6. Computational Experiment

The problem had the following parameters: a number of objects $M = 2$, dimensions of objects $n_1 = 3$, $n_2 = 3$, dimension of state space vector $n = 3 + 3 = 6$, dimensions of control $m_1 = 2$, $m_2 = 2$, dimension of control space $m = 2 + 2 = 4$ dimension of parameter vector $n + 1 + m = 11$.

The following values of parameters of the algorithm were used: $x_0^1 = 0$, $y_0^1 = 0$, $\theta_0^1 = 0$, $x_0^2 = 10$, $y_0^2 = 10$, $\theta_0^2 = 0$, $x_f^1 = 10$, $y_f^1 = 10$, $\theta_f^1 = 0$, $x_f^2 = 0$, $y_f^2 = 0$, $\theta_f^2 = 0$, $u_i^+ = 10$, $u_i^- = -10$, $i = 1, 2$, $t^+ = 3.5$ s, $x_1^* = 5$, $y_1^* = 8$, $r_1 = 2$, $x_2^* = 5$, $y_2^* = 2$, $r_2 = 2$, $d = 2$, $\varepsilon_0 = 0.1$, $a = 2$, $b = 2$, $\varepsilon = 0.01$, $H = 32$, $P = 256$, $P_{length} = 8$, $P_{rt} = 0.33$, $\Delta = 0.22$, $\beta = 0.2$, $\alpha = 0.3$, $K = 7$, constraints on parameter values are $q_i^- = -1$, $q_i^+ = 1$, $i = 1, \ldots, 6$, $q_7^- = -2$, $q_7^+ = 1$, $q_i^- = -10$, $q_i^+ = 10$, $i = 8, \ldots, 11$.

An obtained optimal vector of parameters was

$$\mathbf{q} = [0.7722 \ 0.2142 \ -0.2825 \ -0.2968 \ -0.23 \ 0.3702 \ -1.5112 \ 0.0179 \ 3.3965 \ -2.96 \ -0.5945]^T.$$

This solution provided the value of the goal function (55) $F = 0.1238$.

To obtain the solution of optimal control problem for (33) and (44) by using the Pontryagin maximum principle, the complexity of search was the following: $H = 32$, $P = 256$, $R = H$, $P_{length} = 8$, $step = 0.22$, $n = 8/0.22 = 36$, $H + nRP = 32 + 36 \times 32 \times 256 = 294{,}944$, i.e., the functional was calculated 294,944 times. Simulation was performed in Lazarus, an open-source Free Pascal-based software, on PC with Intel Core i7, 2.8 GHz, OS Win 7. Series of 10 runs was implemented. The CPU time for 10 runs was approx. 20 min, i.e., 1 run was approx. 2 min.

The trajectories of the robots are shown in Figure 1. On Figure 1, red circles present the static constraints. Plots of obtained control are presented on Figures 2–5. Figures 2–5 show that optimal control includes sectors of special control modes [8]. The controls u_2^1 and u_1^2 have sliding modes.

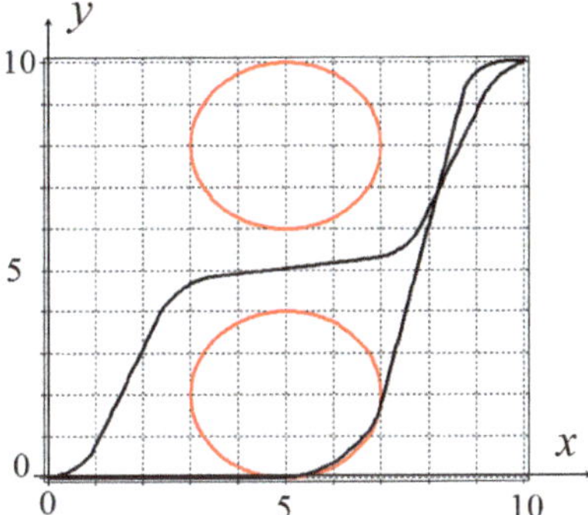

Figure 1. Trajectories of movement of robots.

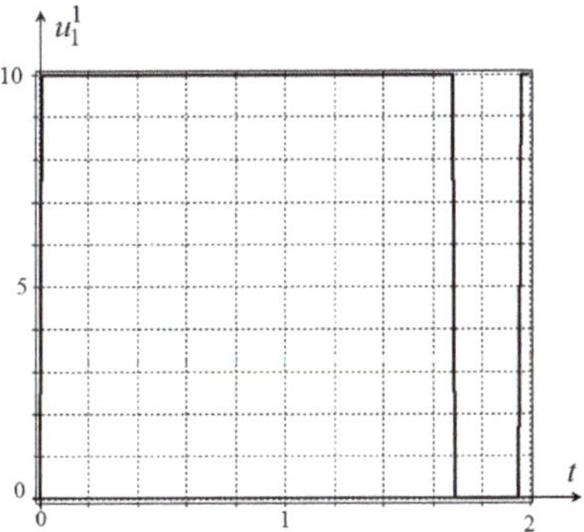

Figure 2. Control u_1^1.

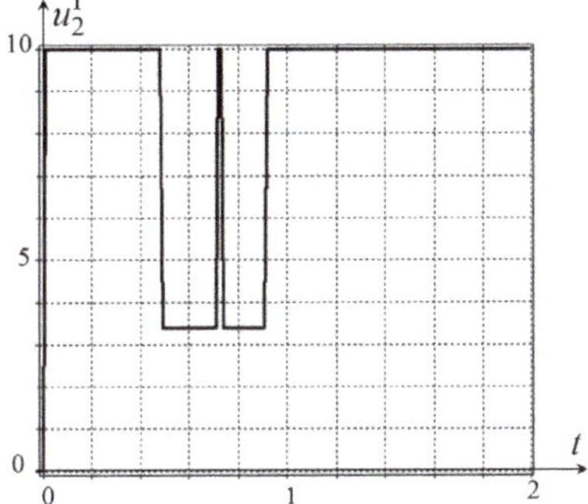

Figure 3. Control u_2^1.

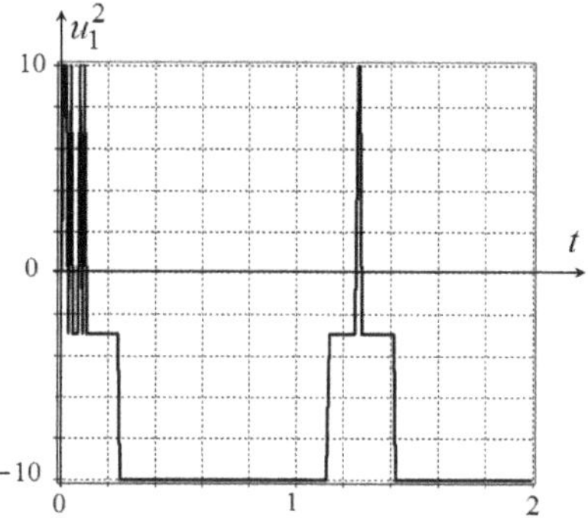

Figure 4. Control u_1^2.

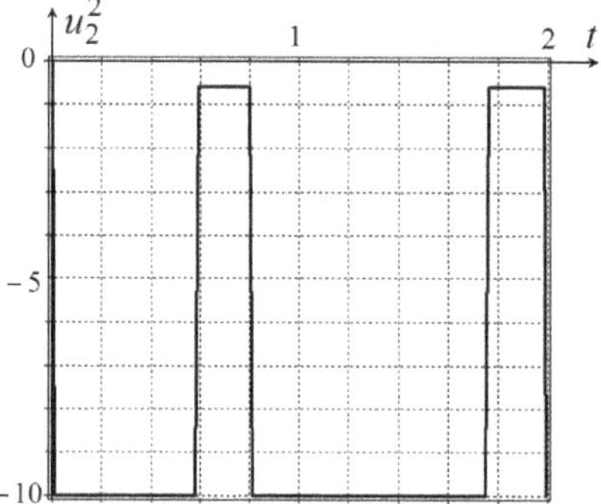

Figure 5. Control u_2^2.

7. Search of Optimal Control by Direct Method

The same problem was solved by direct numerical method. Control for each robot was searched as a piece-wise liner function on interval as follows

$$
u_i^j = \begin{cases} u_i^+, \text{ if } u_i^+ \leq \tilde{u}_i^j \\ u_i^-, \text{ if } \tilde{u}_i^j \leq u_i^-, \\ \tilde{u}_i^j, \text{ otherwise} \end{cases} \tag{56}
$$

where

$$
\tilde{u}_1^1 = q_i + (q_{i+1} - q_i)\frac{(t - i\Delta t)}{\Delta t}, \tag{57}
$$

$$
\tilde{u}_2^1 = q_{i+K} + (q_{i+K+1} - q_{i+K})\frac{(t - i\Delta t)}{\Delta t}, \tag{58}
$$

$$
\tilde{u}_1^2 = q_{i+2K} + (q_{i+2K+1} - q_{i+2K})\frac{(t - i\Delta t)}{\Delta t}, \tag{59}
$$

$$
\tilde{u}_2^2 = q_{i+3K} + (q_{i+3K+1} - q_{i+3K})\frac{(t - i\Delta t)}{\Delta t}, \tag{60}
$$

$i = 1, \ldots, K, t \in [i\Delta t; (i+1)\Delta t), \Delta t = 0.25,$

$$K = \left\lfloor \frac{t^+}{\Delta t} \right\rfloor + 1 = \left\lfloor \frac{2.5}{0.25} \right\rfloor + 1 = 11, \tag{61}$$

Eleven time intervals were used. For each control, it was necessary to find 11 parameters of piece-wise linear function at the boundaries of intervals. Totally, we searched for forty-five parameters $\mathbf{q} = [q_1 \ldots q_{45}]^T$, forty-four parameters were for control of two robots, and q_{45} was for terminal time $t^+ + q_{45}$. Values of parameters were constrained

$$q_i^- \leqslant q_i \leqslant q_i^+, \; i = 1, \ldots, 45, \tag{62}$$

where $q_i^- = -20, q_i^+ = 20, i = 1, \ldots, 44, q_{45}^- = -0.8, q_{45}^+ = 0.8$.

The parameter search was also performed by modified SOMA. Vector of obtained parameters was as follows

$$
\begin{aligned}
\mathbf{q} \;=\; & [15.0129 \; 17.4687 \; 17.6772 \; 2.2532 \; 12.5488 \; 9.0041 \; 0.3886 \; 19.9999 \; 19.3899 \; 19.01849 \\
& -8.8472 \; -15.2669 \; 10.5164 \; 19.9044 \; 16.5724 \; 18.0328 \; 17.5597 \; 18.3563 \; 16.8607 \; 8,2100 \\
& -18.7127 \; 4.3724 \; -8.9377 \; -0.7936 \; 10.6309 \; 18.9660 \; 18.4597 \; 18.9742 \; 17.2781 \; 14.6362 \\
& 18.4152 \; -13.7367 \; -2.8521 \; 17.0837 \; 18.1753 \; 17.5278 \; 9.4618 \; 19.5178 \; 17.6007 \; 11.3479 \\
& -0.6898 \; -5.4015 \; 19.9215 \; 9.6850 \; 0.6628]^T.
\end{aligned}
$$

For direct approach, when we searched for 45 parameters by modified SOMA, the complexity of the algorithm was the following: $H = 32$, $P = 1024$, $R = H$, $P_{length} = 8$, $step = 0.22$, $n = 8/0.22 = 36$, $H + nRP = 32 + 36 \times 32 \times 1024 = 1{,}179{,}680$. Simulation was performed on PC with Intel Core i7, 2.8 GHz. A series of 10 runs was implemented. The CPU time for 10 runs was approx. 3 hours and 10 min, i.e., 1 run was approx. 19 min. We used $P = 1024$ for direct approach, because the number of searched parameters was 45, and it was several times bigger than 11 parameters in the first experiment.

The obtained solution is presented on Figure 6. On Figures 7–10, the plots of direct controls are presented.

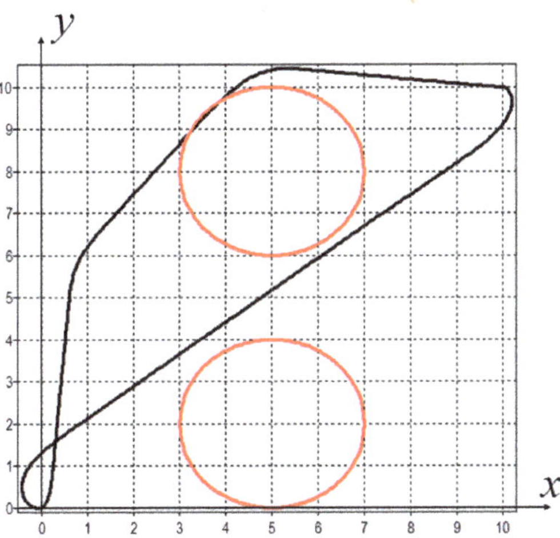

Figure 6. Trajectories of robots obtained by direct method.

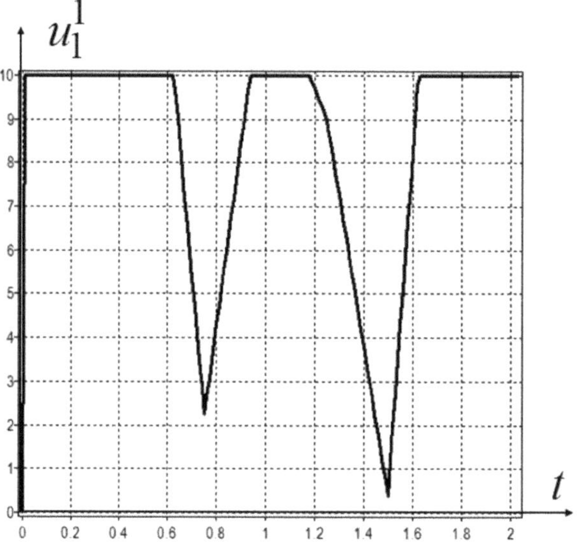

Figure 7. Direct control u_1^1.

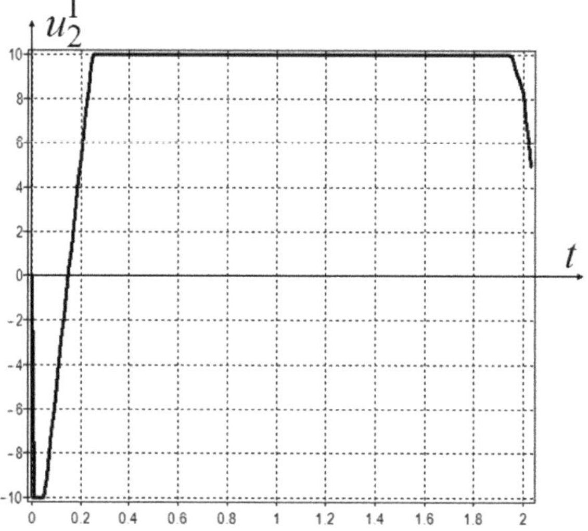

Figure 8. Direct control u_2^1.

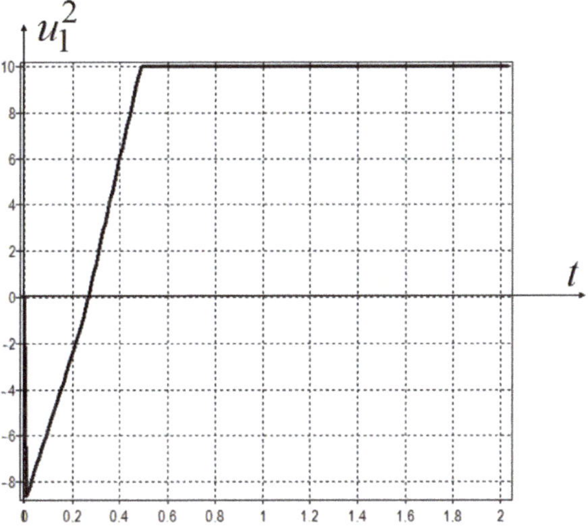

Figure 9. Direct control u_1^2.

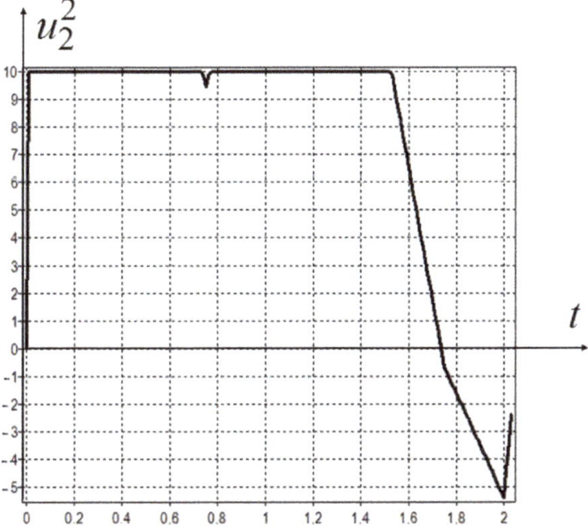

Figure 10. Direct control u_2^2.

8. An Alternative Non-Deterministic Control

One of the most important issues for swarm robotics applications is catching up with moving targets and avoiding multiple dynamic obstacles. It is complicated in that it requires an algorithm to work in real time to avoid obstacles that are standing or moving in an unknown environment, where the robot does not know their position until detecting them by sensors arranged on the robot. As an alternative to the method presented above, the use of swarm intelligence algorithms as reported in [9] can be discussed.

The paper [9] presents a method for swarm robot to catch the moving target and to avoid multiple dynamic obstacles in the unknown environment. An imaginary map is built, representing N targets, M obstacles and N robots and a swarm intelligence algorithm is used to control them so that targets are captured correctly and in the shortest time. The robot dynamics can be viewed as a flow of water moving from high to low. The flow of water is the robot trajectory that is divided into a set of points created by an algorithm called SOMA [5,6]. Simulation results are also presented to show that the obstacle avoidance and catching target task can be reached using this method. All details about those experiments are discussed in [9]. Results are also visualized in selected videos (https://zelinkaivan65.wixsite.com/ivanzelinka/videa). The typical example is in Figure 11.

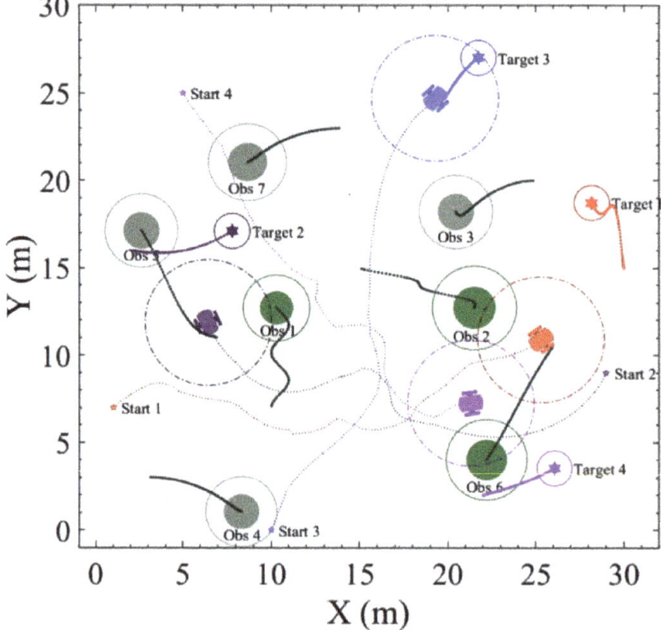

Figure 11. Swarm robot control by SOMA.

Besides the long-standing methods such as potential field method [10,11], and the vector field histogram [12], several new methods such as "follow the gap method" [13], and barrier function [14], or artificial intelligence methods such as genetic algorithm [15], neural network [16], and fuzzy logic [17,18] also demonstrate their effectiveness. Among the methods of artificial intelligence used to solve the problem as a function optimization problem, the self-organizing migrating algorithm (SOMA) emerges as a fast, powerful and efficient algorithm [5,6].

9. Discussion

The optimal control problem for two mobile robots with phase constraints was considered. To solve the problem, an approach based on the Pontryagin maximum principle was used. The mathematical model of robots include linear control in the right parts of differential equations; that is why the optimal control has sectors of special control modes. It should be noted that we used two robots to test the proposed technology and partially to test methodology. A larger group is required to fully test the proposed methodology and it will be our future research, but in the case of many robots, the optimization problem will go on backstage and the collision avoidance will become the real problem.

To solve a boundary-value problem and search of initial conditions of conjugate variables, the modified SOMA was used. Additional parameters for terminal conditions check and control in special modes were introduced.

The optimal control problem was also solved by direct approach. Control time was divided into intervals, and control at each interval was a piece-wise linear function. Additional parameter was also a time of terminal conditions check. The direct approach showed another character of objects movement.

The aim of this paper was to show for the first time how modern evolutionary algorithms can be applied to solution of boundary-value problems that occur when we solve the optimal control problem by an indirect method based on the Pontryagin maximum principle. Other known applications of evolutionary algorithms were mainly with direct approach [4].

Thus, one can conclude that the considered problem is multimodal and application of evolutionary algorithms to both direct and indirect approaches is expedient and prospective. The next research will be focused on an extensive comparative study of classical and swarm control based methods.

10. Patents

Certificate of software registration No.2020619668 Diveev A.I., Sofronova E.A. "Optimal control of group of robots based on Pontryagin maximum principle" 21 August 2020.

Certificate of software registration No.2020619960 Diveev A.I., Sofronova E.A. "Optimal control of group of robots by direct approach based on piece-wise linear approximation", 26 August 2020.

Author Contributions: Formal analysis, A.D.; Investigation, A.D., E.S.; Methodology, I.Z.; Software, E.S.; Supervision, I.Z.; Validation, E.S.; Writing—original draft, A.D.; Writing—review and editing, E.S. All the authors have equal contribution. All authors have read and agreed to the published version of the manuscript.

Funding: This research is supported by the Ministry of Science and Higher Education of the Russian Federation, project No 075-15-2020-799.

References

1. Pontryagin, L.S.; Boltyanskii, V.G.; Gamkrelidze,R.V.; Mishchenko, E.F. *The Mathematical Theory of Optimal Processess*; Interscience: New York, NY, USA, 1962.
2. Arutyunov,A.V.; Karamzin, D.Y.; Pereira, F.L. Maximum principle in problems with mixed constraints under weak assumptions of regularity. *Optimization* **2010**, *59*, 1067–1083. [CrossRef]
3. Karamzin, D.; Pereira, F.L. On a Few Questions Regarding the Study of State-Constrained Problems in Optimal Control. *J. Optim. Theory Appl.* **2019**, *180*, 235–255. [CrossRef]
4. Diveev, A.I.; Konstantinov, S.V. Study of the practical convergence of evolutionary algorithms for the optimal program control of a wheeled robot. *J. Comput. Syst. Sci. Int.* **2018**, *57*, 561–580. [CrossRef]
5. Zelinka, I. SOMA—Self organizing migrating algorithm. In *New Optimization Techniques in Engineering*; Babu, B.V., Onwubolu, G.; Eds.; Springer: Berlin/Heidelberg, Germany, 2004; Volume 33, Chapter 7, ISBN: 3-540-20167X.
6. Zelinka, I. SOMA—Self organizing migrating algorithm. In *Self-Organizing Migrating Algorithm. Methodology and Implementation*; Series: Studies in Computational Intelligence; Davendra, D., Zelinka, I., Eds.; Springer: Cham, Switzerland, 2016; pp. 3–39. ISBN 978-3-319-28161-2.
7. Diveev, A.; Sofronova, E.; Shmalko, E. Modified SOMA for Optimal Control Problem. In Proceedings of the 2019 IEEE Congress on Evolutionary Computation, (CEC 2019), Wellington, New Zealand, 10–13 June 2019; pp. 2894–2899.

8. Gabasov, R.; Kirillova, F.M. Optimal control with special sectors. *Autom. Remote Control* **1969**, *30*, 1554–1563.
9. Diep, Q.B.; Zelinka, I.; Senkerik, R. An algorithm for swarm robot to avoid multiple dynamic obstacles and to catch the moving target. In *Artificial Intelligence and Soft Computing. ICAISC 2019*; Lecture Notes in Computer Science; Rutkowski, L., Scherer, R., Korytkowski, M., Pedrycz, W., Tadeusiewicz, R., Zurada, J.M., Eds.; Springer: Cham, Switzerland, 2019; pp. 666–675.
10. Borenstein, J.; Koren, Y. Real-time obstacle avoidance for fast mobile robots. *IEEE Trans. Syst. Man Cybern.* **1989**, *19*, 1179–1187. [CrossRef]
11. Koren, Y.; Borenstein, J. Potential field methods and their inherent limitations for mobile robot navigation. In Proceedings of the IEEE International Conference on Robotics and Automation, Sacramento, CA, USA, 9–11 April 1991; pp. 1398–1404.
12. Borenstein, J.; Koren, Y. The vector field histogram-fast obstacle avoidance for mobile robots. *IEEE Trans. Robot. Autom.* **1991**, *7*, 278–288. [CrossRef]
13. Sezer, V.; Gokasan, M. A Novel obstacle avoidance algorithm: "Follow the gap method". *Robot. Auton. Syst.* **2012**, *60*, 1123–1134. [CrossRef]
14. Chen, Y.; Peng, H.; Grizzle, J. Obstacle avoidance for low-speed autonomous vehicles with barrier function. *IEEE Trans. Control. Syst. Technol.* **2017**, *99*, 1–13. [CrossRef]
15. Hu, Y.; Yang, S.X. A knowledge based genetic algorithm for path planning of a mobile robot. *IEEE Int. Conf. Robot. Autom.* **2004**, *5*, 4350–4355.
16. Duguleana, M.; Mogan, G. Neural networks based reinforcement learning for mobile robots obstacle avoidance. *Expert Syst. Appl.* **2016**, *62*, 104–115. [CrossRef]
17. Reignier, P. Fuzzy logic techniques for mobile robot obstacle avoidance. *Robot. Auton. Syst.* **1994**, *12*, 143–153. [CrossRef]
18. Zavlangas, P.G.; Tzafestas, S.G.; Althoefer, K. Fuzzy obstacle avoidance and navigation for omnidirectional mobile robots. In Proceedings of the European Symposium on Intelligent Techniques, Aachen, Germany, 14–15 September 2000; pp. 375–382.

Publisher's Note: MDPI stays neutral with regard to jurisdictional claims in published maps and institutional affiliations.

Article

Modular and Self-Scalable Origami Robot: A First Approach

Lisbeth Mena *, Jorge Muñoz , Concepción A. Monje and Carlos Balaguer

Robotics Lab, Carlos III University of Madrid, Avenida de la Universidad 30, Leganés, 28911 Madrid, Spain; jmyanezb@ing.uc3m.es (J.M.); cmonje@ing.uc3m.es (C.A.M.); balaguer@ing.uc3m.es (C.B.)
* Correspondence: lmena@pa.uc3m.es

Abstract: This paper presents a proposal of a modular robot with origami structure. The proposal is based on a self-scalable and modular link made of soft parts. The kinematics of a single link and several links interconnected is studied and validated. Besides, the link has been prototyped, identified, and controlled in position. The experimental data show that the system meets the scalability requirements and that its response is totally reliable and robust.

Keywords: self-scalable robots; modular robots; origami structures

Citation: Mena, L.; Muñoz, J.; Monje, C.A.; Balaguer, C. Modular and Self-Scalable Origami Robot: A First Approach. *Mathematics* **2021**, *9*, 1324. https://doi.org/10.3390/math9121324

Academic Editors: Mikhail Posypkin, Vladimir Titarev and Andrey Gorshenin

Received: 30 April 2021
Accepted: 1 June 2021
Published: 9 June 2021

Publisher's Note: MDPI stays neutral with regard to jurisdictional claims in published maps and institutional affiliations.

1. Introduction

In this paper we propose the design and construction of a modular robot composed by several links which are reconfigurable in shape and size in order to generate different adaptable configurations of the robotic platform. The primary characteristics for this design are the scalability and modularity of the robot. Two designs will be proposed:

1. A single link capable of changing its size individually (self-scalable) is the first proposed design option. This link could be connected to other links with similar features, this way achieving the modularity property.
2. A modular design with several interconnected links is the second design approach, which will improve the scalability of the system and its motion range. This kind of configuration has been studied by several authors since 1988, like CEBOT [1] or CMU RMMS [2].

A Modular Robotic System (MRS) can be defined as link arrays joined together to form a modular structure [3]. MRSs have four interdependent components: Module, Information, Task, and Environment (MITE). MITE allows for the extraction of the characteristics of the MRS, the module properties being the most special features, as other MRS components are transversal to every kind of robot. The module component includes two useful properties for the design of an MRS, these are: class and architecture. The class refers to the different ways in which modularity can be achieved, such as fixed-configuration, manually-reconfigurable [2,4], self-reconfigurable [5,6], and self-replicable [7]. On the other hand, architecture is the hardware categories of configuration: Chain [4,5], Lattice [6,8,9], Mobile [10–12], Hybrid [13,14], Truss [15–17], and Free form [18,19].

Many MRSs change their shape and size through nesting between each module; however, in this case study our goal is to allow the resizing of each module before its connection. This configuration is not often used in the literature. For instance, the closest example is ShapeBots, which is an individual shape-changing link [20] but with no modularity capabilities. A reference work closer to our approach is the Extendable Arm by Matsuo et al. [21], where modular links are connected and each one is scalable. Compared to our approach, the orientation of this platform is limited and its operation is manual. Thanks to the introduction of a three degrees of freedom (DoF) joint connecting each link, our design allows a wider orientation range of the modular robot. Besides, the platform performs automatically thanks to the use of a control system, which avoids the manual operation of the robot and improves its usability.

The initial idea about a flexible structure deforming by sections led us to origami-type constructions. Origami is an ancient technique for paper folding [22], which provides deployable structures that can be reconfigured and change in size and shape. Reconfigurable 3D structures, obtained from a rigid geometric 2D pattern, are booming in designs for engineering applications such as the solar panel surfaces proposed by Miura [23], the modular origami continuous manipulator by Santoso et al. [24], which supports a 1 kg mass at its tip, a gripper with multiple grasp modes [25], and other applications such as biomechanical [26], space [27], or soft robotics [28]. The wide number and type of applications of these designs has motivated us to research this topic and present a different approach in the terms described next.

Our design proposal consists of a modular robot that uses an origami-inspired link-based resizing mechanism. The links can be assembled using a rigid connector or a 3 DoF joint as proposed below. In this study we use the Kresling pattern for the origami structure of the basic link. This pattern is formed by the folding of a thin-walled cylinder when subject to twist buckling under a torsional load. It is characterized by alternating mountain and valley folds angled along the direction of the twist [29,30].

Figure 1a represents an n faces polygon Kresling pattern in planar state, which forms a polyhedral cylinder when assembled. The triangulated polyhedron geometry is resolved by $L_{AB} = a$, $L_{BC} = a \cdot sin(\alpha)/sin(\beta)$, $L_{AC} = a \cdot sin(\alpha + \beta)/sin\beta$ at the planar state, where a, α, and β are constant values. The angles α and β are the main design criteria to create the cylinder, because the strength of the structure depends on them. Zhai et al. suggest that, for small angles around $30°$, the structure is easy to deploy and easy to collapse, and for greater angles around $50°$, the structure is hard to deploy and hard to collapse [31]. For large angles, the structure is stronger and able to support loads. To obtain a symmetric structure we consider $a = r = 30$ mm; therefore, $n = 2\pi$ according to Hunt [32], where $a = 2\pi r/n$ and $\beta = \pi/n$. The angle α has been obtained from the geometric resolution proposed by Jianguo et al. [33]. Here h is considered to be known, $\alpha = asin(d/a)$ and d can be obtained by $ah = d(d \cdot cot(\beta) + \sqrt{a^2 - d^2})$. Consequently, our prototype has been designed with $a = 30$ mm, $h = 34.25$ mm, $\beta = 30°$ and $\alpha = 38°$, thus a flexible deformable link is created, and the unitary ABC triangle angle is >90° to achieve continuous strain at each member tension or compression in the deployed and collapsed states.

The folded cylinder link state generates a twist angle θ with radius r while height h is compressed (Figure 1b). This bistable behavior is due to the change of the lines length during folding (Equation (1)).

$$l_{AB} = 2rsin(\pi/n)$$

$$l_{BC} = \sqrt{h^2 - 2r^2cos\theta + 2r^2} \tag{1}$$

$$l_{AC} = \sqrt{h^2 - 2r^2cos(2\pi/n + \theta) + 2r^2}$$

$$r = \frac{\frac{a}{2}}{sin(\frac{\pi}{n})} \tag{2}$$

$$\theta = \frac{2\pi}{n} - 2asin\left(\frac{l_{BC}cos\delta}{2r}\right) \tag{3}$$

$$h = l_{BC} \cdot sin(\delta) \tag{4}$$

The height value h changes during folding and this change is related to δ angle change, given by Equation (4), as illustrated in Figure 1c. The variable height and bistability allow the self-scaling of the simple link.

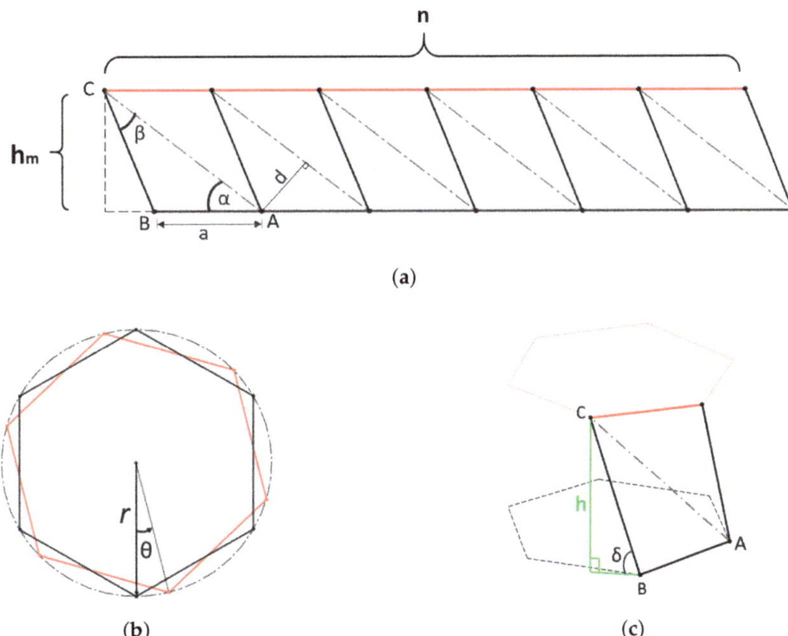

Figure 1. Origamipolyhedron Kresling pattern. (**a**) 2D Kresling pattern. (**b**) Folded cylinder link state. (**c**) Biestable behavior.

The main contributions of this work with respect to the state of the art are the following:

- Design and prototyping of a self-scalable link as a proof of concept. While being inspired by the origami technique, the final prototype integrates both rigid and soft materials in its structure, instead of paper. This novel approach is a real contribution to the state of the art.
- Design of a complete modular robot with interconnected scalable links. A linkage joint is proposed that allows modularity for three DOF configurations, enabling a wider range of applications.
- The final prototype is a 3D printed low cost solution that allows for the validation of the scalability in an autonomous way through the design and implementation of a control system. The control problem of these robotic structures is not generally faced in the majority of the works dealing with these designs, this being another important contribution of this paper. In addition, solutions to common control problems like motor's dead zones or saturation are addressed in this work.

2. Soft Origami-Based Design

An important design parameter of the link is the number of polyhedron faces [34], as they can limit the movement when folding if they are very close, like the case of four faces. To generate a symmetrical model, we decided to build a six face polyhedron as shown in Figure 2 representing every state of folding, from collapse (Figure 2a) to deployment (Figure 2d).

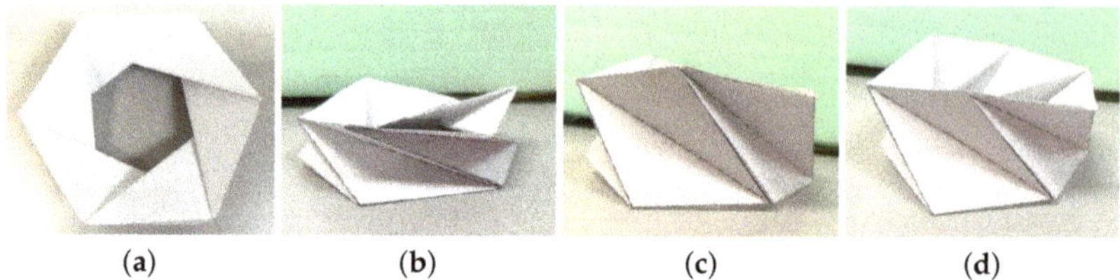

Figure 2. Cylinder polyhedron origami with one section (h_1) and six faces ($n = 6$). (**a**) Top view collapsed state. (**b–d**) Folding state.

A structure having several Kresling layers (for example five) is able to generate a cylinder composed by the same number of sections. The versatility of this design allows each section to be compressed or extended independently, so the five-section cylinder can have a variety of possible lengths, where the maximum height is the extended height of all sections. This cylinder model meets the scalability parameter by its bending property and the number of sections mentioned above. Now, the challenge is to make the cylinder reconfigurable. To achieve this, a number of cylinders have been joined together. Each cylinder is renamed as *link*, regardless of its number of sections, and one layer will be renamed as *single link*. The link connection represents a greater challenge, because it requires a mechanism at each end of the link, as shown in Figure 3a, where the input *IN* and output *OUT* unions of the link are shown in blue and orange, respectively. This allows the link to know which end has been placed in the next link.

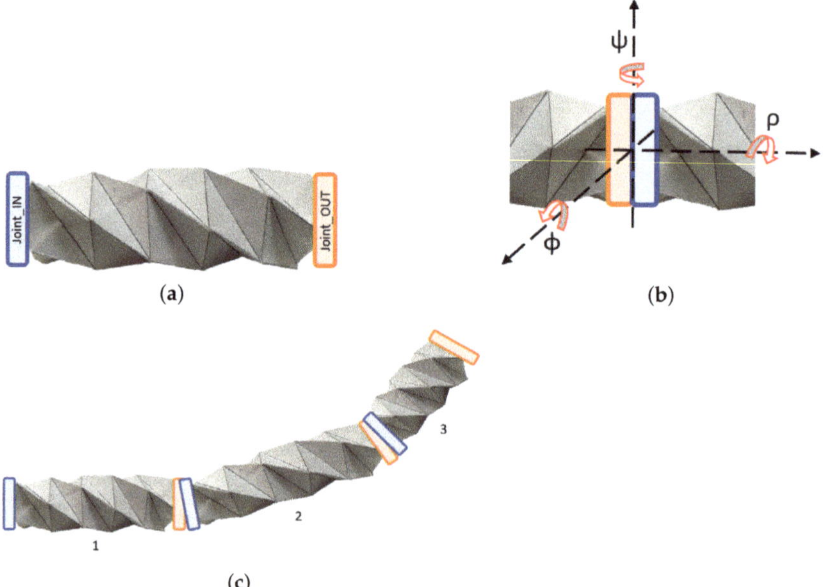

Figure 3. Connection of links. (**a**) Five-sections link with joints. (**b**) Joint between links. (**c**) Joined and reconfigurable links.

The joint between links is very wide, and ideally should rotate along the three axes XYZ and allow mobility in the angles yaw ψ, pitch ρ and roll ϕ (Figure 3b). The ideal joints will enable as many links to be joined as required. The links should always be joined in an orderly sequence, so that there is an *IN joint* at the beginning of the chain and an *OUT joint* at the end. Using this pattern, each link has corresponding position within the chain, with the first link acting as the main or master link.

The ideal case with three rotation axes allows the kinematic chain to move either in a plane or in the three dimensional space. If the yaw angle ψ is rotated in a plane, a snake-like movement will be obtained, while the rotation of roll angle ϕ through space can be assimilated to the behavior of a finger or an arm, according to the number and length of the connected links, as shown in Figure 3c.

Link Prototype

Our aim was to build a prototype to validate the idea of modular and scalable links, designing a paperless origami model. With this purpose, all the parts were modeled using CAD design applications and made using 3D printing technologies. Figure 4 illustrates the basic parts to generate the triangular polyhedron for a cylinder with six faces ($n = 6$). The base with constant length a is shown in Figure 4a. The l_{AC} (Figure 4b) was designed as a variable length piston with spherical bearings at its ends for mobility. Finally, the length l_{BC} is a soft material spring that can be warped with spherical bearings as well (Figure 4c). Values l_{BC} and a have been deemed constant, following Jianguo et al.'s suggestion [33], and l_{AC} is the only variable. In this case $l_{BC} = L_{BC}$. This design allows for operation while keeping constant values, but at the same time, its flexibility enables the free movement of the link. Design dimensions are $a = 35$ mm, $\alpha = 38°$, $\beta = 30°$, $r = 30°$ and planar state lengths $L_{AC} = 64.90$ mm, $L_{BC} = 43.09$ mm. The piston length l_{AC} decreases when the structure deploys and its size increases during the collapse.

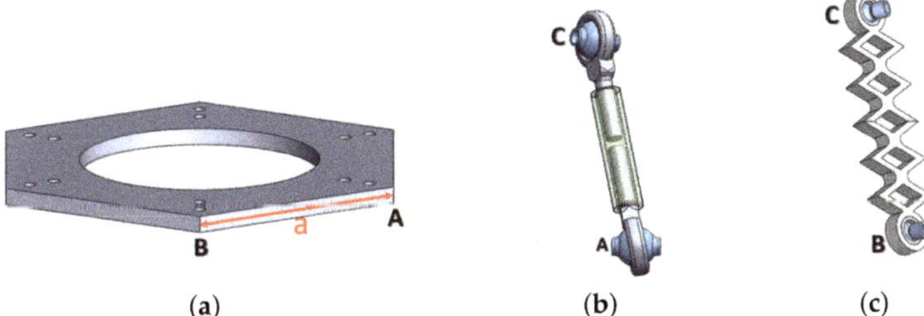

Figure 4. Components of the triangulated polyhedron prototype. (**a**) Constant base a. (**b**) Length l_{AC}, greater displacement. (**c**) Length l_{BC}, minor displacement.

Figure 5 illustrates the single link prototype, which represents an assembly of the components shown in Figure 4. In addition, connecting couplings and pins were required to keep the link assembled but still able to move. The triangles were assembled according to the design in Figure 1, where l_{AC} is folded inside the link, and l_{BC} is outside. Therefore, the bistable movement from the deployed to the collapsed state generates a clockwise rotation of the angle θ.

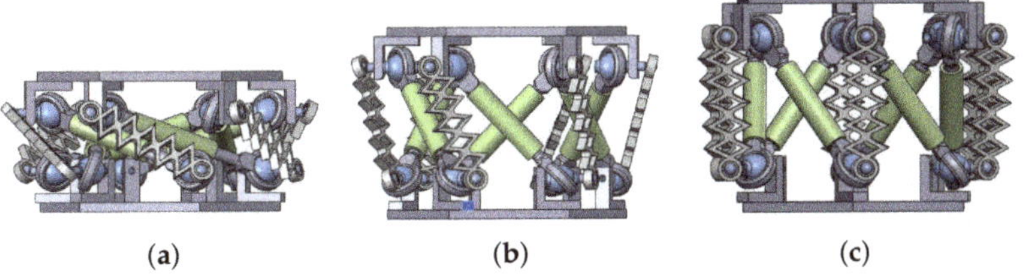

Figure 5. Single link CAD prototype. (**a**) Collapsed state. (**b**) Folding state. (**c**) Deployed state.

Several single links can be nested between them to obtain a cylinder with multiple sections. The union of two (h_2) is shown in Figure 6a, whereas a cylinder with three sections (h_3) is shown in Figure 6b. Each of these groupings constitutes an independent link, which is capable of modifying its length by varying the h value in each section, in an adjustable way. As discussed before, another option providing a relative 3 DoF link movement is the two-part ball socket. This configuration features two ball joints connected through a fixed union, attached to both links. The spherical bearing allows free rotation between the axes. However, for the construction and operation of this coupling, a more complex design is required.

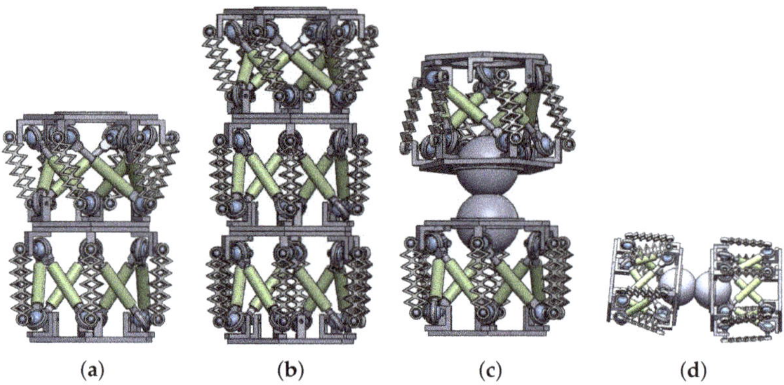

(a)   (b)   (c)   (d)

Figure 6. Nested links CAD prototype. (**a**) two-sections link. (**b**) three-sections link. (**c**) Two single links with a joint. (**d**) Two single links with a joint rotated.

Figure 6c illustrates the union of two links through the spherical joint, where both bodies are aligned with each other in a starting position, with each body consisting of a single link and fully deployed. On the other hand, in Figure 6d the chain of cylinders is horizontal and shows a slight rotation in the roll angle. The double spherical bearing represents the *IN joint* and *OUT joint*, respectively, as described in Figure 3b.

Finally, the prototype components were built in a 3D printer and assembled. The hexagonal bases (length a), the couplings, and the pistons (l_{AC}) were made of Polylactic Acid (PLA) plastic material. The bar l_{BC} was manufactured with a flexible material (NinjaFlex) from the manufacturer NinjaTek, to allow short displacements and keep the structure stable. Metric (M2) screws and 2 mm nuts were used for the final assemble of the prototype.

Figure 7 shows the bistate of the single link prototype assembly. The completely unfolded polyhedron is shown in Figure 7a. In this state the l_{AC} pistons are compressed and the l_{BC} soft links are extended. The final position of the deployment depends on l_{AC}, as mentioned before, and l_{BC} is adapted to that length.

In addition, the nested links were assembled to validate the design, as shown in Figure 8. The changing link size feature has been checked; each single link is able to fold and deploy in a two-sections link according to Figure 8a,b. The spherical joint shown in Figure 8c allows the union and the rotation of two single links while keeping the bistable operation.

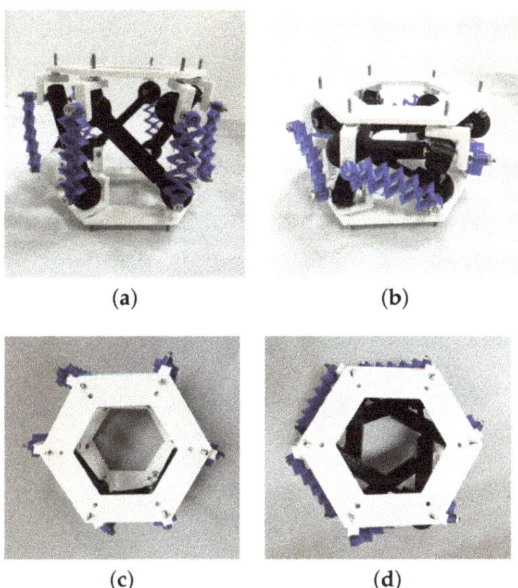

Figure 7. Single link first prototype. (**a**) Deployed single link prototype. (**b**) The single link is in collapsed state, and the height has changed. The l_{AC} pistons are extended and l_{BC} is slightly compressed. (**c**) Top view of the deployed prototype. (**d**) Top view of the collapsed prototype; the condition of the pistons and θ rotation are clearly shown.

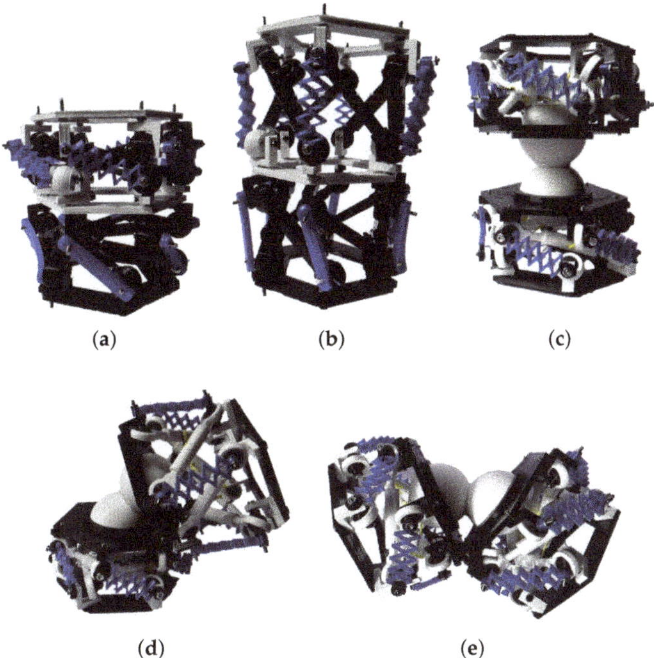

Figure 8. Assembled nested links prototype. (**a**) Two-sections link collapsed. (**b**) Two-sections link deployed. (**c**) Two single links with a joint. (**d**) Two single links with a joint, vertically rotated and one of them extended. (**e**) Two single links with a joint, horizontally rotated and collapsed.

3. Cable-Driven Prototype

The prototypes presented in the last section validate the design of this proposal; however, the bistable behavior is binary. The link has two possible positions, completely collapsed and completely deployed. Therefore, the change of size does not have intermediate steps. Our proposal aims to obtain a self-scaling simple link with a continuous change of the size. For this purpose, a spring and a cable-driven mechanism have been included in the link. The final movement of each cylinder is composed by 2 DoF: displacement in $z(h)$ and rotation in θ. Using three tendons and only one motor provides both movements if attached correctly. The internal spring is needed because of the structure of the link, that is not capable of maintaining an intermediate position and will fold without an external agent providing an extension force. Figure 9 illustrates the simple link prototype with an internal spring and a cable-drive with three tendons. Between the top of the single link and the top of spring, a bearing has been installed, which allows a free spring rotation movement when θ changes during collapse and deployment.

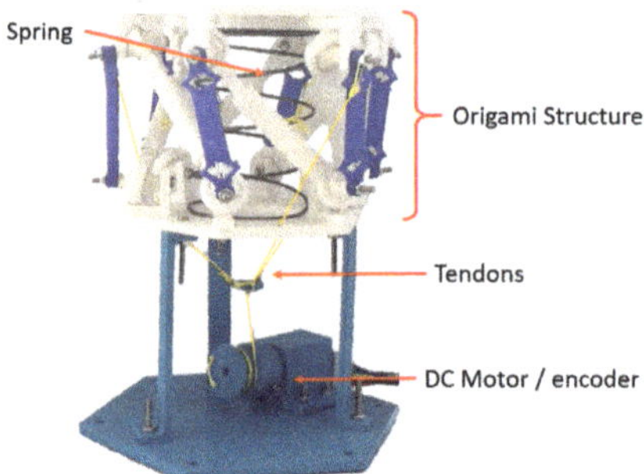

Figure 9. Cable-driven single link prototype.

The cable-drive is actuated by a DC motor with a 210:1 gear and no load speed of $75(RPM)$. It also features an encoder composed by two hall effect sensors displaced 90° between each other and a wheel with seven switching magnets. Therefore, one motor rotation corresponds to 28 quadrature pulses. As the gear ratio is 210:1, a 360° turn in the gear part corresponds to 5880 counts of the encoder. That makes the resolution of the encoder on the outside part 0.06°.

The spring elastic constant has been obtained experimentally. Masses between $0(gr)$ and $400(gr)$ have been placed in the upper base of the spring and the deformation lengths corresponding to the compression have been registered in Table 1, from which the elastic constant has been approximated to a straight line $F = K \cdot x$.

A simple linear regression has been applied to the collected data shown in Figure 10, from which the polynomial in Equation (5) is obtained, where the slope corresponds to the value of the constant K.

Table 1. Experimental data from spring compression.

x (m)	M (kg)
0.13	0
0.128	0.1
0.105	0.2
0.092	0.3
0.082	0.4

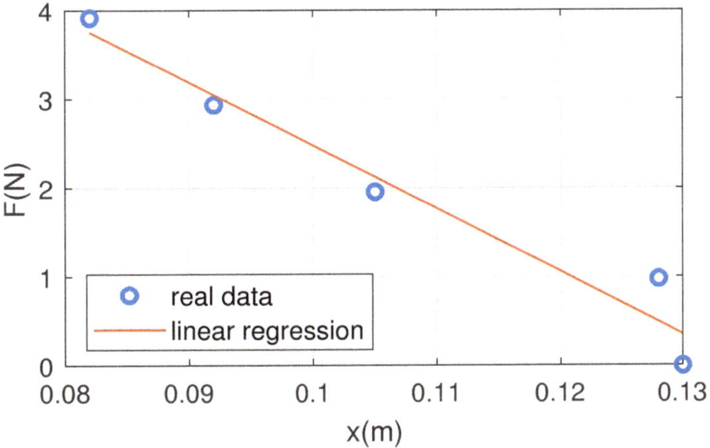

Figure 10. Linear regression to obtain the spring elastic constant K from experimental data.

$$F(x) = -70.9522x + 9.5803 \tag{5}$$

$$K = -70.9522 [N/m] \tag{6}$$

The prototype is expected to validate self-scaling in an autonomous and controlled manner. Given that the considered prototype physical definition is complex and consists of several subsystems, starting from the actuator used for the robot positioning and followed by the complete link, a system identification was performed in order to obtain the plant model.

The origami link is divided into two physical systems, the link itself, and the DC motor driving the mechanism. Given the link geometry described in the previous sections, we can neglect its effects in the final behavior and model the plant based on the DC motor only. Due to the lack of information from the motor provider, the DC motor model was obtained using recursive least squares (RLS) identification to the input-output captured data.

3.1. Motor System Identification

The model considered for identification is the DC motor (and gear) used in the pull mechanism of the robot. Identification data was captured using different input steps of $[1, 2, 3, 4, 5]$ Volts corresponding to throttle input values of $[200, 400, 600, 800, 1023]$. A small gain variation was observed for the different input values, resulting in several transfer functions. In order to use a single model, the average will be considered. The time responses of the identification results and the average transfer function considered are shown in Figure 11 including the identification captured data.

Observe how the maximum possible velocity is close to 6 rad/s, meaning a saturation of the system velocity for inputs of this value and higher. In addition, given the low cost approach of the design, the motor open loop response is noisy and shows dead zones. Therefore, a velocity feedback is proposed to obtain a linear behavior in the motor side.

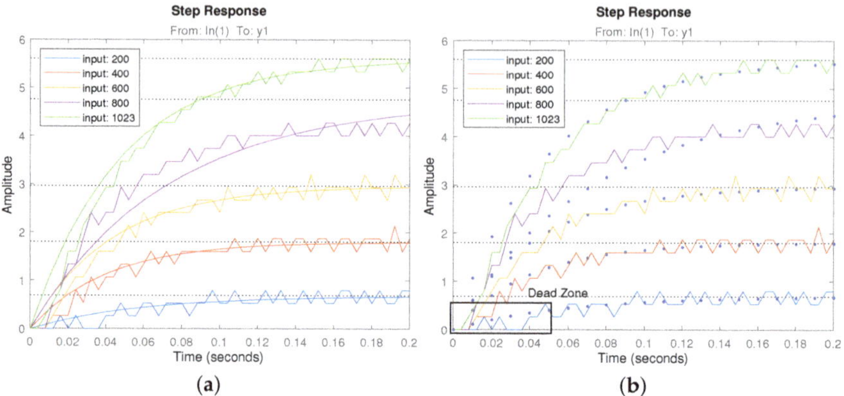

Figure 11. Motor system identification. Different systems identified depending on the inputs (**a**) and average system time response (**b**) compared to the captured data.

3.2. Controller Design

The average transfer function found through RLS identification is shown in Equation (7). This is the low level plant model used for the low level velocity control loop.

$$G_v(s)_{motor} = \frac{0.09991}{s + 19.11} \tag{7}$$

The proposed control scheme is shown in Figure 12. It consists of a feedback loop having a controller with reference in Velocity (rad/s) and output in the same units. As the motor model considered is the one discussed above, the control signal is the motor throttle (0–1023), with a saturation in 1023.

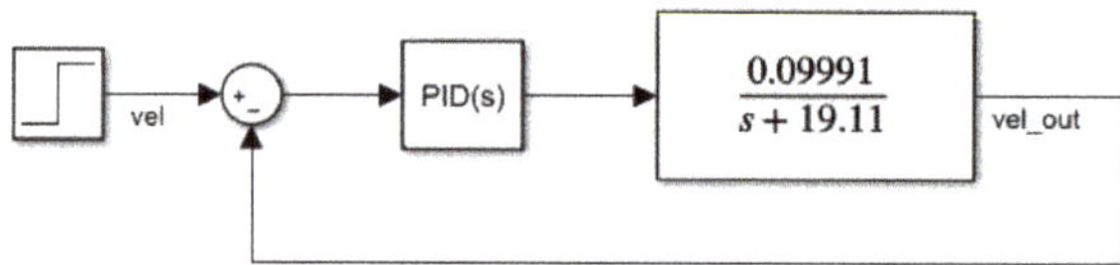

Figure 12. Motor velocity control system.

Given the plant gain variability detected, a robust control is proposed to cope with that plant parameter uncertainty. The controller tuning method proposed is the iso-m described in [35], which includes the robustness conditions in the tuning algorithm. Similar to many fractional order controller tuning methods, the desired performance specifications are based on the phase margin and crossover frequency features of the open loop frequency response. These are related to closed loop features such as bandwidth frequency and resonant peak height, which in turn are related to transient time response properties such as overshoot and peak time. Table 2 shows a summary of the most common constraints used in the frequency domain and time domain to define performance specification.

Table 2. Equivalence between frequency specifications and time response.

Physical Meaning	Effect Defined	Closed Loop Specification	Open Loop Specification
Damping ratio	Overshoot	Resonant peak dB	Phase margin
Response speed	Peak time	Bandwidth	Crossover frequency

It is a common practice to define the system performance by means of the open loop frequency variables (see [36]). In similar works like [37,38], the usual control specifications are crossover frequency (ω_{gc}) and phase margin (ϕ_m). As stated, the first is related to the system responsiveness (peak time) and the second to stability (overshoot). Equations (8) and (9) formulate these specifications, respectively:

$$|C(j\omega_{gc})G(j\omega_{gc})|_{dB} = 0\,\text{dB},\tag{8}$$

$$\arg\left(C(j\omega_{gc})G(j\omega_{gc})\right) = -\pi + \phi_m,\tag{9}$$

where $C(j\omega_{gc})$ is the controller frequency response at ω_{gc}, $G(j\omega_{gc})$ is the plant frequency response at ω_{gc}, and ϕ_m is the desired open loop phase margin for the controlled system.

Once the gain crossover frequency ω_{gc} and the phase margin ϕ_m are set, following the steps described in [35] will provide a solution for the controller parameters using the iso-m method.

Given the method's flexibility, both fractional and integer order controllers can be used, allowing a comparison between their results.

The integer order controller is defined by

$$IOPI(s) = kp + ki/s,\tag{10}$$

kp and ki being the proportional and integral controller gains, while the fractional order controller is defined by

$$FOPI(s) = kp + ka/s^{\alpha},\tag{11}$$

where kp and ka are the proportional and integral controller gains and α the fractional order of the integral operator.

Note that the number of parameters available for tuning while using the IOPI integer controller Equation (10) is not enough to fulfill the three specifications. This restricts the possible tuning inputs in that case, requiring a decision between overshoot (ϕ_m) or responsiveness (ω_{gc}). Then, the remaining specification will be given by the system characteristics and the chosen specification. A controlled overshoot is important to assure a good upper level control loop behavior; therefore, it will be defined using a phase margin of $\phi_m = 80$ deg for the tuning of both controllers.

In the IOPI case, this fully defines the controller using the iso-m method. Using the algorithm described in [35], the tuning parameters obtained were $kp = 163.9$ and $ki = 4462.3$. The responsiveness depends on the other values, resulting $\omega_{gc} = 20$ rad/s in this case. Figure 13 shows the frequency open loop response and the expected closed loop time response for different plant gains using the integer order controller.

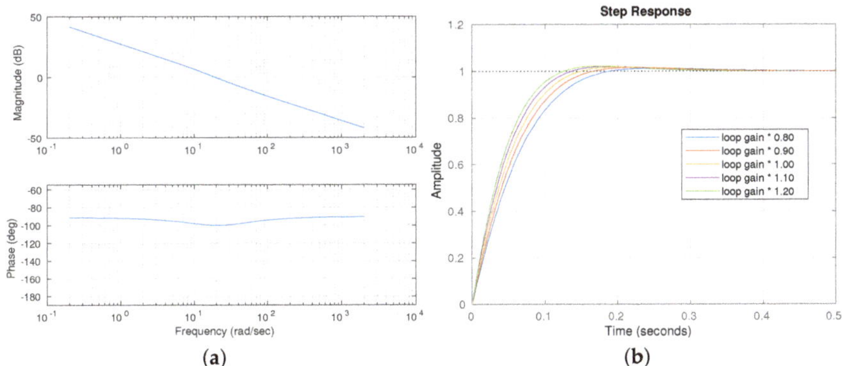

Figure 13. Open loop Bode diagram (**a**) and closed loop time response (**b**) for the integer order (IOPI) controller.

In the case of the FOPI controller, the two specifications described above can be used for controller tuning. The fractional order operator improved flexibility allows us to double the responsiveness while keeping the same robustness compared to the previous results. Therefore, $\phi_m = 80$ and $\omega_{gc} = 40$ rad/s can be used to specify the closed loop behavior. Using the algorithm described in [35], the tuning parameters obtained were $\alpha = -0.9100$, $Kp = 323.9$, $Ka = 7388.5$. Figure 14 shows the frequency open loop response and the expected closed loop time response for different plant gains.

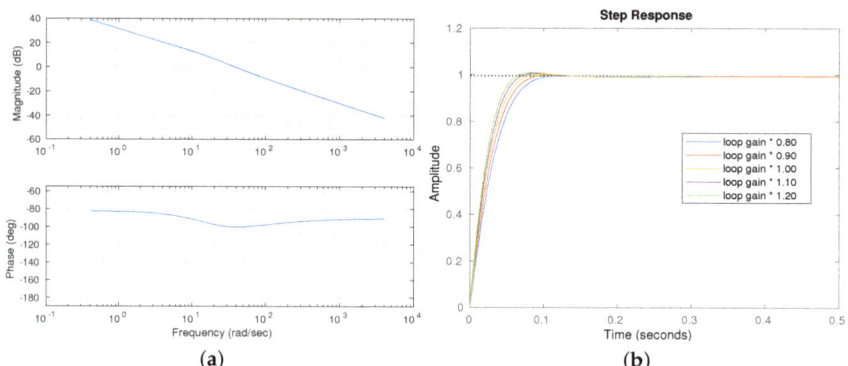

Figure 14. Open loop Bode diagram (**a**) and closed loop time response (**b**) for the fractional order (FOPI) controller.

The resulting plant in closed loop is a velocity reference input, real plant velocity output system described by Equation (12). Both measured and reference value units are rad/s. Therefore, the output obtained from the actuator is also expressed in rad/s with a maximum possible value of 5.5 rad/s.

$$F_v(s)_{motor} = \frac{16.38s + 445.8}{s^2 + 35.49s + 445.8} \tag{12}$$

Using an integrator on $F_v(s)$, the resulting plant $G_p(s) = F_v(s)/s$ is the velocity input, position output system with 1 rad/s crossover frequency.

Using this plant model, a high level position loop was designed. Given the convenient low level system response, we can design our servo-system using a feedback loop with a simple proportional controller. The designed position closed loop is shown in Figure 15.

The expected time response of a controller with a gain of 10 (Kp = 10) is also shown in Figure 15. This control scheme defines the position output of the motor shaft from an input reference (in (rad) units).

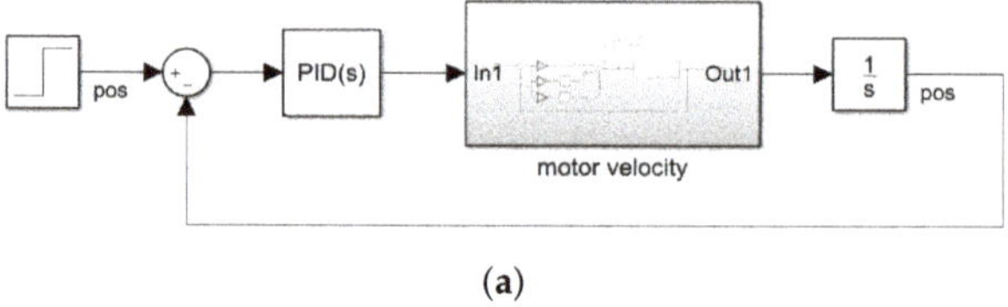

Figure 15. *Cont.*

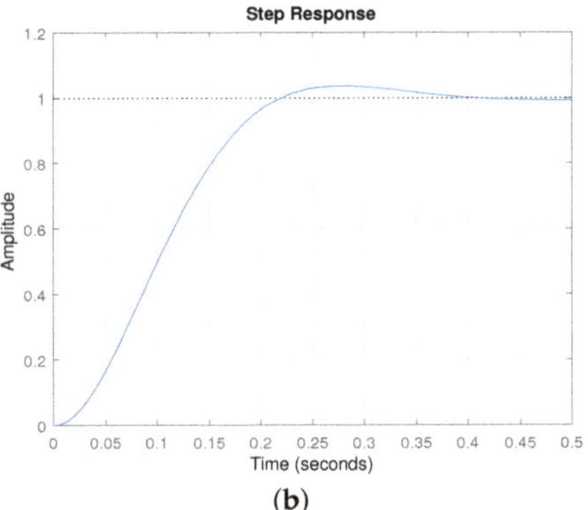

(b)

Figure 15. Motor position control system. Motor position control system. (**a**) Control system diagram. (**b**) Step response.

3.3. Whole System Behavior

Using the actuator described, an input step was performed in the robot. Given the results of the model simulation compared to the real response obtained, we can say that both systems are similar, concluding that the spring and the origami shape are not changing the behavior of the actuator plant. Therefore, we can find a model based on the feedback loop proposed resulting in a transfer function as follows:

$$G_p(s)_{origami} = \frac{163.8s + 4458}{s^3 + 35.49s^2 + 609.6s + 4458} \tag{13}$$

In order to validate the model, a step input of 0.5 rad (saturation will happen in the motor for higher targets) was fed into the system, resulting in the time response shown in Figure 16. The open loop frequency response of the whole system model is also shown in the figure, with a phase margin of $Pm = 65.4$ deg at a gain crossover frequency $\omega_c = 9.62$ rad/s.

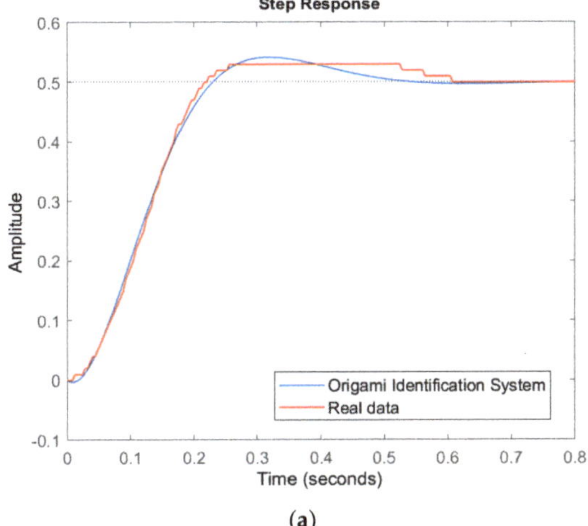

(a)

Figure 16. *Cont.*

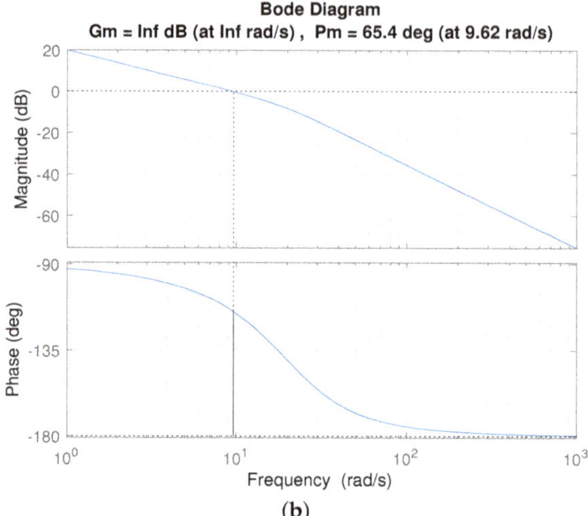

Figure 16. Origami system identification. Step response in closed loop (**a**); Bode diagram in open loop (**b**).

4. Results

A Matlab simulation scheme has been created to validate the kinematics for both simple and nested links with two and three sections. The main parameters a, α and β were used to compute the origami behavior while the height h was the input data to fold or deploy the origami. Taking Equation (4) into account, the maximum height is when $\delta = 90$ and the structure is completely deployed. This position is not achieved in the prototype because the spring force does not generate enough rotation for the links to change position at a positive θ angle and reach $\delta = 90$.

Figure 17 shows the kinematics simulation for a single link with different heights. The change of the rotation angle θ can be seen while the origami is deploying. The simulation results are shown in Table 3.

Table 3. Data from single link kinematics simulation.

	h (mm)	δ (deg)	θ (deg)
Collapsed state	0	0	−13.32
Deploying state	30	54.3	−12.27
Deployed state	36.93	90	1.04

The nested link has been simulated, too. In this case the total link height is the sum of each single link. To achieve a certain height position, we can actuate each individual link or all at once. Figure 18 shows three different configurations: completely deployed link, only one section folding, and three sections folding. The data results from this simulation are shown in Table 4.

Table 4. Three-sections link kinematics simulation data.

	h_1 (mm)	h_2 (mm)	h_3 (mm)	h_{total} (mm)
Completely deployed link	36.93	36.93	36.93	110.8
Only one section folding	36.93	20.55	36.93	94.43
Three sections folding	31.73	25.55	30	87.29

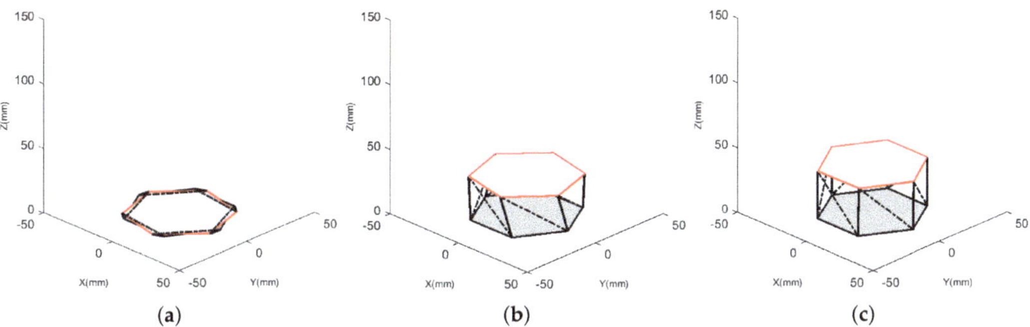

Figure 17. Origami Kresling single link kinematics vadidation, with parameters $\alpha = 38°$, $\beta = 30°$ and $a = 30$ mm. (**a**) Collapsed state. (**b**) Deploying state. (**c**) Deployed state.

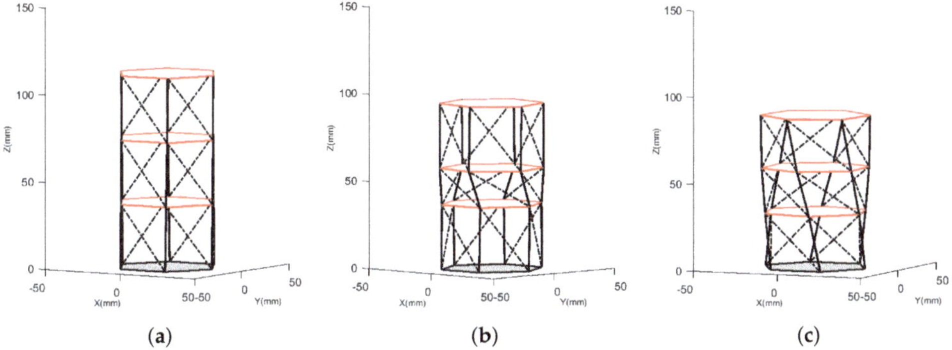

Figure 18. Three-sections link kinematics validation, with parameters $\alpha = 38°$, $\beta = 30°$ and $a = 30$ mm. (**a**) Completely deployed link. (**b**) Only one section folding. (**c**) Three sections folding.

Single Link Cable-Driven Prototype Experimental Results

Position control tests have been carried out with both the integer and the fractional controllers adjusted. The tests were made according to encoder data in *rad*; however, the origami linear displacement is easy to obtain knowing that the motor coupling radius is 7.5 (mm) and the encoder resolution is 5580 counts per turn. The linear displacement corresponds to the origami folding, and height h and rotation angle θ can be indirectly calculated.

Two tests have been designed. The first consists of giving the system individual targets in position: 0.5, 1.0, 1.5, 2.0 and 2.2 (*rad*). The physical behavior of the system can be seen in Figure 19, where the initial reference of the upper part of the origami and the union of the three tendons to visualize the displacement has been marked with a red dashed line.

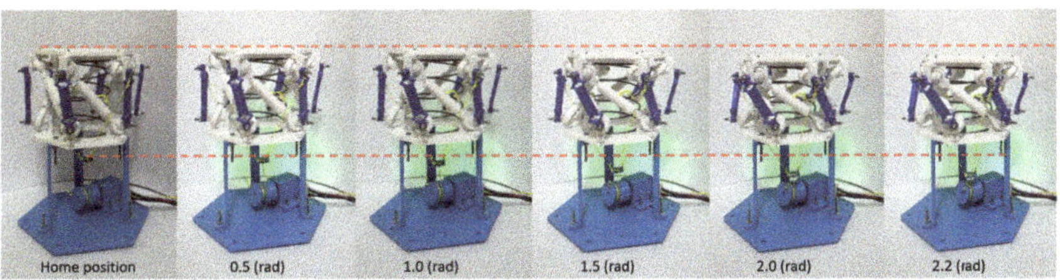

Figure 19. Prototype test results with different target position.

The data results obtained are shown in Figure 20. The saturation of the system is evident in the higher set points, showing an overshoot in the response of the system. The control signals of the internal loop in speed and the external loop in position are shown in Figure 21.

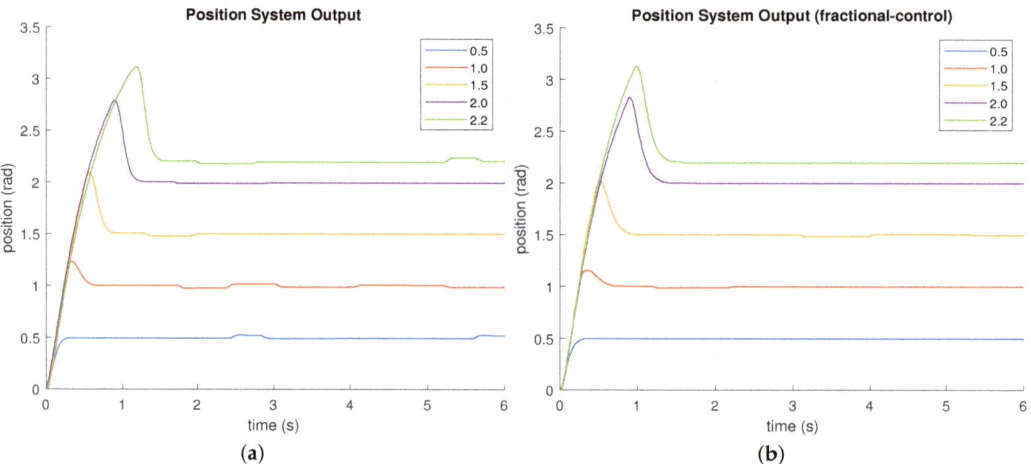

Figure 20. Test results with different target positions. (**a**) Integer controller. (**b**) Fractional controller.

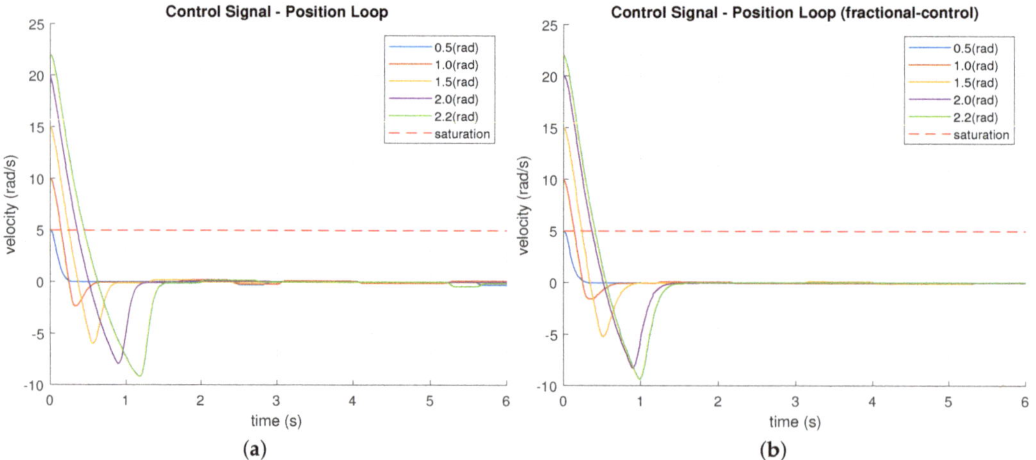

Figure 21. *Cont.*

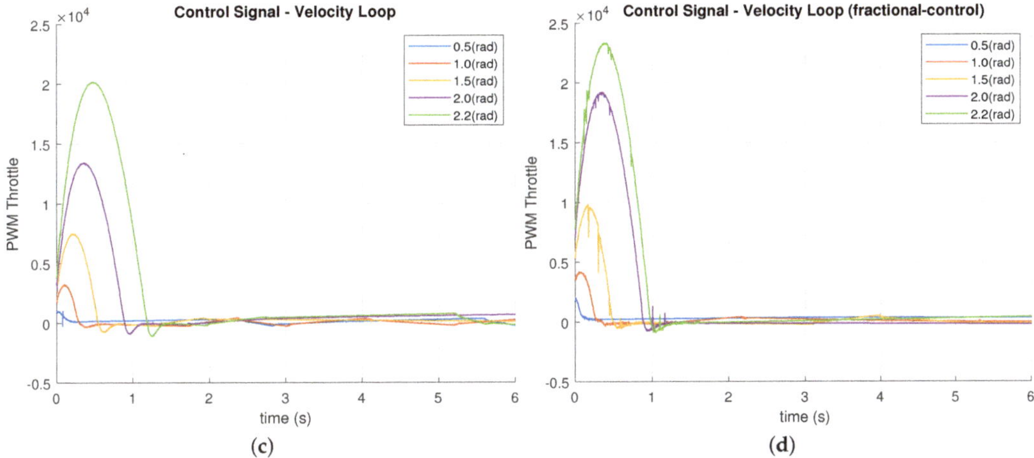

Figure 21. Control signals. (**a**) Position loop control signals with integer controller. (**b**) Position loop control signals with fractional controller. (**c**) Velocity loop control signals with Integer controller. (**d**) Velocity loop control signals with fractional controller.

Table 5 shows the experimental kinematic data, which have been calculated indirectly according to the experimental position changes in the first test. For this purpose, the initial position of the prototype with angle $\theta = 0.0514$ (rad) and initial height $h = 39.44$ (mm) has been considered, resulting in a maximum $\delta = 85.64$ (deg). The position data were measured for all targets once the system reached its permanent state, at time $t = 4$ s.

A simulation was performed with the obtained δ data in order to make a comparison between experimental and simulation data in terms of height h and angle θ. The resulting errors are shown in Table 5. The difference between the real measured and simulated values is clearly the value of l_{BC}, since in the measured value $l_{BCreal} = 39.56$ (mm) and in the simulated value $l_{BCsim} = 43.09$ (mm). This difference is due to the fact that in the assembled prototype the link representing l_{BC} is slightly compressed to maintain the desired position of the structure.

Table 5. Experimental kinematic data indirectly computed.

	Real			Simulation		Error	
Position (rad)	h (mm)	δ (deg)	θ (deg)	h (mm)	θ (deg)	h (mm)	θ (deg)
0.5	35.69	64.46	−12.11	38.88	−12.28	3.18	−0.1635
1	31.94	53.85	−12.72	34.79	−12.89	2.84	−0.1637
1.5	28.19	45.45	−13.06	30.71	−13.23	2.51	−0.1660
2	24.44	38.16	−13.28	26.64	−13.45	2.19	−0.1634
2.2	22.94	35.45	−13.35	24.99	−13.52	2.04	−0.1642

The second test consists in giving the system sequential targets between 0.5 and 2.5 rad with steps of 0.5 rad. The results are shown in Figure 22, where the real position data is in red. Here we can see an expected behavior for the designed controllers. The overshoot in each step is lower than in the first test because the sequential targets are lower than the individual ones.

On the other hand, when the loop is restarted and the position must change from 2.5 to 0.5 rad, the system behavior is the opposite, that is, it must change from folding to deploying. In that case, the position reaches the target with an initial overshoot but quickly stabilizes. In this way, the efficiency and robustness of the control system have been validated.

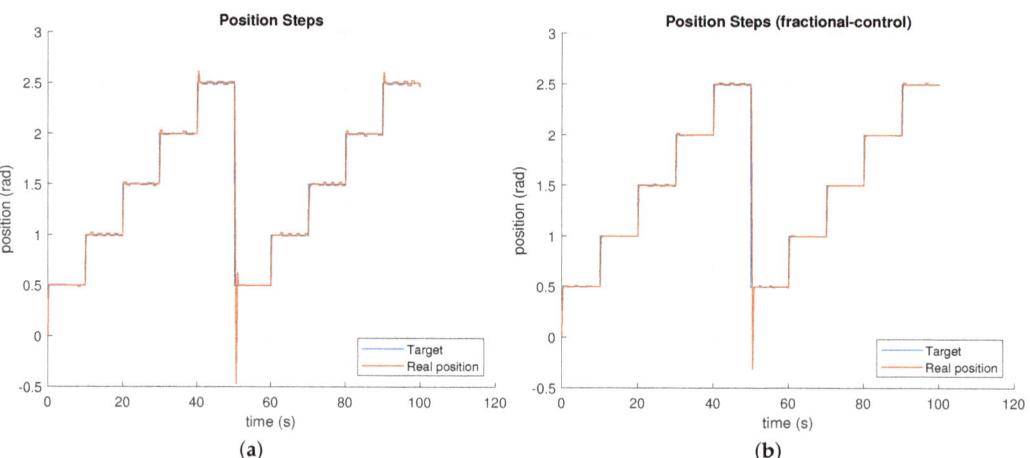

Figure 22. Test results with sequential target positions. (a) Integer controller. (b) Fractional controller.

The video of the performance of this test can be visualized in the following link: https://cutt.ly/rjW0Obi, available since 14 January 2021.

To verify the robustness of both the control and the structure, the steps were tested with different payloads between 100 and 400 g, as shown in Figure 23.

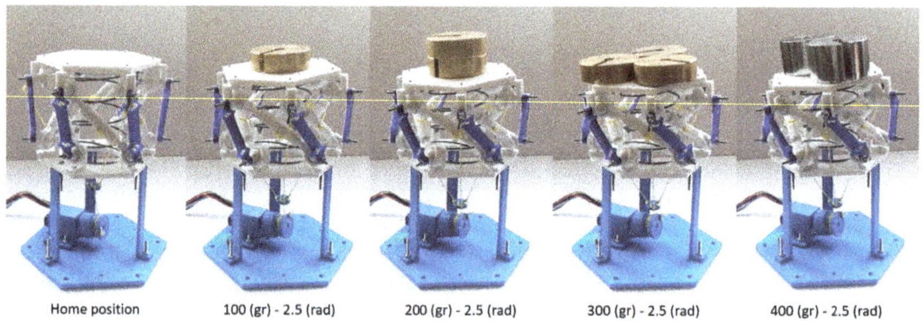

Figure 23. Prototype test results with different payloads in 2.5 (rad) position.

The results obtained allow for the determination of the behavior of the integer and fractional controllers (Figure 24), where the most relevant behavior is shown in the return zone from 2.5 (rad) to 0.5 (rad).

In the case of the integer controller (Figure 24a), the lower peak position reaches -0.54 (rad) with a stabilization time of 0.63 (s) and a maximum overshoot of 16%, while in the case of the fractional controller (Figure 24b), the minimum position is -0.44 (rad); it has no overshoot and the stabilization time is 0.43 (s). Therefore, it can be concluded that the fractional controller is not only robust but also faster than the integer controller.

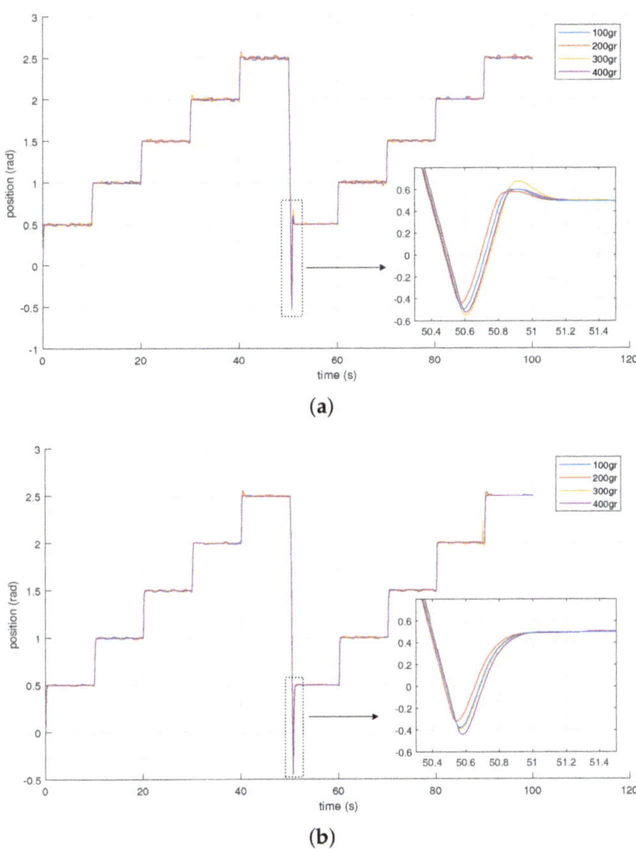

(a)

(b)

Figure 24. Prototype test results with different payloads. (**a**) Integer controller. (**b**) Fractional controller.

The control signals for both controllers are shown in Figure 25.

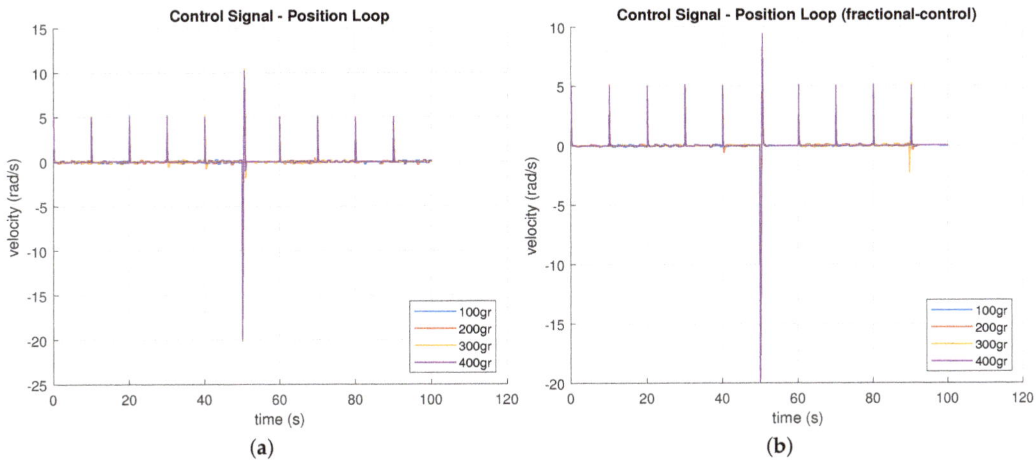

(a)

(b)

Figure 25. *Cont.*

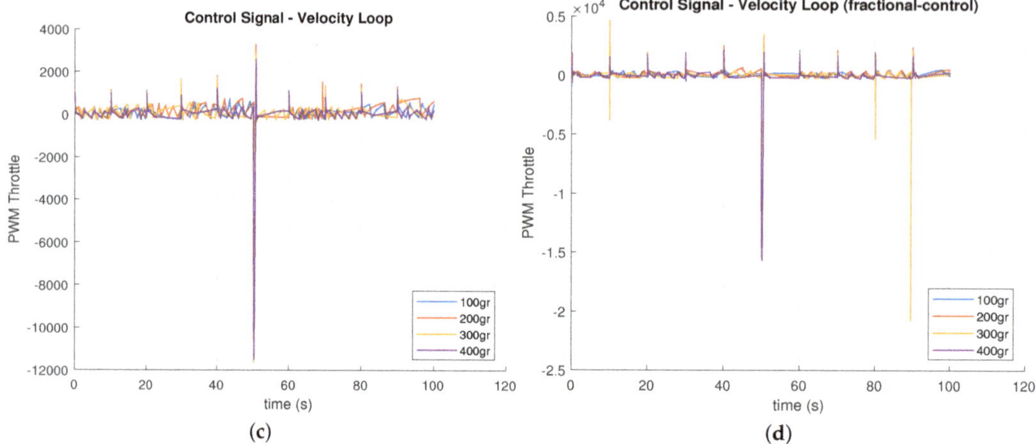

Figure 25. Control signals test results with different payloads. (**a**) Position loop control signals with integer controller. (**b**) Position loop control signals with fractional controller. (**c**) Velocity loop control signals with Integer controller. (**d**) Velocity loop control signals with fractional controller.

It is interesting to mention that in this last test the loads were placed in a distributed way so that the center of mass does not change. In case the loads were placed off-center or unbalanced, the dynamics of the system would change because an additional DoF would be generated, allowing the upper base of the platform to tilt in the direction of the weight. For these scenarios more than one actuator would be required in order to compensate this tilt movement (and other actuators could be included to generate other different DoF). This is an interesting topic to be developed in future works.

5. Conclusions

A design proposal has been presented for a scalable and modular link, inspired by origami structures. The validation of the kinematics for both single and nested links has been successfully carried out. In the case of the nested link, the change in length of the link can be done by completely folding one of the single links or by doing a proportional folding on each single link.

A simple link prototype has been built and experimentally tested to validate its scalability and shape change. The model with three tendons actuated by a motor allows the folding of the origami structure while an internal spring generates the unfolding.

Compared to other platforms such as [21], which are manually controlled, in our study we included system modeling and controller tuning for automatic operation in position control of the prototype.

The single link prototype has been successfully controlled in position mode. The position control has been done with two control loops for the correct operation of the motor. The internal loop allows for the elimination of the dead zones of the motor with a velocity control and with the external loop the origami position is controlled. The internal loop has been designed and tested with two controllers, integer and fractional, where the single link has been tested for correct operation with and without payload.

The identification of the whole system was carried out considering these two control loops; otherwise, the direct identification of the system would have resulted in a nonlinear system, due to the saturation and the dead zone of the motor.

It is also important to remark that the rotational movement of the Kresling pattern can be seen as an advantage that allows the orientation of the platform. However, the rotation can be canceled by coupling two simple links with opposite rotation, if only a prismatic displacement is required.

Some of the main limitations of the system are due to the fact that it is a very low cost 3D printed prototype that needs the adjustment of the mechanical parts and the use of a better motor. However, despite these limitations, the prototype works properly and the design has been validated.

Future works include the improvement of the mechanical and actuation parts of the link and the introduction of distance and rotation sensors to enhance the position accuracy h and rotation angle θ, which are now obtained indirectly. Besides, the development of the three-dimensional joint to interconnect several links is one of our major objectives, which will allow us to implement and test modularity.

Author Contributions: Conceptualization, L.M.; methodology, L.M.; software, L.M. and J.M.; validation, L.M. and J.M.; investigation, L.M., C.A.M., and J.M.; resources, C.A.M. and C.B.; data curation, L.M. and J.M.; writing—original draft preparation, L.M. and J.M.; writing—review and editing, C.A.M.; supervision, C.A.M. and C.B.; project administration, C.A.M. All authors have read and agreed to the published version of the manuscript.

Funding: The research leading to these results has received funding from the project Desarrollo de articulaciones blandas para aplicaciones robóticas, with reference IND2020/IND-1739, funded by the Comunidad Autónoma de Madrid (CAM) (Department of Education and Research), and from RoboCity2030-DIH-CM, Madrid Robotics Digital Innovation Hub (Robótica aplicada a la mejora de la calidad de vida de los ciudadanos, FaseIV; S2018/NMT-4331), funded by "Programas de Actividades I+D en la Comunidad de Madrid" and cofunded by Structural Funds of the EU.

Institutional Review Board Statement: Not applicable.

Informed Consent Statement: Not applicable.

Data Availability Statement: The data presented are available on request from the corresponding author.

Conflicts of Interest: There are no conflicts of interest to declare.

Abbreviations

The following abbreviations are used in this manuscript:

MRS	Modular robotic system
MITE	Module, information, task, and environment
DoF	Degrees of freedom

References

1. Fukuda, T.; Nakagawa, S. Approach to the dynamically reconfigurable robotic system. *J. Intell. Robot. Syst.* **1988**, *1*, 55–72. [CrossRef]
2. Schmitz, D. *The CMU Reconfigurable Modular Manipulator System*; Technical Report; The Robotics Institute, Carnegie Mellon University: Pittsburgh, PA, USA, 1988.
3. Ahmadzadeh, H.; Masehian, E.; Asadpour, M. Modular robotic systems: Characteristics and applications. *J. Intell. Robot. Syst.* **2016**, *81*, 317–357. [CrossRef]
4. Yim, M. A reconfigurable modular robot with multiple modes of locomotion. In Proceedings of the 1993 JSME Conference on Advanced Mechatronics, Tokyo, Japan, August 1993.
5. Qiao, G.; Song, G.; Wang, W.; Zhang, Y.; Wang, Y. Design and implementation of a modular self-reconfigurable robot. *Int. J. Adv. Robot. Syst.* **2014**, *11*, 47. [CrossRef]
6. Murata, S.; Kurokawa, H.; Kokaji, S. Self-assembling machine. In Proceedings of the 1994 IEEE International Conference on Robotics and Automation, San Diego, CA, USA, 8–13 May 1994; IEEE: New York, NY, USA, 1994; pp. 441–448.
7. Murata, S.; Kurokawa, H. Prototypes of self-organizing robots. In *Self-Organizing Robots*; Springer: Tokyo, Japan, 2012; pp. 105–130.
8. Inou, N.; Kobayashi, H.; Koseki, M. Development of pneumatic cellular robots forming a mechanical structure. In Proceedings of the 7th International Conference on Control, Automation, Robotics and Vision, 2002, ICARCV 2002, Singapore, 2–5 December 2002; IEEE: New York, NY, USA, 2002; Volume 1, pp. 63–68.
9. Romanishin, J.W.; Gilpin, K.; Rus, D. M-blocks: Momentum-driven, magnetic modular robots. In Proceedings of the 2013 IEEE/RSJ International Conference on Intelligent Robots and Systems, Tokyo, Japan, 3–8 November 2013; IEEE: New York, NY, USA, 2013; pp. 4288–4295.

10. Wolfe, K.C.; Moses, M.S.; Kutzer, M.D.; Chirikjian, G.S. M 3 Express: A low-cost independently-mobile reconfigurable modular robot. In Proceedings of the 2012 IEEE International Conference on Robotics and Automation, St Paul, MN, USA, 14–18 May 2012; IEEE: New York, NY, USA, 2012; pp. 2704–2710.
11. Hong, W.; Wang, S.; Shui, D. Reconfigurable robot system based on electromagnetic design. In Proceedings of the 2011 International Conference on Fluid Power and Mechatronics, Beijing, China, 17–20 August 2011; IEEE: New York, NY, USA, 2011; pp. 570–575.
12. Sadjadi, H.; Mohareri, O.; Al-Jarrah, M.A.; Assaleh, K. Design and implementation of HexBot: A modular self-reconfigurable robotic system. *J. Frankl. Inst.* **2012**, *349*, 2281–2293. [CrossRef]
13. Davey, J.; Kwok, N.; Yim, M. Emulating self-reconfigurable robots-design of the SMORES system. In Proceedings of the 2012 IEEE/RSJ International Conference on Intelligent Robots and Systems, Vilamoura, Algarve, Portugal, 7–12 October 2012; IEEE: New York, NY, USA, 2012; pp. 4464–4469.
14. Lyder, A.; Garcia, R.F.M.; Stoy, K. Genderless connection mechanism for modular robots introducing torque transmission between modules. In Proceedings of the ICRA Workshop on Modular Robots, State of the Art, Anchorage, Alaska, 3 May 2010; pp. 77–81.
15. Yu, C.H.; Haller, K.; Ingber, D.; Nagpal, R. Morpho: A self-deformable modular robot inspired by cellular structure. In Proceedings of the 2008 IEEE/RSJ International Conference on Intelligent Robots and Systems, Nice, France, 22–26 September 2008; IEEE: New York, NY, USA, 2008; pp. 3571–3578.
16. Galloway, K.C.; Jois, R.; Yim, M. Factory floor: A robotically reconfigurable construction platform. In Proceedings of the 2010 IEEE International Conference on Robotics and Automation, Anchorage, AK, USA, 3–7 May 2010; IEEE: New York, NY, USA, 2010; pp. 2467–2472.
17. Lyder, A.; Garcia, R.F.M.; Stoy, K. Mechanical design of odin, an extendable heterogeneous deformable modular robot. In Proceedings of the 2008 IEEE/RSJ International Conference on Intelligent Robots and Systems, Nice, France, 22–26 September 2008; IEEE: New York, NY, USA, 2008; pp. 883–888.
18. Shimizu, M.; Ishiguro, A.; Kawakatsu, T. A modular robot that exploits a spontaneous connectivity control mechanism. In Proceedings of the 2005 IEEE/RSJ International Conference on Intelligent Robots and Systems, Edmonton, AB, Canada, 2–6 August 2005; IEEE: New York, NY, USA, 2005; pp. 1899–1904.
19. Donald, B.R.; Levey, C.G.; McGray, C.D.; Paprotny, I.; Rus, D. An untethered, electrostatic, globally controllable MEMS micro-robot. *J. Microelectromechan. Syst.* **2006**, *15*, 1–15. [CrossRef]
20. Suzuki, R.; Zheng, C.; Kakehi, Y.; Yeh, T.; Do, E.Y.L.; Gross, M.D.; Leithinger, D. ShapeBots: Shape-changing Swarm Robots. In Proceedings of the 32nd Annual ACM Symposium on User Interface Software and Technology, New Orleans, LA, USA, 20–23 October 2019; pp. 493–505.
21. Matsuo, H.; Asada, H.H.; Takeda, Y. Design of a Novel Mutliple-DOF Extendable Arm With Rigid Components Inspired by a Deployable Origami Structure. *IEEE Robot. Autom. Lett.* **2020**, *5*, 2730–2737. [CrossRef]
22. Hatori, K. History of Origami in the East and the West before Interfusion. In *Origami 5: Fifth International Meeting of Origami Science, Mathematics and Education*; Singapore Management University: Singapore, 2010; pp. 1–13.
23. Miura, K. Method of packaging and deployment of large membranes in space. *Title Inst. Space Astronaut. Sci. Rep.* **1985**, *618*, 1.
24. Santoso, J.; Skorina, E.H.; Luo, M.; Yan, R.; Onal, C.D. Design and analysis of an origami continuum manipulation module with torsional strength. In Proceedings of the 2017 IEEE/RSJ International Conference on Intelligent Robots and Systems (IROS), Vancouver, BC, Canada, 24–28 September 2017; IEEE: New York, NY, USA, 2017; pp. 2098–2104.
25. Firouzeh, A.; Paik, J. An under-actuated origami gripper with adjustable stiffness joints for multiple grasp modes. *Smart Mater. Struct.* **2017**, *26*, 055035. [CrossRef]
26. Kuribayashi, K.; Tsuchiya, K.; You, Z.; Tomus, D.; Umemoto, M.; Ito, T.; Sasaki, M. Self-deployable origami stent grafts as a biomedical application of Ni-rich TiNi shape memory alloy foil. *Mater. Sci. Eng. A* **2006**, *419*, 131–137. [CrossRef]
27. Zirbel, S.A.; Wilson, M.E.; Magleby, S.P.; Howell, L.L. An origami-inspired self-deployable array. In Proceedings of the ASME 2013 Conference on Smart Materials, Adaptive Structures and Intelligent Systems, Snowbird, UT, USA, 16–18 September 2013.
28. Paez, L.; Agarwal, G.; Paik, J. Design and analysis of a soft pneumatic actuator with origami shell reinforcement. *Soft Robot.* **2016**, *3*, 109–119. [CrossRef]
29. Kidambi, N.; Wang, K. Dynamics of Kresling origami deployment. *Phys. Rev. E* **2020**, *101*, 063003. [CrossRef] [PubMed]
30. Kresling, B.; Abel, J.F. Natural twist buckling in shells: From the hawkmoth's bellows to the deployable Kresling-pattern and cylindrical Miura-ori. In Proceedings of the 6th International Conference on Computation of Shell and Spatial Structures, Ithaca, NY, USA, 28–31 May 2008; Volume 11, pp. 12–32.
31. Zhai, Z.; Wang, Y.; Jiang, H. Origami-inspired, on-demand deployable and collapsible mechanical metamaterials with tunable stiffness. *Proc. Natl. Acad. Sci. USA* **2018**, *115*, 2032–2037. [CrossRef] [PubMed]
32. Hunt, G.W.; Ario, I. Twist buckling and the foldable cylinder: An exercise in origami. *Int. J. Non-Linear Mech.* **2005**, *40*, 833–843. [CrossRef]
33. Jianguo, C.; Xiaowei, D.; Ya, Z.; Jian, F.; Yongming, T. Bistable behavior of the cylindrical origami structure with Kresling pattern. *J. Mech. Des.* **2015**, *137*. [CrossRef]
34. Zhang, Q.; Cai, J.; Li, M.; Feng, J. Bistable behaviour of a deployable cylinder with Kresling pattern. In Proceedings of the 7th International Meeting on Origami in Science, Mathematics and Education (7OSME), Oxford, UK, 4–7 September 2018.

35. Muñoz, J.; Monje, C.A.; Nagua, L.F.; Balaguer, C. A graphical tuning method for fractional order controllers based on iso-slope phase curves. *ISA Trans.* **2020**. [CrossRef] [PubMed]
36. Nise, N.S. Frequency response techniques. In *Control Systems Engineering*; Wiley: Pomona, CA, USA, 2019; Chapter 10, pp. 525–612.
37. Chen, Y.; Moore, K.L. Relay Feedback Tuning of Robust PID Controllers with Iso-damping Property. *IEEE Trans. Syst. Man Cybern. Part B* **2005**, *35*, 23–31. [CrossRef] [PubMed]
38. Monje, C.A.; Vinagre, B.M.; Santamaría, G.E.; Tejado, I. Auto-tuning of fractional order $PI^\lambda D^\mu$ controllers using a PLC. In Proceedings of the 2009 IEEE Conference on Emerging Technologies Factory Automation, Palma de Mallorca, Spain, 22–25 September 2009; IEEE: New York, NY, USA, 2009; pp. 1–7. [CrossRef]

 *mathematics*

Article

Fundamentals of Synthesized Optimal Control

Askhat Diveev [1], Elizaveta Shmalko [1,*], Vladimir Serebrenny [2] and Peter Zentay [3]

[1] Federal Research Center "Computer Science and Control" of the Russian Academy of Sciences, 119333 Moscow, Russia; aidiveev@mail.ru

[2] Department of Robotic Systems and Mechatronics, Bauman Moscow State Technical University, 105005 Moscow, Russia; vsereb@bmstu.ru

[3] Faculty of Mechanical Engineering, Budapest University of Technology and Economics, 1111 Budapest, Hungary; zentay.peter@bgk.uni-obuda.hu

* Correspondence: e.shmalko@gmail.com

Abstract: This paper presents a new formulation of the optimal control problem with uncertainty, in which an additive bounded function is considered as uncertainty. The purpose of the control is to ensure the achievement of terminal conditions with the optimal value of the quality functional, while the uncertainty has a limited impact on the change in the value of the functional. The article introduces the concept of feasibility of the mathematical model of the object, which is associated with the contraction property of mappings if we consider the model of the object as a one-parameter mapping. It is shown that this property is sufficient for the development of stable practical systems. To find a solution to the stated problem, which would ensure the feasibility of the system, the synthesized optimal control method is proposed. This article formulates the theoretical foundations of the synthesized optimal control. The method consists in making the control object stable relative to some point in the state space and to control the object by changing the position of the equilibrium points. The article provides evidence that this approach is insensitive to the uncertainties of the mathematical model of the object. An example of the application of the method for optimal control of a group of robots is given. A comparison of the synthesized optimal control method with the direct method on the model without disturbances and with them is presented.

Keywords: optimal control; Lyapunov stability; equilibrium point; symbolic regression; Pontryagin's maximum principle

Citation: Diveev, A.; Shmalko, E.; Serebrenny, V.; Zentay, P. Fundamentals of Synthesized Optimal Control. *Mathematics* **2021**, *9*, 21. https://dx.doi.org/10.3390/math9010021

Received: 3 November 2020
Accepted: 17 December 2020
Published: 23 December 2020

1. Introduction

Object control in the classical mathematical sense is to qualitatively change the right-hand sides of the differential equations describing the mathematical model of the control object, due to the control vector included in them. Thus, the problem of optimal control [1] consists in finding such a control function, as a function of time, which will make the required changes in the right-hand sides of the model of the control object so that, for given initial conditions, the partial solution of the system of differential equations achieves the control goal with the optimal value of the quality criterion.

There are two main directions for solving the problem of optimal control: direct and indirect approaches. The indirect approach based on the Pontryagin's maximum principle [2–4] solves optimal control by formulating it as a boundary-value problem, in which it is necessary to find the initial conditions for a system of differential equations for conjugate variables. Its optimal solution is highly accurate, however, very sensitive to the formulation of additional conditions that the control must satisfy, along with ensuring the maximum of the Hamiltonian, which are generally very difficult to set in practice for problems with complex phase constraints. The direct approach reduces the optimal control problem to a nonlinear programming problem [5–7], that provides the transition from the optimization problem in the infinite-dimensional space to the optimization problem in the finite-dimensional space, so it is more convenient and can be readily solved within a wider convergence region.

However, these works generally focus on the nominal trajectory performance without considering possible uncertainties. In practice, in the right-hand sides of the models, there are objectively some uncertainties of various nature. As a rule, they are not taken into account, but the presence of such uncertainties can lead to the loss of optimality of the obtained control.

There are also approaches when the impact of uncertainties is taken into account during the reference trajectory design beforehand [8,9]. For example, desensitized optimal control [10], modifies the nominal optimal trajectory such that it is less sensitive with respect to uncertain parameters. This involves constructing an appropriate sensitivity cost which, when penalized, provides solutions that are relatively insensitive to parametric uncertainties.

Although in practice such solutions do not guarantee the stability and still require construction of the feedback stabilization control system to eliminate errors [8].

In control theory, there is a field of robust control [11–14], which provides a certain stability coefficient of the control system. Robust control methods generally move the eigenvalues of the linearized system as far as possible to the left of the imaginary axis of the complex plane, so that uncertainties and perturbations do not make the system unstable. These methods are not aimed at solving the optimal control problem.

In practical control system design, the existing uncertainties of the mathematical model of the object, which subsequently cause the discrepancy between the real trajectory of the object and the obtained optimal one, are compensated by the synthesis of a feedback motion stabilization system relative to the optimal trajectory [8,15–17]. But construction of the stabilization system changes the mathematical model of the object and the received control might be not optimal for the new model.

In this paper, uncertainties are included in the problem statement as an additive bounded function. And the optimal control problem is supposed to be solved after ensuring stability to the plant in the state space. This approach was called the method of synthesized optimal control. A control function is found such that the system of differential equations will always have a stable equilibrium point in the state space. With that, the control system contains parameters that affect the position of the equilibrium point. Consequently, the object is controlled by changing the position of the equilibrium point. In this paper, it is shown that such control can also provide the required value of the quality criterion, but the mathematical model of the control object turns out to be insensitive to the existing uncertainties and external disturbances. The approach of synthesized optimal control is new, but we have already managed to obtain good experimental results [18,19] confirming the effectiveness of such control. In this paper, we provide mathematical formulations of the approach and give a theoretical substantiation of the efficiency of the synthesized optimal control. A comparative numerical example of solving the problem of optimal control of two robots under phase constraints by the indirect method of synthesized optimal control and by the direct method based on piecewise linear approximation is given.

2. Problem Statement

The mathematical model of control object with uncertainty is given

$$\dot{\mathbf{x}} = \mathbf{f}(\mathbf{x}, \mathbf{u}) + \mathbf{y}(t), \tag{1}$$

where $\mathbf{x} \in \mathbb{R}^n$, $\mathbf{u} \in U \subseteq \mathbb{R}^m$, U is a compact set, $m \leq n$, $\mathbf{y}$ is a uncertainty function, $\mathbf{y}(t) \in \mathbb{R}^n$,

$$\mathbf{y}^- \leq \mathbf{y}(t) \leq \mathbf{y}^+ \tag{2}$$

$\mathbf{y}^-, \mathbf{y}^+$ are set constant vectors.

Initial conditions are set

$$\mathbf{x}(0) = \mathbf{x}^0. \tag{3}$$

Terminal condition is set

$$\mathbf{x}(t_f) = \mathbf{x}^f, \tag{4}$$

where time t_f of hitting terminal conditions t_f is not given, but is limited

$$t_f \leq t^+, \tag{5}$$

t^+ is a given positive value.

The functional is given

$$J = \int\limits_0^{t_f} f_0(\mathbf{x}(t), \mathbf{u}(t))dt + p_1\|\mathbf{x}^f - \mathbf{x}(t_f)\| \to \min_{\mathbf{u}(\cdot) \in U}, \tag{6}$$

where p_1 is a given positive value.

It is necessary to find a control function

$$\mathbf{u} = \mathbf{h}(\mathbf{x}, t) \tag{7}$$

such that for any partial solution

$$\mathbf{x}(t, \mathbf{x}^0) \tag{8}$$

of the system

$$\dot{\mathbf{x}} = \mathbf{f}(\mathbf{x}, \mathbf{h}(\mathbf{x}, t)) + \mathbf{y}(t) \tag{9}$$

from initial conditions (3) for any uncertainty function (2) value of the functional (6) satisfies inequation

$$J(\mathbf{x}(t, \mathbf{x}^0), \mathbf{y}(t)) \leq J(\mathbf{x}(t, \mathbf{x}^0), 0) + \Delta_y, \tag{10}$$

where $J(\mathbf{x}(t, \mathbf{x}^0), \mathbf{y}(t))$ is a value of functional (6) for the solution (8) with perturbation (2), $J(\mathbf{x}(t, \mathbf{x}^0), 0)$ is a value of functional (6) for the same solution (8) without perturbations, $\mathbf{y}(\cdot) \equiv 0$, Δ_y is a given positive value.

Among possible solutions in the form (7) we consider only such that possess the following properties. Let $\mathbf{x}(t, \mathbf{x}^0)$ be some partial solution of the system (9) with $\mathbf{y}(t) \equiv 0$ and $J(0)$ be a value of criterion (10) for it. Let us denote

$$\tilde{\mathbf{x}} = \mathbf{x}(t, \mathbf{x}^0) + \tilde{\mathbf{z}}(t), \tag{11}$$

$$\tilde{\tilde{\mathbf{x}}} = \mathbf{x}(t, \mathbf{x}^0) + \tilde{\tilde{\mathbf{z}}}(t), \tag{12}$$

and

$$\tilde{\delta} = \max_{t \in [0; t_f]} \|\mathbf{x}(t, \mathbf{x}^0) - \tilde{\mathbf{x}}(t)\|, \tag{13}$$

$$\tilde{\tilde{\delta}} = \max_{t \in [0; t_f]} \|\mathbf{x}(t, \mathbf{x}^0) + \tilde{\tilde{\mathbf{x}}}(t)\|. \tag{14}$$

Then $\tilde{\delta} > 0$ exist, such that $\forall \tilde{\tilde{\delta}} \leq \tilde{\delta}$ conditions are met

$$\tilde{\tilde{\Delta}} \leq \tilde{\Delta}, \tag{15}$$

where

$$\tilde{\Delta} = |J(\mathbf{x}(t, \mathbf{x}^0), 0) - J(\tilde{\mathbf{x}}(t), 0)|, \tag{16}$$

$$\tilde{\tilde{\Delta}} = |J(\mathbf{x}(t, \mathbf{x}^0), 0) - J(\tilde{\tilde{\mathbf{x}}}(t), 0)|. \tag{17}$$

The condition (15) is called the continuous dependence of the functional on perturbations. The goal is to look for solutions in form (7) so that they satisfy condition (15).

3. Theoretical Background and Justifications for the Synthesized Optimal Control Method

Problems with uncertainties are often considered in optimal control, since the question is relevant in the practical implementation of obtained systems. As a rule, uncertain parameters of the right-hand sides or initial conditions are considered as uncertainties, or some random perturbations are introduced. The main direction of solving problems with perturbations is to ensure the stability of the obtained solution. So, firstly, the problem of optimal control is solved without uncertainties, and then, using the stabilization system, an attempt is made to ensure the stability of motion relative to the optimal trajectory. In fact, the creation of a stabilization system is an attempt to ensure the stability of the differential equation solution according to Lyapunov.

Theorem 1. *To perform the condition (10) it is enough that a partial solution (8) of the system (9) without perturbations* $\mathbf{y}(t) \equiv 0$

$$\dot{\mathbf{x}} = \mathbf{f}(\mathbf{x}, \mathbf{h}(\mathbf{x}, t)), \tag{18}$$

was stable according to Lyapunov.

Proof. From differential Equation (1) follows

$$\mathbf{x}(t + \Delta t) = \mathbf{x}(t) + \Delta t \mathbf{f}(\mathbf{x}, \mathbf{h}(\mathbf{x}, t)) + \Delta t \mathbf{y}(t), \tag{19}$$

or

$$\bar{\mathbf{x}}(t) = \mathbf{x}(t, \mathbf{x}^0) + \mathbf{v}(t), \tag{20}$$

where

$$\mathbf{v}(t) = \int\limits_0^t \mathbf{y}(t)dt. \tag{21}$$

Let Δ_y be given. Then according to condition (15) you can always define $\tilde{\Delta}$ and value $\bar{\delta}$ for perturbed solution $\bar{\mathbf{x}}$ such that according to condition of stability on Lyapunov [20,21]

$$\|\mathbf{x}(t, \mathbf{x}^0) - \bar{\mathbf{x}}(t)\| < \bar{\delta}, \ \forall t \in [0; t_f]. \tag{22}$$

For this it is enough to satisfy the inequality

$$0 \leq \|\mathbf{v}(t)\| \leq \bar{\delta}/2, \ \forall t \in [0; t_f]. \tag{23}$$

$\square$

However, to find control function (7) such that partial solution (8) was stable according to Lyapunov is rather difficult and, in fact, it is not always necessary. According to Lyapunov's theorem, a stable solution to a differential equation must have the property of an attractor [20,22], and, therefore, from the mathematical point of view the synthesis of stabilization system is an attempt to give an attractor property to the found optimal trajectory [21,23]. The main problem of unstable solutions is that they are difficult to implement, since small perturbations of the model lead to large errors of the functional, in other words, the solution does not have the attractor property. But in fact, the requirement for the optimal solution to obtain the attractor property or be Lyapunov stable is a fairly strict one and it could be redundant, and other weaker requirements may be enough to implement the resulting solution. For example, the motion of a pendulum is not Lyapunov stable if it is not the zero rest point, but it is physically feasible, since its small perturbations lead to small perturbations of the functional.

In this concern let us introduce the concept of feasibility.

4. Feasibility Property

Based on a qualitative analysis [24] of the solutions of systems of differential equations, the feasibility means that small changes in the model do not lead to a loss of quality. In other words, it is necessary that the solution has the contraction property.

Hypothesis 1. *A mathematical model is feasible, if its errors do not increase in time.*

Definition 1. *The system of differential equations is practically feasible, if this system as a one-parametric mapping obtains a contraction property in the implementation domain.*

Consider a system of differential equations

$$\dot{\mathbf{x}} = \mathbf{f}(\mathbf{x}), \tag{24}$$

where $\mathbf{x} \in \mathbb{R}^n$.

Any ordinary differential equation is a recurrent description of a time function. A solution of the differential equation is a transformation from a recurrent form to a usual time function.

Computer calculation of the differential Equation (24) has a form

$$\mathbf{x}(t + \Delta t) = \mathbf{x}(t) + \Delta t \mathbf{f}(\mathbf{x}(t)), \tag{25}$$

where t is an independent parameter, Δt is a constant parameter, and it is called a step of integration.

The right side of the Equation (25) is a one-parametric mapping from space $\mathbb{R}^n$ to itself

$$F(\mathbf{x}, t) = \mathbf{x}(t) + \Delta t \mathbf{f}(\mathbf{x}(t)) : \ \mathbb{R}^n \to \mathbb{R}^n. \tag{26}$$

Let a compact domain D be set in the space $\mathbb{R}^n$. All solutions of the differential Equations (24), that are of our interest, belong to this domain. Therefore, for the differential Equations (24) the initial and terminal conditions belong to this domain

$$\mathbf{x}(0) \in \mathrm{D} \subseteq \mathbb{R}^n, \ \mathbf{x}(t_f) \in \mathrm{D} \subseteq \mathbb{R}^n, \tag{27}$$

where $\mathbf{x}(t_f)$ is a terminal point of the solution (24).

Theorem 2. *In domain* D *for the mapping* (26), *the following property is performed*

$$\rho(\mathbf{x}^a(t), \mathbf{x}^b(t)) \leq \rho(F(\mathbf{x}^a(t), t), F(\mathbf{x}^b(t), t)), \tag{28}$$

where $\mathbf{x}^a(t) \in \mathrm{D}$, $\mathbf{x}^b(t) \in \mathrm{D}$, $\rho(\mathbf{x}^a, \mathbf{x}^b)$ *is a distance between two points in the space* $\mathbb{R}^n$

$$\rho(\mathbf{x}^a, \mathbf{x}^b) = \left\| \mathbf{x}^a - \mathbf{x}^b \right\|. \tag{29}$$

Then the mathematical model (24) *is feasible if the domain* $\mathrm{D} \subseteq \mathbb{R}^n$ *according to the hypothesis.*

Proof. Let $\mathbf{x}(t) \in \mathrm{D}$ be a known state of the system in the moment t and $\mathbf{y}(t) \in \mathrm{D}$ be a real state of the system in the same moment. The error of the state is

$$\delta(t) = \rho(\mathbf{x}(t), \mathbf{y}(t)). \tag{30}$$

According to the mapping (26)

$$\delta(t + \Delta t) = \rho(F(\mathbf{x}(t), t), F(\mathbf{y}(t))). \tag{31}$$

And according to the condition (28) of the theorem

$$\delta(t) \le \delta(t + \Delta t). \tag{32}$$

This proves the theorem. $\square$

The condition (28) shows that the system of differential equations as a one-parametric mapping has contraction property.

Assume that the system (24) in the neighborhood of the domain D has one stable equilibrium point, and there is no other equilibrium point in this neighborhood

$$\mathbf{f}(\tilde{\mathbf{x}}) = 0, \tag{33}$$

$$\det(\lambda\mathbf{E} - \mathbf{A}(\tilde{\mathbf{x}})) = \lambda^n + a_{n-1}\lambda^{n-1} + \ldots + a_1\lambda + a_0 = \prod_{j=1}^{n}(\lambda - \lambda_j) = 0, \tag{34}$$

where $\mathbf{E}$ is a unit $n \times n$ matrix,

$$\mathbf{A}(\tilde{\mathbf{x}}) = \frac{\partial\tilde{\mathbf{f}}(\mathbf{x})}{\partial\mathbf{x}}, \tag{35}$$

$$\lambda_j = \alpha_j + i\beta_j, \tag{36}$$

$\alpha_j < 0, i = \sqrt{-1}, j = 1, \ldots, n$.

Theorem 3. *If for the system (24) there is a domain D that includes one stable equilibrium point (33)–(36), then the system (24) is practically feasible.*

Proof. According to the Lyapunov's stability theorem on the first approximation the trivial solution of the differential Equation (24)

$$\mathbf{x}(t) = \tilde{\mathbf{x}} = \text{constant} \tag{37}$$

is stable. This means, that, if any solution begins from other initial point $\mathbf{x}^0 \ne \tilde{\mathbf{x}}$, then it will be approximated to the stable solution asymptotically

$$\rho(\mathbf{x}(t + \Delta t, \mathbf{x}^a), \tilde{\mathbf{x}}) \le \rho(\mathbf{x}(t, \mathbf{x}^a), \tilde{\mathbf{x}}), \tag{38}$$

where $\mathbf{x}(t, \mathbf{x}^a)$ is a solution of the differential Equation (24) from initial point $\mathbf{x}^a$.

The same is true for another initial condition $\mathbf{x}^b$

$$\rho(\mathbf{x}(t + \Delta t, \mathbf{x}^b), \tilde{\mathbf{x}}) \le \rho(\mathbf{x}(t, \mathbf{x}^b), \tilde{\mathbf{x}}). \tag{39}$$

From here, it follows that the domain D has a fixed point $\tilde{\mathbf{x}}$ of contraction mapping [24], therefore distance between solutions $\mathbf{x}(t, \mathbf{x}^a)$ and $\mathbf{x}(t, \mathbf{x}^b)$ also tends to zero or

$$\rho(\mathbf{x}(t + \Delta t, \mathbf{x}^a), \mathbf{x}(t + \Delta t, \mathbf{x}^b)) \le \rho(\mathbf{x}(t, \mathbf{x}^a), \mathbf{x}(t, \mathbf{x}^b)). \tag{40}$$

This proves the theorem. $\square$

Following the principle of feasibility, an approach is proposed in which the optimal control problem is solved after ensuring the stability of the object in the state space. This approach is called the method of synthesized optimal control. It includes two stages. In the first stage, the system without perturbations is made stable in some point of the state space. This stage of synthesis of the stabilization system allows to embed the control in the object so that the system of differential equations would have the necessary property of feasibility. In this case, the equilibrium point can be changed after some time, but the object maintains equilibrium at every moment in time. Then we control the position of the stable equilibrium point, as an attractor, to solve the optimal control problem.

5. The Synthesized Optimal Control

According to this approach, it is necessary to find such a control function (7) that the system without perturbations would always have a stable equilibrium point in the state space. Together with that, in the control function a parameter vector is introduced. The value of this parameter vector affects on position of the equilibrium point in the states space

$$\mathbf{u} = \mathbf{g}(\mathbf{x}, \mathbf{q}^*), \tag{41}$$

where $\mathbf{q}^*$ is a parameter vector.

Control function (41) provides for the system without perturbations

$$\dot{\mathbf{x}} = \mathbf{f}(\mathbf{x}, \mathbf{g}(\mathbf{x}, \mathbf{q}^*)) \tag{42}$$

existence of the equilibrium point

$$\mathbf{f}(\mathbf{x}^*(\mathbf{q}^*), \mathbf{g}(\mathbf{x}^*(\mathbf{q}^*), \mathbf{q}^*)) = 0, \tag{43}$$

where $\mathbf{x}^*(\mathbf{q}^*)$ is a vector of coordinates of equilibrium point, depending on the parameter vector $\mathbf{q}^*$. The system (42) satisfies conditions (34)–(36) in the point $\mathbf{x}^*(\mathbf{q}^*)$.

Algorithmically, the method of synthesized optimal control first solves the problem of stabilization system synthesis. For solving the synthesis problem, the functional (6) is not used. Purpose of the control synthesis problem is to receive such control function (41) to provide existence of the stable equilibrium point in the state space.

Once the function (41) is found, the optimal control problem is solved next for the mathematical model (42) with the initial conditions (3) and the terminal conditions (4), and with the quality criterion

$$J_1 = \int\limits_0^{t_f} f_0(\mathbf{x}(t), \mathbf{g}(\mathbf{x}(t), \mathbf{q}^*(t)))dt + p_1 \|\mathbf{x}^f - \mathbf{x}(t_f)\| \rightarrow \min_{\mathbf{q}^* \in Q}, \tag{44}$$

where Q is a compact set in the space of parameters.

In general case, the vector of parameters $\mathbf{q}^*$ can be some function $\mathbf{q}^*(t)$. The properties of this function and methods for finding it requires additional studies. In this work this function is found for the original optimal control problem (1)–(6) as a piece-wise constant one.

Thus, in the synthesized optimal control approach, the uncertainty in the right parts is compensated by the stability of the system relative to a point in the state space. Near the equilibrium point, all solutions converge and feasibility principle is satisfied. This first step of stabilization system synthesis is a key idea of the approach, it provides achievement of better results in the tasks with complex environment and noise. However, this approach could not be previously presented as a single computational method, since there was no general numerical approach for solving the problem of control synthesis. Formally, the problem of synthesis of stabilization system involves the construction of such a feedback control module described by some functions that produces control basing on the received data about the object's state and this control makes the object achieve the terminal goal with the optimal value of some given criterion. In the overwhelming majority of cases, the control synthesis problem is solved analytically or technically taking into account the specific properties of the mathematical model. But now modern numerical methods of symbolic regression can be applied to find a solution without reference to specific model equations. Let us consider the issue in more details.

6. The Problem of Control System Synthesis

Consider the problem statement of the general numerical synthesis of the control system. The mathematical model is

$$\dot{\mathbf{x}} = \mathbf{f}(\mathbf{x}, \mathbf{u}), \tag{45}$$

where $\mathbf{x} \in \mathbb{R}^n$, $\mathbf{u} \in U \subseteq \mathbb{R}^m$.

The domain of initial conditions is given

$$X_0 = \{\mathbf{x}^{0,1}, \dots, \mathbf{x}^{0,K}\} \subseteq \mathbb{R}^n. \tag{46}$$

The terminal condition is given

$$\mathbf{x}^* = [x_1^* \dots x_n^*]^T \in \mathbb{R}^n. \tag{47}$$

The quality criterion is given

$$J_3 = \sum_{i=1}^{K} t_{f,i} + p_1 \|\mathbf{x}^* - \mathbf{x}(t_{f,i}, \mathbf{x}^{0,i})\| \to \min_{\mathbf{u}}, \tag{48}$$

where $t_{f,i}$ is a time of achieving the terminal condition from the initial condition $\mathbf{x}^{0,i}$. It is necessary to find a control in the form (41).

The general formulation of the synthesis problem was posed by V.G. Boltyanskiy in the 60s of the last century [25]. One of the ways to solve it is to reduce the problem to the partial differential equation of Bellman [26,27], who also proposed a method for its solution in the form of a dynamic programming method [26,28]. Bellman's equation in the general case has no solution; therefore, most often it is solved numerically for one initial condition, which in our case is not enough to ensure stability.

To solve the synthesis problem and obtain an equilibrium point, methods of modal control [29] can be applied for linear systems, as well as other analytical methods such as backstepping [30], analytical design of aggregated controllers [31,32], or synthesis based on the application of the Lyapunov function [21,33]. Note that all known analytical synthesis methods for nonlinear systems, when implemented, are associated with a specific type of model, therefore they cannot be considered universal. In practice, linear controllers, such as PID or PI controllers, are often used to ensure stability. Their use is also associated with a specific model, which is linearized in the neighbourhood of the equilibrium point, and their use is not related to the formal statement of the considered synthesis problem.

To solve the synthesis problem in the considered mathematical formulation, it is necessary to find the control function in the form (41). Most of the known methods specify the control function with an accuracy of the parameter values, for example, methods associated with the solution of the Bellman equation, like analytical design of optimal controllers [34], as well as the use of various controllers, including controllers based on very popular now artificial neural networks [35].

This paper proposes to solve the addressed problem numerically. For a solution of the synthesis problem we apply numerical methods of symbolic regression. These methods can look for a structure of the function in the form a special code by some genetic algorithm and also search for the optimal values of parameters in the desired function.

7. Symbolic Regression Methods

To encode a mathematical expression, it is necessary to define sets of arguments of the mathematical expression and elementary functions. To decode a code of the mathematical expression it is enough to know how many arguments has each elementary function. For encoding elementary function, it is enough to use integer vector with two components. The first component is the number of arguments of the elementary function. The second component is the function number. Arguments of mathematical expression are elementary functions without arguments, therefore the first component of an argument code is zero.

For the control synthesis problem (45)–(48) it is necessary to find a mathematical expression of the control function (41).

Let us define sets of elementary functions.

A set of mathematical expression arguments or elementary functions without arguments includes variables, parameters, and unit elements for elementary functions with two
arguments,

$$F_0 = \{f_{0,1} = x_1, \ldots, f_{0,n} = x_n, f_{0,n+1} = c_1, \ldots, f_{0,n+p}, f_{0,n+p+1} = e_1, \ldots, f_{0,n+p+r} = e_V\}, \quad (49)$$

where x_i is a component of the state vector, $i = 1, \ldots, n$, $\mathbf{x} = [x_1 \ldots x_n]^T$, c_i is a component
of the parametric vector, $i = 1, \ldots, p$, $\mathbf{c} = [c_1 \ldots c_p]^p$, e_i is a unit element for function with
two arguments.

A set of functions with one argument includes an identity function

$$F_1 = \{f_{1,1}(z) = z, f_{1,2}(z), \ldots, f_{1,W}(z)\}. \quad (50)$$

A set of functions with two arguments includes such functions, that are associative,
commutative and have a unit element

$$F_2 = \{f_{2,1}(z_1, z_2), \ldots, f_{2,V}(z_1, z_2)\}, \quad (51)$$

where each element from the set F_2 has the following properties:

— associative
$$f_{2,j}(f_{2,j}(z_1, z_2), z_3) = f_{2,j}(z_1, f_{2,j}(z_2, z_3)), \ j = 1, \ldots, V, \quad (52)$$

— commutative
$$f_{2,j}(z_1, z_2) = f_{2,j}(z_2, z_1), \ j = 1, \ldots, V, \quad (53)$$

— existing of a unit element
$$f_{2,j}(z_1, e_j) = z_1, \ f_{2,j}(e_j, z_2) = z_2, \ j = 1, \ldots, V. \quad (54)$$

To describe the most common mathematical expressions, it is enough functions with
one and two arguments. Functions with three and more arguments may not be used.

Any element of the sets (49)–(51) is encoded by integer vector with two arguments

$$\mathbf{s} = [s_1 \ s_2]^T, \quad (55)$$

where s_1 is the number of arguments, s_2 is a function number.

A code of the mathematical expression is a set of codes of elementary functions

$$S = \mathbf{s}^1 \ldots \mathbf{s}^L, \quad (56)$$

where $\mathbf{s}^j = [s_1^j \ s_2^j]^T$, $s_1^j \in \{0, 1, 2\}$,

$$s_2^j \in \begin{cases} \{1, \ldots, n + p + V\}, \text{ if } s_1^j = 0 \\ \{1, \ldots, W\}, \text{ if } s_1^j = 1 \\ \{1, \ldots, V\}, \text{ otherwise} \end{cases} \quad (57)$$

Theorem 4. *For the mathematical expression code (57) with L elements to be correct, it is necessary
and enough that the following formulas are valid*

$$1 + \sum_{i=1}^{j} s_1^i \le L, \ j = 1, \ldots, L - 1, \quad (58)$$

$$1 - L + \sum_{i=1}^{L} s_1^i = 0. \quad (59)$$

Proof. Consider the Formula (58) and add there $-j$ in the left and right sides

$$-j + 1 + \sum_{i=1}^{j} s_1^i \leq L - j. \tag{60}$$

Consider left side of the inequation (60)

$$T(j) = -j + 1 + \sum_{i=1}^{j} s_1^i. \tag{61}$$

This equation calculates how many elements from the set of arguments (49) should be after element j. The value $T(j)$ is increasing on 1 after each $s_1^j = 2$, it is not changing after each $s_1^j = 1$, and it is decreasing on 1 after $s_1^j = 0$.

At $j = L$, we receive the Equation (59). After the last element $j = L$ it must be no elements on the right from element L.

Assume that the inequation (57) fails. Then from (61) we receive for $j = L$

$$T(j) = -L + 1 + \sum_{i=1}^{j} s_1^i > 0. \tag{62}$$

This means, that after the last element there are some elements. This does not allow to decode the code. Therefore conditions (57) and (58) are necessary.

Let the inequation (57) and Equation (58) be satisfied. If the element after the element j is an argument from the set (49), then $T(j)$ is decreasing on 1, if it is the function number with one argument, then $T(j)$ is not changed, if it is the function number with two arguments, then $T(j)$ increases on 1. Equation (58) shows that the last element from the set (49) does not need arguments. The formula is decoded. Therefore, performing the Formulas (57) and (58) is enough. QED. $\square$

From Equation (58) it follows

$$\sum_{i=1}^{L} s_1^i = L - 1. \tag{63}$$

Such direct encoding is in the genetic programming [36]. This method of symbolic regression does not include extra elements, therefore codes of different mathematical expressions have different lengths. It is not very comfortable for programming and implementing crossover in genetic programming. For crossover it is necessary to find in the code (55) the sub-code of mathematical expression with the properties (57) and (58). Crossover operation in genetic programming is performed as exchanging sub-codes of mathematical expressions. Searching for sub-codes and exchanging them takes significant time of the algorithm. Other symbolic regression methods that can be effectively used to find a mathematical expression, such as the network operator method [37,38], or Cartesian genetic programming [39,40] have codes of equal length for different mathematical expressions due to redundant elements.

An effective tool in the search for an optimal mathematical expression is the principle of small variations of the basic solution [41]. According to this principle, the search for the mathematical expression can begin in the neighbourhood of one given basic solution. This solution is coded by some symbolic regression method. Other possible solutions are obtained using sets of codes of small variations of the basic solution. Each small variation slightly modifies the basic solution code so that a new code corresponds to some kind of mathematical expression.

To find the optimal mathematical expression by any method of symbolic regression, a special genetic algorithm is used. Depending on the code of symbolic regression, this genetic algorithm has its own crossover and mutation operations. Using the principle of small variations of the basic solution, crossover and mutation operations are performed on the sets of small variations.

In the numerical solution of control synthesis problems by symbolic regression methods, together with the search of the structure of the mathematical expression, it is advisable to look for the optimal values of the parameter vector $\mathbf{c} = [c_1 \ldots c_p]^T$, which is included in this mathematical expression in the form of its additional arguments (49). For this purpose, it is convenient to use the same genetic algorithm as for finding the structure. In this case, a possible solution is a pair including the code for structure of the mathematical expression and the vector of parameters. When performing a crossover operation, we get not two, but four offsprings. Two offsprings have new mathematical expression structures and new parameter values, and two others inherit parent structures and have only new parameter values. The crossover operation for parameters is performed as in the classical genetic algorithm, by exchanging codes after the crossover point.

It can be seen that the methods of symbolic regression can automate the process of synthesis of control systems, but very little of them are used in this direction. Only few scientific groups [42–44] are developing these approaches for solving the problem of control system synthesis in view of a number of difficulties, such as non-numerical search space and the absence of a metric on it, the complexity of the program code and the absence of publicly available software packages, and so forth.

8. A Computational Example

Let us consider the optimal control problem for two mobile robots. They have to exchange its position on the plane with obstacles.

Mathematical models of mobile robots [45] are given

$$
\begin{aligned}
\dot{x}^j &= 0.5(u_1^j + u_2^j)\cos(\theta^j), \\
\dot{y}^j &= 0.5(u_1^j + u_2^j)\sin(\theta^j), \\
\dot{\theta}^j &= 0.5(u_1^j - u_2^j),
\end{aligned}
\tag{64}
$$

where $\mathbf{u}^j = [u_1^j \ u_2^j]$ is a vector of control, $j = 1, 2$.

Control is restricted

$$
-10 = u_i^- \le u_i^j \le u_i^+ = 10, \ j = 1, 2, \ i = 1, 2.
\tag{65}
$$

The initial conditions are set

$$
x^1(0) = 0, \ y^1(0) = 0, \ \theta^1(0) = 0, x^2(0) = 10, \ y^2(0) = 10, \ \theta^2(0) = 0.
\tag{66}
$$

The terminal conditions are set

$$
x^1(t_f) = 10, \ y^1(t_f) = 10, \ \theta^1(t_f) = 0, x^2(t_f) = 0, \ y^2(t_f) = 0, \ \theta^2(t_f) = 0,
\tag{67}
$$

where

$$
t_f = \begin{cases} t \ , \text{if } t < t^+ \text{and } \Delta_f(t) \le \varepsilon \\ t^+, \text{otherwise} \end{cases}
\tag{68}
$$

$$
\Delta_f(t) = \sqrt{(10 - x^1(t))^2 + (10 - y^1(t))^2 + (\theta^1(t))^2 + (x^2(t))^2 + (y^2(t))^2 + (\theta^2(t))^2},
\tag{69}
$$

$t^+ = 2.4$ s, $\varepsilon = 0.01$.

The quality functional includes the time to reach the terminal state and penalty functions for violation of the accuracy of reaching the terminal state and for violation of static and dynamic phase constraints

$$J_e = t_f + w_1 \Delta_f(t_f) + w_2 \int_0^{t_f} \sum_{i=1}^{2} \sum_{j=1}^{2} \vartheta(\varphi_{i,j}(t)) dt +$$

$$w_3 \int_0^{t_f} \vartheta(d^2 - (x^1(t) - x^2(t))^2 - (y^1(t) - y^2(t))^2) dt \to \min_{u^1, u^2} \tag{70}$$

where $w_1 = 2.5$, $w_2 = 3$, $w_3 = 3$,

$$\vartheta(\alpha) = \begin{cases} 1, \text{ if } \alpha > 0 \\ 0, \text{ otherwise} \end{cases}, \tag{71}$$

$$\varphi_{i,j}(t) = r_i - \sqrt{(x_i - x^j(t))^2 + (y_i - y^j(t))^2}, \ i = 1, 2, \ j = 1, 2, \tag{72}$$

$r_1 = 3$, $r_2 = 3$, $x_1 = 5$, $x_2 = 5$, $y_1 = 9$, $y_2 = 1$, $d = 2$.

It is necessary to find such a control to move all robots from its initial conditions (66) to the terminal conditions (67) with the minimal value of the quality criterion (70).

To solve the optimal control problem (64)–(72) by the proposed synthesized optimal control method it is necessary to initially solve the control synthesis problem (45)–(48) for each robot. Since robots are similar, it is enough to solve the control synthesis problem once for one robot. For the solution of this problem, the symbolic regression method of Cartesian genetic programming is used.

In the result, the following control function was obtained:

$$u_i^j = \begin{cases} u_i^+ = 10, \text{ if } u_i^+ \leq \tilde{u}_i^j \\ u_i^- = -10, \text{ if } \tilde{u}_i^j \leq u_i^- \\ \tilde{u}_i^j, \text{ otherwise} \end{cases}, \ i = 1, 2, \ j = 1, 2, \tag{73}$$

where

$$\tilde{u}_1^j = A + B + \rho_\#(A), \ j = 1, 2, \tag{74}$$

$$\tilde{u}_1^j = B - A - \rho_\#(A), \ j = 1, 2, \tag{75}$$

$$A = c_1(\theta^* - \theta^j) + \sigma_\#((x^* - x^J)(y^* - y^J)), \tag{76}$$

$$B = 2(x^* - x^j) + \text{sgn}(x^* - x^J)c_2, \tag{77}$$

$$\rho_\#(\alpha) = \begin{cases} \text{sgn}(\alpha)B^+, \text{ if } |\alpha| > -\log(\delta^-) \\ \text{sgn}(\alpha)(\exp(|\alpha|) - 1) \end{cases}, \ \sigma_\#(\alpha) = \text{sgn}(\alpha)\sqrt{|\alpha|}, \tag{78}$$

$c_1 = 3.1094$, $c_2 = 3.6289$, $B^+ = 10^8$, $\delta^- = 10^{-8}$.

For solution of the synthesis problem eight initial conditions were used and the quality criterion took into account the speed and the accuracy of terminal position achievement

$$\mathbf{x}^* = [x^* \ y^* \ \theta^*]^T. \tag{79}$$

In the result of the solution of control synthesis problem a stable equilibrium point in the state space is appeared. Position of the equilibrium point depends on the terminal vector (79).

In the second stage the set of four points (79) were searched for each robot on criterion (70)

$$X^* = \{\mathbf{x}^{*,1,1}, \ldots, \mathbf{x}^{*,1,4}, \mathbf{x}^{*,2,1}, \ldots, \mathbf{x}^{*,2,4}\}. \tag{80}$$

These points were switching in some time interval $\Delta t = 0.6$ s for control function (73) of each robot.

To search for the points the evolutionary algorithm of Grey wolf optimizer [46,47] was used. In result, after more than one hundred tests the following best points were found:

$$
\begin{aligned}
\mathbf{x}^{*,1,1} &= [4.0159\ 1.8954\ 1.2397]^T, & \mathbf{x}^{*,1,2} &= [7.0890\ 4.2341\ 0.5270]^T, \\
\mathbf{x}^{*,1,3} &= [7.2194\ -0.4480\ 1.3042]^T, & \mathbf{x}^{*,1,4} &= [11.9722\ 9.4663\ 0.1866]^T, \\
\mathbf{x}^{*,2,1} &= [5.3899\ 4.0791\ -0.1208]^T, & \mathbf{x}^{*,2,2} &= [-0.6401\ 4.3126\ -0.0176]^T, \\
\mathbf{x}^{*,2,3} &= [0.3103\ 0.8955\ 0.6335]^T, & \mathbf{x}^{*,2,4} &= [-0.0791\ -0.1518\ 0.0195]^T.
\end{aligned}
\tag{81}
$$

The algorithm simulated the system (64) with the control (73) for calculation of criterion values (70) in one test more than 500,000 times.

When searching for points, the following constraints were used

$$
-2 \le x^* \le 12,\ -2 \le y^* \le 12,\ -\pi/2 \le \theta^* \le \pi/2.
\tag{82}
$$

In the Figure 1 the projections of optimal trajectories on the plane $\{x, y\}$ are presented. The trajectories are black lines, red circles are obstacles, small black squares are projections of found points (81).

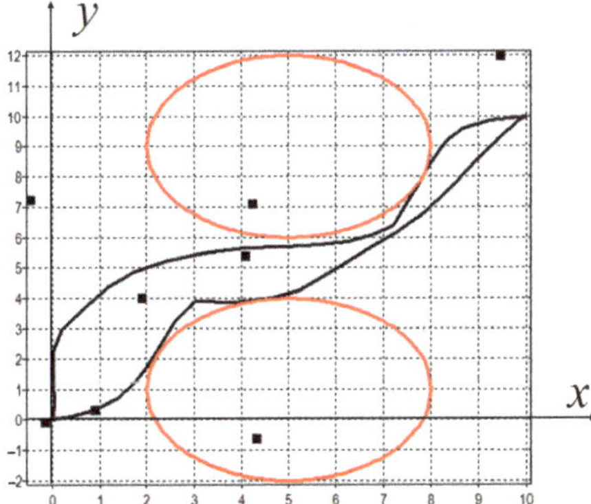

Figure 1. Optimal trajectories of robots on the plane $\{x, y\}$ for synthesized optimal control.

The quality criterion (70) for found control was $J_e = 2.8914$.

For comparative study of the obtained solution, the same optimal control problem was solved by a direct method. For this purpose control functions of robots were approximated by piece-wise linear functions of time. The interval of approximation was $\Delta_d t = 0.4$ s, therefore a number of intervals was

$$
K = \left\lfloor \frac{t^+}{\Delta_d t} \right\rfloor = \left\lfloor \frac{2.4}{0.4} \right\rfloor = 6.
\tag{83}
$$

For the approximation of control function, the values of parameters on the boundaries of intervals were searched. For each one control function it was necessary to find $K + 1 = 7$ parameters. Total vector of parameters had twenty eight components.

$$
\mathbf{q} = [q_1 \ldots q_{28}]^T.
\tag{84}
$$

The direct control has the following form

$$
u_i^j = \begin{cases}
10 = u_i^+, \text{ if } u_i^+ \le \bar{u}_i^j \\
-10 = u_i^-, \text{ if } \bar{u}_i^j \le u_i^- \quad ,i = 1, 2,\ j = 1, 2, \\
\bar{u}_i^j, \text{ otherwise}
\end{cases}
\tag{85}
$$

where

$$\bar{u}_1^1 = q_s + (q_{s+1} - q_s)\frac{(t - s\Delta_d t)}{\Delta_d t}, \tag{86}$$

$$\bar{u}_2^1 = q_{s+L} + (q_{s+L+1} - q_{s+L})\frac{(t - s\Delta_d t)}{\Delta_d t}, \tag{87}$$

$$\bar{u}_1^2 = q_{s+2K} + (q_{s+2L+1} - q_{s+2L})\frac{(t - s\Delta_d t)}{\Delta_d t}, \tag{88}$$

$$\bar{u}_2^2 = q_{s+3L} + (q_{s+3L+1} - q_{s+3L})\frac{(t - s\Delta_d t)}{\Delta_d t}, \tag{89}$$

$s\Delta_d t \le t \le (s+1)\Delta_d t, s \in \{1,\ldots,6\}, L = K + 1 = 7.$

To search for optimal parameters the same evolutionary algorithm of Grey wolf optimizer was used. In the result of more than one hundred tests the following best values of parameters were found:

$$\begin{aligned}
\mathbf{q} \quad = \quad & [19.6125 \; 5.4318 \; 7.5921 \; 19.4020 \; 2.3928 \; 2.1627 \; 1.6976 \\
& 1.4941 \; 5.1828 \; 16.9087 \; 11.2478 \; -2.4499 \; 17.7201 \; -0.6297 \\
& -0.9093 \; -1.6815 \; -19.5283 \; -16.4979 \; -0.2321 \; -11.4719 \; -17.7372 \\
& -1.4218 \; -18.0214 \; -3.7942 \; -3.0899 \; -13.3196 \; -9.7212 \; -0.3233]^T
\end{aligned} \tag{90}$$

The process of searching the parameters had restrictions

$$-20 = q^- \le q_i \le q^+ = 20, \; i = 1,\ldots,28. \tag{91}$$

In one test, the algorithm simulated the system (64) with the control (85) for calculation of criterion values (70) more than 500,000 times. A value of quality criterion (70) for found control was $J_e = 2.5134$.

In Figure 2, the projection of optimal trajectories of mobile robots on the horizontal plane $\{x, y\}$ is presented.

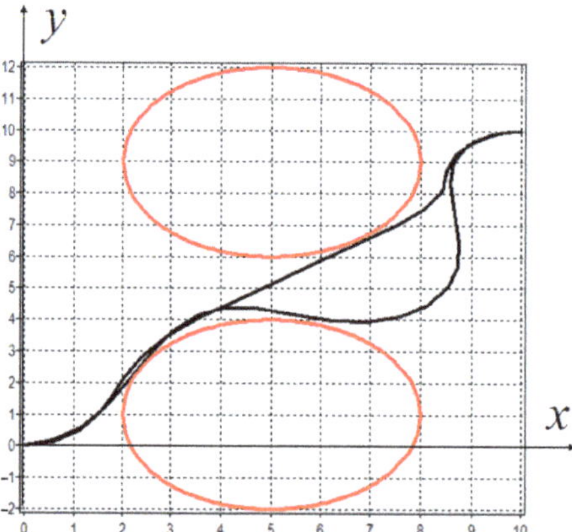

Figure 2. Optimal trajectories of robots on the plane $\{x, y\}$ for direct control.

To check the obtained solutions of sensitivity to perturbations, we included random functions of uncertainty into the model (64)

$$\begin{aligned}
\dot{x}^j &= 0.5(u_1^j + u_2^j)\cos(\theta^j) + B\xi(t), \\
\dot{y}^j &= 0.5(u_1^j + u_2^j)\sin(\theta^j) + B\xi(t), \\
\dot{\theta}^j &= 0.5(u_1^j - u_2^j) + B\xi(t),
\end{aligned} \tag{92}$$

where $j = 1, 2$, $\xi(t)$ generates new random value in interval from -1 to 1 at every call.

Results of simulations with the found optimal controls and different levels of perturbations of the model are presented in the Table 1. The Table 1 includes average values of functional (70) on ten tests. As we can see, the synthesized optimal control is less sensitive to the perturbation of model. For the synthesized control with the level of perturbation $B = 1.5$, the average value of the functional is changed by no more than 30% and, for the direct control with the same level of perturbations, the functional is changed by more than 200%.

Table 1. The average values of functional (70).

Level of Noise B	Synthesized Control	Direct Control
0	2.8914	2.5134
0.1	3.0014	3.0260
0.2	3.0066	3.8571
0.5	3.2141	5.5497
0.8	3.3156	5.8968
1	3.4123	6.7952
1.5	3.6954	8.2654

In Figure 3, the trajectories for synthesized optimal control with model perturbations of level $B = 1.5$ are presented. In Figure 4, the trajectories for the direct control with the same level of perturbation $B = 1.5$ are presented.

As can be seen from Figures 3 and 4, the synthesized control does not change the nature of the motion of objects under large disturbances, and direct control first of all violates the accuracy of achieving the terminal conditions.

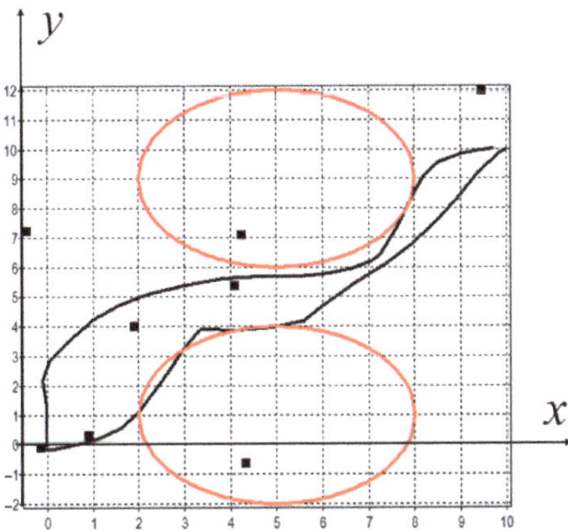

Figure 3. Optimal trajectories of robots on the plane $\{x, y\}$ for synthesized control with $B = 1.5$.

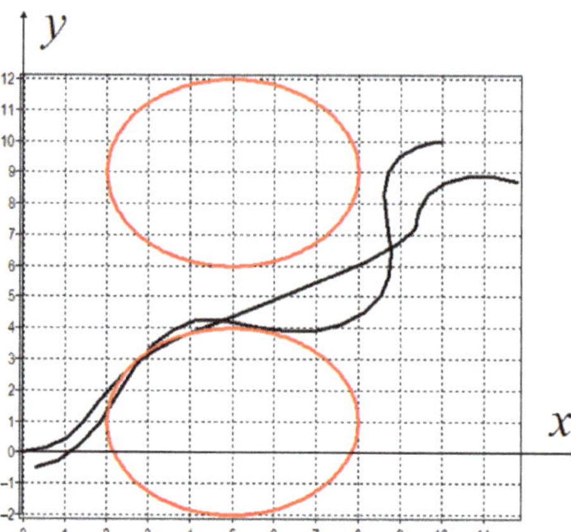

Figure 4. Optimal trajectories of robots on the plane $\{x, y\}$ for direct control with $B = 1.5$.

9. Conclusions

This work presents the statement of the new optimal control problem with uncertainty. In this problem, the mathematical model of the control object includes an additive limited perturbing function simulating possible model inaccuracies. It is necessary to find an optimal control function that provides for limited perturbations bounded variation of functional value. For this purpose, it is proposed to use the synthesized optimal control method. According to this method initially, the control synthesis problem is solved. After that, in the state space a stable equilibrium point appears. In the second stage, the original optimal control problem is solved by searching positions of some stable equilibrium points, which are a control for stabilization system, obtained in the first stage. It is shown that such an approach supplies the property of a contraction mapping for differential equations of the mathematical model of the plant. Such differential equations are quite feasible, and their solutions reduce the errors of determining the state vector. For the solution of the control synthesis problem it is proposed to apply symbolic regression methods. A comparative example is presented. Computational experiments showed that the obtained solution is very less sensitive to perturbations in the mathematical model of the control object than the direct solution of the optimal control problem.

10. Findings/Results

This paper presents a new formulation of the optimal control problem, taking into account the objectively existing uncertainties of the model. The concept of feasibility is introduced, which means that small changes in the model do not lead to a loss of quality. Given the theoretical substantiations (definitions and theorems) that a system of differential equations of the mathematical model is feasible if it obtains, as a one-parametric mapping, a contraction property in the implementation domain. This property is an alternative to Lyapunov stability; it is softer, but sufficient for the development of real stable practical systems. An approach based on the method of synthesized optimal control is proposed, which makes it possible to develop systems that have the property of feasibility.

11. Discussion

According to the method of synthesized optimal control, the stability of the object is first ensured, that is, an equilibrium point appears in the phase space. In the neighbourhood of the stability point, the phase trajectories contract, and this property determines the feasibility of the system. For this, it is necessary to numerically solve the problem of synthesizing the stabilization system in order to obtain expressions for the control and substitute them in the right-hand sides of the object model. The synthesis problem is quite difficult. This paper proposes using numerical methods of symbolic regression to solve it. There are several successful applications, but they are still not very popular due to the complexity of the search area on a non-numerical space of functions where there is no metric. This is the direction for future research.

In the applied method of synthesized optimal control in the second stage we searched positions of equilibrium points as a piece-wise constant function. It is necessary to investigate other types of functions to change the position of the equilibrium point, how many points should be and how often they should be switched.

In further studies it is also necessary to consider solutions of the new optimal control problem for different control objects.

With the numerical solution of the optimal control problem by evolutionary algorithm it was defined that these algorithms can find solutions for complex optimal control problems with static and dynamic phase constraints. It is necessary to continue to research different evolutionary algorithms for the solution of the optimal control problems.

Author Contributions: Conceptualization, A.D. and E.S.; methodology, A.D., E.S.; software, A.D., E.S.; validation, V.S., P.Z.; investigation, E.S.; resources, V.S.; writing—original draft preparation, A.D., E.S.; writing—review and editing, E.S.; supervision, V.S., P.Z. All authors have read and agreed to the published version of the manuscript.

Funding: This research is supported by the Ministry of Science and Higher Education of the Russian Federation, project No. 075-15-2020-799.

Conflicts of Interest: The authors declare no conflict of interest.

References

1. Athans, M.; Falb, P.L. *Optimal Control: An Introduction to the Theory and Its Application*; Dover Publications Inc.: Mineola, NY, USA, 2007; 880p.
2. Pontryagin, L.S.; Boltyanskii, V.G.; Gamkrelidze, R.V.; Mishchenko, E.F. *Pontryagin Selected Works: The Mathematical Theory of Optimal Process*; Gordon and Breach Science Publishers: New York, NY, USA, 1985; Volume 4, p. 360.
3. Chertovskih, R.; Karamzin, D.; Khalil, N.T.; Lobo Pereira, F. Regular path-constrained time-optimal control problems in three-dimensional flow fields. *Eur. J. Control.* **2020**, *56*, 98–106. [CrossRef]
4. Arutyunov, A.; Karamzin, D. A Survey on Regularity Conditions for State-Constrained Optimal Control Problems and the Non-degenerate Maximum Principle. *J. Optim. Theory Appl.* **2020**, *184*, 697–723. [CrossRef]
5. Gill, P.E.; Murray, W.; Wright, M.H. *Practical Optimization*; Academic Press: Cambridge, MA, USA, 1981.
6. Evtushenko, Y.G. *Optimization and Rapid Automatic Differentiation*; Computing Center of RAS: Moscow, Russia, 2013.
7. Betts, J.T. Survey of Numerical Methods for Trajectory Optimization. *J. Guid. Control. Dyn.* **1998**, *21*, 193–207. [CrossRef]
8. Saunders, B.R. Optimal Trajectory Optimization under Uncertainty. Master's Dissertation, Department of Aeronautics and Astronautics, Massachusetts Institute of Technology, Cambridge, MA, USA, 2012.
9. Seywald, H.; Kumar, R. Desensitized Optimal Trajectories. In Proceedings of the AIAA/AAS Spaceflight Mechanics Meeting, Austin, TX, USA, 11–15 February 1996; AAS Paper 96-107:103-115.
10. Makkapati, V.R.; Dor, M.; Tsiotras, P. Trajectory desensitization in optimal control problems. In Proceedings of the IEEE Conference on Decision and Control, Miami, FL, USA, 17–19 December 2018; pp. 2478–2483.
11. Dullerud, G.E.; Paganini, F. *A Course in Robust Control Theory: A Convex Approach*; Springer: New York, NY, USA, 2000; 477p.
12. Calafiore, G.; Dabbene, F. (Eds.) *Probabilistic and Randomized Methods for Design under Uncertainty*; Springer: London, UK, 2006; 458p.
13. Chanthorn, P.; Rajchakit, G.; Thipcha, J.; Emharuethai, C.; Sriraman, R.; Lim, C.P.; Ramachandran, R. Robust Stability of Complex-Valued Stochastic Neural Networks with Time-Varying Delays and Parameter Uncertainties. *Mathematics* **2020**, *8*, 742. [CrossRef]
14. Wu, L.; Zhao, R.; Li, Y.; Chen, Y.-H. Optimal Design of Adaptive Robust Control for the Delta Robot with Uncertainty: Fuzzy Set-Based Approach. *Appl. Sci.* **2020**, *10*, 3472. [CrossRef]
15. Shang, D.; Li, Y.; Liu, Y.; Cui, S. Research on the motion error analysis and compensation strategy of the Delta robot. *Mathematics* **2019**, *7*, 411. [CrossRef]
16. Lu, P. Regulation About Time-Varying Trajectories: Precision Entry Guidance Illustrated. *J. Guid. Control. Dyn.* **1999**, *22*, 784–790, [CrossRef]
17. Angel, L.; Viola, J. Fractional order PID for tracking control of a parallel robotic manipulator type delta. *ISA Trans.* **2018**, *79*, 1–17. [CrossRef]

18. Diveev, A.I. Numerical Method of Synthesized Control for Solution of the Optimal Control Problem. In *Science and Information Conference*; Arai, K., Ed.; Advances in Intelligent Systems and Computing; Springer Nature: Cham, Switzerland, 2020; Volume 1, pp. 137–156.
19. Diveev, A.; Shmalko, E. Comparison of Direct and Indirect Approaches for Numerical Solution of the Optimal Control Problem by Evolutionary Methods. In *Optimization and Applications. OPTIMA 2019. Communications in Computer and Information Science*; Jaćimović, M., Khachay, M., Malkova, V., Posypkin, M., Eds.; Springer: Cham, Switzerland, 2019; Volume 1145, pp. 180–193.
20. Parks, P.C. AM Lyapunov's stability theory—100 years on. *Ima J. Math. Control. Inf.* **1992**, *9*, 275–303. [CrossRef]
21. Clarke, F. Lyapunov Functions and Feedback in Nonlinear Control. In *Optimal Control, Stabilization and Nonsmooth Analysis*; de Queiroz, M., Malisoff, M., Wolenski, P., Eds.; LNCIS 301; Springer: Berlin/Heidelberg, Germany; pp. 267–282.
22. Hahn, W.; Baartz, A. *Stability of Motion*; Springer: Berlin, Germany, 1967.
23. Diveev, A.I.; Shmalko, E.Y.; Sofronova, E.A. Multipoint numerical criterion for manifolds to guarantee attractor properties in the problem of synergetic control design. *ITM Web Conf.* **2018**, *18*, 01001. [CrossRef]
24. Kolmogorov, A.N.; Fomin, S.V. *Elements of the Theory of Functions and Functional Analysis*; Metric and Normed Spaces; Graylock Press: Rochester, NY, USA, 1957; Volume 1, 130p.
25. Boltyansky, V.G. *Mathematical Methods of Optimal Control*; Holt, Rinehart and Winston: New York, NY, USA, 1971; 272p.
26. Bellman, R.E.; Dreyfus, S.E. *Applied Dynamic Programming*; Princeton University Press: Princeton, NJ, USA, 1971; 364p.
27. Afanasiev, V.N.; Kolmanovskii, V.; Nosov, V.R. *Mathematical Theory of Control Systems Design*; Springer: Berlin/Heidelberg, Germany, 2014; 700p.
28. Bertsecas, D. *Dynamic Programming and Optimal Control*; Athena Scientific: Bellmont, MA, USA, 1995; 387p.
29. Simon, J.D.; Mitter, S.K. A theory of modal control. *Inf. Control.* **1968**, *13*, 316–353. [CrossRef]
30. Khalil, H.K. *Nonlinear Systems*; Prentice Hall: Upper Saddle River, NJ, USA, 2002; 750p.
31. Kolesnikov, A.A.; Kuz'menko, A.A. Backstepping and ADAR Method in the Problems of Synthesis of the Nonlinear Control Systems. *Mekhatronika Avtom. Upr.* **2016**, *17*, 435–445. (In Russia) [CrossRef]
32. Podvalny, S.L.; Vasiljev, E.M. Analytical synthesis of aggregated regulators for unmanned aerial vehicles. *J. Math. Sci.* **2019**, *239*, 135–145. [CrossRef]
33. Agarwal, R.; O'Regan, D.; Hristova, S. Stability by Lyapunov like functions of nonlinear differential equations with non-instantaneous impulses. *J. Appl. Math. Comput.* **2017**, *53*, 147–168. [CrossRef]
34. Mizhidon, A.D. On a Problem of Analytic Design of an Optimal Controller. *Autom. Remote Control.* **2011**, *72*, 2315–2327. [CrossRef]
35. Yang, J.; Lu, W.; Liu, W. PID Controller Based on the Artificial Neural Network. In *Advances in Neural Networks—Lecture Notes in Computer Science*; Yin, F.L., Wang, J., Guo, C., Eds.; Springer: Berlin/Heidelberg, Germany, 2004; Volume 3174.
36. Koza, J.R. *Genetic Programming: On the Programming of Computers by Means of Natural Selection*; MIT Press: Cambridge, UK, 1992; 819p.
37. Diveev, A.I.; Sofronova, E.A. The Network Operator Method for Search of the Most Suitable Mathematical Equation. In *Bio-Inspired Computational Algorithms and Their Applications*; Gao, S., Ed.; Intech: Rijeka, Croatia, 2012; pp. 19–42.
38. Diveev, A.I. A Numerical Method for Network Operator for Synthesis of a Control System with Uncertain Initial Values. *J. Comput. Syst. Sci. Int.* **2012**, *51*, 228–243. [CrossRef]
39. Miller, J.; Thomson, P. Cartesian Genetic Programming. In *Proceedings of the European Conference on Genetic Programming (EuroGP2000)*; Springer: Milan, Italy, 2000; Volume 1802, pp. 121–132.
40. Diveev, A.I. Cartesian Genetic Programming for Synthesis of Control System for Group of Robots. In Proceedings of the 2020 28th Mediterranean Conference on Control and Automation (MED), Saint-Raphaël, France, 15–18 September 2020; pp. 972–977.
41. Diveev, A. Small Variations of Basic Solution Method for Non-numerical Optimization. *IFAC-PapersOnLine* **2015**, *48*, 28–33. [CrossRef]
42. Duriez, T.; Brunton, S.L.; Noack, B.R. Taming nonlinear dynamics with MLC. In *Machine Learning Control—Taming Nonlinear Dynamics and Turbulence*; Springer: Berlin/Heidelberg, Germany, 2017.
43. Derner, E.; Kubalík, J.; Ancona, N.; Babuška, R. Symbolic Regression for Constructing Analytic Models in Reinforcement Learning. *Appl. Soft Comput.* **2020**, *94*, 1–12. [CrossRef]
44. Diveev, A.; Hussein, O.; Shmalko, E.; Sofronova, E. Synthesis of Control System for Quad-Rotor Helicopter by the Network Operator Method. In *Proceedings of SAI Intelligent Systems Conference*; Advances in Intelligent Systems and Computing; Springer: Cham, Switzerland, 2020; pp. 246–263.
45. Šuster, P.; Jadlovská, A. Tracking Trajectory of the Mobile Robot Khepera II Using Approaches of Artificial Intelligence. *Acta Electrotech. Inform.* **2011**, *11*, 38–43. [CrossRef]
46. Diveev, A.I.; Konstantinov, S.V. Study of the Practical Convergence of Evolutionary Algorithms for the Optimal Program Control of a Wheeled Robot. *J. Comput. Syst. Sci. Int.* **2018**, *57*, 561–580. [CrossRef]
47. Mirjalili, S.; Mirjalili, S.M.; Lewis, A. Grey Wolf Optimizer. *Adv. Eng. Softw.* **2014**, *69*, 46–61. [CrossRef]

 *mathematics*

MDPI

Article

Rock Segmentation in the Navigation Vision of the Planetary Rovers

Boyu Kuang [1,*], **Mariusz Wisniewski** [1], **Zeeshan A. Rana** [1] and **Yifan Zhao** [2]

[1] Centre for Computational Engineering Sciences (CES), School of Aerospace, Transport and Manufacturing (SATM), Cranfield University, Bedfordshire MK43 0AL, UK; m.wisniewski@cranfield.ac.uk (M.W.); zeeshan.rana@cranfield.ac.uk (Z.A.R.)

[2] Centre for Life-Cycle Engineering and Management, School of Aerospace, Transport and Manufacturing (SATM), Cranfield University, Bedfordshire MK43 0AL, UK; yifan.zhao@cranfield.ac.uk

* Correspondence: neil.kuang@cranfield.ac.uk; Tel.: +44-7988-477406

Citation: Kuang, B.; Wisniewski, M.; Rana, Z.A.; Zhao, Y. Rock Segmentation in the Navigation Vision of the Planetary Rovers. *Mathematics* **2021**, *9*, 3048. https://doi.org/10.3390/math9233048

Academic Editors: Andrey Gorshenin, Mikhail Posypkin and Vladimir Titarev

Received: 17 September 2021
Accepted: 24 November 2021
Published: 27 November 2021

Publisher's Note: MDPI stays neutral with regard to jurisdictional claims in published maps and institutional affiliations.

Abstract: Visual navigation is an essential part of planetary rover autonomy. Rock segmentation emerged as an important interdisciplinary topic among image processing, robotics, and mathematical modeling. Rock segmentation is a challenging topic for rover autonomy because of the high computational consumption, real-time requirement, and annotation difficulty. This research proposes a rock segmentation framework and a rock segmentation network (NI-U-Net++) to aid with the visual navigation of rovers. The framework consists of two stages: the pre-training process and the transfer-training process. The pre-training process applies the synthetic algorithm to generate the synthetic images; then, it uses the generated images to pre-train NI-U-Net++. The synthetic algorithm increases the size of the image dataset and provides pixel-level masks—both of which are challenges with machine learning tasks. The pre-training process accomplishes the state-of-the-art compared with the related studies, which achieved an accuracy, intersection over union (IoU), Dice score, and root mean squared error (RMSE) of 99.41%, 0.8991, 0.9459, and 0.0775, respectively. The transfer-training process fine-tunes the pre-trained NI-U-Net++ using the real-life images, which achieved an accuracy, IoU, Dice score, and RMSE of 99.58%, 0.7476, 0.8556, and 0.0557, respectively. Finally, the transfer-trained NI-U-Net++ is integrated into a planetary rover navigation vision and achieves a real-time performance of 32.57 frames per second (or the inference time is 0.0307 s per frame). The framework only manually annotates about 8% (183 images) of the 2250 images in the navigation vision, which is a labor-saving solution for rock segmentation tasks. The proposed rock segmentation framework and NI-U-Net++ improve the performance of the state-of-the-art models. The synthetic algorithm improves the process of creating valid data for the challenge of rock segmentation. All source codes, datasets, and trained models of this research are openly available in Cranfield Online Research Data (CORD).

Keywords: image segmentation; remote sensing; terrain identification; data synthesis; transfer learning

1. Introduction

Planetary rovers integrate various sensors and computing units, making the study an interdisciplinary research topic of subjects such as mathematics, human–robot interaction, and computer vision [1–3]. The *Spirit* rover endured the Martian winter, survived 1000 Martian days (*sols*), and traveled more than 6876 m, while the *Opportunity* rover traveled more than 9406 m [4]. However, the space environment poses challenges to the planetary rover operation [5]. The *Spirit* and *Opportunity* rovers experienced communication and function failures during their explorations [6,7]. To prevent this, automating onboard systems is essential for future planetary rovers [3,8]. This research focuses on the semantic terrain segmentation from the monocular navigation vision of the planetary rovers [8], which can provide support for the high-level planetary rover functionalities.

Semantic segmentation is an important research topic in computer vision [9]. Semantic segmentation can be achieved using either traditional computer vision or deep learning [10]. Traditional computer vision solutions utilize probabilistic models to predict pixels [11,12]. Deep learning-based solutions can be further classified into two categories: one-stage pipelines and two-stage pipelines [10]. One-stage pipelines provide End-to-End (E2E) [13] pixel-level predictions for each pixel [14,15]. Popular architectures include DeepLab [16], SSD [17], and U-Net [14]. Two-stage pipelines detect the bounding box of the target and then conduct pixel-level segmentations. Popular two-stage pipelines include RCNN [18], SDS [19], and Mask-RCNN [20].

Semantic segmentation plays an essential role in autonomous driving. Dewan et al. and Badrinarayanan et al. conducted multi-classification for each pixel (road, car, bicycle, column-pole, tree, and sky) [21,22]. Teichmann et al. committed to the road segmentation [23]. He et al. and Wu et al. focused on various traffic participants (vehicles and people) [20,24]. However, autonomous driving operates in a structured environment, while rover navigation, the focus of this research, operates in an unstructured environment. A structured environment refers to a scene with prior knowledge, while an unstructured environment refers to a scene without prior knowledge [25].

Rocks are typical semantic targets in planetary environments [26,27]. The jet propulsion laboratory (JPL) in the *National Aeronautics and Space Administration* (NASA) studied the terrain classification for the planetary rovers [6,28]. Rocks play a significant role in the planetary rovers' autonomy [26]. For example, the *Curiosity* Mars rover involves a generally flat plain with about 5% of the area covered by small (tens of cm size or smaller) rocks [26]. The *Spirit*, *Curiosity*, and *Opportunity* all occurred challenges because of rock-related terrain [6,7,29]. However, existing geometric hazard detection methods cannot detect all of the rocks [28].

The related studies on rock segmentation for planetary rovers can be divided into the following five categories. Table 1 summarizes the discussions in a tabular form, while their results have been summarized in Table 1 in the Appendix A.

Table 1. The summary of the related studies on rock segmentation for planetary rovers.

Category [1]	Explanation	Machine Learning-Based	Reference Index [2]
i	3D point cloud	No	[30–32]
ii	Edge-based method	No (except [33])	[4,5,33–36]
iii	Outstanding rocks	No	[5,37,38]
iv	Other non-machine learning studies	No	[32,39–41]
v	Machine learning studies	Yes	[8,27,28,35,42–44]

[1] "i", "ii", "iii", "iv", and "v" correspond to the same index of category in the context. [2] "Reference index" refers to the same citation index in References.

Category-i refers to the studies that use 3D point clouds [30–32]. The 3D point cloud is generally obtained through LIDAR or stereo cameras, which requires considerable computing resources and storage space. This research applies a less computing and lighter weight solution through 2D images and the monocular camera.

Category-ii refers to the studies that use texture and boundary-based image processing methods [4,5,33–36]. The *Rockster* [36] and *Rockfinder* [34] are popular software packages in this category. However, some image conditions (such as skylines, textures, backgrounds, and unclosed contours) can significantly affect their performance [4]. This research has better robustness on image conditions by applying the various brightness, contrast, and resolution to the input images.

Category-iii refers to the studies focusing on rock identification [5,37,38], while the rock segmentation is only a sub-session of the identification studies. However, this research focuses on pixel-level segmentation, which can achieve more accurate segmentation results.

Category-iv refers to all the rest of the studies using non-machine learning-based methods. Virginia et al. committed to using shadows to find rocks [39]. Li et al. built detailed topographic information of the area between two sites based on rock peak and surface points [40]. Xiao et al. focus on reducing computational cost [32]. Yang and Zhang proposed a gradient-region constrained level set method [41]. In general, they applied artificial features, which usually require significant manual adjustments. This research uses learning-based features, which can intelligently learn the optimized feature from the image and annotations.

Category-v refers to the studies using machine learning methods. Dunlop et al. used a superpixel-based supervised learning method [35]. Ono et al. used Random Forest for terrain classification [28]. Ding Zhou et al. and Feng Zhou et al. focused on the mechanical properties corresponding to different terrain types [27,42]. Gao et al. reviewed the related results of monocular terrain segmentation [8]. Furlan et al. conducted a deeplabv3plus-based rock segmentation solution [43], and Chiodini et al. proposed a fully convolutional network-based rock segmentation solution [44]. Although their performance is much better than Category-i/ii/iii/iv, their training dataset is very small because the annotation costs significant time and effort. This research proposes a synthetic algorithm that can generate a large amount of data and corresponding annotations with very limited manual annotation.

Pixel-level rock segmentation is a challenging task. The shape of rocks in an unstructured planetary exploration environment is hard to predict [5]. Identifying the boundary of the rocks can be made difficult by the low resolution of the navigation camera and the blurred outlines between background and rocks. Furthermore, most rock segmentation datasets for the planetary rovers are confidential to the public or only in the form of images instead of video [7,45].

A solution based on generating synthetic data addresses these problems. Data synthesis produces pixel-level data annotation and image generation. Therefore, synthetic data can generate a large amount of images and corresponding annotations for the pre-training process [46]. Furthermore, the synthetic process is based on the practical video stream, which guarantees good transferability in the following transfer-training process. Then, the model can be transfer-trained to the convergence based on the prior knowledge from the pre-training process.

The contributions of this research include the following:

(i)   This research proposed a synthetic algorithm and transfer learning-based framework, which provides a labor-saving solution for the rock segmentation in the navigation vision of the planetary rovers.
(ii) This research proposed a synthetic algorithm and a synthetic dataset, which aid the research into the rock segmentation in the navigation vision of the planetary rovers.
(iii) This research came up with an end-to-end (E2E) network (NI-U-Net++) for the pixel-level rock segmentation, which achieved state-of-the-art in the synthetic dataset.

All source codes, datasets, and trained models of this research are openly available in Cranfield Online Research Data (CORD) at https://doi.org/10.17862/cranfield.rd.16958728, accessed on 26 November 2021.

The article is arranged as follows. Section 2 depicts the proposed synthetic algorithm and rock segmentation network. Section 3 discusses the experimental results. Conclusions and future work are placed in Section 4.

2. Methods

The proposed rock segmentation framework is based on the transfer learning process (see Figure 1). Transfer learning is a typical solution for the data-limited situation [47,48]. The overall framework can be divided into the following.

(1)   The framework can be divided into two processes. Figure 1 identifies the pre-training process and the transfer-training process with the blue and green frames, respectively. Rock segmentation in an unannotated scenario is significantly difficult, and the transfer learning strategy divides the learning process into two steps. Although the synthetic dataset can generate large amount of pixel-level annotated data, they inevitably have a significant difference from the real-life data. The real-life data represent the practical mission, while its annotation corresponds to an expensive

cost. Therefore, a cooperated solution between the synthetic data and real-life images becomes very promising. The pre-training process aims to achieve prior knowledge from a similar scene, and then, the transfer-training process fine-tunes the pre-trained weight to fit the real-life images.

(2)   In the pre-training process:

    (a)   The purple ellipse with "Annotation-1" refers to the first manual annotation, which aims to acquire the backgrounds and rock samples for the synthetic algorithm.

    (b)   Then, the synthetic algorithm utilizes these backgrounds and rock samples to generate the synthetic dataset. The synthetic dataset contains 14,000 synthetic images and corresponding annotations.

    (c)   The orange solid round frame refers to the proposed rock segmentation network (NI-U-Net++). The blue dash arrow refers to the pre-training, which aims to achieve prior knowledge from the synthetic dataset.

    (d)   The pre-training process eventually accomplishes the pre-trained weights of the NI-U-Net++, and these pre-trained weights refer to the prior knowledge from the synthetic dataset.

(3)   In the transfer-training process:

    (a)   The purple ellipse with "Annotation-2" refers to the second manual annotation, which aims to produce some pixel-level annotations (see the green round frame with "Annotated visual dataset"). The "Annotated visual dataset" contains 183 real-life images and corresponding pixel-level annotations.

    (b)   The green dash arrow refers to the transfer training, which aims to fine-tune the pre-trained weights to fit the "Annotated visual dataset".

    (c)   (iii–iii) The transfer-training process comes up with the final weights of the NI-U-Net++.

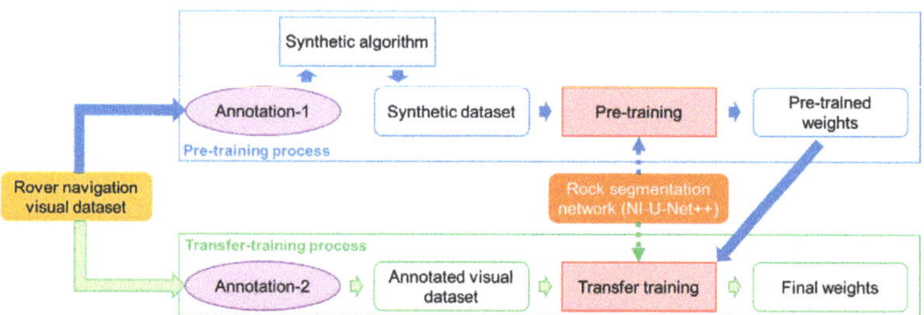

Figure 1. The pipeline of the proposed rock segmentation framework. The rover navigation visual dataset used in this research is the Katwijk beach planetary rover dataset [49], while it can be different in other scenarios. The synthetic dataset for the pre-training is not augmented, while the annotated visual dataset for the transfer training is applied augmentation to extend the dataset.

2.1. The Real-Life Visual Navigation Dataset for the Planetary Rovers

The visual navigation dataset of the planetary rovers used in this research is part1 and part2 of the *Katwijk* beach planetary rover dataset [49] from the European Space Agency (ESA) [50–53], which contains 2250 frames of the image. The *Katwijk* dataset is a professional open dataset for the navigation vision of the planetary rover research, and many studies use the *Katwijk* dataset as the planetary environment [44,52,54]. The *Katwijk* dataset is achieved at the site where is near the heavy-duty planetary rover (HDPR) platform project of the European Space and Technology Research Center [49].

The reasons for adopting the *Katwijk* dataset are as follows: (i) The focus of this research is to integrate a real-time and E2E rock segmentation framework into the navigation vision of planetary rovers. Thus, a navigation vision stream for evaluating the real-time performance is essential. (ii) The *Katwijk* dataset involves all relevant landmarks supported in the research of Ono et al. [28]. (iii) Other datasets are not suitable for this research. For example, [54] involves some targets that are less likely to appear in planetary exploration (such as the tree, wall, and people). (iv) Other datasets (such as NASA raw images [55]) contain many different types of rock samples, introducing a more complex marginal probability distribution (this research utilizes the concept about task, domain, and marginal probability distribution from [56] as the fundaments). However, rock diversity (or even new rocks [38]) is not the focus of this research but an entirely new discipline.

2.2. The Synthetic Dataset

The proposed synthetic algorithm aims to generate a large amount of images and the corresponding pixel-level annotations with limited manual annotations. Although planetary exploration provides numerous visual data, they have barely been pixel-level annotated. Labor-saving annotation is a vital and usual challenge for planetary visual data. The target of the synthetic algorithm is to build a labor-saving solution to generate a large amount of images and corresponding pixel-level annotations for the pre-training process. Planetary explorations are expensive regarding labor, time, and resource, while the synthetic approach aims to minimize the associated costs. Although multi-labeler seems a promising solution for suppressing human errors, it will further increase the labor and time required. The proposed synthetic algorithm can generate pixel-level annotations while generating synthesized images. To maintain the labor-saving and annotation quality, the following four highlights are essential for designing the synthetic algorithm.

(1) The synthetic algorithm also prepares data for the pre-training process. Therefore, the materials utilized in the synthetic algorithm should come from the real-life images.
(2) Another target is to generate images and annotations synchronously through the synthesis algorithm, thereby significantly reducing the cost of manual intervention.
(3) The target is to ensure the diversity of the synthetic dataset. The pre-training dataset can determine the robustness and generalization ability of the segmentation framework for the navigation visions. The data diversity introduced through morphology, brightness, and contrast transformations are significantly important to the above end.
(4) The embedded rock samples require further processing to simulate the visual comfortable images.

2.2.1. The Proposed Synthetic Algorithm

The synthetic algorithm uses image processing technology and the illumination intensity-based assumption. Equations (1)–(9) and Figure 2 depict the illumination intensity-based assumptions and the corresponding process based on the geometrics and mathematics. Figure 2a abstracts a typical navigation scenario of the planetary rovers using a sketch. The light source (I) can be approximated as the sun in the scenario. The angles between the rays i_1, i_2, and i_3 of the light and the horizontal ground (g) are θ_1, θ_2, and θ_3, respectively. When I is significantly far away from the ground g, this research considers that all light rays are parallel to each other, so the angles θ_1, θ_2, and θ_3 of i_1, i_2, and i_3 and the horizontal ground are equal (see Equation (1)).

$$\begin{cases} i_1 \parallel i_2 \parallel i_3, \\ \theta_1 = \theta_2 = \theta_3, \end{cases} \quad if\ I \to +\infty. \tag{1}$$

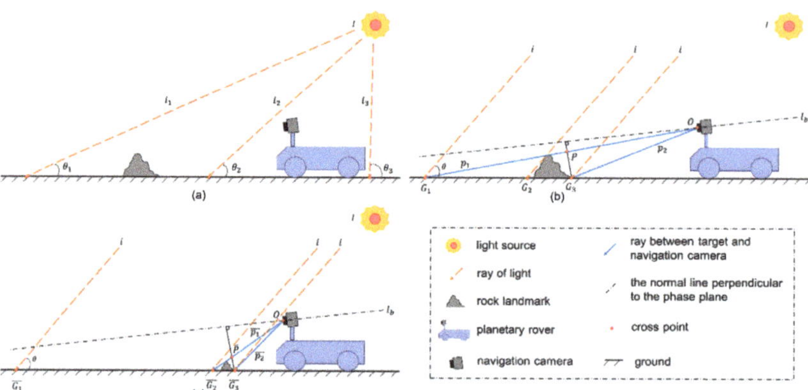

Figure 2. The sketches of the planetary rover navigations. (**a**) refers to the typical scenario of the planetary rover. (**b**) refers to the abstracted scenario through applying Equation (1) to (**a**). (**c**) refers to the abstracted scenario with a small and closer rock landmark compared to (**b**). G_1, G_2, G_3, P, p_1, and p_2 in the (**b**) scenario correspond to $\overline{G_1}$, $\overline{G_2}$, $\overline{G_3}$, $\overline{P}$, $\overline{p_1}$, and $\overline{p_2}$ in the (**c**) scenario, respectively.

Figure 2b shows the abstracted sketch of Figure 2a through applying Equation (1). The angles between all rays (i) and g all equal to θ. This research defines ρ to refer to the density of rays, which also refers to the illumination intensity (L) in the unit area on the ground. Therefore, the L on a specific ground area equals the multiplication between the area of the region (S) and ρ (see Equation (2)).

$$L = \rho * S \tag{2}$$

The solid blue lines (p_1 and p_2) in Figure 2b refer to the rock area captured by the navigation camera. The dashed line (l_b) refers to the normal line perpendicular to the phase plane. The solid black line segment (PG_3) refers to the corresponding rock on the image. Although the rock occupies the same image region as the ground $G_1 G_3$, the L of the rock is different than the ground without rock because of the difference between $G_2 G_3$ and $G_1 G_3$. In Equation (3), $L_{G_1 G_3}$ refers to the L in the $G_1 G_3$ area, and PG_3 refers to the PG_3 area.

$$\rho = \frac{L_{G_1 G_3}}{PG_3} \tag{3}$$

Notably, all images involved in this section refer to the grayscale images. Thus, PG_3 is a grayscale image. This research assumes the image grayscale value of the PG_3 area relates to two parameters, corresponding density (ρ) and the surface optical properties (P_{opt}) of the object (c_T).

i. The above discussion uses Equation (2) to achieve the desired illumination intensity, while ρ is difficult to obtain from a grayscale image. However, the known information is the corresponding image grayscale value ($G_1 G_3$) and the area of PG_3. It is noteworthy that $G_1 G_3$ and $G_2 G_3$ appear in the same image region. This research assumes that the ratio ($\overline{\rho}$) between the sum grayscale in $G_1 G_3$ and the area of PG_3 can approximate the value of ρ (see Equation (4)).

$$\rho \approx \overline{\rho} = \frac{L_{G_1 G_3}}{PG_3} = \sum_{(x,y)\,\in\,T} \left[\frac{pixel_{img}(x,\,y)}{N_{pixel}} \right] \tag{4}$$

However, Figure 2c shows another scenario. A pronounced difference between $G_1 G_2$ (Figure 2b) and $\overline{G_1 G_2}$ (Figure 2c) comes from a smaller and closer rock landmark. Therefore, the difference ($\Delta \rho$) between ρ and $\overline{\rho}$ is located on $G_1 G_2$ (equivalent to

$\overline{G_1 G_2}$). It is noteworthy that ρ is the ratio between the sum grayscale of $G_1 G_3$ and PG_3, whereas $\overline{\rho}$ is the ratio between the sum grayscale of $G_2 G_3$ to PG_3 (see Equation (5)).

$$\Delta\rho = \overline{\rho} - \rho = \frac{L_{G_1 G_3}}{PG_3} - \frac{L_{G_2 G_3}}{PG_3} = \frac{L_{G_1 G_3} - L_{G_2 G_3}}{PG_3} \tag{5}$$

Substituting Equation (2) into Equation (5) can produce Equation (6), so $\Delta\rho$ is a value related to $L_{G_1 G_2}$.

$$\Delta\rho = \overline{\rho} - \rho = \frac{\rho * G_1 G_3 - \rho * G_2 G_3}{PG_3} = \frac{\rho * G_1 G_2}{PG_3} = \frac{L_{G_1 G_2}}{PG_3} \tag{6}$$

ii. The optical properties of the object surface are complex (such as surface reflectance, refracting, and absorptivity), and they do not belong to the scope of this research. Here, we use a variable c_T to pack all factors related to optical properties. Equation (7) depicts the grayscale change caused through the optical properties.

$$P_{opt} = f_1(c_T) \tag{7}$$

Recalling the objective of the synthetic algorithm, Equation (7) can only correlate the optical properties and image grayscales implicitly. Thus, this research proposes Equation (8) to approach Equation (7) artificially. Equation (8) assumes that the grayscale distribution in the target region (rock in this research) is a function of the coordinates when ρ is constant. This research calculates the averaged grayscale value (img_{mean}) for the corresponding image area. Then, it subtracts the grayscale values (img) to img_{mean} to obtain a differential grayscale "image" (img_Δ), which is a statistical result only related to the coordinates.

$$P_{opt} \approx img_\Delta = img - img_{mean} \tag{8}$$

The synthetic algorithm corresponding to the rock-embedded area can be depicted using Equation (9):

$$\overline{L} = \overline{\rho} * img_\Delta - C. \tag{9}$$

The C refers to the constants used to correct the distance between ρ and $\overline{\rho}$. Recalling Equation (6), $\Delta\rho$ positively correlates to the $L_{G_1 G_2}$. The practical area of $L_{G_1 G_2}$ is a varying value that is dependent on the appearance of the target. Measuring $L_{G_1 G_2}$ is challenging, but $L_{G_1 G_2}$ positively correlates to img_{mean} (a brighter image causes a higher $L_{G_1 G_2}$). Thus, this research assumes C is a constant that depends on img_{mean}. Table 2 depicts the values of C, while the detailed experiments for deciding C can be found in Appendix A.2 in the Appendix A. It is noteworthy that L, $\overline{L}$, and img_Δ all contain multiple values, which correspond to the coordinates.

Table 2. The constant C to correct $\overline{\rho}$ from ρ.

Conditions	Value [1]
$img_{mean} \leq 25$	0
$25 < img_{mean} \leq 50$	5
$50 < img_{mean} \leq 75$	10
$75 < img_{mean} \leq 100$	15
$100 < img_{mean} \leq 125$	20
$125 < img_{mean} \leq 150$	25
$150 < img_{mean} \leq 175$	30
$175 < img_{mean} \leq 225$	35
$200 < img_{mean} \leq 225$	40
$225 < img_{mean} \leq 250$	45
$250 < img_{mean}$	50

[1] The values correspond to the grayscale metric with 256 scales.

2.2.2. Implementation

Figure 3 and Algorithm 1 show the implementation process of the proposed synthetic algorithm.

i. This research randomly picks up 35 images from the *Katwijk* dataset for "Annotation-1". The number of 35 images is arbitrary; it needs to be large enough to get a sufficient dataset of rock annotations but not too large that it takes a long time to annotate the images. Furthermore, this research focuses on exploring a feasible framework so that the upper and lower limits of the image number in "Annotation-1" are not studied thoroughly.

ii. Then, the synthetic algorithm conducts the "Annotation-1" to these images (see Figure 3). The red mask refers to the rock sample, and the green masks refer to other rocks. It is noteworthy that each image only includes the largest rock in the rock samples. Before embedding into a new background, a morphological transformation is necessary to ensure the variant of the synthetic dataset. However, the enlarged morphological transformations can bring a significant resolution change if the rock sample is too small.

iii. The algorithm also utilizes the images in "Annotation-1" as backgrounds for the synthetic algorithm. The annotation rule for "Annotation-1" is: if a rock cannot be identified with the three to six times enlargement, this research decides to abandon it as a part of the background.

iv. The above three steps finish the data preparation for the synthetic algorithm. The *rocks* refer to rock samples, and *scenes* refer to backgrounds. Then, the algorithm conducts Algorithm 1 to generate the synthetic dataset.

v. Morphological transformations can increase the number and diversity of the synthetic dataset. The morphological transformation schemes for rock samples (aug_{rock}) come from the combinations using mirror, flatten, narrowing, and zooming. The morphological transformation schemes for backgrounds (aug_{scene}) further include the adjustments of brightness, contrast, and sharpness.

vi. Then, Algorithm 1 traverses each background with all aug_{scene} to achieve the morphologically transformed images ($scene_{aug}$ in Algorithm 1) (see row 3 and 4 in Algorithm 1). Meanwhile, the sky and ground segmentation model is applied to identify the ground pixels, and the rock samples are only embedded into the ground region. The sky and ground segmentation model comes from [57].

vii. For each $scene_{aug}$ the synthetic algorithm embeds a random number of $rock_{aug}$ (see row 11 in Algorithm 1).

viii. Each $rock_{aug}$ comes from a random selection from the rocks ($rock_{select}$). The algorithm also randomly selects a morphological transformation scheme (aug_r) from aug_{rock}. The algorithm conducts aug_r to $rock_{select}$, which results in a morphologically transformed rock ($rock_{aug}$) (see rows 9, 10, and 11 in Algorithm 1).

ix. The algorithm adopts Equation (8), Equation (4), Table 2, and Equation (9) to achieve img_Δ, $\bar{\rho}$, the correction constant for the corresponding $\bar{\rho}$ (C_{select}), and the grayscale values of the embedded rock ($rock_{replace}$) (see rows 12, 14, 15, and 16 in Algorithm 1). The further discussion of the values in Table 2 can be found in Appendix A.2.

x. Finally, the synthetic images that correspond to the $scene_{aug}$ are saved as the synthetic dataset.

Algorithm 1: Synthetic algorithm

	Input:	rock samples: $rock = [rock_1, rock_2, \ldots, rock_{35}]$
		practical sense: $sense = [scene_1, scene_2, \ldots, scene_{35}]$
		correction constant: $C = [C_1, C_2, \ldots, C_{11}]$
		scene augmentation: $aug_{scene} = [s_1, s_2, \ldots, s_8]$
		rock augmentation: $aug_{rock} = [r_1, r_2, \ldots, r_9]$
	Output:	Synthetic dataset: $img = [img_1, img_2, \ldots, img_n]$

1	**for** img_{idx} **in** $range(n)$ **do**	
2	**for** $scene$ **in** $scenes$ **do**	
3	**for** aug_s **in** aug_{scene} **do**	
4	$scene_{aug} = aug_s(scene)$	
5	**for** i **in** $range(50)$ **do**	
6	$N_{rocks} \leftarrow$ **a random integer between 5 and 20;**	
7	**for** j **in** $range(N_{rocks})$ **do**	
8	$(x_a, y_a) \leftarrow$ **random anchor point for rock;**	
9	$rock_{select} \leftarrow$ **random select in** $rocks$;	
10	$aug_r \leftarrow$ **random select in** aug_{rock};	
11	$rock_{aug} = aug_r(rock_{select})$	
12	$img_\Delta \leftarrow rock_{aug}$;	Equation (8)
13	$img_{mean} \leftarrow scene_{arg}$ & (x_a, y_a);	
14	$\bar{\rho} \leftarrow img_{mean}$;	Equation (4)
15	$C_{select} \leftarrow$ **find in** C;	Table 2
16	$rock_{replace} \leftarrow img_\Delta$ & $\bar{\rho}$ & C_{select};	Equation (9)
17	$img_{idx} \leftarrow$ **embed** $rock_{replace}$ **in** $scene_{arg}$ **at** (x_a, y_a)	
18	**end**	
19	**end**	
20	**end**	
21	**end**	
22	**end**	

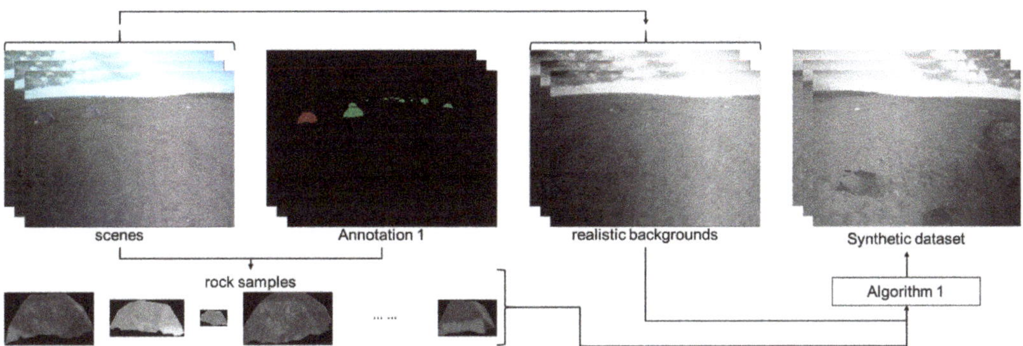

Figure 3. The preparation part in the implementation of the proposed synthetic algorithm. "Annotation 1" refers to the same "Annotation-1" as in Figure 1. The red and green pixels in "Annotation 1" refer to the rock samples and other rocks, respectively.

It is noteworthy that the proposed synthetic algorithm is a typical incremental method through embedding new rock samples into the original image, which inevitably adds many large and obvious rocks. Thus, the synthetic algorithm may lead the quantitative metrics to a better result in the pre-training process than the transfer-training process. In addition, the metrics adopted in this research include the accuracy, intersection over union (IoU), and Dice score.

2.3. Proposed Rock Segmentation Network

This section discusses the modified rock segmentation network (named the NI-U-Net++). Figure 4 depicts the proposed NI-U-Net++, which is a modified U-Net++ [15] through modifying the overall architecture and integrating some modified micro-networks. It is noteworthy that this research has been inspired by the U-Net++ [15] and NIN [58].

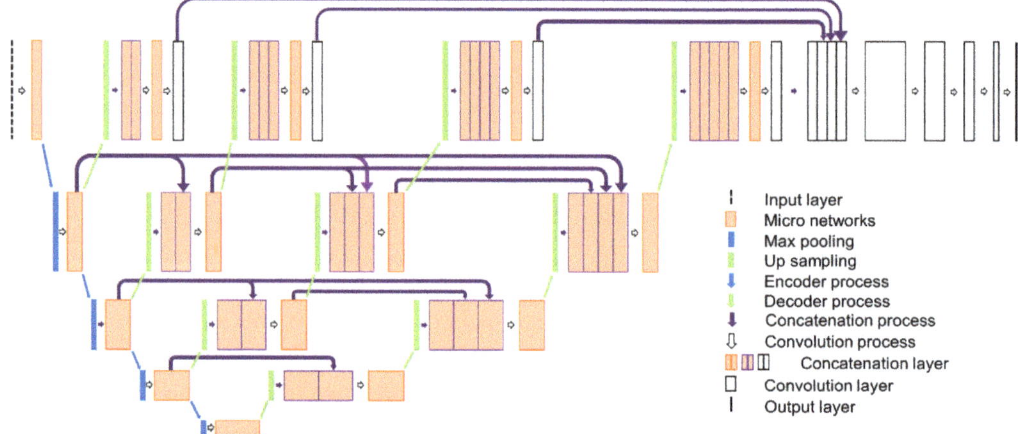

Figure 4. The proposed rock segmentation network (NI-U-Net++).

The U-Net network uses the encoder–decoder configuration and concatenation layer to configure a deep network [14,59], which provides an efficient and effective structure for feature extraction and backpropagation. U-Net++ is an updated U-Net, which adopts a new encoder–decoder network with a series of nested, dense skip pathways. U-Net++ further applies deep supervision to avoid the skips of the shallow sub-U-Nets [15].

The proposed NI-U-Net++ adopts a similar overall structure of the encoder–decoder design and deep supervision as the U-Net++. The blue and green solid arrows in Figure 4 refer to the encoder and decoder part, respectively. The encoder part in the NI-U-Net++ has four scale reductions (see the four blue arrows in Figure 4). Deep supervision is implemented using the concatenate and convolutional layers (see the purple arrows and white blocks at the top of Figure 4). Moreover, the purple arrows refer to the "highway" using the concatenate layers to connect the front and back layers. These highways can pass the backpropagation gradients in the front layers, thereby avoiding the gradient vanishing.

The NIN refers to the micro-block of networks assembled in another neural network. The 1×1 convolutions play an essential role in NIN. The 1×1 convolutions have low computational consumption, while they can integrate cross-channel information. Furthermore, 1×1 convolutions can transform the number of channels without changing the tensor scale [58].

This research proposes a modified NIN network as a micro-network to integrate into the NI-U-Net++. Figure 5 depicts the structure of the proposed micro-network, which is the orange squares in Figure 4. The channel of the micro-network input tensor is N channels, and the first 3×3 convolution decreases it to $N/4$ channels. Then, the following two 1×1 convolutions can be understood as the fully connected layers along the channel axis. Finally, another 3×3 convolution restores the tensor channels to N channels. Thus, the micro-network ensures the proposed NI-U-Net++ can adopt a deep structure with a small computational graph.

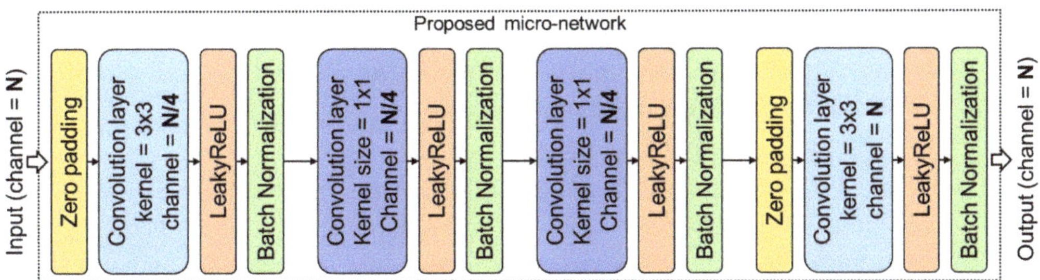

Figure 5. The layer configuration of the proposed micro-network. The yellow, light blue, orange, green, and dark blue squares refer to the zero-padding layer, convolution layer with 3×3 kernel size, LeakyReLU activation layer, and batch normalization layer, respectively.

There are three highlights in the proposed NI-U-Net++ rock segmentation network. (1) NI-U-Net++ does not determine the image scale-change in NI-U-Net++. NI-U-Net++ provides more flexible freedom of the scale-change than U-Net, and the task can automatically find the optimal scale. The scale-change refers to the optimal number of continuous downsampling operations before the decoder. (2) The strategy of deep supervision is adopted in the proposed NI-U-Net++. Zhou et al. mentioned that the shallow sub-U-Nets might be disconnected when the deep supervision is not activated [15]. To this end, deep supervision can provide the backpropagation to any sub-U-Nets. (3) The micro-network establishes the cross-channel data relevance in each scale of the segmentation network. (The further pairwise comparisons between proposed NI-U-Net++ and related studies can be found in Appendix A.4.)

2.4. The Pre-Training Process

The pre-training process aims to provide efficient prior knowledge for rock segmentation. The pre-training process divides the synthetic dataset into a training, validation, and testing set according to the ratios of 80%, 10%, and 10%. The hyperparameters are listed in Table 3. The number of epochs is set to 50 epochs, the batch size is set to 5 samples per batch, the learning rate is set to 0.00005, the optimizer adopts the Adam, and the binary cross-entropy loss is chosen as the loss function. The pixels of the rocks are annotated using value one, and the background pixels use value zero. Furthermore, the pre-training process uses six usual metrics to compare the proposed NI-U-Net++ to the related studies. The six metrics are accuracy, intersection over union (IoU), Dice score, root mean squared error (RMSE), and receiver operating characteristic curve (ROC). The related studies correspond to U-Net [14], U-Net++ [15], NI-U-Net [57], Furlan2019 [50], and Chiodini2020 [44].

Table 3. The hyperparameters of the pre-training process.

Hyperparameter	Setting	Hyperparameter	Setting
Epoch	50 epochs	Batch size	5 sample per batch
Learning rate	0.00005	Optimizer	Adam
Loss function	Binary cross-entropy	Training set ratio	80% of the synthetic dataset
Validation set ratio	10% of the synthetic dataset	Testing set ratio	10% of the synthetic dataset
Evaluation metrics	Accuracy, intersection over union (IoU), Dice score, root mean squared error (RMSE), and receiver operating characteristic curve (ROC)		

The chosen evaluation metrics come from the following reasons. (i) Loss function decides the learning gradient, and it is the specific factor for fitting conditions, converges, and the learning process. (ii) Accuracy refers to a very intuited indicator for knowing performance. (iii) IoU is a prevalent and influential metric in semantic segmentation studies, but it is also based on the confusion matrix as the accuracy. (iv) Dice score is a similar metric. Thus, this research puts the Dice score in the Appendix A as additional results. (v) ROC indicates the sensitivity for different thresholds of positive and negative prediction.

It is noteworthy that the training, validation, and testing sets are saved to local storage to prevent the potential uncertainty from the dataset shuffle. Thus, any synthetic dataset mentioned in this study refers to the same data distribution. Some details of the related studies have been discussed as following:

(i)   U-Net is proposed by Ronneberger et al. [14], which is a very popular one-stage image segmentation network [60,61]. The applied U-Net references the high-starred implementations on GitHub [62,63]. The encoder of U-Net contains four downsampling layers, the decoder contains four upsampling layers, and the activation uses the "ReLU" function. The size of each convolution kernel is 3×3.

(ii) U-Net++ is proposed by Zhou et al. [15] in 2018, which is an undated U-shaped network based on the U-Net. The applied U-Net++ references the high-stared implementation on GitHub [64]. The applied U-Net++ contains four downsampling layers, and the deep supervision has been activated.

(iii) The NI-U-Net [57] shares the same architecture as the sky and ground segmentation network used in Section 2.2. NI-U-Net only contains a single U-shaped encoder-decoder design, and the micro-networks have also been applied.

(iv) Furlan et al. proposed a deeplabv3plus-based rock segmentation solution in 2019, and the implementation of Furlan2019 referenced the study in [43].

(v)   Chiodini et al. proposed a fully convolutional network-based rock segmentation solution in 2020; the implementation of Chiodini2020 referenced the study in [44].

2.5. The Transfer-Training Process

The aim of the transfer-training process is to fine-tune the NI-U-Net++ from the "Pre-trained weights" to the "Final weights" for the real-life images (see Figure 1). The "Annotated visual dataset" is divided into training, validation, and testing sets according to the ratio of 80%:10%:10% (similar to the pre-training process). The hyperparameters have been depicted in Table 4: the number of epochs is set to 50 epochs, the batch size is set to 5 samples per batch, the learning rate is set to 0.00005, the optimizer uses the Adam, and the loss function uses the binary cross-entropy. The evaluation also uses the three popular metrics, accuracy, IoU, and Dice score.

Table 4. The hyperparameters of the transfer-training process.

Hyperparameter	Setting	Hyperparameter	Setting
Epoch	50 epochs	Batch size	5 sample per batch
Learning rate	0.00005	Optimizer	Adam
Loss function	Binary cross-entropy	Training set ratio	80% of the synthetic dataset
Validation set ratio	10% of the synthetic dataset	Testing set ratio	10% of the synthetic dataset
Evaluation metrics	Accuracy, intersection over union (IoU), Dice score, root mean squared error (RMSE), and receiver operating characteristic curve (ROC)		

The data for the transfer-training process comes from "Annotation-2" in Figure 1. "Annotation-2" can be composed of the following four steps.

(1)   "Annotation-2" randomly re-selects 150 images from the *Katwijk* dataset.

(2)   "Annotation-2" performs pixel-level annotations on these images.

(3)   The images annotated in "Annotation-1" can also be used for the transfer-training process, so "Annotation-2" merges 35 images in "Annotation-1" with the 150 images. It is noteworthy that there are two duplicate images, so the final number of images for "Annotation-2" is 183 images (The 183 images are only about 8% of the *Katwijk* dataset)

(4)   "Annotation-2" uses data augmentation to simulate possible situations for the planetary rover operations. For example, rotations simulate the pose changes, brightness changes simulate changes in illumination conditions, and contrast changes simulate

changes in imaging conditions. The data augmentation eventually achieves about 4000 images.

3. Results and Discussion

All experiments in this research were conducted on the same data, hardware, and software. This research saved the random-shuffled dataset to ensure the repeatability for any experiment. The CPU, GPU, and memory size are Core i7-7700, NVIDIA RTX1080, and 32 GB. The deep learning platform, GPU parallel computing support, programming language, and operating system are TensorFlow 2.1, CUDA 10.1, Python 3.6, and Ubuntu 18.04.

3.1. The Results of the Proposed Synthetic Algorithm

The proposed synthetic algorithm (Section 2.2) generates 14,000 synthetic images as the synthetic dataset using the rock samples and real-life backgrounds from Section 2.2. Figure 6a visualizes an example in the synthetic dataset. The grayscale distributions between the rock samples and the real-life backgrounds can be significantly different. For example, directly embedding a rock sample extracted from a dark region to a bright region of the real-life background is not visually comfortable. The solid blue frames in Figure 6a refer to the embedded rocks, and the green dashed frames refer to the original rocks. The grayscale distributions of the embedded rocks are visually comfortable. Furthermore, Figure 6 illustrates some complex cases that usually appear in the practical planetary explorations (such as occlusion, unclosed outline, far and small target, etc.). These complex cases can significantly enforce the robustness and generalization-ability of the synthetic dataset. Figure 6b refers to the corresponding annotation of Figure 6a, which is the synthetic image.

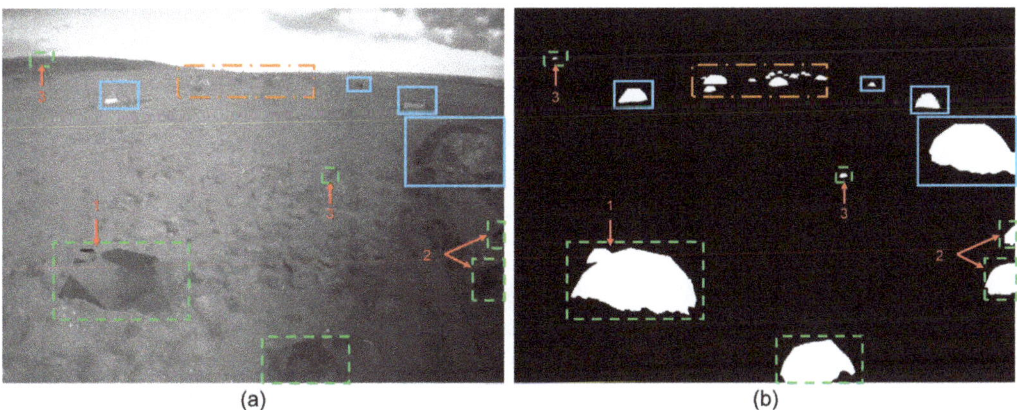

(a)   (b)

Figure 6. A typical example in the synthetic dataset. (**a**,**b**) refer to the synthetic image (from the proposed synthetic algorithm) and the simultaneously generated annotation. Blue solid frames, green dash frames, and orange dot-dash frames refer to original rocks, embedded synthetic rocks, and un-highlighted rocks, respectively. The reason for the un-highlighted rocks is their small and dense distribution, which can cause a bad visualization. "1", "2", and "3" highlight the complex cases of occlusion, unclosed outline, far, and small target, respectively. (**b**) uses white pixels to refer to the rocks, while black pixels refer to the background.

The target of the synthetic algorithm is to simulate real-life images as much as possible when generating the synthetic data. The difference between synthetic and real-life images comes from different imaging sources. Figure A1 in the Appendix A shows that the synthetic algorithm without well-optimization can cause an apparent visual difference. The materials used in the synthetic algorithm are all derived from real-life images to ensure visual comfort (such as rock samples and backgrounds). Furthermore, the synthetic algorithm further optimizes visual comfort through the illumination intensity assumption. It is noteworthy that using synthetic data aims to assist rock segmentation in real-life images. Therefore, this research utilizes the results in real-life images to verify the capacity of the proposed synthetic algorithm (see Figure A2 and the demo video in the supplementary material).

3.2. The Results of the Pre-Training Process

This section compares the proposed NI-U-Net++ with five related studies. Table 5 describes the quantitative comparisons of the pre-training process. Figure 7 depicts the loss and accuracy curves of the training and validation sets for the proposed NI-U-Net++. Figures A4–A6 describe the loss and accuracy curves of U-Net, U-Net++, NI-U-Net, Furlan2019, and Chiodini2020, respectively. Dice scores have been described in Table A2 in the Appendix A. Figure 8 compares the ROC curve of the proposed NI-U-Net++ with the advanced studies from Furlan2019 [43] and Chiodini2020 [44].

Table 5. The results of the pre-training process.

Network	Loss			Accuracy			IoU			RMSE		
	Train	Valid	Test	Train	Valid	Test	Train	Valid	Test	Train	Valid	Test
U-Net	0.0360	0.0393	0.0397	99.13%	98.96%	98.95%	0.8446	0.8248	0.8255	0.1027	0.1039	0.1043
U-Net++	0.0121	0.0211	0.0209	99.56%	99.28%	99.28%	0.9182	0.8769	0.8783	0.0668	0.0744	0.0743
NI-U-Net	0.0102	0.0281	0.0280	99.63%	99.25%	99.24%	0.9313	0.8715	0.8720	0.0665	0.0775	0.0776
Furlan2019	0.0273	0.0307	0.0308	99.04%	98.86%	98.86%	0.9125	0.9005	0.9001	0.0912	0.0924	0.0926
Chiodini2020	0.0108	0.1724	0.1692	99.38%	97.98%	98.00%	0.9423	0.8299	0.8330	0.1298	0.1336	0.1328
NI-U-Net++	0.0117	0.0175	0.0173	99.58%	99.40%	99.41%	0.9209	0.8972	0.8991	0.0665	0.0775	0.0775

The "loss" refers to the binary cross-entropy used for training. The "accuracy", "IoU", and "RMSE" refer to the adopted evaluation metrics. The "train", "valid", and "test" refer to the results from the training, validation, and testing sets. U-Net, U-Net++, NI-U-Net, Furlan2019, and Chiodini2020 refer to the related studies [14,15,43,44,57], respectively. NI-U-Net++ refers to the proposed network. Gray shadings indicate the lowest loss, highest accuracy, highest IoU, and lowest RMSE.

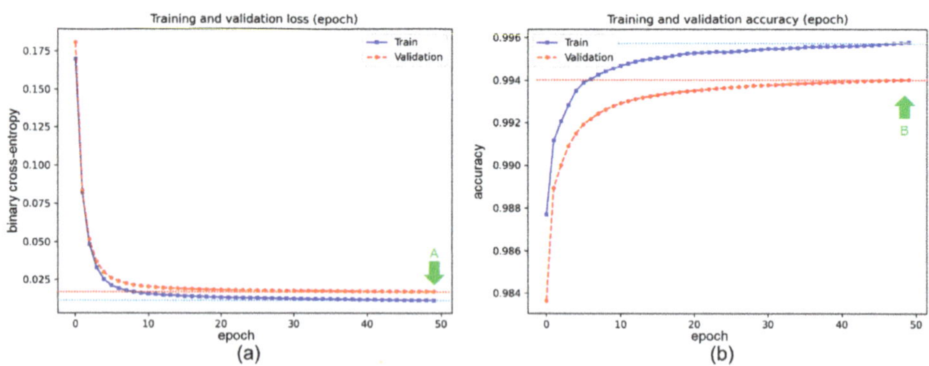

Figure 7. The loss and accuracy curves of NI-U-Net++ using the synthetic dataset. The green "A" and "B" correspond to the two highlights mentioned in the content of the NI-U-Net++ curves. (**a**) refers to the epoch-wised loss curves in the training and validation sets. (**b**) refers to the epoch-wised accuracy curves in the training and validation sets. The horizontal dash lines refer to the references of final converge status.

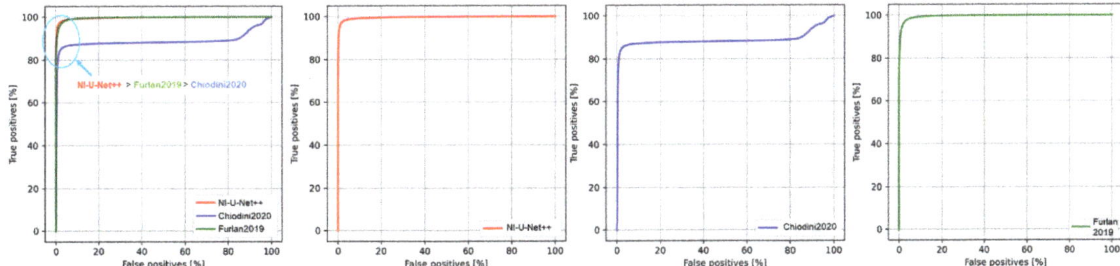

Figure 8. The ROC curves of the proposed NI-U-Net++, Furlan2019 [43], and Chiodini2020 [44].

The gray shadings in Tables 5 and A2 highlight the best results in each column. NI-U-Net and NI-U-Net++ show better performances than the U-Net and U-Net++ with a lower "loss" value and higher "accuracy", "IoU", and "Dice" values. This suggests that the proposed micro-network helps to improve the performance of rock segmentation. Moreover, Figures 6 and A6 both appear to have a more rapid initial learning speed compared to Figures A4 and A5. Thus, the proposed micro-network can accelerate the learning efficiency.

The NI-U-Net achieves the highest training accuracy (see Table 5). Arrow "A" in Figure A6a highlights a U-shaped rise that appears on the validation loss curve, while the training loss curve keeps decreasing. These indicate that overfitting occurs for NI-U-Net. This can explain that NI-U-Net achieved the lowest training loss and highest training accuracy, but the validation and testing loss and accuracy were poorer than others. The green arrow "B" in Figure A6b indicates that NI-U-Net produces the largest distance in accuracy between the training and validation sets. NI-U-Net is a modified U-Net using the micro-network. Compared with U-Net, all the results of NI-U-Net achieve improvements. Therefore, the proposed micro-network can also suppress the overfitting level.

Table 5 and arrow "A" in Figure A4a find that U-Net achieves a higher loss and lower accuracy. Thus, U-Net has the highest level of underfitting. Arrow "B" in Figure A4b highlights that accuracy curves keep flat at the first two epochs. This indicates that the learning process of U-Net is difficult. This comes from a fixed and high encoder ratio. The down-sampling operations in the encoder can cause significant information loss, especially for small targets.

U-Net++ also appears to have overfitting in Table 5. The U-Net++ training curves and the horizontal reference lines depict that the training curves keep learning throughout the pre-training process, while the validation curves come to the convergence (see the arrows "A" in Figure A5a and "B" in Figure A5b).

Table 5 shows that the proposed NI-U-Net++ achieves the lowest validation loss, lowest validation and testing loss, highest validation and testing accuracy, as well as lowest RMSE. The curves in Figure 6a,b appear to be promising learning trends. In the initial stage of training, it drops rapidly and then slowly converges. The arrows "A" and "B" in Figure 6a,b indicate that NI-U-Net++ stays stable on both the training and validation sets, and the overfitting level is low. The outstanding evaluation results indicate that the risk of underfitting is also low. NI-U-Net++ achieved the best pre-training results by improving the overall configuration and introducing the micro-network.

This research further applied two advanced related studies as the comparisons. (i) The "Chiodini2020" in Table 5 and Figure A7 indicates the results using Chiodini et al. [44]. The proposed NI-U-Net++ suppresses all qualitative results of Chiodini2020. Moreover, Chiodini2020 appears to have significant overfitting and unstable conditions on the validation set. (ii) The "Furlan2019" in Table 5 and Figure A8 indicates the results using Furlan et al. [43]. Furlan et al. applied a fully convolutional network (FCN)-based rock segmentation solution. Although Furlan2019 achieves higher IoU than the proposed

NI-U-Net++, it is only 0.1–0.3% higher than the proposed NI-U-Net. Furthermore, the proposed NI-U-Net++ achieves significantly better results in loss, accuracy, and RMSE.

Figure 9 depicts the visualizations of NI-U-Net++ from the pre-training process. Table A3 indicates the quantitative results of using different numbers of synthetic images, and the further discussion can be found in Appendix A.5.

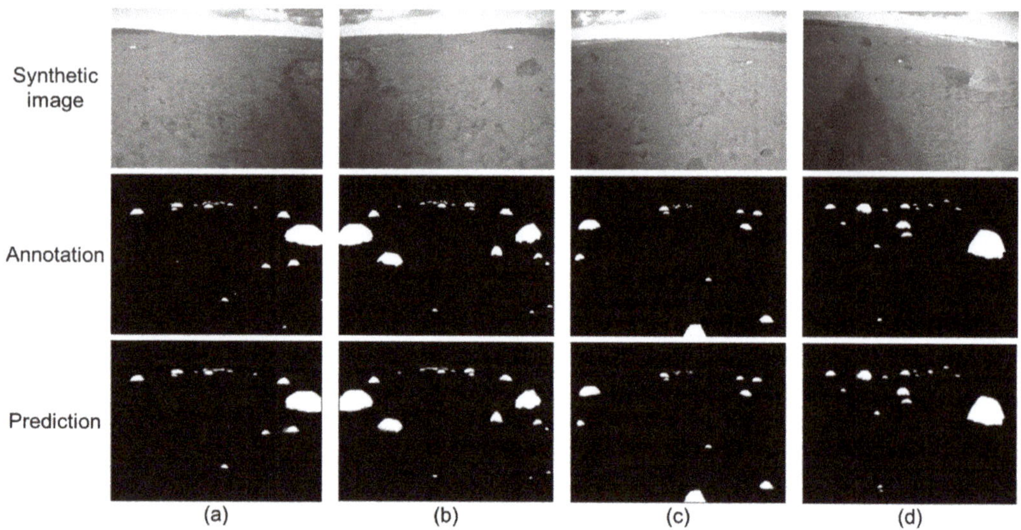

Figure 9. The example results of the NI-U-Net++ rock segmentation network in the pre-training process. "Synthetic image", "Annotation", and "Prediction" refer to the synthetic input images, the simultaneously generated ground truth annotations, and the predictions from the pre-trained NI-U-Net++, respectively. (**a–d**) correspond to four examples.

3.3. The Results of the Transfer-Training Process

The results of transfer learning are presented in Table 6. Figure 10 depicts the loss, accuracy, IoU, and Dice score curves on training and validation sets. Each curve comes to convergence with a smooth and stable trend. Thus, the model does not appear to be overfitting. Although transfer learning only used 183 images from the *Katwijk* dataset, the proposed synthetic algorithm and the transfer learning strategy accomplish a significantly low loss value, high accuracy, high IoU, and high Dice score. It is noteworthy that the used navigation vision has about 2500 images from the *Katwijk* dataset, and the transfer learning only uses about 8%. Furthermore, the good results of the metrics indicate that the NI-U-Net++ does not appear to be underfitting either.

Table 6. Result of transfer-training using the proposed NI-U-Net++.

Loss			Accuracy			IOU			Dice			RMSE		
Train	Valid	Test	Train	Valid	Test	Train	Valid	Test	Train	Valid	Test	Train	Valid	Test
0.0061	0.0183	0.0151	99.74%	99.54%	99.58%	0.8841	0.7223	0.7476	0.9384	0.8387	0.8556	0.0499	0.0594	0.0557

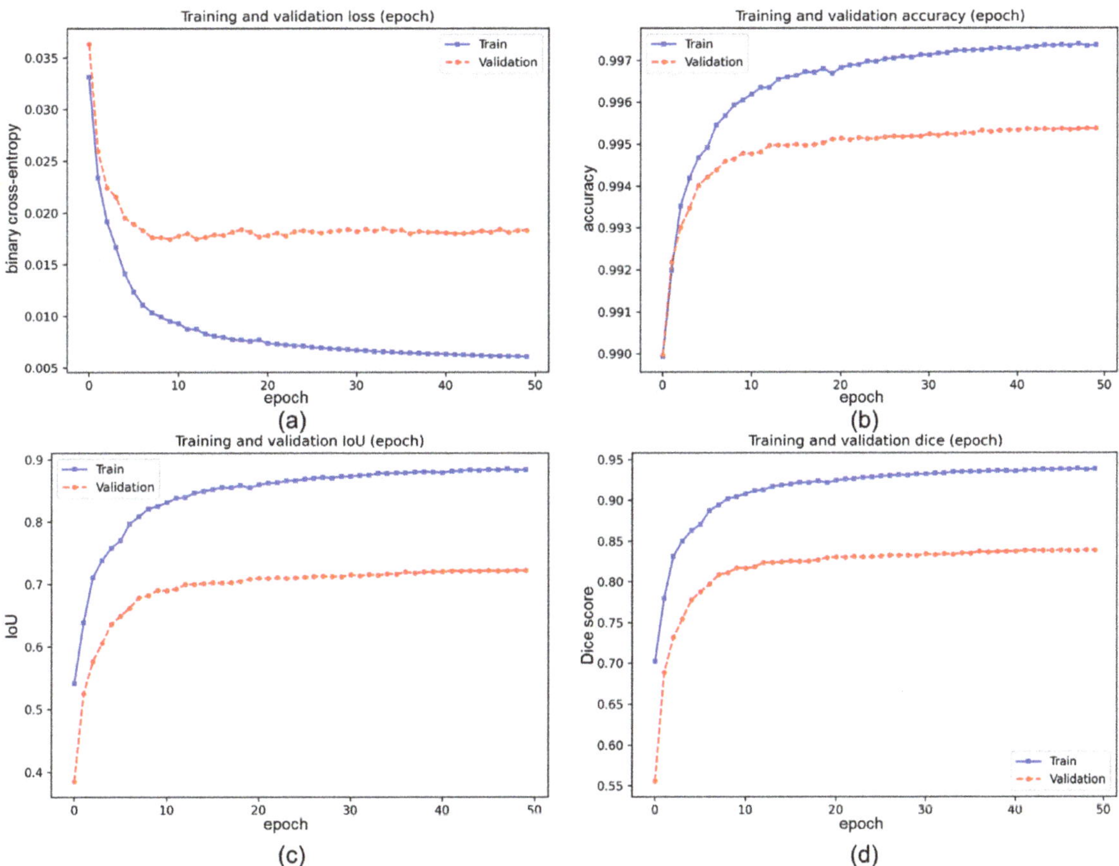

Figure 10. The transfer training curves using the "Annotation-2" dataset. (**a–d**) refer to the transfer training curves of the loss, accuracy, IoU, and Dice score, respectively. The blue solid curves and red dash curves refer to the training records from the training and validation sets.

Table 6 provides the quantitative records of the transfer learning process (the green frame in Figure 1). The loss value in Table 6 has reached a small magnitude, and the accuracy reaches a high level. Although IoU is not as high as in the pre-training process (see Table 5), it is already a considerably high value in the image segmentation topic (see the IoU level in [16,65,66]). The performance of the Dice score and RMSE are good. Figure 11 indicates the qualitative results of transfer learning. Figure 11 also involves the results using the pre-trained model. The pre-trained model can achieve highly similar predictions, which justified the help using the transfer learning strategy. The Supplementary Video S1 depicts the integration of the transfer learning achievement into the navigation vision of the planetary rovers. Compared with the frame rate of the original navigation vision (8 FPS), the processing speed of the proposed NI-U-Net++ is 32.57 FPS (or the inference time is 0.0307 s per frame), which is 4.071 times the frame rate in the original video. The details of the inference time can be found in Appendix A.6 in the Appendix A, which shows that the real-time performance of the proposed NI-U-Net++ appears excellent on the tested device.

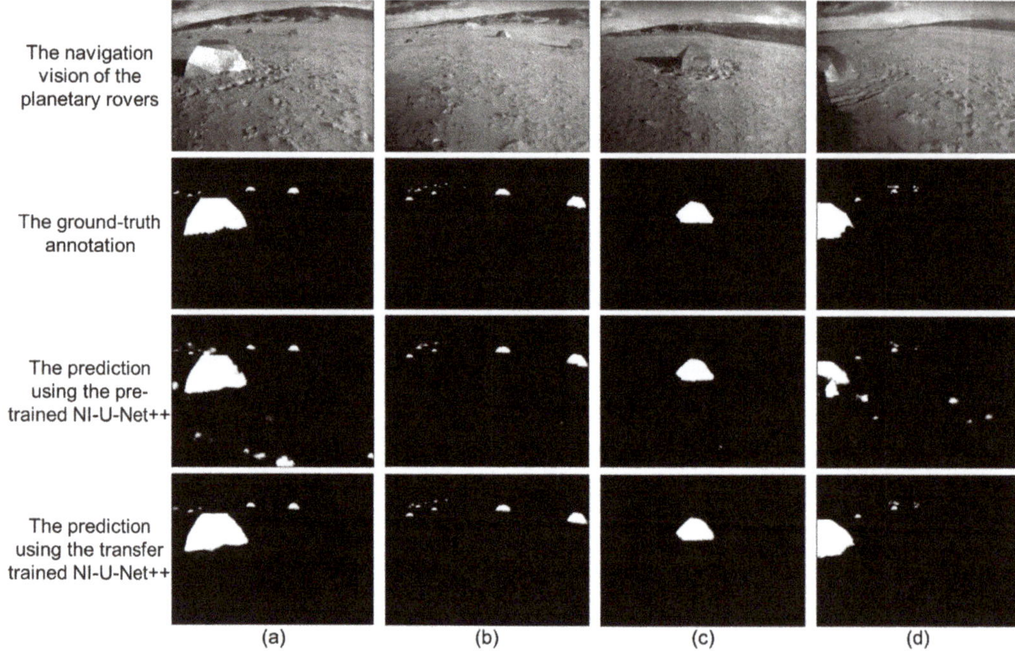

Figure 11. The visualized results of the proposed NI-U-Net++ in the transfer-training process. The navigation vision of the planetary rovers refers to the images from the Katwijk dataset. (**a**–**d**) refer to four variant selected images.

Notably, the quantitative results of the metrics between the transfer learning and the pre-training are not directly comparable. Compared with pre-training, the result of transfer learning is low (such as IoU in Table 5). As discussed in Section 2.2, the synthetic dataset is essentially generated using the incremental approach. The synthetic algorithm sets the scaling to be 0.6 to 1.0. The evaluation metrics (accuracy, IoU, and Dice) are all based on the statistical results of pixels. The embedded synthetic rock samples can be divided into two categories: the clustered pixels (that are easy to determine) and the edge pixels (that are not easy to determine). As the target size increases, the clustered pixels pull the overall metrics to a high level. Moreover, many situations do not appear in the pre-training dataset (such as significant changes in pose, brightness, illumination, sharpness, etc.), which enlarges the marginal probability distribution of the transfer-training process.

4. Conclusions and Future Works

This research proposed a rock segmentation framework for the navigation vision of the planetary rovers using the synthetic algorithm and transfer learning. This framework provided an end-to-end rock segmentation solution for the future planetary rover autonomy. Furthermore, the proposed synthetic algorithm provided a new idea for handling the challenge of the lack of pixel-level semantic annotations in the planetary explorations. The synthetic dataset also provided a valid dataset and benchmark for the related research. The proposed NI-U-Net++ achieved the best results (see Section 3.2) in all three popular metrics compared to the state-of-the-art (the accuracy, IoU, Dice score, and RMSE are 99.41%, 0.8991, 0.9459, and 0.0075, respectively). Moreover, both the pre-training and transfer-training processes achieved outstanding training curves and results (the accuracy, IoU, Dice score, and RMSE are 99.58%, 0.7476, 0.8556, and 0.0557, respectively), which proved the assumptions (of the proposed synthetic algorithm) in Section 2.2.

The proposed framework made a significant step in the semantic segmentation of unstructured planetary explorations. As a cheap and extensive sensor, the monocular camera generates a large amount of data for planetary rover navigation. The proposed framework can efficiently conduct a semantic analysis for the planetary rover. These rocks can be integrated into the visual navigation system to further assist various advanced functions, such as path planning, localization, scene matching, etc.

The future works include transfering the proposed framework to the onboard device. The proposed framework uses the normal TensorFlow library, while only TensorFlow lite can operate on the onboard device. The potential action may also include the network slimming to fit the specific onboard device. Furthermore, the proposed NI-U-Net++ requires optimizations for the targeted system, hardware, and software.

Supplementary Materials: The following are available online at https://www.mdpi.com/article/10.3390/math9233048/s1, Video S1: The demo video of the proposed rock segmentation solution.

Author Contributions: Conceptualization, B.K.; methodology, B.K.; software, B.K. and M.W.; validation, B.K.; investigation, B.K., Z.A.R. and Y.Z.; resources, Z.A.R.; writing—original draft preparation, B.K.; writing—review and editing, B.K., M.W., Z.A.R. and Y.Z.; visualization, B.K., M.W., Z.A.R. and Y.Z.; supervision, Z.A.R. and Y.Z.; project administration, Z.A.R.; funding acquisition, Z.A.R. All authors have read and agreed to the published version of the manuscript.

Funding: The Future Aviation Security Solutions (FASS) Programme, a joint Department for Transport and Home Office initiative with support from Connected Places Catapult (CPC) part funded this research.

Data Availability Statement: The proposed dataset is openly available in Cranfield Online Research Data (CORD) at https://doi.org/10.17862/cranfield.rd.16958728. The Katwijk beach planetary rover dataset is available at https://robotics.estec.esa.int/datasets/katwijk-beach-11-2015/.

Acknowledgments: All simulations have been carried out using the HPC facility (HILDA) at Digital Aviation Research and Technology Centre (DARTeC), Cranfield.

Conflicts of Interest: The authors declare no conflict of interest.

Nomenclature

$X, Y, \overline{X}, \overline{Y}$	Formal parameters.
I	Light source.
$i_1 - i_3, i$	Rays of light.
g	Horizontal ground.
$\theta_1, \theta_2, \theta_3, \theta$	Angles between the corresponding ray of the Light and the horizontal ground.
ρ	The density of rays in the unit ground area.
L	Light intensity.
S	Area of a ground region.
p_1, p_2	The boundary rays between object and camera.
l_b	The normal line perpendicular to the phase plane.
XY	The area between X and Y cross-points.
$G_1 - G_3, \overline{G_1} - \overline{G_3}$	Cross points on the ground.
P	Cross point between p_1 and PG_3.
O	The origin of image plane.
L_{XY}	The light intensity in the area between X and Y cross-points in the sketch.
P_{opt}	Abstracted value of the optical properties.
c_T	A variable to pack all factors related to optical properties.
$\overline{\rho}$	An approximate value of ρ.
T	The target (rocks in this research) in the sketch.
(x, y)	Coordinate.
$pixel_{img}(x, y)$	Grayscale value at coordinate (x, y).
N_{pixel}	The number of pixels in a specific region.
$\Delta\rho$	The difference between ρ and $\overline{\rho}$.

$\overline{XY}$	The area between $\overline{X}$ and $\overline{Y}$ cross-points.
f_1	An implicit function to correlate the optical properties and image grayscales.
img_{mean}	The averaged grayscale value for the corresponding image area.
img	A set of the grayscale values for the corresponding image area.
img_Δ	A set of the differential values between img and img_{mean} (only related to the coordinates).
C	The constants to correct $\bar{\rho}$ from ρ.
$\overline{L}$	An approximation of L using the proposed synthetic algorithm.

Appendix A

Appendix A.1 Further Details of the Related Studies

Table 1. The detailed results of the related studies of Table 1.

Reference	Category in Table 1 [1]	Results [2]
[30]	i	Only the qualitative segmentation results.
[31]	i	Only the qualitative segmentation results.
[32]	i	Only the qualitative segmentation results.
[4]	ii	Fit error = 1.504~114.934.
[5]	ii and iii	Only the qualitative segmentation results.
[33]	ii	Only the qualitative segmentation results.
[34]	ii	(1) Average precision = 89% (the center matching method); (2) Average precision = 87% (the overlap method); (3) Average precision $\geq$ 90% = 83 images.
[35]	ii and v	(1) Standard deviation of recall = 0.2–0.3; (2) Standard deviation of precision = 0.2–0.3; (3) Recall and precision are modestly improved.
[36]	ii	Only the qualitative segmentation results.
[37]	iii	Only the qualitative segmentation results.
[38]	iii	(1) RMS error (X) = 0.22–0.93 (HiRISE pixel), RMS error (Y) = 0.22–0.97 (HiRISE pixel); (2) RMS error (X) = 0.23–0.70 (HiRISE pixel), RMS error (Y) = 0.23–0.89 (HiRISE pixel).
[32]	iv	CPU time (seconds): 0.2214–0.7484 (MAD); 0.1966–0.6955 (LMedsq); 0.5994–2.2033 (IKOSE); 0.2931–0.9633 (PDIMSE); 0.0380–0.1238 (RANSAC); 106.4747–236.2487 (RECON).
[39]	iv	(1) Processing time: 2–3 s for 256 * 256 images; 20–45 s for 640 * 480 images (2) Only the qualitative segmentation results.
[40]	iv	Medium rock match is successful (up to 26 m).
[41]	iv	The proposed method is robust and efficient for small- and large-scale rock detection.
[8]	v	A survey for terrain classification (including rock segmentation).
[27]	v	(1) Pixel-wise accuracy = 99.69% (background); 97.89% (sand); 89.33% (rock); 96.33% (gravel); 89.73% (bedrock). (2) Mean intersection-over-union (mIoU) = 0.9459.
[28]	v	(1) Accuracy = 76.2% (derivable terrain comprising sand, bedrock, and loose rock); (2) Accuracy = 89.2% (embedded pointy rocks).
[42]	v	mIoU = 0.93; recall = 96%; frame rate = 116 frame per second
[43]	v	F-score = 78.5%
[44]	v	Accuracy = 90~96%; IoU = 0.21~0.58.

[1] "i", "ii", "iii", "iv", and "v" in column "Category in Table 1" correspond to the same category index in Table 1. [2] The "Results" column only provides a statistic summary among the results of related studies. The exact values have no comparability either between each other or with this research. The reason comes from the different research focus, applied data, and experimental environments. The valid quantitative comparisons can be found in Section 3.2.

A.2. The Experiments of the Values in Table 2

Figure A1 illustrates the examples using different settings for the constant value C. It is noteworthy that C in Table 2 aims to correct the difference from the " $\rho \approx \bar{\rho}$" in Equation (4). According to the assumption in Section 2.2.1, this difference is small but sensitive to rock property. The goal of C is to optimize the visual comfort mentioned in Section 3.1. Therefore, C is affected by two settings, range and scale.

The range of the pixel value is between 0 and 256. (i) In Table 2, the range of C is set from 0 to 50. Thus, the maximum adjustment is less than 20% of the pixel value. Figure A1b shows a synthetic example using Table 2, and the white pixels in Figure A1a highlight the rocks. Figure A1a,b depict that Table 2 is a visually comfortable setting. Figure A1c,d respectively increase the range of C by three times and five times, and the embedded rock samples are very unreal to the background. Figure A1e reduces the range of C to about half of Figure A1b. The inserted rock is too bright compared to the background. Therefore, the range setting of C in Table 2 is in a reasonable range. (ii) C in Table 2 is divided into 11 scales according to the corresponding conditions (img_{mean}). A higher img_mean corresponds to a higher C. Figure A1f doubles the scale-setting to 21 scales, but there is no significant change compared to Figure A1b. Therefore, the classification method in Table 2 is also reasonable.

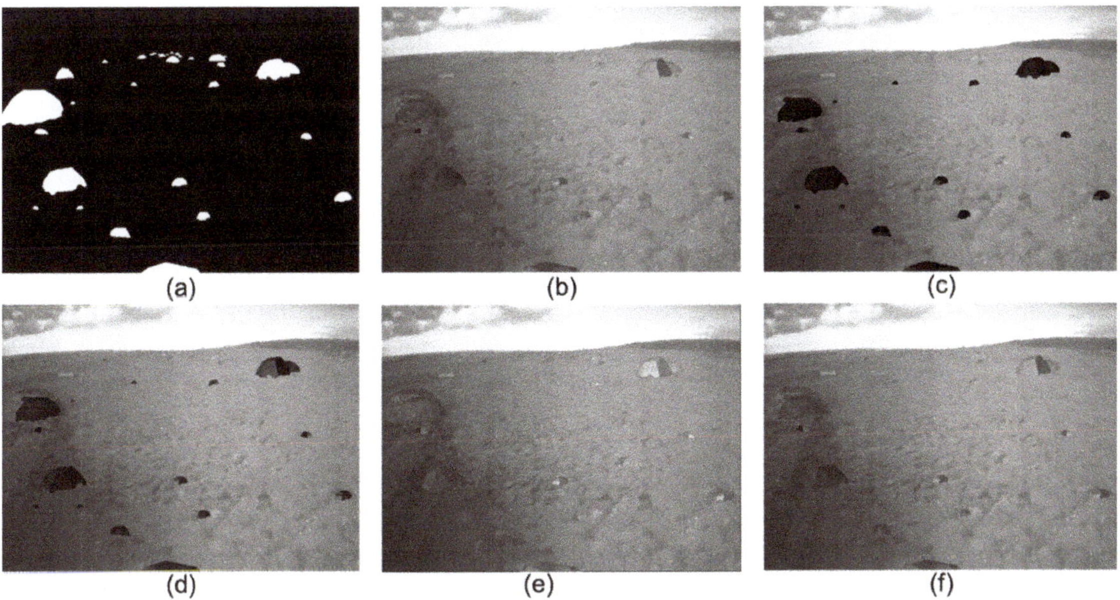

Figure A1. The visualized results of the experiments for the constant C in Table 2. (**a**) refers to the synthetic annotation, while (**b–f**) corresponds to the synthetic images through different settings of C. (**b**) applies the same setting as Table 2. (**c**) keeps the grade setting but increases the range of the C, the maximum C is set to 250. (**d**) refers to the results of only increasing maximum C to 150. (**e**) refers to the results of decreasing maximum C to 20. (**f**) keeps the maximum C as the same as (**b**), while the grade setting applies 21 grades.

Appendix A.3 Qualitative Examples of the Proposed Synthetic Dataset

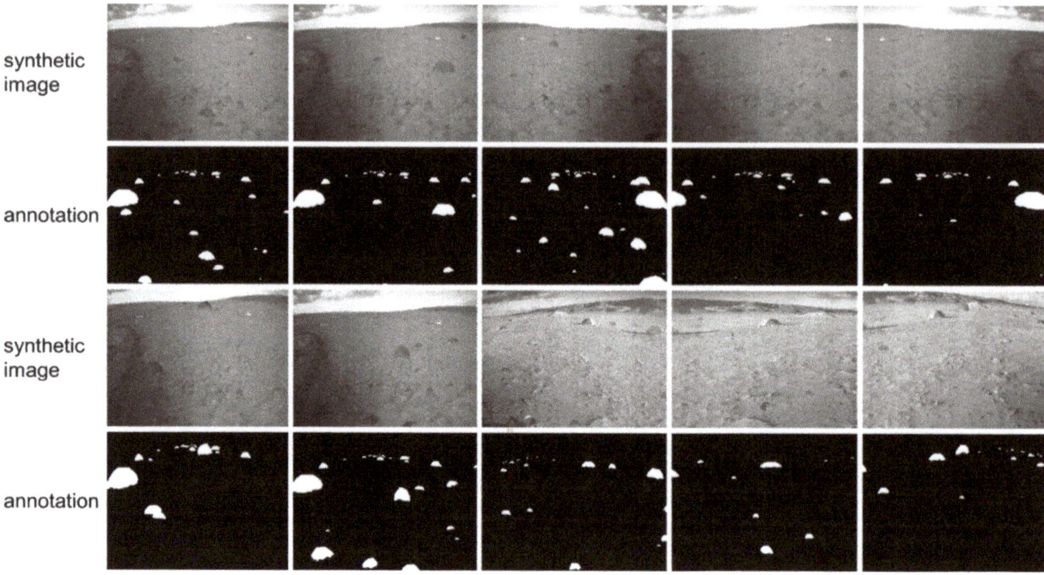

Figure A2. Some examples from the synthetic dataset. "Synthetic image" and "annotation" refer to the synthetic images and corresponding annotations, respectively. Annotations use white and black pixels to represent the rock and background pixels.

Appendix A.4 Pairwise Comparisons between Proposed NI-U-Net++ and Related Studies

This research uses Figures 3 and A3 in Section 2.3 to discuss the pairwise comparison between NI-U-Net++ and related studies in Table 5. Figure A3 uses NI-U-Net++ as background, but some highlights have been added for further comparison. The red arrows refer to the sub-U-Nets; each of them has a complete encoder–decoder process. Here defines a concept of compression ratio, which is the ratio between the input and output size (height or weight) of the encoder. "Sub-U-Net No.1" has the highest compression ratio, while "Sub-U-Net No.4" has the lowest compression ratio. The blue dash frame highlights the deep supervision mentioned in Section 2.3, and the orange frames refer to the micro-networks.

i. NI-U-Net++ with U-Net [14,63]:

    a. U-Net only has the "Sub-U-Net No. 1". Therefore, the compression ratio is constant at a high level.

    b. U-Net does not have deep supervision design.

    c. U-Net utilizes the 3×3 convolution layers and "Relu" activation instead of the micro-network in Figures 3, 4 and A3.

ii. NI-U-Net++ with U-Net++ [15]:

    a. U-Net++ also has four sub-U-Nets as in the NI-U-Net++.

    b. U-Net++ also has the deep supervision as in the NI-U-Net++.

    c. However, the U-Net++ applies the 3×3 convolution layer and "Relu" activation as in U-Net instead of the micro-network in NI-U-Net++.

iii. NI-U-Net++ with NI-U-Net [57]:

    a. NI-U-Net only has the "Sub-U-Net No. 1". Therefore, the compression ratio is constant at a high level.

    b. NI-U-Net has not deep supervision design.

    c. NI-U-Net utilizes the same micro-network as in NI-U-Net++.

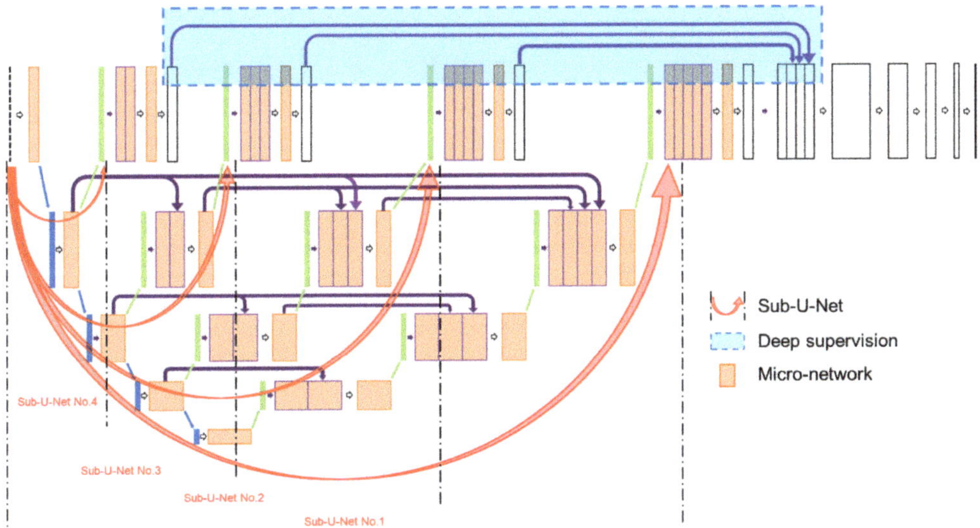

Figure A3. The pairwise comparisons for U-Net, U-Net++, NI-U-Net, and proposed NI-U-Net++.

Appendix A.5 Additional Results of the Pre-Training Process

Table A2. The Dice score of U-Net, U-Net++, NI-U-Net, and NI-U-Net++.

Networks	Dice Score		
	Train	**Valid**	**Test**
U-Net	0.9158	0.9040	0.9044
U-Net++	0.9574	0.9344	0.9352
NI-U-Net	0.9644	0.9313	0.9316
NI-U-Net++	0.9588	0.9458	0.9469

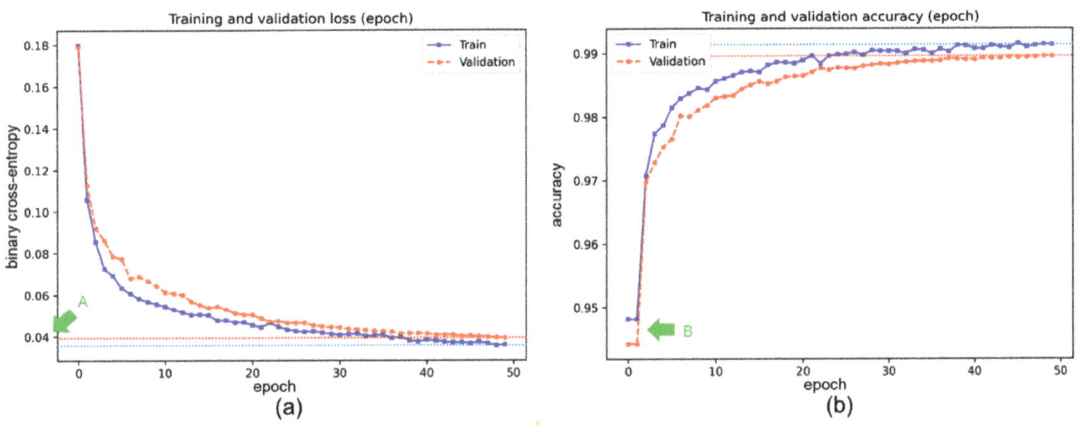

Figure A4. The loss and accuracy curves of U-Net [14] using the synthetic dataset. The green "A" and "B" correspond to the two highlights mentioned in Section 3.2. (**a**) Refers to the epoch-wised loss curves in the training and validation sets. (**b**) Refers to the epoch-wised accuracy curves in the training and validation sets. The horizontal dash lines refer to the references of final converge status.

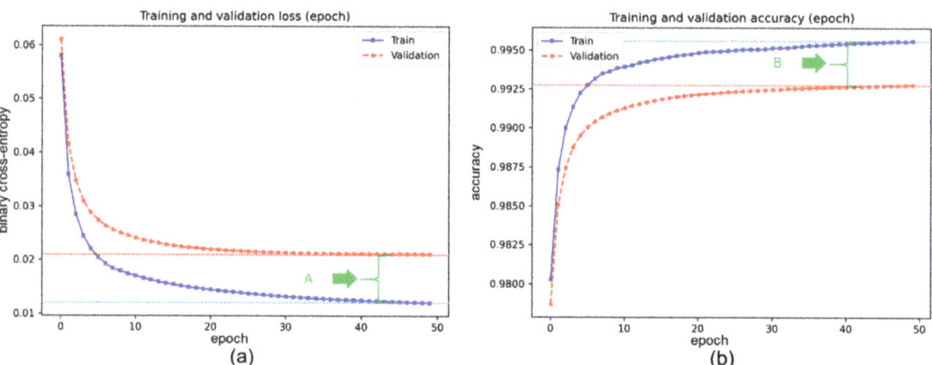

Figure A5. The loss and accuracy curves of U-Net++ [15] using the synthetic dataset. The green "A" and "B" correspond to the two highlights mentioned in Section 3.2. (**a**) Refers to the epoch-wised loss curves in the training and validation sets. (**b**) Refers to the epoch-wised accuracy curves in the training and validation sets. The horizontal dash lines refer to the references of final converge status.

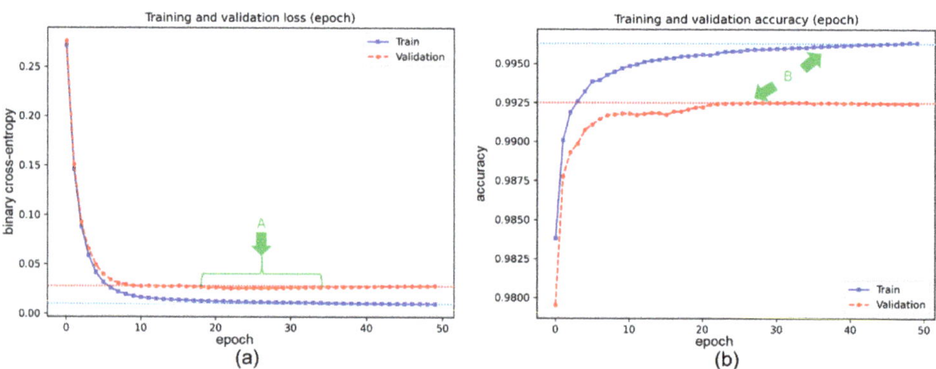

Figure A6. The loss and accuracy curves of NI-U-Net [57] using the synthetic dataset. The green "A" and "B" correspond to the two highlights mentioned in Section 3.2. (**a**) Refers to the epoch-wised loss curves in the training and validation sets. (**b**) Refers to the epoch-wised accuracy curves in the training and validation sets. The horizontal dash lines refer to the references of final converge status.

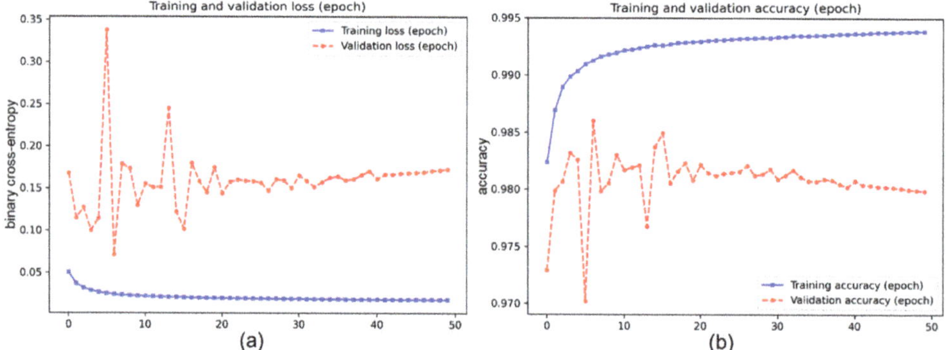

Figure A7. The loss and accuracy curves of Chiodini2020 [44] using the synthetic dataset. (**a**) Refers to the epoch-wised loss curves in the training and validation sets. (**b**) Refers to the epoch-wised accuracy curves in the training and validation sets.

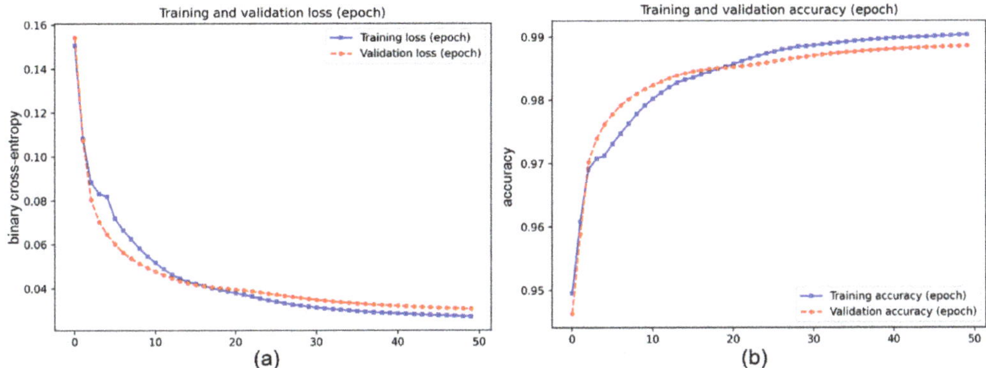

Figure A8. The loss and accuracy curves of Furlan2019 [43] using the synthetic dataset. (**a**) Refers to the epoch-wised loss curves in the training and validation sets. (**b**) Refers to the epoch-wised accuracy curves in the training and validation sets.

Table A3 refers to the results of training NI-U-Net++ using different numbers of synthetic images. This research chooses about 50% (7000 images) and 10% (1000 images) as two experiment settings to evaluate the impact when the number of synthetic images decreases. All results decrease when the images number decreases. The synthetic algorithm aims to generate a large amount of valid data, so applying all available data is more fitted to the target of this research.

Table A3. The quantitative results of NI-U-Net++ tested using a different number of synthetic images.

Number [1] (Images)	Loss			Accuracy			IoU			Dice Score		
	Train	**Valid**	**Test**	**Train**	**Valid**	**Test**	**Train**	**Valid**	**Test**	**Train**	**Valid**	**Test**
7000	0.0137	0.0189	0.0199	99.49%	99.39%	99.37%	0.9164	0.8919	0.8876	0.9564	0.9429	0.9405
1000	0.0273	0.0618	0.0580	99.53%	99.02%	99.03%	0.9175	0.8374	0.8389	0.9570	0.9115	0.9124

[1] "Number" refers to the number of synthetic images used in corresponding experiment.

Appendix A.6 Additional Results of the Transfer-Training Process

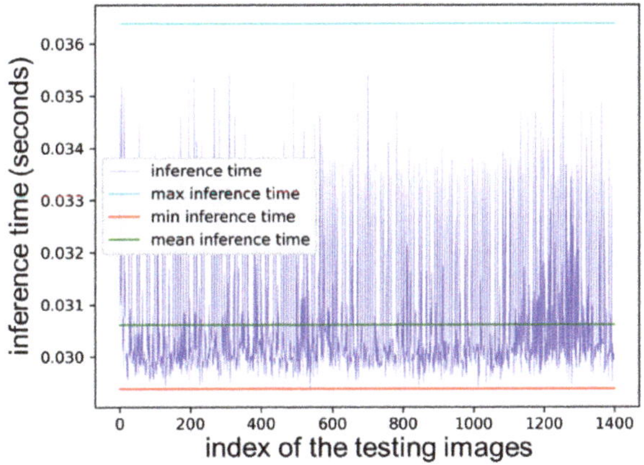

Figure A9. The inference time record. The max, min, and mean inference time is 0.0364, 0.0307, and 0.0294 s.

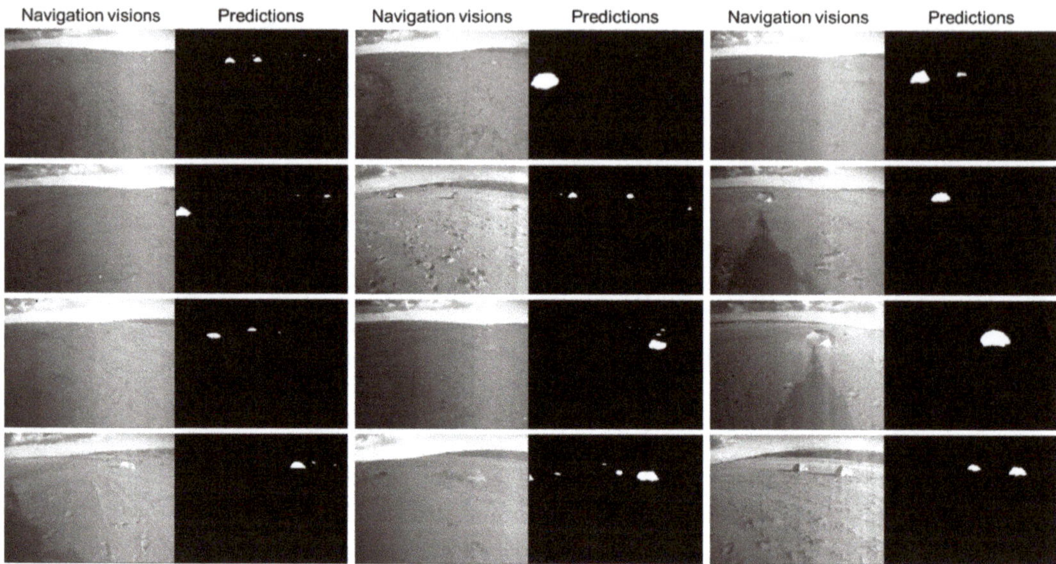

Figure A10. Some examples of the real-life rover vision and corresponding predictions.

References

1. Privitera, C.M.; Stark, L.W. Human-vision-based selection of image processing algorithms for planetary exploration. *IEEE Trans. Image Process.* **2003**, *12*, 917–923. [CrossRef] [PubMed]
2. Kim, W.S.; Diaz-Calderon, A.; Peters, S.F.; Carsten, J.L.; Leger, C. Onboard centralized frame tree database for intelligent space operations of the Mars Science Laboratory rover. *IEEE Trans. Cybern.* **2014**, *44*, 2109–2121. [CrossRef]
3. Gao, Y.; Chien, S. Review on space robotics: Toward top-level science through space exploration. *Sci. Robot.* **2017**, *2*, eaan5074. [CrossRef]
4. Castano, R.; Estlin, T.; Gaines, D.; Chouinard, C.; Bornstein, B.; Anderson, R.C.; Burl, M.; Thompson, D.; Castano, A.; Judd, M. Onboard autonomous rover science. In Proceedings of the 2007 IEEE Aerospace Conference, Big Sky, MT, USA, 3–10 March 2007; pp. 1–13.
5. Estlin, T.A.; Bornstein, B.J.; Gaines, D.M.; Anderson, R.C.; Thompson, D.R.; Burl, M.; Castaño, R.; Judd, M. AEGIS automated science targeting for the MER opportunity rover. *ACM Trans. Intell. Syst. Technol.* **2012**, *3*, 1–19. [CrossRef]
6. Otsu, K.; Ono, M.; Fuchs, T.J.; Baldwin, I.; Kubota, T. Autonomous terrain classification with co- and self-training approach. *IEEE Robot. Autom. Lett.* **2016**, *1*, 814–819. [CrossRef]
7. Swan, R.M.; Atha, D.; Leopold, H.A.; Gildner, M.; Oij, S.; Chiu, C.; Ono, M. AI4MARS: A dataset for terrain-aware autonomous driving on Mars. In Proceedings of the 2021 IEEE/CVF Conference on Computer Vision and Pattern Recognition Workshops (CVPRW), Nashville, TN, USA, 19–25 June 2021.
8. Gao, Y.; Spiteri, C.; Pham, M.-T.; Al-Milli, S. A survey on recent object detection techniques useful for monocular vision-based planetary terrain classification. *Robot. Auton. Syst.* **2014**, *62*, 151–167. [CrossRef]
9. Minaee, S.; Boykov, Y.; Porikli, F.; Plaza, A.; Kehtarnavaz, N.; Terzopoulos, D. Image segmentation using deep learning: A survey. *IEEE Trans. Pattern Anal. Mach. Intell.* **2020**, 1–22. [CrossRef]
10. Liu, D.; Bober, M.; Kittler, J. Visual semantic information pursuit: A survey. *IEEE Trans. Pattern Anal. Mach. Intell.* **2021**, *43*, 1404–1422. [CrossRef]
11. Zoller, T.; Buhmann, J.M. Robust image segmentation using resampling and shape constraints. *IEEE Trans. Pattern Anal. Mach. Intell.* **2007**, *29*, 1147–1164. [CrossRef]
12. Alpert, S.; Galun, M.; Brandt, A.; Basri, R. Image segmentation by probabilistic bottom-up aggregation and cue integration. *IEEE Trans. Pattern Anal. Mach. Intell.* **2012**, *34*, 315–327. [CrossRef]
13. Saltzer, J.H.; Reed, D.P.; Clark, D.D. End-to-end arguments in system design. *ACM Trans. Comput. Syst.* **1984**, *2*, 277–288. [CrossRef]
14. Ronneberger, O.; Fischer, P.; Brox, T. U-Net: Convolutional networks for biomedical image segmentation. In *Lecture Notes in Computer Science (Including Subseries Lecture Notes in Artificial Intelligence and Lecture Notes in Bioinformatics)*; Springer: Berlin/Heidelberg, Germany, 2015; Volume 9351, pp. 234–241. ISBN 9783319245737.

15. Zhou, Z.; Rahman Siddiquee, M.M.; Tajbakhsh, N.; Liang, J. Unet++: A nested u-net architecture for medical image segmentation. In *Lecture Notes in Computer Science (Including Subseries Lecture Notes in Artificial Intelligence and Lecture Notes in Bioinformatics)*; Springer: Berlin/Heidelberg, Germany, 2018; Volume 11045, pp. 3–11. [CrossRef]
16. Chen, L.-C.; Papandreou, G.; Kokkinos, I.; Murphy, K.; Yuille, A.L. Semantic image segmentation with deep convolutional nets and fully connected CRFs. *arXiv* **2014**, arXiv:1412.7062.
17. Liu, W.; Anguelov, D.; Erhan, D.; Szegedy, C.; Reed, S.; Fu, C.-Y.; Berg, A.C. SSD: Single shot multibox detector. In *Lecture Notes in Computer Science (Including Subseries Lecture Notes in Artificial Intelligence and Lecture Notes in Bioinformatics)*; Springer: Berlin/Heidelberg, Germany, 2016; Volume 9905, pp. 21–37. ISBN 9783319464473.
18. Gupta, S.; Girshick, R.; Arbeláez, P.; Malik, J. Learning rich features FROM RGB-D images for object detection and segmentation. In *Lecture Notes in Computer Science*; Springer: Berlin/Heidelberg, Germany, 2014; Volume 8695, pp. 345–360. ISBN 9783319105833.
19. Hariharan, B.; Arbeláez, P.; Girshick, R.; Malik, J. Simultaneous detection and segmentation. In *Lecture Notes in Computer Science*; Springer: Berlin/Heidelberg, Germany, 2014; Volume 8695, pp. 297–312. ISBN 9783319105833.
20. He, K.; Gkioxari, G.; Dollár, P.; Girshick, R. Mask R-CNN. *IEEE Trans. Pattern Anal. Mach. Intell.* **2017**, *42*, 386–397. [CrossRef]
21. Dewan, A.; Oliveira, G.L.; Burgard, W. Deep semantic classification for 3D LiDAR data. In Proceedings of the 2017 IEEE/RSJ International Conference on Intelligent Robots and Systems (IROS), Vancouver, BC, Canada, 24–28 September 2017; Volume 2017, pp. 3544–3549.
22. Badrinarayanan, V.; Kendall, A.; Cipolla, R. SegNet: A deep convolutional encoder-decoder architecture for image segmentation. *IEEE Trans. Pattern Anal. Mach. Intell.* **2017**, *39*, 2481–2495. [CrossRef] [PubMed]
23. Teichmann, M.; Weber, M.; Zollner, M.; Cipolla, R.; Urtasun, R. MultiNet: Real-time joint semantic reasoning for autonomous driving. In Proceedings of the 2018 IEEE Intelligent Vehicles Symposium (IV), Suzhou, China, 26–30 June 2018; Volume 2018, pp. 1013–1020.
24. Wu, B.; Wan, A.; Yue, X.; Keutzer, K. SqueezeSeg: Convolutional neural nets with recurrent CRF for real-time road-object segmentation from 3D LiDAR point cloud. In Proceedings of the 2018 IEEE International Conference on Robotics and Automation (ICRA), Brisbane, Australia, 21–25 May 2018; pp. 1887–1893.
25. Busquets, D.; Sierra, C.; López de Màntaras, R. A multiagent approach to qualitative landmark-based navigation. *Auton. Robots* **2003**, *15*, 129–154. [CrossRef]
26. Kovács, G.; Kunii, Y.; Maeda, T.; Hashimoto, H. Saliency and spatial information-based landmark selection for mobile robot navigation in natural environments. *Adv. Robot.* **2019**, *33*, 520–535. [CrossRef]
27. Zhou, R.; Ding, L.; Gao, H.; Feng, W.; Deng, Z.; Li, N. Mapping for planetary rovers from terramechanics perspective. In Proceedings of the 2019 IEEE/RSJ International Conference on Intelligent Robots and Systems (IROS), Macau, China, 3–8 November 2019; pp. 1869–1874.
28. Ono, M.; Fuchs, T.J.; Steffy, A.; Maimone, M.; Jeng, Y. Risk-aware planetary rover operation: Autonomous terrain classification and path planning. In Proceedings of the 2015 IEEE Aerospace Conference, Big Sky, MT, USA, 7–14 March 2015; pp. 1–10.
29. Zhou, F.; Arvidson, R.E.; Bennett, K.; Trease, B.; Lindemann, R.; Bellutta, P.; Iagnemma, K.; Senatore, C. Simulations of Mars rover traverses. *J. Field Robot.* **2014**, *31*, 141–160. [CrossRef]
30. Pedersen, L. Science target assessment for Mars rover instrument deployment. In Proceedings of the IEEE/RSJ International Conference on Intelligent Robots and System, Lausanne, Switzerland, 30 September–4 October 2002; Volume 1, pp. 817–822.
31. Di, K.; Yue, Z.; Liu, Z.; Wang, S. Automated rock detection and shape analysis from mars rover imagery and 3D point cloud data. *J. Earth Sci.* **2013**, *24*, 125–135. [CrossRef]
32. Xiao, X.; Cui, H.; Tian, Y. Robust plane fitting algorithm for landing hazard detection. *IEEE Trans. Aerosp. Electron. Syst.* **2015**, *51*, 2864–2875. [CrossRef]
33. Dunlop, H.; Thompson, D.R.; Wettergreen, D. Multi-scale features for detection and segmentation of rocks in Mars images. In Proceedings of the 2007 IEEE Conference on Computer Vision and Pattern Recognition, Minneapolis, MN, USA, 18–23 June 2007; pp. 1–7.
34. Castano, R.; Judd, M.; Estlin, T.; Anderson, R.C.; Gaines, D.; Castano, A.; Bornstein, B.; Stough, T.; Wagstaff, K. Current results from a rover science data analysis system. In Proceedings of the 2005 IEEE Aerospace Conference, Big Sky, MT, USA, 5–12 March 2005; Volume 2005, pp. 356–365.
35. Castano, R.; Mann, T.; Mjolsness, E. Texture analysis for Mars rover images. In *Applications of Digital Image Processing XXII*; Tescher, A.G., Ed.; Society of Photo-optical Instrumentation Engineers: Bellingham, WA, USA, 1999; Volume 3808, pp. 162–173.
36. Burl, M.C.; Thompson, D.R.; DeGranville, C.; Bornstein, B.J. Rockster: Onboard rock segmentation through edge regrouping. *J. Aerosp. Inf. Syst.* **2016**, *13*, 329–342. [CrossRef]
37. Castafio, R.; Anderson, R.C.; Estlin, T.; DeCoste, D.; Fisher, F.; Gaines, D.; Mazzoni, D.; Judd, M. Rover traverse science for increased mission science return. In Proceedings of the 2003 IEEE Aerospace Conference Proceedings, Big Sky, MT, USA, 8–15 March 2003; Volume 8, pp. 8_3629–8_3636. Available online: https://ieeexplore.ieee.org/document/1235546 (accessed on 26 November 2021).
38. Di, K.; Liu, Z.; Yue, Z. Mars rover localization based on feature matching between ground and orbital imagery. *Photogramm. Eng. Remote Sens.* **2011**, *77*, 781–791. [CrossRef]
39. Gulick, V.C.; Morris, R.L.; Ruzon, M.A.; Roush, T.L. Autonomous image analyses during the 1999 Marsokhod rover field test. *J. Geophys. Res. Planets* **2001**, *106*, 7745–7763. [CrossRef]

40. Li, R.; Di, K.; Howard, A.B.; Matthies, L.; Wang, J.; Agarwal, S. Rock modeling and matching for autonomous long-range Mars rover localization. *J. Field Robot.* **2007**, *24*, 187–203. [CrossRef]

41. Yang, J.; Kang, Z. A gradient-region constrained level set method for autonomous rock detection from Mars rover image. *Int. Arch. Photogramm. Remote Sens. Spat. Inf. Sci. ISPRS Arch.* **2019**, *42*, 1479–1485. [CrossRef]

42. Zhou, R.; Feng, W.; Yang, H.; Gao, H.; Li, N.; Deng, Z.; Ding, L. Predicting terrain mechanical properties in sight for planetary rovers with semantic clues. *arXiv* **2020**, arXiv:2011.01872.

43. Furlán, F.; Rubio, E.; Sossa, H.; Ponce, V. Rock detection in a Mars-like environment using a CNN. In *Lecture Notes in Computer Science (Including Subseries Lecture Notes in Artificial Intelligence and Lecture Notes in Bioinformatics)*; Springer: Berlin/Heidelberg, Germany, 2019; Volume 11524, pp. 149–158. [CrossRef]

44. Chiodini, S.; Torresin, L.; Pertile, M.; Debei, S. Evaluation of 3D CNN semantic mapping for rover navigation. In Proceedings of the 2020 IEEE International Workshop on Metrology for AeroSpace, Pisa, Italy, 22 June–5 July 2020; pp. 32–36. [CrossRef]

45. Pessia, R. Artificial Lunar Landscape Dataset. Available online: https://www.kaggle.com/romainpessia/artificial-lunar-rocky-landscape-dataset (accessed on 22 June 2021).

46. Bonechi, S.; Bianchini, M.; Scarselli, F.; Andreini, P. Weak supervision for generating pixel–level annotations in scene text segmentation. *Pattern Recognit. Lett.* **2020**, *138*, 1–7. [CrossRef]

47. Nalepa, J.; Myller, M.; Kawulok, M. Transfer learning for segmenting dimensionally reduced hyperspectral images. *IEEE Geosci. Remote Sens. Lett.* **2020**, *17*, 1228–1232. [CrossRef]

48. Li, J.; Zhang, L.; Wu, Z.; Ling, Z.; Cao, X.; Guo, K.; Yan, F. Autonomous Martian rock image classification based on transfer deep learning methods. *Earth Sci. Inform.* **2020**, *13*, 951–963. [CrossRef]

49. Hewitt, R.A.; Boukas, E.; Azkarate, M.; Pagnamenta, M.; Marshall, J.A.; Gasteratos, A.; Visentin, G. The Katwijk beach planetary rover dataset. *Int. J. Robot. Res.* **2018**, *37*, 3–12. [CrossRef]

50. Sánchez-Ibáñez, J.R.; Pérez-del-Pulgar, C.J.; Azkarate, M.; Gerdes, L.; García-Cerezo, A. Dynamic path planning for reconfigurable rovers using a multi-layered grid. *Eng. Appl. Artif. Intell.* **2019**, *86*, 32–42. [CrossRef]

51. Gerdes, L.; Azkarate, M.; Sánchez-Ibáñez, J.R.; Joudrier, L.; Perez-del-Pulgar, C.J. Efficient autonomous navigation for planetary rovers with limited resources. *J. Field Robot.* **2020**, *37*, 1153–1170. [CrossRef]

52. Furlán, F.; Rubio, E.; Sossa, H.; Ponce, V. CNN based detectors on planetary environments: A performance evaluation. *Front. Neurorobot.* **2020**, *14*, 1–9. [CrossRef]

53. Meyer, L.; Smíšek, M.; Fontan Villacampa, A.; Oliva Maza, L.; Medina, D.; Schuster, M.J.; Steidle, F.; Vayugundla, M.; Müller, M.G.; Rebele, B.; et al. The MADMAX data set for visual-inertial rover navigation on Mars. *J. Field Robot.* **2021**, *38*, 833–853. [CrossRef]

54. Lamarre, O.; Limoyo, O.; Marić, F.; Kelly, J. The Canadian planetary emulation terrain energy-aware rover navigation dataset. *Int. J. Robot. Res.* **2020**, *39*, 641–650. [CrossRef]

55. NASA. NASA Science Mars Exploration Program. Available online: https://mars.nasa.gov/mars2020/multimedia/raw-images/ (accessed on 29 May 2021).

56. Pan, S.J.; Yang, Q. A survey on transfer learning. *IEEE Trans. Knowl. Data Eng.* **2010**, *22*, 1345–1359. [CrossRef]

57. Kuang, B.; Rana, Z.A.; Zhao, Y. Sky and ground segmentation in the navigation visions of the planetary rovers. *Sensors* **2021**, *21*, 6996. [CrossRef] [PubMed]

58. Lin, M.; Chen, Q.; Yan, S. Network in Network. In Proceedings of the 2nd International Conference on Learning Representations ICLR 2014, Banff, AB, Canada, 14–16 April 2014; pp. 1–10.

59. Gurita, A.; Mocanu, I.G. Image segmentation using encoder-decoder with deformable convolutions. *Sensors* **2021**, *21*, 1570. [CrossRef]

60. Marcinkiewicz, M.; Nalepa, J.; Lorenzo, P.R.; Dudzik, W.; Mrukwa, G. Segmenting brain tumors from MRI using cascaded multi-modal U-nets. In *International MICCAI Brainleison Workshop*; Springer: Berlin/Heidelberg, Germany, 2019; pp. 13–24.

61. Tarasiewicz, T.; Nalepa, J.; Kawulok, M. Skinny: A lightweight U-net for skin detection and segmentation. In Proceedings of the 2020 IEEE International Conference on Image Processing (ICIP), Abu Dhabi, United Arab Emirates, 25–28 October 2020; pp. 2386–2390.

62. Zhixuhao. Unet. Available online: https://github.com/zhixuhao/unet (accessed on 23 July 2021).

63. Mulesial. Pytorch-UNet. Available online: https://github.com/milesial/Pytorch-UNet (accessed on 23 July 2021).

64. 4uiiurz1. Pytorch-Nested-Unet. Available online: https://github.com/4uiiurz1/pytorch-nested-unet (accessed on 26 November 2021).

65. Lin, C.H.; Kong, C.; Lucey, S. Learning efficient point cloud generation for dense 3D object reconstruction. In Proceedings of the 32nd AAAI Conference on Artificial Intelligence, New Orleans, LA, USA, 2–7 February 2018; pp. 7114–7121.

66. Zuo, J.; Xu, G.; Fu, K.; Sun, X.; Sun, H. Aircraft type recognition based on segmentation with deep convolutional neural networks. *IEEE Geosci. Remote Sens. Lett.* **2018**, *15*, 282–286. [CrossRef]

 *mathematics*

Article

3D Model Identification of a Soft Robotic Neck

Fernando Quevedo *, Jorge Muñoz, Juan Alejandro Castano Pena and Concepción A. Monje

RoboticsLab, University Carlos III of Madrid, Avenida Universidad 30, 28911 Madrid, Spain;
jmyanezb@ing.uc3m.es (J.M.); jucastan@ing.uc3m.es (J.A.C.P.); cmonje@ing.uc3m.es (C.A.M.)
* Correspondence: fquevedo@ing.uc3m.es

Abstract: Soft robotics is becoming an emerging solution to many of the problems in robotics, such as weight, cost and human interaction. In order to overcome such problems, bio-inspired designs have introduced new actuators, links and architectures. However, the complexity of the required models for control has increased dramatically and geometrical model approaches, widely used to model rigid dynamics, are not enough to model these new hardware types. In this paper, different linear and non-linear models will be used to model a soft neck consisting of a central soft link actuated by three motor-driven tendons. By combining the force on the different tendons, the neck is able to perform a motion similar to that of a human neck. In order to simplify the modeling, first a system input–output redefinition is proposed, considering the neck pitch and roll angles as outputs and the tendon lengths as inputs. Later, two identification strategies are selected and adapted to our case: set membership, a data-driven, nonlinear and non-parametric identification strategy which needs no input redefinition; and Recursive least-squares (RLS), a widely recognized identification technique. The first method offers the possibility of modeling complex dynamics without specific knowledge of its mathematical representation. The selection of this method was done considering its possible extension to more complex dynamics and the fact that its impact in soft robotics is yet to be studied according to the current literature. On the other hand, RLS shows the implication of using a parametric and linear identification in a nonlinear plant, and also helps to evaluate the degree of nonlinearity of the system by comparing the different performances. In addition to these methods, a neural network identification is used for comparison purposes. The obtained results validate the modeling approaches proposed.

Keywords: mathematical modeling of complex systems; non-linear models; soft robotics; soft robotic neck; tendon-driven actuators

Citation: Quevedo, F.; Muñoz, J.; Castano Pena, J.A.; Monje, C.A. 3D Model Identification of a Soft Robotic Neck. *Mathematics* **2021**, *9*, 1652. https://doi.org/10.3390/math9141652

Academic Editors: Mikhail Posypkin, Andrey Gorshenin and Vladimir Titarev

Received: 3 June 2021
Accepted: 9 July 2021
Published: 13 July 2021

1. Introduction

Soft robotics has been gaining importance in the robotics research field. The intrinsic compliance and adaptable properties of this hardware are pushing them into many areas. The purpose of these technologies is to overcome some of the problems found in the current robotic platforms. These include weight, cost, versatility and more importantly, safe human-to-robot interaction.

Different soft robotics technologies have emerged. These include pneumatic muscles with rigid links [1], pneumatic materials that deform according to their strain field [2], robots with fully inflatable links [3], fully inflatable robots [4], plant-based structures [5] and many other technologies [6,7]. In particular, we are interested in tendon-driven soft robots, a bio-inspired model scheme, as those in [8–10]. However, the kinematic models, unlike rigid ones, are not yet well-understood. Given the high non-linearity and physical characteristics, several assumptions and numeric simplifications are considered to actuate. Therefore, they are not as reliable and have lower versatility in comparison with their counterpart, thus limiting their impact on robotics [11]. These drawbacks are stopping soft robotics to enter fields such as industrial robotics or manufacturing. However, where precision is not mandatory or humans might apply proper correction to achieve the desired goal, they have found a niche [12,13], such as rehabilitation and prosthetics.

In [8], the authors developed a mathematical model for the tendon-driven robotic arm. In particular, the authors approximated the elasticity of the tendons as a mass-less spring, given that their mass is many times smaller than the other parts (motors, gears, and loads). This enables them, on one side, to neglect coupling effects over different links, and also to assume rigid motions of the particular link to be modeled. Notice that even though the motion of the tendons is aligned with the arm motion, obtaining such a model is troublesome and requires further developments to increase the accuracy of the final result. To overcome the modeling problem for control purposes, the authors in [10] used reinforcement-learning to control the tendon-driven ACT hand synergies. This robotic hand has 24 motor-driven tendons that mimic the human hand biomechanics. Therefore, dynamic interaction with the hand skeleton results in redundant motions and other non-linear characteristics of the hardware that should be considered if a mathematical model is required. By using reinforcement learning, the authors are able to capture the desired dynamics over a set of motions that derive into a control strategy over the 24 tendons in a reduced state-space. However, as pointed out by [9], data-driven control algorithms on tendon-based robots or soft robotics have not yet been explored, and model-based control strategies are still preferred. Considering the previous statement, the authors in [9] analyzed an autonomous learning algorithm to obtain the model of a tendon-driven leg when different stiffness is used.

From the modeling perspective, [14] proposed a finite element model (FEM) for a glove with pneumatic bending actuators. The authors worked in a two-dimensional space, neglecting the dynamic energy from the model. In further research, a black-box model identification was given by [15] for a fluidic actuator. This allows the authors to introduce the shear deformation into the model, which in their previous work was not considered. The maximum parametric variations reached 36%, which was compensated by a back-stepping controller. In the present paper, black-box data-driven modeling will be used. Therefore, the overall dynamics of the given neck will be considered and modeling results will be compared with standard linear and non-linear modeling techniques, that is, Recursive Least Square and Neural Networks. This provides an overview of alternative modeling possibilities and their implications over a non-linear system as the tendon-driven neck.

In [16], a geometrical model and a two-dimensional FEM model for a soft fluidic actuator were studied. The geometrical model considered a uniform bending curvature of the link, while the FEM model showed a linear trend on the link behaviour. A new approach was proposed in [17] in order to obtain a pneumatic soft-arm 3D model, based on a constant link's bending curvature and neglecting the gravity or payload effects. Another geometrical approach for modeling a soft link is presented in [18]. In this case, the approached model neglects the effects of gravity or internal elastic forces. Regarding tendon-based robots, in the hand exoskeleton given in [19,20], each finger is considered as a three-link kinematic chain and all the joints are considered to be pure revolute. Friction and cable guide deformation were neglected. As shown in the cases above, geometric modeling requires several constraints and assumptions to reduce the model complexity, which allow the designers to cope with the complex system mechanics. Nonetheless, the black-box modeling approach will include the whole system dynamics, which led to the proposed methods in this work.

Modeling of soft robotic links is of particular interest, given the coupled dynamics that arise when actuating the robots. In this sense, different approaches are presented as well. Geometrical approaches expose their limitations when the modeling space increases. Therefore, sensor-based approaches are being used, although their results are limited to the sensor's range and capabilities. In [21], textile strain sensors are embedded into the robot structure to calculate the link deflection state and position. A similar approach is presented in [22,23]. In this last one, the authors describe the implementation of a soft hand where each finger uses an elastic joint with an embedded piezo-electric transducer to sense the deflection of the joint. In this case, the curvature is given by the sensor but is assumed to be continuous through the link. A different sensor technique for embedded deflection modeling is presented in [24], where photo-sensing is used to determine the deflection angle of the link. A 3D modeling approach is given in [25], where embedded cameras for self-observing of the robot configuration are synchronized to obtain the final soft body (robot) shape through learning algorithms. The named references imply additional hardware but allow for rigid modeling based on sensor information. However, their effectiveness is limited to the sensor's accuracy and the validity of the hypothesis over the soft link, such as continuous link curvature. Furthermore, to obtain the mathematical model, it is still required to neglect certain dynamics, and in some cases, only the 2D motion of the soft link is considered. In this work, the soft link is aimed to move in 3D and it is not desired to add additional hardware to the system.

This work aims to characterize the 3D motion of a tendon-driven soft neck described in [26]. An improved version of the initial version was later proposed in [27]. This new design features a soft bendable spine that replaces the central spring. The replaced structure decreases the overall weight and increases the system robustness. An inclination sensor was also introduced on the top platform for extracting the current pitch and roll angles, and enables feedback control.

Although the central structure introduced an already non-linear behaviour, as seen in [27], the new material adds other non-linearity mechanics. Some previous works already tackle system identification. Firstly, in [26] for control design, the study was limited to actuators and ignored the dynamics of the link. The resulting theoretical model is outside the standard modeling methods. As a consequence, additional methodology is required to extract a simulation and control model for the platform. An initial identification exploration on 2D was presented in [28]. In that work, which this paper is a continuation of, we identified the soft link dynamics considering the actuators and the soft link. However, only the front inclination was considered, neglecting at that time the interactions that occur when all the soft neck degrees of freedom are used.

In this work, the proposed models are improved and extended to the entire robot motion range. Set membership and Recursive least-squares identification methods are used for modeling as in [28]. As the recursive least-squares method is only valid for linear plants, the non-linear behavior will not be captured. The selected methods do not need hardware modifications nor neglected dynamics. Therefore, physical effects, such as gravity, elasticity, and plasticity will be considered by the obtained 3D models when possible. These models are compared with a neural network model identification as ground comparison. As an important contribution, no modeling technique selected relies on local deformation sensors, and they do not require additional external hardware for possible neck control considered in the future.

The remaining parts of this paper are organized as follows. In Section 2, the platform to be identified is described. Sections 3 and 4 present the different methods used for identification. In Section 5 the experimental procedures are described and Section 6 shows the resulting models. Then, in Section 7, different tests are performed for validation and comparison purposes. Finally, in Section 8, the main conclusions are discussed.

2. Soft Neck Description

The mechanism that enables soft neck operation is the central soft link, which acts as a spine. It is made with bendable material and actuated with a parallel mechanism driven by cables, which produce a tilt in the upper platform. Figure 1 shows the soft neck prototype and its parts.

The neck is composed of a base, a mobile platform, a central soft link, tendons (cables), and motors, as shown in Figure 1. All parts were built using a 3D printer, including the soft link, which weighs 100 gr (excluding motors and hardware).

Combining the actions of the three actuators, any position or orientation can be reached inside the bounded space. As the robot workspace is three-dimensional, the final rotation can be defined using three Euler angles. The Z-axis rotation (yaw) is neglected since it cannot change due to the configuration of the link; therefore, two rotations around the X- and Y-axes are enough to fully define the robot position and orientation. System output will be defined through an X-axis rotation, roll(ϕ), and a Y-axis rotation, pitch (θ), as shown in Figure 2.

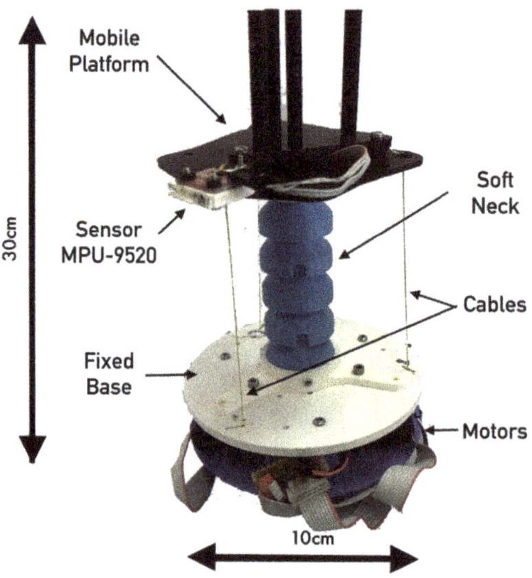

Figure 1. Soft neck platform.

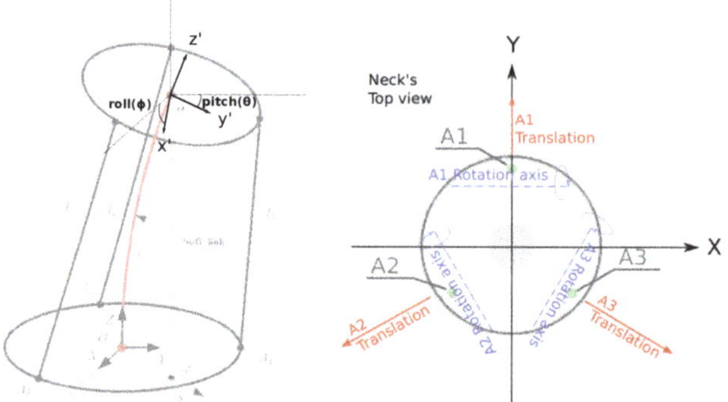

Figure 2. Soft neck kinematics. Orientation and inclination variables [27].

According to [29,30], the soft neck is a hyper-redundant robot. Therefore, the term degrees of freedom (DOF) is not applicable in the usual sense. Nevertheless, there is a connection between the three tendon lengths and the neck's final angular position.

The three tendon actuators are located at the base, each composed with a motor, gear, encoder, and a driver, with the characteristics shown in Table 1.

Table 1. Platform hardware specifications.

Driver	Technosoft iPOS4808 MX-CAN; 400 W, 12–50 Volt, 8 Amp (intelligent motor driver)
Motor	Maxon RE 16-118739; graphite brushes, 48 Volt, 4 Watt
Gear	Maxon 134777 (24 : 1)
Encoder	Maxon mr201937

There exists low-level control managed by the motors' drivers, which satisfies all the platform's needs. For this reason, all system data are captured as an open-loop plan, with the actuator position and velocity as input and the inclinations roll and pitch as output.

2.1. Geometric Simplification

The described plant input and output variables are coupled, defining a Multiple Inputs Multiple Outputs (MIMO) system, which makes the system identification more difficult. Fortunately, there is a way to simplify the system, decoupling these variables, allowing to analyze its behavior through simpler Single-Input Single-Output (SISO) models. Using this scheme, the inverse kinematics described in [31] will not be necessary, making the model identification easier.

The angle combination produced by each actuator effect is a final rotation that can be defined or measured by two angles. A more detailed analysis of the robot's geometry will show the connection between the inputs and these final angle outputs. Since the inputs and outputs of the system are coupled in a MIMO system of three inputs and three outputs, it is desirable to rearrange the original input scheme using a linear combination of them. In this way, three new inputs will be obtained, having a direct action with respect to the outputs. Note that the aim is not to simplify the system, but to study the effects of the different inputs in the neck output variables. To simplify this operation, we will consider the system in the resting position. In this state, the single effect of the $A1$ actuator (reducing l_1) results in a rotation aligned with the X-axis of the base frame (see Figure 2). This results in an output angle directly related to the length of its tendon, and therefore, the motor position. Given that motor angles can be negative, we will consider the neck's rest position ($pitch = 0, roll = 0$) as the initial zero value for all tendons, resulting in positive values when tendon lengths increase, and negative otherwise. Considering just the first actuator with the index number 1, a possible equation describing pitch angle θ in X is the following:

$$\theta_1 = f(P_1) \tag{1}$$

where θ_1 is the angle contribution from the first actuator to the final pitch angle (θ), P_1 is the actuator input position, and f is a nonlinear function describing the relation between both. Although it is considered that just P_1 can change the angle θ_1 as shown in Equation (1), given the neck's nonlinear nature, the other inputs may have a tiny effect on that angle, too, but they are considered too small and will be neglected in this case. The other actuators' effects (θ_2, θ_3) on the final angle θ are the following:

$$\theta_2 = \cos(\gamma_2)f(P_2) \tag{2}$$
$$\theta_3 = \cos(\gamma_3)f(P_3) \tag{3}$$

Given the proposed vertical robot setup, and using the same actuators, we can assume that the functions f are similar. Nevertheless, a projection factor needs to be considered, which depends on the actuator's relative angle (γ). We can generalize the previous functions in the following equation:

$$\theta_i = \cos(\gamma_i)f(P_i) \tag{4}$$

Keeping in mind that we are not modeling the system but proposing an alternative input–output scheme, we can consider these input angles additive. Again, it is not a model simplification, but an input redefinition.

$$\theta = \theta_1 + \theta_2 + \theta_3 = \cos(\gamma_{11})f(P_1) + \cos(\gamma_{12})f(P_2) + \cos(\gamma_{13})f(P_3) \tag{5}$$

According to Figure 2, the three actuators are symmetrically arranged, and the angles are $\gamma_{11} = 0$ deg, $\gamma_{12} = 120$ deg and $\gamma_{13} = 240$ deg. Therefore, Equation (5) results in:

$$\theta = f(P_1) - 0.5f(P_2) - 0.5f(P_3) = f(P_1) - 0.5[f(P_2) + f(P_3)]. \tag{6}$$

This result shows how both A_2 and A_3 actuator effects on the angle *pitch* are divided by two, with an opposite direction to actuator A_1. This leads to the first result of this approach. The *pitch* angle is defined by the length difference, being positive when P_1 is larger than $0.5(P_2 + P_3)$, and negative otherwise. In the case of $P_1 = P_2 = P_3$, angle $\theta = 0$, leading to different robot compression states depending on the tendon lengths, form zero ($P_1 = P_2 = P_3 = 0$) to full compression ($P_1 = P_2 = P_3 = P_{max}$). This feature could be used to change the neck stiffness, although this is not discussed in this paper, where the soft link length is considered constant.

Now, roll angle (ϕ) is defined as the rotation around the Y-axis. Using the previous reasoning but projecting in the Y-axis (using $\sin(\gamma)$):

$$\phi = \phi_1 + \phi_2 + \phi_3 = \sin(\gamma_1)f(P_1) + \sin(\gamma_2)f(P_2) + \sin(\gamma_3)f(P_3) \tag{7}$$

In the case of $\gamma_1 = 0$ deg, $\gamma_2 = 120$ deg and $\gamma_3 = 240$ deg, Equation (7) results in:

$$\phi = 0.866f(P_2) - 0.866f(P_3) = 0.866[f(P_2) - f(P_3)] \tag{8}$$

Note that in this case, the value of the ϕ angle just depends on the difference between P_2 and P_3, and that the A_1 actuator has no effect. Again, the angle just depends on their difference, and the compression is an average function of the tendon lengths. For the case $P_1 = P_2 = P_3$, angle $\phi = 0$, leading to the same previous result regarding soft link compression. Additionally, note that θ and ϕ angles depend on the tendon length difference, and the compression (δ) depends on the tendon lengths' average. Based on this, we can define the new input variables θ_i, ϕ_i and δ_i as a linear combination of the motor position inputs.

Using the results from Equations (6) and (8), and considering the link compression input as the motor positions' average, the following input redefinition is proposed:

$$\theta_i = P_1 - 0.5(P_2 + P_3) \tag{9}$$

$$\phi_i = 0.866(P_2 - P_3) \tag{10}$$

$$\delta_i = \frac{P_1 + P_2 + P_3}{3} \tag{11}$$

Using this input redefinition, we can decouple and simplify the system considering ϕ_i as an input, which provides a change exclusively in the ϕ output angle. Therefore, a nonlinear single-input single-output (SISO) system can be defined, having ϕ_i inputs and ϕ outputs. Likewise, θ_i and δ_i inputs will affect only the output values of θ and δ, respectively, defining another two SISO systems.

Based on this, the soft neck can be modeled as three decoupled SISO systems. The transfer functions G_θ, G_ϕ, and G_δ will model the actual outputs (θ,ϕ,δ) as a function of the new inputs (θ_i,ϕ_i,δ_i), defined by Equations (9)–(11). Given the simplifications we have considered, the real behavior will be different in several aspects, like showing interference between actuators and a nonlinear plant response. These effects will be discussed in the Experiments section.

Two different system identification methods are used. First, the set membership method as described in [32] is used for nonlinear identification, and second, recursive least-squares (RLS), as described in [33], is applied for different tilt configurations, which will result in a linear system for each RLS identification performed. The evolution of these systems, according to the inclination, will be studied.

In the case of RLS system identification, the new redefined inputs (θ_i, ϕ_i and l_i) were considered instead of motor position inputs. Note that these are just the input redefinition, and the output angles still depend on the system dynamics. Although f functions are unknown, they are considered within the resulting models, although the nonlinear part may be neglected depending on the identification method.

3. Set Membership Non-Linear Identification

This section briefly describes the Non-Linear Set Membership (NLSM) identification method proposed in [32].

Consider a system that has a Nonlinear AutoRegressive with eXogenous input (NARX) structure, as

$$y(k) = f_o(\omega(k)) + e(k) \tag{12}$$

where $\omega(k)$ is the system's regressor formed by past samples of the system inputs $u1, u2$ and the output $y1, y2$, as:

$$\omega(k) = [y_i(k-1), \ldots, y_i(k-n_y), u_i(k-1), \ldots, u_i(k-n_u)]' \tag{13}$$

$$\omega(k) \in W \subseteq \mathcal{R}^n, n = \sum_i n_{y_i} + n_{u_i} \tag{14}$$

where $e(k)$ represents the measurement noise and W is the function domain.

The NARX regressor is widely used in system identification considering its capacity of representing nonlinear dynamics and developing estimation algorithms which are computationally cost-efficient.

If f_o is unknown, but a set of measurements of $y_i(k)$ and $\omega(k)$ are available for $k - 1, \ldots, N$ and considering that the noise magnitude is bounded by ϵ:

$$|e(k)| \leq \epsilon \tag{15}$$

and no statistical assumption on its behavior is made. The goal is to estimate $\hat{f}$ of f_o, where $\hat{f}$ is the estimation of f.

Even though f is unknown, the following information is available:

$$f_o \in \mathcal{F} \doteq \left\{ f \in C^1(W) : \|f'(\omega)\| \leq \gamma, \forall \omega \in W \right\} \tag{16}$$

where $f'(\omega)$ denotes the gradient of $f(\omega)$ and $\|x\|$ is the Euclidean norm. Therefore, we assume that the identified system is continuous on its first derivative and has maximum growth of γ for all the regressors applied to the function of interest.

On the other hand, if there is a Feasible System Set (FSS), which is the set of all systems in the space $\mathcal{F}$ which satisfies the following conditions:

$$FSS \doteq \left\{ \begin{array}{c} f \in \mathcal{F} : |y(k) - f(\omega(k))| \leq \epsilon, \\ \text{and} \\ f \in \mathcal{F} : \frac{y(k) - y(k+1)}{\delta_T} \leq \gamma \end{array} \right\}, k = 1, 2, \ldots, N \tag{17}$$

therefore, there always exists a non-empty FSS and $f_o \in FSS$ when both assumptions on f_o and e are true. Then, if we guarantee the validity of the conditions γ and ϵ over a set of measurements generated by the system to be identified, we will find a $FSS \neq \emptyset$. In [32], the procedure to guarantee conditions γ and ϵ over a data set is presented. For the following sections, prior assumptions are considered to be true.

Given that the aim of the model is to find the output generated by the system for a new input, it is necessary to distinguish the identification data set, k, and the new inputs x. Hence, for a given input $x \in W$, the optimal NLSM estimate of $f_o(x)$ is:

$$f_c(x) \doteq \frac{f_u(x) + f_l(x)}{2} \tag{18}$$

where:

$$f_u(x) = min_{1<k<N} y(k) + \epsilon + \gamma \|x - \omega(k)\| \tag{19}$$
$$f_l(x) = max_{1<k<N} y(k) - \epsilon - \gamma \|x - \omega(k)\| \tag{20}$$

As presented in [32],

- $f_u(x)$ and $f_l(x)$ are optimal upper and lower bounds for $f_o(x)$, respectively.
- $f_u(x)$ and $f_l(x)$ are Lipschitz-continuous on W; therefore, they belong to the FSS.
- $f_c(x)$ is an optimal approximation of $f_o(x)$ for any $L_p(W)$ norm, with $p \in [1, \infty]$, with an optimality criterion as:

$$f_{opt} = \arg\inf_{\hat{f}} \sup_{f \in FSS} \left\| f - \hat{f} \right\|_p$$

The NLSM algorithm produces a non-linear, non-parametric model which is embedded on the data set. That is, there is no explicit equation that represents the input–output or physical variables relation.

For a new regressor value $x \in \mathcal{R}^n$, the NLSM model output $f_c(x)$ is evaluated through Algorithm 1.

Algorithm 1: Set membership algorithm.

$F_{NLSM}(x)$
Set $f_u(x) = +\infty$
Set $f_l(x) = -\infty$
for $k = 1$ *to* N **do**
    Calculate the distance between x and $\omega(k)$ as
    $Distance(k) = \|x - \omega(k)\|$.
    Obtain the upper bound on $f_o(x)$ guaranteed by $\omega(k)$ as the projection
    $P_u(k) = y(k) + \epsilon + \gamma * Distance(k)$.
    Obtain the lower bound on $f_o(x)$ guaranteed by $\omega(k)$ as the projection
    $P_l(k) = y(k) - \epsilon - \gamma * Distance(k)$.
    Choose the lowest upper bound
    if $P_u(k) \leq f_u(x)$ **then**
        $f_u(x) = y(k) + \epsilon + \gamma \|x - \omega(k)\| = P_u(k)$
    end
    Choose the highest lower bound
    if $P_l(k) \geq f_l(x)$ **then**
        $f_l(x) = y(k) - \epsilon - \gamma \|x - \omega(k)\| = P_l(k)$
    end
end
Calculate the estimation
$f_c(x) = \frac{f_u(x) + f_l(x)}{2}$
return $f_c(x)$

In order to obtain the FSS, as described in [32,34], it is possible to execute the Algorithm 1 over the identification data set, updating the variable γ whenever the positive or negative projections $f_u(i)$, $f_l(i)$, over each data point $\omega(i) \in \omega(k) \forall k \neq i$ produces a greater, $f_u(i) < y(i)$, or lower, $f_l(i) > y(i)$, value.

3.1. Non-Linear Set Membership Data Set Generation

In our specific problem, as described in Section 2, we have three motors that drive three tendons to actuate over the soft link and provide the desired pitch-roll motion. As described in Algorithm 1, to provide an estimation using Set Membership, we need to construct the FSS for a defined regressor that contains enough information so that all the identified system behaviors are contained in the FSS.

For this purpose, we define our regressor empirically since there are no standard methodologies to do so. Therefore, for simplicity, we run several system identifications using a neural networks MATLAB toolbox providing non-linear data-driven models for different regressor sizes. Once the NN is trained, we assume that the best neural network model uses the most informative regressor and corresponds to the original regressor selection. Later, to improve the computational time, the regressor is reduced by running different estimations modifying the number of elements in the regressor. In this way, less operations are required for each of the estimated data [35]. The chosen regressor is:

$$
\begin{aligned}
\omega(k) \;=\; & [y(k-1), u_1(k-2), u_1(k-3), \\
& u_2(k-2), u_2(k-3), \\
& u3(k-2), u3(k-3), \\
& M_1(k-3), \\
& M_2(k-3), M_3(k-3)]
\end{aligned}
\tag{21}
$$

where $u_i(k)$ is the desired motor position for motor i at sample k, $M_i(K)$ is the measured motor position at discrete time k, and y is the measured output at sample k when an estimator and control model is generated. Therefore, if noise or disturbances are detected in the measured output, the model aligns its dynamics using this information with the true model dynamics. On the other hand, if the required model is generated for prediction and simulation, the signal in (22) will be replaced by the previous model estimations at time $k - j$ $y(k - j)$. In this case, errors and disturbances detected at the output will not be perceived by the model unless a closed-loop control action modifies the input components of the regressor. In this case, if the model diverges from the real dynamics, they will not align with each other. The model architectures are given in Figure 3.

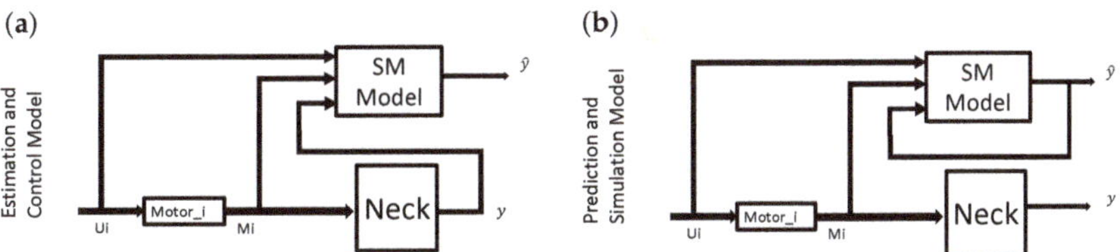

Figure 3. Model architectures. (**a**) An estimation and control model. (**b**) A prediction and simulation model.

With the regressor being defined as in (22), we generate our FSS by applying a sum of sinusoidals to each of the three motors such that the signals are not correlated and they give us a wide spectrum of the neck behavior. We capture the real motor positions, desired motor positions and, as output, the neck pitch and roll angles. Then, two separate models are generated.

The signal used for each motor $MP(i)$ to create the FSS is described in Equation (22). The values used for the specific motor are listed in Table 2.

$$MP(i) = (0.6sin(2sin(\omega_1 t + \phi_1) + cos(\omega_1 t + \phi_2))) * \ldots$$

$$* abs \left[3 + sin(\omega 2t) + sin(\omega_3 t + \phi_3) + sin(\omega_1 t - \phi_4) + \ldots \right.$$

$$\left. \ldots + sin(\omega_4 t) + sin(\omega_5 t + \phi_5) + sin(\omega_6 t + \phi_6)\frac{sin(\omega_7 t + \phi_7)}{2} \right]$$

(22)

As it can be seen, the different signals are non-linear and have different frequencies and phases. This provides a pseudo-random interaction and covers a wide range of operational modes of the neck. The frequency spectrum that was chosen is coherent with the system bandwidth, which is 4 (rad/s), generating soft, continuous, and human-like motion in the axes of interest. By modifying the phase and mixing the minimum 0.25 (rad/s) and maximum rad/s frequencies, we aim to explore in a single experiment a wide range of motions providing sufficient information for the FSS. However, it is necessary to point out that some system dynamics did not occur during the proposed study scenario, such as the three tendons pulling at the same time with the same force, which keeps a static neck position with different stiffness, as well as continuous single tendon activation, to name some. Even if the proposed FSS does not cover the full system dynamics, the chosen signal should cover the normal operational range for the soft neck.

Table 2. Values used for the identification data set creation.

Variable	PositionM1	PositionM2	PositionM3
ω_1 rad/s	1	1	1
ϕ_1 rad	0	2.09	4.18
ω_2 rad/s	0.25	0.25	0.25
ϕ_2 rad	0	2.09	4.18
ω_3 rad/s	1.5	1.5	1.5
ϕ_3 rad	0.32	0.32	0.32
ω_4 rad/s	2.56	2.56	2.56
ϕ_4 rad	0.095	0.095	0.95
ω_5 rad/s	1.75	1.75	1.75
ϕ_5 rad	0.09	0.09	0.09
ω_6 rad/s	1.66	1.66	1.66
ϕ_6 rad	0.29	0.29	0.29
ω_7 rad/s	4	4	4
ϕ_7 rad	0.67	0.67	0.67

The identification and validation data sets are given in Figure 4, where 10,000 samples were taken, 7000 for the FSS (Identification Data Set) and 3000 for the validation set.

As seen in the Figure, the rotational position of the tendon is maximum 6 rad. Having a pulley diameter of 15 mm, each tendon has linear displacement of the tendon 7.5 mm/rad, and therefore, a maximum linear displacement of $\approx$45 mm. This generates inclinations of ±20 deg for the pitch and $[-20, 40]$ deg for the roll. This provides a wide dynamic range of motion. In addition, the motion frequency was set to replicate a human-like motion which is the region of interest.

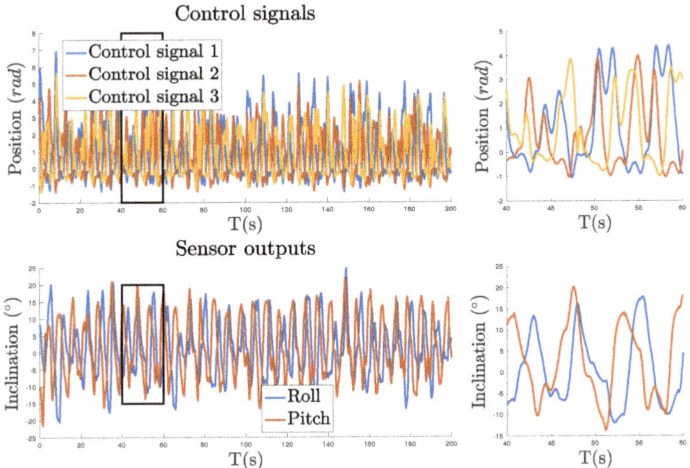

Figure 4. Input and output signals.

4. Recursive Least-Squares Linear Identification

Despite the nonlinear nature of the plant, a simple recursive least-squares (RLS) identification was performed. On the one hand, it will show a qualitative estimation of the system's nonlinearity degree, and on the other hand, a linear model could be used to solve the nonlinearity issues by means of robust or adaptive control strategies.

The RLS identification algorithm can be described using an ARX structure:

$$\hat{y}(t) = -a_1 y(t-1) - .. - a_{na} y(t-na) + b_1 u(t-1) + .. + b_{nb} u(t-nb), \tag{23}$$

with $y(t)$ and $u(t)$ being the plant output and input variables, with a matrix representation as follows:

$$\hat{y}(t) = \theta \phi'(t-1) \tag{24}$$

$$\theta = [a_1, .., a_{na}, b_1, .., b_{nb}] \tag{25}$$

$$\phi(t-1) = [-y(t-1), .., -y(t-na), u(t-1), .., u(t-nb)] \tag{26}$$

Increasing one time-index ($\hat{y}(t+1) = \theta \phi'(t)$), Equations (24)–(26) provide the output prediction, based on the model parameters (θ), and the set of past inputs and outputs ($\phi(t-1)$). Comparing the next actual system output with this predicted value results in the prediction error:

$$\epsilon(t) = y(t) - \hat{y}(t) \Rightarrow \epsilon(t+1) = y(t+1) - \hat{y}(t+1) \tag{27}$$

In order to minimize this error, different algorithms can be used. In the least-squares case, the squared sum of all errors is the variable to be minimized. Since the parameters that minimize the error produced by the least-squares solution can also be obtained from the preceding parameters (recursively), the algorithm can be expressed using recursion, as shown below:

$$\hat{\theta}(t+1) = \hat{\theta}(t) + F(t+1)\phi(t)\epsilon(t+1) \tag{28}$$

$$F(t+1) = F(t) - \frac{F(t)\phi'(t)\phi(t)F(t)}{1 + \phi(t)F(t)\phi'(t)} \tag{29}$$

$$\epsilon(t+1) = y(t+1) - \hat{\theta}(t)\phi'(t) \tag{30}$$

These equations define the operations needed to find $\hat{\theta}(t+1)$ based on the previous parameters and captured inputs and outputs. An improved method is described in [33] as RLS with a constant forgetting factor (CFF-RLS). It will not be necessary at this point, as the soft neck system identification will be done offline, but it can be used in the future, if an adaptive scheme is proposed as a solution to the nonlinearity issues. See [33] or [36] for a more detailed discussion about RLS and other identification methods.

Using the described inputs and outputs definition of Section 2, the same data captured in the identification experiments were used in order to obtain a plant model. As the data capture is based on the motor positions, we can find the equivalent input values using Equations (9) and (10), and consider these inputs. The outputs will be the same as in the other cases, the neck pitch and roll angles.

For example, Figure 5 shows part of the inputs and outputs considered for the pitch and roll RLS identification.

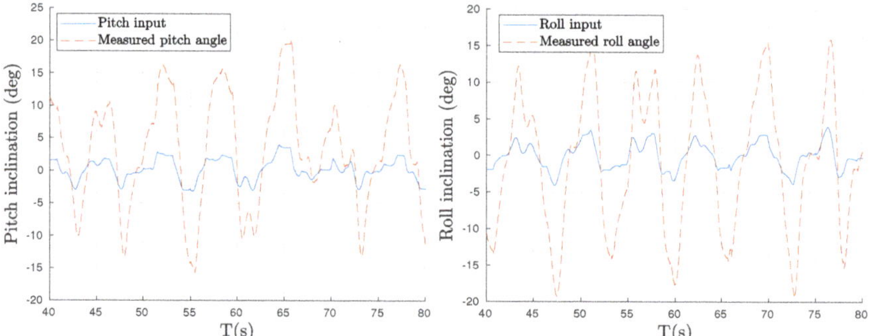

Figure 5. Examples of decoupled identification datasets. Redefined input targets compared to measured angles for pitch (**left**), and roll (**right**).

A small delay can be observed in the data set example shown in that Figure. This delay must be considered during the system identification process. The resulting transfer functions corresponding to the pitch dynamics, $G_\theta(s)$, and roll dynamics, $G_\phi(s)$, obtained using the RLS algorithm through the entire data set, are:

$$G_\theta(s) = e^{-0.08s}\frac{27.691}{(s+5.293)} \quad G_\phi(s) = e^{-0.08s}\frac{25.424}{(s+4.938)}. \tag{31}$$

The model unit input time responses are shown in Figure 6 for the described system model. Note how both systems' ($G_\theta(s)$, $G_\phi(s)$) static gains are close to 5, showing a stationary response above the unit input level, as expected from Figure 5.

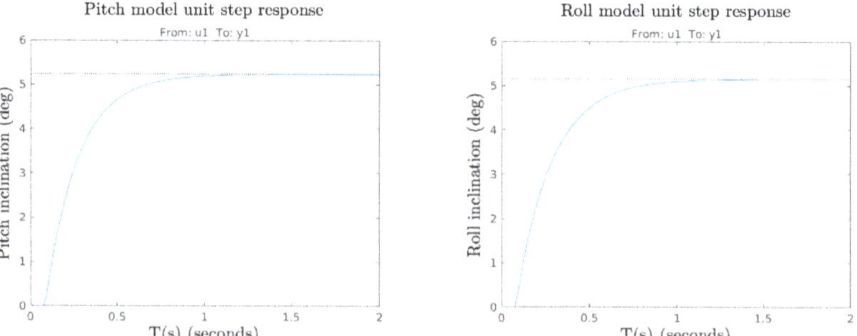

Figure 6. Unit input time response for $G_\theta(s)$ (**left**) and $G_\phi(s)$ (**right**).

Once the linear models of the soft neck decoupled system are determined, a new input response simulation was performed using those models, together with a new data set for validation and accuracy check. A partial plot of these results is shown in Figure 7 for the pitch and roll angles.

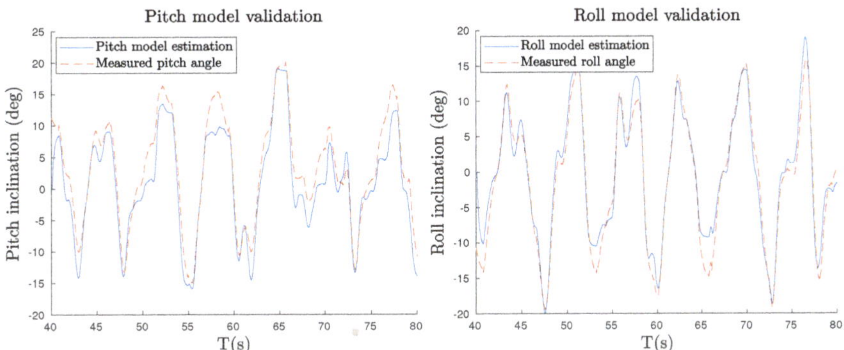

Figure 7. Validation example of the identified models for $G_\theta(s)$ (**left**) and $G_\phi(s)$ (**right**).

Note how although the linear model captures the system behavior quite well, there are mismatches due to plant non-linearity. In order to deal with these problems, a robust controller could be used in the future, since it will provide a constant behavior despite plant parameter changes or non-linearities.

5. Experimental Setup

The main objective of this work was to extract a 3D model for the soft neck platform. The selected identifications were done in an offline configuration, with an open-loop data capture scheme. In this sense, a set of experiments has been designed for data capture.

As stated before, as we expected a correlation between the motor position and the inclination of the top platform, the motors' states are therefore considered as inputs, while the measured sensor angles are used as system outputs. The captured data involve the following inputs and outputs:

- Motor input position (*rad*)
- Motor current position (*rad*)
- Motor current velocity ($\frac{rad}{s}$)
- Platform roll or model output (°)
- Platform pitch or model output (°)

Neck actuator motion was programmed to follow a composition of sinusoidal functions, as described in Section 3.1. The captured motion describes human-like movement. Input and output sets can be seen in Figure 4.

All models used the same data for modeling the system, enabling direct comparisons of the models. Additional tests were also captured for validation purposes.

6. Model Results

This section presents the different model behaviors for the validation data. Figure 8 represents 30% of the data set described in Equation (22). All the results will be compared to those obtained by a NLARX NN with two hidden layers and 25 neurons each. To train the neural network, the 70% of the FSS data set described in Equation (22) was used.

As a form of comparison, the fitting value for the Normalized Root Mean Squared Error (NRMSE) will be taken into consideration. This tool finds the difference between the measured data and the model response as the sum of the squared individual errors throughout the entire signal. Using this method, the large errors will have a bigger quantitative penalization than small errors.

Finally, to validate the results, three independent different tests will be conducted that compare the methodologies used for static movement, dynamic movement, and normal operation mode.

6.1. Set Membership

The set membership model was able to follow the system output with high accuracy (see Table 3). However, in some peaks, especially for the pitch output, it failed to reach the maximum value (an error of around 2 degrees) (see Figures 9 and 10). SM scores a high fit for both pitch, 93.9794%, and roll, 96.8854%. The values reached by the model show possible over-fitting to the training data. This means that the identification data set almost explicitly contains the validation set.

6.2. Neural Network

The neural network used is an NLARX with two hidden layers of 25 neurons each. The output for the validation can be found in Figures 9 and 10. Like the SM case, the resulting fit value obtained exceeds expectations and some concerns of over-fitting arise. The fitted values for pith and roll are 99.0162% and 99.2027%, respectively (see Table 3). Similarly to the behavior of the SM case, the training data for the neural network covers the validation data with high precision. Therefore, additional tests are required to properly evaluate the model performance.

6.3. Recursive Least-Squares

The RLS model proposed in Section 4 was fed with the validation data in order to be compared with both previous models. The model output can be seen in Figures 9 and 10. RLS captured the overall behaviour of the neck within acceptable tolerance. The mismatch observed is attributed to the plant non-linearity. The fit values are 78.0448% for pitch and 82.7217% for roll. An overall comparison of the results can be found in Table 3.

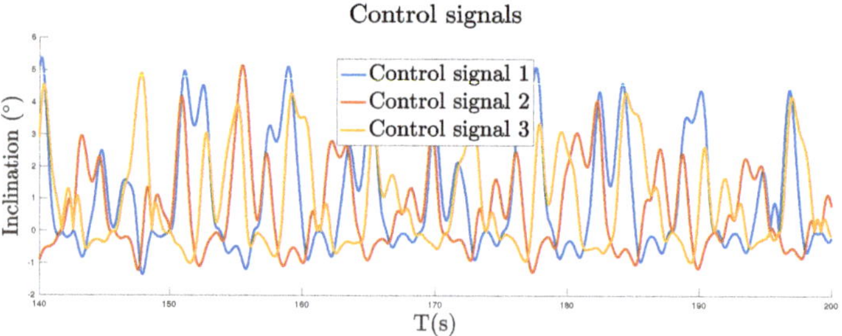

Figure 8. Control signal for the validation test.

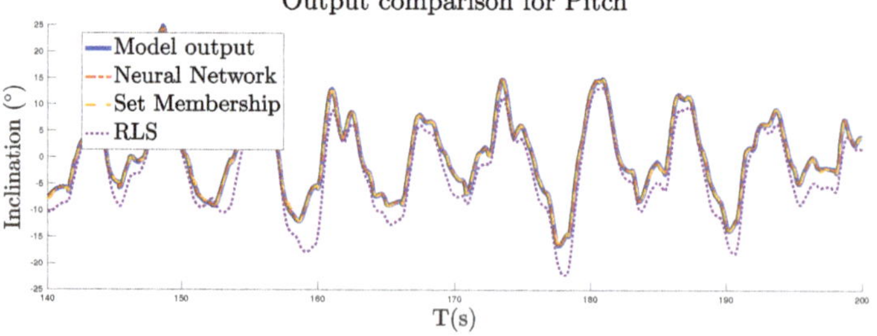

Figure 9. Validation of the pitch output.

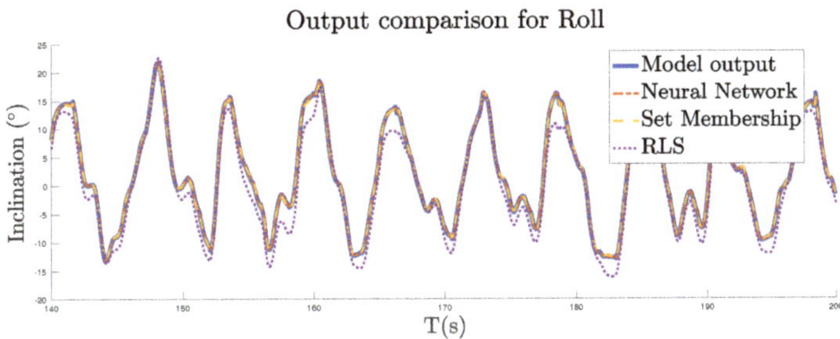

Figure 10. Validation of the roll output.

Table 3. Fitness of models on the validation data.

	Pitch	Roll
SM	93.9794%	96.8854%
NN	99.0162%	99.2027%
RLS	78.0448%	82.7217%

7. Methods Comparison

With the models already trained and properly adjusted, three different tests in the estimation configuration were conducted to validate proper behaviour of the systems and compare the outputs for the different models.

7.1. Test 1: Step Inputs

This test consists of three separated step-waves with a duration of 8 seconds, each independently activating the neck tendons, as shown in Figure 11. The aim of this test was to validate the models' capability of responding to a static input. Since the dataset for the training and NN which corresponds to the FSS lacks individual tendon actuation, some error in the models is expected. Figures 12 and 13 show the outputs.

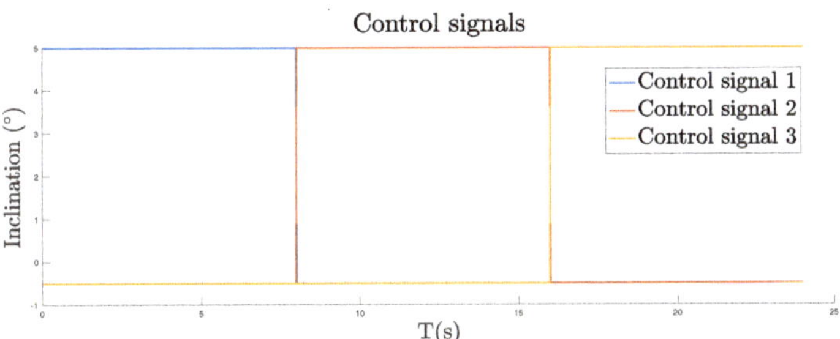

Figure 11. Test 1 input signal.

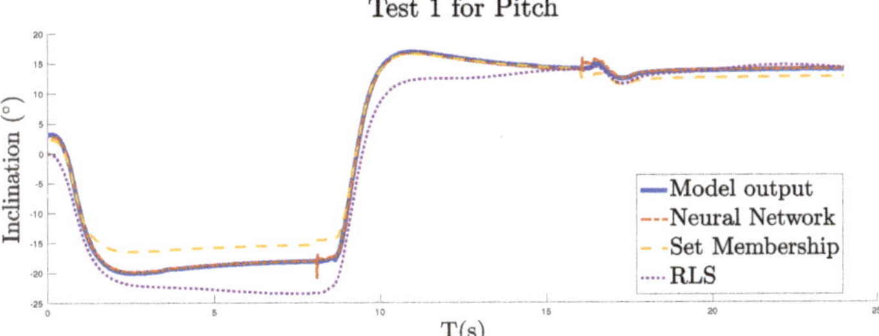

Figure 12. Test 1 results for pitch.

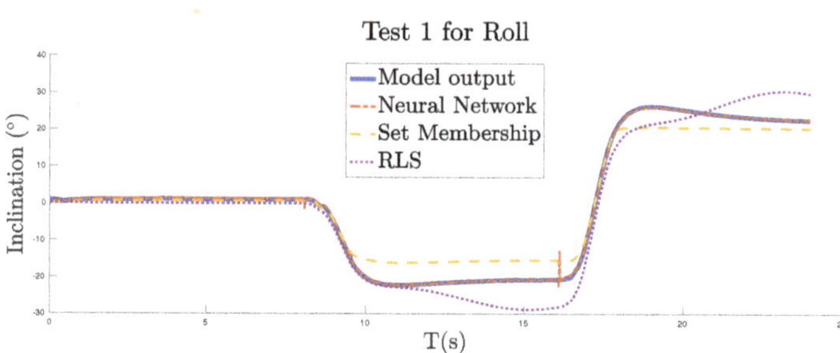

Figure 13. Test 1 results for roll.

Set membership scored 87.6260% in the NRMSE test for pitch and 79.3195% for roll. NN followed the output better and scored 97.9574% for pitch and 98.5654% for roll. The SM response did not settle at the appropriated inclination, lagging out before the maximum inclinations were reached. As can be seen, the model does not reach the negative inclinations properly. However, in Figure 12, the dynamics for negative and positive inclinations are followed as desired. It is seen that the existing bias in the time windows $[3, 5]$ s follows the output dynamics. In the roll axis case, the same bias appears with the negative inclination angles, while in the positive case, it stabilizes at time 17 s in the final value. However, it does not properly capture that dynamic, neither. The maximum errors for the NN appear at 8 and 16 seconds, when the signal is changed from one tendon to the next; this is probably due to a lack of information in the data set. Meanwhile, RLS scored 79.9230% in pitch and 76.0284% in roll. This can be due to the fact that the initial conditions do not match the real model ones.

7.2. Test 2: Sine Inputs

The next test feeds a more complex signal composed of a sine wave with increasing frequency instead of a step signal, as shown in Figure 14. The test is conducted in order to validate the models for simple dynamic movements. As mentioned before, these cases are not explicitly captured by the FSS or training data. Figures 15 and 16 show the outputs.

The Set Membership followed the output of the system closer than in the previous test. It scored 93.0012% for pitch and 93.8389% for roll, much closer to the validation results. It is important to mention that the SM follows the dynamics and does not have the bias error observed in Test 1. Therefore, the FSS properly captures the continuous dynamic behavior, but it requires additional information to capture static behaviors, as required in Test 1. This is true also for the NN model, which also improved. It scored 98.1058% in pitch and 98.3087% in roll. The RLS roll output shows the disadvantages of this model. Due to the decoupling of the signal, while the initial movement causes little movement on the roll axis, RLS cannot process them and scores a worse fit than in the rest of the test. The fit scores are 78.4813% in pitch and 48.5090% in roll.

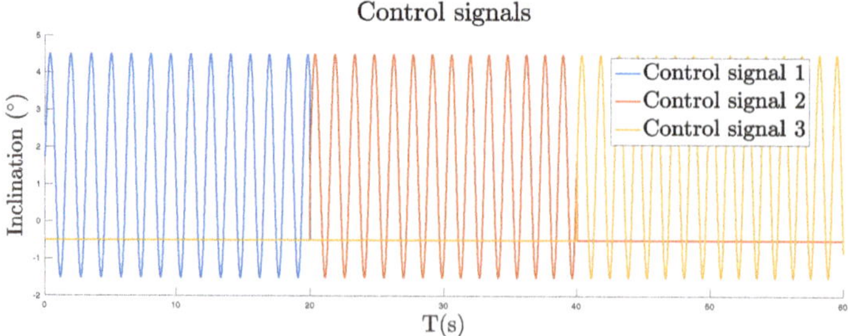

Figure 14. Test 2 input signal.

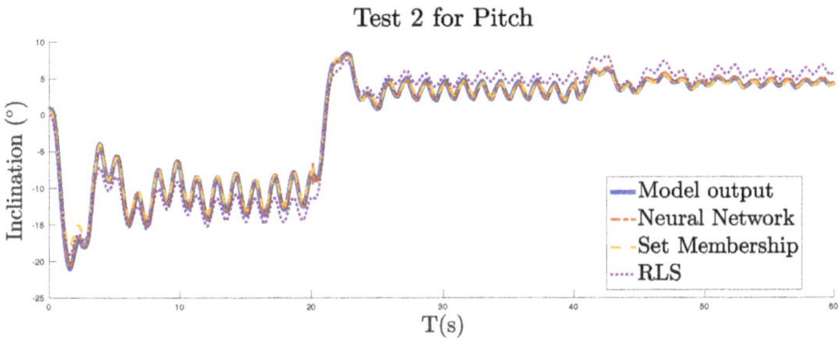

Figure 15. Test 2 results for pitch.

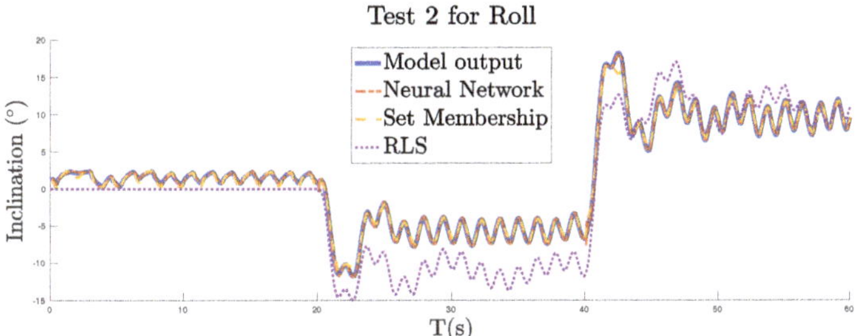

Figure 16. Test 2 results for roll.

7.3. Test 3: Neck Rotation

The final test combines multiple sine and cosine waves in order to create a rotatory motion on the neck, Figure 17. This test simulates normal operation for the neck, where a circular motion is described. Figures 18 and 19 show the outputs.

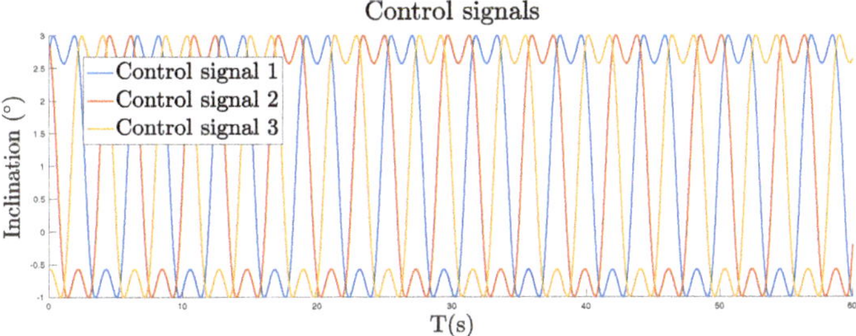

Figure 17. Test 3 input signal.

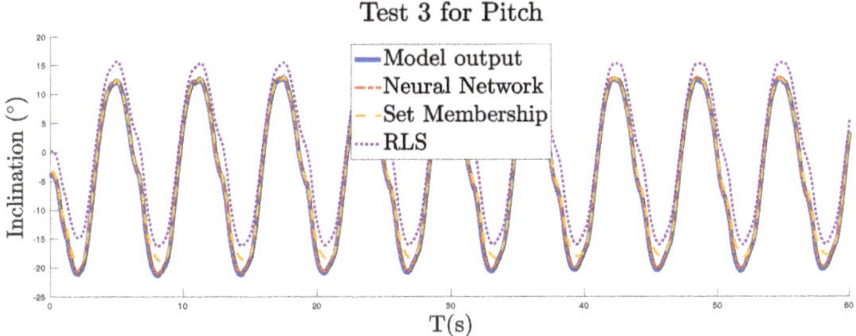

Figure 18. Test 3 results for pitch.

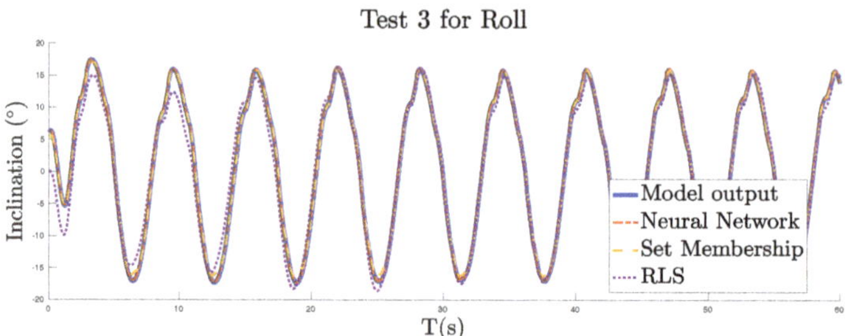

Figure 19. Test 3 results for roll.

Table 4. Fitness on validation data.

	Test 1		Test 2		Test 3	
	Pitch	**Roll**	**Pitch**	**Roll**	**Pitch**	**Roll**
SM	87.6260%	79.3195%	93.0012%	93.8389%	90.2614%	96.7512%
NN	97.9574%	98.5654%	98.1058%	98.3087%	98.5191%	99.1767%
RLS	79.9230%	76.0284%	78.4813%	48.5090%	63.1412%	83.2230%

SM scored 90.2614% on pitch and 96.7512% on roll, while NN scored 98.5191% for pitch and 99.1767% for roll. NN captures the dynamics of the neck both in pitch and roll. SM also closely resembles the output for roll, but on pitch, lags behind the real value. RLS also resembles the real output, but with an offset in pitch. The final scores for RLS are 63.1412% in pitch and 83.2230% in roll.

Table 4 shows a summary of all model scores for all previous tests.

7.4. Prediction and Simulation Configuration

In the previous Sections 7.1–7.3, we evaluated the performance for the NN and SM models using the measured output in the model regressor. This configuration can be used for control or estimation applications, to control the plant using the future predicted behaviour. Alternatively, prediction control techniques are desirable. These models are limited to short prediction horizons. On the contrary, if the model is aimed for simulation or pure prediction over long horizons, parallel architecture has to be used as the one in Figure 3. In that case, the model is fed with the previous estimations, and therefore, it can model the whole system's behavior. If the output is disturbed during simulation, the model will not be aligned and will not provide information in this regard.

In order to evaluate the performance of the obtained NN and SM models as predictors, we used Experiments 2 and 3 from Sections 7.2 and 7.3, respectively.

7.4.1. Neck Rotation

When these experiments are applied using the parallel architecture, we can see in Figure 20 corresponding to the pitch that both models decrease in performance. However, the dynamics are still well-captured by both models. In the SM case, the limit values are not reached properly with an error of ≈5 deg for the negative picks and ≈3 deg for positive ones. However, the overall dynamics are captured with a fit that marks 77%. For the NN model, the fit marks 58%. As can be seen, there are important dynamic errors in the negative sinusoidal cycle. Regarding the roll, as shown in Figure 21, both models properly capture the dynamics with fits that mark 86.5% for the SM model and 87.5% for the NN model. RLS results are unchanged, since no feedback is used in the regressor.

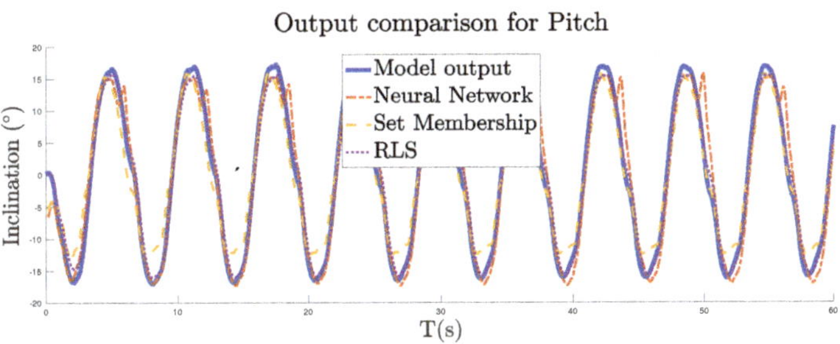

Figure 20. Prediction configuration results for pitch in Test 3.

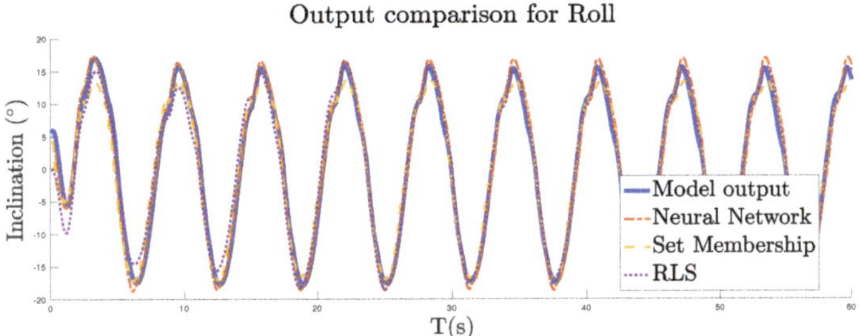

Figure 21. Prediction configuration results for roll in Test 3.

7.4.2. Sine Wave

Unlike the last results, in Section 7.4.1, as expected, they are not as clean as desired, considering that the FSS lacks these behaviors and therefore, the predictor does not emulate the given dynamics. As can be seen in Figures 22 and 23, the SM stays closer to the measured values. However, there are important gain errors and the model dynamics do not resemble the expected one, even if the results are better than those obtained by the NN model. The final fit values in these cases were: for pitch, NN = 13.5% and SM = 60%; for roll, NN = 60% and SM = 37%. These results confirm that in order to model static and non-coupled behaviours, additional dynamic signals should be considered in the FSS so that the identification data provide reliable information to increase the performance to the one shown in the experiment of Section 7.4.1.

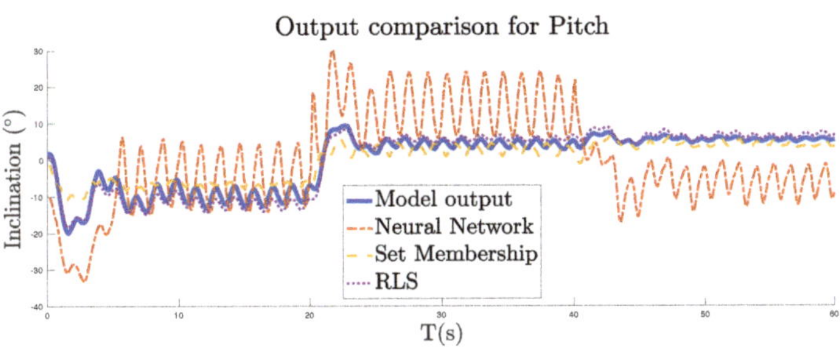

Figure 22. Prediction configuration results for pitch in Test 2.

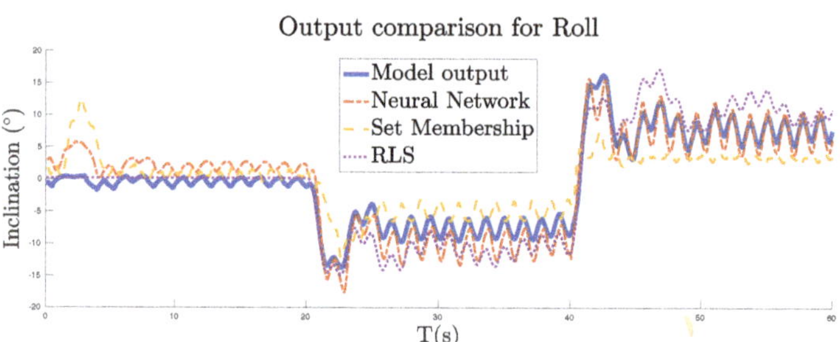

Figure 23. Prediction configuration results for roll in Test 2.

8. Conclusions

In this work, an improved mathematical model for a robotic soft neck has been presented. The whole soft-neck actuation range was modeled, resulting in a multi-input multi-output (MIMO) system showing a total of three inputs and two outputs. In particular, a nonlinear data-driven identification model using Set Membership, a linear model using Recursive least-squares, and a Neural Network model have been developed and discussed in this paper.

The outstanding results show that the proposed methods are suitable for estimation and control purposes when measures from the output are available to align the models. As shown, given the high level of correlation that the identification data set has over the NN training and the FSS for the set membership, additional identification data are required to use the methods as predictors over long prediction horizons, although results show that the proposed models are viable in soft nonlinear dynamics with multiple inputs and outputs.

A shown advantage of the SM identification stands in the possibility of incorporating additional signal dependency, delays, and unknown dynamics through a richer identification data set which derives from better and more complex modeling without explicit knowledge of the system. Even though the computational time might be a future consideration, there already exist approximation methods to overcome this drawback.

The accuracy difference found between the linear and nonlinear models suggests an important plant non-linearity, as expected. This issue can lead to problems at the time of defining a control strategy, although there are several options which will be explored in upcoming studies.

From the control point of view, the self-aligning characteristic of the given methods provide further knowledge on forecasting in short horizons, which is interesting for predictive and robust control techniques. Besides, the linear model accuracy is good enough to propose solutions like adaptive or robust control, which can provide excellent results. The predictive models' performance shown allows the use of the system for some applications. However, it is limited to continuous mode operation, which yet limits its utility. To overcome this issue, a more informative data set should be constructed that contains additional system behaviors to the continuous operation mode.

Author Contributions: Conceptualization, F.Q., J.M., J.A.C.P. and C.A.M.; methodology, F.Q., J.M., J.A.C.P. and C.A.M.; software, F.Q., J.M. and J.A.C.P.; validation, F.Q., J.M. and J.A.C.P.; formal analysis, F.Q., J.M. and J.A.C.P.; investigation, F.Q., J.M., J.A.C.P. and C.A.M.; resources, C.A.M.; data curation, F.Q., J.M. and J.A.C.P.; writing—original draft preparation, F.Q., J.M. and J.A.C.P.; writing—review and editing, F.Q., J.M., J.A.C.P. and C.A.M.; visualization, F.Q., J.M. and J.A.C.P.; supervision, C.A.M.; project administration, C.A.M.; funding acquisition, C.A.M. All authors have read and agreed to the published version of the manuscript.

Funding: The research leading to these results has received funding from the project Desarrollo de articulaciones blandas para aplicaciones robóticas, with reference IND2020/IND-1739, funded by the Comunidad Autónoma de Madrid (CAM) (Department of Education and Research), and from RoboCity2030-DIH-CM, Madrid Robotics Digital Innovation Hub (Robótica aplicada a la mejora de la calidad de vida de los ciudadanos, FaseIV; S2018/NMT-4331), funded by "Programas de Actividades I+D en la Comunidad de Madrid" and cofunded by Structural Funds of the EU.

Institutional Review Board Statement: Not applicable.

Informed Consent Statement: Not applicable.

Data Availability Statement: Not applicable.

Conflicts of Interest: The authors declare no conflict of interest.

References

1. Ohta, P.; Valle, L.; King, J.; Low, K.; Yi, J.; Atkeson, C.G.; Park, Y.L. Design of a Lightweight Soft Robotic Arm Using Pneumatic Artificial Muscles and Inflatable Sleeves. *Soft Robot.* **2018**, *5*, 204–215. [CrossRef]
2. Ding, L.; Dai, N.; Mu, X.; Xie, S.; Fan, X.; Li, D.; Cheng, X. Design of soft multi-material pneumatic actuators based on principal strain field. *Mater. Des.* **2019**, *182*, 108000. [CrossRef]
3. Oliveira, J.; Ferreira, A.; Reis, J.C. Design and experiments on an inflatable link robot with a built-in vision sensor. *Mechatronics* **2020**, *65*, 102305. [CrossRef]
4. Pawlowski, B.; Sun, J.; Xu, J.; Liu, Y.; Zhao, J. Modeling of Soft Robots Actuated by Twisted-and-Coiled Actuators. *IEEE/ASME Trans. Mechatron.* **2019**, *24*, 5–15. [CrossRef]
5. Mazzolai, B.; Beccai, L.; Mattoli, V. Plants as Model in Biomimetics and Biorobotics: New Perspectives. *Front. Bioeng. Biotechnol.* **2014**, *2*, 2. [CrossRef] [PubMed]
6. Shintake, J.; Cacucciolo, V.; Floreano, D.; Shea, H. Soft Robotic Grippers. *Adv. Mater.* **2018**, *30*, 1707035. [CrossRef]
7. Walker, J.; Zidek, T.; Harbel, C.; Yoon, S.; Strickland, F.S.; Kumar, S.; Shin, M. Soft Robotics: A Review of Recent Developments of Pneumatic Soft Actuators. *Actuators* **2020**, *9*, 3. [CrossRef]
8. Lens, T.; von Stryk, O. Design and dynamics model of a lightweight series elastic tendon-driven robot arm. In Proceedings of the 2013 IEEE International Conference on Robotics and Automation, Karlsruhe, Germany, 6–10 May 2013; pp. 4512–4518. [CrossRef]
9. Marjaninejad, A.; Tan, J.; Valero-Cuevas, F. Autonomous Control of a Tendon-driven Robotic Limb with Elastic Elements Reveals that Added Elasticity can Enhance Learning. In Proceedings of the 2020 42nd Annual International Conference of the IEEE Engineering in Medicine & Biology Society (EMBC), Montreal, QC, Canada, 20–24 July 2020; Volume 2020, pp. 4680–4686. [CrossRef]
10. Rombokas, E.; Malhotra, M.; Theodorou, E.A.; Todorov, E.; Matsuoka, Y. Reinforcement Learning and Synergistic Control of the ACT Hand. *IEEE/ASME Trans. Mechatron.* **2013**, *18*, 569–577. [CrossRef]
11. Rus, D.; Tolley, M.T. Design, fabrication and control of soft robots. *Nature* **2015**, *521*, 467–475. [CrossRef]
12. Villoslada, A.; Rivera, C.; Escudero, N.; Martín, F.; Blanco, D.; Moreno, L. Hand Exo-Muscular System for Assisting Astronauts During Extravehicular Activities. *Soft Robot.* **2018**, *6*. [CrossRef]
13. Long, Y.; Du, Z.; Cong, L.; Wang, W.; Zhang, Z.; Dong, W. Active disturbance rejection control based human gait tracking for lower extremity rehabilitation exoskeleton. *ISA Trans.* **2017**, *67*, 389–397. [CrossRef]
14. Wang, J.; Fei, Y.; Pang, W. Design, Modeling, and Testing of a Soft Pneumatic Glove with Segmented PneuNets Bending Actuators. *IEEE/ASME Trans. Mechatron.* **2019**, *24*, 990–1001. [CrossRef]
15. Wang, T.; Zhang, Y.; Chen, Z.; Zhu, S. Parameter Identification and Model-Based Nonlinear Robust Control of Fluidic Soft Bending Actuators. *IEEE/ASME Trans. Mechatron.* **2019**, *24*, 1346–1355. [CrossRef]
16. Polygerinos, P.; Wang, Z.; Overvelde, J.T.; Galloway, K.C.; Wood, R.J.; Bertoldi, K.; Walsh, C.J. Modeling of soft fiber-reinforced bending actuators. *IEEE Trans. Robot.* **2015**, *31*, 778–789. [CrossRef]
17. Gong, Z.; Xie, Z.; Yang, X.; Wang, T.; Wen, L. Design, fabrication and kinematic modeling of a 3D-motion soft robotic arm. In Proceedings of the 2016 IEEE International Conference on Robotics and Biomimetics (ROBIO), Qingdao, China, 3–7 December 2016; pp. 509–514.
18. Chen, X.; Guo, Y.; Duanmu, D.; Zhou, J.; Zhang, W.; Wang, Z. Design and Modeling of an Extensible Soft Robotic Arm. *IEEE Robot. Autom. Lett.* **2019**, *4*, 4208–4215. [CrossRef]
19. Xiloyannis, M.; Cappello, L.; Khanh, D.B.; Yen, S.C.; Masia, L. Modeling and design of a synergy-based actuator for a tendon-driven soft robotic glove. In Proceedings of the 2016 6th IEEE International Conference on Biomedical Robotics and Biomechatronics (BioRob), Singapore, 26–29 June 2016; pp. 1213–1219.
20. Nycz, C.J.; Delph, M.A.; Fischer, G.S. Modeling and design of a tendon actuated soft robotic exoskeleton for hemiparetic upper limb rehabilitation. In Proceedings of the 2015 37th Annual International Conference of the IEEE Engineering in Medicine and Biology Society (EMBC), Milan, Italy, 25–29 August 2015; pp. 3889–3892.
21. Yuen, M.C.; Tonoyan, H.; White, E.L.; Telleria, M.; Kramer, R.K. Fabric sensory sleeves for soft robot state estimation. In Proceedings of the 2017 IEEE International Conference on Robotics and Automation (ICRA), Singapore, 29 May–3 June 2017; pp. 5511–5518. [CrossRef]
22. Elgeneidy, K.; Lohse, N.; Jackson, M. Data-Driven Bending Angle Prediction of Soft Pneumatic Actuators with Embedded Flex Sensors. *IFAC-PapersOnLine* **2016**, *49*, 513–520. [CrossRef]

23. She, Y.; Li, C.; Cleary, J.; Su, H.J. Design and Fabrication of a Soft Robotic Hand With Embedded Actuators and Sensors. *J. Mech. Robot.* **2015**, *7*. [CrossRef]

24. Dobrzynski, M.K.; Pericet-Camara, R.; Floreano, D. Contactless deflection sensor for soft robots. In Proceedings of the 2011 IEEE/RSJ International Conference on Intelligent Robots and Systems, San Francisco, CA, USA, 25–30 September 2011; pp. 1913–1918. [CrossRef]

25. Wang, R.; Wang, S.; Du, S.; Xiao, E.; Yuan, W.; Feng, C. Real-Time Soft Body 3D Proprioception via Deep Vision-Based Sensing. *IEEE Robot. Autom. Lett.* **2020**, *5*, 3382–3389. [CrossRef]

26. Mena, L.; Monje, C.A.; Nagua, L.; Muñoz, J.; Balaguer, C. Sensorización de un sistema de eslabón blando actuando como cuello robótico. In *Actas de las Jornadas Nacionales de Robótica*; Universidad de Alicante: Alicante, Spain, 2019; pp. 98–102.

27. Nagua, L.; Monje, C.; Muñoz Yañez-Barnuevo, J.; Balaguer, C. Design and performance validation of a cable-driven soft robotic neck. In *Actas de las Jornadas Nacionales de Robótica*; Universidad de Valladolid: Valladolid, Spain, 2018.

28. Quevedo, F.; Yañez-Barnuevo, J.M.; Castano, J.A.; Monje, C.A.; Balaguer, C. Model Identification of a Soft Robotic Neck. In Proceedings of the 2020 IEEE/RSJ International Conference on Intelligent Robots and Systems (IROS), Las Vegas, NV, USA, 24 October–24 January 2020; pp. 8640–8645. [CrossRef]

29. Martín Barrio, A.; Terrile, S.; Barrientos, A.; del Cerro, J. Robots Hiper-Redundantes: Clasificación, Estado del Arte y Problemática. *Rev. Iberoam. Automática e Inf. Ind.* **2018**, *15*, 351–362. [CrossRef]

30. Martin, A.; Barrientos, A.; del Cerro, J. The Natural-CCD Algorithm, a Novel Method to Solve the Inverse Kinematics of Hyper-redundant and Soft Robots. *Soft Robot.* **2018**, *5*, 242–257. [CrossRef]

31. Nagua, L.; Muñoz, J.; Monje, C.A.; Balaguer, C. A first approach to a proposal of a soft robotic link acting as a neck. In *Actas de las Jornadas de Automática*; Área de Ingeniería de Sistemas y Automática; Universidad de Extremadura: Badajoz, Spain, 2018; pp. 522–529.

32. Milanese, M.; Novara, C. Set Membership identification of nonlinear systems. *Automatica* **2004**, *40*, 957–975. [CrossRef]

33. Landau, I.D.; Lozano, R.; M'Saad, M.; Karimi, A. Parameter Adaptation Algorithms—Deterministic Environment. In *Adaptive Control: Algorithms, Analysis and Applications*; Springer: London, UK, 2011; pp. 55–120. [CrossRef]

34. Castaño, J.; Ruiz, F.; Régnier, J. A Fast Approximation Algorithm for Set-Membership System Identification. *IFAC Proc. Vol.* **2011**, *44*, 4410–4415. [CrossRef]

35. Castano, J.; Ruiz, F. Set membership identification of an excimer lamp for fast simulation. *Control Eng. Pract.* **2013**, *21*, 96–104. [CrossRef]

36. Åström, K.; Eykhoff, P. System identification—A survey. *Automatica* **1971**, *7*, 123–162. [CrossRef]

Article

Automatic Convexity Deduction for Efficient Function's Range Bounding

Mikhail Posypkin [1,*] and Oleg Khamisov [2]

[1] Federal Research Center "Computer Science and Control" of the Russian Academy of Sciences, Vavilova 44-2, 119333 Moscow, Russia

[2] Melentiev Energy Systems Institute of Siberian Branch of the Russian Academy of Sciences, Lermontov St., 130, 664033 Irkutsk, Russia; globopt@mail.ru

* Correspondence: mposypkin@gmail.com

Abstract: Reliable bounding of a function's range is essential for deterministic global optimization, approximation, locating roots of nonlinear equations, and several other computational mathematics areas. Despite years of extensive research in this direction, there is still room for improvement. The traditional and compelling approach to this problem is interval analysis. We show that accounting convexity/concavity can significantly tighten the bounds computed by interval analysis. To make our approach applicable to a broad range of functions, we also develop the techniques for handling nondifferentiable composite functions. Traditional ways to ensure the convexity fail in such cases. Experimental evaluation showed the remarkable potential of the proposed methods.

Keywords: interval analysis; function approximation; global optimization; convexity evaluation; overestimators; underestimators

Citation: Posypkin, M.; Khamisov, O. Automatic Convexity Deduction for Efficient Function's Range Bounding. *Mathematics* **2021**, *9*, 134. https://doi.org/10.3390/math9020134

Received: 2 December 2020
Accepted: 7 January 2021
Published: 10 January 2021

1. Introduction

Reliable bounding of univariate functions is one of the primary techniques in global optimization, i.e., finding the solution for the following problem:

$$f(x) \to \min, \; x \in [a, b]. \tag{1}$$

The problem (1) has many practical applications [1–6]. Besides solving problems of one variable, univariate search serves as an auxiliary method in multivariate global optimization. A promising optimization technique known as space-filling curves reduces an optimization [7,8] or approximation [9] problem of multiple variables to a sequence of univariate problems. Univariate optimization techniques are widely used in separable programming [10], where an objective and constraints are sums of functions of one variable. Many univariate optimization methods are directly extended to the multivariate case [11,12].

Univariate global optimization has been intensively studied last decades. The first results date back to the early 1970s. Seminal works in this area [13–16] relied on the Lipschitzian property of a function:

$$|f(x) - f(y)| \leq L|x - y|, \; \text{for any } x, y \in [a, b]. \tag{2}$$

In [14,15] the "saw-tooth cover" lower and upper bounding functions for Lipschitzian objectives were proposed. The lower (upper) bounding functions were defined as $\max_{i \in 1, \ldots, n} f(x_i) - L|x - x_i|$ ($\min_{i \in 1, \ldots, n} f(x_i) + L|x - x_i|$), where L is a Lipschitz constant and $\{x_1, \ldots, x_n\}$ is a set of function evaluation points. Since the functions are piecewise linear, their range can be easily computed. This makes such estimates attractive for bounding an objective from below and/or above. Other approaches exploiting the property (2) were studied in numerous papers [17–19]. In papers [20–22], the Lipschitzian first derivatives were used to facilitate the global search. Good surveys on Lipschitzian optimization can be found in [7,23–25].

Interval analysis [26,27] is another powerful technique for global optimization. The goal of interval analysis is to find the tightest enclosing interval for a range of a function. The left end of the enclosing interval provides a lower bound for a function over an interval that can be used to reduce the search space in global optimization methods. Most promising approaches are based on interval arithmetic, and more advanced techniques based on interval Taylor expansions [26,28]. Promising approaches based on combining Lipschitzian optimization and interval analysis ideas were proposed in [29]. Efficient optimization algorithms based on piecewise linear [30,31], piecewise convex [32], slopes techniques [33], and DC-decomposition [34,35] should also be mentioned.

The approaches outlined above apply various methods to obtain bounds on a range of a function. However, they do not analyze the convexity of the objective function. Meanwhile, the convexity plays an essential role in global optimization. If the objective is proved to be convex, then efficient local search techniques can be applied to locate its minimum. For example, the univariate convexification technique developed in [36] even sacrifices the dimensionality of the problem for convexity.

The convexity test [26] helps to reduce the search region by pruning areas where a function is proved to be nonconvex. Usually, the convexity is checked by analyzing the range of the second derivative. If this range lies above (below) zero, the function is convex (concave). This approach works only for functions with continuous second derivatives.

Checking convexity is, in general, an NP-hard problem (see [37]) and references therein. Approaches based on the symbolical proof and the numerical disproof of convexity are described in [38]. In the context of convexity checking, it is necessary to mention the disciplined convex programming [39,40], which also relies on a set of rules for proving the convexity of the problem under consideration. However, authors limit their techniques to proving the convexity of the entire mathematical programming problem for a subsequent use of convex programming methods. As we show below, monotonicity, convexity and concavity properties can also remarkably improve the accuracy of interval bounds when applied to subexpression of the function's algebraic representation.

The main contribution of our paper is the novel techniques for bounding the function's range by accounting monotonicity, convexity or concavity of subexpressions of its algebraic expression. This approach efficiently restricts the objective function's range even if the latter is not convex neither concave. We proved experimentally that the introduced techniques can significantly reduce the bounds on the function's range and remarkably enhance the conventional interval global search procedures. A set of rules for deducing monotonicity, concavity and convexity properties of a univariate function from its algebraic expression is clearly and concisely formulated and proved. These rules complement the traditional ways of establishing the properties of the objective function based on evaluating its derivatives' ranges.

Notation:

$\mathbb{R}$ — the set of real numbers;

$\mathbb{Z}$ — the set of integers;

$\mathbb{N}$ — the set of positive integers (natural numbers);

$\mathbb{IR}$ — the set of all intervals in $\mathbb{R}$;

$\mathbf{x} = [\underline{x}, \overline{x}]$ — intervals are denoted with bold font;

$\mathcal{R}_f([a,b]) = \{y \in \mathbb{R} : y = f(x) \text{ for some } x \in [a,b]\}$ — the range of function $f \colon \mathbb{R} \to \mathbb{R}$ over interval $[a,b]$;

$\mathbf{f}$—an interval extension of a function $f : \mathbb{R} \to \mathbb{R}$, i.e., a mapping $\mathbf{f} \colon \mathbb{IR} \to \mathbb{IR}$ such that $\mathcal{R}_f([a,b]) \subseteq \mathbf{f}([a,b])$ for any $[a,b] \in \mathbb{IR}$, notice, there may be many different interval extensions for a function $f(x)$;

$f(x) \nearrow$—$f(x)$ is non-decreasing monotonic on $\mathbb{R}$ or an interval if additionally specified;

$f(x) \searrow$—$f(x)$ is non-increasing monotonic on $\mathbb{R}$ or an interval if additionally specified.

By elementary functions we mean commonly used mathematical functions, i.e., power exponential, logarithmic and trigonometric functions. We distinguish smooth elementary functions that have derivatives of any order in the domain of the definition and nonsmooth functions, which are nondifferentiable at some points. The list of elementary functions supported by our method is given in Table 1. Notice that other elementary functions can be expressed as algebraic expressions over the functions listed in the table and thus omitted. We consider only univariate functions in what follows. Thus, we do not mention it in each statement. We restrict our study to the case of continuous functions.

Table 1. Supported elementary functions.

Type	Smooth	Non-Smooth
One variable	x^n, $\sqrt[n]{x}$, $1/x$, $\ln(x)$, e^x $\sin(x)$, $\arcsin(x)$, $\arctan(x)$	$\lvert x \rvert$
Two variables	$x + y$, $x \cdot y$	$\max(x, y)$, $\max(x, y)$

The paper is organized as follows. Section 2 describes the deduction techniques to evaluate the convexity/concavity of a function automatically. Then, in Section 3 it is shown how this technique is used to bound the range of a function. Section 4 contains the experimental results demonstrating the the the proposed approach's efficiency. Section 5 concludes the paper and discusses possible future research directions.

2. Automatic Deduction of the Convexity and Concavity of a Function

2.1. Deducing Monotonicity

The monotonicity significantly helps in global optimization. If a function $f(x)$ is monotonically nondecreasing on a segment $[a, b]$, then $\min_{x \in [a,b]} f(x) = f(a)$, $\max_{x \in [a,b]} f(x) = f(b)$ and the segment $[a, b]$ can be eliminated from further consideration after updating the record (best known solution so far). A similar statement is valid for a nonincreasing function. This techniques is known as the monotonicity test [26,41,42]. Moreover, as it is shown below, the monotonicity is crucial for evaluating the convexity/concavity of a composite function.

The usual way to ensure the monotonicity of a differentiable univariate function $f(x)$ on an interval $[a, b]$ is to compute an interval extension for its derivative $[c, d] = \mathbf{f}'([a, b])$. If $c \geq 0$, then the function is nondecreasing monotonic on $[a, b]$. Similarly, if $d \leq 0$, then the function is nonincreasing monotonic on $[a, b]$.

If a function is not differentiable, its monotonicity can still be evaluated using the rules described below. The Proposition 1 lists rules for evaluating an expression's monotonicity composed with the simple arithmetic operations.

Proposition 1. *The following rules hold:*

1. *if $f(x) \nearrow$ on $[a, b]$ then $-f(x) \searrow$ on $[a, b]$;*
2. *if $f(x) \searrow$ on $[a, b]$ then $-f(x) \nearrow$ on $[a, b]$;*
3. *if $f(x) \nearrow$ and $g(x) \nearrow$ on $[a, b]$ then $f(x) + g(x) \nearrow$ on $[a, b]$;*
4. *if $f(x) \nearrow$, $f(x) \geq 0$ and $g(x) \nearrow$, $g(x) \geq 0$ on $[a, b]$ then $f(x) \cdot g(x) \nearrow$ on $[a, b]$;*
5. *if $f(x) \nearrow$ and $g(x) \nearrow$ on $[a, b]$ then $\min(f(x), g(x)) \nearrow$ on $[a, b]$;*
6. *if $f(x) \nearrow$ and $g(x) \nearrow$ on $[a, b]$ then $\max(f(x), g(x)) \nearrow$ on $[a, b]$.*

The proof of Proposition 1 is obvious. The rules for evaluating the monotonicity of the composition of functions are summarized in Proposition 2. The proof is intuitive and not presented here.

Proposition 2. *Let $f(x)$ be a composition of univariate functions $g(x)$ and $h(x)$: $f(x) = g(h(x))$. Then, the following four statements hold.*

1. *If $h(x) \nearrow$ on $[a, b]$, $g(x) \nearrow$ on $[c, d]$ and $\mathcal{R}_h([a, b]) \subseteq [c, d]$ then $f(x) \nearrow$ on $[a, b]$.*

2. If $h(x) \searrow$ on $[a,b]$, $g(x) \nearrow$ on $[c,d]$ and $\mathcal{R}_h([a,b]) \subseteq [c,d]$ then $f(x) \searrow$ on $[a,b]$.
3. If $h(x) \nearrow$ on $[a,b]$, $g(x) \searrow$ on $[c,d]$, $\mathcal{R}_h([a,b]) \subseteq [c,d]$ then $f(x) \searrow$ on $[a,b]$.
4. If $h(x) \searrow$ on $[a,b]$, $g(x) \searrow$ on $[c,d]$, $\mathcal{R}_h([a,b]) \subseteq [c,d]$ then $f(x) \nearrow$ on $[a,b]$.

The monotonicity of elementary univariate functions on a given interval can easily be established as these functions' behavior is well-known (Table 2).

Table 2. The monotonicity of elementary functions.

Function	Increase	Decrease
$\lvert x \rvert$	$[0,\infty)$	$(-\infty, 0]$
$x^{2n+1}, n \in \mathbb{N}, e^x,$	$(-\infty, \infty)$	—
$x^{2n}, n \in \mathbb{N}$	$[0,\infty)$	$(-\infty, 0]$
$\sqrt[n]{x}$	$[0,\infty)$	—
$\ln(x)$	$(0,\infty)$	—
$1/x$	—	$(-\infty, 0) \cup (0, \infty)$
$\sin(x)$	$[-\pi/2 + 2\pi k, \pi/2 + 2\pi k], k \in \mathbb{Z}$	$[\pi/2 + 2\pi k, 3\pi/2 + 2\pi k], k \in \mathbb{Z}$
$\arcsin(x)$	$[-1,1]$	—
$\arctan(x)$	$(-\infty, \infty)$	—

The monotonicity of a composite function defined by an arbitrary complex algebraic expression can be evaluated automatically using Propositions 1 and 2 and the data from the Tables 2. Let us consider an example.

Example 1. *Evaluate the monotonicity of the function* $f(x) = \max(3 - x, 1/\ln(x+1))$, *where* $x \in [0.1, 3]$. *This function is nonsmooth: it can be easily shown that* $f(x)$ *does not have derivatives in two points on* $[0.1, 3]$. *Apply rules from Propositions 1 and 2:*

$$x \nearrow \text{ on } [0.1, 3], 1 \nearrow \text{ on } [0.1, 3] \;\Rightarrow\; x + 1 \nearrow \text{ on } [0.1, 3],$$

$$x + 1 \nearrow \text{ on } [0.1, 3], \ln(x) \nearrow \text{ on } [1.1, 4] \;\Rightarrow\; \ln(x+1) \nearrow \text{ on } [0.1, 3],$$

$$\ln(x+1) \nearrow \text{ on } [0.1, 3], \ln(x+1) > 0 \text{ on } [0.1, 3] \;\Rightarrow\; 1/\ln(x+1) \searrow \text{ on } [0.1, 3].$$

Thus, $1/\ln(x+1)$ *is nonincreasing monotonic on* $[0.1, 3]$. *In the same way, it can be established that* $3 - x$ *is nonincreasing monotonic on* $[0.1, 3]$. *From the Proposition 1, it follows that* $f(x) = \max(3 - x, 1/\ln(x+1))$ *is also nonincreasing monotonic on* $[0.1, 3]$.

It is worth noting that the rules outlined above help to prove the monotonicity of nondifferentiable functions. However, for differentiable functions, the analysis of the the range of the first derivative is a better way to establish monotonicity. For example, a function $f(x) = e^x + \sin(x)$ is monotonic on an interval $[0, 2\pi]$. Indeed, the range $[0, e^{2\pi} + 1]$ of its first derivative $f'(x) = e^x + \cos(x)$ computed by the natural interval expansion is non-negative. However, its monotonicty cannot be established by the outlined rules since $\sin(x)$ is not monotonic on $[0, 2\pi]$. The general recommendation is to compute the first derivative's range when the function is smooth and use Propositions 1 and 2 otherwise.

Monotonicity itself plays a vital role in optimization. The following obviously valid Proposition shows how the interval bounds can be computed for a monotonic function.

Proposition 3. *Let* $f(x)$ *be a monotonic function on an interval* $[a,b]$. *Then*

$$\min_{x \in [a,b]} f(x) = \min(f(a), f(b)),$$

$$\max_{x \in [a,b]} f(x) = \max(f(a), f(b)).$$

2.2. Deducing Convexity

First, we recall some well-known mathematical notions used in the rest of the paper. A function $f(x)$ is *convex on an interval* $[a, b]$ if

$$f(\lambda x_1 + (1 - \lambda)x_2) \le \lambda f(x_1) + (1 - \lambda)f(x_2). \tag{3}$$

for any $x_1, x_2, a \le x_1 \le x_2 \le b$ and any $\lambda, 0 \le \lambda \le 1$. A function $f(x)$ is called concave on the interval $[a, b]$ if $-f(x)$ is convex on $[a, b]$.

Convexity plays an important role in optimization due to the following two observations. If a function is convex on some interval, then a minimum point of $f(x)$ can be efficiently found by well elaborated local search techniques [43,44]. If a function $f(x)$ is concave on $[a, b]$, then $\min_{x \in [a,b]} f(x) = \min(f(a), f(b))$.

If the function is two times differentiable, the convexity can be deduced from the second derivative. If one can prove that $f''(x) \ge 0 (\le 0)$ on a segment $[a, b]$, then $f(x)$ is convex (concave) on this segment. However, if the function is nonsmooth, the convexity property should be computed in some other way. Even if $f(x)$ is smooth, the accurate bounding of its second derivative can be a complicated task, and the convexity test becomes difficult.

The conical combination and the maximum of two functions are known to preserve convexity. The proof can be found in seminal books on convex analysis, e.g., [43]. For the sake of completeness, we reproduce these rules in the following Proposition 4.

Proposition 4. *Let $f(x)$ and $g(x)$ be convex functions on an interval $[a, b]$. Then, the following statements hold:*

1. $f(x) + g(x)$ *is convex on* $[a, b]$,
2. $\alpha f(x)$ *is convex on* $[a, b]$ *if* $\alpha > 0$,
3. $\max(f(x), g(x))$ *is convex on* $[a, b]$.

The product of two convex functions is not always a convex function. For example, $(x - 1)(x^2 - 4)$ is not convex while both $x - 1$ and $x^2 - 4$ are convex functions on $\mathbb{R}$. In [45], it is proved that if f and g are two positive convex functions defined on an interval $[a, b]$, then their product is convex provided that they are synchronous in the sense that

$$(f(x) - f(y))(g(x) - g(y)) \ge 0$$

for all $x, y \in I$. However checking this general property automatically is difficult. Instead, we propose the following sufficient condition that can be effectively evaluated.

Proposition 5. *Let $f(x)$ and $g(x)$ be convex positive functions on an interval $[a, b]$ such that $f(x)$ and $g(x)$ are both nonincreasing or both nondecreasing. Then, the function $h(x) = f(x)g(x)$ is convex on $[a, b]$.*

Proof. Consider $\lambda, 0 < \lambda < 1$ and $y = \lambda a + (1 - \lambda)b$. Since $f(x)$ and $g(x)$ are convex, we get

$$f(y) \le f(b) + \lambda(f(a) - f(b)),$$
$$g(y) \le g(b) + \lambda(g(a) - g(b)).$$

Since $f(y) \ge 0$ and $g(y) \ge 0$, we get

$$h(y) = f(y)g(y) \le q(\lambda),$$

where

$$q(\lambda) = (f(b) + \lambda(f(a) - f(b)))(g(b) + \lambda(g(a) - g(b))))$$

is a quadratic function. Since $f(x)$ and $g(x)$ are both nonincreasing or both nondecreasing, we have that $(f(a) - f(b))(g(a) - g(b)) \geq 0$. Therefore $q(\lambda)$ is convex. Note that $q(0) = h(b), q(1) = h(a)$. From convexity of $q(\lambda)$, we obtain the following inequality:

$$q(\lambda) = q((1 - \lambda) \cdot 0 + \lambda \cdot 1) \leq (1 - \lambda)q(0) + \lambda q(1) = \lambda h(a) + (1 - \lambda)h(b).$$

This completes the proof. $\square$

Propositions 4 and 5 can be readily reformulated for concave functions. The following Proposition gives rules for evaluating the convexity of a composite function.

Proposition 6. *Let $f(x) = g(h(x))$ and there be intervals $[a, b]$, $[c, d]$ such that $\mathcal{R}_h([a, b]) \subseteq [c, d]$. Then, the following holds:*

1. *g is convex and nondecreasing on $[c, d]$, h is convex on $[a, b]$, then f is convex on $[a, b]$,*
2. *g is convex and nonincreasing on $[c, d]$, h is concave on $[a, b]$, then f is convex on $[a, b]$,*
3. *g is concave and nondecreasing on $[c, d]$, h is concave on $[a, b]$, then f is concave on $[a, b]$,*
4. *g is concave and nonincreasing on $[c, d]$, h is convex on $[a, b]$, then f is concave on $[a, b]$.*

The proof of the Proposition 6 can be found in numerous books for convex analysis, e.g., [43].

Many elementary functions are convex/concave on a whole domain of the definition, e.g., e^x, $\ln x$, x^n for even natural n. For other functions, the intervals of concavity/convexity can be efficiently established as these function's behavior is well-known (Table 3).

Table 3. The convexity/concavity of elementary functions.

Function	Convex	Concave
$\lvert x \rvert, x^{2n}, n \in \mathbb{N}, e^x$	$(-\infty, \infty)$	—
$x^{2n+1}, n \in \mathbb{N},$	$[0, \infty)$	$(-\infty, 0]$
$\sqrt[n]{x}$	—	$[0, \infty)$
$\ln(x)$	—	$(0, \infty)$
$1/x$	$(0, \infty)$	$(-\infty, 0)$
$\sin(x)$	$[-\pi + 2\pi k, 2\pi k], k \in \mathbb{Z}$	$[2\pi k, \pi + 2\pi k], k \in \mathbb{Z}$
$\arcsin(x)$	$[0, 1]$	$[-1, 0]$
$\arctan(x)$	$(-\infty, 0]$	$[0, \infty)$

Propositions 4–6 enable an automated convexity deduction for composite functions, as the following examples show.

Example 2. *Consider the function $f(x) = 2^x + 2^{-x}$ on the interval $[-1, 1]$. The function 2^x is convex on $[-1, 1]$ and nondecreasing. The function $-x$ is convex on $[-1, 1]$. According to the Proposition 6 function, 2^{-x} is convex. Since 2^x is also convex, we conclude (Proposition 4) that $2^x + 2^{-x}$ is convex.*

It is worth noting that the convexity can be proved by computing the interval bounds for the second derivative in the considered example. Indeed, $f''(x) = \ln^2(2) \times 2^x + \dfrac{\ln^2(2)}{2^x}$ is obviously positive on $[-1, 1]$. Since there are plenty of tools for automatic differentiation and interval computations, the convexity can be proved automatically.

However, a convex function does not necessarily have derivatives in all points. Moreover, even if it is piecewise differentiable, locating the points where the function is not continuously differentiable can be difficult. Fortunately, the theory outlined above efficiently copes with such situations.

Example 3. *Consider the following function*

$$f(x) = \max(x, 2 - \sin(x)) + e^{-x}$$

on an interval $[0, \pi]$. Since $\sin(x)$ is concave on $[0, \pi]$, we conclude that $2 - \sin(x)$ is convex on $[0, \pi]$. The convexity of e^{-x} follows from the convexity of the linear function $-x$ and the Proposition 6. From the convexity of x, $2 - \sin(x)$, e^{-x} and Proposition 4 we derive that $f(x)$ is convex.

Notice that automatic symbolic differentiation techniques cannot compute the derivative of $f(x)$ because it involves computing the intersection points of x and $2 - \sin(x)$ functions, which is a rather complex problem.

3. Application to Bounding the Function's Range

An obvious application of the proposed techniques is the convexity/concavity test [26] that helps to eliminate the interval from the further consideration and reduce the number of steps of branch-and-bound algorithms. Consider the following problem:

$$f(x) \rightarrow \min, x \in [a, b]. \tag{4}$$

If the objective $f(x)$ is concave on $[a, b]$, then the global minimum can be easily computed as follows: $f(x_*) = \min(f(a), f(b))$. If the concavity does not hold for the entire search region, the test can be used in branch-and-bound, interval Newton or other global minimization methods by applying it to subintervals of $[a, b]$ processed by the algorithm.

However, if the objective is convex on $[a, b]$, then any local minimum in $[a, b]$ is a global minimum and can be easily found by a local search procedure. Since any continuously differentiable function is convex or concave on a sufficiently small interval, the convexity/concavity test can tremendously reduce the number of algorithm's steps by preventing excessive branching.

Another situation commonly encountered in practice occurs when a subexpression represents a convex/concave function while the entire function is not convex neither concave. For example, the function $0.5 - cos(x)$ is convex on interval $[-\pi/2, \pi/2]$ while $(0.5 - cos(x))^3$ is not. In such cases, the interval cannot be discarded by the convexity/concavity test. Nevertheless, the convexity and concavity can be used to compute tight upper and lower bounds for the sub-expression yielding better bounds for the entire function.

For computing upper and lower bounds, recall that a convex function graph always lies above any of its tangents. This property and the convexity definition yield the Proposition 7.

Proposition 7. *Let $f(x)$ be a convex function on $[a, b]$. Then*

$$\underline{f}(x) \leq f(x) \leq \overline{f}(x), \text{ for all } x \in [a, b], \tag{5}$$

where

$$\underline{f}(x) = \max\left(f(a) + f'(a)(x - a), f(b) + f'(b)(x - b)\right),$$
$$\overline{f}(x) = f(a) + (f(b) - f(a))\frac{x - a}{b - a}. \tag{6}$$

Proof. First, prove that $\underline{f}(x)$ is an underestimator for $f(x)$. For a function $f(x)$ convex on an interval $[a, b]$ and a point $t \in [a, b]$, the following inequality holds [43]:

$$f(x) \geq f(t) + f'(t)(x - t), \text{ for all } x \in [a, b]. \tag{7}$$

Substituting t with a and b in (7), we get the following system of valid inequalities:

$$f(x) \geq f(a) + f'(a)(x - a), \text{ for all } x \in [a, b],$$
$$f(x) \geq f(b) + f'(b)(x - b), \text{ for all } x \in [a, b].$$
$$(8)$$

From (8), it directly follows that

$$f(x) \geq \max\left(f(a) + f'(a)(x - a), f(b) + f'(b)(x - b)\right), \text{ for all } x \in [a, b].$$

The right part is $\underline{f}(x)$ from (6).

Now prove that $\overline{f}(x)$ is the overestimator for $f(x)$. Taking $x_1 = a$, $x_2 = b$, $\lambda = \frac{b-x}{b-a}$ in the definition of a convex function (3) we obtain:

$$f(x) \leq \frac{b-x}{b-a} f(a) + \left(1 - \frac{b-x}{b-a}\right) f(b) = \left(1 - \frac{x-a}{b-a}\right) f(a) + \frac{x-a}{b-a} f(b)$$
$$= f(a) + (f(b) - f(a)) \frac{x-a}{b-a}.$$

The rightmost part is $\overline{f}(x)$ from (6). This completes the proof. $\square$

Proposition 7 is illustrated in Figure 1. The figure shows the original function $f(x)$ (blue curve), its overestimator consisting of one green line segment and the underestimator consisting of two connected line segments AC and CB marked with red. The estimators are constructed by following (6).

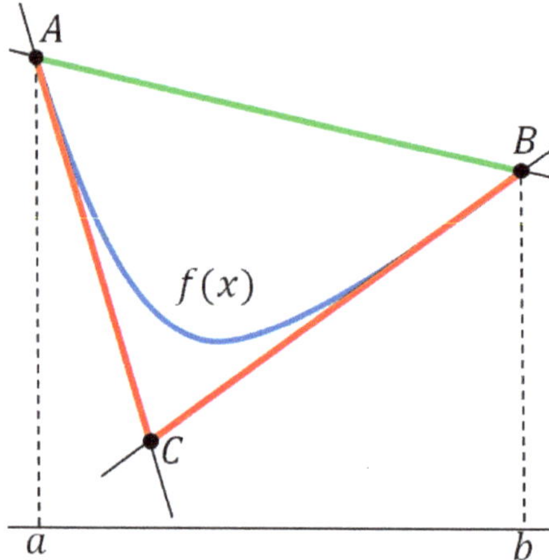

Figure 1. The overestimator (green) and the underestimator (red) of a convex function $f(x)$ on an interval $[a, b]$.

The similar proposition holds for concave functions.

Proposition 8. *Let $f(x)$ be a concave function over on $[a, b]$. Then*

$$\underline{f}(x) \leq f(x) \leq \overline{f}(x), \text{ for all } x \in [a, b],$$
$$(9)$$

where

$$\underline{f}(x) = f(a) + (f(b) - f(a)) \frac{x-a}{b-a},$$
$$\overline{f}(x) = \min\left(f(a) + f'(a)(x - a), f(b) + f'(b)(x - b)\right).$$
$$(10)$$

Proof. This statement is a straightforward corollary of Proposition 7. Indeed, if $f(x)$ is concave then $-f(x)$ is convex and one can apply Formula (6) to obtain its estimators. After changing the sign and reversing the inequalities we get (10). $\square$

Fortunately, the minimum and maximum of estimators $\underline{f}(x)$ and $\overline{f}(x)$ can be found analytically as stated by the following propositions.

Proposition 9. *If a function f is convex on an interval $[a,b]$ then*

$$\max_{x\in[a,b]} f(x) = \max(f(a), f(b)), \tag{11}$$

$$\min_{x\in[a,b]} f(x) = f(a), \ \text{if } f'(a) \geq 0, \tag{12}$$

$$\min_{x\in[a,b]} f(x) = f(b), \ \text{if } f'(b) \leq 0, \tag{13}$$

$$\min_{x\in[a,b]} f(x) \geq \frac{f'(b)f(a) - f'(a)f(b)}{f'(b) - f'(a)} + f'(a)f'(b)\frac{b-a}{f'(b) - f'(a)} \tag{14}$$

otherwise.

Proof. Equation (11) is obviously valid. Denote $\alpha = f'(a)$, $\beta = f'(b)$. Equation (12) follows from the fact the function $f(x)$ lies above its tangent $f(a) + \alpha(x - a)$, coincides with it at $x = a$ and the tangent is a monotonically nondecreasing function. In the same way, Equation (13) is proved.

For the remaining case $\alpha < 0 < \beta$ the minimum of the underestimator is achieved at the intersection point of lines defined by $f(a) + \alpha(x - a)$, $f(b) + \beta(x - b)$ (point C in the Figure 1). This point is the solution of the following equation:

$$f(a) + \alpha(x - a) = f(b) + \beta(x - b).$$

Simple transformations yield:

$$f(a) - f(b) + \beta b - \alpha a = x(\beta - \alpha).$$

Since $\alpha \neq \beta$ the minimum of the underestimator is achieved at the point

$$x = \frac{f(a) - f(b) + \beta b - \alpha a}{\beta - \alpha}.$$

Substituting this value to $f(a) + \alpha(x - a)$ we obtain:

$$\min_{x\in[a,b]} \underline{f}(x) = \frac{\beta f(a) - \alpha f(b)}{\beta - \alpha} + \alpha\beta\frac{b-a}{\beta - \alpha}.$$

This concludes the proof. $\square$

Similarly, the validity of the following Proposition giving bounds for a concave function is justified.

Proposition 10. *If a function f is concave over an interval $[a,b]$ then*

$$\min_{x\in[a,b]} f(x) = \min(f(a), f(b)), \tag{15}$$

$$\max_{x\in[a,b]} f(x) = f(a), \ \text{if } f'(a) \leq 0, \tag{16}$$

$$\max_{x\in[a,b]} f(x) = f(b), \ \text{if } f'(b) \geq 0, \tag{17}$$

$$\max_{x\in[a,b]} f(x) \le \frac{f'(b)f(a) - f'(a)f(b)}{f'(b) - f'(a)} + f'(a)f'(b)\frac{b-a}{f'(b) - f'(a)} \tag{18}$$

otherwise.

Proof. This statement is a straightforward corollary of Proposition 9. Indeed, if $f(x)$ is concave then $-f(x)$ is convex and one can apply Formulas (11)–(14) to obtain its estimators. After changing the sign and reversing the inequalities, we get Formulas (15)–(18). $\square$

The bounds computed with the help of the Propositions 9 and 10 are often more precise with respect to other bounds. Below we compare the ranges computed according to Propositions 9 and 10 with the results of interval analysis techniques.

4. Numerical Experiments

In this section, we experimentally evaluate the proposed approach. First, in Section 4.1 the interval bounds and bounds computed with the proposed techniques are compared for a set of functions. In Section 4.2, we study the impact of the accounting of the monotonicity and convexity properties on global optimization algorithms' performance.

4.1. Comparison with Interval Bounds

We selected two well-known [26,28] interval analysis techniques for computing the range of a function. The first is the *natural interval expansion* that computes the interval bounds of a function's range by applying interval arithmetic rules according to the function's expression. The second approach is so-called first-order Taylor expansion:

$$\mathcal{R}_f([a,b]) \subseteq f(c) + [a - c, b - c] \cdot \mathbf{f}'([a,b]), \tag{19}$$

where $c = (a+b)/2$ and $\mathbf{f}'([a,b])$ denotes the natural interval expansion for the derivative of $f(x)$. The detailed proof of (19) can be found in [26].

Example 4. *Let $f(x) = -\cos(x) + e^{-x}$ and $a = 0, b = 1$. The convexity of $f(x)$ can easily be established by applying evaluation rules introduced in the previous section:*

1. *$\cos(x)$ is concave on $[0,1]$,*
2. *$-\cos(x)$ is convex on $[0,1]$ (by definition),*
3. *x is concave on $[0,1]$,*
4. *$-x$ is convex on $[0,1]$ (by definition),*
5. *e^{-x} is convex on $[0,1]$ (by Proposition 6),*
6. *$-\cos(x) + e^{-x}$ is convex on $[0,1]$ (by Proposition 4).*

Applying (9), we get the following enclosing interval for $f(x)$ on $[0,1]$:

$$f([0,1]) \subseteq [-0.438, 0],$$

with the width 0.438. Natural interval expansion gives:

$$f([0,1]) \subseteq [-0.632, 0.46],$$

with the width 1.092 and the first order Taylor expansion produces

$$f([0,1]) \subseteq [-0.77, 0.23]$$

with the width 1.092. Thus, the interval computed with the proposed techniques is nearly 2.5 times narrower than produced by the natural interval and Taylor expansions.

It is worth noting that the bounds provided by Propositions 9 and 10 can be computed for functions that are not differentiable at a set of points. It suffices that a function has its derivatives at the ends of the interval. The latter can be computed using the *forward mode automatic differentiation* [28], which is merely the application of differentiation rules at a point.

Table 4 compares bounds computed with the interval analysis techniques and the bounds computed by the proposed method for five convex functions. The convexity of these functions can be easily deduced by the introduced convexity evaluation rules. For an interval $[a, b]$, three bounds are presented in the respective columns:

> **Natural**—a bound computed by the natural interval expansion techniques,
> **Taylor**—a bound computed by the 1st order Taylor expansion,
> **Convex**—a bound computed according to Propositions 9 and 10.

Table 4. Comparison of natural interval expansion (Natural) Taylor expansion (Taylor) and bounds produced by the proposed techniques (Convex).

No	$f(x)$	$[\mathbf{a}, \mathbf{b}]$	Natural	Taylor	Convex
1	$-\cos(x) + e^{-x}$	$[0, 1]$	$[-0.632, 0.46]$	$[-0.77, 0.23]$	$[-0.438, 0]$
2	$e^x + e^{-x}$	$[-0.5, 0.5]$	$[1.21, 3.29]$	$[1.48, 2.52]$	$[1.73, 2.26]$
3	$0.2x^2 - \sin(x)$	$[0, \pi/2]$	$[-1, 0.49]$	$[-1.37, 0.2]$	$[-0.92, 0]$
4	$2(x-3)^2 + e^{0.5x^2}$	$[1, 3]$	$[1.65, 98.02]$	$[-260.66, 279.44]$	$[-0.92, 90.02]$
5	$(x-4)^2 + (x+4)^2 + e^{|x|}$	$[-2, 2]$	$[9, 79.39]$	—	$[16.61, 47.39]$

For all functions except No. 4, the bound produced by the proposed techniques contain both intervals produced by interval techniques and significantly more tight. For function number 4, the interval computed by the Convex method is narrower than the natural interval expansion but does not enclose it. However, as neither of these intervals contains each other, they can be intersected to obtain a better enclosing interval $[1.65, 90.02]$. The 5th function is non-differentiable in $x = 0$. Thus the symbolic differentiation does not give a meaningful result, and the Taylor expansion cannot be applied in this case. For that reason, the respective cell is marked with "$-$".

4.2. Impact on the Performance of Global Search

In Section 4.1, we observed that accounting convexity can significantly improve the interval bounds. As expected, the application of these bounds entails reducing the number of steps of the global search algorithm.

We implemented a standard branch-and-bound algorithm that uses the lower-bound test to discard subintervals from the further search. The description of this algorithm can be found elsewhere [26,41]. For completeness, we outline it here (Figure 2).

```
01: Algorithm BnB

02: input: f(x), [a, b]

03: begin
04:    L := {[a, b]}
05:    x_r := (a + b)/2
06:    while L ≠ ∅ do
07:        take (and remove) interval x from L
08:        x_c := (x + x̄)/2
09:        if f(x_c) < f(x_r) then
10:            x_r := x_c
11:        endif
12:        compute interval y := f(x)
13:        if y < f(x_r) − ε then
14:            put [x, x_c] and [x_c, x̄] to L
15:        endif
16:    end
17:    return x_r
18: end
```

Figure 2. The standard branch-and-bound algorithm.

The algorithm operates over a list L of intervals, initialized with the feasible set $[a, b]$ (line 04). The record point (incumbent solution) is initialized with the center of the interval $[a, b]$ (line 05). The main loop (lines 06—16) iterates until the list L is not empty. At each iteration one of the intervals from this set is taken (line 07) and examined. First, the value in the middle of this interval is computed, and if necessary, the record is updated (lines 08–11). The interval extension $\mathbf{y} = \mathbf{f}(\mathbf{x})$ is computed at the line 12. The interval lying above $f(x_r) - \varepsilon$ is discarded from the further search. Otherwise, it is partitioned into two smaller intervals. The obtained intervals are added to the list L (line 14).

We consider three variants of computing the interval extension:

1. **Natural**—the natural interval expansion techniques,
2. **Taylor**—the 1-st order Taylor expansion,
3. **Convex**—the range is computed according to Propositions 3, 9 and 10.

The described methods can be applied in combination, when the intervals computed by several methods are intersected to obtain the resulting range. We considered four different combinations of the range bounding techniques to compute the enclosing interval of the objective function:

1. **Natural**—pure natural interval expansion;
2. **Natural + Convex**—the natural interval expansion combined with the proposed techniques;
3. **Natural + Taylor**—the natural interval expansion combined with the first-order Taylor expansion;
4. **Natural + Taylor + Convex**—the natural interval expansion combined with the first-order Taylor expansion and the proposed techniques.

The convexity and the monotonicity are detected by analyzing the ranges of the first/second derivatives in differentiable cases or by using the introduced evaluation rules for the non-differentiable expressions.

Table 5 lists the set of test problems used in the experiments. For each problem, the objective function ($f(x)$), the interval ($[a, b]$), and the global optimum value ($f(x_*)$) are presented. The first ten problems are taken from [29]. The objective functions in these problems have both first and second derivatives.

To demonstrate the applicability of the proposed automatic convexity deduction techniques, we also have added four nondifferentiable problems. Test cases 11 and 12 were proposed by us, and 13 and 14 were taken from [33].

Table 5. Test problems.

No	$f(\mathbf{x})$	$[\mathbf{a}, \mathbf{b}]$	$f(x_*)$
1	$(x-1)^2 + \left(-x^2+x\right)^2$	$[-10, 10]$	0
2	$24x^4 - 142x^3 + 303x^2 - 276x + 3$	$[0, 3]$	1
3	$x^4 - 12x^3 + 47x^2 - 60x - 20e^{-x}$	$[-1, 7]$	-32.781261
4	$x^4 - 10x^3 + 35x^2 - 50x + 24$	$[-10, 20]$	-1
5	$-1.5\sin^2(x) + \sin(x)\cos(x) + 1.2$	$[0.2, 7]$	-0.451388
6	$-x + \sin(3x) + 1$	$[0.2, 7]$	-5.815675
7	$x + \sin(5x)$	$[0.2, 7]$	-0.07759
8	$-\sin(5x) + \cos(x) + 1$	$[0.2, 7]$	-0.952897
9	$2\cos(x) + \cos(2x) + 5$	$[0.2, 7]$	3.5
10	$2e^{-x}\sin(x)$	$[0.2, 7]$	-0.027864
11	$|x| + |x-4| + |x+4|$	$[-8, 8]$	8
12	$(x-4)^2 + (x+4)^2 + e^{|x|}$	$[-4, 8]$	33
13	$|(x-1)/4| + |\sin(\pi(1+(x-1)/4))| + 1$	$[-10, 10]$	1
14	$(10|\sin(x+1)| + 1)|x-1| + 1$	$[-10, 10]$	1

The results of numerical experiments are summarized in Table 6. The cells contain the number of steps performed by the branch-and-bound method. Columns correspond to different ways for computing the range of the objective functions, and rows correspond to test problems. The Taylor expansion cannot be applied to nondifferentiable problems 11–14, and the respective cells are blank.

Table 6. Testing results.

No	Natural	Natural + Convex	Natural + Taylor	Natural + Taylor + Convex
1	35	15	29	15
2	135,043	199	267	81
3	98,995	107	269	79
4	72,953	151	311	91
5	443	39	83	39
6	187	19	47	19
7	183	39	69	39
8	189	49	91	49
9	857	31	75	31
10	51	19	27	19
11	55	5	—	—
12	579	23	—	—
13	35	27	—	—
14	125	125	—	—

Experimental results demonstrate that the proposed techniques tremendously improve the standard branch-and-bound algorithm's performance that uses the natural interval expansion for the majority of the test problems. The combination of the natural interval expansion and the proposed method always outperform the combination of the natural and the first-order Taylor interval expansion. The comparison of the last two columns of Table 6 indicates that the Taylor expansion version of branch-and-bound can be further improved when combined with the proposed techniques. However, for problems 1 and 5–10, the proposed method does not benefit from the Taylor expansion.

5. Discussion

The standard way to ensure the convexity is to bound the range of the function's second derivative. However, this approach is only applicable to smooth functions. We defined a set of rules that can efficiently handle nonsmooth functions. The algebraic representation for the function, however, should be available.

It is worth noting that the proposed approach can be efficiently coded in modern programming languages supporting the operator's overloading techniques. To run the experiments presented in Tables 4 and 6 we have implemented our approach in Python. The elementary functions and operators were overloaded to support a particular data type that carries monotonicity and convexity information and the range of the function. The overloaded methods work according to the rules described in Section 2 and interval arithmetic.

As we have shown above, evaluating convexity can improve interval bounds on the function's range and accelerate the global optimization algorithms. Moreover, the over- and underestimators defined by the Propositions 7 and 8 enable efficient reduction techniques. The reduction techniques are widely used to accelerate the search for a global minimum of a function or a root of an equation.

We believe that the proposed approach has great potential as it can be extended to various generalized notions of convexity, e.g., quasiconvexity [46]. Quasiconvex functions possess the unimodality property, and thus recognizing the quasiconvexity (quasiconcavity) can tremendously enhance global optimization algorithms.

Author Contributions: Investigation: both authors. All authors contributed equally to this work. All authors have read and agreed to the published version of the manuscript.

Funding: This research was supported by the Ministry of Science and Higher Education of the Russian Federation, project No 075-15-2020-799.

Institutional Review Board Statement: Not applicable.

Informed Consent Statement: Not applicable.

Data Availability Statement: Not applicable.

Conflicts of Interest: The authors declare no conflict of interest.

References

1. Johnson, D.E. *Introduction to Filter Theory*; Prentice Hall: Englewood Cliffs, NJ, USA, 1976.
2. Zilinskas, A. Optimization of one-dimensional multimodal functions. *J. R. Stat. Soc. Ser. C Appl. Stat.* **1978**, *27*, 367–375.
3. Kvasov, D.; Menniti, D.; Pinnarelli, A.; Sergeyev, Y.D.; Sorrentino, N. Tuning fuzzy power-system stabilizers in multi-machine systems by global optimization algorithms based on efficient domain partitions. *Electr. Power Syst. Res.* **2008**, *78*, 1217–1229. [CrossRef]
4. Bedrosian, D.; Vlach, J. Time-domain analysis of networks with internally controlled switches. *IEEE Trans. Circuits Syst. I Fundam. Theory Appl.* **1992**, *39*, 199–212. [CrossRef]
5. Femia, N.; Tucci, V. On the modeling of PWM converters for large signal analysis in discontinuous conduction mode. *IEEE Trans. Power Electron.* **1994**, *9*, 487–496. [CrossRef]
6. Lassere, J.B. Connecting optimization with spectral analysis of tri-diagonal matrices. *Math. Program.* **2020**, doi:10.1007/s10107-020-01549-3. [CrossRef]
7. Strongin, R.G.; Sergeyev, Y.D. *Global Optimization with Non-Convex Constraints: Sequential and Parallel Algorithms*; Springer Science & Business Media: Berlin/Heidelberg, Germany, 2013; Volume 45.
8. Lera, D.; Sergeyev, Y.D. GOSH: Derivative-free global optimization using multi-dimensional space-filling curves. *J. Glob. Optim.* **2018**, *71*, 193–211. [CrossRef]
9. Lera, D.; Posypkin, M.; Sergeyev, Y.D. Space-filling curves for numerical approximation and visualization of solutions to systems of nonlinear inequalities with applications in robotics. *Appl. Math. Comput.* **2021**, *390*, 125660. [CrossRef]
10. Jensen, P.A.; Bard, J.F.; Jensen, P. *Operations Research Models and Methods*; John Wiley & Sons: Hoboken, NJ, USA, 2003.
11. Pintér, J. Extended univariate algorithms for n-dimensional global optimization. *Computing* **1986**, *36*, 91–103. [CrossRef]
12. Sergeyev, Y.D.; Kvasov, D.E. *Deterministic Global Optimization: An Introduction to the Diagonal Approach*; Springer: Berlin/Heidelberg, Germany, 2017.

13. Evtushenko, Y.G. Numerical methods for finding global extrema (case of a non-uniform mesh). *USSR Comput. Math. Math. Phys.* **1971**, *11*, 38–54. [CrossRef]

14. Pijavskij, S. An algorithm for finding the global extremum of function. *Optim. Decis.* **1967**, *2*, 13–24.

15. Shubert, B.O. A sequential method seeking the global maximum of a function. *SIAM J. Numer. Anal.* **1972**, *9*, 379–388. [CrossRef]

16. Timonov, L. Algorithm for search of a global extremum. *Eng. Cybern.* **1977**, *15*, 38–44.

17. Jones, D.R.; Perttunen, C.D.; Stuckman, B.E. Lipschitzian optimization without the Lipschitz constant. *J. Optim. Theory Appl.* **1993**, *79*, 157–181. [CrossRef]

18. Kvasov, D.E.; Sergeyev, Y.D. A univariate global search working with a set of Lipschitz constants for the first derivative. *Optim. Lett.* **2009**, *3*, 303–318. [CrossRef]

19. Lera, D.; Sergeyev, Y.D. Acceleration of univariate global optimization algorithms working with Lipschitz functions and Lipschitz first derivatives. *SIAM J. Optim.* **2013**, *23*, 508–529. [CrossRef]

20. Gergel, V.P. A global optimization algorithm for multivariate functions with Lipschitzian first derivatives. *J. Glob. Optim.* **1997**, *10*, 257–281. [CrossRef]

21. Sergeyev, Y.D. Global one-dimensional optimization using smooth auxiliary functions. *Math. Program.* **1998**, *81*, 127–146. [CrossRef]

22. Sergeyev, Y.D.; Nasso, M.C.; Mukhametzhanov, M.S.; Kvasov, D.E. Novel local tuning techniques for speeding up one-dimensional algorithms in expensive global optimization using Lipschitz derivatives. *J. Comput. Appl. Math.* **2020**, *383*, 113134. [CrossRef]

23. Hansen, P.; Jaumard, B.; Lu, S.H. Global optimization of univariate Lipschitz functions: I. Survey and properties. *Math. Program.* **1992**, *55*, 251–272. [CrossRef]

24. Hansen, P.; Jaumard, B.; Lu, S.H. Global optimization of univariate Lipschitz functions: II. New algorithms and computational comparison. *Math. Program.* **1992**, *55*, 273–292. [CrossRef]

25. Pintér, J.D. *Global Optimization in Action: Continuous and Lipschitz Optimization: Algorithms, Implementations and Applications*; Springer Science & Business Media: Berlin/Heidelberg, Germany, 2013; Volume 6.

26. Hansen, E.; Walster, G.W. *Global Optimization Using Interval Analysis: Revised and Expanded*; CRC Press: Boca Raton, FL, USA, 2003; Volume 264.

27. Moore, R.E.; Kearfott, R.B.; Cloud, M.J. *Introduction to Interval Analysis*; SIAM: Philadelphia, USA: 2009.

28. Kearfott, R.B. *Rigorous Global Search: Continuous Problems*; Springer Science & Business Media: Berlin/Heidelberg, Germany, 2013; Volume 13.

29. Casado, L.G.; Martínez, J.A.; García, I.; Sergeyev, Y.D. New interval analysis support functions using gradient information in a global minimization algorithm. *J. Glob. Optim.* **2003**, *25*, 345–362. [CrossRef]

30. Fasano, G.; Pintér, J.D. Efficient piecewise linearization for a class of non-convex optimization problems: Comparative cesults and extensions. In *Springer Proceedings in Mathematics & Statistics*; Pintér, J., Terlaky, T., Eds.; Springer: Berlin/Heidelberg, Germany, 2019; Volume 279, pp. 39–56.

31. Posypkin, M.; Usov, A.; Khamisov, O. Piecewise linear bounding functions in univariate global optimization. *Soft Comput.* **2020**, *24*, 17631–17647. [CrossRef]

32. Floudas, C.; Gounaris, C. Tight convex underestimators for C2-continuous functions: I. Univariate functions. *J. Glob. Optim* **2008**, *42*, 51–67.

33. Ratz, D. A nonsmooth global optimization technique using slopes: The one-dimensional case. *J. Glob. Optim.* **1999**, *14*, 365–393. [CrossRef]

34. Tuy, H.; Hoang, T.; Hoang, T.; Mathématicien, V.N.; Hoang, T.; Mathematician, V. *Convex Analysis and Global Optimization*; Springer: Berlin/Heidelberg, Germany, 1998.

35. Strekalovsky, A.S. On local search in dc optimization problems. *Appl. Math. Comput.* **2015**, *255*, 73–83.

36. Arıkan, O.; Burachik, R.; Kaya, C. Steklov regularization and trajectory methods for univariate global optimization. *J. Glob. Optim.* **2020**, *76*, 91–120. [CrossRef]

37. Ahmadi, A.; Hall, G. On the complexity of detecting convexity over a box. *Math. Program.* **2020**, *182*, 429–443. [CrossRef]

38. Fourer, R.; Maheshwari, C.; Neumaier, A.; Orban, D.; Schichl, H. Convexity and concavity detection in computational graphs: Tree walks for convexity assessment. *Informs J. Comput.* **2010**, *22*, 26–43. [CrossRef]

39. Grant, M.; Boyd, S. CVX: MATLAB Software for Disciplined Convex Programming. Version 1.21. 2010. Available online: http://cvxr.com/cvx (accessed on 9 January 2020) .

40. Grant, M.C.; Boyd, S.P. Graph implementations for nonsmooth convex programs. In *Recent Advances in Learning and Control*; Springer: Berlin/Heidelberg, Germany, 2008; pp. 95–110.

41. Ratschek, H.; Rokne, J. *New Computer Methods for Global Optimization*; Horwood: Chichester, UK, 1988.

42. Nataraj, P.S.; Arounassalame, M. A new subdivision algorithm for the Bernstein polynomial approach to global optimization. *Int. J. Autom. Comput.* **2007**, *4*, 342–352. [CrossRef]

43. Boyd, S.; Vandenberghe, L. *Convex Optimization*; Cambridge University Press: Cambridge, UK, 2004.

44. Nesterov, Y. *Introductory Lectures on Convex Optimization: A Basic Course*; Springer Science & Business Media: Berlin/Heidelberg, Germany, 2013; Volume 87.

45. Niculescu, C.; Persson, L.-E. *Convex Functions and their Applications. A Contemporary Approach*; Springer International Publishing: Berlin/Heidelberg, Germany, 2018.

46. Hadjisavvas, N.; Komlósi, S.; Schaible, S.S. *Handbook of Generalized Convexity and Generalized Monotonicity*; Springer Science & Business Media: Berlin/Heidelberg, Germany, 2006; Volume 76.

Article

Application of Mathematical Models to Assess the Impact of the COVID-19 Pandemic on Logistics Businesses and Recovery Solutions for Sustainable Development

Han Khanh Nguyen

Faculty of Economics, Thu Dau Mot University, Number 6, Tran Van On Street, Phu Hoa Ward, Thu Dau Mot 590000, Vietnam; khanhnh@tdmu.edu.vn

Abstract: The logistics industry can be considered as the economic lifeline of each country because of its role in connecting production and business activities of enterprises and promoting socio-economic development between regions and countries. However, the COVID-19 pandemic, which began at the end of 2019, has seriously affected the global supply chain, causing heavy impacts on the logistics service sector. In this study, the authors used the Malmquist productivity index to assess the impact of the pandemic on logistics businesses in Vietnam. Moreover, the authors used a super-slack-based model to find strategic alliance partners for enterprises. The authors also used the Grey forecasting model to forecast the business situation for enterprises during the period 2021–2024, in order to provide the leaders of these enterprises with a complete picture of their partners as a solid basis for making decisions to implement alliances that will help logistics enterprises in Vietnam to develop sustainably. The results have found that the alliance between LO_7 and LO_{10} is the most optimal, as this alliance can exploit freight in the opposite direction and reduce logistics costs, creating better competitiveness for businesses.

Keywords: mathematical modelling; modelling in economics; impact of the COVID-19; logistics businesses

Citation: Nguyen, H.K. Application of Mathematical Models to Assess the Impact of the COVID-19 Pandemic on Logistics Businesses and Recovery Solutions for Sustainable Development. *Mathematics* **2021**, *9*, 1977. https://doi.org/10.3390/math9161977

Academic Editor: Mikhail Posypkin

Received: 20 July 2021
Accepted: 14 August 2021
Published: 18 August 2021

1. Introduction

According to the General Statistics Office of Vietnam's logistics industry, in the first 10 months of 2020, 4513 transport and warehousing enterprises were newly established (down 5.5% compared to 2019). A total of 2366 transport and warehousing enterprises dissolved. Cargo transport reached 1.43 billion tons of goods, (down 7.5% compared to 2019) [1]. The COVID-19 pandemic had many negative effects on businesses, industries, countries, and the whole world. Specifically, when the COVID-19 pandemic occurred, infected workers had to take leaves of absence for treatment, which affected the production and business situation of factories that were halted. In addition, the most impactful factor is the social distancing orders of localities. This complicated the situation of transporting goods and materials in factories, causing supply chain disruptions and breach of contracts with partners, seriously affecting the logistics industry of countries.

The logistics chain involves sea transport, rail transport, water transport, and road transport; and activities in transportation, loading, unloading, forwarding, and storage (shown in Figure 1) [2]. If managers can come up with solutions to reduce these costs by maximizing both directions of routes and improving the occupancy rate at warehouses, it will help businesses improve results. Considering those problems, the questions are: How does the COVID-19 pandemic affect the business situation of logistics enterprises in Vietnam? The pandemic affects which areas in logistics activities? Are there any solutions to help logistic businesses grow after the pandemic? Are there any cost-saving solutions for logistics businesses? In this context, the authors realize that it is necessary to specifically assess the impact of the pandemic on the business performance of logistics enterprises, and it is necessary to find solutions to limit the risks of the epidemic to all stakeholders. It is necessary to research and propose solutions to help logistics enterprises in Vietnam restore and stabilize their business situations, help businesses ensure reasonable growth, stabilize jobs for employees, and create a foundation for rapid and sustainable economic growth.

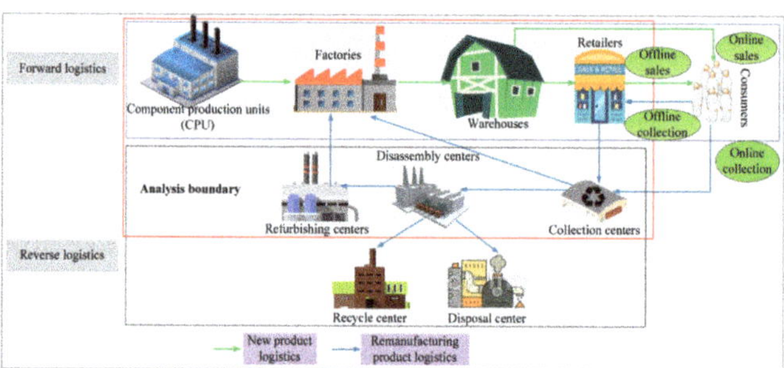

Figure 1. Dual channel network structure in Logistics (Liu et al., 2020).

2. Materials and Methods

2.1. Overview of Vietnam's Logistics

Vietnam's logistics industry has been heavily affected by the pandemic in all forms of transport: road, sea, rail, and especially air.

Road traffic: According to the Directorate for Roads of Vietnam, currently more than 1800 km of expressways are in operation; 16,000 km of roads and nearly 600,000 km of national highways. The system of rural roads has been built, upgraded, and expanded [3]. This helps meet the needs of the freight transport of domestic and foreign enterprises, promoting production and business development and, thereby, improving competitiveness of the economy (proportion of road types shown in Figure 2) [4].

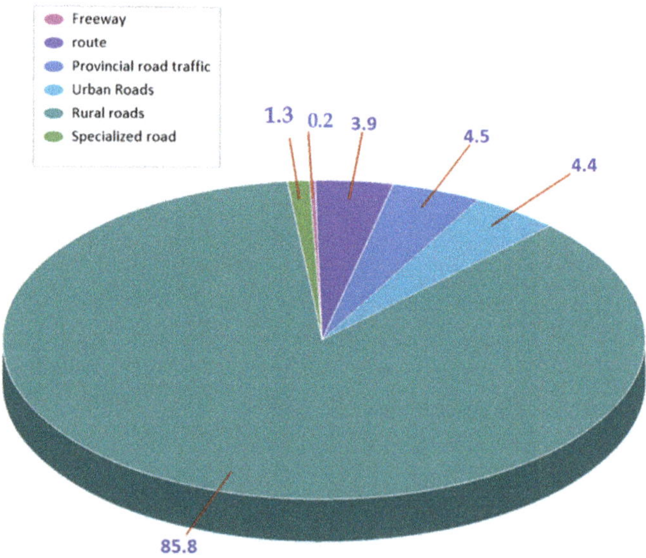

Figure 2. Proportion of road types in Vietnam (Vietnam Logistics Report 2020).

In Vietnam, domestic road freight transport still accounts for the highest proportion of all modes of transport (76.8% in 2019) (weight of goods transported by road shown in Figure 3). Meanwhile, the cost of transporting goods by road is still high, because about

70–75% of vehicles carry only one-way goods; the high costs of road use and fuel increase logistics costs dramatically [4].

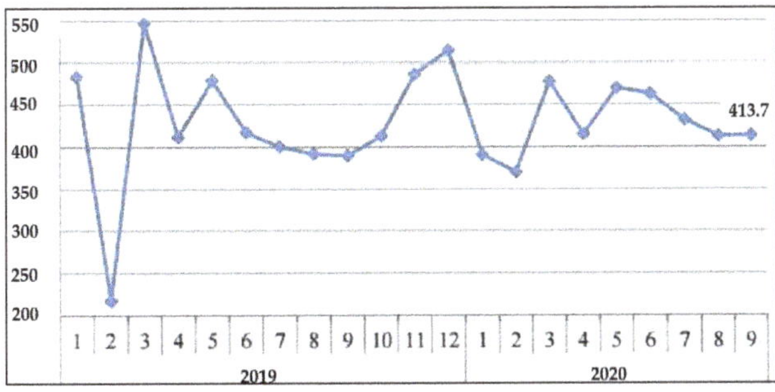

Figure 3. Weight of goods transported by road (Million tons) (Vietnam Logistics Report 2020).

Railway transport: The railway system in Vietnam includes 7 main lines and 12 branch lines with a total length of 3143 km, stretching across 34 provinces and cities. The railway system includes 277 stations, including 3 types of gauges: 1000 mm gauge (85%), 1435 mm gauge (6%), and cage gauges of 1000 mm and 1435 mm (accounting for 9%). The railway density is about 7.9 km/1000 km². Vietnam's railway system was built a long time ago. The infrastructure is outdated with no modern technology; the trains are loud and of low service quality. Therefore, the proportion of passenger and freight transport by rail is lower than that of other forms of transport (weight of goods transported by railway shown in Figure 4) [4]. The railway industry has not kept up with the development of other modes of transport. The railway industry focuses on exploiting short segments, from 800 km to 1200 km, and places where it has more advantages than sea routes [4].

Figure 4. Weight of goods transported by railway (thousand tons) (Vietnam Logistics Report, 2020).

Sea transport: With the advantage of geographical location, Vietnam is located on an important sea route for continents and regions in the world. This favorable condition for domestic and international transportation of goods has led to development of the shipping industry to promote economic development. In 2019, the transport volume reached 49.2 million tons of goods (weight of goods transported by seaway shown in Figure 5); 43,150 ferry boats used seaports and inland waterways and average growth rate of goods reached 204% (from July 2014 to 2019) [4].

Inland waterway transport: In 2019, inland waterway freight transport in Vietnam reached 303.4 million tons with an increase of 5.6%. In the first 9 months of 2020, inland waterway cargo transport reached 238.1 million tons with a decrease of 7.6% over the same period in 2019 (weight of goods transported by inland waterways shown in Figure 6). As of 2020, there are a total of 1786 VR-SB-class vehicles in operation, of which 839 are cargo vehicles with a tonnage of 1,742,834 tons, accounting for 0.5% of inland waterway vehicles [4].

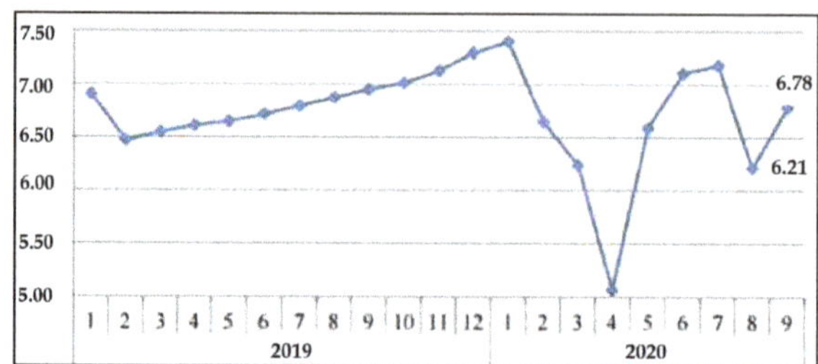

Figure 5. Weight of goods transported by seaway (million tons) (Vietnam Logistics Report 2020).

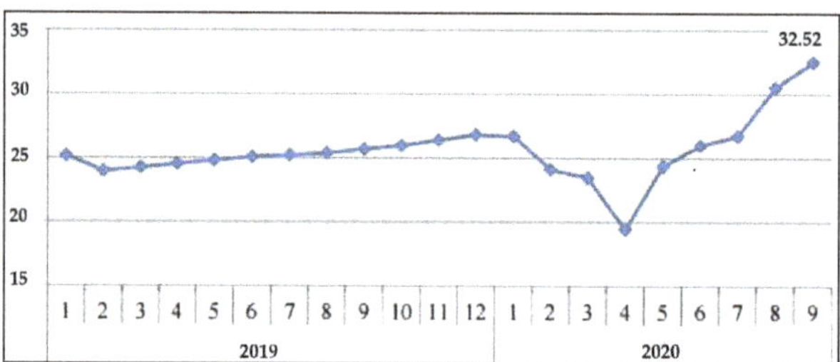

Figure 6. Weight of goods transported by inland waterways (million tons) (Vietnam Logistics Report 2020).

Air traffic: As of 2020, there are a total of 22 airports in Vietnam with civil aviation operations, including 11 international airports and 11 domestic airports. According to the Civil Aviation Authority of Vietnam, as of the first quarter of 2020, Vietnam has 235 registered civil aircraft and 32 helicopters [4].

Although air transport only accounts for a small part of the total volume of goods transported in Vietnam (0.23%), it accounts for 25% of the total export value of the country (weight of goods transported by airline shown in Figure 7) [4]. This is a feature that should be taken into account when planning development. It is necessary to orient investment in aviation infrastructure to increase the service capacity of airports and shorten the time for cargo services.

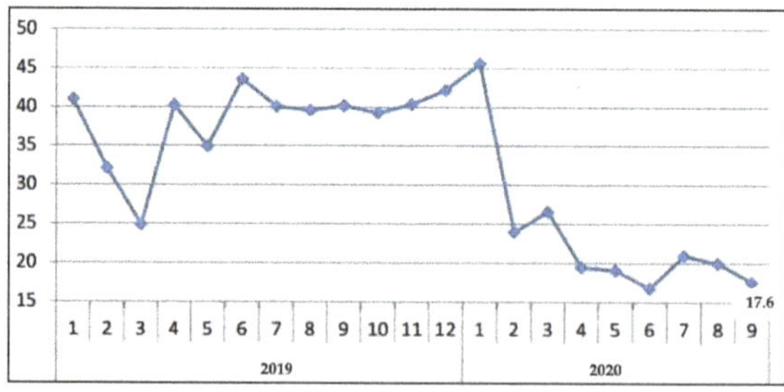

Figure 7. Weight of goods transported by airline (thousand tons) (Vietnam Logistics Report 2020).

2.2. Literature Review

Data envelopment analysis (DEA) is a linear programming method for measuring the performance of multiple industry players (DMUs) when a production process presents a structure of multiple inputs and multiple outputs. DEA has been widely applied by many scientists in many different scientific disciplines [5–8]. Chowdhury et al., (2011) used the Malmquist productivity index to evaluate the performance of hospitals in Ontario between 2003–2006 [9]. In that study, the authors did an in-depth analysis of the efficiency of technical and technological investment in hospitals in Ontario. The researchers pointed out the limitations of technical and technology investment in these hospitals, and proposed solutions to improve the efficiency of technology investment. Abbas et al., (2015) used the Malmquist productivity index to evaluate and compare the performance of Islamic banks and conventional commercial banks [10]. The results show that Islamic banks have higher operational efficiency than conventional commercial banks. The reason is that, in Muslim countries, Islamic banks are sponsored.

Bahrini et al., (2015) used the Malmquist productivity index to evaluate the performance of 33 Islamic banks in 10 countries around the world for the period 2006–2011 [11]. The results show that Islamic banks were hit hard by the 2008 global financial crisis. In that study, the researchers also proposed solutions to help Islamic commercial banks' recovery and growth. Lee et al., (2017) used DEA models to evaluate the performance of 18 banks in Korea in three categories: National Bank, Regional Bank, and Special Bank [12]. The authors found that special banks have the highest business efficiency compared to other types of banks. Wang et al., (2017) used DEA models to evaluate the performance of infrastructure investment and development companies in Vietnam [13]. The authors evaluated and selected good investors and suggested that the Vietnamese government establish appropriate policies when selecting contractors for infrastructure investment projects to achieve good results on time and on budget.

Grey system theory was introduced by Professor Julong Deng in 1982 [14]. Grey prediction theory is a multidisciplinary forecasting science that has been applied in almost all sciences. Since its introduction, it has been applied by scientific works around the world [15–19]. Fan et al., (2018) used a Grey forecasting model to forecast natural gas demand in China [20]. The results of that research helped the Chinese government to develop and issue energy policies to ensure a stable supply of natural gas for production and daily life. Nguyen (2020) used the super-slack-based model to select partners for construction companies in Vietnam [21]. After selecting an alliance partner, the author used two forecasting methods, the Grey forecasting model and ARIMA model, to forecast the business situation of construction companies. Wang et al., (2021) used the Grey forecasting model to predict the number of railway passengers by quarter (period 2020–2022) in China. This result helps railway management companies create plans to meet the travel needs of customers.

In this study, the Malmquist productivity index (MPI) is used to evaluate the business performance of logistics enterprises in Vietnam from 2017 to 2020. The authors continue to use the super-slack-based model to select optimal partners to enter strategic alliances with businesses to help businesses recover and develop sustainably after the pandemic. In addition, in this study, the authors used the Grey forecasting model simultaneously to forecast and provide a post-pandemic picture of businesses participating in the alliance, giving managers a solid basis when making decisions about implementing alliances.

2.3. Theoretical Fundamentals

2.3.1. Research Development

The authors found that the COVID-19 pandemic negatively impacted most businesses, sectors, and industries in Vietnam's economy [1]. In particular, the logistics industry was most affected because localities and countries implemented social distancing orders to limit the movement of people and goods. Therefore, the author realizes that it is necessary to assess the impacts of the epidemic on logistics enterprises and propose solutions to help businesses recover and develop. The research process is carried out by the authors according to the steps shown in Figure 8 below:

After determining the research objectives, the authors selected enterprises to conduct the research. These enterprises must use the same operations in the logistics industry, have similarity of scale, and have appropriate geographical locations to ensure feasible transportation.

After selecting businesses that fulfill the conditions to carry out the research objectives, the authors selected factors to analyze the business situations of logistics enterprises before and during the pandemic. Then, the authors checked the correlation of these factors to ensure the appropriateness of the data included in analysis and processing.

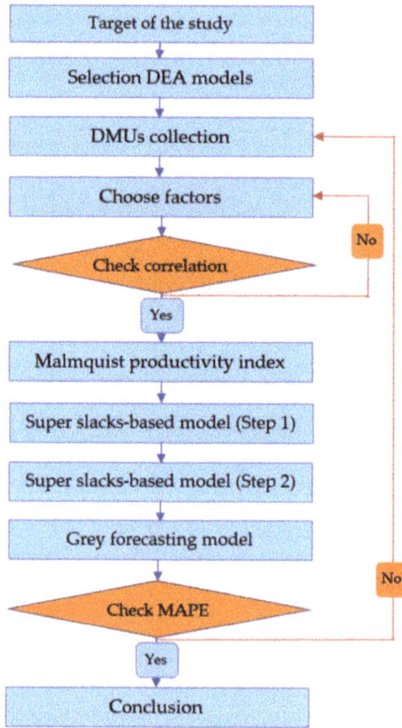

Figure 8. Research process (Source: Researcher).

After examining the correlation between the factors used in the study, the authors used the Malmquist productivity index to assess the impact of the pandemic on the business situation of Vietnamese logistics enterprises for the period 2017–2020. Then, the authors used a super-slack-based model to rank these enterprises, as a basis for choosing the optimal alliance partner to improve business efficiency for logistics enterprises in the future.

After evaluating and ranking the logistics enterprises, the authors used the rankings to make alliances for enterprises. Then, the authors used the Grey forecasting model (GFM) to forecast the business situation of enterprises in the alliance. This forecast aims to provide managers with a complete picture of their alliances as a solid basis for decision making to enable sustainable development.

2.3.2. Research Methods

Malmquist Productivity Index

DEA is a linear programming method for measuring the effectiveness of multiple decision-making units (DMUs) when a production process presents a structure of multiple inputs and outputs. This method relies on the past business data of the enterprise to construct the production boundary in the non-parametric plane (the production boundary). In which, the Malmquist index (MI) evaluates the efficiency of a business at $t_1(x_0^1, y_0^1)$ and $t_2(x_0^2, y_0^2)$. This efficiency is assessed through the catch-up (CU) and frontier-shift (FS) indicators of that business [22].

$$CU = \frac{\text{Efficiency of } t_2(x_0^2, y_0^2) \text{ with respect to the period 2 frontier}}{\text{Efficiency of } t_1(x_0^1, y_0^1) \text{ with respect to the period 1 frontier}} \tag{1}$$

A specific example of evaluating the effectiveness of an element in the above model is shown in Figure 9:

$$CU = \frac{BD}{BQ} \times \frac{AP}{AC} \tag{2}$$

$$\varphi_1 = \frac{AC}{AP} \times \frac{AP}{AE} = \frac{AC}{AE} = \frac{\text{Efficiency of } (x_0^1, y_0^1) \text{ with respect to the period 1 frontier}}{\text{Efficiency of } (x_0^1, y_0^1) \text{ with respect to the period 2 frontier}} \tag{3}$$

$$\varphi_2 = \frac{BF}{BQ} \times \frac{BQ}{BD} = \frac{BF}{BD} = \frac{\text{Efficiency of } (x_0^2, y_0^2) \text{ with respect to the period 1 frontier}}{\text{Efficiency of } (x_0^2, y_0^2) \text{ with respect to the period 2 frontier}} \tag{4}$$

$$FS = \varphi = \sqrt{\varphi_1 \varphi_2} \tag{5}$$

$$MI = CU \times FS \tag{6}$$

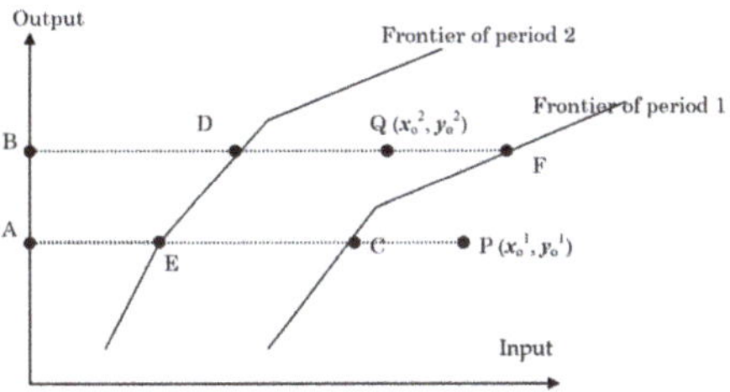

Figure 9. Catch-up (Le et al., 2020) [23].

The efficiency score of the DMU at point $(x_0, y_0)^{t_1}$ measured by frontier technology t_2 as follows [22]:

$$\delta^{t_2}(x_0, y_0)^{t_1}; \ (t_1 = 1, 2; \ t_2 = 1, 2)$$

$$CU = \frac{\delta^2(x_0, y_0)^2}{\delta^1(x_0, y_0)^1} \tag{7}$$

$$FS = \left[\frac{\delta^1(x_0, y_0)^1}{\delta^2(x_0, y_0)^1} \times \frac{\delta^1(x_0, y_0)^2}{\delta^2(x_0, y_0)^2} \right]^{\frac{1}{2}} \tag{8}$$

$$MI = CU \times FS = \left[\frac{\delta^1(x_0, y_0)^2}{\delta^1(x_0, y_0)^1} \times \frac{\delta^2(x_0, y_0)^2}{\delta^2(x_0, y_0)^1} \right]^{\frac{1}{2}} \tag{9}$$

If :

$$\begin{cases} MI < 1 : \text{The relative efficiency drops.} \\ MI = 1 : \text{The relative efficiency } t_1(x_0^1, y_0^1) \text{ equivalent } t_2(x_0^2, y_0^2). \\ MI > 1 : \text{The relative efficiency increases from } t_1(x_0^1, y_0^1) \text{ to } t_2(x_0^2, y_0^2). \end{cases}$$

Super-Slack-Based Model

In 2001, Tone introduced the slack-based measure model to evaluate the production and business efficiency of enterprises based on changes in production factors causing changes in corporate profits. The introduction is described as follows [24,25]:

$$\text{Min} \rho = \frac{1 - \frac{1}{m} \sum_{i=1}^{m} \frac{s_i^-}{x_{ik}}}{1 + \frac{1}{s} \sum_{r=1}^{s} \frac{s_r^+}{y_{rk}}} \tag{10}$$

Subject to :

$$x_{ik} = \sum_{j=1; j \neq k}^{n} \lambda_j x_{ij} - s_i^- \ (i = 1, 2, \ \ldots, n) \tag{11}$$

$$y_{rk} = \sum_{j=1; j \neq k}^{n} \lambda_j y_{ij} - s_i^+ \ (r = 1, 2, \ \ldots, s) \tag{12}$$

$$s^- \geq 0, \ s^+ \geq 0, \ \lambda_j \geq 0 \ (j = 1, 2, \ \ldots, n, j \neq k) \tag{13}$$

ρ shows the relative business performance of the enterprise. If $0 < \rho < 1$, this reflects that the enterprise is not operating efficiently. If $\rho = 1$, it reflects that the enterprise is relatively efficient. However, there are many businesses in the same business field that achieve relative efficiency. Therefore, to evaluate and rank these enterprises, Tone introduced the super-slack-based model to evaluate the ranking of enterprises in the same industry. The super-slack-based model is described as follows:

$$\text{Min}\rho = \frac{\frac{1}{m} \sum_{i=1}^{m} \frac{\bar{x}_i}{x_{ik}}}{\frac{1}{s} \sum_{r=1}^{s} \frac{\bar{y}_r}{y_{rk}}} \tag{14}$$

Subject to :

$$\bar{x} \geq \sum_{j=1; j \neq k}^{n} \lambda_j x_{ij} \tag{15}$$

$$\bar{y} \leq \sum_{j=1; j \neq k}^{n} \lambda_j y_j \tag{16}$$

$$\bar{x} \geq x_k; \bar{y} \leq y_k \tag{17}$$

$$\lambda_j \geq 0 \ (j = 1, 2, \ \ldots, n, j \neq k) \tag{18}$$

In which :

$\left\{ \begin{array}{l} \text{n : Denotes the number of DMUs.} \\ \text{m : Denotes the number of input indexes.} \\ \text{s : denotes the number of output indexes.} \\ s^+, s^- : \text{Are the output and the input relaxation variables.} \\ \lambda : \text{Denotes the weight vector.} \\ x_{ik}, y_{rk} : \text{Denote the ith input and the rth output of the DMU}_k \end{array} \right.$

Grey Forecasting Model

GFM was first introduced by Professor Julong Deng in 1982. GFM focuses on the study of uncertain information systems and incomplete data sources in decision making. Grey system theory can perform research with a small sample size data set. Therefore, Grey system theory overcomes the inherent disadvantages of other forecasting methods. The authors used Grey system theory to conduct this study. After being introduced and published in the journal System & Control Letters, GFM has been successfully applied by many scientists around the world in most fields of economy and society. The process of calculating the GM (1, 1) model of GFM is shown in 6 steps in Figure 10 below:

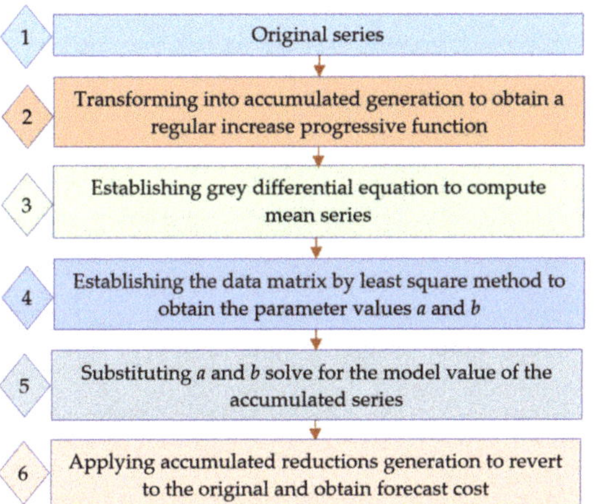

Figure 10. Forecasting process (Nguyen Han Khanh 2021) [26].

Correlation Coefficient and Error

As mentioned, the authors used 4 inputs and 2 outputs to assess the impact of the pandemic on the business situation of logistics companies in Vietnam in the period 2017–2020. To test the correlation between factors, the authors used Pearson correlation coefficient (r). Testing the correlation coefficient through (r) is the best method to measure the relationship between factors used in the study because it is based on the covariance method. (r) is calculated by following formula [27]:

$$r = \frac{\sum\limits_{i=1}^{n} (a_i - \overline{a})(b_i - \overline{b})}{\left[\sum\limits_{i=1}^{n} (a_i - \overline{a})^2 \sum\limits_{i=1}^{n} (b_i - \overline{b})^2 \right]^{\frac{1}{2}}} \tag{19}$$

The authors used the GM (1, 1) model to forecast the business situation of logistic enterprises in the period of 2021–2024. To evaluate the quality and fit of the GM (1, 1) model used in this study, the authors used MAPE to calculate error. MAPE is calculated according to the following formula [28]:

$$\begin{cases} \delta = \frac{1}{n} \left[\sum\limits_{i=1}^{n} \left| \frac{A_i - F_i}{A_i} \right| \times 100 \right]; \\ \delta \leq 10\% : \text{Excellent} \\ 10\% < \delta \leq 20\% : \text{Good} \\ 20\% < \delta \leq 50\% : \text{Qualified} \\ \delta > 50\% : \text{Unqualified} \end{cases} \tag{20}$$

2.4. Data

The authors selected typical logistic enterprises that are suitable for this research objective. Specifically, the enterprises must fulfill the following conditions: they are of appropriate size; they have geographical concordance to exploit potential customers of partners and save the cost of reverse traffic; and they must be in the same industry and field of operation to optimize available infrastructure, technical support, and transportation without having to invest in any additional equipment. Based on those conditions, the authors selected enterprises summarized in Table 1 below [29].

Table 1. List of LOs (Statistics 2021).

LOs	Name of Companies
LO1	GMD corporation
LO2	HA transport & stevedoring
LO3	HT transport joint stock company
LO4	S & A freight international
LO5	DHMM transport joint stock company
LO6	TC warehousing joint stock company
LO7	TRA corporation
LO8	VIN joint stock company
LO9	VIN logistics joint stock company
LO10	VCS joint stock corporation

To assess the impact of the COVID-19 pandemic on the business situation of logistics enterprises in Vietnam, the authors used four input factors and two output factors:

- Equity is the total net assets of the business; these assets are owned by shareholders.
- Total asset is the entire set of assets and valuable papers of an enterprise used for production and business activities.
- Cost of goods sold includes cost of purchasing machinery, raw materials, cost of goods production, labor cost, administrative expenses, etc.
- General and administrative expenses are expenses used to operate an enterprise's activities.
- Net revenue is the amount earned by the business after all deductions have been deducted.
- Profit after tax is the amount obtained after taking total sales revenue minus all costs of logistics services.

The indicators on Total Assets and Equity are the main items in the balance sheet. These indicators show an overview of the assets situation of the enterprise. Based on these indicators, it is possible to assess the business situation and the ability to use the capital of the enterprise. Factors on the cost of goods sold; management costs; net revenue and profit after tax are the main indicators in the income statement of an enterprise. These indicators reflect the business results and development trends of the enterprise as a basis for making strategic financial decisions. These financial indicators reflect the business situation of a logistics enterprise. The data source is actual data on the business situation of enterprises in the period 2017–2020. The data were collected through the website of the General Statistics Office and are summarized in Tables 2–5 below [29].

3. Research Results

3.1. Check Correlation Coefficient

The correlation coefficient is a statistical quantity that measures the degree of correlation between two factors. If the correlation coefficient has a value in the range $[-1, 0)$, that indicates the negative correlation between those two factors (that is, if this value increases, the other value decreases, and vice versa). If the correlation coefficient has a value in the range $(0, 1]$, that indicates the positive correlation between the two factors (that is, the value of one factor increases, the value of the other factor also increases and vice versa)) The correlation coefficient has a value of 0, indicating that the two factors are independent of each other.

Table 2. Data of 10 LOs in 2017 (Statistics 2021).

LOs	IN1	IN2	IN3	IN4	OU1	OU2
LO1	7,094,537	11,291,217	2,954,817	344,481	3,990,532	581,436
LO2	836,177	1,309,071	574,311	45,393	777,930	152,573
LO3	320,833	377,548	144,037	15,200	181,182	21,162
LO4	353,880	570,430	172,822	70,447	716,293	40,947
LO5	211,893	232,389	121,307	19,214	159,959	17,665
LO6	322,166	676,834	539,185	42,987	679,417	62,766
LO7	1,421,715	2,737,361	1,882,482	59,715	2,136,424	211,414
LO8	260,283	736,057	1,806,305	24,310	1,886,382	44,213
LO9	201,262	340,814	797,138	14,774	824,846	24,904
LO10	1,709,546	2,479,002	895,119	60,881	1,302,883	263,828

Table 3. Data of 10 LOs in 2018 (Statistics 2021).

LOs	IN1	IN2	IN3	IN4	OU1	OU2
LO1	6,528,982	9,984,063	1,739,451	320,526	2,707,556	1,900,250
LO2	1,218,676	1,655,980	834,979	61,303	1,054,283	158,895
LO3	330,438	392,029	175,367	16,914	219,561	27,751
LO4	407,014	707,326	202,781	71,644	869,055	54,172
LO5	208,490	226,436	121,974	19,810	158,488	14,726
LO6	340,517	609,841	528,232	42,381	659,418	60,549
LO7	1,625,789	3,166,212	2,089,885	68,910	2,333,136	235,012
LO8	340,219	744,914	1,608,770	21,849	1,676,896	33,710
LO9	210,991	354,157	907,519	13,078	941,690	24,372
LO10	1,944,570	2,489,083	1,198,472	63,187	1,694,460	354,245

Table 4. Data of 10 LOs in 2019 (Statistics 2021).

LOs	IN1	IN2	IN3	IN4	OU1	OU2
LO1	6,567,257	10,119,907	1,630,141	330,636	2,642,914	613,569
LO2	1,254,682	1,827,544	889,647	67,209	1,108,933	132,739
LO3	335,807	427,116	225,370	20,254	271,911	29,377
LO4	445,005	538,935	136,653	14,237	845,985	44,877
LO5	195,483	213,861	125,466	18,317	161,096	16,251
LO6	359,439	626,332	548,740	54,609	701,657	68,593
LO7	1,947,165	3,310,259	2,067,261	80,137	2,348,544	225,324
LO8	356,345	716,298	1,463,866	19,708	1,519,304	19,795
LO9	211,456	340,901	871,202	14,559	899,915	18,788
LO10	2,070,078	2,393,245	1,355,854	65,611	1,792,751	285,795

Table 5. Data of 10 LOs in 2020 (Statistics 2021).

LOs	IN1	IN2	IN3	IN4	OU1	OU2
LO1	6,594,929	9,834,544	1,656,082	341,474	2,605,666	440,476
LO2	1,335,797	2,094,551	952,285	67,886	1,191,667	146,598
LO3	338,248	418,484	237,067	24,904	282,084	26,660
LO4	482,381	702,041	171,784	19,294	1,203,173	82,333
LO5	200,204	220,371	134,019	19,509	170,252	17,861
LO6	356,895	652,319	601,216	57,627	768,721	78,060
LO7	2,346,510	3,919,585	3,111,468	98,228	3,421,254	321,629
LO8	355,180	917,042	2,420,329	24,450	2,471,666	8557
LO9	220,936	402,607	1,162,837	20,349	1,202,207	23,191
LO10	2,170,698	2,458,144	1,239,556	73,458	1,688,865	296,404

Based on the results obtained in Table 6, the values of correlation coefficients between factors are all positive (+). This result reflects that the factors used in the study have a positive relationship with each other (that is, when the input factors increase, the output factors also increase accordingly). In particular, the values of the correlation coefficients in this study are mostly greater than 0.5, showing that the factors have a strong correlation with each other [25]. This result confirms that the factors used in the study satisfy the correlation conditions to serve as a basis for research and analysis.

Table 6. Correlation coefficient (calculated by researcher).

	IN1	IN2	IN3	IN4	OU1	OU2	IN1	IN2	IN3	IN4	OU1	OU2
	2017						2018					
IN1	1.0000						1.0000					
IN2	0.9979	1.0000					0.9948	1.0000				
IN3	0.7858	0.8175	1.0000				0.5549	0.6024	1.0000			
IN4	0.9800	0.9793	0.7424	1.0000			0.9732	0.9734	0.4506	1.0000		
OU1	0.8780	0.9022	0.9762	0.8546	1.0000		0.7591	0.7937	0.9340	0.6936	1.0000	
OU2	0.9655	0.9652	0.7909	0.9183	0.8771	1.0000	0.9893	0.9835	0.4880	0.9829	0.7005	1.0000
	2019						2020					
IN1	1.0000						1.0000					
IN2	0.9953	1.0000					0.9938	1.0000				
IN3	0.5761	0.5944	1.0000				0.3875	0.4404	1.0000			
IN4	0.9809	0.9866	0.5046	1.0000			0.9798	0.9832	0.3235	1.0000		
OU1	0.7904	0.7977	0.9237	0.7164	1.0000		0.5850	0.6282	0.9349	0.5102	1.0000	
OU2	0.9859	0.9717	0.6146	0.9500	0.8191	1.0000	0.9128	0.8955	0.4863	0.8391	0.6714	1.0000

3.2. Malmquist Productivity Index Results

The authors use the Malmquist productivity index to assess the impact of the COVID-19 pandemic on the business situation of logistics enterprises in Vietnam in the period 2017–2020. The results are as shown in Table 7 and Figure 11 below.

Since the end of 2019, the COVID-19 pandemic has forced countries around the world to apply measures to prevent the spread of the disease. These include restricting logistics activities, including the export and import activities at borders. This has had a heavy impact on logistics activities, disrupting supply chains and international trade flows. Many businesses had to suspend operations, causing a backlog of goods in warehouses, factories, and distribution centers, and reduced volume of goods in circulation. At the same time, the storage costs of goods increased, especially goods in cold storage and fresh food. This made the cost of transportation and logistics services more expensive.

Table 7. Malmquist results (calculated by researcher).

Malmquist	2017 => 2018	2018 => 2019	2019 => 2020	Average
LO1	1.1643	0.7163	0.7235	0.8680
LO2	0.7853	0.8382	1.0542	0.8926
LO3	0.9747	0.9007	0.9371	0.9375
LO4	1.0368	1.5156	1.2058	1.2527
LO5	1.0256	1.1056	0.9853	1.0388
LO6	0.9705	1.0628	1.1078	1.0470
LO7	1.0054	0.9615	1.4105	1.1258
LO8	0.8538	0.9284	1.1514	0.9779
LO9	1.0732	0.9243	0.9857	0.9944
LO10	1.1240	1.0037	0.9866	1.0381
Average	1.0014	0.9957	1.0548	1.0173
Max	1.1643	1.5156	1.4105	1.2527
Min	0.7853	0.7163	0.7235	0.8680
SD	0.1149	0.2134	0.1824	0.1132

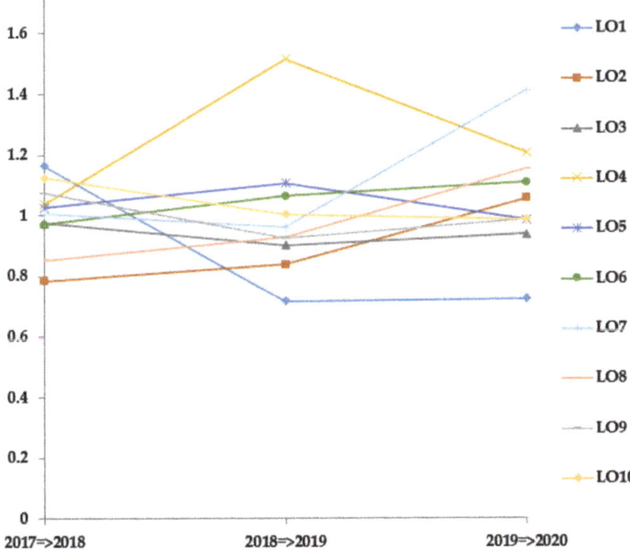

Figure 11. Malmquist results (source: researcher).

Research results show that logistics businesses operating in the field of transportation have been heavily affected by the COVID-19 pandemic, so the business situation fluctuates sharply. Specifically, Malmquist LO_1 decreased from 1.1643 in the period 2017–2018 to 0.7235 in the period 2019–2020; Malmquist LO_5 decreased from 1.0256 for 2017–2018 to 0.9853 for 2019–2020; Malmquist LO_9 decreased from 1.0732 for the period 2017–2018 to 0.9857 for the period 2019–2020; Malmquist LO_{10} decreased from 1.1240 for 2017–2018 to 0.9866 for 2019–2020. However, there are a number of logistics enterprises still operating effectively, including $Malmquist_{LO4(2019–2020)} = 1.2058$; $Malmquist_{LO6(2019–2020)} = 1.1078$; $Malmquist_{LO7(2019–2020)} = 1.4105$; $Malmquist_{LO8(2019–2020)} = 1.1514$. Basic logistics service businesses include the management of freight services, warehousing services, and logistics network design. Therefore, depending on the line of each business, the level of impact of the COVID-19 pandemic is different. According to the business profile, the above businesses all have the following main areas: bonded warehouse services, container freight station warehouses, cold storage, warehousing, loading and unloading, storage of import and export goods and services, freight forwarding, customs clearance, shipping agents and cargo brokers. Some logistics enterprises have large warehouse systems, and a cold storage system to store fresh food and special goods.

3.3. Super-Slacks-Based Model Results

3.3.1. Results before Alliance

In this study, the authors used the Super-SBM model to evaluate efficiency and rank the logistics enterprises in Vietnam in the period of 2019–2020. The results show that, even during the pandemic, there are still businesses that operate very effectively: $Rank_{LO4} = 1$ ($Score_{LO4} = 3.2525$), $Rank_{LO9} = 2$ ($Score_{LO9} = 1.5320$), $Rank_{LO8} = 3$ ($Score_{LO8} = 1.3031$). However, there are businesses that have been heavily affected by the COVID-19 pandemic, so their operations are not effective: $Rank_{LO2} = 9$ ($Score_{LO2} = 0.5554$); $Rank_{LO3} = 10$ ($Score_{LO3} = 0.4432$).

The authors used the results in Table 8 and Figure 12 as a basis for selecting enterprises to make alliances with other enterprises. If we choose businesses that have not achieved business efficiency in this period (LO_2, LO_3), it is difficult to convince other businesses to implement the alliance. Therefore, the authors have chosen LO_{10} (Vietnam container shipping joint stock corporation) as a target enterprise to engage in negotiations with other enterprises to implement alliances in order to realize strategic goals and support each other for mutual development. The authors chose LO_{10} as the target enterprise. In 2020, LO_{10} still had good business results: Rank $LO_{10} = 5$ (Score $LO_{10} = 1.2242$). LO_{10} in Hai Phong city was established in 1985, specializing in logistics and container agency services, shipping agents, warehouse business, yards, transport of import and export goods, cargo projects, goods in transit, and so on. When participating in negotiations to form alliances with other businesses, this enterprise will have many advantages and a high probability of success.

3.3.2. Results after Alliance

After selecting LO_{10} as the target enterprise, the authors combined it with nine other businesses to create virtual alliances. Then, the authors evaluated the business performance of these alliances.

From the results in Table 9 and Figure 13, it is shown that, when implementing the LO_{10} alliance with other enterprises, it can bring better business performance for those enterprises. However, there are also alliances of LO_{10} with other businesses that do not achieve better business performance. The authors divided enterprises into two groups of alliances as follows:

Group 1: The alliances are not really suitable, as they have not brought good business results (shown in Table 10). Specifically, those alliances are: $LO_9 + LO_{10}$; $LO_2 + LO_{10}$; $LO_5 + LO_{10}$; $LO_3 + LO_{10}$. These alliances make businesses less efficient. Therefore, these alliances are not recommended.

Group 2: These alliances bring good business results for enterprises (shown in Table 11). Specifically, those alliances are: $LO_7 + LO_{10}$; $LO_1 + LO_{10}$; $LO_4 + LO_{10}$; $LO_8 + LO_{10}$; $LO_6 + LO_{10}$. These alliances are therefore encouraged.

Among the above alliances, the alliance between LO_7 and LO_{10} achieved the highest business efficiency ($Rank_{LO7+LO10} = 4/19$) ($Score_{LO7+LO10} = 1.2060$). LO_7 (Transimex corporation transimex) in Ho Chi Minh City was established in 1983, specializing in import and export goods transportation, bonded warehouse services, CFS warehouse, cold storage, warehousing, loading and unloading, and storing goods. The location is convenient; so, in the future, LO_7 will become one of the most competitive enterprises in the market. Moreover, the geographical advantage of these enterprises can help the parties save many logistical costs (LO_{10} in the north, LO_7 in the south). These two businesses have the advantage of all forms of transportation.

Table 8. Rank and score before alliances (calculated by researcher).

LOs	Score	Rank
LO1	1.1969	6
LO2	0.5554	9
LO3	0.4432	10
LO4	3.2525	1
LO5	1.0729	8
LO6	1.1042	7
LO7	1.2964	4
LO8	1.3031	3
LO9	1.5320	2
LO10	1.2242	5
Average		1.2981
Max		3.2525
Min		0.4432
St Dev		0.7646

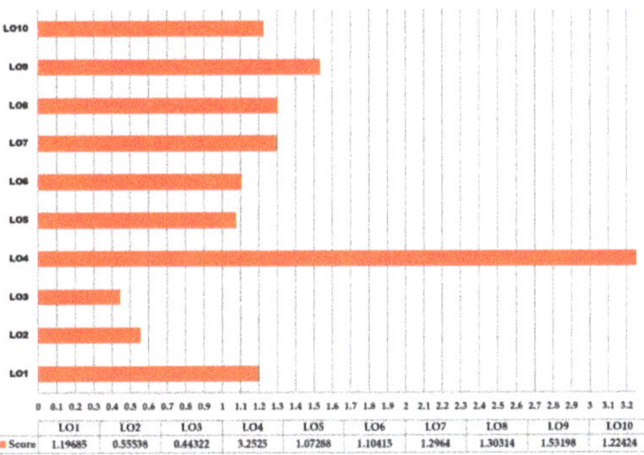

Figure 12. Score efficiency of LOs before alliances (source: researcher).

By road: LO_{10} in Hai Phong City–LO_7 in HCM City which is 1654.3 km apart (via National Highway 1A).

Waterway: LO_{10} is near Hai Phong port; LO_7 is near Cat Lai port in Ho Chi Minh City.

By air: LO_{10} is near Cat Bi airport, while LO_7 is near Tan Son Nhat airport.

By railway: LO_{10} is near Hai Phong station, LO_7 is near Saigon station.

Therefore, the alliance of LO_{10} and LO_7 is very convenient regarding all forms of transportation. These businesses can maximize each other's advantages, forming a win–win relationship.

According to statistics, logistics costs in Vietnam are still very high because about 70–75% of transport routes only carry one-way goods. When LO_7 and LO_{10} create an alliance, they can exploit freight in the opposite direction and save a lot of costs, such as material costs, personnel costs, road and bridge costs, and the cost of vehicle wear and tear. The alliance helps businesses access and share customers, increase revenue, and take advantage of economies of scale. This alliance will increase the competitive advantage for both parties. This is considered a reasonable tactic for LO_7 and LO_{10} during this pandemic period, and today's rapidly changing era of science, technology, and engineering. When implementing the alliance, businesses will solve difficult problems during and after the pandemic, aiming for sustainable development together. As every business is a cell of the economy, any business that survives and prospers will create a great impetus for the national and world economy to recover and develop rapidly.

Table 9. Performance ranking of virtual LOs (calculated by researcher).

DMU	Score	Rank
LO4	3.1323	1
LO9	1.5320	2
LO8	1.2891	3
LO7 + LO10	1.2060	4
LO1 + LO10	1.1506	5
LO4 + LO10	1.1447	6
LO6	1.1042	7
LO5	1.0729	8
LO8 + LO10	1.0569	9
LO6 + LO10	1.0098	10
LO7	1.0051	11
LO10	1.0019	12
LO1	1.0009	13
LO9 + LO10	0.8816	14
LO2 + LO10	0.8149	15
LO5 + LO10	0.7543	16
LO3 + LO10	0.7444	17
LO2	0.4930	18
LO3	0.4432	19

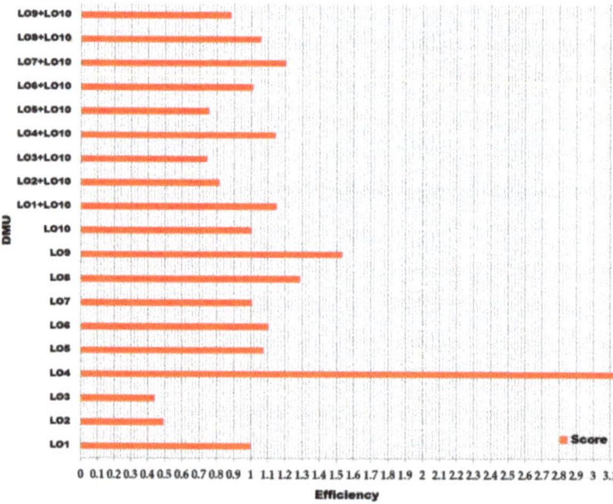

Figure 13. Score efficiency of virtual alliances (source: researcher).

Table 10. The alliances are not really suitable (calculated by researcher).

Virtual Alliance	Rank of LO Objectives (1)	Rank of Virtual Alliance (2)	Difference (1)–(2)
LO9 + LO10	12	14	(−2)
LO2 + LO10	12	15	(−3)
LO5 + LO10	12	16	(−4)
LO3 + LO10	12	17	(−5)

Table 11. The good alliances (calculated by researcher).

Virtual Alliance	Rank of LO Objectives (1)	Rank of Virtual Alliance (2)	Difference (1)–(2)
LO7 + LO10	12	4	8
LO1 + LO10	12	5	7
LO4 + LO10	12	6	6
LO8 + LO10	12	9	3
LO6 + LO10	12	10	2

3.4. Grey Forecasting Results

In this study, the authors used the GM (1, 1) model to forecast the business situation of two enterprises selected to implement a strategic alliance. This forecast result provides a solid basis for managers to make decisions using a complete picture of the business situation of partners in the period 2021–2024. The authors used the data of IN_1 of LO_7 to explain in detail the calculation steps of the forecast data of enterprises. The steps to calculate the total forecast are performed as follows:

The statistics on IN_1 of LO_7 in the period 2017–2020 were used to build the original value chain as follows:

$$X^{(0)} = (1,421,715,\ 1,625,789,\ 1,947,165,\ 2,346,510)$$

The authors use the cumulative addition method to build the value chain of $X^{(1)}$:

$$\begin{cases} X^{(1)}_{(1)} = X^{(0)}_{(1)} = 1,421,715 \\ X^{(1)}_{(2)} = X^{(0)}_{(1)} + X^{(0)}_{(2)} = 3,047,504 \\ X^{(1)}_{(3)} = X^{(1)}_{(2)} + X^{(0)}_{(3)} = 4,994,669 \\ X^{(1)}_{(4)} = X^{(1)}_{(3)} + X^{(0)}_{(4)} = 7,341,179 \end{cases}$$

$$X^{(1)} = (1,421,715,\ 3,047,504,\ 4,994,669,\ 7,341,179)$$

The authors use the value chain of $X^{(1)}$ to calculate the mean $Z^{(1)}$:

$$\begin{cases} Z^{(1)}_{(2)} = (1,421,715 + 3,047,504) \times 0.5 = 2,234,609.5 \\ Z^{(1)}_{(3)} = (3,047,504 + 4,994,669) \times 0.5 = 4,021,086.5 \\ Z^{(1)}_{(4)} = (4,994,669 + 7,341,179) \times 0.5 = 6,167,924.0 \end{cases}$$

After calculating the mean $Z^{(1)}$, the authors set up the following system of equations:

$$\begin{cases} 3,047,504 + 2,234,609.5 \times a = b \\ 4,994,669 + 4,021,086.5 \times a = b \\ 7,341,179 + 6,167,924.0 \times a = b \end{cases}$$

From the values in the above system of equations, the authors set up the matrices and find the coefficients a, b by the method of least squares:

$$B = \begin{bmatrix} -2,234,609.5 & 1 \\ -4,021,086.5 & 1 \\ -6,167,924.0 & 1 \end{bmatrix};\ Y_N = \begin{bmatrix} 3,047,504 \\ 4,994,669 \\ 7,341,179 \end{bmatrix};\ \begin{bmatrix} a \\ b \end{bmatrix} = (B^T B)^{(-1)} B^T \overline{Y}_N = \begin{bmatrix} -0.1833 \\ 1,213,958 \end{bmatrix}$$

With the coefficients a, b, the authors built the equation of the GM (1, 1) model:

$$\frac{dx^{(1)}_{(k)}}{d_{(k)}} - 0.1833x^{(1)}_{(k)} = 1,213,958$$

The formula for calculating the forecast values is set up as follows:

$$\hat{X}^{(1)}_{(k+1)} = 8,043,514.77 \times e^{0.1833k} - 6,621,799.77$$

Substituting the values of k in turn, the authors obtain the values of $\hat{X}^{(1)}_{(k+1)}$ as in Table 12.

Table 12. Values of $\hat{X}^{(1)}_{(k+1)}$.

k	0	1	2	3	4	5	6	7
$\hat{X}^{(1)}_{(k+1)}$	1,421,715	3,040,132.07	4,984,187.10	7,319,400.97	10,124,477.83	13,493,957.75	17,541,402.96	22,403,225.28

By the same calculation methods, the authors obtain forecast values that reflect the business situation of logistics enterprises participating in the strategic alliance in the period 2021–2024, which are shown in Tables 13 and 14, below.

To ensure the reliability of the forecast results, the authors used MAPE to recheck and the results are as follows: $MAPE_{LO7} = 3.96\%$; $MAPE_{LO10} = 2.06\%$. This result shows that the predictive values have very high accuracy (<10%). The forecast results provide managers of enterprises with an overview of the business situation of enterprises in the period 2021–2024. Therefore, managers of enterprises can use the forecast results in this study as a solid basis for making decisions about implementing alliances to bring high results for the business and sustainable development.

The cumulative method is used to calculate the forecast values below:

$$\hat{X}^{(0)}_{(1)} = X^{(1)}_{(1)} = 1,421,715$$
$$\hat{X}^{(0)}_{(2)} = \hat{X}^{(1)}_{(2)} - \hat{X}^{(1)}_{(1)} = 1,618,417.07$$
$$\hat{X}^{(0)}_{(3)} = \hat{X}^{(1)}_{(3)} - \hat{X}^{(1)}_{(2)} = 1,944,055.03$$
$$\hat{X}^{(0)}_{(4)} = \hat{X}^{(1)}_{(4)} - \hat{X}^{(1)}_{(3)} = 2,335,213.87$$
$$\hat{X}^{(0)}_{(5)} = \hat{X}^{(1)}_{(5)} - \hat{X}^{(1)}_{(4)} = 2,805,076.87$$
$$\hat{X}^{(0)}_{(6)} = \hat{X}^{(1)}_{(6)} - \hat{X}^{(1)}_{(5)} = 3,369,479.92$$
$$\hat{X}^{(0)}_{(7)} = \hat{X}^{(1)}_{(7)} - \hat{X}^{(1)}_{(6)} = 4,047,445.21$$
$$\hat{X}^{(0)}_{(8)} = \hat{X}^{(1)}_{(8)} - \hat{X}^{(1)}_{(7)} = 4,861,822.33$$

Table 13. Forecast results of LO7 (calculated by researcher).

Year	IN1	IN2	IN3	IN4	OU1	OU2
2021	2,805,076.87	4,303,481.46	3,711,574.61	1,16,408.90	4,053,514.37	3,66,039.62
2022	3,369,479.92	4,808,990.52	4,654,061.51	1,39,347.27	5,023,131.95	4,37,167.59
2023	4,047,445.21	5,373,879.28	5,835,875.82	1,66,805.63	6,224,686.10	5,22,116.97
2024	4,861,822.33	6,005,122.78	7,317,790.39	1,99,674.67	7,713,657.04	6,23,573.51

Table 14. Forecast results of LO10 (calculated by researcher).

Year	IN1	IN2	IN3	IN4	OU1	OU2
2021	1,719,878.32	1,304,769.41	78,465.61	256,273.93	2,415,700.90	2,297,303.85
2022	1,717,145.55	1,325,379.86	84,760.31	232,672.22	2,400,308.87	2,426,501.12
2023	1,714,417.13	1,346,315.89	91,559.99	211,244.13	2,385,014.91	2,562,964.27
2024	1,711,693.04	1,367,582.62	98,905.16	191,789.47	2,369,818.40	2,707,101.93

4. Conclusions

The COVID-19 pandemic has greatly affected the production and business situation of enterprises around the world. Enterprises in different industries and of different sizes have different levels of influence. In this study, the authors used the Malmquist productivity index to assess the impact of the pandemic on logistics enterprises in Vietnam and the super-slack-based model to evaluate the rankings for businesses in two steps before and after alliance implementation. The rankings are used to choose the optimal alliances for logistics enterprises in Vietnam. The alliances can help businesses save on transportation costs, loading and unloading costs, storage costs, and labor costs, while helping businesses increase revenue and profit. The alliances can help businesses promote their strengths and create competitive advantages. In addition, the authors used the Grey forecasting model to provide managers of enterprises with a complete picture of their partners' business situation in the period 2021–2024 as a solid basis for decision making.

5. Discussion

The research has some limitations, due to legal policies, environmental conditions, and weather, which affect the business situation of logistics enterprises. In addition, the business strategy of an enterprise also depends on the cultural characteristics, the owner's views on the development strategy and the resources of the enterprise. So, in practice, to implement this alliance, it is necessary to closely consider combining the above factors. In the future, it will be necessary to combine these factors with the models used in the research to obtain more comprehensive results.

Funding: This research received no external funding.

Institutional Review Board Statement: Not applicable.

Informed Consent Statement: Informed consent was obtained from all subjects involved in the study.

Data Availability Statement: Not applicable.

Conflicts of Interest: The author declares no conflict of interest.

References

1. Loan, H. The Picture of the Logistics Industry Is Not Uniform. VnEconomy. Available online: https://vneconomy.vn/ (accessed on 25 May 2021).
2. Liu, A.; Zhang, Y.; Luo, S.; Miao, J. Dual-Channel Global Closed-Loop Supply Chain Network Optimization Based on Random Demand and Recovery Rate. *Int. J. Environ. Res. Public Health* **2020**, *17*, 8768. [CrossRef]
3. Van, N. Vietnam's Transport Infrastructure after 35 Years of Renovation: One Step Ahead to Promote Economic Development. Labour Online. Available online: https://laodong.vn/ (accessed on 27 June 2021).
4. Vietnam Logistics Report 2020. Ministry of Industry and Trade. Available online: https://moit.gov.vn/ (accessed on 25 June 2021).
5. Toloo, M. An Equivalent Linear Programming Form of General Linear Fractional Programming: A Duality Approach. *Mathematics* **2021**, *9*, 1586. [CrossRef]
6. Wong, W.-P. A Global Search Method for Inputs and Outputs in Data Envelopment Analysis: Procedures and Managerial Perspectives. *Symmetry* **2021**, *13*, 1155. [CrossRef]
7. Parte, L.; Alberca, P. Business Performance and Sustainability in Cultural and Rural Tourism Destinations. *Mathematics* **2021**, *9*, 892. [CrossRef]
8. Lacko, R.; Hajduová, Z.; Zawada, M. The Efficiency of Circular Economies: A Comparison of Visegrád Group Countries. *Energies* **2021**, *14*, 1680. [CrossRef]

9. Chowdhury, H.; Wodchis, W.; Laporte, A. Efficiency and technological change in health care services in Ontario: An application of Malmquist Productivity Index with bootstrapping. *Int. J. Product. Perform. Manag.* **2011**, *60*, 721–745. [CrossRef]

10. Abbas, M.; Hammad, R.S.; Elshahat, M.F.; Azid, T. Efficiency, productivity and Islamic banks: An application of DEA and Malmquist index. *Humanomics* **2015**, *31*, 118–131. [CrossRef]

11. Bahrini, R. Productivity of MENA Islamic banks: A bootstrapped Malmquist index approach. *Int. J. Islamic Middle East. Financ. Manag.* **2015**, *8*, 508–528. [CrossRef]

12. Lee, Y.J.; Joo, S.-J.; Park, H.G. An application of data envelopment analysis for Korean banks with negative data. *Benchmarking Int. J.* **2017**, *24*, 1052–1064. [CrossRef]

13. Wang, C.-N.; Nguyen, H.-K. Enhancing Urban Development Quality Based on the Results of Appraising Efficient Performance of Investors—A Case Study in Vietnam. *Sustainability* **2017**, *9*, 1397. [CrossRef]

14. Deng, J.L. Introduction to Grey system theory. *J. Grey Syst.* **1989**, *1*, 1–24.

15. Stanujkić, D.; Karabašević, D.; Popović, G.; Stanimirović, P.S.; Saračević, M.; Smarandache, F.; Katsikis, V.N.; Ulutaş, A. A New Grey Approach for Using SWARA and PIPRECIA Methods in a Group Decision-Making Environment. *Mathematics* **2021**, *9*, 1554. [CrossRef]

16. Gerus-Gościewska, M.; Gościewski, D. Grey Systems Theory as an Effective Method for Analyzing Scarce, Incomplete and Uncertain Data on the Example of a Survey of Public Perceptions of Safety in Urban Spaces. *Land* **2021**, *10*, 73. [CrossRef]

17. Wu, X.; Zhou, J.; Yu, H.; Liu, D.; Xie, K.; Chen, Y.; Hu, J.; Sun, H.; Xing, F. The Development of a Hybrid Wavelet-ARIMA-LSTM Model for Precipitation Amounts and Drought Analysis. *Atmosphere* **2021**, *12*, 74. [CrossRef]

18. Kokocińska, M.; Nowak, M.; Łopatka, P. Measuring the Efficiency of Economic Growth towards Sustainable Growth with Grey System Theory. *Sustainability* **2020**, *12*, 10121. [CrossRef]

19. Gligorić, Z.; Gligorić, M.; Halilović, D.; Beljić, Č.; Urošević, K. Hybrid Stochastic-Grey Model to Forecast the Behavior of Metal Price in the Mining Industry. *Sustainability* **2020**, *12*, 6533. [CrossRef]

20. Fan, G.-F.; Wang, A.; Hong, W.-C. Combining Grey Model and Self-Adapting Intelligent Grey Model with Genetic Algorithm and Annual Share Changes in Natural Gas Demand Forecasting. *Energies* **2018**, *11*, 1625. [CrossRef]

21. Nguyen, H.-K. Combining DEA and ARIMA Models for Partner Selection in the Supply Chain of Vietnam's Construction Industry. *Mathematics* **2020**, *8*, 866. [CrossRef]

22. Wang, G.; Qian, Z.; Deng, X. Analysis of Environmental Policy and the Performance of Sustainable Agricultural Development in China. *Sustainability* **2020**, *12*, 10453. [CrossRef]

23. Le, T.; Wang, C.; Nguyen, H. Using the optimization algorithm to evaluate and predict the business performance of logistics companies—A case study in Vietnam. *Appl. Econ.* **2020**, *52*, 4196–4212. [CrossRef]

24. Liu, Y.; Sun, H.; Shi, L.; Wang, H.; Xiu, Z.; Qiu, X.; Chang, H.; Xie, Y.; Wang, Y.; Wang, C. Spatial-Temporal Changes and Driving Factors of Land-Use Eco-Efficiency Incorporating Ecosystem Services in China. *Sustainability* **2021**, *13*, 728. [CrossRef]

25. Nguyen, H.-K. Applications Optimal Math Model to Solve Difficult Problems for Businesses Producing and Processing Agricultural Products in Vietnam. *Axioms* **2021**, *10*, 90. [CrossRef]

26. Hou, J.; Ruan, X.; Lv, J.; Guo, H. Two-Stage Super-Efficiency Slacks-Based Model to Assess China's Ecological Wellbeing. *Int. J. Environ. Res. Public Health* **2020**, *17*, 7045. [CrossRef] [PubMed]

27. Ebtehaj, I.; Soltani, K.; Amiri, A.; Faramarzi, M.; Madramootoo, C.A.; Bonakdari, H. Prognostication of Shortwave Radiation Using an Improved No-Tuned Fast Machine Learning. *Sustainability* **2021**, *13*, 8009. [CrossRef]

28. Lin, Z.; Guo, W. Cotton Stand Counting from Unmanned Aerial System Imagery Using MobileNet and CenterNet Deep Learning Models. *Remote Sens.* **2021**, *13*, 2822. [CrossRef]

29. Statistics. General Statistics Office of Vietnam. Available online: https://www.gso.gov.vn/ (accessed on 25 May 2021).

Article

Qualitative Properties of Randomized Maximum Entropy Estimates of Probability Density Functions

Yuri S. Popkov [1,2,3]

[1] Federal Research Center "Computer Science and Control" of Russian Academy of Sciences, 119333 Moscow, Russia; popkov@isa.ru
[2] Institute of Control Sciences of Russian Academy of Sciences, 117997 Moscow, Russia
[3] Department of Software Engineering, ORT Braude College, 2161002 Karmiel, Israel

Abstract: The problem of randomized maximum entropy estimation for the probability density function of random model parameters with real data and measurement noises was formulated. This estimation procedure maximizes an information entropy functional on a set of integral equalities depending on the real data set. The technique of the Gâteaux derivatives is developed to solve this problem in analytical form. The probability density function estimates depend on Lagrange multipliers, which are obtained by balancing the model's output with real data. A global theorem for the implicit dependence of these Lagrange multipliers on the data sample's length is established using the rotation of homotopic vector fields. A theorem for the asymptotic efficiency of randomized maximum entropy estimate in terms of stationary Lagrange multipliers is formulated and proved. The proposed method is illustrated on the problem of forecasting of the evolution of the thermokarst lake area in Western Siberia.

Keywords: randomized maximum entropy estimation; probability density functions; Lagrange multipliers; Lyapunov-type problems; implicit function; rotation of vector field; asymptotic efficiency; thermokarst lakes; forecasting

Citation: Popkov, Y.S. Qualitative Properties of Randomized Maximum Entropy Estimates of Probability Density Functions. *Mathematics* **2021**, *9*, 548. https://doi.org/10.3390/math9050548

Academic Editors: Mikhail Posypkin, Andrey Gorshenin and Vladimir Titarev

Received: 28 January 2021
Accepted: 2 March 2021
Published: 5 March 2021

Publisher's Note: MDPI stays neutral with regard to jurisdictional claims in published maps and institutional affiliations.

1. Introduction

Estimating the characteristics of models is a very popular and, at the same time, important problem of science. This problem arises in applications with unknown parameters, which have to be estimated somehow using real data sets. In particular, such problems have turned out to be fundamental in machine learning procedures [1–5]. The core of these procedures is a parametrized model trained by statistically estimating the unknown parameters based on real data. Most of the econometric problems associated with reconstructing functional relations and forecasting also reduce to estimating the model parameters; for example, see [6,7].

The problems described above are solved using traditional mathematical statistics methods, such as the maximum likelihood method and its derivatives, the method of moments, Bayesian methods, and their numerous modifications [8,9].

Among the mathematical tools for parametric estimation mentioned, a special place is occupied by entropy maximization methods for finite-dimensional probability distributions [10,11].

Consider a random variable x taking discrete values $x_1, \ldots, x_n$ with probabilities $p_1, \ldots, p_n$, respectively, and r functions $f_1(x), \ldots, f_r(x)$ of this variable with discrete values. The discrete probability distribution function $\mathbf{p}(x) = \{p_1(x_1), \ldots, p_n(x_n)\}$ is defined as the solution of the problem

$$H(\mathbf{p}) = -\sum_{i=1}^{n} p_i \ln p_i, \quad \sum_{i=1}^{n} p_i f_k(x_i) \le q_k, \quad k = 1, \ldots, r,$$

where $q_1, \ldots, q_r$ are given constants.

If $f_k(x_i) \equiv x_i^k$, then the system of equalities specifies constraints on the kth moments of the discrete random variable x. In the case of equality constraints, some modifications of this problem adapted to different applications were studied in [10–13]. Since this problem is conditionally extremal, it can be solved using the Lagrange method, which leads to a system of equations for Lagrange multipliers. The latter often turn out to be substantially nonlinear functions, and hence, rather sophisticated techniques are needed for their numerical calculation [14,15].

In the case of inequality constraints, this problem belongs to the class of mathematical programming problems [16].

The entropy maximization principle is adopted to estimate the parameters of a priori distributions when constructing Bayesian estimates [17,18] or maximum likelihood estimates.

The parameters of probability distributions (continuous or discrete) can be estimated using various mathematical statistics methods, including the method of entropy maximization. Their efficiency in hydrological problems was compared in [19]. Apparently, the method of entropy maximization yields the best results in such problems due to the structure of hydrological data.

The problem of estimating some model characteristics on real data was further developed in connection with the appearance of new machine learning methods, called randomized machine learning (RML) [20]. They are based on models with random parameters, and it is necessary to estimate the probability density functions of these parameters. The estimation algorithm (RML algorithm) is formulated in terms of functional entropy-linear programming [21].

The original statement of this problem was to estimate probability density functions (PDFs) in RML procedures. However, in recent times, a more general context has been assumed—the method of maximizing entropy functionals for constructing estimates of continuous probability density functions using real data (randomized maximum entropy (RME) estimation).

In this paper, the general RME estimation problem is formulated; its solutions, numerical algorithms, and the asymptotic properties of the solutions are studied. The theoretical results are illustrated by an important application—estimating the evolution of the thermokarst lake area in Western Siberia.

2. Statement of the RME Estimation Problem

Consider a scalar continuous function $\varphi(x, \theta)$ with parameters $\theta = \{\theta_1, \ldots, \theta_n\}$. Assume that this function is a characteristic of an object's model with an input x and an output $\hat{y}$. Let $\mathbf{x}^{(r)} = \{x[1], \ldots, x[r]\}$ and $\mathbf{y}^{(r)} = \{y[1], \ldots, y[r]\}$ be given measurements at time $t = 1, \ldots, r$. Note that the latter measurements are obtained with random vector errors $\xi = \{\xi[1], \ldots, \xi[r]\}$, which are generally different for different time points.

Thus, after r measurements, the model and observations are described by the equations

$$
\begin{aligned}
\hat{\mathbf{y}} &= \Gamma(\mathbf{x}^{(r)}, \theta), \\
\hat{\mathbf{v}} &= \hat{\mathbf{y}} + \xi,
\end{aligned}
\tag{1}
$$

where the vector function $\Gamma(\mathbf{x}^{(r)}, \theta)$ has the components $\varphi(x[t], \theta)$, where $t = 1, \ldots, r$ are the time points; $\hat{\mathbf{v}}$ denotes the observed output of the model containing measurement noises of the object's output.

Let us introduce a series of assumptions necessary for further considerations.

- The random parameters are $\theta \in \Theta \subset R^n$, $\Theta = [\theta^-, \theta^+]$, where $[\bullet, \bullet]$ is a vectorial segment in the space R^n [22].
- The PDF $P(\theta)$ of the parameters is continuously differentiable on its support Θ.

- The random noise is $\xi \in \Xi \subset R^r$, where

$$\Xi = \bigotimes_{t=1}^{r} \Xi_t, \qquad \Xi_t = [\xi_t^-, \xi_t^+]. \tag{2}$$

- The PDF $Q(\xi)$ of the measurement noises is continuously differentiable on the support Ξ and also has the multiplicative structure

$$Q(\xi) = \prod_{t=1}^{r} Q_t(\xi[t]). \tag{3}$$

The estimation problem is stated as follows: Find the estimates of the PDFs $P^*(\theta)$ and $Q^*(\xi)$ that maximize the generalized information entropy functional

$$\mathcal{H}[P(\theta), Q(\xi)] = -\int_Q P(\theta)\ln P(\theta)d\theta - \sum_{t=1}^{r}\int_{\Xi_t} Q_t(\xi[t])\ln Q_t(\xi[t]) \Rightarrow \max \tag{4}$$

subject to
—the normalization conditions of the PDFs given by

$$\int_\Theta P(\theta)d\theta = 1; \quad \int_{\Xi_t} Q_t(\xi[t])d\xi[t] = 1, \quad t = 1,\ldots,r; \tag{5}$$

and
—the empirical balance conditions

$$\begin{aligned}
\Phi[P(\theta), Q(\xi)] &= \mathbf{y}^{(r)}, \\
\Phi[P(\theta), Q(\xi)] &= \{\Phi_1[P(\theta), Q(\xi)], \ldots, \Phi_r[P(\theta), Q(\xi)]\} \\
\Phi_t[P(\theta), Q(\xi)] &= \int_\Theta \varphi(x[t], \theta)P(\theta)d\theta + \int_{\Xi_t} Q_t(\xi[t])\xi[t]d\xi[t], \quad t = 1,\ldots,r,
\end{aligned} \tag{6}$$

where $\mathbf{y}^{(r)} = \{y[1],\ldots,y[r]\}$ are the measured data on the object's output. We will denote the problems (4)–(6) as the RME estimate.

Problems (4)–(6) are of the Lyapunov type [23,24], as they have an integral functional and also integral constraints.

3. Optimality Conditions

The optimality conditions in optimization problems of the Lyapunov type are formulated in terms of Lagrange multipliers. In addition, the Gâteaux derivatives of the problem's functionals are used [25].

The Lagrange functional is defined by

$$\begin{aligned}
\mathcal{L}[P(\theta), Q(\xi), \mu, \eta, \lambda] &= \mathcal{H}[P(\theta), Q(\xi)] + \mu\left(1 - \int_\Theta P(\theta)d\theta\right) + \\
&+ \sum_{t=1}^{r}\eta_t\left(1 - \int_{\Xi_t} Q_t(\xi[t])d\xi[t]\right) + \\
&+ \sum_{t=1}^{r}\lambda_t\left(y[t] - \int_\Theta P(\theta)\varphi(x[t], \theta)d\theta - \int_{\Xi_t} Q_t(\xi[t])\xi[t]d\xi[t]\right).
\end{aligned} \tag{7}$$

Let us recall the technique for obtaining optimality conditions in terms of the Gâteaux derivatives [26].

The PDFs $P(\theta)$ and $Q_t(\xi[t])$, $(t = 1, \ldots, r)$, are continuously differentiable, i.e., belong to the class C^1. Choosing arbitrary functions $h(\theta)$ and $w_t(\xi[t])$, $(t = 1, \ldots, r)$, from this class, we represent the PDFs as

$$P(\theta) = P^*(\theta) + \alpha h(\theta); \quad Q_t(\xi[t]) = Q_t^*(\xi[t]) + \beta_t w_i(\xi[t]), \quad t = 1, \ldots, r,$$

where the PDFs $P^*(\theta)$ and $Q_t^*(\xi[t])$ are the solutions of problems (4)–(6), and α and $\beta_1, \ldots, \beta_r$ are parameters.

Next, we substitute the above representations of the PDFs into (7). If all functions from C^1 are assumed to be fixed, the Lagrange functional depends on the parameters α and $\beta_1, \ldots, \beta_r$. Then, the first-order optimality conditions for the functional (7) in terms of the Gâteaux derivative take the form

$$\frac{d\mathcal{L}}{d\alpha}\bigg|_{(\alpha,\beta)=0} = 0, \quad \frac{\partial\mathcal{L}}{\partial\beta_t}\bigg|_{(\alpha,\beta)=0} = 0, \quad t = 1, \ldots, r.$$

These conditions lead to the following system of integral equations:

$$\int_\Theta h(\theta)\Omega(\theta)d\theta = 0, \quad \int_{\Xi_t} w_t(\xi[t])Y_t(\xi[t])d\xi[t] = 0, \quad t = 1, \ldots, r,$$

which are satisfied for any functions $h(\theta)$ and $w_1(\xi[1]), \ldots, w_r(\xi[r])$ from C^1 if and only if

$$\Omega(\theta) = 0, \quad Y_t(\xi[t]) = 0, \quad t = 1, \ldots, r.$$

The optimality conditions for problems (4)–(6) are given by

$$\Omega(\theta) = \ln P^*(\theta) + 1 - \mu - \sum_{t=1}^{s} \lambda_t \varphi(x[t], \theta) = 0, \tag{8}$$

$$Y_t(\xi[t]) = \ln Q_t^*(\xi[t]) + 1 - \eta_t - \lambda_t \xi[t] = 0, \quad t = 1, \ldots, r. \tag{9}$$

Hence, the entropy-optimal PDFs of the model parameters and measurement noises have the form

$$P^*(\theta \mid \mathbf{y}^{(r)}, \mathbf{x}^{(r)}) = \frac{\exp\left(-\sum_{j=1}^{r} \lambda_j(\mathbf{y}^{(r)}, \mathbf{x}^{(r)})\varphi(x[j], \theta)\right)}{\mathcal{P}(\lambda(\mathbf{y}^{(r)}, \mathbf{x}^{(r)}))},$$

$$Q_t^*(\xi[t] \mid \mathbf{y}^{(r)}, \mathbf{x}^{(r)}) = \frac{\exp\left(\lambda_t(\mathbf{y}^{(r)}, \mathbf{x}^{(r)})\xi[t]\right)}{\mathcal{Q}_t(\lambda_t(\mathbf{y}^{(r)}, \mathbf{x}^{(r)}))}, \quad t = 1, \ldots, r, \tag{10}$$

where

$$\mathcal{P}(\lambda(\mathbf{y}^{(r)}, \mathbf{x}^{(r)})) = \int_\Theta \exp\left(-\sum_{j=1}^{r} \lambda_j(\mathbf{y}^{(r)}, \mathbf{x}^{(r)})\varphi(x[j], \theta)\right)d\theta,$$

$$\mathcal{Q}_t(\lambda_t(\mathbf{y}^{(r)}, \mathbf{x}^{(r)})) = \int_{\Xi_t} \exp\left(\lambda_t(\mathbf{y}^{(r)}, \mathbf{x}^{(r)})\xi[t]\right)d\xi[t], \quad t = 1, \ldots, r. \tag{11}$$

Due to equalities (10) and (11), the entropy-optimal PDFs are parametrized by the Lagrange multipliers $\lambda_1, \ldots, \lambda_r$, which represent the solutions of the empirical balance equations

$$\frac{\mathcal{G}(\lambda(\mathbf{y}^{(r)}, \mathbf{x}^{(r)}))}{\mathcal{P}(\lambda(\mathbf{y}^{(r)}, \mathbf{x}^{(r)}))} + \frac{\mathcal{E}_t(\lambda_t(\mathbf{y}^{(r)}, \mathbf{x}^{(r)}))}{\mathcal{Q}_t(\lambda_t(\mathbf{y}^{(r)}, \mathbf{x}^{(r)}))} = y[t], \quad t = 1, \ldots, r, \tag{12}$$

where

$$\mathcal{G}(\lambda(\mathbf{y}^{(r)}, \mathbf{x}^{(r)})) = \int_{\Theta} \varphi(x[t], \theta) \exp\left(-\sum_{j=1}^{r} \lambda_j(\mathbf{y}^{(r)}, \mathbf{x}^{(r)}) \varphi(x[j], \theta)\right) d\theta,$$

$$\mathcal{E}_t(\lambda_t(\mathbf{y}^{(r)}, \mathbf{x}^{(r)})) = \int_{\Xi_t} \xi[t] \exp\left(-\lambda_t(\mathbf{y}^{(r)}, \mathbf{x}^{(r)}) \xi[t]\right) d\xi[t], \quad t = 1, \ldots, r. \tag{13}$$

The solution $\lambda^*(\mathbf{y}^{(r)}, \mathbf{x}^{(r)})$ of these equations depends on the sample $(\mathbf{y}^{(r)}, \mathbf{x}^{(r)})$ used for constructing the RME estimates of the PDFs.

4. Existence of an Implicit Function

The second term in the balance Equations (12) and (13) is the mean value of the noise in each measurement t. The noises and their characteristics are often assumed to be equal over the measurements:

$$\xi^- \leq \xi[t] \leq \xi^+, \quad t = 1, \ldots, r. \tag{14}$$

Therefore, the mean value of the noise is given by

$$\bar{\xi} = \frac{\mathcal{E}_t(\lambda_t(\mathbf{y}^{(r)}, \mathbf{x}^{(r)}))}{\mathcal{Q}_t(\lambda_t(\mathbf{y}^{(r)}, \mathbf{x}^{(r)}))}, \quad \xi^- \leq \bar{\xi} \leq \xi^+. \tag{15}$$

The balance equations can be written as

$$W_t(\lambda \mid \tilde{y}[t], \mathbf{x}^{(r)}) = \int_{\Theta} (\varphi(x[t], \theta) - \tilde{y}[t]) \exp\left(-\sum_{j=1}^{r} \lambda_j(\tilde{\mathbf{y}}^{(r)}, \mathbf{x}^{(r)}) \varphi(x[j], \theta)\right) d\theta = 0,$$

$$t = 1, \ldots, r, \tag{16}$$

where

$$\tilde{y}[t] = y[t] - \bar{\xi}, \qquad \tilde{\mathbf{y}}^{(r)} = \{\tilde{y}[1], \ldots, \tilde{y}[r]\}. \tag{17}$$

In the vector form, Equation (16) is described by

$$\mathbf{W}(\lambda \mid \tilde{\mathbf{y}}^{(r)}, \mathbf{x}^{(r)}) = \mathbf{0}. \tag{18}$$

Equation (21) defines an implicit function $\lambda(\tilde{\mathbf{y}}^{(r)}, \mathbf{x}^{(r)})$. The existence and properties of this implicit function depend on the properties of the Jacobian matrix

$$J_\lambda(\lambda \mid \tilde{\mathbf{y}}^{(r)}, \mathbf{x}^{(r)}) = \left[\frac{\partial W_t}{\partial \lambda_i} \mid (t, i) = 1, \ldots, r\right], \tag{19}$$

which has the elements

$$\frac{\partial W_t}{\partial \lambda_i} = \int_{Q} (\varphi(x[t], \theta) - \tilde{y}[t]) \varphi(x[i], \theta) \sum_{j=1}^{r} \exp\left(-\sum_{j=1}^{r} \lambda_j \varphi(x[j], \theta)\right) d\theta. \tag{20}$$

Theorem 1. *Let the next conditions be valid (assume that):*
- *The function $\varphi(\mathbf{x}^{(r)}, \theta)$ is continuous in all variables.*
- *For any $(\mathbf{x}^{(r)}, \tilde{\mathbf{y}}^{(r)}) \in R^r \times R^r$,*

$$\det J_\lambda(\lambda \mid \tilde{\mathbf{y}}^{(r)}, \mathbf{x}^{(r)}) \neq 0, \tag{21}$$

$$\lim_{\|\lambda\| \to \infty} \mathbf{W}(\lambda \mid \tilde{\mathbf{y}}^{(r)}, \mathbf{x}^{(r)}) = \pm\infty. \tag{22}$$

Then, there exists a unique implicit function $\lambda(\tilde{\mathbf{y}}^{(r)}, \mathbf{x}^{(r)},)$ defined on $R^r \times R^r$.

Proof of Theorem 1. Due to the first assumption, the continuous function $\mathbf{W}(\lambda \mid \tilde{\mathbf{y}}^{(r)}, \mathbf{x}^{(r)})$ induces the vector field $\Phi_{(\tilde{\mathbf{y}}^{(r)}, \mathbf{x}^{(r)})}(\lambda) = \mathbf{W}(\lambda \mid \tilde{\mathbf{y}}^{(r)}, \mathbf{x}^{(r)})$ in the space $R^r \times R^r$.

We choose an arbitrary vector $\mathbf{u}$ in R^r and define the vector field

$$\Pi_{\mathbf{u}}(\lambda) = \Phi_{(\tilde{\mathbf{y}}^{(r)}, \mathbf{x}^{(r)})}(\lambda) - \mathbf{u}.$$

By condition (22), the field $\Pi_{\mathbf{u}}(\lambda)$ with a fixed vector $\mathbf{u}$ has no zeros on the spheres $\|\lambda\| = \varrho$ of a sufficiently large radius ϱ.

Hence, a rotation is well defined on the spheres $\|\lambda\| = \varrho$ of a sufficiently large radius ϱ. For details, see [27].

Consider the two vector fields

$$\Pi_{\mathbf{u}^{(1)}}(\lambda) = \Phi_{(\tilde{\mathbf{y}}^{(r)}, \mathbf{x}^{(r)})}(\lambda) - \mathbf{u}^{(1)}, \quad \Pi_{\mathbf{u}^{(2)}}(\lambda) = \Phi_{(\tilde{\mathbf{y}}^{(r)}, \mathbf{x}^{(r)})}(\lambda) - \mathbf{u}^{(2)}.$$

These vector fields are homotopic on the spheres of a sufficiently large radius, i.e., the field

$$\Omega(\lambda) = \alpha \Pi_{\mathbf{u}^{(1)}}(\lambda) + (1 - \alpha)\Pi_{\mathbf{u}^{(2)}}(\lambda) = \Phi_{(\tilde{\mathbf{y}}^{(r)}, \mathbf{x}^{(r)})}(\lambda) - [\alpha \mathbf{u}^{(1)} + (1 - \alpha)\mathbf{u}^{(2)}]$$

has no zeros on the spheres of a sufficiently large radius for any $\alpha \in [0, 1]$. Homotopic fields have identical rotations [27]:

$$\gamma(\Pi_{\mathbf{u}^{(1)}}(\lambda)) = \gamma(\Pi_{\mathbf{u}^{(2)}}(\lambda)).$$

The vector fields $\Pi_{\mathbf{u}^{(1)}}(\lambda)$ and $\Pi_{\mathbf{u}^{(2)}}(\lambda)$ are nondegenerate on the spheres of a sufficiently large radius; in the ball $\|\lambda\| \leq \varrho_1 < \varrho$, however, each of them may have a number of singular points. We denote by $\kappa(\mathbf{u}^{(1)})$ and $\kappa(\mathbf{u}^{(2)})$ the numbers of singular points of the vector fields $\Pi_{\mathbf{u}^{(1)}}(\lambda)$ and $\Pi_{\mathbf{u}^{(2)}}(\lambda)$, respectively. As the vector fields are homotopic,

$$\kappa(\mathbf{u}^{(1)}) = \kappa(\mathbf{u}^{(2)}) = \kappa.$$

In view of (21), these singular points are isolated.

Now, let us utilize the index of a singular point introduced in [27]:

$$\mathrm{ind}\,(\lambda^0) = (-1)^{\beta(\lambda^0)},$$

where $\beta(\lambda^0)$ is the number of eigenvalues of the matrix $\Pi'_{\mathbf{u}}(\lambda^0) = J_\lambda(\lambda^0 \mid, \tilde{\mathbf{y}}^{(r)}, \mathbf{x}^{(r)})$ with the negative real part. By definition, the value of this index depends not on the magnitude of $\beta(\lambda^0)$, but on its parity. Due to condition (21), all singular points have the same parity. Really, $J_\lambda(\lambda^0 \mid \tilde{\mathbf{y}}^{(r)}, \mathbf{x}^{(r)}) \neq 0$, and hence, for any $\tilde{\mathbf{y}}^{(r)}, \mathbf{x}^{(r)} \in R^r \times R^r$, the eigenvalues of the matrix $J_\lambda(\lambda^0 \mid \tilde{\mathbf{y}}^{(r)}, \mathbf{x}^{(r)})$ may move from the left half-plane to the right one in pairs only: Real eigenvalues are transformed into pairs of complex–conjugate ones, passing through the imaginary axis.

In view of this fact, the rotation of the homotopic fields (20) is given by

$$\gamma(\Pi_{\mathbf{u}}) = \kappa(-1)^\beta,$$

where β is the number of eigenvalues of the matrix $\Pi'_{\mathbf{u}}(\lambda)$ for some singular point.

It remains to demonstrate that the vector field $\Pi_{\mathbf{u}}(\lambda)$ has a unique singular point in the ball $\|\lambda\| \leq \varrho_1 < \varrho$. Consider the equation

$$\Pi_{\mathbf{u}}(\lambda) = \Phi_{(\tilde{\mathbf{y}}^{(r)}, \mathbf{x}^{(r)})}(\lambda) - \mathbf{u} = 0.$$

Assume that for each fixed pair $(\tilde{\mathbf{y}}^{(r)}, \mathbf{x}^{(r)})$, this equation has κ singular points, i.e., the functions $\lambda^{(1)}(\tilde{\mathbf{y}}^{(r)}, \mathbf{x}^{(r)}), \ldots, \lambda^{(\kappa)}(\tilde{\mathbf{y}}^{(r)}, \mathbf{x}^{(r)})$. Therefore, it defines a multivalued function $\lambda(\tilde{\mathbf{y}}^{(r)}, \mathbf{x}^{(r)})$, whose κ branches are isolated (the latter property follows from the isolation of the singular points). Due to condition (21), each of the branches $\lambda^{(i)}(\tilde{\mathbf{y}}^{(r)}, \mathbf{x}^{(r)})$ defines an open set in the space R^r, and

$$\bigcup_{i=1}^{\kappa} \lambda^{(i)}(\tilde{\mathbf{y}}^{(r)}, \mathbf{x}^{(r)}) = R^r.$$

This is possible if and only if $\kappa = 1$. Hence, for each pair $(\tilde{\mathbf{y}}^{(r)}, \mathbf{x}^{(r)})$ from $R^r \times R^r$, there exists a unique function $\lambda^*(\tilde{\mathbf{y}}^{(r)}, \mathbf{x}^{(r)})$ for which the function $\mathbf{W}(\lambda \,|\, \tilde{\mathbf{y}}^{(r)}, \mathbf{x}^{(r)})$ will vanish. $\square$

Theorem 2. *Under the assumptions of Theorem 1, the function $\lambda(\tilde{\mathbf{y}}^{(r)}, \mathbf{x}^{(r)})$ is real analytical in all variables.*

Proof of Theorem 2. From (15), it follows that the function $\mathbf{W}(\lambda \,|\, \tilde{\mathbf{y}}^{(r)}, \mathbf{x}^{(r)})$ is analytical in all variables. Therefore, the left-hand side of Equation (15) can be expanded into the generalized Taylor series [26], and the solution can be constructed in the form of the generalized Taylor series as well. The power elements of this series are determined using a recursive procedure. $\square$

5. Asymptotic Efficiency of RME Estimates

The RME estimate yields the entropy-optimal PDFs (10) for the arrays of input and output data, each of size r. For the sake of convenience, consider the PDFs parametrized by the exponential Lagrange multipliers $z = \exp(-\lambda)$. Then, equalities (10) take the form

$$P^*\left(\theta, \mathbf{z}(\mathbf{y}^{(r)}, \mathbf{x}^{(r)})\right) = \frac{\prod_{j=1}^{r}[z_j(\mathbf{y}^{(r)}, \mathbf{x}^{(r)})]^{\varphi(x[j],\theta)}}{\int_{\Theta} \prod_{j=1}^{r}[z_j(\mathbf{y}^{(r)}, \mathbf{x}^{(r)})]^{\varphi(x[j],\theta)} d\theta},$$

$$Q_t^*(\xi[t], z_t(\mathbf{y}^{(r)}, \mathbf{x}^{(r)})) = \frac{[z_t(\mathbf{y}^{(r)}, \mathbf{x}^{(r)})]^{\xi[t]}}{\int_{\Xi_t} [z_t(\mathbf{y}^{(r)}, \mathbf{x}^{(r)})]^{\xi[t]} d\xi[t]}, \quad t = 1, \ldots, r. \qquad (23)$$

Consequently, the structure of the PDF significantly depends on the values of the exponential Lagrange multipliers $\mathbf{z}$, which, in turn, depend on the data arrays $\mathbf{y}^{(r)}$ and $\mathbf{x}^{(r)}$.

Definition 1. *The estimates $P^*(\theta, \mathbf{z}^*)$ and $Q_t^*(\xi[t], z_t^*)$ are said to be asymptotically efficient if*

$$\lim_{r \to \infty} P^*\left(\theta, \mathbf{z}(\mathbf{y}^{(r)}, \mathbf{x}^{(r)})\right) = P^*(\theta, \mathbf{z}^*),$$

$$\lim_{r \to \infty} Q_t^*(\xi[t], z_t(\mathbf{y}^{(r)}, \mathbf{x}^{(r)})) = Q_t^*(\xi[t], z_t^*), \quad t = 1, \ldots, r; \qquad (24)$$

where

$$\mathbf{z}^* = \lim_{r \to \infty} \mathbf{z}(\mathbf{y}^{(r)}, \mathbf{x}^{(r)}). \qquad (25)$$

Consider the empirical balance Equation (21), written in terms of the exponential Lagrange multipliers:

$$\Phi_t(\mathbf{z}, \tilde{\mathbf{y}}^{(r)}, \mathbf{x}^{(r)}) = \int_{\Theta} \prod_{j=1}^{r}[z_j(\tilde{\mathbf{y}}^{(r)}, \mathbf{x}^{(r)})]^{\varphi(x[j],\theta)} (\varphi(x[t], \theta) - \tilde{y}[t]) d\theta = 0, \quad t = 1, \ldots, r. \qquad (26)$$

As has been demonstrated above, Equation (26) defines an implicit analytical function $\mathbf{z} = \mathbf{z}(\tilde{\mathbf{y}}^{(r)}, \mathbf{x}^{(r)})$ for $(\tilde{\mathbf{y}}^{(r)}, \mathbf{x}^{(r)}) \in R^r \times R^r$.

Differentiating the left- and right-hand sides of these equations with respect to $\tilde{\mathbf{y}}^{(r)}$ and $\mathbf{x}^{(r)}$ yields

$$\frac{\partial \mathbf{z}}{\partial \tilde{\mathbf{y}}^{(r)}} = -\left[\frac{\partial \Phi}{\partial \mathbf{z}}\right]^{-1}\frac{\partial \Phi}{\partial \tilde{\mathbf{y}}^{(r)}},$$

$$\frac{\partial \mathbf{z}}{\partial \mathbf{x}^{(r)}} = -\left[\frac{\partial \Phi}{\partial \mathbf{z}}\right]^{-1}\frac{\partial \Phi}{\partial \mathbf{x}^{(r)}}. \tag{27}$$

Then, passing to the norms and using the inequality for the norm of the product of matrices [28], we obtain the equalities

$$0 \le \left\|\frac{\partial \mathbf{z}}{\partial \tilde{\mathbf{y}}^{(r)}}\right\| \le \left\|\left[\frac{\partial \Phi}{\partial \mathbf{z}}\right]^{-1}\right\|\left\|\frac{\partial \Phi}{\partial \tilde{\mathbf{y}}^{(r)}}\right\|, \tag{28}$$

$$0 \le \left\|\frac{\partial \mathbf{z}}{\partial \mathbf{x}^{(r)}}\right\| \le \left\|\left[\frac{\partial \Phi}{\partial \mathbf{z}}\right]^{-1}\right\|\left\|\frac{\partial \Phi}{\partial \mathbf{x}^{(r)}}\right\|.$$

Both of the inequalities incorporate the norm of the inverse matrix $\left\|\left[\frac{\partial \Phi}{\partial \mathbf{z}}\right]^{-1}\right\|$.

Lemma 1. *Let a square matrix A be nonsingular, i.e., $\det A \ne 0$. Then, there exists a constant $\alpha > 1$ such that*

$$\frac{1}{\|A\|} \le \|A^{-1}\| \le \frac{\alpha}{\|A\|}. \tag{29}$$

Proof of Lemma 1. Since the matrix A is nondegenerate, the elements $a_{ik}^{(-1)}$ of the inverse matrix A^{-1} can be expressed in terms of the algebraic complement (adjunct) of the element a_{ki} in the determinant of the matrix A [28]:

$$a_{ik}^{(-1)} = \frac{A_{ki}}{\det A}, \qquad (k,i) = 1,\ldots,r,$$

and they are bounded:

$$a_{ik}^{(-1)} \le M < \infty, \qquad \|A^{-1}\| < \infty.$$

Hence, there exists a constant $\alpha > 1$ for which inequality (29) is satisfied. $\square$

Lemma 1 can be applied to the norm $\left\|\left[\frac{\partial \Phi}{\partial \mathbf{z}}\right]^{-1}\right\|$ of the inverse matrix. As a result,

$$\left(\left\|\frac{\partial \Phi}{\partial \mathbf{z}}\right\|\right)^{-1} \le \left\|\left[\frac{\partial \Phi}{\partial \mathbf{z}}\right]^{-1}\right\| \le \alpha\left(\left\|\frac{\partial \Phi}{\partial \mathbf{z}}\right\|\right)^{-1}, \tag{30}$$

where

$$\left\|\frac{\partial \Phi}{\partial \mathbf{z}}\right\| = r\max_{t,j}\left|\frac{\partial \Phi_t}{\partial z_j}\right|. \tag{31}$$

Lemma 2. *Let*

$$\left\|\frac{\partial \Phi}{\partial \tilde{\mathbf{y}}^{(r)}}\right\| \le \varrho < \infty, \qquad \left\|\frac{\partial \Phi}{\partial \mathbf{x}^{(r)}}\right\| \le \omega < \infty. \tag{32}$$

Then,

$$\lim_{r\to\infty}\left\|\frac{\partial \mathbf{z}}{\partial \tilde{\mathbf{y}}^{(r)}}\right\| = \lim_{r\to\infty}\left\|\frac{\partial \mathbf{z}}{\partial \mathbf{x}^{(r)}}\right\| = 0. \tag{33}$$

Proof of Lemma 2. According to (28), (31), and (32) we have:

$$\|\frac{\partial \mathbf{z}}{\partial \tilde{\mathbf{y}}^{(r)}}\| \le \frac{1}{r}\left(\frac{\varrho}{b}\right), \quad \|\frac{\partial \mathbf{z}}{\partial \tilde{\mathbf{x}}^{(r)}}\| \le \frac{1}{r}\left(\frac{\omega}{b}\right),$$

where $b = \max_{t,j}\left|\frac{\partial \Phi_t}{\partial z_j}\right|$.

Whence, it follows that for the sample length $r \to \infty$, the norms of relevant Jacobians tend to zero, and function $\mathbf{z} = \mathbf{z}(\tilde{\mathbf{y}}^{(r)}, \mathbf{x}^{(r)})$ tends to the vector $\mathbf{z}^*$ (25). $\square$

6. Thermokarst Lake Area Evolution in Western Siberia: RME Estimation and Testing

Permafrost zones, which occupy a significant part of the Earth's surface, are the locales of thermokarst lakes, which accumulate greenhouse gases (methane and carbon dioxide). These gases make a considerable contribution to global climate change.

The source data in studies of the evolution of thermokarst lake areas are acquired through remote sensing of the Earth's surface and ground measurements of meteorological parameters [29,30].

The state of thermokarst lakes is characterized by their total area $S[t]$ in a given region, measured in hectares (ha), and the factors influencing thermokarst formations—the average annual temperatures $T[t]$, measured in Celsius ($C°$), and the annual precipitation $R[t]$, measured in millimeters (mm), where t denotes the calendar year.

We used the remote sensing data and ground measurements of the meteorological parameters for a region of Western Siberia between 65° N–70° N and 65° E–95° E that were presented in [31]. We divided the available time series into two groups, which formed the training collection $\mathcal{L}$ ($t = 0, \ldots, 24$) and the testing collection $\mathcal{T}$ ($t = 25, \ldots, 35$).

6.1. RME Estimation of Model Parameters and Measurement Noises

The temporal evolution of the lake area $S[t]$ is described by the following dynamic regression equation with two influencing factors, the average annual temperature $T[t]$ and the annual precipitation $R[t]$:

$$\begin{aligned}
\hat{S}[t] &= a_0 + \sum_{k=1}^{p} a_k \hat{S}[t-k] + a_{(p+1)} T[t] + a_{(p+2)}(R[t], \\
\hat{v}[t] &= \hat{S}[t] + \xi[t].
\end{aligned} \tag{34}$$

The model parameters and measurement noises are assumed to be random and of the interval type:

$$a_k \in \mathcal{A}_k = [a_k^-, a_k^+], \quad k = 0, dots, p+2,$$

$$\mathbf{a} = \{a_0, \ldots, a_p, a_{p+1}, a_{p+2}\} \in \mathcal{A} = \bigcup_{k=0}^{p+2} \mathcal{A}_k.$$

The probabilistic properties of the parameters are characterized by a PDF $P(\mathbf{a})$.

The variable $\hat{v}[t]$ is the observed output of the model, and the values of the random measurement noise $\xi[t]$ at different time instants t may belong to different ranges:

$$\xi[t] \in \Xi_t = [\xi^-[t], \xi^+[t]], \tag{35}$$

with a PDF $Q_t(\xi[t])$, $(t = 0, \ldots, N)$, where N denotes the length of the observation interval. The order $p = 4$ and the parameter ranges for the dynamic randomized regression model (34) (see Table 1 below) were calculated based on real data using the empirical correlation functions and the least-square estimates of the residual variances.

Table 1. Parameter ranges for the model.

a	a_0	a_1	a_2	a_3	a_4	a_5	a_6
$\mathbf{a}^-$	-0.50	-0.14	-0.49	-0.53	-0.44	0.46	0.19
$\mathbf{a}^+$	0.07	0.52	0.20	0.19	0.19	1.14	0.88

For the training collection $\mathcal{L}$, the model can be written in the vector–matrix form

$$
\begin{aligned}
\hat{\mathbf{S}} &= \hat{\mathbb{S}}\mathbf{a} + a_5\mathbf{T} + a_6\mathbf{R}, \\
\hat{\mathbf{v}} &= \hat{\mathbf{S}} + \xi,
\end{aligned}
\tag{36}
$$

with the matrix

$$
\hat{\mathbb{S}} =
\begin{pmatrix}
1 & \hat{S}[3] & \cdots & \hat{S}[0] \\
1 & \hat{S}[4] & \cdots & \hat{S}[1] \\
\cdots & \cdots & \cdots & \cdots \\
1 & \hat{S}[23] & \cdots & \hat{S}[20]
\end{pmatrix}
\tag{37}
$$

and the vectors $\hat{\mathbf{S}} = [\hat{S}[4],\dots,\hat{S}[24]]$, $\mathbf{T} = [T[4],\dots,T[24]]$, $\mathbf{R} = [R[4],\dots,R[24]]$, and $\hat{\mathbf{v}} = [v[4],\dots,v[24]]$; $\xi = [\xi[4],\dots,\xi[24]]$.

The RME estimation procedure yielded the following entropy-optimal PDFs of the model parameters (36) and measurement noises:

$$
P^*(\mathbf{a},\lambda) = \prod_{k=0}^{6} \frac{\exp(-q_k a_k)}{\mathcal{P}_k(\lambda)}, \quad \mathcal{P}_k(\lambda) = \int_{\mathcal{A}_\|} \exp(-q_k a_k)\,da_k,
$$

$$
q_0 = \sum_{t=4}^{24} \lambda_n, \quad q_k = \sum_{t=p}^{24} \lambda_n\, S[t-k], \quad k = 1,\dots,4,
\tag{38}
$$

$$
q_5 = \sum_{t=4}^{24} \lambda_t\, T[t], \quad q_6 = \sum_{t=p}^{24} \lambda_t\, R[t],
$$

$$
Q^*(\xi,\bar{\lambda}) = \frac{\exp(-\bar{\lambda}\,\xi)}{\mathcal{Q}}, \quad \mathcal{Q} = \int_{\Xi} \exp(-\bar{\lambda}\,\xi)\,d\xi, \quad \bar{\lambda} = \frac{q_0}{20}.
$$

Note that $S[t-k]$, $T[t]$, and $R[t]$ are the data from the collection $\mathcal{L}$. The two-dimensional sections of the function $P^*(\mathbf{a})$ and the function $Q^*(\xi)$ are shown in Figure 1.

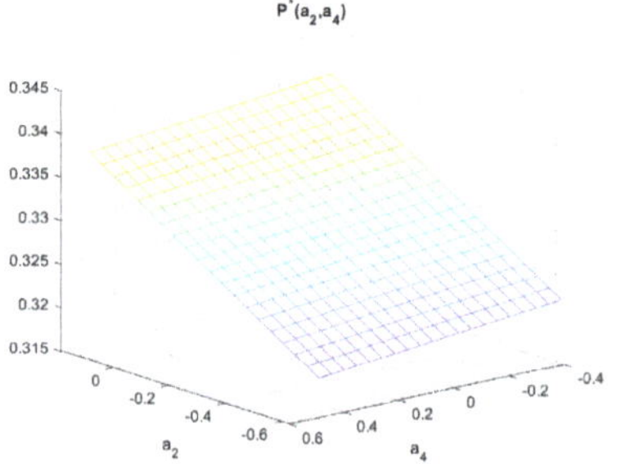

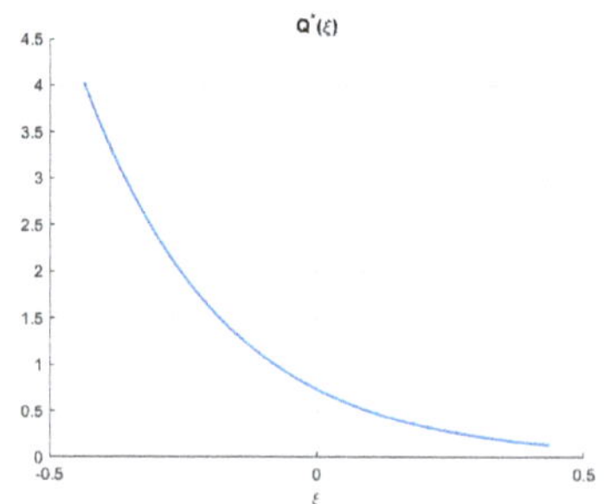

(**a**) Two-dimensional section of function $P^*(\mathbf{a})$ (**b**) Function $Q^*(\xi)$.

Figure 1. Two-dimensional section of the function P^* and the function Q^*.

6.2. Testing

Testing was performed using the data from the collection $\mathcal{T}$, which included the lake area $S[t]$, the average annual temperature $T[t]$, and the annual precipitation $R[t]$, $t = 25,\dots,35$. An ensemble of trajectories of the model's observed output $v[t]$ was generated using Monte Carlo simulations and sampling of the entropy-optimal PDFs

$P^*(\mathbf{a})$, $Q^*\zeta$ on the testing interval. In addition, the trajectory of the empirical means $\bar{v}[t]$ and the dimensions of the empirical standard deviation area were calculated.

The quality of RME estimation was characterized by the absolute and relative errors:

$$AbsErr = \sqrt{\sum_{t=26}^{35} (S[t] - \bar{v}[t])^2} = 0.3446, \tag{39}$$

$$RelErr = \frac{\sqrt{\sum_{t=26}^{35} (S[t] - \bar{v}[t])^2}}{\sqrt{\sum_{t=26}^{35} S^2[t]} + \sqrt{\sum_{t=26}^{35} \bar{v}^2[t]}} = 0.0089. \tag{40}$$

The generated ensemble of the trajectories is shown in Figure 2.

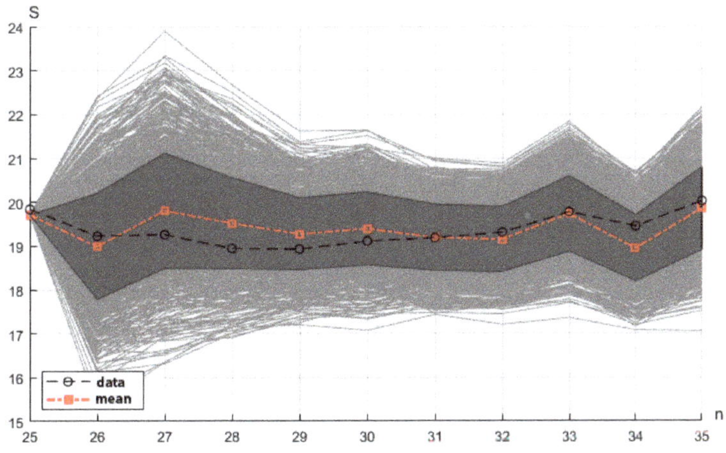

Figure 2. Ensemble of the trajectories (gray domain), the standard deviation area (dark gray domain), the empirical mean trajectory, and the lake area data.

7. Discussion

Given an available data collection, the RME procedure allows estimation of the PDFs of a model's random parameters under measurement noises corresponding to the maximum uncertainty (maximum entropy). In addition, this procedure needs no assumptions about the structure of the estimated PDFs or the statistical properties of the data and measurement noises.

An entropy-optimal model can be simulated by sampling the PDFs to generate an empirical ensemble of a model's output trajectories and to calculate its empirical characteristics (the mean and median trajectories, the standard deviation area, interquartile sets, and others).

The RME procedure was illustrated with an example of the estimation of the parameters of a linear regression model for the evolution of the thermokarst lake area in Western Siberia. In this example, the procedure demonstrated a good estimation accuracy.

However, these positive features of the procedure were achieved with computational costs. Despite their analytical structure, the RME estimates of the PDFs depend on Lagrange multipliers, which are determined by solving the balance equations with the so-called integral components (the mathematical expectations of random parameters and measurement noises). Calculating the values of multidimensional integrals may require appropriate computing resources.

8. Conclusions

The problem of randomized maximum entropy estimation of a probability density function based on real available data has been formulated and solved. The developed estimation algorithm (the RME algorithm) finds the conditional maximum of an information entropy functional on a set of admissible probability density functions characterized by the empirical balance equations for Lagrange multipliers. These equations define an implicit dependence of the Lagrange multipliers on the data collection. The existence of such an implicit function for any values in a data collection has been established. The function's behavior for a data collection of a greater size has been studied, and the asymptotic efficiency of the RME estimates has been proved.

The positive features of RME estimates have been illustrated with an example of estimation and testing a linear dynamic regression model of the evolution of the thermokarst lake area in Western Siberia with real data.

Funding: This research was funded by the Ministry of Science and Higher Education of the Russian Federation, project no. 075-15-2020-799.

Institutional Review Board Statement: Not applicable.

Informed Consent Statement: Not applicable.

Conflicts of Interest: The author declares no conflict of interest.

References

1. Vapnik, V.N. *Statistical Learning Theory*; Wiley: New York, NY, USA, 1998.
2. Witten, I.H.; Eibe, F. *Data Mining: Practical Machine Learning Tools and Techniques*; Morgan Kaufmann: Heidelberg, Germany, 2005.
3. Bishop, C.M. *Pattern Recognition and Machine Learning. Series: Information Theory and Statistics*; Springer: New York, NY, USA, 2006.
4. Hastie, T.; Tibshirani, R.; Friedman, J. *The Elements of Statistical Learning*; Springer: New York, NY, USA, 2001.
5. Vorontsov, K.V. *Mathematical Methods of Learning by Precedents: A Course of Lectures*; Moscow Institute of Physics and Technology: Moscow, Russia, 2013.
6. Goldberger, A.S. *A Course in Econometrics*; Harvard University Press: Cambridge, UK, 1991.
7. Aivazyan, S.A.; Enyukov, I.S.; Meshalkin, L.D. *Prikladnaya Statistika: Issledovanie Zavisimostei (Applied Statistics: Study of Dependencies)*; Finansy i Statistika: Moscow, Russia, 1985.
8. Lagutin, M.B. *Naglyadnaya Matematicheskaya Statistika (Visual Mathematical Statistics)*; BINOM, Laboratoriya Znanii: Moscow, Russia, 2013.
9. Roussas, G. *A Course of the Mathematical Statistics*; Academic Press: San Diego, CA, USA, 2015.
10. Malouf, R. A comparison of algorithms for maximum entropy parameters estimation. In Proceedings of the 6th Conference on Natural Language Learning 2002 (CoNLL-2002), Taipei, Taiwan, 31 August–1 September 2002; Volume 20, pp. 1–7.
11. Borwein, J.; Choksi, R.; Marechal, P. Probability distribution of assets inferred from option prices via principle of maximum entropy. *SIAM J. Optim.* **2003**, *14*, 464–478. [CrossRef]
12. Golan, A.; Judge, G.; Miller, D. *Maximum Entropy Econometrics: Robust Estimation with Limited Data*; John Wiley & Sons: New York, NY, USA, 1997.
13. Golan, A. Information and Entropy econometrics—A review and synthesis. *Found. Trends Econom.* **2008**, *2*, 1–145. [CrossRef]
14. Csiszar, I.; Matus, F. On minimization of entropy functionals under moment constraints. In Proceedings of the IEEE International Symposium on Information Theory, Toronto, ON, Canada, 6–11 July 2008.
15. Loubes, J.-M. Approximate maximum entropy on the mean for instrumental variable regression. *Stat. Probab. Lett.* **2012**, *82*, 972–978. [CrossRef]
16. Borwein, J.M.; Lewis, A.S. Partially-finite programming in L_1 and existence of maximum entropy estimates. *SIAM J. Optim.* **1993**, *3*, 248–267. [CrossRef]
17. Burg, J.P. The relationship between maximum entropy spectra and maximum likelihood spectra. *Geophysics* **1972**, *37*, 375–376. [CrossRef]
18. Christakos, G. A Bayesian/maximum entropy view to the spatial estimation problem. *Math. Geol.* **1990**, *22*, 763–777. [CrossRef]
19. Singh, V.P.; Guo H. Parameter estimation for 3-parameter generalized Pareto distribution by the principle of maximum entropy. *Hydrol. Sci. J.* **1994**, *40*, 165–181. [CrossRef]
20. Popkov, Y.S.; Dubnov, Y.A.; Popkov, A.Y. Randomized machine learning: Statement, solution, applications. In Proceedings of the 2016 IEEE 8th International Conference on Intelligent Systems (IS), Sofia, Bulgaria, 4–6 September 2016. [CrossRef]
21. Popkov, A.Y.; Popkov, Y.S. New methods of entropy-robust estimation for randomized models under limited data. *Entropy* **2014**, *16*, 675–698. [CrossRef]
22. Krasnosel'skii, M.A.; Vainikko, G.M.; Zabreyko, R.P.; Ruticki, Y.B.; Stet'senko, V.V. *Approximate Solutions of Operator Equations*; Wolters-Noordhoff Publishing: Groningen, The Netherlands, 1972. [CrossRef]

23. Ioffe, A.D.; Tikhomirov, V.M. *Theory of Extremal Problems*; Elsevier: New York, NY, USA, 1974.
24. Alekseev, V.M.; Tikhomirov, V.M.; Fomin, S.V. *Optimal Control*; Springer: Boston, MA, USA, 1987.
25. Kaashoek, M.A.; van der Mee, C. *Recent Advances in Operator Theory and Its Applications*; Birkhäuser Basel: Basel, Switzerland, 2006.
26. Kolmogorov, A.N.; Fomin, S.V. *Elements of the Theory of Functions and Functional Analysis*; Dover Publication: New York, NY, USA, 1999.
27. Krasnoselskii, M.A.; Zabreiko, P.P. *Geometrical Methods of Nonlinear Analysis*; Springer: Berlin, Germany; New York, NY, USA, 1984.
28. Gantmacher, F.R.; Brenner, J.L. *Applications of the Theory of Matrices*; Dover: New York, NY, USA, 2005.
29. Riordan, B.; Verbula, D.; McGruire, A.D. Shrinking ponds in subarctic Alaska based on 1950–2002 remotely sensed images. *J. Geophys. Res.* **2006**, *111*, G04002. [CrossRef]
30. Kirpotin, S.; Polishchuk, Y.; Bruksina, N. Abrupt changes of thermokarst lakes in Western Siberia: Impacts of climatic warming on permafrost melting. *Int. J. Environ. Stud.* **2009**, *66*, 423–431. [CrossRef]
31. Western Siberia Thermokarsk Lakes Dataset. Available online: https://cloud.uriit.ru/index.php/s/0DOrxL9RmGqXsV0 (accessed on 20 February 2021).

mathematics

MDPI

Article

Minimax Estimation in Regression under Sample Conformity Constraints

Andrey Borisov [1,2,3,4]

1 Federal Research Center "Computer Science and Control" of the Russian Academy of Sciences, 44/2 Vavilova Str., 119333 Moscow, Russia; ABorisov@frccsc.ru
2 Moscow Aviation Institute, 4, Volokolamskoe Shosse, 125993 Moscow, Russia
3 Faculty of Computational Mathematics and Cybernetics, Lomonosov Moscow State University, GSP-1, 1-52 Leninskiye Gory, 119991 Moscow, Russia
4 Moscow Center for Fundamental and Applied Mathematics, Lomonosov Moscow State University, GSP-1, Leninskie Gory, 119991 Moscow, Russia

Abstract: The paper is devoted to the guaranteeing estimation of parameters in the uncertain stochastic nonlinear regression. The loss function is the conditional mean square of the estimation error given the available observations. The distribution of regression parameters is partially unknown, and the uncertainty is described by a subset of probability distributions with a known compact domain. The essential feature is the usage of some additional constraints describing the conformity of the uncertain distribution to the realized observation sample. The paper contains various examples of the conformity indices. The estimation task is formulated as the minimax optimization problem, which, in turn, is solved in terms of saddle points. The paper presents the characterization of both the optimal estimator and the set of least favorable distributions. The saddle points are found via the solution to a dual finite-dimensional optimization problem, which is simpler than the initial minimax problem. The paper proposes a numerical mesh procedure of the solution to the dual optimization problem. The interconnection between the least favorable distributions under the conformity constraint, and their Pareto efficiency in the sense of a vector criterion is also indicated. The influence of various conformity constraints on the estimation performance is demonstrated by the illustrative numerical examples.

Keywords: mathematical modeling; estimation; minimax techniques; pareto optimization; regression analysis; statistical uncertainty

Citation: Borisov, A. Minimax Estimation in Regression under Sample Conformity Constraints. *Mathematics* **2021**, *9*, 1080. https://doi.org/10.3390/math9101080

Academic Editors: Mikhail Posypkin, Andrey Gorshenin and Vladimir Titarev

Received: 6 April 2021
Accepted: 6 May 2021
Published: 11 May 2021

Publisher's Note: MDPI stays neutral with regard to jurisdictional claims in published maps and institutional affiliations.

1. Introduction

The problems of the heterogeneous parameter estimation in the regression under the model uncertainty are considered intensively from the various points of view. The guaranteeing (or minimax) approach gives one of the most prospective tools to solve these problems. For the proper formulation of an estimation problem in minimax terms one usually needs:

- A description of the uncertainty set in the observation model;
- A class of the admissible estimators;
- An optimality criterion (a loss function) as a function of the argument pair "estimator–uncertain parameter value".

The problem is to find the estimator that minimizes the maximal losses over the whole uncertainty set.

In the related literature, the parametric uncertainty set is specified either by geometric [1–7], or by statistical [8–15] constraints. In the former case, the uncertain parameters are treated as nonrandom but unknown ones lying within the fixed uncertainty set. In the latter case, the parameters are supposed to be random with unknown distribution, and the uncertainty set is formed by all the admissible distributions. In both cases, the guaranteeing estimation presumes a solution to a two-person game problem: the first player is "a statistician", and the performer of the second, "external" player role is dictated by the problem statement—it might be nature, another human or device. Nevertheless, the guaranteeing approach suggests the unified prescription: finding the best estimator under the worst behavior of the uncertainty. In practice, such a universality leads to a loss of some prior information.

Let us explain this point by an example: the statistician knows that the source of the uncertainty is nature. This means he/she "should bear in mind that nature, as a player, is not aiming for a maximal win (that is, does not want us to suffer a maximal loss), and in this sense, it is 'impartial' in the choice of strategies" [12]. Hence, in this case, the minimax approach is too pessimistic and leads to cautious and coarse estimates. Even if we know the second player is a human, this does not imply his/her "bad will" towards the statistician. Hopefully, the second player has goal other than maximizing the loss of the statistician. If the goal of the second player is known, one can change the estimation criterion and transform the initial problem into a non-antagonistic game [16]. Otherwise, the statistician can identify the goal indirectly, relying on the available observations. Hence, in the latter case, it seems natural to introduce additional constraints to the uncertainty set, depending on the realized observations.

The paper aims to present a solution to the minimax estimation problem under additional constraints, which are determined by a conformity index of the uncertain parameters to the available observations.

The paper is organized as follows. Section 2 contains the formal problem statement with the conformity index based on the likelihood function. The section presents the assumptions concerning the observation model, which guarantee the correctness of the stated estimation problem and the existence of its solution. It also contains the comparison of the problem with the recent investigations.

Section 3 provides the main result: the initial estimation problem is reformulated as a game problem, which has a saddle point, defining the minimax estimator completely. Moreover, the point is a solution to a dual finite-dimensional constrained optimization problem, which is simpler than the initial minimax problem. The form of the minimax estimator and properties of the least favorable distributions (LFD) is also included in the section.

Section 4 is devoted to the analysis of the obtained results. First, a numerical algorithm for the dual optimization problem solution is presented along with its accuracy characterization. Second, some other conformity indices based on the empirical distribution function (EDF) and sample mean are also introduced. Third, a new concept of the uncertain distribution choice under a vector criterion is considered. The first criterion component, being the loss function introduced in Section 2, describes the influence of the uncertainty on the estimation quality. The second component is the conformity index, which characterizes the accordance of the unknown distribution of γ and the realized observations $Y = y$. We present an assertion that the LFD in the minimax estimation problem is Pareto-efficient in the sense of the introduced vector criterion.

Section 5 presents the numerical examples, which illustrate the influence of various conformity constraints on the estimation performance. Section 6 contains concluding remarks.

The following notations are used in this manuscript:

- $\mathcal{B}(S)$ is the Borel σ-algebra of the topological space S (is S is the whole space) or its contraction to the set S (if S is a set of the topological space);
- $\mathrm{col}(A_1, \ldots, A_n)$ is a column vector formed by the ordinary or block components $A_1, \ldots, A_n$;
- $\mathrm{row}(A_1, \ldots, A_n)$ is a row vector formed by the ordinary or block components $A_1, \ldots, A_n$;
- $\langle a, b \rangle$ is a scalar product of two finite-dimensional vectors;
- $\mathcal{C}(\mathcal{X})$ is a set of all continuous real-valued functions with the domain $\mathbb{X}$;
- $\|x\|$ is the Euclidean norm of the vector x;
- $\mathsf{P}_F\{A\}$ is the probability of the event A corresponding to the distribution F;
- $\mathsf{E}_F\{X\}$ is a mathematical expectation of the random vector X with the distribution F;

- conv$(\mathbb{S})$ is a convex hull of the set $\mathbb{S}$.

2. Statement of Problem

2.1. Formulation

Let us consider the following observation model:

$$Y = A(X, \gamma) + B(X, \gamma)V. \tag{1}$$

Here:

- $\gamma \in \mathcal{C} \in \mathcal{B}(\mathbb{R}^m)$ is an unobservable random vector, having an unknown cumulative distribution function (cdf) F;
- $X \in \mathbb{R}^n$ is a random unobservable vector with a known cdf $\Psi(dx|\gamma)$ dependent on the value of γ;
- $Y \in \mathbb{R}^k$ is a vector of observations;
- $V \in \mathbb{R}^k$ is a random vector of observation errors with the known probability density function (pdf) $\phi_V(v)$;
- $A(\cdot) : \mathcal{C} \times \mathbb{R}^n \to \mathbb{R}^k$ is a nonrandom function characterizing the observation plant;
- $B(\cdot) : \mathcal{C} \times \mathbb{R}^n \to \mathbb{R}^{k \times k}$ is a nonrandom function characterizing the observation error intensity.

The observation model is defined on the family of the probability triplets $\{(\Omega, \mathcal{F}, \mathsf{P}_F)\}_{F \in \mathbb{F}}$, where:

- The outcome space $\Omega \triangleq \mathcal{C} \times \mathbb{R}^m \times \mathbb{R}^k$ contains all admissible values of the compound vector $\mathrm{col}(\gamma, X, V)$;
- σ-algebra is determined as $\mathcal{F} \triangleq \mathcal{B}(\mathcal{C} \times \mathbb{R}^m \times \mathbb{R}^k)$;
- The probability measures P_F are determined as:

$$\mathsf{P}_F\{\gamma \in dq, \ X \in dx, \ V \in dv\} \triangleq \Psi(dx|q)F(dq)\varphi_V(v)dv. \tag{2}$$

Using the generalized Bayes rule [17], it is easy to verify that the function:

$$\mathcal{L}(y|q) \triangleq \int_{\mathbb{R}^n} |\det(B(q, x))|^{-1}\phi_V(B^{-1}(q, x)(y - A(q, x)))\Psi(dx|q) \tag{3}$$

is the conditional pdf of the observation Y given γ: $\mathsf{P}_F\{Y \in dy|\gamma = q\} = \mathcal{L}(y|q)dy$. Furthermore, the function:

$$\mathfrak{L}(y, F) \triangleq \int_{\mathcal{C}} \mathcal{L}(y|q)F(dq) \tag{4}$$

defines the pdf of the observation Y under the assumption that the distribution law of γ equals F:

$$\mathfrak{L}(y, F) = \frac{\mathsf{P}_F\{Y \in dy\}}{dy} = \int_{\mathcal{C}} \mathcal{L}(y|q)F(dq). \tag{5}$$

Below in the paper we refer to the function $\mathfrak{L}(y, F)$ as *the sample conformity index based on the likelihood function*.

Our aim is to estimate the function $h(\gamma, X) : \mathcal{C} \times \mathbb{R}^m \to \mathbb{R}^l$ of (γ, X), and the admissible estimators are the functions $\overline{h}(Y) : \mathbb{R}^k \to \mathbb{R}^l$ of the available observations.

The loss function is a conditional mean square of estimate error given the available observations:

$$J(\overline{h}, F|y) \triangleq \mathsf{E}_F\left\{\|h(\gamma, X) - \overline{h}(Y)\|^2|Y = y\right\}, \tag{6}$$

and the corresponding estimation criterion:

$$J^*(\overline{h}|y) \triangleq \sup_{F \in \mathbb{F}_L} J(\overline{h}, F|y) \tag{7}$$

characterizes the maximal loss for a fixed estimator $\overline{h}$ within the class $\mathbb{F}_L$ of the uncertain distributions of γ, for which $\mathfrak{L}(y, F) \geqslant L$.

The minimax estimation problem for the vector h is to find an estimator $\widehat{h}(\cdot)$, such that:

$$\widehat{h}(y) \in \underset{\overline{h} \in \mathbb{H}}{\operatorname{Argmin}} J^*(\overline{h}|y), \tag{8}$$

where $\mathbb{H}$ is a class of admissible estimators.

2.2. Necessary Assumptions Concerning Observation Model

To state the minimax estimation problem (8) properly and guarantee the existence of its solution we have to make additional assumptions concerning the uncertainty of γ, the observation model (1) and the estimated vector h:

(i) The set $\mathcal{C}$ is compact.
(ii) Let $\mathbb{F}$ be a family of all probability distributions with a support lying within the set $\mathcal{C}$. The set $\mathbb{F}_L$ is itself a convex $*$–weakly compact [18] subset of $\mathbb{F}$.
(iii) The constraint

$$\mathfrak{L}(y, F) \geqslant L \tag{9}$$

holds for all $F \in \mathbb{F}_L$. The inequality (9) is called *the conformity constraint of the level L based on the likelihood function* (or, shortly, likelihood constraint).
(iv) The set $\mathbb{F}_L$ is nonempty.
(v) $A(\cdot, \cdot), B(\cdot, \cdot), h(\cdot, \cdot) \in \mathbf{C}(\mathcal{C} \times \mathbb{R}^n)$.
(vi) pdf $\phi_V(v) > 0$ for $\forall v \in \mathbb{R}^k$; $\phi_V(v) \in \mathbf{C}(\mathbb{R}^k)$; the function $\Psi(dx|q)$ is a regular version of the conditional distribution for $\forall\, q \in \mathcal{C}$.
(vii) The observation noise is uniformly non-degenerate, i.e.,

$$\min_{(q,x) \in \mathcal{C} \times \mathbb{R}^n} B(q, x) B^T(q, x) \geqslant \lambda_0 I > 0.$$

(viii) The inequalities

$$\int_{\mathbb{R}^k} \|v\|^2 \phi_V(v) dv < \infty,$$

$$\sup_{q \in \mathcal{C}} \int_{\mathbb{R}^n} \|A(q, x)\|^2 \Psi(dx|q) \triangleq K_A < \infty,$$

$$\sup_{q \in \mathcal{C}} \int_{\mathbb{R}^n} \|h(q, x)\|^2 \Psi(dx|q) \triangleq K_h < \infty$$

are true.
(ix) The set of admissible estimators $\mathbb{H}$ contains only the functions $\overline{h}(\cdot) : \mathbb{R}^k \to \mathbb{R}^l$, for which:

$$\sup_{q \in \mathcal{C}} \int_{\mathbb{R}^k} \|\overline{h}(y)\|^2 \mathcal{L}(y|q) dy < \infty. \tag{10}$$

2.3. Argumentation

First, we discuss the sense of the assumptions in the subsection above.

Conditions (i)–(iv), describing the set $\mathbb{F}_L$, have the following interpretation.

The requirement for $\mathcal{C}$ to be compact (i.e., fulfillment of condition (i)) is standard for the minimax estimation problems (see, e.g., [2,3]). In the case the prior information about the vector γ limited by the knowledge of its domain $\mathcal{C}$ only, it is rather natural to treat γ as a random vector with an unknown distribution $F \in \mathbb{F}$. In practice we often have some additional prior information concerning the moment characteristics of γ, hence the entire uncertainty set $\mathbb{F}$ can be significantly reduced. If, for example, $\mu(q) = \operatorname{col}(\mu_1(q), \ldots, \mu_N(q)) : \mathcal{C} \to \mathbb{R}^N$ is a vector of convex moment functions, and we know the vector $\overline{\mu} \triangleq \operatorname{col}(\overline{\mu}_1, \ldots, \overline{\mu}_N) \in \mathbb{R}^N$ of their upper bounds, then the set of admissible distributions takes the form $\left\{F \in \mathbb{F} : \int_{\mathcal{C}} \mu_j(q) F(dq) \leqslant \overline{\mu}_j, \ j = \overline{1, N}\right\}$. The $*$-weak compactness and convexity can be easily verified for this subset. Further in the presentation, we do not stress the explicit form of the "total" constraints other than (9) forming the subset $\mathbb{F}_L$: they should just guarantee the closure and convexity for $\mathbb{F}_L$. That is the sense of condition (ii).

The conditional pdf $\mathcal{L}(y|q)$ (3) can also be treated as the likelihood function of the parameter γ, calculated at the point q given the observed sample $Y = y$. This likelihood value reflects the relevance of the parameter value q to the realized observation y. By analogy, the function $\mathfrak{L}(y, F)$ can be considered as some generalization of the likelihood function that evaluates the correspondence between the uncertain distribution F and the realized observation y. The following lower and upper bounds for this value are obvious:

$$0 < \underline{\mathcal{L}}(y) \triangleq \min_{q \in \mathcal{C}} \mathcal{L}(y|q) \leqslant \mathfrak{L}(y, F) \leqslant \max_{q \in \mathcal{C}} \mathcal{L}(y|q) \triangleq \overline{\mathcal{L}}(y).$$

Below in the paper we suppose that the likelihood level L lies in $[\underline{\mathcal{L}}(y), \overline{\mathcal{L}}(y)]$. The subset formed by constraint $\{F \in \mathbb{F} : \int_{\mathcal{C}} \mathcal{L}(y|q) F(dq) \geqslant L\}$ is called *a distribution subset satisfying the likelihood conformity constraint of the level L*. It is nonempty because it contains at least all distributions with the support lying within the set $\{q \in \mathcal{C} : \mathcal{L}(y|q) \geqslant L\}$.

Adjusting the level L, we can vary the uncertainty set $\mathbb{F}_L$, choosing the distributions F, which are more or less relevant to the realized observations $Y = y$. That is an essence of condition (iii). Condition (iv) is obvious: all the constraints, defining the set $\mathbb{F}_L$, should be feasible.

Condition (v) is technical: it provides correctness of a subsequent change of measure. The condition is non-restricting because the broad class of the functions A, B and h can be approximated by the continuous functions. Conditions (vi) and (vii) guarantee correct utilization of the Fubini theorem and an abstract variant of the Bayes formula [19]. In practice these conditions are usually valid. Condition (viii) guarantees finite variance for both the observations and estimated vector independently of the distribution F.

Condition (ix) guarantees a finite variance of the estimate $\overline{h}(Y)$ independently of $F \in \mathbb{F}_L$.

The solution to (8) is obvious in the case of the one-point set $\mathbb{F}_L = \{F\}$. This means the distribution F of the parameter γ is known, and the initial problem is reduced to the traditional optimal in the mean square sense (MS-optimal) estimation problem. The case of the one-point set $\mathcal{C} = \{q\}$ is quite similar. In both cases the optimal estimator is completely defined by the conditional expectation (CE): $\widehat{h}(y) = \mathsf{E}_F\{h(\gamma, X)|Y = y\}$ in the case of a known distribution F, and $\widehat{h}(y) = \mathsf{E}_{\{q\}}\{h(q, X)|Y = y\}$ in the "one point" case.

In the general case of $\mathbb{F}_L$ this result is inapplicable, because the CE $\mathsf{E}_F\{h(\gamma, X)|Y = y\}$ is a functional of the unknown distribution F.

The stated estimation problem has a transparent interpretation. First, under prior uncertainty of the distribution F the replacement of the loss function (6) by guaranteeing analog looks natural. Second, utilization of the CE in the criterion means that the desired estimate should be calculated optimally for each observed sample. The criteria in the form of the CE appear often in estimation and control problems [11,17,20–22]. Mostly, the estimation is the preliminary stage in the solution to the optimization and/or control problem under incomplete information. The random disturbances/noises in such observation systems represent:

- A result of natural (non-human) impacts;
- A randomized (or generalized) control [23,24], used in the dynamic system;
- A result of some uncontrollable (parasitic) input signals of "the external players".

The impact of the two latter types is not necessarily the nonrandom functions of available observations, but some "extra generated" random processes with distributions dependent on the observations. This type of control is used in the areas of telecommunications [25,26], cellular networks [27], technical systems [28], etc. The proposed minimax criterion allows inhibiting the negative effect of the "additional randomness" in the external signals (the third type of disturbances mentioned above) to the estimation quality.

The additional comprehension of the natural gaps, which are inherent to the minimax estimation paradigm, and the ways of their partial coverage can be revealed by the following interpretation. It is well-known that in the case a minimax estimation problem can be reduced to a two-person game with a saddle point, the minimax estimator is the best one calculated for the LFD. The form of the LFD can be very strange and artificial. Moreover, the conformity degree of the LFD to the realized observations can be too low. Thus, the utilization of various sample conformity indices (particularly the ones based on the likelihood function) admits all to describe this degree, restrict it from below, implicitly reduce the distribution uncertainty set and exclude "exotic" variants of the LFDs.

Minimax estimation of the regression parameters is an investigation object in the various settings. Mostly, the observation model is a linear function of the estimated parameters corrupted by an additive Gaussian noise. The optimality criterion is a mathematical expectation of some loss function. In [29], the problem is solved by engaging the framework of the fuzzy sets. The authors of [30,31] used the criterion other than the traditional mean square one, and the estimated vector was random with the uncertain discrete distribution. In [32], the Gaussian noises have an uncertain but bounded covariance matrix. The papers [33–35] are also devoted to the minimax Bayesian estimation in the regression under various geometric and moment constraints of the estimated parameters. The criterion functions are ℓ_p norms of the estimation errors.

The optimality criterion in the form of CE and the admissibility of nonlinear estimates distinguish the proposed estimation problem from the recently considered ones [2,3,5–7,9]. A closely related problem considered in [11] has an essential difference. The uncertain parameter in [11] was treated as unknown and nonrandom, and hence the initial minimax problem could not be solved in terms of the saddle points. Moreover, the statistic uncertainty in [11] gave no possibility to take into account any additional prior and posterior information about the moment characteristics, conformity indices, etc. The paper [14] was devoted to the particular case of the likelihood constraints only. An idea to use confidence sets, calculated by the available statistical data, as the uncertainty sets of the distribution moments was used in [36] for the conditionally-minimax prediction.

3. The Main Result

As is known, the CE is determined in a non-unique way, hence we should specify a version of the CE so as to use it in further inferences. If the distribution F of the vector γ is known, then the CE of an integrable random value $h(\gamma, X) : C \times \mathbb{R}^m \to \mathbb{R}$ can be calculated by the abstract variant of the Bayes formula:

$$\widehat{h}^F(y) = \frac{\int_{C \times \mathbb{R}^n} h(q, x)| \det(B(q, x))|^{-1}\phi_V(B^{-1}(q, x)(y - A(q, x)))\Psi(dx|q)F(dq)}{\int_{C \times \mathbb{R}^n} | \det(B(q', x'))|^{-1}\phi_V(B^{-1}(q', x')(y - A(q', x')))\Psi(dx'|q')F(dq')}, \tag{11}$$

i.e., $\mathsf{E}_F\{h(\gamma, X)|Y = y\} = \widehat{h}^F(y)$ (11) P_F − a.s. Below in the presentation we use the CE version, defined by (11). It should also be noted that if $\widehat{h}(\cdot)$ is the desired minimax estimator, then the inclusion (8) must be satisfied point-wise for any sample $y \in \mathbb{R}^k$.

Further in the paper the function:

$$J_*(F|y) \triangleq \min_{\overline{h} \in \mathbb{H}} J(\overline{h}, F|y) = J(\widehat{h}^F, F|Y) = \widehat{\|h\|^2}^F (y) - \|\widehat{h}^F(y)\|^2 \tag{12}$$

is called *the dual criterion* for J^* (7). All CEs in (12) are calculated by (11).

Using (3) for the calculation of $\mathcal{L}$, the notation:

$$v(q, x|y) \triangleq | \det B(q, x)|^{-1}\phi_V(B(q, x)^{-1}(y - A(q, x))), \tag{13}$$

and the CE version (11), the loss function (6) can be rewritten in the form:

$$J(\overline{h}, F|y) = \frac{\int_{C \times \mathbb{R}^n} \|h(q, x) - \overline{h}(y)\|^2 v(q, x|y) \Psi(dx|y) F(dq)}{\int_C \mathcal{L}(y|q') F(dq')}. \tag{14}$$

As can be seen from (14), the function $J(\overline{h}, F|y)$ is neither convex nor concave in F, which complicates the solution to the estimation problem (8). Moreover, the argument F lies in the abstract infinite-dimensional space of the probability measures. Nevertheless, the problem can be reduced to a standard finite-dimensional minimax problem with a convex–concave criterion.

First, we introduce a new reference measure F' and verify that the loss function (14) represents a functional, which is linear in F'.

Let:

$$F'(F, dq|y) \triangleq \frac{\mathcal{L}(y|q) F(dq)}{\int_C \mathcal{L}(q'|y) F(dq')}. \tag{15}$$

Lemma 1. *If conditions (i)–(ix) are satisfied, then the following assertions are true.*

1. *$F'(F, dq|y)$ is a probability measure for $\forall\, y \in \mathbb{R}^k$, and $F'(F, \cdot|y) \sim F(\cdot)$. The transformation (15) is a bijection of $\mathbb{F}$ into itself, and its inversion F'' has the form:*

$$F''(F', dq|y) \triangleq \frac{\mathcal{L}^{-1}(y|q) F'(dq)}{\int_C \mathcal{L}^{-1}(q'|y) F'(dq')}. \tag{16}$$

2. *The set $\mathbb{F}'_L$ of all distributions obtained from $\mathbb{F}_L$ by the transformation (15):*

$$\mathbb{F}'_L \triangleq \{\overline{F}(\cdot) : \ \exists\, F \in \mathbb{F}_L, \ \overline{F}(\cdot) = F'(F, \cdot|y)\} \tag{17}$$

is convex and $*$-weakly closed.

The proof of Lemma 1 is given in Appendix A.

Applying the Fubini theorem and keeping in mind (11) and (15), we can rewrite the loss function (14) in the form:

$$J(\overline{h}, F|y) = \frac{\int_C \frac{\int_{\mathbb{R}^n} \|h(q,x) - \overline{h}(y)\|^2 v(q,x|y)\Psi(dx|y)}{\mathcal{L}(y|q)} \mathcal{L}(y|q) F(dq)}{\int_C \mathcal{L}(q'|y) F(dq')}$$

$$= \int_C \frac{\int_{\mathbb{R}^n} \|h(q, x) - \overline{h}(y)\|^2 v(q, x|y) \Psi(dx|y)}{\mathcal{L}(y|q)} F'(F, dq|y) = J(\overline{h}, F'|y). \tag{18}$$

To reduce the initial problem to some finite-dimensional equivalent, we also introduce the vectors:

$$w(y|q) \triangleq \mathrm{col}(w_1(y|q), w_2(y|q)) \in \mathbb{R}^{\ell+1} :$$

$$w_1(y|q) \triangleq \mathsf{E}_F\Big\{ \|h(\gamma, X)\|^2 | Y = y, \ \gamma = q \Big\} = \frac{\int_{\mathbb{R}^n} \|h(q, x)\|^2 v(q, x) \Psi(dx|y)}{\mathcal{L}(y|q)}, \tag{19}$$

$$w_2(y|q) \triangleq \mathsf{E}_F\{ h(\gamma, X) | Y = y, \ \gamma = q \} = \frac{\int_{\mathbb{R}^n} h(q, x) v(q, x) \Psi(dx|y)}{\mathcal{L}(y|q)};$$

$$w(F|y) \triangleq \mathrm{col}(w_1(F|y), w_2(F|y)) \in \mathbb{R}^{\ell+1} :$$

$$w_1(F|y) \triangleq \mathsf{E}_F\Big\{ \|h(\gamma, X)\|^2 | Y = y \Big\} = \int_C w_1(y|q) F'(F, dq|y), \tag{20}$$

$$w_2(F|y) \triangleq \mathsf{E}_F\{ h(\gamma, X) | Y = y \} = \int_C w_2(y|q) F'(F, dq|y),$$

and their collections generated by the subsets $\mathcal{C}$ and $\mathbb{F}_L$:

$$W(\mathcal{C}|y) \triangleq \{w(y|q) : q \in \mathcal{C}\},$$
$$W(\mathbb{F}_L|y) \triangleq \{w(F|y) : F \in \mathbb{F}_L\}. \tag{21}$$

Here and below the notation $\mathbb{H}(y)$ also stands for the whole set of the estimate values $\overline{h} \in \mathbb{H}$ calculated for the fixed argument y.

The set $W(\mathbb{F}_L|y) \in \mathcal{B}(\mathbb{R}^{\ell+1})$ is compact; moreover (see [37]), the inclusion $W(\mathbb{F}_L|y) \subseteq \mathrm{conv}(W(\mathcal{C}|y))$ holds.

On the set $\mathbb{R}^{\ell} \times \mathbb{R}^{\ell+1}$ we prepare the new loss function:

$$\mathbf{J}(\eta, w) \triangleq w_1 - 2\langle \eta, w_2 \rangle + \|\eta\|^2 = w_1 - \|w_2\|^2 + \|\eta - w_2\|^2. \tag{22}$$

It is easy to verify that the loss function (18) can be expressed via (22):

$$J(\overline{h}, F|y) = \int_{\mathcal{C}} \mathbf{J}(\overline{h}(y), w(y|q)) F'(F, dq|y) = \mathbf{J}(\overline{h}(y), w(F|y)).$$

The corresponding guaranteeing criterion takes the form:

$$\mathbf{J}^*(\eta|y) \triangleq \sup_{w \in W(\mathbb{F}_L|y)} \mathbf{J}(\eta, w), \tag{23}$$

and its dual can be determined as:

$$\mathbf{J}_*(w) \triangleq \min_{\eta \in \mathbb{H}(y)} \mathbf{J}(\eta, w) = J(w_2, w) = w_1 - \|w_2\|^2. \tag{24}$$

The finite-dimensional minimax problem is to find:

$$\widehat{\mathbf{h}}(y) \in \mathrm{Argmin}_{\eta \in \mathbb{H}(y)} \mathbf{J}^*(\eta|y). \tag{25}$$

From the definitions of $W(\mathbb{F}_L|y)$, $\mathbb{H}(y)$ and criterion (23) it follows that the problem (25) is equivalent to the initial minimax estimation problem (8):

$$\min_{\overline{h} \in \mathbb{H}} J^*(\overline{h}|y) = \min_{\eta \in \mathbb{H}(y)} \mathbf{J}^*(\eta|y) \triangleq \mathcal{J}(y), \tag{26}$$

$$\left. \mathrm{Argmin}_{\overline{h} \in \mathbb{H}} J^*(\overline{h}|y) \right|_y \triangleq \{\widehat{h}(y) : J^*(\widehat{h}|y) = \mathcal{J}(y)\} = \mathrm{Argmin}_{\eta \in \mathbb{H}(y)} \mathbf{J}^*(\eta|y) \tag{27}$$

for $\forall y \in \mathbb{R}^k$.

The following theorem characterizes the solution to the finite-dimensional minimax problem in terms of a saddle point of the loss function $\mathbf{J}$.

Theorem 1. *For $\forall y \in \mathbb{R}^k$, the loss function $\mathbf{J}(\eta, w)$ (22) has the unique saddle point $(\widehat{\mathbf{h}}(y), \widehat{\mathbf{w}}(y))$ on the set $\mathbb{H}(y) \times W(\mathbb{F}_L|y)$. The second block subvector $\widehat{\mathbf{w}}(y) = \mathrm{col}(\widehat{\mathbf{w}}_1(y), \widehat{\mathbf{w}}_2(y)) \in W(\mathbb{F}_L|y)$ of the saddle point is the unique solution to the finite-dimensional dual problem:*

$$\{\widehat{\mathbf{w}}(y)\} = \mathrm{Argmax}_{w \in W(\mathbb{F}_L|y)} \mathbf{J}_*(w), \tag{28}$$

and $\widehat{\mathbf{h}}(y) = \widehat{\mathbf{w}}_2(y)$ is the second sub-vector of this optimum $\widehat{\mathbf{w}}(y)$.

The proof of Theorem 1 is given in Appendix B.

By the definition of $\mathbb{W}(\mathbb{F}_L|y)$, for any vector $\widehat{\mathbf{w}}(y)$ there exists at least one distribution $\widehat{F}$ such that:

$$\widehat{\mathbf{w}}_1(y) = \mathsf{E}_{\widehat{F}}\{\|h(\gamma, X)\|^2|Y = y\}, \quad \widehat{\mathbf{w}}_2(y) = \mathsf{E}_{\widehat{F}}\{h(\gamma, X)|Y = y\}. \tag{29}$$

$\widehat{F}$ is an LFD, and the whole set of the distributions satisfying (29) is denoted by $\widehat{\mathbb{F}}_L$.

Theorem 1 allows to obtain a solution to the initial minimax estimation problem. The result is formulated as:

Corollary 1. *The estimator $\widehat{\mathbf{w}}_2(y)$ introduced in Theorem 1 is a solution to the minimax estimation problem (8), i.e., $\widehat{h}(y) = \widehat{\mathbf{w}}_2(y)$ point-wise. The set $\{(\widehat{h}, \widehat{F})\}_{\widehat{F} \in \widehat{\mathbb{F}}_L}$ presents the saddle points of the loss function J (6) on the set $\mathbb{H} \times \widehat{\mathbb{F}}_L$. The estimator $\widehat{\mathbf{h}}(y)$ is invariant to the LFD choice: if $\widehat{F}'$ and $\widehat{F}''$ are different LFDs then $\mathsf{E}_{\widehat{F}'}\{h(\gamma, X)|Y = y\} = \mathsf{E}_{\widehat{F}''}\{h(\gamma, X)|Y = y\} = \widehat{\mathbf{w}}_2(y)$.*

The following assertion characterizes the key property of the LFD set $\widehat{\mathbb{F}}_L$.

Corollary 2. *There exists a variant of the LFD $\widehat{F}_L \in \widehat{\mathbb{F}}$ concentrated at most at $\dim(\mathbb{W}(\mathbb{F}_L|y)) + 1$ points of the set $\mathcal{C}$.*

The proof of Corollary 2 is given in Appendix C.

The presence of the discrete version of LFD is a remarkable fact. Let us remind the reader that initially, we suppose that the uncertain vector γ lies in the set $\mathcal{C}$. The deterministic hypothesis concerning γ hopelessly obstructed the solution to the minimax estimation problem. To overcome this obstacle we provide the randomness of γ: the vector keeps constant during the individual observation experiment, and the stochastic nature of γ appears from experiment to experiment only. The existence of a discrete LFD returns us partially to the primordial situation. The point is that there exists a set of γ values that are the most difficult for estimation. Tuning to these parameters we can obtain estimates of γ with the guaranteed quality.

Theorem 1 and Corollary 1 simplify the solution to the initial problem (8), reducing it to the maximization of the finite-dimensional quadratic function (28) over the convex compact set.

4. Analysis and Extensions

4.1. Dual Problem: A Numerical Solution

To simplify presentation of the numerical algorithm of problem (28)'s solution, we suppose that the uncertainty set $\mathbb{F}_L$ takes the form $\mathbb{F}_L = \{F \in \mathbb{F} : \mathfrak{L} \geqslant L\}$, i.e., it is restricted by the conformity constraint only.

Let us consider the case $\mathcal{C} \triangleq \{q_j\}_{j=\overline{1,M}} \subset \mathbb{R}^m$, which corresponds to the practical problem of Bayesian classification [10,38]. Here the dual problem (28) has the form $\widehat{\mathbf{w}}(y) = \underset{w \in \mathrm{conv}(\mathbb{W}(\mathcal{C}|y))}{\mathrm{Argmax}} \mathbf{J}_*(w)$. Its solution can be represented as $\widehat{\mathbf{w}}(y) = \sum_{j=1}^{M} \widehat{\mathsf{P}}_j(y)w(q_j|y)$, where $\widehat{\mathsf{P}}(y) \triangleq \mathrm{row}(\widehat{\mathsf{P}}_1(y), \ldots, \widehat{\mathsf{P}}_M(y))$ is a solution to the standard quadratic programming problem (QP problem):

$$\widehat{\mathsf{P}}(y) \in \underset{\substack{p_1,\ldots,p_M \geqslant 0: \\ \Sigma_{j=1}^{M} p_j = 1}}{\mathrm{Argmin}} \left(\sum_{j=1}^{M} p_j w_1(q_j|y) - \sum_{j,j'=1}^{M} p_j p_{j'} \langle w_2(q_j|y), w_2(q_{j'}|y) \rangle \right). \tag{30}$$

Consequently, in the case of finite $\mathcal{C}$ the minimax estimation problem can be reduced to the standard QP problem with well-investigated properties and advanced numerical procedures.

Utilization of the finite subsets $\mathcal{C}(\cdot)$ instead of the original domain $\mathcal{C}$ allows to calculate the "mesh" approximations for the solution to (8).

Let:

- $\epsilon_n \downarrow 0$ be a decreasing nonrandom sequence characterizing the approximation accuracy;
- $\{\mathcal{C}(\epsilon_n)\}_{n\in\mathbb{N}}$: $\mathcal{C}(\epsilon_1) \subseteq \mathcal{C}(\epsilon_2) \subseteq \mathcal{C}(\epsilon_3) \subseteq \ldots \subseteq \mathcal{C}$ be a sequence of embedded subdivisions;
-

$$\omega_1^\epsilon(y) \triangleq \max_{\substack{q_1,q_2\in\mathcal{C}:\\ \|q_1-q_2\|<\epsilon}} |w_1(q_1|y) - w_1(q_2|y)|,$$

$$\omega_2^\epsilon(y) \triangleq \max_{\substack{q_1,q_2\in\mathcal{C}:\\ \|q_1-q_2\|<\epsilon}} \|w_2(q_1|y) - w_2(q_2|y)\| \tag{31}$$

be modulus of continuity for $w_1(y|q)$ and $w_2(y|q)$.

The assertion below characterizes the divergence rate of the approximating solutions to the initial minimax estimate.

Lemma 2. *If $\{\widehat{\mathbf{w}}(n|y)\}_{n\in\mathbb{N}}$ are corresponding solutions to the problems:*

$$\widehat{\mathbf{w}}^n(y) = \underset{w\in\mathrm{conv}(\mathbb{W}(\mathcal{C}(\epsilon_n)|y))}{\mathrm{Argmax}} \mathbf{J}_*(w)$$

then the following sequences are convergent as $\epsilon_n \downarrow 0$:

$$\widehat{\mathbf{w}}^n(y) \to \widehat{\mathbf{w}}(y),$$

$$\mathcal{J}(y) - \max_{w\in\mathrm{conv}(\mathbb{W}(\mathcal{C}(\epsilon_n)|y))} \mathbf{J}_*(w) \leqslant \omega_1^{\epsilon_n}(y) + K[\omega_2^{\epsilon_n}(y)]^2 \downarrow 0 \tag{32}$$

with some constant $0 < K < \infty$.

The proof of Lemma 2 is given in Appendix D.

4.2. The Least Favorable Distribution in the Light of the Pareto Efficiency

The minimax estimation problem under the conformity constraints is tightly interconnected with the choice of the distribution $\widehat{F}$ that is optimal in the sense of a vector-valued criterion. On the one hand, the solution to the considered estimation problem is grounded on the evaluation of the distribution $\widehat{F}$, maximizing the dual criterion (12): $\mathbf{I}_1(F|y) \triangleq J_*(F|y) \to \max_F$. On the other hand, the distribution F should conform to the realized sample $Y = y$, and the maximization of the conformity index leads to the following optimization problem: $\mathbf{I}_2(F|y) \triangleq \mathfrak{L}(y, F) \to \max_F$.

Obviously, the criteria $\mathbf{I}_1$ and $\mathbf{I}_2$ are conflicting; hence the proper choice of F requires the application of the vector optimization techniques.

Let:

- $\widehat{\mathbb{F}}_0$ be a set of the LFDs in the estimation problem (8) without conformity constrains (i.e., as $L = 0$);
- $\widetilde{\mathcal{L}}(y) \triangleq \max_{F\in\widehat{\mathbb{F}}_0} \mathfrak{L}(y, F)$;
- $M \in [\widetilde{\mathcal{L}}(y), \overline{\mathcal{L}}(y)]$ be an arbitrary fixed conformity level;
- $\widehat{\mathbf{w}}(y) = \mathrm{Argmax}_{w\in\mathbb{W}(\mathbb{F}_M|y)} \mathbf{J}_*(w)$ be a solution to the finite-dimensional dual problem;
- $\widehat{\mathbb{F}}_M$ be the set of corresponding LFDs.

Lemma 3. *Any least favorable distribution $\widehat{F}_M \in \widehat{\mathbb{F}}_M$ is Pareto-efficient with respect to the vector-valued criterion $(\mathbf{I}_1, \mathbf{I}_2)$.*

The proof of Lemma 3 follows directly from the Germeyer theorem [16].

Consideration of the constrained minimax estimation problem in light of the optimization by the vector criterion is somehow close to the one investigated in [31], where the estimation quality is characterized by the ℓ_2 norm of the error, and the Shannon entropy is characterized as a measure of the statistical uncertainty of the estimated vector.

4.3. Other Conformity Indices

First, we consider the conformity constraint (9) thoroughly. It admits the following treatment. Let $\widetilde{F} \in \mathbb{F}$ be some reference distribution. The constraint $\mathfrak{L}(y, F) \geqslant \mathfrak{L}(y, \widetilde{F})$ is a specific case of (9); the feasible distributions F should be relevant to the available observations $Y = y$ no less than the reference distribution $\widetilde{F}$ is. One more treatment is also acceptable. Let $\widetilde{q} \in \mathcal{C}$ be some "guess" value of the uncertain parameter γ, and $\alpha > 0$ be a fixed value. The constraint:

$$\frac{\mathfrak{L}(y, F)}{\mathcal{L}(y|\widetilde{q})} \geqslant \alpha \tag{33}$$

is a specific case of (9): it means that the likelihood ratio of any feasible distribution F to the one-point distribution at $\widetilde{q}$ should be no less that the level α. Obviously, the guess value $\widetilde{q}$ could be chosen from the maxima of the function $\mathcal{L}$, i.e., $\widetilde{q} \in \mathrm{Argmax}_{q \in \mathcal{C}} \mathcal{L}(y|q)$, but calculation of these maxima is itself a nontrivial problem of likelihood function maximization. In Section 5 we use some modification of (33):

$$\frac{\mathfrak{L}(y, F) - \min_{q \in \mathcal{C}_n} \mathcal{L}(y|q)}{\max_{q \in \mathcal{C}_n} \mathcal{L}(y|q) - \min_{q \in \mathcal{C}_n} \mathcal{L}(y|q)} \geqslant r \tag{34}$$

where $\mathcal{C}_n \subseteq \mathcal{C}$ is a known subset, and $r \in (0, 1)$ is a fixed parameter. This form is important, because in the case of $\mathcal{C} = \mathcal{C}_n$ it guarantees for the constraint (34) to be active in the considered minimax optimization problem for each $r \in (0, 1)$.

Furthermore, the proposed conformity index $\mathfrak{L}(y, F)$ (9) is a non-unique numerical characteristic that describes the interconnection between F and Y. For example, an alternative conformity index can be defined as $\int_{\mathcal{C}} f(\mathcal{L}(y|q)) F(dq)$, where $f(\cdot) : \mathbb{R} \to \mathbb{R}$ is some continuous nondecreasing function. Another way to introduce this index is to set it as $\int_{\mathcal{S}(y)} \mathfrak{L}(y', F) dy' = \mathsf{P}_F\{Y \in \mathcal{S}(y)\}$, i.e., as a probability that the observation Y lies in the confidence set $\mathcal{S}(y) \in \mathcal{B}(\mathbb{R}^k)$.

For a particular case of the observation model (1) we can propose one more conformity index that is based on the EDF. Let us consider the observation model with the "pure uncertain" estimated parameter γ:

$$Y_t = A(\gamma) + B(\gamma) V_t, \quad t = \overline{1, T}. \tag{35}$$

Here:

- $\mathbf{Y}_T \triangleq \mathrm{col}(Y_1, \ldots, Y_T)$ are available observations;
- $\gamma \in \mathcal{C} \in \mathbb{R}^m$ is a random vector with unknown distribution F;
- $\mathbf{V}_T \triangleq \mathrm{col}(V_1, \ldots, V_T)$ are the observation errors that are i.i.d. centered normalized random values with the pdf $\phi_V(v)$.

If the value γ is known, the observations $\{Y_t\}_{t=\overline{1,T}}$ can be considered as i.i.d. random values, whose pdf is equal to $\phi_V(v)$ after some shifting and scaling. The EDF of the sample $\{Y_t\}_{t=\overline{1,T}}$ has the form:

$$F_T^*(y) \triangleq \frac{1}{T} \sum_{t=1}^{T} \mathbf{I}(y - Y_t). \tag{36}$$

On the other hand, the cdf $F^Y(y)$ of any observation Y_t for a fixed distribution F can be calculated as:

$$F^Y(y) \triangleq \int_{-\infty}^{y} \int_{\mathcal{C}} \phi_V\left(\frac{u - A(q)}{B(q)}\right) F(dq) du. \tag{37}$$

The sample conformity index based on the EDF is the following value:

$$\mathfrak{M}(\mathbf{Y}_T, F) \triangleq \|F_T^* - F^Y\|_\infty = \sup_{y \in \mathbb{R}} |F_T^*(y) - F^Y(y)|. \tag{38}$$

The new uncertainty set $\mathbb{F}_M$ describing all admissible distributions F satisfies conditions (i), (ii) and (iv) above, but condition (iii) is replaced by the following one:

(x) the constraint

$$\mathfrak{M}(\mathbf{Y}_T, F) \leqslant M \tag{39}$$

This holds for all $F \in \mathbb{F}_M$ and some fixed level $M > 0$. It is called *the constraint based on the EDF.*

The proposed conformity index represents the well known Kolmogorov distance used in the goodness-of-fit test. One also knows the asymptotic characterization of $\mathfrak{M}(\mathbf{Y}_T, F)$:

$$\lim_{T \to \infty} \mathsf{P}\left\{ \mathfrak{M}(\mathbf{Y}_T, F) < \frac{x}{\sqrt{T}} \right\} = \sum_{-\infty}^{+\infty} (-1)^j e^{-2j^2 x^2}.$$

Furthermore, the value $\mathfrak{M}(\mathbf{Y}_T, F)$ can be easily calculated, because the function F_T^* is piece-wise constant while F^Y is continuous:

$$\mathfrak{M}(\mathbf{Y}_T, F) = \max_{1 \leqslant t \leqslant T} \max(|F_T^*(Y_t) - F^Y(Y_t-)|, |F_T^*(Y_t) - F^Y(Y_t)|),$$

and the cdf F^Y is calculated by (37).

The distribution set determined by (39) takes the form:

$$\left\{ F \in \mathbb{F} : -M + F_T^*(Y_t) \leqslant \int_{-\infty}^{Y_t} \int_{\mathcal{C}} \phi_V\left(\frac{u - A(q)}{B(q)} \right) F(dq) du \leqslant M + F_T^*(Y_t-), \quad t = \overline{1, T} \right\}. \tag{40}$$

Using the variational series $\mathbf{Y}_{(T)} \triangleq \mathrm{col}(Y_{(1)}, \ldots, Y_{(T)})$ of the sample $\mathbf{Y}_T$, and recalling $F_T^*(Y_{(t)}) = \frac{t}{T}$, $F_T^*(Y_{(t)}-) = \frac{t-1}{T}$, (40) can be rewritten in the form:

$$\left\{ F \in \mathbb{F} : -M + \frac{t}{T} \leqslant \int_{-\infty}^{Y_{(t)}} \int_{\mathcal{C}} \phi_V\left(\frac{u - A(q)}{B(q)} \right) F(dq) du \leqslant M + \frac{t-1}{T}, \quad t = \overline{1, T} \right\}. \tag{41}$$

It can be seen that this set is a convex closed polyhedron, lying in $\mathbb{F}$, with at most $2T$ facets. All assertions formulated in Section 3 are valid after replacing the uncertainty set $\mathbb{F}_L$, generated by the likelihood function, by the set $\mathbb{F}_M$, generated by the EDF. Moreover, the mesh algorithm for the dual optimization problem solution, presented above in Section 4.1, can also be applied to this case.

Let us consider the observation model (35) again. We can use the sample mean $\overline{Y} \triangleq \frac{1}{T} Y_t$ as one more conformity index. Let us remind the reader that due to the model property, the random parameter $\gamma(\omega)$ is constant for each sample $\mathbf{Y}_T$. For rather large T values, the central limit theorem allows to treat the normalized value $\frac{\sqrt{T}(\overline{Y} - A(\gamma))}{|B(\gamma)|}$ as a standard Gaussian random one. We then fix a standard Gaussian quantile c_α of the confidence level α and exscind the subset:

$$\mathcal{C}_\alpha \triangleq \left\{ q \in \mathcal{C} : \overline{Y} - \frac{c_\alpha |B(\gamma)|}{\sqrt{T}} \leqslant A(q) \leqslant \overline{Y} + \frac{c_\alpha |B(\gamma)|}{\sqrt{T}} \right\} \subseteq \mathcal{C}.$$

If $\mathcal{C}_\alpha$ is compact then the set $\mathbb{F}_\alpha$ of all probability distributions with the domain lying in $\mathcal{C}_\alpha$ is called *the set of admissible distributions satisfying the sample mean conformity constraint of the level α.*

The comparison of the minimax estimates, calculated under various types of the conformity constraints, is presented in the next section.

5. Numerical Examples

5.1. Parameter Estimation in the Kalman Observation System

Let us consider the linear Gaussian discrete-time (Kalman) observation system:

$$
\begin{cases}
X_t = aX_{t-1} + bV_t, & t = \overline{1,T}, \quad x_0 \sim \mathcal{N}(0, P_0), \\
Y_t = cX_t + fW_t, & t = \overline{0,T},
\end{cases}
\tag{42}
$$

where:

- $\mathbf{X}_T \triangleq \mathrm{col}(X_0, \ldots, X_T)$ is an unobservable state trajectory (the autoregression X_t is supposed to be stable);
- $\mathbf{Y}_T \triangleq \mathrm{col}(Y_0, \ldots, Y_T)$ are available observations;
- $\mathbf{V}_T \triangleq \mathrm{col}(V_1, \ldots, V_T)$ and $\mathbf{W}_T \triangleq \mathrm{col}(W_0, \ldots, W_T)$ are vectorizations of independent standard Gaussian discrete-time white noises;
- P_0, c and f are known parameters;
- $\gamma \triangleq \mathrm{col}(a, b)$ is an uncertain vector lying in the fixed rectangle $\mathcal{C} \triangleq [\underline{a}, \overline{a}] \times [\underline{b}, \overline{b}]$.

Our goal is to calculate the proposed minimax estimates of the uncertain vector γ and analyze their performance depending on the specific form of the loss function (6). To vary the loss function we can either specify the estimated test signal $h(\cdot)$ or determine different Euclidean weighted norms. We choose the second approach and define the following norm $\|\cdot\|_{\xi_X, \xi_\gamma}$ for the compound vector: $Z \triangleq \mathrm{col}(\mathbf{X}_T, \gamma)$:

$$
\|Z\|_{\xi_X, \xi_\gamma} \triangleq \sqrt{\xi_X^2 \sum_{t=1}^{T} X_t^2 + \xi_\gamma^2 (a^2 + b^2)},
$$

and the corresponding loss function takes the form:

$$
J_{\xi_X, \xi_\gamma}(\overline{Z}, F|\mathbf{Y}_T) \triangleq \mathsf{E}_F \left\{ \|Z - \overline{Z}(\mathbf{Y}_T)\|_{\xi_X, \xi_\gamma}^2 | \mathbf{Y}_T \right\}.
\tag{43}
$$

In the case $\xi_\gamma = 1$ and $\xi_X = 0$ we obtain "the traditional" case of the mean-square loss conditional function $J_{0,1}(\overline{Z}, F|\mathbf{Y}_T) = \mathsf{E}_F\{\|\gamma - \overline{\gamma}(\mathbf{Y}_T)\|^2 | \mathbf{Y}_T\}$, and the estimation quality of $\overline{\gamma}(\cdot)$ is determined directly through the loss function. Using $\xi_\gamma = 0$ and $\xi_X = 1$ we transform the loss function into $J_{1,0}(\overline{Z}, F|\mathbf{Y}_T) = \mathsf{E}_F\{\|X - \overline{X}(\mathbf{Y}_T)\|^2 | \mathbf{Y}_T\}$, and the estimation of γ appears indirectly via the estimation of the state trajectory $\mathbf{X}_T$.

The minimax estimation is calculated by the numerical procedure introduced in Section 4.1 with the uniform mesh $\mathcal{C}_{h_a, h_b}$ of the uncertainty set $\mathcal{C}$; h_a and h_b are corresponding mesh steps along each coordinate.

We calculate the minimax estimate with the likelihood conformity constraint of the form:

$$
\frac{\mathfrak{L}(\mathbf{Y}_T, F) - \min_{(a,b) \in \mathcal{C}_{h_a, h_b}} \mathcal{L}(\mathbf{Y}_T|(a,b))}{\max_{(a,b) \in \mathcal{C}_{h_a, h_b}} \mathcal{L}(\mathbf{Y}_T|(a,b)) - \min_{(a,b) \in \mathcal{C}_{h_a, h_b}} \mathcal{L}(\mathbf{Y}_T|(a,b))} \geq r,
$$

where $r \in (0, 1)$ is a confidence ratio.

We compare the proposed minimax estimate with some known alternatives.

The calculations have been executed with the following parameter values: $\mathcal{C} = [-0.1; 0.1] \times [0.1; 1]$, $a = -0.1$, $b = 0.1$, $P_0 = 0.5$, $c = 1$, $f = 0.5$, $T = 1000$, $h_a = 0.01$, $h_b = 0.045$. The choice of the parameters can be explained by the following facts. First, the point $(-0.1; 0.1)$ of actual parameter values belongs to the domain of the LFD for both loss functions $J_{0,1}$ and $J_{1,0}$. This means the appearance of just the LFD for both cases. Second, in spite of sufficient observation length, the signal-to-noise ratio is rather small, which prevents high performance of the asymptotic estimation methods.

Figure 1 presents the evolution of the minimax estimates $\widehat{a}_{0,1}(r)$ and $\widehat{a}_{1,0}(r)$ of a drift coefficient depending on the confidence ratio $r \in (0, 1)$. The minimax estimates are compared with;

- The estimate $\bar{a}^{MS}(Y_T)$ calculated by the moment/substitution method [12]:

$$\bar{a}^{MS} = \sum_{t=1}^{T} y_{t-1}y_t \Big/ \Big(\sum_{t=1}^{T} y_t^2 - Tf^2\Big), \quad \bar{b}^{MS} = \sqrt{\frac{1}{c^2}\Big(1 - (\bar{a}^{MS})^2\Big)\Big(\sum_{t=1}^{T} y_t^2 - Tf^2\Big)};$$

- The Bayesian estimate $\hat{a}^{F_1}(\mathbf{Y}_T)$ (11) calculated under the assumption that prior distribution F_1 of γ is uniform over the whole uncertainty set $\mathcal{C}$;
- The Bayesian estimate $\hat{a}^{F_2}(\mathbf{Y}_T)$ (11) calculated under the assumption that the prior distribution F_2 of γ is uniform over the vertices of $\mathcal{C}$;
- The estimate $\bar{a}^{EKF}(\mathbf{Y}_T)$ calculated by *the extended Kalman filter* (EKF) algorithm [39] and subsequent residual processing;
- The *maximum likelihood estimate* (MLE) $\bar{a}^{MLE}(\mathbf{Y}_T)$ calculated by *the expectation/maximization algorithm* (EM algorithm) [17].

Figure 2 contains a similar comparison of the diffusion coefficient estimates $\hat{b}_{0,1}(r)$ and $\hat{b}_{1,0}(r)$.

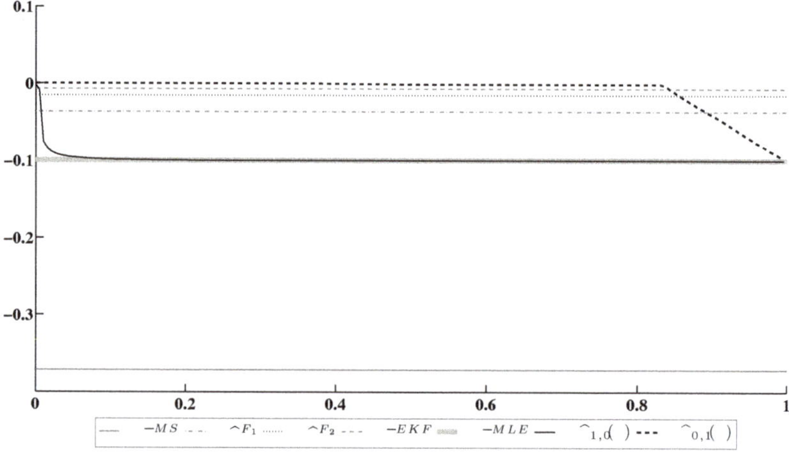

Figure 1. Estimation of the drift coefficient *a*.

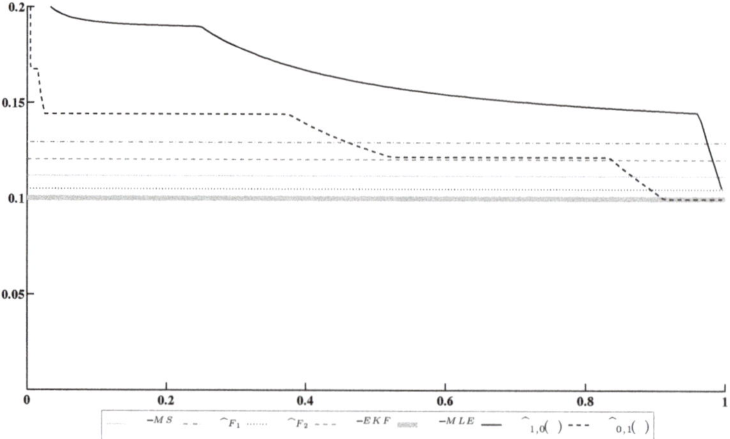

Figure 2. Estimation of the diffusion coefficient *b*.

The results of this experiment allow us to make the following conclusions.

1. Both minimax estimates $(\widehat{a}_{0,1}(r), \widehat{b}_{0,1}(r))$ and $(\widehat{a}_{1,0}(r), \widehat{b}_{1,0}(r))$ converge to the MLE $(\overline{a}^{MLE}, \overline{b}^{MLE})$ as $r \to 1$. Nevertheless, the rate of convergence depends on the specific choice of the loss function ($J_{0,1}$ or $J_{1,0}$ in the considered case).
2. Both minimax estimates are more conservative than the MLE, because they take into account a chance for other points of the LFD domain to be realized.
3. Under an appropriate choice of the confidence ratio r, both minimax estimates become more accurate than other candidates, except for the MLE.

5.2. Parameter Estimation under Additive and Multiplicative Observation Noises

We consider the observations $\mathbf{Y}_T \triangleq \mathrm{col}(Y_1, \ldots, Y_T)$:

$$Y_t = aX_t + V_t, \qquad t = \overline{1, T}. \tag{44}$$

Here:

- a is an estimated value;
- $\mathbf{X}_T \triangleq \mathrm{col}(X_1, \ldots, X_T)$ is a vector of the i.i.d. unobservable random values (multiplicative noise): $X_1 \sim \mathcal{R}[0, 1]$;
- $\mathbf{V}_T \triangleq \mathrm{col}(V_1, \ldots, V_T)$ is a vector of the i.i.d. unobservable random values (additive noise): $V_1 \sim \mathcal{N}(0, \sigma)$.

We assume that the parameter a is random with unknown distribution, whose support set lies within the known set $\mathcal{C} \triangleq [c^1, c^2]$. The loss function has the form:

$$J(\overline{a}, F|\mathbf{Y}_T) = \mathsf{E}_F\left\{ \|a - \overline{a}(\mathbf{Y}_T)\|^2 |\mathbf{Y}_T \right\}.$$

In this example our goal is to compare the minimax estimates of the parameter a under conformity constraint based either on the likelihood function or on the EDF.

The minimax estimations are calculated for the following parameter values: $a = 2$, $T = 20$, $\mathcal{C} = [2, 3]$, $\sigma = 0.1$. We use the proposed numerical procedure under a uniform mesh $\mathcal{C}_h$ of the set $\mathcal{C}$ with the step $h = 0.005$. The example has some features. First, the observation model contains both the additive ($\mathbf{V}_T$) and multiplicative ($\mathbf{X}_T$) heterogeneous noises. Second, the available observed sample is not too long to provide the high quality for the consistent estimates. Third, the exact value of a is equal 2; meanwhile under the constraint absence there exists a discrete variant of the LFD with the finite support set $\{2, 3\}$. This means that the LFD is realized only in the considered observation model.

The likelihood conformity constraint looks similar to the one from the previous subsection:

$$\frac{\mathfrak{L}(\mathbf{Y}_T, F) - \min_{q \in \mathcal{C}_h} \mathcal{L}(\mathbf{Y}_T|q)}{\max_{q \in \mathcal{C}_h} \mathcal{L}(\mathbf{Y}_T|q) - \min_{q \in \mathcal{C}_h} \mathcal{L}(\mathbf{Y}_T|q)} \geqslant r, \tag{45}$$

where $r \in (0, 1)$ is a confidence ratio.

Figure 3 contains comparison of the minimax estimate $\widehat{a}(r)$ with its actual value a, the (consistent asymptotically Gaussian) M-estimate $\overline{a}^{sub} \triangleq \frac{2}{T} \sum_{t=1}^{T} Y_t$, obtained by the moment/substitution method [12] and the MLE $\overline{a}^{MLE}$.

Next, we investigate minimax posterior estimates under the conformity constraint based on the EDF. The constraint is of the form:

$$\frac{\max_{F \in \mathbb{F}_{\mathcal{C}_h}} \mathfrak{M}(\mathbf{Y}_T, F) - \mathfrak{M}(\mathbf{Y}_T, F)}{\max_{F \in \mathbb{F}_{\mathcal{C}_h}} \mathfrak{M}(\mathbf{Y}_T, F) - \min_{F \in \mathbb{F}_{\mathcal{C}_h}} \mathfrak{M}(\mathbf{Y}_T, F)} \geqslant r, \tag{46}$$

where $r \in (0, 1)$ is some fixed confidence ratio, and $\mathbb{F}_{\mathcal{C}_h}$ is a "mesh" approximation of the set $\mathbb{F}_{\mathcal{C}}$ corresponding to the uniform "mesh" $\mathcal{C}_h$. The form (46) of the conformity constraint provides that it is active in the minimax optimization problem for any $r \in (0, 1)$.

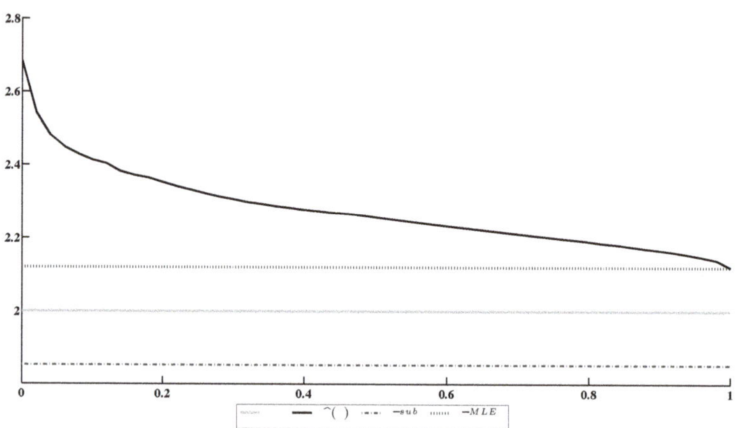

Figure 3. Estimation of the coefficient a under conformity constraint based on the likelihood function.

Figure 4 contains:

- The EDF $F_Y^*(y)$ calculated by the sample $\mathbf{Y}_T$;
- The cdf's $F_Y^q(y) = \int_{-\infty}^y \phi_V\left(\frac{u-A(q)}{B(q)}\right) du$ of Y, corresponding to the one-point distribution concentrated at the point q ($q = 2, 3$);
- The cdf $\overline{F}_Y(y)$ $\overline{F}_Y(y) \in \text{Argmin}_{F \in \mathbb{F}_{\mathcal{C}_h}} \mathfrak{M}(\mathbf{Y}_T, F)$, closest to the EDF $F_Y^*(y)$ within the set $\mathbb{F}_{\mathcal{C}_h}$.

Note that $F_Y^2(y)$ is a cdf of Y corresponding to the actual value of a.

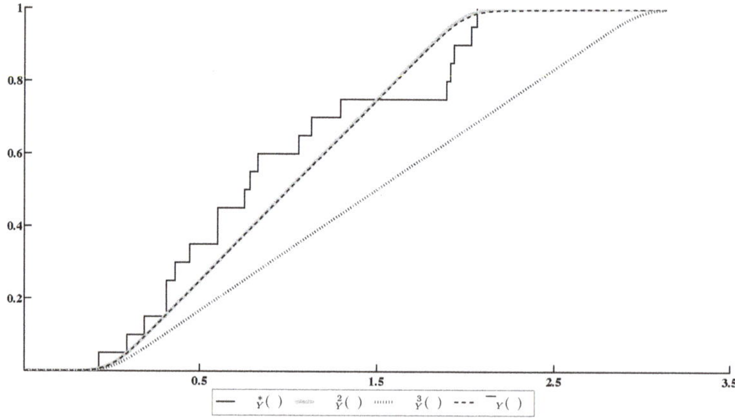

Figure 4. The EDF of Y and different cdf's of Y under various choices of a.

Figure 5 contains a comparison of the minimax estimate $\widehat{a}(r)$ under the conformity constraint, based on the EDF, with its actual value a, the moment/substitution estimate $\overline{a}^{sub}$ and the MLE $\overline{a}^{MLE}$.

The results of this experiment allow us to make the following conclusions.

1. The minimax estimate $\widehat{a}(r)$ under the conformity constraint, based on the EDF, does not converge to the MLE $\overline{a}^{MLE}$ as $r \to 1$.
2. Under an appropriate choice of the confidence ratio r, the minimax estimate under the EDF constraint becomes more accurate than other candidates, including the MLE.

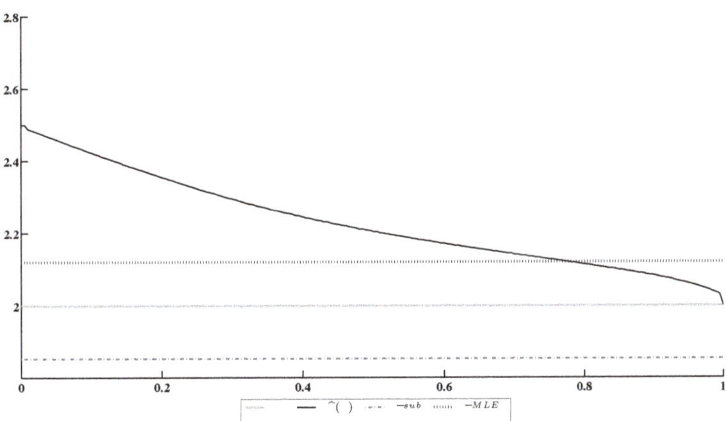

Figure 5. Estimation of the coefficient a under conformity constraint based on the EDF.

6. Conclusions

The paper contains the statement and solution to a new minimax estimation problem for the uncertain stochastic regression parameters. The optimality criterion is the conditional mean square of the estimation error given the realized observations. The class of admissible estimators contains all (linear and nonlinear) statistics with finite variance. The a priori information concerning the estimated vector is incomplete: the vector is random and the part of its components lies in the known compact. The key feature of the considered problem is the presence of the additional constraints for the statistical uncertainty, restricting from below the correspondence degree between the uncertainty and realized observations. The paper presents various indices, characterizing this conformity via the likelihood function, the EDF and the sample mean.

We propose a reduction of the initial optimization problem in the abstract infinite-dimensional spaces to the standard finite-dimensional QP problem with convex constraints along with an algorithm of its numerical realization and precision analysis.

The minimax estimation problem is solved in terms of the saddle points, i.e., besides the estimators with the guaranteed quality, we have a description of the LFDs. First, the investigation of the LFDs' domains allowed us the detection of the uncertain parameter values, which are the worst for the estimation. Second, the consideration of the performance index pair "conformity index–guaranteed estimation quality" uncovered rather a new conception of the parameter estimation under a vector optimality criterion. The paper contains an assertion, which states that the LFDs are Pareto-optimal for the vector-valued criterion above.

The paper focuses mostly on the conformity indices related to the likelihood function; thus, it is obvious that the performance of the minimax estimate is compared with the one of the MLE. In general, the MLE has several remarkable properties, in particular the asymptotic minimaxity under some additional restrictions [12]. However, the estimate is non-robust to the prior statistical uncertainty. The proposed minimax estimate can be considered as a robustified version of the MLE, which is ready for application in the cases of the short non-asymptotic samples or the violation of the conditions for the MLE asymptotic minimaxity.

The conformity constraints are not exhausted by the likelihood function. In the paper, we present other conformity indices based on the EDF and sample mean. We demonstrate that the minimax estimates with the EDF conformity constraint are better than the MLE. One of the points of the paper is that the flexible choice of the conformity indices and design of the additional conformity constraints for each individual applied estimation problem allows obtaining a tradeoff between the prior uncertainty and available observations.

The reason to choose one or another conformity index depends not only on the conditions of the specific practical estimation problem solved under the minimax settings. One of the essential conditions is the possibility of its quick computation for the subsequent verification of the conformity constraint. For example, calculation of the likelihood conformity constraint (33) with the guess value $\mathcal{L}(y|\bar{q}) = \max_q \mathcal{L}(y|q)$ tends to necessarily solve the auxiliary maximization problem for the likelihood function, which is nontrivial itself. Thus, the conformity indices based on the EDF or sample moments look more prospective from the computational point of view.

The applicability of the proposed minimax estimate also depends on the presence of the analytical formula of the estimates $w(y|q)$, or the fast numerical algorithms of its calculation. In turn, this possibility is a base for the subsequent effective solution to the QP problem and specification of the LFD.

Finally, the key indicator affecting the estimate calculation process and its precision is the number of the mesh nodes in the approximation $\mathcal{C}(\epsilon_n)$ of the uncertainty set $\mathcal{C}$. It is a function of "the size of $\mathcal{C}$ / the mesh step ϵ_n" ratio and dimensionality m of $\mathcal{C}$.

All of the factors above characterize the limits of possible applicability of the proposed minimax estimation method for the solution to one or another practical problem.

Funding: The research was supported by the Ministry of Science and Higher Education of the Russian Federation, project No. 075-15-2020-799.

Institutional Review Board Statement: Not applicable.

Informed Consent Statement: Not applicable.

Data Availability Statement: Data sharing is not applicable to this article.

Conflicts of Interest: The author declares no conflict of interest.

Abbreviations

The following abbreviations are used in this manuscript:

cdf	cumulative distribution function
CE	conditional expectation
EDF	empirical distribution function
EKF	extended Kalman filter
EM algorithm	expectation/maximization algorithm
LFD	least favorable distribution
MLE	maximum likelihood estimate
MS-optimal	optimal in the mean square sense
pdf	probability density function
QP problem	quadratic programming problem

Appendix A

Proof of Lemma 1. Conditions (v)—(viii) imply fulfillment of the inequalities:

$$\mathcal{L}(y|q) \leqslant \sup_{x \in \mathbb{R}^n} v(q, x|y) \leqslant \frac{1}{\lambda_0^{k/2}} \max_{x \in \mathbb{R}^n} \phi_V(x) \triangleq M < \infty.$$

Furthermore, for $\forall\, \epsilon\ (0 < \epsilon < 1)$ there exists a compact set $S(\epsilon) \in \mathcal{B}(\mathbb{R}^n)$, such that $\int_{S(\epsilon)} \Psi(dx|q) \geqslant 1 - \epsilon$, and by the Weierstrass theorem $m(y) \triangleq \min_{(q,x) \in \mathcal{C} \times S(\epsilon)} v(q, x|y) > 0$. Each measure $F \in \mathbb{F}$ can be associated with the measure $\mu_F(dq|y) \triangleq \mathcal{L}(y|q)F(dq)$. Obviously, $\mu_F \ll F$, and μ_F is finite, i.e., $0 < m(y) \leqslant \int_{\mathcal{C}} \mu_F(dq|y) \leqslant M < \infty$. Hence, $\forall\, y \in \mathbb{R}^k$ and $\forall\, F \in \mathbb{F}$. The measure $F'(F, dq|y)$ (15) is probabilistic; moreover $F' \ll F$. The measure $F''(F', dq|y)$ (16) is also a probabilistic one defined on $(\mathcal{C}, \mathcal{B}(\mathcal{C}))$, $F'' \ll F$, and the denominator in (16) has the following lower and upper bounds:

$$0 < \frac{1}{M} \leqslant \int_{\mathcal{C}} \mathcal{L}^{-1}(y|q)F(dq) \leqslant \frac{1}{m(y)} < \infty.$$

From (15) and (16) it follows that $F \sim F'$, and the corresponding measure transformations are mutually inverse, i.e., $\forall\, F \in \mathbb{F}$ the identity $F''(F'(F)) \equiv F'(F''(F)) \equiv F$ holds, and, moreover, $\{F'(F) : F \in \mathbb{F}\} = \{F''(F) : F \in \mathbb{F}\} = \mathbb{F}$. Assertion (1) of Lemma 1 is proven.

The set $\mathbb{F}'_L$ is $*$-weakly closed, because the set $\mathbb{F}'_L$ is, and the function $\mathcal{L}(y|q)$ is non-negative, continuous and bounded in $q \in \mathcal{C}$.

Let $F'_1, F'_2 \in \mathbb{F}'_L$ be two arbitrary distributions from $\mathbb{F}'_L$, and $F'_\alpha \triangleq \alpha F'_1 + (1 - \alpha)F'_2$ be its convex linear combination with a fixed parameter $\alpha \in [0, 1]$. We should prove that $F'_\alpha \in \mathbb{F}'_L$. By the definition of $\mathbb{F}'_L$ there exist distributions $F_1, F_2 \in \mathbb{F}_L$ such that $F'_1 = F'(F_1)$ and $F'_2 = F'(F_2)$. Furthermore, for the convex combination $F_\beta = \beta F_1 + (1 - \beta)F_2$ with

$$\beta \triangleq \frac{\alpha \mathcal{L}(F_2|y)}{\alpha \mathcal{L}(F_2|y) + (1 - \alpha)\mathcal{L}(F_1|y)} \in [0, 1],$$

we can verify easily that $F'_\alpha = F'(F_\beta)$, i.e., $F'_\alpha \in \mathbb{F}'_L$. Assertion (2) of Lemma 1 is proven. $\square$

Appendix B

Proof of Theorem 1. The set $\mathbb{H}(y) = \mathbb{R}^\ell$ by condition (ix); thus it is convex and closed. The set $\mathbb{F}'_L$ is convex and $*$-weakly closed due to Lemma 1. From this fact and (20) it follows that $\mathbb{W}(\mathbb{F}_L|y)$ is also a convex closed set. Moreover, it is bounded due to condition (viii). The function $\mathbf{J}$ (22) is strictly convex in η and concave (affine) in w. These conditions are sufficient for the existence of a saddle point [40]. It should be noted that both the set $\mathbb{H}(y) \times \mathbb{W}(\mathbb{F}_L|y)$ and the saddle point $(\widehat{\mathbf{h}}(y), \widehat{\mathbf{w}}(y))$ depend on the observed sample y. For the saddle point the following equalities are true:

$$\mathbf{J}(\widehat{\mathbf{h}}(y), \widehat{\mathbf{w}}(y)) = \min_{\eta \in \mathbb{H}(y)} \max_{w \in \mathbb{W}(\mathbb{F}_L|y)} \mathbf{J}(\eta, w) = \max_{w \in \mathbb{W}(\mathbb{F}_L|y)} \min_{\eta \in \mathbb{H}(y)} \mathbf{J}(\eta, w) = \max_{w \in \mathbb{W}(\mathbb{F}_L|y)} \mathbf{J}_*(w),$$

i.e., $\widehat{\mathbf{w}}(y) \in \underset{w \in \mathbb{W}(\mathbb{F}_L|y)}{\mathrm{Argmax}}\, \mathbf{J}_*(w).$

Now we prove the uniqueness of the saddle point $\widehat{\mathbf{w}}(y)$. Let $w'(y) = \mathrm{col}(w'_1(y), w'_2(y))$ and $w''(y) = \mathrm{col}(w''_1(y), w''_2(y))$ be two different saddle points, and $\mathcal{J}(y) \triangleq \mathbf{J}_*(w'(y)) = \mathbf{J}_*(w''(y))$ and $w'''(y) \triangleq \alpha w'(y) + (1 - \alpha)w''(y)$ be arbitrary convex combinations of the chosen points $(0 < \alpha < 1)$. After elementary algebraic transformations we have:

$$\mathbf{J}_*(w'''(y)) = \mathcal{J}(y) + \alpha(1 - \alpha)\|w'(y)_2 - w''_2(y)\|^2 > \mathcal{J}(y),$$

which contradicts our assumption that $w'(y)$ and $w''(y)$ are two different solutions to the finite-dimensional dual problem. Theorem 1 is proven. $\square$

Appendix C

Proof of Corollary 2. The set $\mathbb{W}(\mathbb{F}_L|y) \in \mathcal{B}(\mathbb{R}^{\ell+1})$ is compact, and $\mathbb{W}(\mathbb{F}_L|y) \subseteq \mathrm{conv}(\mathbb{W}(\mathcal{C}|y))$. By the Krein–Milman theorem [37], *each* point of the set $\mathbb{W}(\mathbb{F}_L|y)$ can be represented as a convex combination at most of $\dim(\mathbb{W}(\mathbb{F}_L|y)) + 1$ extreme points of the set $\mathbb{W}(\mathbb{F}_L|y)$.

Obviously, all extreme points of $\mathbb{W}(\mathbb{F}_L|y)$ belong to the set $\mathbb{W}(\mathcal{C}|y)$. Hence, for the point $\widehat{\mathbf{w}}(y)$ which is a solution to the finite-dimensional dual problem (28), there exists a finite set $\{\mathbf{q}_s(y)\}_{s=\overline{1,S}} \subseteq \mathcal{C}, 1 \leqslant S \leqslant \dim(\mathbb{W}(\mathbb{F}_L|y)) + 1$ of parameters, and weights $\{\mathsf{P}_s(y)\}_{s=\overline{1,S}}\ (\mathsf{P}_s(y) \geqslant 0, \sum_{s=1}^{S} \mathsf{P}_s(y) = 1)$ such that:

$$\widehat{\mathbf{w}}(y) = \sum_{s=1}^{S} \mathsf{P}_s(y)w(\mathbf{q}_s(y)|y). \tag{A47}$$

The parameters and weights define the reference measure (15) on the space $(\mathcal{C}, \mathcal{B}(\mathcal{C}))$:

$$\widehat{F}'(dq|y) \triangleq \sum_{s=1}^{S} \mathsf{P}_s(y)\delta_{\mathbf{q}_s(y)}(dq).$$

We can establish the initial measure by (16):

$$\widehat{F}(dq|y) = \frac{\sum_{s=1}^{S} \mathcal{L}^{-1}(\mathbf{q}_s(y)|y)\mathsf{P}_s(y)\delta_{\mathbf{q}_s(y)}(dq)}{\sum_{s'=1}^{S} \mathcal{L}^{-1}(\mathbf{q}_{s'}(y)|y)\mathsf{P}_{s'}(y)}.$$

It is easy to verify that $\mathsf{E}_{\widehat{F}}\{\|h(\gamma, X)\|^2|Y = y\} = \mathbf{w}_1(y)$ and $\mathsf{E}_{\widehat{F}}\{h(\gamma, X)|Y = y\} = \mathbf{w}_2(y)$, i.e., $\widehat{F}$ is the required LFD. Corollary 2 is proven. $\square$

Appendix D

Proof of Lemma 2. Without loss of generality we suppose each ϵ_n-mesh contains at least $\dim(\mathbb{W}(\mathbb{F}|y)) + 2$ points. By Corollary 2 the solution to problem (28) can be represented in form (A1). By the condition of Lemma 2 there exists a set $\{\widehat{q}_s(\epsilon_n|y)\}_{s=\overline{1,S}} \subseteq \mathcal{C}(\epsilon_n)$, such that $\max_{1\leqslant s\leqslant S} \|\widehat{\mathbf{q}}_s(y) - q_s(\epsilon_n|y)\| \leqslant \epsilon_n$. For the vector $w(\epsilon_n|y) \triangleq \sum_{s=1}^{S} \widehat{\mathsf{P}}_s(y)w(q_s(\epsilon_n|y)|y)$ the inequalities

$$|\widehat{\mathbf{w}}_1(y) - w_1(\epsilon_n|y)| \leqslant \sum_{s=1}^{S} \widehat{\mathsf{P}}_s(y)|w_1(\widehat{\mathbf{q}}_s(y)|y) - w_1(q_s(\epsilon_n|y)|y)| \leqslant \omega_1(\epsilon_n|y),$$

$$\|\widehat{\mathbf{w}}_2(y) - w_2(\epsilon_n|y)\| \leqslant \sum_{s=1}^{S} \widehat{\mathsf{P}}_s(y)\|w_1(\widehat{\mathbf{q}}_s(y)|y) - w_1(q_s(\epsilon_n|y)|y)\| \leqslant \omega_2(\epsilon_n|y)$$

hold. Furthermore, the sequence of inequalities

$$\max_{w\in\mathrm{conv}(\mathbb{W}(\mathcal{C}(\epsilon_n)|y))} \mathbf{J}_*(w) = \mathcal{J}(y) - \min_{w\in\mathrm{conv}(\mathbb{W}(\mathcal{C}(\epsilon_n)|y))} (\widehat{\mathbf{w}}_1(y) - w_1 + \|w_2\|^2 - \|\widehat{\mathbf{w}}_2(y)\|^2) \geqslant$$

$$\geqslant \mathcal{J}(y) - \left[|\widehat{\mathbf{w}}_1(y) - w_1(\epsilon_n|y)| + \|\widehat{\mathbf{w}}_2(y) - w_2(\epsilon_n|y)\|^2 - 2\langle\widehat{\mathbf{w}}_2(y), \widehat{\mathbf{w}}_2(y) - w_2(\epsilon_n|y)\rangle\right] \geqslant$$

$$\geqslant \mathcal{J}(y) - \left[\omega_1(\epsilon_n|y) + \left(\omega_2(\epsilon_n|y) + 2\frac{M}{m(y)}K_h\right)\omega_2(\epsilon_n|y)\right]$$

proves the convergence $\max_{w\in\mathrm{conv}(\mathbb{W}(\mathcal{C}(\epsilon_n)|y))} \mathbf{J}_*(w) \uparrow \mathcal{J}(y)$ as $\epsilon_n \downarrow 0$.

Let $\widehat{\mathbf{w}}(n|y) \nrightarrow \widehat{\mathbf{w}}(y)$ as $\epsilon_n \downarrow 0$. Then there exists a subsequence $\{\epsilon_{n_k}\}_{n_k\in\mathbb{N}}$, such that $\widehat{\mathbf{w}}(n_k|y) \to \overline{\mathbf{w}}(y) \neq \widehat{\mathbf{w}}(y)$. This means that $\mathbf{J}_*(\widehat{\mathbf{w}}(y)) = \mathbf{J}_*(\overline{\mathbf{w}}(y))$, which contradicts the uniqueness of the solution to the finite-dimensional dual problem (28). Lemma 2 is proven. $\square$

References

1. Calafiore, G.; El Ghaoui, L. Robust maximum likelihood estimation in the linear model. *Automatica* **2001**, *37*, 573–580. [CrossRef]
2. Kurzhanski, A.B.; Varaiya, P. *Dynamics and Control of Trajectory Tubes*; Birkhäuser: Basel, Switzerland, 2014.
3. Matasov, A. *Estimators for Uncertain Dynamic Systems*; Kluwer: Dortrecht, The Netherlands, 1998.
4. Borisov, A.V.; Pankov, A.R. Optimal filtering in stochastic discrete-time systems with unknown inputs. *IEEE Trans. Autom. Control* **1994**, *39*, 2461–2464. [CrossRef]
5. Pankov, A.R.; Semenikhin, K.V. Minimax identification of a generalized uncertain stochastic linear model. *Autom. Remote Control* **1998**, *59*, 1632–1643.
6. Poor, V.; Looze, D. Minimax state estimation for linear stochastic systems with noise uncertainty. *IEEE Trans. Autom. Control* **1981**, *26*, 902–906. [CrossRef]
7. Soloviev, V. Towards the Theory of Minimax-Bayesian Estimation. *Theory Probab. Its Appl.* **2000**, *44*, 739–754. [CrossRef]
8. Blackwell, D.; Girshick, M. *Theory of Games and Statistical Decisions*; Wiley: New York, NY, USA, 1954.

9. Martin, C.; Mintz, M. Robust filtering and prediction for linear systems with uncertain dynamics: A game-theoretic approach. *IEEE Trans. Autom. Control* **1983**, *28*, 888–896. [CrossRef]

10. Berger, J.O. *Statistical Decision Theory and Bayesian Analysis*; Springer: Berlin/Heidelberg, Germany, 1985.

11. Anan'ev, B. Minimax Estimation of Statistically Uncertain Systems Under the Choice of a Feedback Parameter. *J. Math. Syst. Estim. Control* **1995**, *5*, 1–17.

12. Borovkov, A. *Mathematical Statistics*; Australia Gordon & Breach: Blackburn, Australia, 1998.

13. Epstein, L.; Ji, S. Ambiguous volatility, possibility and utility in continuous time. *J. Math. Econ.* **2014**, *50*, 269–282. [CrossRef]

14. Borisov, A.V. A posteriori minimax estimation with likelihood constraints. *Autom. Remote Control* **2012**, *73*, 1481–1497. [CrossRef]

15. Arkhipov, A.; Semenikhin, K. Minimax Linear Estimation with the Probability Criterion under Unimodal Noise and Bounded Parameters. *Autom. Remote Control* **2020**, *81*, 1176–1191. [CrossRef]

16. Germeier, Y. *Non-Antagonistic Games*; Springer: New York, NY, USA, 1986.

17. Elliott, R.J.; Moore, J.B.; Aggoun, L. *Hidden Markov Models: Estimation and Control*; Springer: New York, NY, USA, 1995.

18. Yosida, K. *Functional Analysis*; Grundlehren der Mathematischen Wissenschaften; Springer: Berlin/Heidelberg, Germany, 2013.

19. Liptser, R.; Shiryaev, A. *Statistics of Random Processes: I. General Theory*; Springer: Berlin/Heidelberg, Germany, 2001.

20. Kats, I.; Kurzhanskii, A. Estimation in Multistep Systems. *Proc. USSR Acad. Sci.* **1975**, *221*, 535–538.

21. Petersen, I.R.; James, M.R.; Dupuis, P. Minimax optimal control of stochastic uncertain systems with relative entropy constraints. *IEEE Trans. Autom. Control* **2000**, *45*, 398–412. [CrossRef]

22. Xie, L.; Ugrinovskii, V.A.; Petersen, I.R. Finite horizon robust state estimation for uncertain finite-alphabet hidden Markov models with conditional relative entropy constraints. In Proceedings of the 2004 43rd IEEE Conference on Decision and Control (CDC) (IEEE Cat. No.04CH37601), Nassau, Bahamas, 14–17 December 2004; Volume 4, pp. 4497–4502. [CrossRef]

23. El Karoui, N.; Jeanblanc Picque, M. Contrôle de processus de Markov. *Séminaire Probab. Strasbg.* **1988**, *22*, 508–541.

24. Lee, E.; Markus, L. *Foundations of Optimal Control Theory*; SIAM Series in Applied Mathematics; Wiley: Hoboken, NJ, USA, 1967.

25. Floyd, S.; Jacobson, V. Random early detection gateways for congestion avoidance. *IEEE/ACM Trans. Netw.* **1993**, *1*, 397–413. [CrossRef]

26. Low, S.H.; Paganini, F.; Doyle, J.C. Internet congestion control. *IEEE Control Syst. Mag.* **2002**, *22*, 28–43. [CrossRef]

27. Altman, E.; Avrachenkov, K.; Menache, I.; Miller, G.; Prabhu, B.J.; Shwartz, A. Dynamic Discrete Power Control in Cellular Networks. *IEEE Trans. Autom. Control* **2009**, *54*, 2328–2340. [CrossRef]

28. Perruquetti, W.; Barbot, J.P. *Sliding Mode Control in Engineering*; Marcel Dekker, Inc.: New York, NY, USA, 2002.

29. Arnold, B.F.; Stahlecker, P. Fuzzy prior information and minimax estimation in the linear regression model. *Stat. Pap.* **1997**, *38*, 377–391. [CrossRef]

30. Donoho, D.; Johnstone, I.; Stern, A.; Hoch, J. Does the maximum entropy method improve sensitivity? *Proc. Natl. Acad. Sci. USA* **1990**, *87*, 5066—5068. [CrossRef] [PubMed]

31. Donoho, D.L.; Johnstone, I.M.; Hoch, J.C.; Stern, A.S. Maximum Entropy and the Nearly Black Object. *J. R. Stat. Society. Ser. B* **1992**, *54*, 41–81. [CrossRef]

32. Pham, D.S.; Bui, H.H.; Venkatesh, S. Bayesian Minimax Estimation of the Normal Model with Incomplete Prior Covariance Matrix Specification. *IEEE Trans. Inf. Theory* **2010**, *56*, 6433–6449. [CrossRef]

33. Donoho, D.L.; Johnstone, I.M. Minimax risk over l_p-balls for l_q-error. *Probab. Theory Relat. Fields* **1994**, *99*, 277–303. [CrossRef]

34. Donoho, D.L.; Johnstone, I.M. Minimax estimation via wavelet shrinkage. *Ann. Stat.* **1998**, *26*, 879–921. [CrossRef]

35. Donoho, D.L.; Johnstone, I.; Montanari, A. Accurate Prediction of Phase Transitions in Compressed Sensing via a Connection to Minimax Denoising. *IEEE Trans. Inf. Theory* **2013**, *59*, 3396–3433. [CrossRef]

36. Bosov, A.; Borisov, A.; Semenikhin, K. Conditionally Minimax Prediction in Nonlinear Stochastic Systems. *IFAC-PapersOnLine* **2015**, *48*, 802–807. [CrossRef]

37. Kadets, V. *A Course in Functional Analysis and Measure Theory*; Springer: Berlin/Heidelberg, Germany, 2018.

38. Gelman, A.; Carlin, J.B.; Stern, H.S.; Rubin, D.B. *Bayesian Data Analysis*, 2nd ed.; Chapman and Hall/CRC: London, UK, 2004.

39. Anderson, B.; Moore, J. *Optimal Filtering*; Prentice-Hall: Upper Saddle River, NJ, USA, 1979.

40. Grabiner, J.; Balakrishnan, A. *Applications of Mathematics: Applied Functional Analysis*; Applications of Mathematics; Springer: New York, NY, USA, 1981.

Article

Study of Synergistic Effects in Complex Stochastic Systems

Gurami Tsitsiashvili

Institute for Applied Mathematics, Far Eastern Branch of Russian Academy Sciences, Radio Str. 7, IAM FEB RAS, 690041 Vladivostok, Russia; guram@iam.dvo.ru; Tel.: +89146932749

Abstract: In this paper, a method for detecting synergistic effects of the interaction of elements in multi-element stochastic systems of separate redundancy, multi-server queuing, and statistical estimates of nonlinear recurrent relations parameters has been developed. The detected effects are quite strong and manifest themselves even with rough estimates. This allows studying them with mathematical methods of relatively low complexity and thereby expand the set of possible applications. These methods are based on special techniques of the structural analysis of multi-element stochastic models in combination with majorant asymptotic estimates of their performance indicators. They allow moving to more accurate and rather economical numerical calculations, as they indicate in which direction it is most convenient to perform these calculations.

Keywords: complex system; synergistic effect; performance indicator; structure change

MSC: 60J28

Citation: Tsitsiashvili, G. Study of Synergistic Effects in Complex Stochastic Systems. *Mathematics* **2021**, *9*, 1396. https://doi.org/10.3390/math9121396

Academic Editors: Mikhail Posypkin, Andrey Gorshenin, Vladimir Titarev and Jaan Janno

Received: 23 March 2021
Accepted: 13 June 2021
Published: 16 June 2021

Publisher's Note: MDPI stays neutral with regard to jurisdictional claims in published maps and institutional affiliations.

1. Introduction

Questions of composition and decomposition in multi-element stochastic systems are relevant for solving a number of problems. These include paralleling of algorithms and programs, modeling of supercomputers, the Internet, computer networks, mobile telephone communication systems, development of software packages for modeling catastrophic events in complex systems, design and improvement of technological and economic processes, and so on.

The term "synergy" (the result of the interaction of many elements of the system) originated in statistical physics, but recently it has been used by specialists from other fields: economics, biology, engineering, etc. Furthermore, research in these areas no longer leads to microscopic, but to phenomenological considerations. Here are some examples, taken from science history and devoting the detection of synergistic effects in complex systems, which have been obtained by famous researchers in their objective areas, using observation and mathematical intuition.

The economist A. Smith investigated the transition from shop production to manufacturing on the example of the production of safety pins. In the workshop method, the pin was made entirely by one master, performing all the operations sequentially. In manufacturing, each operation was performed by a separate master, which significantly increased labor productivity.

The physiologist I.P. Pavlov discovered the conditioned reflex by detecting feedback in the nervous system of the body. Stochastic feedback theory was developed by N. Wiener. A detailed study of the conditioned reflex led to the creation by P.K. Anokhin of the concept of a functional system that is urgently formed in the body when it is necessary to achieve the desired result and quickly disintegrates after it is achieved. N. Wiener and P.K. Anokhin collaborated in the development of this scientific direction, actively discussing the possibilities of mathematical methods in this area.

The physicist E. Rutherford discovered the atomic nucleus and proposed to P.L. Kapitsa to create an installation for the effect of a strong magnetic field on the atomic nucleus. Long-running installations were melted under the influence of a strong magnetic field. P.L. Kapitsa constructed an installation that creates a strong magnetic field for a short time, which turned out to be long enough for the processes occurring in the atomic nucleus.

Synergistic effects are a source of explicit dependencies between the characteristics of the system against the background of sufficiently large random perturbations. To study them, it was necessary to develop special techniques based on the structural analysis of multi-element stochastic models in combination with majorant asymptotic estimates of their performance indicators. This, in turn, required new techniques for working with statistical data, as well as skills in using the limit theorems of probability theory and the accompanying asymptotic expansions and estimates.

According to the author, many works on the analysis of complex multi-element systems require at the initial stage the construction of simpler models that allow you to determine the main performance indicators and the main parameters with which you can influence these indicators. For this purpose, it is very convenient to build procedures for comparing systems with different (alternative) structures to study their effectiveness with a large number of elements, with a large load, etc. For this purpose, schemes and/or modes of complex systems, computational algorithms, etc. can be used as objects of comparison. At the same time, at the initial stage of the study, a reasonable proportion should be observed between the accuracy of the calculations, which may be relatively small; the complexity of the calculations, which also should not be large; and the significance of the obtained results, which should be sufficiently large. Comparing systems with an alternative structures allows us to take these requirements into account, as with an increase in the number of elements, the differences between systems with an alternative structures are quite large.

The first author's works, devoted to the study of synergistic effects, are analytical generalizations of the results of numerical and field experiments conducted by his colleagues in the modeling of telecommunications systems, container terminals, etc. In this connection, it should be remembered that in hydrodynamics, nonlinear soliton waves were also first discovered in the course of numerical experiments, and then their analytical theory was constructed. The use of computational experiments allows to obtain more accurate estimates of the synergistic effects. This can be used when working with models used in the programs "digital economy", "smart city", when modeling remote modes of operation that have become popular, on-line conferences, when using smart phones, etc. Currently, new information technologies are rapidly entering our life and their research helps us to adapt to them and to adapt these technologies themselves to the needs of potential users (for example, the use of smart phones by aged users). Nevertheless, analytical research helps to determine the direction of such research and to carry them out. In a sense, this avoids very complex structural optimization problems, a significant part of which are NP problems. Along with this, it becomes possible to use observations of complex systems, which also contributes to the study of synergistic effects in them.

In this paper, the synergistic effect is understood as a significant change in the performance indicators of a complex system when its structure changes, i.e., the connections between its elements. The complexity issues play an important role in modern systems analysis [1,2]. To reduce complexity, various techniques are used, among which the structural transformation of the system plays an important role [3,4]. This methodological technique is closely linked to the issues of the stability of a complex system [5].

Such a statement of the problem can be the comparing the reliability of separate and block reserving elements of a two-pole with unreliable edges [6]. This result is a classic in the mathematical theory of reliability and its refinement or amplification can be significant in itself. Note that the study of the reliability of two poles is widely used in various theoretical and applied studies (see, for example, in [7–10], etc. However, such a comparative analysis made in the monograph [6] of Barlow and Proshan did not develop in subsequent works, while the synergistic effects identified in this paper were very significant.

The peculiarity of this task is the use of probabilistic models, which, at first glance, complicate the task. This transition requires the selection of a new performance indicator—the required amount of reserve, which reflects the content of the reservation procedure and the novelty of the proposed approach. On the other hand, it is also necessary to construct sufficiently weak (logarithmic) dependencies of the so-introduced indicator on a number of the scheme elements. When selecting a new reserve efficiency indicator, its analogy with probabilistic metrics [11] is used. Therefore, the results obtained in this section are new, original, and significant.

Another problem considered in this paper and connected with synergistic effects appeared at the ITMM 2018 and ITMM 2020 conferences, when discussing the multi-server model of the RQ queuing system [12–14]. The Conference ITMM 2018 was held in conjunction with 12th International Workshop on Retrial Queues (RQ) and Related Topics with a wide representation of queuing theory researchers from Russia, India, Bulgaria, the Netherlands, and other countries. A good source of recent works on this topic is a collection of articles on RQ systems [15].

The RQ queuing system is a system in which a customer received in the presence of busy servers is not rejected, but is sent to the so-called orbit, from where it is extracted in accordance with some protocol for queuing, when one of the servers is released. A.N. Dudin remarked that it is most often assumed Poisson input flow to such a system. However, this requirement is not met because there is a dependence and even a long range dependence between the random variables, characterizing numbers of arrived customers in disjoint time intervals. Moreover, despite the large number of analytical results in which the distributions in RQ systems are calculated in formula form, their use for numerical calculations is difficult due to the high complexity of such calculations, especially for multi-server RQ systems.

The novelty of the proposed approach is that instead of a stationary distribution of the process describing a multi-server RQ system, the probability of customers appearing in the orbit of this system for a fixed period of time is investigated and the convergence of this indicator to zero is established when the number of channels proportional to the intensity of the input flow tends to infinity. Secondly, with an increase in the number of servers, even in a system with a Poisson input flow and exponentially distributed service times, the computational complexity of the problem of calculating the limit distribution in an RQ system increases quite strongly.

Thus, a new problem arises for calculating the RQ queuing system with a large number of servers and a non-Poisson input flow. Using asymptotic theorems for multichannel queuing systems, it is possible, on the contrary, to simplify the problem of analyzing RQ systems. For this purpose, it is convenient to use limit theorems based on topological concepts of convergence in the space of random processes defined on a finite time interval [16]. The significance of this approach lies in the broad scope of its application and in the ability to circumvent the computational complexity of the problem by reducing it to the limit theorems of probability theory.

A continuation of the study of multi-server queuing systems in this paper is the analysis of a system with failures. This system arises when modeling modern data transmission networks (of fifth generation), formulated by leading Russian specialists in the mathematical theory of communication [17]. This task is quite important and leading Russian specialists in modeling of transmission networks Samouylov K.E. and Gaidamaka Yu.V. even organized a seminar with the author's participation to find alternative approaches to this problem solution with publishing of obtained results [18]. The solution to this problem is based on the recently installed a synergistic effect in multi-server queuing system with failures, when the stationary probability of failure tends to zero as the number of servers and proportionally the input flow intensity tend to infinity. Moreover, the obtained asymptotic results were quite accurate.

This study is based on the classical Erlangian model of loss multi-server system (see, for example, in [19,20]). Asymptotic behaviors of the blocking probability and parameters of the Equivalent Random Theory method was analyzed in [21] for the case when both the number of servers and the input flow intensity tend to infinity.

However, the inclusion in this model of the assumption that load factor equals one, the intensity of the input flow is proportional to the number of servers n, and the tendency of n to infinity allowed us to establish that the probability of failure tends to zero also. The exact asymptotic rate of this convergence is established. Moreover, when the load factor is less than one, it is possible to construct an upper estimate of the rate of convergence to zero in the form of a geometric progression. Therefore, the synergistic effect found in this paper is very strong and so can be used in the design of data transmission systems of the fifth generation.

The features of probabilistic models of complex systems discovered in this way can also be used in the estimation of their parameters. In particular, in the deterministic model of logistic growth [22] (which is very important and classical in mathematical biology), the problem of estimating the growth parameter from inaccurate observations arises and attracts specialists again and again. The solution of this problem by the method of least squares leads to quite large errors. In this paper, the unknown growth parameter is expressed in terms of the trajectory averages of the deterministic sequence of the model. In turn, the trajectory averages are estimated from observations over a sufficiently long period of time, which leads to the leveling of observation errors. These estimates are based on the use of probabilistic metrics developed in [11] and are new.

Thus, the solution of the above problems of system analysis required a combination of probabilistic and deterministic methods of system analysis, among which the methods of studying the synergistic effects arising from the structural restructuring of a complex system play a decisive role. The benefit of received results is to establish sufficiently strong dependencies of performance indicators on changes in the system structure. This approach opens up new opportunities in solving problems of structural optimization of stochastic systems: queuing, reliability, etc.

2. Separate Redundancy in a Two-Pole System

Consider m sequentially connected and independently operating elements with a failure-free probability of p, $0 < p < 1$. The probability of failure-free operation of such a chain is p^m. Let us focus on two alternative ways to reserve this network. In the first method, n independently functioning duplicates are connected in parallel (see Figure 1).

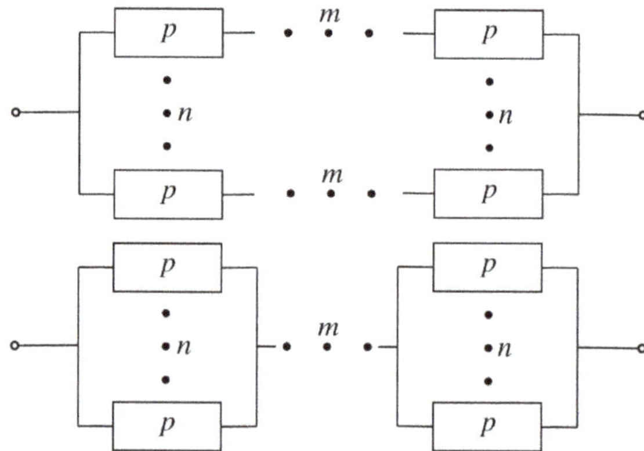

Figure 1. n-multiple block redundancy (**top**), split redundancy (**bottom**) of a chain of length m.

Reliability of the network obtained in this way is $H^n(m) = 1 - (1 - p^m)^n$. In the second method, each element of the original chain is n-multiple reserved separately (see Figure 1). Reliability of the newly formed network $H_n(m) = (1 - q^n)^m$, $q = 1 - p$.

From the results of the monograph [6], it follows that $H_n(m) \geq H^n(m)$ (this inequality is valid for any bipolar). However, this inequality gives only a qualitative idea of the possibilities of separate reservation. To give a quantitative assessment, it is convenient to move from the reliability function to the required amount of reserve.

For $\delta > 0$, denote $n^*(m, \delta) = \min(n : H^n(m) \geq 1 - \delta)$, $n_*(m, \delta) = \min(n : H_n(m) \geq 1 - \delta)$ the required volume of reserve, in which the reliability exceeds $1 - \delta$. To calculate the reliability of general type two-pole, it is necessary to solve an NP-complex problem. However, to compare the different ways of reserving a chain of the length m, it is necessary only to solve a few simple inequalities. Moreover, the results of this comparison are very contrasting and the most interesting consideration of a separate reserve may be applied to general type two-pole also. Let us denote $[a]$ the integer part of the real number a.

Proposition 1. *The following inequalities are met:*

$$n^*(m, \delta) \geq \left[\frac{1-\delta}{p^m}\right] + 1, \; n_*(m, \delta) \leq \left[\frac{\ln(\delta/m)}{\ln q}\right] + 1. \tag{1}$$

Proof. Indeed, for all a, $0 < a < 1$, the inequality holds

$$(1-a)^m \geq 1 - ma, \; m = 1, 2, \ldots, \; \Rightarrow \; H^n(m) = 1 - (1 - p^m)^n \leq np^m, \; \Rightarrow$$

$$n^*(m, \delta) \geq \min(n : np^m \geq 1 - \delta) = \min\left(n : n \geq \frac{1-\delta}{p^m}\right) \geq \left[\frac{1-\delta}{p^m}\right] + 1,$$

so the first relation in Formula (1) takes place. In turn,

$$H_n(m, \delta) \geq (1 - q^n)^m \geq 1 - mq^n, \; \Rightarrow \; n_*(m, \delta) \leq \min(n : mq^n \leq \delta) \; \Rightarrow$$

$$n_*(m, \delta) \leq \min(n : \ln m + n \ln q \leq \ln \delta) \leq \left[\frac{\ln(\delta/m)}{\ln q}\right] + 1.$$

Therefore, the second relation in Formula (1) is valid.
Table 1 demonstrates how much $n^*(m, \delta)$ is greater than $n_*(m, \delta)$. $\square$

Table 1. Meanings of $n^*(m, \delta)$, $n_*(m, \delta)$ for $p = 0,7$, $\delta = 0,1$.

m	1	2	3	4	53	6	7	8	9	10	11	12	13	14	15
$n^*(m, \delta)$	2	4	6	9	13	19	27	39	56	81	116	166	237	339	484
$n_*(m, \delta)$	2	3	3	4	4	4	4	4	4	4	4	4	5	5	5

A comparison of these relations shows that for a large chain length of m, the split-reservation scheme provides special advantages, as the lower bound, which grows as a geometric progression, is replaced by the upper logarithmic bound. Note that the upper estimate of the required reserve in the scheme of separate reservation of a sequential chain is logarithmic in m and can be easily extended to the general case.

Indeed, consider a two-pole consisting of m independently operating edges with probabilities of operation $p_1, \ldots, p_m \geq 1 - q$, $0 < q < 1$. Let us construct a two-pole in which each edge of the original two-pole is a reserve of n identical elements and denote $H_n(p_1, \ldots, p_m)$ the probability of the existence of a working path from the initial to the final vertex in this two-pole.

Proposition 2. *For the value $n_*(p_1, \ldots, p_m, \delta)$, the relation is valid*

$$n_*(p_1, \ldots, p_m, \delta) \leq \left[\frac{\ln(\delta/m)}{\ln q}\right] + 1.$$

Proof. The proof of this statement is based on the inequality $H_n(p_1, \ldots, p_n) \geq (1 - (1 - p_1)^n) \cdot \ldots \cdot (1 - (1 - p_m)^n) \geq (1 - q^n)^m \geq 1 - mq^n$. This inequality follows from the fact that the reliability of an arbitrary two-pole with m independently functioning elements is not less than the reliability of a chain of m elements connected in series. Therefore, the second inequality in the formula (1) is true also. $\square$

For an arbitrary two-pole, a logarithmic by m upper estimate of the value of the required reserve in the separate reservation scheme is performed. Note that this result is obtained using trivial inequalities and does not require calculating the reliability of $H_n(p_1, \ldots, p_m)$, which in general is an NP-problem.

Indeed, if $\alpha_1, \ldots, \alpha_m$ are independent boolean random variables which describe states of two-pole elements and boolean function $A(\alpha_1, \ldots, \alpha_m)$ describes a workability of two-pole dependently on states of its elements then its reliability

$$H_A(p_1, \ldots, p_m) = \sum_{\alpha_1, \ldots, \alpha_m = 0}^{1} A(\alpha_1, \ldots, \alpha_m) \prod_{j=1}^{m} p_j^{\alpha_j}, \text{ with } p_j^1 = p_j, \; p_j^0 = 1 - p_j, \; j = 1, \ldots, m.$$

Calculation of the reliability $H(p_1, \ldots, p_m)$ formally requires performing of 2^m arithmetical operations.

Thus, a convenient choice of the reserve efficiency indicator in the form of the required reserve volume solves two problems. It allows us to obtain a strong (logarithmic) dependence of the chosen efficiency indicator on the number of edges of the two-pole m and makes it possible to abandon the solution of the NP-problem of calculating the reliability of the two-pole.

3. RQ-Queuing Systems with a Large Number of Servers

Consider an RQ-system, i.e., a queuing system, in which, if there is a free server, the customer that has come to the system immediately begins to be served on it. If there are no free servers, then the customer is sent to the orbit, from where it can return to the newly released server in accordance with some protocol [12–14]. A good source for RQ systems in recent years has been Conference ITMM 2018 in Tomsk, which was held in conjunction with 12th International Workshop on Retrial Queues and Related Topics (WRQ 2018).

To solve this problem, we propose to use the theorem on the asymptotic behaviour of an n-server queuing system for $n \to \infty$. In this theorem, we prove that at $T > 0$ for $n \to \infty$, the probability $P_n(T)$ that on the segment $[0, T]$ in the system there will be customers going into orbit tends to zero. Already in this result, the transition from the limit distribution to the above probability is made. Moreover, this characteristic becomes a new indicator of efficiency, which is convenient to use when analyzing a multichannel RQ queuing system.

Consider the series scheme in which the characteristics of n-server queuing systems are defined by the parameter $n \to \infty$, which characterizes an intensity of input flow tending to infinity. Denote $e_n(t)$ a number of input flow customers arriving before the moment t, $e_n(0) = 0$. Assume that $q_n(t)$ is a number of busy servers in this system at the moment t, $q_n(0) = 0$, τ_j is the service time of j input flow customer and τ_j, $j \geq 1$, is a sequence of independent and identically distributed random variables (s.i.i.d.r.v.'s) with the distribution function (d.f.) $F(t)$ ($\overline{F} = 1 - F$), which has continuous and bounded by $\bar{f} > 0$ density $f(t)$. All results of this section are based on ([16], Chapter II, § 1, Theorem 1):

Theorem 1. *Assume that the following conditions are true.*

(1) *For some $a > 0$ the equality $Ee_n(t) = nat$, $t \geq 0$, takes place.*
(2) *There is the function $B(n)$ such that for $A(n) = \max(n^{1/2}, B(n))$ the limit relations take place for $n \to \infty$*

$$\frac{B(n)}{A(n)} \to B \geq 0, \; \frac{\sqrt{n}}{A(n)} \to K \geq 0, \; \frac{n}{A(n)} \to \infty.$$

    so that $\max(B, K) = 1$).

(3)   *The sequence of random processes* $x_n(t) = \dfrac{e_n(t) - Ee_n(t)}{B(n)}$ *for* $n \to \infty$ *C-converges to the centred Gaussian process* $z(t)$.

(4)   *Random process* $\zeta(t) = \displaystyle\int_0^t \overline{F}(t - u)dz(u) + K\Theta(t)$, $0 \le t \le T$, *where* $\Theta(t)$ *is centred Gaussian process independent with* $z(t)$, *which has the covariance function* $R(t, t + u) = \displaystyle\int_0^t \overline{F}(v + u)F(v)adv$ *and satisfies the relation* $P(\sup\limits_{0 \le t \le T} \zeta(t) > L) \to 0$, $L \to \infty$.

(5)   *If the inequality* $\rho = aE\tau_j < 1$ *is true then for any* $T > 0$ *we have the relation*
$$P\left(\sup_{0 \le t \le T} q_n(t) \ge n \right) \to 0, \; n \to \infty.$$

Here, the concept of C-convergence used in Theorem 1 is defined as follows. Denote by $\mathcal{F}_1$ the space of deterministic functions on the segment $[0, T]$ with uniform metric ρ. Designate by $\mathcal{F}$ the set of bounded functionals f defined on $\mathcal{F}_1$ and continuous in the metric ρ : if $z = z(t), z_1 = z_1(t), z_2 = z_2(t), \dots \in \mathcal{F}_1$ and $\rho(z, z_n) \to 0$, $n \to \infty$, then $f(z_n) \to f(z)$, $n \to \infty$. Say that the sequence of random processes $z_n = z_n(t)$, $n \ge 1$, C-converges to the random process $z = z(t)$ if for any functional $f \in \mathcal{F}$ we have that $Ef(z_n) \to Ef(z)$, $n \to \infty$.

Deterministic input flow of customer groups. Let at times $1, 2, \dots$ in n-server RQ-queuing system come groups of customers of the size of $\eta_1 \ge 0, \eta_2 \ge 0, \dots$, where $\eta_1, \eta_2, \dots$ – i.i.d.r.v.'s with integer values, $E\eta_1 = a$, $Var\ \eta_1 < \infty$. Define the input flow by the equality
$$e_n(t) = \sum_{k=1}^{[nt+\psi]} \eta_k, \; t \ge 0,$$
where ψ – independent of η_k, $k \ge 1$, τ_j, $j \ge 1$, a random variable with a uniform distribution on the segment $[0, 1]$ ($[d]$ is the integer part of the real number d). Here and in two next models random variable ψ has uniform distribution to ensure the proportionality t of the mathematical expectation $Ee_n(t)$.

Theorem 2. *Suppose that, for some* $D > 0$, *almost certainly* $\eta_1 < D$ *and the inequality* $aE\tau_1 < 1$ *is true. Then for any* $T > 0$ *the relation* $P_n(T) \to 0$, $n \to \infty$, *is valid.*

Proof. In [23] it is proved that under the conditions of this theorem,
$$P\left(\sup_{0 \le t \le T} q_n(t) \ge n \right) \to 0, \; n \to \infty. \tag{2}$$

Connecting this relation with the inequality $P_n(T) \le P\left(\sup\limits_{0 \le t \le T} q_n(t) \ge n \right)$, $n \ge 1$, one obtains the proof of the theorem. $\square$

Alternating input flow. Consider a n-server RQ-queuing system, assuming $n = n(N) \to \infty$, $N \to \infty$. Let us define the input flow to this system using the following construction. Following the works in [24,25], we define a continuous random flow defined by ON and OFF periods. Let a sequence of i.i.d.r.v's $X_0 \ge 0$, $X_1 \ge 0, X_2 \ge 0, \dots$ consists of lengths of ON-periods, the sequence of i.i.d.r.v.'s $Y_0 \ge 0$, $Y_1 \ge 0$, $Y_2 \ge 0, \dots$ consists of the lengths of OFF-periods and these random sequences are independent. Denote $F_1(t) = P(X_1 < t)$, $F_2(t) = P(Y_1 < t)$, $t \ge 0$, and suppose that
$$\overline{F}_1(t) = t^{-\alpha_1} L_1(t), \; \overline{F}_2(t) = t^{-\alpha_2} L_2(t), \; 1 < \alpha_1 < \alpha_2 < 2,$$

where the function $L_1(t) \to l_1 > 0$, $t \to \infty$, and $L_2(t)$ is a slowly varying function. Let $b(t)$ is the inverse of the function $1/\overline{F}_1(t)$: $b(1/\overline{F}_1(t)) = t$.

We introduce independent r.v.'s B, X, Y, which are independent of X_n, Y_n, $n \geq 1$, and Y_0 with distributions

$$P(B=1) = \frac{\mu_1}{\mu}, \ P(B=0) = \frac{\mu_2}{\mu}, \ \mu=\mu_1+\mu_2, \ \mu_1 = EX_1, \ \mu_2 = EY_1,$$

$$P(X\leq x) = \frac{1}{\mu_1} \int_0^x \overline{F}_1(s)ds, \ P(Y\leq x) = \frac{1}{\mu_2} \int_0^x \overline{F}_2(s)ds.$$

Then, a random sequence

$$T_0 = B(X + Y_0) + (1 - B)Y, \ T_n = T_0 + \sum_{i=1}^n (X_i + Y_i), \ n \geq 1,$$

generates an ON–OFF process

$$W(t) = BI_{[0,X)}(t) + \sum_{n=0}^{\infty} I_{[T_n, T_n+X_{n+1})}(t), \ t \geq 0$$

(here $I_A(t)$ is the indicator function of a random event $t \in A$). The random process $W(t)$ is binary: $W(t) = 1$, if t is contained in an ON-period, $W(t) = 0$, if t is contained in the OFF-period and stationary, and $EW(t) = \mu_1/\mu = \alpha$.

Denote $A(t) = \int_0^t W(s)ds$, then $EA(t) = \alpha t$, $t \geq 0$. Let $n = n(N) = NM(N)$, $M = M(N) = [N^\gamma]$, $\gamma > 0$, and random functions $A_m(t)$, $m = 1, ..., M$, are independent copies of a random function $A(t)$. We introduce the function $e_n(t) = \left[\sum_{m=1}^M A_m(Nt) + \psi \right]$, specifying the alternating input flow.

Theorem 3. *If $\gamma > \alpha_1 - 1$ and $\alpha E\tau_j < 1$, then for any $T > 0$ the relation $P_n(T) \to 0$, $n \to \infty$, is true.*

The proof of Theorem 3 repeats the proof of Theorem 2 verbatim.

Erlangian input flow. Let $E_n(t)$ a Poisson flow of customers with intensity $n\alpha$. Define the input flow to the n-server system described above by the equality

$$e_n(t) = \left[\frac{E_n(t)}{r} + \psi \right], \ t \geq 0,$$

where ψ is a random variable independent of η_k, $k \geq 1$, τ_j, $j \geq 1$, with a uniform distribution on the segment $[0, 1]$, and the fixed r takes natural values. It is obvious that for any fixed ψ, $0 \leq \psi \leq 1$, the moments of single jumps of the process $e_n(t)$ form an Erlangian flow. Here, the Erlangian flow is obtained from $E_n(t)$ by allocation of moments with numbers that are multiples of r.

Theorem 4. *If $\alpha E\tau_j < 1$, then for any $T > 0$ the relation $P_n(T) \to 0$, $n \to \infty$, holds.*

Proof. In [26] it is proved that Formula (2) is valid under the conditions of the theorem. Connecting it with inequality $P_n(T) \leq P\left(\sup_{0 \leq t \leq T} q_n(t) \geq n \right)$, one obtains the proof of the theorem. $\square$

The choice of the probability $P_n(T)$ as an efficiency indicator allows us to apply the known theorems to the analysis of a multi server RQ-system with a fairly general protocol for the transfer of customers from orbit to the vacated server almost without additional consideration.

4. Multiserver Loss Systems

Consider n-server queuing system $M|M|n|0$ with a Poisson input flow of intensity $n\lambda$ and exponentially distributed service times having intensity μ on all n servers, $\rho = \lambda/\mu$. This system can be considered as combining n single-server systems with input flow intensities λ (see Figure 2).

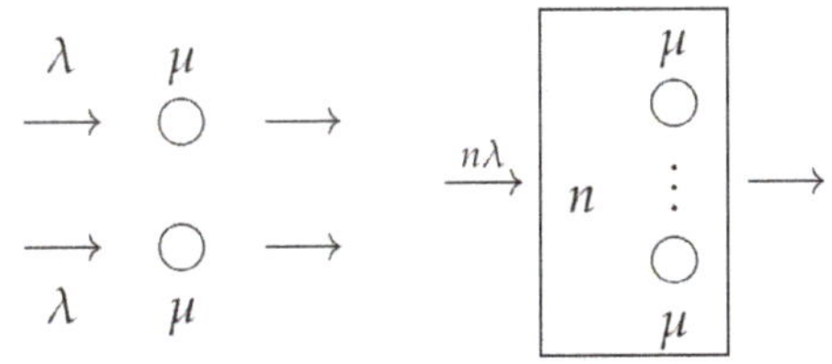

Figure 2. n isolated $M|M|1|0$ systems (**left**), aggregated $M|M|n|0$ system (**right**). $\widehat{b}_n$.

The number of customers in the system $M|M|n|0$ describes the process of death and birth with the intensities of birth and death $\lambda_n(k) = n\lambda$, $0 \le k < n$, $\mu_n(k) = k\mu$, $0 < k \le n$.

Let us denote $P_n(\rho)$ the stationary probability of failure in the system A_n for a given ρ. It is not difficult to establish that $P_1(1) = 1/2$. However, the combined system A_n satisfies new relation, which characterizes the synergistic effect of such a combination.

Theorem 5. *The following limit ratio is true:* $P_n(1) \sim \sqrt{\dfrac{2}{\pi n}}$, $n \to \infty$.

Proof. Let $\delta > 0$, consider the function $f(x) = 1 - x - \exp(-(1+\delta)x)$. The $f(x)$ function satisfying the condition: $f(0) = 0$, $f(1) < 0$, and such that the inequalities

$$f'(x) > 0, \ 0 < x < \frac{\ln(1+\delta)}{1+\delta}, \ f'(x) < 0, \ \frac{\ln(1+\delta)}{1+\delta} < x \le 1$$

hold. Therefore, on the half interval $[0,1)$ there exists a single $x(\delta)$, satisfying the condition $f(x(\delta)) = 0$ and such that the inequalities $1 - x \ge \exp(-(1+\delta)x)$, $0 \le x \le x(\delta) < 1$ hold. Let $p_n(k) = \lim\limits_{t \to \infty} P(x_n(t) = k)$, $0 \le k \le n$, then in force [16] [Chapter 2, § 1]

$$p_n(n-1) = p_n(n)\frac{\mu}{\lambda}\frac{n}{n}, \ p_n(n-2) = p_n(n)\left(\frac{\mu}{\lambda}\right)^2 \frac{n(n-1)}{n^2}, \ldots$$

Therefore, the stationary blocking probability in virtue of the integral theorems of recovery and the law of large numbers for the recovery process [1] [Chapter 9, § 4, 5] satisfies the equality

$$P_n(\rho) = p_n(n) = \left(\sum_{k=0}^{n} \rho^{-k} \prod_{j=0}^{k-1}\left(1 - \frac{j}{n}\right)\right)^{-1}, \tag{3}$$

where $\prod_{j=0}^{-1}$ equals 1. From Formula (3), we obtain the inequality

$$P_n^{-1}(1) \ge \sum_{0 \le k \le nx(\delta)} \prod_{j=0}^{k-1}\left(1 - \frac{j}{n}\right) \ge \sum_{0 \le k \le nx(\delta)} \prod_{j=0}^{k-1} \exp(-(1+\delta)j/n) \ge$$

$$\ge \sum_{1 \le k \le nx(\delta)} \exp(-(1+\delta)k^2/2n).$$

This implies that

$$P_n^{-1}(1) \geq \int_1^{nx(\delta)} e^{-(1+\delta)x^2/2n} dx = \sqrt{\frac{n}{1+\delta}} \int_{\sqrt{\frac{1+\delta}{n}}}^{x(\delta)\sqrt{n(1+\delta)}} e^{-y^2/2} dy,$$

consequently

$$P_n(1)\sqrt{n} \leq (1+\delta) \left(\int_{\sqrt{\frac{1+\delta}{n}}}^{x(\delta)\sqrt{n(1+\delta)}} e^{-y^2/2} dy \right)^{-1} \to (1+\delta)\sqrt{\frac{2}{\pi}}, \quad n \to \infty.$$

and so $\limsup\limits_{n\to\infty} P_n(1)\sqrt{\dfrac{\pi n}{2}} \leq 1+\delta$.

Using Formula (3) and the inequality $1 - x \leq \exp(-x)$, $0 \leq x \leq 1$, we obtain

$$P_n^{-1}(1) \leq \sum_{1\leq k\leq n} e^{-k(k-1)/2n} \leq \sum_{1\leq k\leq n} e^{-(k-1)^2/2n} \leq \int_0^{\infty} e^{-x^2/2n} dx,$$

thus it follows that $1 \leq \liminf\limits_{n\to\infty} P_n(1)\sqrt{\dfrac{\pi n}{2}}$. Obtained above inequalities for upper and lower limits lead to the statement of Theorem 5. $\square$

Remark 1. *In aggregated $M|M|n|0$ system at $\rho < 1$ following relations are valid [18]:*

$$e^{-n\ln^2\rho/2}\sqrt{\frac{2}{\pi n}}\sqrt{\frac{\rho}{8}} \preceq P_n(\rho) \preceq (e^{-n\ln^2\rho/2})^{(\rho-1)/\ln\rho}\sqrt{\frac{2}{\pi n}}\sqrt{\frac{\ln\rho}{\rho-1}}. \tag{4}$$

And if $\rho = \rho(n) = 1 - n^{-\gamma}$, $\gamma > 0$, then Theorem 5 gives

$$\frac{1}{2}\sqrt{\frac{1}{\pi n}} \preceq P_n(\rho) \preceq \sqrt{\frac{2}{\pi n}}, \quad \gamma \geq \frac{1}{2},$$

$$\frac{1}{2}\sqrt{\frac{1}{\pi n}} \preceq P_n(\rho)\exp\left(\frac{n^{1-2\gamma}}{2}\right) \preceq \sqrt{\frac{2}{\pi n}}, \quad \gamma < \frac{1}{2}.$$

Similar results were obtained for Erlang's loss function in [27,28] but in a more complex way.

Remark 2. *In aggregated $M|M|n|\infty$ system following relations are valid [29] for A_n—stationary mean waiting time and B_n—stationary mean queue length:*
(1) *If $\rho < 1$, then for some $c < \infty$, $q < 1$ the relation holds $A_n \leq c\, q^n$, $n \geq 1$.*
(2) *If $\rho = 1 - n^{-\alpha}$, $0 < \alpha < \infty$, then for $n \to \infty$*

$$A_n \to \begin{cases} 0, & \alpha < 1, \\ 1/\mu, & \alpha = 1, \\ \infty, & \alpha > 1. \end{cases} \qquad B_n \to \begin{cases} 0, & \alpha < 1/2, \\ \infty, & \alpha \geq 1/2. \end{cases}$$

Suppose that we have m independently functioning n_k-server queuing systems with Poisson input flows of intensity λ_k, $k = 1,\ldots,m$. In the k-th system, the customer of the input flow is served exponentially distributed time simultaneously on c_k channels with intensity μ_k. Let $l_k = n_k/c_k$ be a natural number and the equality $\rho_k = \lambda_k/(l_k\mu_k) = 1$ holds.

We combine n copies of each of the n_k-server systems under consideration, denoting P_n^k stationary probability of failure in each of the combined systems, $k = 1,\ldots,m$. Using Theorem 5, it is not difficult to obtain the following limit relations

$$P_n^1 \sim \sqrt{\frac{2}{\pi n l_1}}, \ldots, P_n^m \sim \sqrt{\frac{2}{\pi n l_m}}, \ n \to \infty.$$

This solution allows us to distribute the total number of $n(n_1 + \ldots + n_m)$ servers between flows so that the failure probabilities of customers of different flows tend to zero with the growth of a large parameter n. To solve this problem, one could use the exact multiplicative formula obtained in [17], but this would lead to significantly more complex calculations.

5. Parameter Estimation in the Logistics Growth Model

The recurrent model of logistic growth

$$x_0 = a, \ x_{n+1} = bx_n(1 - x_n), \ n = 0, 1, \ldots, \tag{5}$$

where the parameters a, b satisfy the conditions $0 < a < 1$, $1 < b < 4$, attracts increased attention from biologists and physicists. For this model, both practically and theoretically, it is important to evaluate the parameter b based on inaccurate observations. Due to the nonlinearity of the recurrence relation (5), the least squares method applied to the estimation of the parameter b seems somewhat unnatural, which is confirmed by numerous computational experiments that give quite large errors. It seems more natural to apply such qualitative properties of the sequence, as the existence of its limit cycle or limit distribution [30] depending on the value of b in combination with the method of probability metrics [11].

Consider an additive model for introducing errors in observations $y_n = x_n + \varepsilon_n$, $n = 1, \ldots$ Here, ε_n, $n = 1, \ldots$, is a sequence of i.i.d.r.v.'s having a distribution with mean zero and variance σ^2. We introduce the following notation

$$X_n = \sum_{i=0}^{n-1} \frac{x_i}{n}, \ Y_n = \sum_{i=0}^{n-1} \frac{y_i}{n}, \ X_n' = \sum_{i=0}^{n-1} \frac{x_i^2}{n}, \ Y_n' = \sum_{i=0}^{n-1} \frac{y_i^2}{n}.$$

Using the results of [30], it is possible to establish that for the deterministic sequence x_n, $n = 1, \ldots$, with a given b there are limits

$$\lim_{n \to \infty} X_n = \bar{x} \quad \lim_{n \to \infty} X_n' = \overline{x^2}. \tag{6}$$

Indeed, say that the sequence x_n, $n = 1, \ldots$, has a limit cycle $x^{(1)}, \ldots, x^{(q)}$ of length $q \geq 1$, if $\lim_{k \to \infty} x_{qk+j} = x^{(j)}$, $j = 1, \ldots, q$. Denote $\bar{x} = \frac{1}{q} \sum_{j=1}^{q} x^{(j)}$, $\overline{x^2} = \frac{1}{q} \sum_{j=1}^{q} [x^{(j)}]^2$, then we have

$$X_{Nq} = \frac{1}{Nq} \sum_{i=1}^{Nq} x_i \to \bar{x}, \ X_{Nq}' = \frac{1}{Nq} \sum_{i=1}^{Nq} x_i^2 \to \overline{x^2}, \ N \to \infty,$$

so Formula (6) is true in the case, when the sequence x_n, $n = 1, \ldots$, has limit cycle.

Let $p(dx)$ be a probability measure on the σ-algebra of Lebesgue-measurable subsets of the segment $[0, 1]$. Let us say that $p(dx)$ is the limiting distribution of the sequence x_n, $n = 1, \ldots$, if for any Lebesgue-measurable set $C \subseteq [0, 1]$ the equality holds $\lim_{n \to \infty} \dfrac{k(C, n)}{n} = \int_C p(dx) = p(C)$, where $k(C, n)$ is the number of x_i satisfying the inclusion $x_i \in C$, $i = 1, \ldots, n$. Then, we define $\bar{x} = \int_0^1 xp(dx)$, $\overline{x^2} = \int_0^1 x^2 p(dx)$ and prove Formula (6) as follows.

Let us take an arbitrary $\delta > 0$ and put $m = \left[\frac{2}{\delta}\right] + 1$, $\gamma = \delta\left(2 + \left[\frac{2}{\delta}\right]\right)^{-1}$. Divide the half interval $[0, 1)$ into disjoint segments

$$C_1 = \left[0, \frac{1}{m}\right), \quad C_2 = \left[\frac{1}{m}, \frac{2}{m}\right), \ldots, \quad C_m = \left[\frac{m-1}{m}, 1\right).$$

Choose $N(\delta)$ so that for any $n > N(\delta)$ we have $\left[\frac{k(C_j, n)}{n}\right] \leq \gamma$, $j = 1, \ldots, m$. It is sufficiently simple to prove for $n \geq N(\delta)$ the following inequalities

$$\frac{1}{n} \cdot \sum_{x_i \in C_j, \, i=1,\ldots,n} x_i \leq \frac{j}{m} \cdot \frac{k(C_j, n)}{n} \leq \frac{j}{m}(p(C_j) + \gamma) \leq$$

$$\leq \frac{\gamma j}{m} + \int_{C_j}\left(x + \frac{1}{m}\right)p(dx) = \frac{\gamma j}{m} + \frac{p(C_j)}{m} + \int_{C_j} xp(dx).$$

Summing these inequalities by $j = 1, \ldots, m$, and using the equality for m we get for $n \geq N(\delta)$ the inequality

$$X_n \leq \frac{\gamma(m+1)}{2} + \frac{1}{m} + \overline{x} = \overline{x} + \delta.$$

Analogously it is possible to obtain

$$\frac{1}{n} \cdot \sum_{x_i \in C_j, \, i=1,\ldots,n} x_i \geq \frac{j-1}{m} \cdot \frac{k(C_j, n)}{n} \geq \frac{j-1}{m}(p(C_j) - \gamma) \geq$$

$$\geq \int_{C_j}\left(x - \frac{1}{m}\right)p(dx) - \frac{\gamma(j-1)}{m} = \int_{C_j} xp(dx) - \frac{1}{m} - \frac{\gamma(m-1)}{2} \geq \overline{x} - \delta,$$

consequently $X_n \to \overline{x}$, $n \to \infty$. Similarly we have the relation $X'_n \to \overline{x^2}$, $n \to \infty$, so Formula (6) is true in the case, when the sequence x_n, $n = 1, \ldots$, has limit distribution also.

Note that formally the limits $\overline{x}, \overline{x^2}$ may depend on the initial state x_0. However, in the logistics growth model there is no such dependence.

We will evaluate the parameter b in two stages. First, we express b in terms of the path averages: $b = \overline{x}/(\overline{x} - \overline{x^2})$. Using the ratio

$$EY_n = \frac{1}{n}\sum_{i=0}^{n-1} E(x_i + \varepsilon_i) = X_n \to \overline{x},$$

$$EY'_n = \frac{1}{n}\sum_{i=0}^{n-1} E(x_i + \varepsilon_i)^2 = \frac{1}{n}\sum_{i=0}^{n-1}(x_i^2 + \sigma^2) = X'_n + \sigma^2 \to \overline{x^2} + \sigma^2, \, n \to \infty,$$

let us estimate the parameter b by the formula

$$b_n = \frac{EY_n}{EY_n - (EY'_n - \sigma^2)} \to b, \, n \to \infty.$$

As a result, the parameter b is evaluated by the formula $\hat{b}_n = \dfrac{Y_n}{Y_n - (Y'_n - \sigma^2)}$. The convergence in probability $\hat{b}_n \to b$, $n \to \infty$, follows from the relations

$$VarY_n = \frac{1}{n^2}\sum_{i=0}^{n-1} Var(x_i + \varepsilon_i) = \frac{1}{n^2}\sum_{i=0}^{n-1} Var\varepsilon_i = \frac{\sigma^2}{n} \to 0;$$

$$VarY'_n = \frac{1}{n^2}\sum_{i=0}^{n-1} Var(x_i + \varepsilon_i)^2 = \frac{1}{n^2}\sum_{i=0}^{n-1} Var(2x_i\epsilon_i + \epsilon_i^2) \le \frac{4}{n}(4\sigma^2 + \sigma^4) \to 0, \; n \to \infty.$$

The following is an illustrative example of estimating parameter b for a logistic growth model. Calculations of $\widehat{b}_n$ were performed for the case $x_0 = 0.75$; $a = 0.5$; $b = 3$ at $n = 1000$ (see Figure 3). An additive model of introducing errors was considered under the assumption that ε_i, $i = 0, .., n-1$, have a uniform distribution on the segment $[-1/4, 1/4]$.

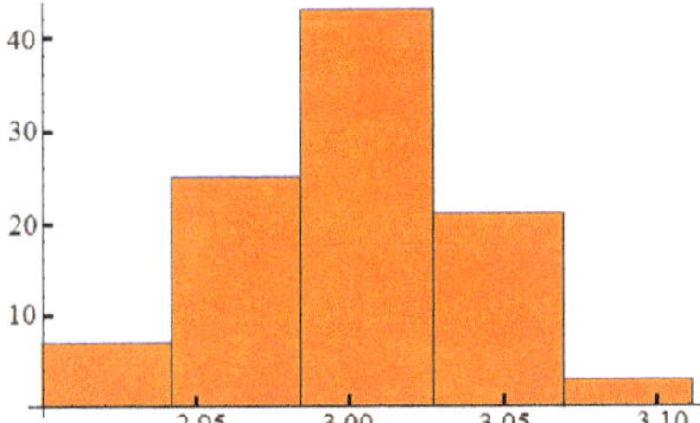

Figure 3. Frequency histogram for $\widehat{b}_n$.

This method can be applied to the estimation of the parameters of the Rikker model (see, for example, in [22]). Here, the Rikker model is described by recurrent relation

$$x_0 = 1, \; x_{n+1} = ax_n \exp(-bx_n), \; a,b > 0,$$

and observations are following: $y_n = x_n \exp(\varepsilon_n)$, where ε_n has normal distribution with zero mean and known variation, $n \ge 0$. Another application of described method is the finite-difference approximation of the system of Lorentz differential equations (see, for example, in [31]), etc.

6. Discussion

All the problems of system analysis considered in this paper are based on the choice of changes in the structure of the system, the efficiency indicator, and the computational algorithm with an assessment of its complexity. In some cases, it is possible to replace the NP-problem with a fairly simple computational procedure, abandoning the high accuracy of the resulting solution in favor of a significant change in the performance indicator. Apparently, such problems require a certain proportion between the accuracy and efficiency of the resulting solution.

The proposed approach to the study of synergistic effects in complex systems can be applied to the construction of queuing systems with a large load and a small queue, to backup systems with recovery, to insurance models and other stochastic systems. It allows you to explore and find the main parameters in such popular technologies in applications as powder metallurgy, 3-D printing, fast mixing of fuel in engines, etc. The emphasis on economical, but not highly accurate calculations, makes it possible at the initial stage to correctly select the main parameters of the analyzed systems before performing more detailed and accurate calculations. This property of the proposed approach to the analysis of complex systems can be used in programs of digital economy, smart city, etc., when at the initial stage of the study it is important to determine the main indicators of the effectiveness of a complex system.

Funding: This research received no external funding.

Institutional Review Board Statement: Not applicable.

Informed Consent Statement: Not applicable.

Data Availability Statement: Data sharing is not applicable to this article.

Acknowledgments: The author thanks Marina Osipova for her help in the design of the work.

Conflicts of Interest: The authors declare no conflict of interest.

References

1. Skrimizea, E.; Haniotou, H.; Parra, C. On the complexity turn in planning: An adaptive rationale to navigate spaces and times of uncertainty. *Plan. Theory* **2019**, *18*, 122–142. [CrossRef]
2. Battiston, S.; Caldarelli, G.; May, R.; Roukny, T.; Stiglitz, J. The price of complexity in financial networks. *Proc. Natl. Acad. Sci. USA* **2016**, *113*, 10031–10036. [CrossRef] [PubMed]
3. Majdandzic, A.; Braunstein, L.; Curme, C.; Vodenska, I.; Levy-Carciente, S.; Eugene, S.; Havlin, S. Multiple tipping points and optimal repairing in interacting networks. *Nat. Commun.* **2016**, *7*, 1–10. [CrossRef] [PubMed]
4. Lever, J.; Leemput, I.; Weinans, E.; Quax, R.; Dakos, V.; Nes, E.; Bascompte, J.; Scheffer, M. Foreseeing the future of mutualistic communities beyond collapse. *Ecol. Lett.* **2020**, *23*, 2–15. [CrossRef] [PubMed]
5. Limiao, Z.; Guanwen, Z.; Daqing, L.; Hai-Jun, H.; Eugene, S.; Shlomo, H. Scale-free resilience of real traffic jams. *Proc. Natl. Acad. Sci. USA* **2019**, *116*, 8673–8678.
6. Barlow, R.; Proshan, F. *Mathematical Theory of Reliability*; John Wiley and Sons: New York, NY, USA, 1965.
7. Ryabinin, I.A. *Reliability and Safety of Structurally Complex Systems*; St. Petersburg University Press: Saint-Petersburg, Russia, 2007. (In Russian)
8. Solojentsev, E.D. *Scenario Logic and Probabilistic Management of Risk in Business and Engeneering*; Springer: Berlin/Heidelberg, Germany, 2004.
9. Gertsbakh, I. *Statistical Reliability Theory*; Marcel Dekker: New York, NY, USA, 1989.
10. Rocchi, P. *Reliability Is A New Science. Gnedenko Was Right*; Springer: Berlin/Heidelberg, Germany, 2017.
11. Zolotarev, V. *Modern Theory of Summation of Random Variables*; VSP: Utrecht, The Netherlands, 1997.
12. Dudin, A.; Nazarov, A. On a tandem queue with retrials and losses and state dependent arrival, service and retrial rates. *Int. J. Oper. Res.* **2017**, *29*, 170–182. [CrossRef]
13. Artalejo, J.; Gomez-Corral, A. *Retrial Queueing Systems. A Computational Approach*; Springer: Berlin/Heidelberg, Germany, 2008.
14. Nazarov, A.; Moiseeva E. Investigation of the RQ-system $MMPP|M|1$ by the method of asymptotic analysis in the condition of a large load. *Izv. Tomsk. Polytech. Univ.* **2013**, *322*, 19–23. (In Russian)
15. Information Technologies and Mathematical Modelling-Queueing Theory and Applications. In Proceedings of the 17th International Conference, ITMM 2018, Named After A.F. Terpugov, and 12th Workshop on Retrial Queues and Related Topics, WRQ 2018, Tomsk, Russia, 10–15 September 2018; Volume 912. Communications in Computer and Information Science Series.
16. Borovkov, A. *Asymptotic Methods in Queueing Theory*; John Wiley and Sons: New York, NY, USA, 1984.
17. Basharin, G.P.; Gaidamaka, Yu.V.; Samouylov, K.E. Mathematical Theory of Teletraffic and Its Applications to the Analysis of Multiservice Communication of Next Generation Networks. *Autom. Control. Comput. Sci.* **2013**, *47*, 62–69. [CrossRef]
18. Tsitsiashvili, G.S.; Osipova, M.A.; Samoulov, K.E.; Gaidamaka, Y.V. Synergetic effects in multiserver loss systems. In Proceedings of the VIII Moscow International Conference on Operations Research for the Centenary of Yu. B. Hermeyer at the Moscow State University and the VC RAS, Moscow, Russia, 17–21 October 2016; Volume I, pp. 350–355.
19. Gnedenko, B.V.; Kovalenko, I.N. *Introduction to Queuing Theory*; Nauka: Moscow, Russia, 1966. (In Russian)
20. Ivchenko, G.I.; Kashtanov, V.A.; Kovalenko, I.N. *Queuing Theory*; Visshaya Shkola: Moscow, Russia, 1982. (In Russian)
21. Naumov, V.A. On the behavior of the parameters of the Equivalent Random Theory method at low load. In *Numerical Methods and Informatics*; RUDN Publisher: Moscow, Russia, 1988. (In Russian)
22. Geritz, S.; Kisdi, E. On the mechanistic underpinning of discrete-time population models with complex dynamics. *J. Theor. Biol.* **2004**, *228*, 261–269. [CrossRef] [PubMed]
23. Tsitsiashvili, G.; Osipova M. Synergetic effects for number of busy servers in multiserver queuing systems. *Commun. Comput. Inf. Sci. Ser.* **2015**, *564*, 404–414.
24. Heath, D.; Resnick, S.; Samorodnitsky, G. Heavy tails and long range dependence in on/off processes and associated fluid models. *Math. Oper. Res.* **1998**, *23*, 145–165. [CrossRef]
25. Mikosch, T.; Resnick, S.; Rootzen, H. Stegeman A. Is network traffic approximated by stable Levy motion or fractional Brownian motion? *Ann. Appl. Probab.* **2002**, *12*, 23–68. [CrossRef]
26. Tsitsiashvili, G.; Markova, N. Synergistic effects in a multi-channel queuing system with an Erlangian input flow. *Bull. Pac. State Univ.* **2015**, *4*, 17–22. (In Russian)
27. Jagerman, D.L. Some Properties of the Erlang Loss Function. *Bell Syst. Tech. J.* **1974**, *53*, 525–551. [CrossRef]
28. Mitra, D.; Weiss, A. The Transient Behavior in Erlang's Model for Large Trunk Groups and Various Traffic Conditions. *Proc. 1988 Int. Teletraffic Congr.* **1988**, *26*, 223. [CrossRef]
29. Tsitsiashvili, G.S.; Osipova, M.A. Phase Transitions in Multiserver Queuing Systems. *Inf. Technol. Math. Model. Queueing Theory Appl.* **2016**, *638*, 341–353.
30. Sharkovskiy, A.; Sharkovskiy A.N. *Difference Equations and Population Dynamics*. Preprint 82.18; Institute of mathematics of the Academy of Sciences of the Ukrainian SSR: Kiev, Ukraine, 1982. (In Russian)
31. Leonov, G.; Kuznetsov, N.; Korzhemanova, N.; Kusakin, D. Lyapunov dimension formula for the global attractor of the Lorenz system. *Commun. Nonlinear Sci. Numer. Simul.* **2016**, *41*, 84–103. [CrossRef]

Review

Review of the Latest Progress in Controllability of Stochastic Linear Systems and Stochastic GE-Evolution Operator

Zhaoqiang Ge

School of Mathematics and Statistics, Xi'an Jiaotong University, No. 28, Xianning West Road, Xi'an 710049, China; gezqjd@mail.xjtu.edu.cn

Abstract: According to the spatial dimension, equation type, and time sequence, the latest progress in controllability of stochastic linear systems and some unsolved problems are introduced. Firstly, the exact controllability of stochastic linear systems in finite dimensional spaces is discussed. Secondly, the exact, exact null, approximate, approximate null, and partial approximate controllability of stochastic linear systems in infinite dimensional spaces are considered. Thirdly, the exact, exact null and impulse controllability of stochastic singular linear systems in finite dimensional spaces are investigated. Fourthly, the exact and approximate controllability of stochastic singular linear systems in infinite dimensional spaces are studied. At last, the controllability and observability for a type of time-varying stochastic singular linear systems are studied by using stochastic GE-evolution operator in the sense of mild solution in Banach spaces, some necessary and sufficient conditions are obtained, the dual principle is proved to be true, an example is given to illustrate the validity of the theoretical results obtained in this part, and a problem to be solved is introduced. The main purpose of this paper is to facilitate readers to fully understand the latest research results concerning the controllability of stochastic linear systems and the problems that need to be further studied, and attract more scholars to engage in this research.

Keywords: controllability; observability; stochastic linear systems in finite and infinite dimensional spaces; stochastic singular linear systems in finite and infinite dimensional spaces; semigroup; evolution operator; GE-semigroup; GE-evolution operator; stochastic GE-evolution operator

Citation: Ge, Z. Review of the Latest Progress in Controllability of Stochastic Linear Systems and Stochastic GE-Evolution Operator. *Mathematics* **2021**, *9*, 3240. https://doi.org/10.3390/math9243240

Academic Editors: Mikhail Posypkin, Andrey Gorshenin and Vladimir Titarev

Received: 15 November 2021
Accepted: 11 December 2021
Published: 14 December 2021

1. Introduction

Since Kalman published the seminal paper [1], the controllability of stochastic systems has become a central problem in the study of mathematical control theory, a large number of academic papers have been published. For representative papers, see references [1–73]. However, even for the controllability of stochastic linear systems, there are still many important problems to be solved. In this paper, we discuss the latest development of controllability of stochastic linear systems and raise some unsolved issues. According to the spatial dimension, equation type and time sequence, the rest of the paper is organized as follows. In Section 2, the following contents are introduced concerning the controllability of stochastic linear systems in finite dimensional spaces: (i) The L^p−exact controllability and exact observability are discussed; (ii) The exact controllability by feedback controller is considered; (iii) The exact controllability of the stochastic linear systems with memory is investigated; (iv) Some theoretical results for these concepts are given and four important problems to be solved are put forward. In Section 3, the controllability of stochastic linear systems in infinite dimensional spaces is considered: (i) The null controllability is investigated by using C_0−semigroup in the sense of mild solution in Hilbert spaces; (ii) The approximate controllability and approximate null controllability are discussed by using C_0−semigroup in the sense of mild solution in Hilbert spaces; (iii) The partial approximate controllability is studied by using evolution operator in the sense of mild solution in Hilbert spaces; (iv) According to these theories, three problems that need to be studied are raised. In Section 4, the controllability of stochastic singular linear systems in finite dimensional spaces is dealt with: (i) The exact controllability is considered by using Gramian matrix; (ii) The exact null controllability is studied by using Gramian matrix; (iii) The impulse controllability and impulse observability are investigated in the sense of impulse solution; (iv) A problem that needs to be discussed is put forward. In Section 5, the controllability of stochastic singular linear systems in infinite dimensional spaces is studied: (i) The exact controllability for a type of time invariant systems is considered by using C_0-semigroup in the sense of strong solution in Hilbert spaces; (ii) The exact controllability and approximate controllability for a type of time invariant systems are investigated by using GE-semigroup in the sense of mild solution in Banach and Hilbert spaces, respectively; (iii) The exact controllability and approximate controllability for a type of time-varying systems are dealt with by using GE-evolution operator in the sense of mild solution in Hilbert spaces; (iv) The exact controllability and approximate controllability for a type of time invariant systems are considered by using stochastic GE-evolution operator in the sense of mild solution in Banach spaces; (v) The exact controllability, approximate controllability, exact observability, and approximate observability for a type of time-varying systems are studied by using stochastic GE-evolution operator in the sense of mild solution in Banach spaces. Some necessary and sufficient conditions concerning these concepts are obtained, the dual principle is proved to be true, an example is given to illustrate the validity of the theoretical results obtained in this part, and a problem to be solved is raised.

The main idea of this paper is to introduce the latest progress for the controllability of stochastic linear systems and the mathematical methods applied in this field, including GE-semigroup, GE-evolution operator, stochastic GE-evolution operator and so on. The main purpose of this paper is to facilitate readers to fully understand the latest research results concerning the controllability of stochastic linear systems and the problems that need to be further studied, and attract more scholars to engage in this research.

Notations. $(\Omega, F, \{F_t\}, P)$ is a complete probability space with filtration $\{F_t\}$ satisfying the usual condition (i.e., the filtration contains all $P-$null sets and is right continuous); all processes are $\{F_t\}-$adapted; $w(t)$ is a standard Wiener process defined on $(\Omega, F, \{F_t\}, P)$; E denotes the mathematical expectation; $\mathbb{R}^n$ is the $n-$dimensional real Euclidean space with the standard norm $\|\cdot\|_{\mathbb{R}^n}$, $\mathbb{R}^{n\times m}$ is the space of all $(n \times m)$ real matrices; $I_n \in \mathbb{R}^{n\times n}$ denotes the identical matrix; T denotes the transpose of a vector or a matrix; $H = \mathbb{R}^n, \mathbb{R}^{n\times m}$, etc, and $p \in [1, \infty)$; $L^p([0, \tau]; H)$ denotes the set of all functions $f : [0, \tau] \to H$ satisfying $\|f(\cdot)\|_{L^p([0,\tau];H)} = (\int_0^\tau \|f(t)\|_H^p dt)^{1/p} < \infty$; $L^\infty([0, \tau]; H)$ denotes the subset of $L^p([0, \tau]; H)$ whose element is essentially bounded; $C([0, \tau]; H)$ denotes the set of all functions $f : [0, \tau] \to H$, which are continuous on $[0, \tau]$ in the sense of $\|f(\cdot)\|_{C([0,\tau];H)} = \max_{t\in[0,\tau]} \|f(t)\|_H$; $L^p(\Omega, F_t, P, H)$ denotes the set of all random variables $\eta \in H$, such that η is F_t-measurable and $\|\eta\|_p = (E(\|\eta\|_H^p))^{1/p} < +\infty$; $L^p([0, \tau], \Omega, F_t, H)$ denotes the set of all processes $x(t) \in H$ such that $\|x(t)\|_p < +\infty, \forall t \in [0, \tau]$; $L^p([0, \tau], \Omega, H)$ denotes the set of all processes $x(t) \in L^p([0, \tau], \Omega, F_t, H)$ such that $E \int_0^\tau \|x(t)\|_H^p d\tau < +\infty$; $L^\infty([0, \tau], \Omega, H)$ is the subset of $L^2([0, \tau], \Omega, H)$ where each element $x(\cdot)$ is essentially bounded; Let A be a linear operator. $\mathrm{dom}(A), \ker(A)$ and $\mathrm{ran}(A)$ denote its domain, kernel and range, respectively; I denotes the identical operator. Other mathematical symbols involved in this paper will be properly explained in the discussion.

2. Exact Controllability of Finite Dimensional Stochastic Linear Systems

In this section, we discuss the latest development of exact controllability of finite dimensional stochastic linear systems.

2.1. L^p-Exact Controllability

In 2017, Wang et al. consider the controllability of the following stochastic linear differential equation in [59]:

$$dx(t) = [A(t)x(t) + B(t)u(t)]dt + \sum_{k=1}^{d}[C_k(t)x(t) + D_k(t)u(t)]dw_k(t), t \geq 0, \tag{1}$$

where $A, C_k: [0,\tau] \times \Omega \to \mathbb{R}^{n\times n}$ and $B, D_k: [0,\tau] \times \Omega \to \mathbb{R}^{n\times m}(k = 1,2,\cdots,d)$ are suitable matrix-valued processes; $x(t)$ is the state process valued in $\mathbb{R}^n$ and $u(t)$ is the control process valued in $\mathbb{R}^m$; $\{w_k(t): (k = 1,2,\cdots,d)\}$ is a system of independent one-dimensional standard Wiener processes, $w(t) = (w_1(t),\cdots,w_d(t))$. We will denote system (1) by $[A(\cdot),C(\cdot);B(\cdot),D(\cdot)]$, with $C(\cdot) = (C_1(\cdot),\cdots,C_d(\cdot))$ and $D(\cdot) = (D_1(\cdot),\cdots,D_d(\cdot))$.

For the convenience of narration, the following notations and concepts are introduced. $L_F^p(\Omega; L^q([0,\tau]; H))$ is the set of all processes $x(\cdot)$ valued in H, such that

$$\|x(\cdot)\|_{L_F^p(\Omega;L^q([0,\tau];H))} = [E(\int_0^\tau \|x(t)\|_H^q dt)^{p/q}]^{1/p} < \infty,$$

$$L_F^p(\Omega; L^p([0,\tau]; H)) = L_F^p([0,\tau]; H), p \in [1,\infty].$$

$L_F^p(\Omega; C([0,\tau]; H))$ is the set of all processes $x(\cdot)$ valued in H, such that for almost $\omega \in \Omega, t \to x(t,\omega)$ is continuous and

$$\|x(\cdot)\|_{L_F^p(\Omega;C([0,\tau];H))} = [E(\sup_{t\in[0,\tau]}\|x(t)\|_H^p)]^{1/p} < \infty.$$

In the similar manner, one can define $L_F^\infty(\Omega; L^\infty([0,\tau]; H))$ and $L_F^\infty(\Omega; C([0,\tau]; H))$.

Hypothesis 1. *The $\mathbb{R}^{n\times n}-$valued processes $A(\cdot), C_k(\cdot)$ satisfy*

$$A(\cdot), C_k(\cdot) \in L_F^\infty(\Omega; L^\infty([0,\tau]; \mathbb{R}^{n\times n}))(k = 1,\cdots,d).$$

Hypothesis 2. *For some $\mu \in (1,\infty]$ and $\sigma \in (2,\infty]$, the following hold:*

$$B(\cdot) \in L_F^\mu(\Omega; L^{\frac{2\sigma}{\sigma+2}}([0,\tau]; \mathbb{R}^{n\times m})), \mu \in (1,\infty], \sigma \in (2,\infty),$$

$$B(\cdot) \in L_F^\mu(\Omega; L^2([0,\tau]; \mathbb{R}^{n\times m})), \mu \in (1,\infty], \sigma = \infty,$$

$$D_1(\cdot),\cdots,D_d(\cdot) \in L_F^\mu(\Omega; L^\sigma([0,\tau]; \mathbb{R}^{n\times m})).$$

Now, we introduce the following definition.

Definition 1. *(i) A process $u(t)(t \in [0,\tau])$ is called a feasible control of system (1) if under $u(t)$, for any $x_0 \in \mathbb{R}^n$, system (1) admits a unique strong solution $x(t) \in L_F^1(\Omega; C([0,\tau]; \mathbb{R}^n))$ satisfying $x(0) = x_0$. The set of feasible controls is denoted by $U[0,\tau]$;*
(ii) A control $u(t) \in U[0,\tau]$ is said to be L^p-feasible for system (1) if

$$p \geq 1, B(\cdot)u(\cdot) \in L_F^p(\Omega; L^1([0,\tau]; \mathbb{R}^n)), D_k(\cdot)u(\cdot) \in L_F^p(\Omega; L^2([0,\tau]; \mathbb{R}^{n\times n}))$$

holds true. The set of L^p-feasible controls is denoted by $U^p[0,\tau]$;
(iii) System (1) is said to be L^p-exactly controllable by $U[0,\tau]$ on $[0,\tau]$, if for any $x_0 \in \mathbb{R}^n$ and $\zeta \in L^p(\Omega, F_\tau, P, \mathbb{R}^n)$, there exists a $u(\cdot) \in U[0,\tau]$ such that the solution $x(\cdot) \in L_F^1(\Omega; C([0,\tau]; \mathbb{R}^n))$ of (1) with $x(0) = x_0$ satisfies $x(\tau) = \zeta$.

2.1.1. The Case $D(\cdot) = 0$

In this case, we consider system $[A(\cdot), C(\cdot); B(\cdot), 0]$, i.e., the state equation is

$$dx(t) = [A(t)x(t) + B(t)u(t)]dt + \sum_{k=1}^{d} C_k(t)x(t)dw_k(t), t \geq 0. \tag{2}$$

Thus, the control $u(\cdot)$ does not appear in the diffusion. The L^p-exact controllability of system (2) was discussed and the following results were obtained in [59].

Theorem 1 ([59]). *Let Hypothesis 1 hold. Let*

$$B(t)B(t)^T \geq \delta I_n, t \in [0, \tau], a.s.,$$

for some $\delta > 0$. Then for any $p > 1$, system (2) is L^p-exactly controllable on $[0, \tau]$ by $U^{p-} = \cap_{q \in (0,p)} U^q[0, \tau]$.

Theorem 2 ([59]). *Let Hypothesis 1 hold. Suppose there exists a continuous differentiable function $f : [0, \tau] \to \mathbb{R}^n, \|f(t)\|_{\mathbb{R}^n} = 1$, for all $t \in [0, \tau]$ such that $f(t)^T B(t) = 0$. Additionally, let*

$$C_k(\cdot) \in L_F^\infty(\Omega; C([0, \tau]; \mathbb{R}^{n \times n})), 1 \leq k \leq d. \tag{3}$$

Then for any $p > 1$, system (2) is not L^p-exactly controllable on $[0, \tau]$ by $U^p[0, \tau]$.

Corollary 1 ([59]). *Let Hypothesis 1 and (3) hold. Let $B \in \mathbb{R}^{n \times m}$.*
(i) If for some $p > 1$, system $[A(\cdot), C(\cdot); B, 0]$ is L^p-exactly controllable on $[0, \tau]$ by $U^p[0, \tau]$, then

$$\text{rank} B = n, \tag{4}$$

where $\text{rank} B$ denotes the rank of B;
(ii) If (4) holds, then for any $p > 1$, system $[A(\cdot), C(\cdot); B, 0]$ is L^p-exactly controllable on $[0, \tau]$ by $U^{p-}[0, \tau]$.

The above result shows that the gap between condition (4) and the L^p-exact controllability of system $[A(\cdot), C(\cdot); B, 0]$ (by $U^p[0, \tau]$, or $U^{p-}[0, \tau]$) is very small.

2.1.2. The Case $\text{rank} D(\cdot) = n$

In this case, we let $d = 1$, i.e., the Wiener process is one-dimensional. The case $d > 1$ can be discussed similarly. For system $[A(\cdot), C(\cdot); B(\cdot), D(\cdot)]$, we assume the following:

$$D(t)D(t)^T \geq \delta I_n, a.s., a.e.t \in [0, \tau]. \tag{5}$$

In this case, $[D(t)D(t)^T]^{-1}$ exists and uniformly bounded. We define

$$\tilde{A}(t) = A(t) - B(t)D(t)^T[D(t)D(t)^T]^{-1}C(t),$$

$$\tilde{B}(t) = B(t)\{I_n - D(t)^T[D(t)D(t)^T]^{-1}D(t)\}, \tilde{D}(t) = B(t)D(t)^T[D(t)D(t)^T]^{-1},$$

and introduce the following controlled system:

$$dx(t) = [\tilde{A}(t)x(t) + \tilde{B}(t)v(t) + \tilde{D}(t)z(t)]dt + z(t)dw(t), t \in [0, \tau], x(0) = x_0, \tag{6}$$

with $x(t)$ being the state and $(v(\cdot), z(\cdot))$ being the control. For system (6), we need the following set and definition:

$$\tilde{U}^p[0, \tau] = \{v(\tau) : \tilde{B}(\tau)v(\tau) \in L_F^p(\Omega; L^1([0, \tau]; \mathbb{R}^n)).$$

Definition 2. *System (6) is said to be exactly null-controllable by*

$$\tilde{U}^p[0,\tau] \times L_F^p(\Omega; L^2([0,\tau]; \mathbb{R}^n))$$

on the $[0,\tau]$, if for any $x_0 \in \mathbb{R}^n$, there exists a pair

$$(v(\cdot), z(\cdot)) \in \tilde{U}^p[0,\tau] \times L_F^p(\Omega; L^2([0,\tau]; \mathbb{R}^n)),$$

such that the solution $x(\cdot)$ to

$$dx(t) = [\tilde{A}(t)x(t) + \tilde{B}(t)v(t) + \tilde{D}(t)z(t)]dt + z(t)dw(t), t \in [0,\tau],$$

$$x(0) = x_0, x(\tau) = \xi, \tag{7}$$

under $(v(\tau), z(\tau))$ satisfies $x(\tau) = 0$.

The following results were obtained in [59].

Theorem 3 ([59])**.** *Let Hypothesis 1 and (5) hold. Suppose*

$$\tilde{A}(t) \in L_F^\infty(\Omega; L^{1+\epsilon}([0,\tau]; \mathbb{R}^{n \times n})), \tilde{D}(t) \in L_F^\infty(\Omega; L^2([0,\tau]; \mathbb{R}^{n \times n})),$$

where $\epsilon > 0$ is a given constant. Then system (1) is L^p-exactly controllable on $[0,\tau]$ by $U^p[0,\tau]$ if and only if system (6) is L^p-exactly controllable on $[0,\tau]$ by $\tilde{U}^p[0,\tau] \times L_F^p(\Omega; L^2([0,\tau]; \mathbb{R}^n))$.

Theorem 4 ([59])**.** *Let Hypothesis 1 and (5) hold. Suppose*

$$\tilde{A}(t) \in L_F^\infty(\Omega; L^{1+\epsilon}([0,\tau]; \mathbb{R}^{n \times n})), \tilde{B}(t) \in L_F^{\max\{2,p\}+\epsilon}(\Omega; L^{2+\xi}([0,\tau]; \mathbb{R}^{n \times m})),$$

$$\tilde{D}(t) \in L_F^\infty(\Omega; L^{2+\epsilon}([0,\tau]; \mathbb{R}^{n \times n})), \tag{8}$$

where $\epsilon > 0$ is a given constant. Then the following are equivalent:
(i) System (6) is L^p-exactly controllable on $[0,\tau]$ by $\tilde{U}^p[0,\tau] \times L_F^p(\Omega; L^2([0,\tau]; \mathbb{R}^n))$;
(ii) System (6) is exactly null-controllable on $[0,\tau]$ by $\tilde{U}^p[0,\tau] \times L_F^p(\Omega; L^2([0,\tau]; \mathbb{R}^n))$;
(iii) Matrix G defined below is invertible:

$$G = E \int_0^\tau Y(t)\tilde{B}(t)\tilde{B}(t)^T Y(t)^T dt, \tag{9}$$

where $Y(\cdot)$ is the adapted solution to the following stochastic linear equation:

$$dY(t) = -Y(t)\tilde{A}(t)dt - Y(t)\tilde{D}(t)dw(t), t \geq 0, Y(0) = I_n.$$

Theorem 5 ([59])**.** *Let Hypothesis 1, (5), and (8) hold. Then system (1) is L^p-exactly controllable on $[0,\tau]$ by $U^p[0,\tau]$ if and only if G defined by (9) is invertible.*

In the above, we have discussed the two extreme cases: either $D(\cdot) = 0$ or $\mathrm{rank}D(\cdot) = n$. The case in between remains open. Therefore, we have the following open problem.

Problem 1. *If $0 < \mathrm{rank}D(\cdot) < n$, what are the conditions under which system (1) can be L^p-exactly controlled?*

2.1.3. Duality and Observability Inequality

In this subsection, we introduce the dual principle for system (1). The following result was obtained in [59].

Theorem 6 ([59])**.** *Let hypotheses 1 and 2 hold. Then system (1) is L^p-exactly controllable on $[0, \tau]$ by $U^{p,\mu,\sigma}[0, \tau]$ if and only if there exists a $\delta > 0$ such that the following, called an observability inequality holds:*

$$\|B(\cdot)^T y(\cdot) + \sum_k^d D_k(\cdot) z_k(\cdot)\|_{U^{p,\mu,\sigma}[0,\tau]^*} \geq \delta \|\eta\|_{L^q(\Omega, F_\tau, P, \mathbb{R}^n)}, \forall \eta \in L^q(\Omega, F_\tau, P, \mathbb{R}^n),$$

where

$$U^{p,\mu,\sigma}[0, \tau] = L_F^{\frac{\mu p}{\mu - p}}(\Omega; L^{\frac{2\sigma}{\sigma-2}}([0, \tau]; \mathbb{R}^m)), p \in [1, \mu), \mu \in (1, \infty], \sigma \in (2, \infty),$$

$$U^{p,\mu,\sigma}[0, \tau] = L_F^{p}(\Omega; L^{\frac{2\sigma}{\sigma-2}}([0, \tau]; \mathbb{R}^m)), p \in [1, \mu), \mu = \infty, \sigma \in (2, \infty),$$

$$U^{p,\mu,\sigma}[0, \tau] = L_F^{\frac{\mu p}{\mu - p}}(\Omega; L^{2}([0, \tau]; \mathbb{R}^m)), p \in [1, \mu), \mu \in [1, \infty], \sigma = \infty,$$

$$U^{p,\mu,\sigma}[0, \tau] = L_F^{p}(\Omega; L^{2}([0, \tau]; \mathbb{R}^m)), p \in [1, \mu), \mu = \sigma = \infty;$$

$U^{p,\mu,\sigma}[0, \tau]^*$ denotes the adjoint space of $U^{p,\mu,\sigma}[0, \tau]$; $(y(\cdot), z(\cdot))$ (with $z(\cdot) = (z_1(\cdot), \cdots, z_d(\cdot))$) is the unique adapted solution to the following system:

$$dy(t) = -[A(t)^T y(t) + \sum_{k=1}^d C_k(t)^T z_k(t)]dt + \sum_{k=1}^d z_k(t)dw_k(t), t \in [0, \tau], y(\tau) = \eta. \quad (10)$$

Now, we introduce the following definition which makes the name "observability inequality" aforementioned meaningful.

Definition 3. *Let Hypothesis 1 hold and $(y(t), z(t))$ be the adapted solution to system (10) with $\eta \in L^q(\Omega, F_\tau, P, \mathbb{R}^n)$. (i) For the pair $(B(\cdot), D(\cdot))$ with $B(\cdot), D_k(\cdot) \in L_F^1([0, \tau]; \mathbb{R}^{n \times m})(k = 1, 2, \cdots, d)$ and $D(\cdot) = (D_1(\cdot), \cdots, D_d(\cdot))$, the map*

$$\eta \to K^* \eta = B(\cdot)^T y(\cdot) + \sum_k^d D_k(\cdot)^T z_k(\cdot)$$

is called an $Y[0, \tau]-$observer of (10) if $K^* \eta \in Y[0, \tau], \forall \eta \in L^q(\Omega, F_\tau, P, \mathbb{R}^m)$, where $Y[0, \tau]$ is a subspace of $L_F^1([0, \tau]; \mathbb{R}^m)$. System (10), together with the observer of (10) is denoted by $[A(\cdot)^T, C(\cdot)^T; B(\cdot)^T, D(\cdot)^T]$;
(ii) Subsystem $[A(\cdot)^T, C(\cdot)^T; B(\cdot)^T, D(\cdot)^T]$ is said to be L^q-exactly observable by $Y[0, \tau]$ observations if from the observation $K^* \in Y[0, \tau]$, the terminal value $\eta \in L^q(\Omega, F_\tau, P, \mathbb{R}^n)$ of $y(\cdot)$ at τ can be uniquely determined, i.e., the map $K^* : L^q(\Omega, F_\tau, P, \mathbb{R}^n) \to Y[0, \tau]$ admits a bounded inverse.

With the above definition, the following result was obtained in [59]:

Theorem 7 ([59])**.** *Let Hypotheses 1 and 2 hold true. Then, system (1) is L^p-exactly controllable on $[0, \tau]$ by $U^{p,\mu,\sigma}[0, \tau]$ if and only if system $[A(\cdot)^T, C(\cdot)^T; B(\cdot)^T, D(\cdot)^T]$ is L^p-exactly observable by $U^{p,\mu,\sigma}[0, \tau]^*$ observations.*

2.2. Exact Controllability by Feedback Controller

In 2018, Barbu and Tubaro consider the exact controllability by feedback controller of the following stochastic linear system in [60]:

$$dx(t) + A(t)x(t)dt = B(t)u(t)dt + \sum_{k=1}^d C_k x(t)dw_k(t), x(0) = x_0, \quad (11)$$

with the final target $x(\tau) = \xi$, where $A(\cdot), B(\cdot) \in C([0, \infty); \mathbb{R}^{n \times m})$; for some $\gamma > 0$, $B(t)B(t)^T \geq \gamma^2 I_n, \forall t \in [0, \infty); C_k \in \mathbb{R}^{n \times n}$;

$$x(\cdot) \in L^2([0, \tau], \Omega, \mathbb{R}^n), u(\cdot) \in L^2([0, \tau], \Omega, \mathbb{R}^m); x_0, \xi \in \mathbb{R}^n.$$

The problem we address here is the following.

Problem 2. *Given* $x_0, \xi \in \mathbb{R}^n$ *find an* F_t-*adapted feedback controller* $u = f(x)$ *and* $u \in L^2([0, \tau], \Omega, \mathbb{R}^m)$, *such that the solution* $x(t)$ *to system (11) satisfies* $x(0) = x_0, x(\tau) = \xi$.

Let $F \in C([0, \tau]; \mathbb{R}^{n \times n})$ be the solution to equation

$$dF(t) = \sum_{k=1}^{d} C_k F(t) dw_k(t), t \geq 0, F(0) = I_n.$$

By the substitution $x(t) = F(t)z(t)$ one transforms via Ito's formula equation (see [60] for details) (11) into stochastic differential equation

$$\frac{dz(t)}{dt} + F(t)^{-1} A(t) F(t) z(t) = F(t)^{-1} B(t) u(t), z(0) = x_0. \tag{12}$$

In (12), we take as u the feedback controller

$$u(t) = -\tilde{\alpha} \mathrm{sign}(F(t)^{-1} B(t))^T (z(t) - z_\tau)), t \geq 0, \tag{13}$$

where $\tilde{\alpha} \in L^2(\Omega, F_T, P, \mathbb{R}), z_\tau \in L^2(\Omega, F_T, P, \mathbb{R}^n)$ are given and $z_\tau = F(\tau)^{-1}\xi$; $\mathrm{sign} : \mathbb{R}^n \to \mathbb{R}^n$ is the multivalued mapping $\mathrm{sign} y = \frac{y}{\|y\|_{\mathbb{R}^n}}$ if $y \neq 0, \mathrm{sign} y = \{\beta \in \mathbb{R}^n : \|\beta\|_{\mathbb{R}^n} \leq 1\}$ if $y = 0$. Arguing as in the proof of Proposition 3.1 in [60], it follows that (12) has unique absolutely continuous solution $z(t)$. We note that if $z(t)$ is an F_t-adapted solution to (12) and (13) then $x(t) = F(t)z(t)$ is the solution to closed loop system (11) with feedback control

$$u(t) = -\tilde{\alpha} \mathrm{sign}((F(t)^{-1} B(t))^T F(t)^{-1}(x(t) - F(t)F(\tau)^{-1} x(\tau))).$$

The following results were obtained in [60].

Theorem 8 ([60]). *Let* $\tau > 0, x_0 \in \mathbb{R}^n$ *and* $\xi \in L^2(\Omega, F_\tau, P, \mathbb{R}^n)$ *be arbitrary but fixed. Then there is* $\tilde{\alpha} \in L^2(\Omega, F_T, P, \mathbb{R})$, *such that the controller (13) steers* x_0 *in* z_τ, *in time* τ, *with probability one.*

Remark 1. *It should be noted that, under the assumption of the Theorem 8, the solution* $z(t)$ *to (12) is not adapted. Therefore, the solution* $x(t) = F(t)z(t)$ *to system (11) is not* F_t-*adapted. Hence, further research is needed on Problem 2.*

Theorem 9 ([59]). *Consider system (11) where* $A \in \mathbb{R}^{n \times n}, B \in \mathbb{R}^{n \times m}, 1 \leq m \leq n$ *is time independent and satisfy the Kalman rank condition* $\mathrm{rank}[B, AB, \cdots, A^{n-1}B] = n$. *Assume also that* $d = 1, C_1 = C$ *and* $C^2 = aC, C(\mathbb{R}^n) \subset B(\mathbb{R}^m)$ *for some* $a \in \mathbb{R}$. *Let* $\tau > 0$ *and* $x_0 \in \mathbb{R}^n$ *be arbitrary but fixed. Then there is an* F_t-*adapted controller* $u \in L^2([0, \tau], \Omega, \mathbb{R}^m)$ *which steers* x_0 *in origin, in time* τ, *with probability one.*

Remark 2. *One might suspect that the controller* u *steering* x_0 *in origin can be found in feedback form but the problem is open.*

See [60] (p. 22) for example of this part.

2.3. Exact Controllability of Stochastic Differential Equation with Memory

In 2020, Wang and Zhou consider the exact controllability of the following controlled stochastic linear differential equation with a memory in [61].

$$dx(t) = [A(t)x(t)dt + B(t)u(t) + \int_0^t M(t,s)x(s)ds]dt$$

$$+ [C(t)x(t) + D(t)u(t)]dw(t), t \geq 0, \tag{14}$$

where $x(\cdot), u(\cdot)$ are the state variable, control variable which take values in $\mathbb{R}^n, \mathbb{R}^m$, respectively; for any $t, s \in [0, \tau]$ with $\tau \in [0, \infty)$, $A(t), M(t,s), C(t) \in \mathbb{R}^{n \times n}$, and $B(t), D(t) \in \mathbb{R}^{n \times m}$; $w(t)$ is 1-dimensional Wiener process. System (14) is denoted by $[A(\cdot), M(\cdot, \cdot), C(\cdot); B(\cdot), D(\cdot)]$.

The following is definition of controllability for system (14).

Definition 4. *For any $\tau_0, \tau (\tau_0 \leq \tau)$, the following system*

$$dx(t) = [A(t)x(t)dt + B(t)u(t) + \int_{\tau_0}^t M(t,s)x(s)ds]dt$$

$$+ [C(t)x(t) + D(t)u(t)]dw(t), t \geq 0, \tag{15}$$

$\tau_0 \in L^2(\Omega, F_{\tau_0}, P, \mathbb{R}^n)$, *is called exactly controllable on* $[\tau_0, \tau]$, *if for any* $\tau_0 \in L^2(\Omega, F_{\tau_0}, P, \mathbb{R}^n)$, $\tau \in L^2(\Omega, F_\tau, P, \mathbb{R}^n)$, *there exists a control* $u(\cdot) \in L^2([\tau_0, \tau], \Omega, \mathbb{R}^m)$, *such that the solution* $x(\cdot, \tau_0, x_{\tau_0}, u(\cdot))$ *to system (15) with initial condition* $x(\tau_0) = x_{\tau_0}$ *satisfies* $x(\tau, \tau_0, x_{\tau_0}, u(\cdot)) = x_\tau$ *a.s.*

Throughout this subsection, we introduce the following basic hypothesis:

$$A(\cdot), C(\cdot) \in L^\infty([0, \tau], \Omega, \mathbb{R}^{n \times n}), M(\cdot, \cdot) \in L^\infty([0, \tau]; L^\infty([0, \tau], \Omega, \mathbb{R}^{n \times n})),$$

$$B(\cdot), D(\cdot) \in L^\infty([0, \tau], \Omega, \mathbb{R}^{n \times m}).$$

2.3.1. Time Invariant Systems

In this subsection, we discuss system (14) with time invariant matrices: i.e.,

$$[A(\cdot), M(\cdot, \cdot), C(\cdot); B(\cdot), D(\cdot)] = [A, M, C; B, D].$$

To consider the exact controllability of system $[A, M, C; B, D]$, we adopt the partial controllability of controlled system as follows:

$$dx(t) = [A_0(t)x(t)dt + B_0(t)u(t)]dt + [A_1(t)x(t)dt + B_1(t)u(t)]dw(t), t \geq 0. \tag{16}$$

For fixed $\tau \geq 0$ and a matrix $Q \in \mathbb{R}^{l \times n}$, define $X_\tau = \{\xi \in L^2(\Omega, F_\tau, P, \mathbb{R}^l) : \xi(\omega) \in \text{ran}(Q)\}$.

Definition 5. *Let a matrix $Q \in \mathbb{R}^{l \times n}$ be given. System (16) is called $Q-$partially controllable on* $[0, \tau]$, *if for any $x_0 \in \mathbb{R}^n, \xi \in X_\tau$, there exists a $u(\cdot) \in L^2([\tau_0, \tau], \Omega, \mathbb{R}^m)$, such that the solution* $x(\cdot, x_0, u(\cdot))$ *to system (16) with the initial condition* $x(0) = x_0$ *satisfies* $Qx(\tau, x_0, u(\cdot)) = \xi$ *a.s.*

Setting

$$\eta(\cdot) = \int_0^\cdot x(s)ds, y(\cdot) = \begin{bmatrix} x_1(\cdot) \\ \eta(\cdot) \end{bmatrix}, A_0 = \begin{bmatrix} A & M \\ I_n & 0 \end{bmatrix},$$

$$B_0 = \begin{bmatrix} B \\ 0 \end{bmatrix}, C_0 = \begin{bmatrix} C & 0 \\ 0 & 0 \end{bmatrix}, D_0 = \begin{bmatrix} B \\ 0 \end{bmatrix},$$

we can rewrite system $[A, M, C; B, D]$ as follows:

$$dy(t) = [A_0(t)y(t)dt + B_0(t)u(t)]dt + [C_0 y(t)dt + D_0 u(t)]dw(t), t \geq 0. \qquad (17)$$

The following results were obtained in [61].

Theorem 10 ([61]). *System $[A, M, C; B, D]$ is exactly controllable on $[0, \tau]$ with $x(0) = x_0$ if and only if system (17) is $[I_n, 0]-$partially controllable on $[0, \tau]$ with $y(0) = [x_0^T, 0^T]^T$.*

Theorem 11 ([61]). *If system $[A, M, C; B, D]$ is exactly controllable on $[0, \tau]$, then $\mathrm{rank} D = n$.*

In what follows, we tend to present a rank criterion ensuring system $[A, M, C; B, D]'s$ exact controllability. By Theorem 11, from now on, we suppose that $\mathrm{rank} D = n$. Then, there exists an invertible $K \in \mathbb{R}^{m \times m}$, such that $DK = [I_n, 0]$. Set

$$u(\cdot) = K \begin{bmatrix} u_1(\cdot) \\ u_2(\cdot) \end{bmatrix} + Jy(\cdot), BK = [B_1, B_2],$$

where $B_1 \in R^{n \times n}, B_2 \in R^{n \times (m-n)}$, and $J \in R^{m \times 2n}$. Then, system (17) turns to

$$dy(t) = \{[A_0 + \begin{bmatrix} BJ - B_1([C, 0] + DJ) \\ 0 \end{bmatrix}]y(t)$$

$$+ \begin{bmatrix} B_1 \\ 0 \end{bmatrix} [u_1(t) + ([C, 0] + DJ)y(t)] + \begin{bmatrix} B_2 \\ 0 \end{bmatrix} u_2(t)\}dt$$

$$+ \begin{bmatrix} I_n \\ 0 \end{bmatrix} [u_1(t) + ([C, 0] + DJ)y(t)]dw(t). \qquad (18)$$

Take

$$\tilde{A}_0 = A_0 + \begin{bmatrix} BJ - B_1([C, 0] + DJ) \\ 0 \end{bmatrix}, v(\cdot) = u(\cdot) + ([C, 0] + DJ)y(\cdot).$$

Then, system (17) or (18) can be rewritten as

$$d \begin{bmatrix} x(t) \\ \eta(t) \end{bmatrix} = [\tilde{A}_0 \begin{bmatrix} x(t) \\ \eta(t) \end{bmatrix} + \begin{bmatrix} B_1 \\ 0 \end{bmatrix} v(t) + \begin{bmatrix} B_2 \\ 0 \end{bmatrix} u_2(t)]dt$$

$$+ \begin{bmatrix} I_n \\ 0 \end{bmatrix} v(t)dw(t), t \geq 0. \qquad (19)$$

In order to discuss the exact controllability of (19), we need to introduce the following stochastic linear differential equation

$$d \begin{bmatrix} x(t) \\ \eta(t) \end{bmatrix} = [\tilde{A}_0 \begin{bmatrix} x(t) \\ \eta(t) \end{bmatrix} + \begin{bmatrix} B_1 \\ 0 \end{bmatrix} v(t) + \begin{bmatrix} B_2 \\ 0 \end{bmatrix} u_2(t)]dt$$

$$+ \begin{bmatrix} I_n \\ 0 \end{bmatrix} v(t)dw(t), t \in [0, \tau], x(\tau) = 0, \eta(0) = 0. \qquad (20)$$

Let

$$L = -([0, I_n]e^{-\tilde{A}_0^T \tau}[0, I_n]^T)^{-1}[0, I_n]e^{-\tilde{A}_0^T \tau}[I_n, 0]^T,$$

$$L_0 = [I_n, L^T], B_0 = \begin{bmatrix} B_2 \\ 0 \end{bmatrix}, \tilde{B}_0 = \begin{bmatrix} B_1 & 0 \\ 0 & 0 \end{bmatrix}.$$

The determinant of a square matrix F will be denoted by $\det F$.
The following result was obtained in [61].

Theorem 12 ([61]). *Suppose that for any $u_2(\cdot) \in L^2([0, \tau], \Omega, \mathbb{R}^{m-n})$ system (20) admits a unique solution, and*

$$\det([0, I_n]e^{-\tilde{A}_0^T \tau}[0, I_n]^T) \neq 0, \forall t \in [0, \tau]$$

holds. Then system $[A, M, C; B, D]$ is exactly controllable if, and only if, the following rank condition holds:

$$\text{rank}[L_0 B_0, L_0 \tilde{A}_0 B_0, L_0 \tilde{B}_0 B_0, L_0 \tilde{A}_0 \tilde{B}_0 B_0, L_0 \tilde{B}_0 \tilde{A}_0 B_0, \cdots] = n.$$

2.3.2. Time Varying System

In this part, we discuss time varying stochastic linear system with memory terms, and tend to to provide some criteria. In Section 2.3.1, we can present some criteria ensuring system $[A, M, C; B, D]'$s exact controllability. However, for time variant systems even for systems without memory terms, it is difficult to list those criteria. However, for some special systems, we still can make a try.

Case I. $M(t, s) = M_1(t)M_2(s), 0 \leq s \leq t \leq \tau$, and

$$M_1(\cdot), M_2(\cdot) \in L^\infty([0, \tau], \Omega, \mathbb{R}^{n \times n}).$$

In this case, we can set

$$\eta(\cdot) = \int_0^\cdot M_2(s)x(s)ds, y(\cdot) = \begin{bmatrix} x_1(\cdot) \\ \eta(\cdot) \end{bmatrix}, A_0(\cdot) = \begin{bmatrix} A(\cdot) & M_1(\cdot) \\ M_2(\cdot) & 0 \end{bmatrix},$$

$$B_0(\cdot) = \begin{bmatrix} B(\cdot) \\ 0 \end{bmatrix}, C_0(\cdot) = \begin{bmatrix} C(\cdot) & 0 \\ 0 & 0 \end{bmatrix}, D_0(\cdot) = \begin{bmatrix} B(\cdot) \\ 0 \end{bmatrix}.$$

Hence, time varying system $[A(\cdot), M(\cdot, \cdot), C(\cdot); B(\cdot), D(\cdot)]'$s exact controllability turns to the $[I_n, 0]-$partial controllability of the following linear system without memory term:

$$dy(t) = [A_0(t)y(t)dt + B_0(t)u(t)]dt + [C_0 y(t) + D_0 u(t)]dw(t), t \geq 0. \tag{21}$$

The following result provides an equivalent condition ensuring system (21)'s $[I_n, 0]-$partial controllability (see [61] (Theorem 3.1)).

Theorem 13 ([61]). *Assume that $M(t, s) = M_1(t)M_2(s), 0 \leq s \leq t \leq \tau$. Then the following two statements are equivalent:*
(i) System (21) is $[I_n, 0]-$partially controllable on $[0, \tau]$;
(ii) There exists a positive c such that the following observability inequality holds

$$\|\zeta\|_{L^2(\Omega, F_\tau, P, \mathbb{R}^n)} \leq c\|B_0(\cdot)^T Y(\cdot) + D_0(\cdot)^T Z(\cdot)\|_{L^2([0,\tau], \Omega, \mathbb{R}^m)},$$

for all $\zeta \in L^2([0, \tau], \Omega, \mathbb{R}^n)$, and $(Y(\cdot), Z(\cdot))$ solve the following equation:

$$dY(t) = [A_0(t)^T Y(t)dt + C_0(t)^T Z(t)]dt + Z(t)dw(t), t \in [0, \tau], Y(\tau) = [I_n, 0]^T \zeta.$$

Remark 3. *Theorem 13 can be used to determine some stochastic system's exact controllability (see [61] (Example 3.2)).*

Case II. $M(t, s) = M(t - s), 0 \leq s \leq t \leq \tau$, and $M(\tau) \in L^\infty([0, \tau], \Omega, \mathbb{R}^{n \times n})$.
In this case, for the stochastic system $[A(\cdot), M(\cdot, \cdot), C(\cdot); B(\cdot), D(\cdot)]$, we can present the following sufficient condition (see [61] (Proposition 3.4)).

Theorem 14 ([61]). *Assume that $M(t, s) = M(t - s), 0 \leq s \leq t \leq \tau$, and*

$$M(\tau) \in L^\infty([0, \tau], \Omega, \mathbb{R}^{n \times n}).$$

If system $[A(\cdot), M(\cdot, \cdot), C(\cdot); B(\cdot), D(\cdot)]$ is exactly controllable on $[\tau_0, \tau]$, for some $\tau_0 \in (0, \tau)$, then system $[A(\cdot), M(\cdot, \cdot), C(\cdot); B(\cdot), D(\cdot)]$ is exactly controllable on $[0, \tau]$.

The applicable example of this part can be found in [61] (p. 9).

According to the above discussion, further research is needed on the following problems.

Problem 3. *Find a $u(\cdot) \in L^2([0, \tau], \Omega, \mathbb{R}^m)$ in general case such that the system (14) is exactly controllable.*

Problem 4. *How to discuss the L^p-exact controllability for system (14)?*

3. Controllability of Infinite Dimensional Stochastic Linear Systems

In this section, we discuss the latest development of controllability of infinite dimensional stochastic linear systems.

In 2001, Sirbu and Tessitore discussed the null controllability of the following general infinite dimensional linear stochastic differential equation in [62]:

$$dx(t) = [Ax(t) + Bu(t)]dt + \sum_{k=1}^{\infty} C_k x(t) dw_{1,k}(t) + \sum_{j=1}^{\infty} D_j u(t) dw_{2,j}(t), x(0) = x_0, \quad (22)$$

where $x(\cdot)$ is the state process valued in H, $u(\cdot)$ is the control process valued in H, $A : \text{dom}(A) \subseteq H \to H$ is the infinitesimal generator of a C_0-semigroup in H (the Hilbert space with product $< \cdot, \cdot >$), $B \in B(H)$ (the space of all bounded linear operators on H); $C_k, D_k \in B(H)$ for each $i \in \mathbb{N}$ and

$$\sum_{k=1}^{\infty} \|C_k\|_{B(H)}^2 < +\infty, \sum_{k=1}^{\infty} \|D_k\|_{B(H)}^2 < +\infty;$$

the countable set $\{w_{1,k}, w_{2,j}, k, j \in \mathbb{N}\}$ consists of independent standard Wiener processes defined on the stochastic basis $(\Omega, F, \{F_t\}, P)$.

Given any Hilbert space H, We denote by $C^2([0, \tau], \Omega, F_t, H)$ the space of all $\xi \in L^2([0, \tau], \Omega, F_t, H)$ such that ξ has a modification in $C([0, \tau]; L^2(\Omega, F, P, H))$, where
$$L^2(\Omega, F, P, H) = \{x : x \text{ is } F-\text{adapted process valued in } H \text{ with norm}$$

$$(E(\|x\|_H^2))^{1/2} < +\infty\}.$$

As it is well known (see for instance [62]) for any initial data $x_0 \in L^2(\Omega, F_0, P, H)$ and any control $u \in L^2([0, \tau], \Omega, F_t, H)$ there exists a unique mild solution $x \in C^2([0, \tau], \Omega, F_t, H)$ of (22). When needed, we will denote the mild solution of (22) by $x(\cdot, x_0, u)$ (the definition of mild solution is in the ordinary sense).

Definition 6. *For $\tau > 0$, the state system (22) is $\tau-$null controllable if for each $x_0 \in L^2(\Omega, F_0, P, H)$ there exists $u \in L^2([0, \tau], \Omega, F_t, H)$ such that the solution $x(\tau, x_0, u) = 0, P-$almost surely. Moreover, the system is null controllable if it is $\tau-$null controllable for each $\tau > 0$.*

We recall a classical result on linear quadratic games for Equation (22). By $\Sigma^+(H)$ we denote the space of all self-adjoint, non-negative, bounded linear operators on H. Moreover, if $J \subset \mathbb{R}^+$ is an interval (bounded or unbounded), we denote by $C_s(J; \Sigma^+(H))$ the space of all maps $Q : J \to \Sigma^+(H)$, such that $Q(\cdot)v$ is continuous in H for every $v \in H$.

Definition 7. *We say that $Y \in C_s((0, \infty); \Sigma^+(H))$ is a mild solution of the Riccati equation*

$$\frac{dY(t)}{dt} = A^*Y(t) + Y(t)A - Y(t)B[I + \sum_{j=1}^{\infty} D_j^*Y(t)D_j]^{-1}B^*Y(t)$$

$$+ \sum_{j=1}^{\infty} C_j^* Y(t) C_j + S, Y(0) = +\infty \tag{23}$$

if

(i) For each $\delta \in (0, +\infty), Y(\cdot + \delta)$ is a mild solution of

$$\frac{dY(t)}{dt} = A^* Y(t) + Y(t) A - Y(t) B[I + \sum_{j=1}^{\infty} D_j^* Y(t) D_j]^{-1} B^* Y(t)$$

$$+ \sum_{j=1}^{\infty} C_j^* Y(t) C_j + S, Y(0) = Y(\delta) \in \Sigma^+(H);$$

(ii) $\lim_{(t,z) \to (0,v)} < Y(t)z, z >= +\infty$ for all $v \in H, v \neq 0$.

The following result was obtained in [62]:

Theorem 15 ([62]). *The following conditions are equivalent:*
(i) The Riccati Equation (23) has a mild solution;
(ii) The state system (22) is null controllable.

We assume that $F_t = \sigma \, w_{1,k}(s), w_{2,k}(s), s \in [0, t], k \in \mathbb{N}$ and introduce the following backward stochastic differential equation:

$$dp(t) = -[A^* p(t) + + \sum_{k=1}^{\infty} C_k^* q_{1,k}(t)]dt + \sum_{k=1}^{\infty} q_{1,k}(t)dw_{1,k}(t)$$

$$+ \sum_{j=1}^{\infty} q_{2,k}(t)dw_{2,j}(t), p(\tau) = p_\tau.$$

The following duality approach was obtained in [62]:

Theorem 16 ([62]). *The following statements are equivalent:*
(i) System (1) is $\tau-$null controllable;
(ii) There exists a constant $C_\tau > 0$, such that for all $p_\tau \in L^2(\Omega, F_\tau, P, H)$ the following observability relation holds:

$$\|p(0)\|_{L^2(\Omega, F_0, P, H)}^2 \leq C_\tau E \int_0^\tau \|B^* p(t) + \sum_{k=1}^{\infty} D_k^* q_{2,k}(t)\|_{L^2(\Omega, F_t, P, H)}^2 dt.$$

Remark 4. *We can give the similar characterization for the exact controllability on the interval $[0, \tau]$. This is equivalent to the stronger observability inequality*

$$\|p(\tau)\|_{L^2(\Omega, F_\tau, P, H)}^2 \leq C_\tau E \int_0^\tau \|B^* p(t) + \sum_{k=1}^{\infty} D_k^* q_{2,k}(t)\|_{L^2(\Omega, F_t, P, H)}^2 dt.$$

See [62] (p. 392) for the applicable example.

Problem 5. *How about the controllability of the following system?*

$$dx(t) = [A(t)x(t) + B(t)u(t)]dt + \sum_{k=1}^{\infty} C_k(t)x(t)dw_{1,k}(t)$$

$$+ \sum_{j=1}^{\infty} D_j(t)u(t)dw_{2,j}(t), x(0) = x_0,$$

where $A(t) : \mathrm{dom}(A(t)) \subseteq H \to H$ is the generator of an evolution operator in the Hilbert space H, $B(t) : \mathrm{dom}(B(t)) \subset U \to H$ is unbounded, U is a Hilbert space; $C_k(t) \in P([0,\tau], B(H))$, $D_k(t) \in P([0,\tau], B(U,H))$, for each $i \in \mathbb{N}$, $P([0,\tau], B(U,H)) = \{C(\cdot) \in B(U,H) : C(\cdot)z$ is continuous for every $z \in U$ and $\sup_{0 \leq t \leq \tau} \|C(t)\|_{B(U,H)} < +\infty\}$; and

$$\sum_{k=1}^{\infty} \sup_{0 \leq t \leq \tau} \|C_k(t)\|_{B(H)}^2 < +\infty, \; \sum_{k=1}^{\infty} \sup_{0 \leq t \leq \tau} \|D_k(t)\|_{B(U,H)}^2 < +\infty,$$

$B(U,H)$ denotes the set of all bounded linear operators from U to H; the countable set

$$\{w_{1,k}, w_{2,j}, k, j \in \mathbb{N}\}$$

consists of independent standard Wiener processes defined on the stochastic basis $(\Omega, F, \{F_t\}, P)$.

In 2015, Shen et al. studied the exact null controllability, approximate controllability and approximate null controllability of the following linear stochastic system in [63]:

$$dx(t) = [Ax(t) + Bu(t)]dt + Cx(t)dw(t), x(0) = x_0, \tag{24}$$

where $x(t)$ is the state process valued in H, $u(t)$ is the control process valued in U, $x(0) = x_0 \in L^2(\Omega, F_0, P, H)$, $w(t)$ is a standard Wiener process valued in W, and $A : D(A) \subseteq H \to H$ is the infinitesimal generator of a C_0−semigroup on H; $B \in B(U,H)$, $C \in B(H, B(W,H))$; H, U, W are separable Hilbert spaces. System (24) admits a unique mild solution $x(t, x_0, u) \in L_F^2(\Omega; C([0,\tau]; H))$.

We introduce the following backward stochastic system as our adjoint system to obtain sufficient conditions.

$$dy(t) = -[A^*y(t) + C^*z(t)]dt + z(t)dw(t), y(\tau) = \eta, \tag{25}$$

where A^*, C^* denote the adjoint operators of A, C, respectively.

For any $\eta \in H$, system (25) admits a unique mild solution $(y(t), z(t))$. In (25) $y(t)$ can be interpreted as an evolution process of the fair price, whereas $z(t)$ as the related consumption and portfolio process.

Remark 5. *When C is unbounded, the situation will be more complex.*

The closure of a set S will be denoted by $\overline{S}$.

Definition 8. *For $\tau > 0$, system (24) is null controllable at τ if for each $x_0 \in L^2(\Omega, F_0, P, H)$, there exists $u \in U$ such that $x(\tau, x_0, u) = 0, P - a.s.$*

System (24) is approximately controllable at τ if for each $x_0 \in L^2(\Omega, F_0, P, H)$, there exists $u \in U$ such that $\overline{\{x(\tau, x_0, u), u \in U\}} = L^2(\Omega, F_\tau, P, H), P - a.s.$

System (24) is approximately null controllable at τ if for each $x_0 \in L^2(\Omega, F_0, P, H)$, there exists $u \in U$ such that $x(\tau, x_0, u)$ can be arbitrarily close to 0, $P - a.s.$

The following results were obtained in [63].

Theorem 17 ([63])**.** *System (24) is null controllable if, and only if, there exists a positive constant c, such that*

$$\|y(0)\|_{L^2(\Omega, F_0, P, H)}^2 \leq c \int_0^\tau \|B^*y(s)\|_{L^2(\Omega, F_\tau, P, H)}^2 ds.$$

Theorem 18 ([63])**.** *Let $(y(t), z(t))$ denote the solution of (25).*

(i) System (24) is approximate controllable at τ if and only if for every $(y(t), z(t))$ such that $B^*y(t) = 0$ we have $(y(t), z(t)) = 0, t \in [0, \tau], P - a.s.$;

(ii) System (24) is approximate null controllable at τ if, and only if, for every $y(t)$ such that $B^*y(t) = 0$ we have $y(0) = 0, t \in [0,\tau], P - a.s.$;

The illustrative example can be found in [63] (p. 601).

Problem 6. *If A, B, C are $A(t), B(t), C(t)$, respectively, and $A(t) : \mathrm{dom}(A(t)) \subseteq H \to H$ is the generator of an evolution operator; $B(t), C(t)$ are unbounded in (24), how about the controllability of this system?*

In 2019, Dou and Lu studied the partial approximate controllability for the following system in [64]:

$$dy(t) - A(t)y(t)dt = (A_1(t)y(t) + Bu(t))dt$$
$$+ A_2(t)y(t)dw(t), t \in (0,\tau], y(0) = y_0, \tag{26}$$

here $A(t)$ is a linear operator on H, which generates strongly continuous evolution operator; $A_1(t), A_2(t) \in L^\infty([0,\tau]; B(H)), B \in B(U, H); U, H$ are separable Hilbert spaces; $u \in L^2([0,\tau], F_t, P, U), y_0 \in H, w(t)$ is a one-dimensional standard Wiener process. In (26), y is the state process valued in H and u is the control process valued in U. In what follows, $y(\cdot, y_0, u)$ denotes the mild solution to (26).

In order to discuss the partial approximate controllability of (26), we introduce the following equations and concepts.

$$dz(t) - A(t)^*z(t)dt = -(A_1^*z(t) + A_2^*Z(t))dt + Z(t)dw(t), t \in (0,\tau], z(\tau) = z_\tau, \tag{27}$$

where the final datum $z_\tau \in L^2(\Omega, F_\tau, P, H)$.

In what follows, we denoted by (z,Z) the mild solution to (27) (the definition of mild solution is in the ordinary sense).

Definition 9. *We say that (27) fulfills the unique continuation property (UCP) with respect to B^* if $z = Z = 0$ in H for a.e. $(t, \omega) \in [0, \tau] \times \Omega$, provided that $B^*z = 0$ in U for a.e. $(t, \omega) \in [0, \tau] \times \Omega$.*

$$\tilde{z}(t) + A(t)^*\tilde{z}(t) = -A_1(t)^*\tilde{z}(t), t \in [t_0, \tau], \tilde{z}(\tau) = \tilde{z}_\tau, \tag{28}$$

where the final data $\tilde{z}_\tau \in H$ and $t_0 \in [0, \tau]$.

Definition 10. *We say that (28) fulfills UCP if $\tilde{z} = 0$ in H for a.e. $t \in [t_0, \tau]$, provided that $B^*\tilde{z} = 0$ for a.e. $t \in [t_0, \tau]$.*

Hypothesis 3. *Solutions to (28) fulfill the UPC for any $t_0 \in [0, \tau]$.*

Denoted by $h_k(x)$ the kth Hermite polynomial (see [64]). For $k \in \mathbb{N} \cup \{0\}$, let

$$H_k = \mathrm{span}\{h_k\Big(\int_0^\tau l(t)dw(t)\Big) : l \in L^2([0,\tau], \mathbb{R}), \|l\|_{L^2([0,\tau],\mathbb{R})} = 1\}.$$

We have that $H_0 = \mathbb{R}, H_k$ and H_r are orthogonal subspaces of $L^2(\Omega, F_\tau, P, \mathbb{R})$ for $k \neq r$ and

$$L^2(\Omega, F_\tau, P, \mathbb{R}) = \oplus_{k=0}^\infty H_k.$$

For $k \in \mathbb{N} \cup \{0\}$, denote by $H_k(H)$ the closed subspace of $L^2(\Omega, F_\tau, P, H)$ generated by H valued random variable of the form $\sum_{j=1}^r l_j v_j (r \in \mathbb{N}), l_j \in H_k$, and $v_j \in H$. Let $\{e_j\}_{j=1}^\infty$ be an orthonormal basis of H. It is easy to see that

$$H_k(H) = \{\sum_{j=1}^\infty l_j e_j : \{l_j\}_{j=1}^\infty \subset H_k, E\sum_{j=1}^\infty |l_j|^2 < +\infty\}.$$

$H_0(H) = H, H_k(H)$ and $H_r(H)$ are orthogonal subspaces of $L^2(\Omega, F_\tau, P, H)$ for $k \neq r$ and

$$L^2(\Omega, F_\tau, P, H) = \oplus_{k=0}^\infty H_k(H).$$

Write

$$L_m^2(\Omega, F_\tau, P, H) = \oplus_{k=0}^m H_k(H).$$

Clearly $L_m^2(\Omega, F_\tau, P, H)$ is a closed subspace of $L^2(\Omega, F_\tau, P, H)$. Denote by Γ_m the orthogonal projection from $L^2(\Omega, F_\tau, P, H)$ to $L_m^2(\Omega, F_\tau, P, H)$.

Definition 11. *System (26) is said to be $m-$approximately controllable if for any $\epsilon > 0, y_0 \in H$ and $y_1 \in L_m^2(\Omega, F_\tau, P, H)$, there is a control $u \in L^2([0, \tau], \Omega, U)$, such that the corresponding mild solution fulfills that $\|\Gamma_m(y(\tau, y_0, u) - y_1)\|_{L^2(\Omega, F_\tau, P, H)} < \epsilon$.*
The system (26) is said to be partially approximately controllable if it is $m-$approximately controllable for all $m \in \mathbb{N}$.

To study the above controllability problem, we need the following notion.

Definition 12. *Equation (27) is said to fulfill the m-unique continuation property (m-UCP) if $z = Z = 0$ in H for a.e. $(t, \omega) \in [0, \tau] \times \Omega$, provided that $z_\tau \in L_m^2(\Omega, F_\tau, P, H)$ and $B^* z = 0$ in U for a.e. $(t, \omega) \in [0, \tau] \times \Omega$.*
Equation (27) is said to fulfill the partial UCP if it fulfills m-UCP for all $m \in \mathbb{N}$.

The following results were obtained in [64].

Theorem 19 ([64]). *(i) System (26) is m-approximately controllable if and only if (27) fulfills the m-UCP;*
(ii) System (26) is partially approximately controllable if and only if (27) fulfills the partial UCP.

Theorem 20 ([64]). *Suppose that Hypothesis 3 holds. Then system (26) is partially approximate controllable.*

Problem 7. *If B is $B(t)$, and $A_1(t), B(t), A_2(t)$ are unbounded in (26), how about the controllability of this system?*

4. Controllability of Finite Dimensional Stochastic Singular Linear Systems

Stochastic singular linear systems are also called stochastic implicit systems, stochastic differential algebraic systems, stochastic descriptor systems, stochastic degenerate systems, and stochastic generalized systems, etc. Controllability is the important concept for stochastic singular linear systems. So far, however, few results have been obtained. In this section, we discuss the latest development of controllability of finite dimensional stochastic singular linear systems.

In 2013, Gashi and Pantelous studied the exact controllability of the following stochastic singular linear system in [65,66].

$$Ldx(t) = [Mx(t) + Bu(t)]dt + [Cx(t) + Du(t)]dw(t), x(0 = x_0), \qquad (29)$$

where $L, M, C \in \mathbb{R}^{n \times n}, \det L = 0; B, D \in \mathbb{R}^{n \times m}$, $x(t)$ is the state process valued in $\mathbb{R}^n$, $u(t)$ is the state process valued in $\mathbb{R}^m$, $w(t)$ is a one-dimensional standard Wiener process, (L, M) is regular, i.e., matrix pencil $\det(sL - M)$ is not identically zero $(s \in \mathbb{R})$. Let us begin by stating the definition of exact controllability.

Definition 13. *System (29) is called exactly controllable at time τ if for any $x_0 \in \mathbb{R}^n$ and $\xi \in L^2(\Omega, F_\tau, P, \mathbb{R}^n)$, there exists at least one admissible control $u(\cdot) \in L^2([0, \tau], \Omega, \mathbb{R}^m)$, such* *that the corresponding trajectory $x(\cdot)$ satisfies the initial condition $x(0) = x_0$ and the terminal condition $x(\tau) = \xi$, a.s.*

The following result was obtained in [65,66].

Theorem 21 ([65,66]). *(i) A necessary condition for exact controllability of (29) is*

$$\mathrm{rank}\tilde{K}_1 = n - \sigma; \tag{30}$$

(ii) Let the condition (30) hold. A necessary and sufficient condition for exact controllability of (29) is

$$\mathrm{rank}G_\tau = n - \sigma.$$

Here, G_τ is the Gramian matrix defined as

$$G_\tau = E \int_0^\tau \Phi(t)\tilde{K}_{12}\tilde{K}_{12}^T\Phi(t)^T dt,$$

where $\Phi(t)$ is the unique solution to the matrix stochastic differential equation

$$d\Phi(t) = -\Phi(t)[\tilde{N}dt + \tilde{K}_{11}dw(t)], \Phi(0) = I.$$

For the detail see [65] (Theorem 4) and [65] (Theorem 2).

In 2015, Gashi and Pantelous studied the exact controllability of the stochastic singular linear system (29) on the basis of [65,66] in [67], in which L is skew-symmetric and M is symmetric. The following result was obtained in [67].

Theorem 22 ([67]). *(i) A necessary condition for exact controllability of (29) is*

$$\mathrm{rank}\tilde{K}_1 = n - q - 2p; \tag{31}$$

(ii) Let the condition (31) hold. A necessary and sufficient condition for exact controllability of (29) is

$$\mathrm{rank}G_\tau = n - q - 2p.$$

Here, G_τ is the Gramian matrix defined as

$$G_\tau = E \int_0^\tau \Phi(t)\tilde{K}_{12}\tilde{K}_{12}^T\Phi(t)^T dt,$$

where $\Phi(t)$ is the unique solution to the matrix stochastic differential equation

$$d\Phi(t) = -\Phi(t)[\tilde{N}dt + \tilde{K}_{11}dw(t)], \Phi(0) = I.$$

For the detail see [67] (Theorem 5).

See [67] (p. 9) for practical example.

In 2021, Ge and Ge considered the exact null controllability of stochastic singular linear system (29).

Here, we assume that there are a pair of nonsingular deterministic and constant matrices $P_1, Q \in \mathbb{R}^{n\times n}$ such that the following condition is satisfied:

$$P_1LQ = \begin{bmatrix} I_{n_1} & 0 \\ 0 & N \end{bmatrix}, P_1MQ = \begin{bmatrix} B_1 & 0 \\ 0 & I_{n_2} \end{bmatrix},$$

$$P_1B = \begin{bmatrix} C_1 \\ C_2 \end{bmatrix}, P_1CQ = \begin{bmatrix} D_1 & 0 \\ 0 & 0 \end{bmatrix}, P_1D = \begin{bmatrix} G_1 \\ 0 \end{bmatrix}, \tag{32}$$

where $N \in \mathbb{R}^{n_2 \times n_2}$ denotes a nilpotent matrix with order h, i.e., $h = \min\{k : k \geq 1, N^k = 0\}$; $B_1, D_1 \in \mathbb{R}^{n_1 \times n_1}, C_1, G_1 \in \mathbb{R}^{n_1 \times m}, C_2 \in \mathbb{R}^{n_2 \times m}$, and $n_1 + n_2 = n$. Let $\begin{bmatrix} x_1 \\ x_2 \end{bmatrix} = Q^{-1}x$, system (29) is equivalent to

$$dx_1(t) = (B_1 x_1(t) + C_1 u(t))dt + (D_1 x_1(t) + G_1 u(t))dw(t), x_1(0) = x_{10}, \tag{33}$$

$$Ndx_2(t) = x_2(t)dt + C_2 u(t)dt, x_2(0) = x_{20}. \tag{34}$$

Now, we consider the initial value problem (34). In the following, assume that the solution to (33) is the strong solution in the ordinary sense and (34) admits the stochastic Laplace transform (see [68]). Applying the stochastic Laplace transform to (34), we have

$$(sN - I_{n_2})X_2(s) = Nx_{20} + C_2 U(s). \tag{35}$$

Definition 14. *(Impulse Solution) Suppose that $x_2(t)$ is the inverse stochastic Laplace transform of $X_2(s)$ obtained from (35). Then, $x_2(t)$ is the impulse solution to (34) in the sense of the stochastic Laplace transform, or simply, the impulse solution to (34). In this case, if $x_1(t)$ denotes the solution to (33), then $x(t) = Q\begin{bmatrix} x_1(t) \\ x_2(t) \end{bmatrix}$ is called the impulse solution of Equation (29).*

Let $\Phi(t)$ be the solution of system

$$d\Phi(t) = (B_1 dt + D_1 dw(t))\Phi(t), \Phi(0) = I_{n_1}, \tag{36}$$

Definition 15. *(Exact Null Controllability) System (33) and (34) is said to be exactly null controllable on $[0, \tau]$ if for any $\begin{bmatrix} x_{10} \\ x_{20} \end{bmatrix} \in R^n$, there exists $u \in L^2([0, \tau], \Omega, R^m)$, such that (33) and (34) has a unique solution $\begin{bmatrix} x_1(t) \\ x_2(t) \end{bmatrix}$ satisfying the initial condition $\begin{bmatrix} x_1(0) \\ x_2(0) \end{bmatrix} = \begin{bmatrix} x_{10} \\ x_{20} \end{bmatrix}$ in addition to the terminal condition $\begin{bmatrix} x_1(\tau) \\ x_2(\tau) \end{bmatrix} = 0.$*

It is obvious that if (33) and (34) is exactly null controllable, so is (33) and (34). In general, if $N \neq 0$, then (33) and (34) is not necessarily exactly null controllable. Consequently, we assume that $N = 0$ in the following.

The following result was obtained in [68].

Theorem 23 ([68]). *If $G_1 = 0$, then the necessary condition for (33) to be exactly null controllable on $[0, \tau]$ is that*

$$E(\int_0^\tau f^2(t)\Phi^{-1}(t)C_1(\Phi^{-1}(t)C_1)^{\mathrm{T}}dt) \tag{37}$$

is invertible for any real valued polynomial $f(t)$ not identical zero.

Let $\mathrm{rank} G_1 = n_1$; let $u(t) = M_1 \begin{bmatrix} 0 \\ v(t) \end{bmatrix}, z(t) = D_1 x_1(t)$, where M_1 denotes an $m \times m$ matrix, which satisfies $G_1 M_1 = [I_{n_1} \quad 0]$, and $v(t)$ denotes an $(m - n_1)$-dimension vector. For the above $u(t)$, system (33) and (34) is equivalent to

$$- dx_1(t) = (F_1 x_1(t) + F_2 z(t) + F_3 v(t))dt - z(t)dw(t), x_1(0) = x_{10}, \tag{38}$$

$$x_2(t) = -C_2 M_1 \begin{bmatrix} 0 \\ v(t) \end{bmatrix}, t > 0, \tag{39}$$

where

$$F_1 = D_1 - B_1, F_2 = -I_{n_1}, F_3 v(t) = -C_1 M_1 \begin{bmatrix} 0 \\ v(t) \end{bmatrix}.$$

Let $\Psi(t)$ denote the solution of system

$$d\Psi(t) = \Psi(t)(F_1 dt + F_2 dw(t)), \Psi(0) = I_{n_1}.$$

The following result was obtained in [68].

Theorem 24 ([68]). *System (38) and (39) is exactly null controllable on $[0, T]$ if, and only if,*

$$E\left(\int_0^\tau f^2(t)\Psi^{-1}(t)F_3(\Psi^{-1}(t)F_3)^\mathrm{T} dt\right)$$

is invertible for any real valued polynomial $f(t)$ not identical to zero.

The practical example can be found in [68] (supplementary file).

In 2021, Ge considered the impulse controllability and impulse observability of the following stochastic singular linear system in [69].

$$Adx(t) = Bx(t)dt + Cu(t)dt + Dx(t)dw(t), x(0) = x_0, \tag{40}$$

$$y(t) = Gx(t), \tag{41}$$

where $x(t) \in L^2([0,\tau], \Omega, \mathbb{R}^n)$ is the state vector, $u(t) \in L^2([0,\tau], \Omega, \mathbb{R}^m)$ is the control vector, $w(t)$ is one dimensional standard Wiener process, $x_0 \in L^2(\Omega, F_0, P, \mathbb{R}^n)$ is a given random variable, $y(t) \in L^2([0,\tau], \Omega, \mathbb{R}^l)$ is the measurement output.

For a stochastic singular system, impulse terms may exist in the solution. In a practical system, the impulse terms are generally undesirable because strong impulse behavior may impede the working of the system or even damage the system. Therefore, the impulse terms must be eliminated by imposing appropriate controls. In view of this fact, in this part, the concepts of impulse controllability and impulse observability for stochastic singular system (40) is considered.

In order to discusses the impulse controllability and impulse observability for stochastic singular system (40), let us introduce the class H_n of all processes $f(t) \in L^2([0, +\infty), \Omega, \mathbb{R}^n)$, such that

(i) $f(t)$ is mean square locally integrable;
(ii) There exist constants $a \geq 0$ and $M_0 > 0$ such that

$$(E\|f(t)\|_{\mathbb{R}^n}^2)^{1/2} \leq M_0 e^{at}, t \geq 0.$$

In the following, $C^k(J, \Omega, \mathbb{R}^n)$ denotes the set of all k times continuously differentiable stochastic processes $x(t) \in L^2(J, \Omega, \mathbb{R}^n)$, such that $x^{(i)}(t) \in L^2(J, \Omega, \mathbb{R}^n)(i = 0, 1, \cdots, k)(J = [0, \tau]or[0, +\infty)$; we assume that there are a pair of non-singular matrices $P_1, Q \in \mathbb{R}^{n \times n}$, such that the following condition is satisfied

$$\begin{cases} P_1 AQ = \begin{bmatrix} I_{n_1} & 0 \\ 0 & N \end{bmatrix}, P_1 BQ = \begin{bmatrix} B_1 & 0 \\ 0 & I_{n_2} \end{bmatrix}, \\ P_1 C = \begin{bmatrix} C_1 \\ C_2 \end{bmatrix}, P_1 DQ = \begin{bmatrix} D_1 & 0 \\ 0 & 0 \end{bmatrix}, GQ = [G_1 \quad G_2], \end{cases} \tag{42}$$

where $N \in \mathbb{R}^{n_2 \times n_2}$ is a nilpotent, the index of nilpotency of N is denoted by h, i.e., $h = \min\{k : k \text{ is a positive integer}, k \geq 1, N^k = 0\}$, $B_1 \in \mathbb{R}^{n_1 \times n_1}, C_1 \in \mathbb{R}^{n_1 \times m}, C_2 \in \mathbb{R}^{n_2 \times m}, D_1 \in \mathbb{R}^{n_1 \times n_1}, G_1 \in \mathbb{R}^{l \times n_1}, G_2 \in \mathbb{R}^{l \times n_2}, n_1 + n_2 = n$. Let $\begin{bmatrix} x_1(t) \\ x_2(t) \end{bmatrix} = Q^{-1}x(t)$, system (40) and (41) is equivalent to

$$dx_1(t) = (B_1 x_1(t) + C_1 u(t))dt + D_1 x_1(t)dw(t), x_1(0) = x_{10}, \tag{43}$$

$$y_1(t) = G_1 x_1(t), \tag{44}$$

$$Ndx_2(t) = x_2(t)dt + C_2u_2(t)dt, x_2(0) = x_{20}, \tag{45}$$

$$y_2(t) = G_2x_2(t). \tag{46}$$

Let $\Phi(t)$ be the solution of system

$$d\Phi(t) = (B_1dt + D_1dw(t))\Phi(t), \Phi(0) = I_{n_1},$$

the following results were obtained in [69]

Theorem 25 ([69]). *If $u \in L^2([0,\tau], \Omega, \mathbb{R}^m)$ is a bounded Borel measurable function, then subsystem (43) has a unique solution on $[0, \tau]$ with any $x_{10} \in L^2(\Omega, F_0, P, \mathbb{R}^{n_1})$, and the solution is given by the stochastic process*

$$x_1(t) = \Phi(t)x_{10} + \Phi(t) \int_0^t \Phi^{-1}(s)C_1u(s)ds. \tag{47}$$

Theorem 26 ([69]). *For any $x_{20} \in L^2(\Omega, F_0, P, \mathbb{R}^{n_2}), u \in C^{h-1}([0, +\infty), \Omega, \mathbb{R}^m)$ and $u^{(i)} \in H_m(i = 0, 1, \cdots, h - 1)$, subsystem (45) has a unique impulse solution, which is given by*

$$x_2(t) = -\sum_{i=1}^{h-1} \delta^{(i-1)}(t)[N^i x_{20} + \sum_{k=i}^{h-1} N^k C_2 u^{(k-i)}(0)] - \sum_{i=0}^{h-1} N^i C_2 u^{(i)}(t), \tag{48}$$

where $\delta(t)$ is the Dirac function, $\delta^{(i-1)}(t)$ is the $(i-1)$th derivative of $\delta(t)$.

Theorem 27 ([69]). *Assume that (40) and (41) is equivalent to (43)–(46),*

$$u \in C^{h-1}([0, +\infty), \Omega, \mathbb{R}^m)$$

is a bounded Borel measurable function, and $u^{(i)} \in H_m(i = 0, 1, \cdots, h - 1)$. Then, for any $x_0 \in L^2(\Omega, F_0, P, \mathbb{R}^n)$, system (40) has a unique impulse solution on $[0, \tau]$, which is given by

$$x(t) = Q\begin{bmatrix} x_1(t) \\ x_2(t) \end{bmatrix}, \tag{49}$$

where $x_1(t)$ and $x_2(t)$ are given by (47) and (48), respectively.

Definition 16. *System (40) is called impulse controllable, if for any $x_0 \in L^2(\Omega, F_0, P, \mathbb{R}^n)$, there exists a bounded Borel measurable function $u \in C^h([0, +\infty), \Omega, \mathbb{R}^m)$ and $u^{(i)} \in H_m(i = 0, 1, \cdots, h - 1)$, such that the coefficient vectors of $\delta^{(i)}(t), i = 0, 1, \cdots, h - 2$, in the solution formula (49) are all zero.*

The following results were obtained in [69].

Theorem 28 ([69]). *System (40) is impulse controllable if, and only if, subsystem (45) is impulse controllable.*

Theorem 29 ([69]). *Subsystem (45) is impulse controllable if and only if for any*

$$x_{20} \in L^2(\Omega, F_0, P, \mathbb{R}^{n_2}),$$

there exists a bounded Borel measurable function $u \in C^{h-1}([0, +\infty), \Omega, \mathbb{R}^m)$ and $u^{(i)} \in H_m(i = 0, 1, \cdots, h - 1)$, such that

$$Nx_{20} + \sum_{i=0}^{h-2} N^{i+1}C_2u^{(i)}(0) = 0.$$

Theorem 30 ([69]). *System (40) is impulse controllable if, and only if,*

$$\mathrm{ran}(N) = \mathrm{ran}([NC_2 \quad \cdots \quad N^{h-1}C_2]),$$

where $\mathrm{ran}(N) = \{y : y = Nz, z \in L^2(\Omega, F_0, P, \mathbb{R}^{n_2})\}$, $\mathrm{ran}([NC_2 \quad \cdots \quad N^{h-1}C_2]) = \{y : \exists \alpha_k \in L^2(\Omega, F_0, P, \mathbb{R}^m), k = 1, 2, \cdots, h - 1, y = \sum_{k=1}^{h-1} N^k C_2 \alpha_k\}$.

Now, we discuss the impulse observability of system (40) and (41). Without loss of generality, let $u(t) \equiv 0$.

Definition 17. *System (40) and (41) with subsystem (43)–(46) is called impulse observable if,* $y_2(t)|_{t=0} = 0$ *implies* $x_2(t)|_{t=0} = 0$.

Impulse observability guarantees the ability to uniquely determine the impulse behavior in solution from information of the impulse behavior in output, and focuses on the impulse terms that take infinite values in the solution.

The following results were obtained in [69].

Theorem 31 ([69]). *Subsystem (43) and (44) is always impulse observable.*

Theorem 32 ([69]). *System (40) and (41) is impulse observable if, and only if, one of the following conditions holds:*

(i) Subsystem (45) and (46) is impulse observable;
(ii)

$$\ker\left(\begin{bmatrix} G_2 N \\ G_2 N^2 \\ \vdots \\ G_2 N^h \end{bmatrix}\right) = \ker(N).$$

where $\ker(N) = \{x : Nx = 0, x \in L^2(\Omega, F_0, P, R^{n_2})\}$,

$$\ker\left(\begin{bmatrix} G_2 N \\ G_2 N^2 \\ \vdots \\ G_2 N^h \end{bmatrix}\right) = \left\{x : \begin{bmatrix} G_2 N \\ G_2 N^2 \\ \vdots \\ G_2 N^h \end{bmatrix} x = 0, x \in L^2(\Omega, F_0, P, R^{n_2})\right\}.$$

For the impulse observability and impulse controllability, the so-called dual principle holds, which reveals the close relation between impulse observability and impulse controllability.

In order to introduce the dual principle for system (40) and (41), let us first introduce the dual system.

Definition 18. *The following system*

$$\begin{cases} A^T dz(t) = B^T z(t)dt + G^T v(t)dt + D^T z(t)dw(t), \\ w_0(t) = C^T z(t), \end{cases} \tag{50}$$

is called the dual system of the system (40) and (41).

The following dual principle was obtained in [69].

Theorem 33 ([69]). *Let (50) be the dual system of system (40) and (41). Then, system (40) and (41) is impulse observable (impulse controllable) if, and only if, its dual system (50) is impulse controllable (impulse observable).*

An illustrative example is given in [69] (p. 908).

Furthermore, in 2021, Ge discussed the exact observability for a kind of stochastic singular linear systems in the sense of impulse solution. Some necessary and sufficient conditions were obtained. See [70] (Theorems 3.1 and 3.3) for details.

Problem 8. *How to discuss the L^p—exact controllability for the following stochastic singular linear system?*

$$Ldx(t) = [A(t)x(t) + B(t)u(t)]dt + \sum_{k=1}^{d}[C_k(t)x(t) + D_k(t)u(t)]dw_k(t), t \geq 0, x(0) = x_0.$$

where L as defined in (29); $A(t), B(t), C_k(t), D_k(t)$ as defined in (1).

5. Controllability of Infinite Dimensional Stochastic Singular Linear Systems

In this section the latest development of the controllability of infinite dimensional stochastic singular linear systems is discussed by using the methods of C_0—semigroup, GE-semigroup, GE-evolution operator, and stochastic GE-evolution operator, respectively. Some necessary and sufficient conditions concerning the controllability are introduced.

5.1. C_0—Semigroup Method for a Class of Time Invariant Systems in Hilbert Spaces

In 2015, Liaskos et al. studied the exact controllability of the following stochastic singular linear system by using the C_0—semigroup method in the sense of strong solution in Hilbert spaces in [71].

$$dLx(t) = [Mx(t) + Cu(t) + f(t)]dt + Bdw(t), t \in [0, \tau], x(0) = \zeta. \tag{51}$$

In order to introduce the exact controllability, make the following assumptions and preparations.

Let H, U, K be separable and infinite dimensional Hilbert spaces, $x(t)$ be the state process valued in H, $u(t)$ be the control process valued in U, and $w(t)$ be a U—valued standard Wiener process in (51). The closure of an operator S will be denoted by $\overline{S}$. We use the notation $S^\perp$ for the orthogonal complement of a set S and for the restriction of the operator A to a linear subset S the symbol $A|_S$. For the coefficients L, M, C, f, B, ζ involved in (51), the following assumptions and definitions should be considered.

(A_1) (i) $L \in B(H), \ker(L) \neq \{0\}$. (ii) $\overline{\ker(L)} = \ker(L)$.

(A_2) (i) $M : \text{dom}(M) \subseteq H \to H$ is a linear, densely defined and closed operator.

(ii) For the linear subspace $D = \{x \in \text{dom}(M) : Mx + f(t) \in \text{ran}(L)\}$, we assume that $D \cap \ker(L) = \{0\}$ and $P_1^\perp D$ is dense in $P_1^\perp H$, where $P_1, P_1^\perp$ are the projections onto $\ker(L)$ and $(\ker(L))^\perp$, respectively.

(A_3) (i) The operator pencil $\lambda L - M : \text{dom}(M) \to H$ is of parabolic type, i.e., the restriction of the pencil $\lambda L - M : D \to \text{ran}(L)$ is invertible with a bounded inverse $(\lambda L - M)^{-1}$, for all $\lambda > \omega$, where ω is a negative real constant. This regularity on the pencil also implies that $M(D) = \text{ran}(L)$ and $M|_D : D \to \text{ran}(L)$ is invertible with a bounded inverse M^{-1}.

(ii) The bounded pseudo-resolvent operators $R_1(\lambda) = (\lambda L - M)^{-1}L : H \to D$ and $R_2(\lambda) = L(\lambda L - M)^{-1} : \text{ran}(L) \to L(D)$ satisfy $\|U(\lambda)\|_{B(H)} \leq \frac{c}{\lambda - \omega}$, for all $\lambda > \omega, 0 < c < 1$, where $U(\lambda)$ stands for both $R_1(\lambda), R_2(\lambda)$.

(A_4) $f \in L^1([0, \tau]; H) \cap L^2([0, \tau], \Omega, F_t, H)$, satisfying $f(t) \in L(D), P - a.s., a.e.$ in $[0, \tau]$.

(A_5) $B : U \to H$ is a linear operator with $\text{ran}(B) \subseteq L(D)$, such that $B \in B(U, H)$.

(A_6) ζ is a D—valued random variable $P - a, s.$, with $\zeta \in L^2(\Omega, F_0, P, H)$.

(A_7) $C \in B(K, H)$, with $\text{ran}(C) \subseteq L(D)$, such that for any $u \in L^2([0, \tau], \Omega, K)$, the stochastic process $Cu(t), t \in [0, \tau]$ satisfies

$$E\left[\int_0^\tau \int_0^t \|(L^\perp)^{-1}M_0S_1(s - t)(L^\perp)^{-1}(Cu(s) + f(s))\|_H dsdt\right] < \infty,$$

where $L^{\perp} = L|_{P_1^{\perp}H} : P_1^{\perp}H \to Q^{\perp}H, Q$ is the projection onto $\ker(L^*)$; $M_0 = M(P_1^{\perp}|_D)^{-1}$, $S_1(t)$ is the C_0-semigroup in the closed subspace $P_1^{\perp}H$ generated by the operator $(L^{\perp})^{-1}M_0$.

Definition 19. *An $H-$valued stochastic process $x(t), t \in [0, \tau]$, is called a strong solution of the initial value problem (51), if*
(i) $x \in D, P - a.s., a.e.$ in $[0, \tau]$ and $x \in L^1([0, \tau]; H), P - a.s.$
(ii) $Lx, Mx \in L^1([0, \tau]; H), P - a.s.$
(iii) $Lx(t) = L\xi + \int_0^t [Mx(s) + Cu(t) + f(s)]ds + Bw(t), P - a.s., a.e.$ in $[0, \tau]$.

From the above, the controlled stochastic singular linear system (51) has a unique strong solution $x_u(t), t \in [0, \tau]$, which admits the form:

$$x_u(t) = \overline{(P_1^{\perp}|_D)^{-1}}S_1(t)P_1^{\perp}\xi + \int_0^t \overline{(P_1^{\perp}|_D)^{-1}}S_1(t-s)(L^{\perp})^{-1}[Cu(s) + f(s)]ds$$

$$+ \int_0^t \overline{(P_1^{\perp}|_D)^{-1}}S_1(t-s)(L^{\perp})^{-1}Bdw(s), t \in [0, \tau]. \tag{52}$$

Definition 20. *Stochastic singular linear system (51) is called exactly controllable at time $\tau > 0$, if for any ξ which is $D-$valued random variable $P - a.s.$, with $\xi \in L^2(\Omega, F_0, PH)$ and for any ξ_τ which is also a $D-$valued random variable $P - a.s.$, with $\xi \in L^2(\Omega, F_\tau, P, H)$, there exists at least one control $u \in L^2([0, \tau], \Omega, K)$, such that the corresponding strong solution $x_u(t)$, which admits the form of (52), satisfies the initial condition $x_u(0) = \xi$ and the terminal condition $x_u(\tau) = \xi_\tau$.*

The following result was obtain in [71].

Theorem 34 ([71]). *Suppose that $L^{\perp}S_1(t)v(t) - f(t) \in \mathrm{ran}(C), P - a.s., a.e.$ in $[0, \tau]$. Then there exists at least one $u \in L^2([0, \tau], \Omega, K)$, such that the corresponding strong solution $x_u(t)$, which admits the form of (52), satisfies the initial condition $x_u(0) = \xi$ and the terminal condition $x_u(\tau) = \xi_\tau$ and hence stochastic singular linear system (51) is exactly controllable.*

See [71] for the details of practical example.

In 2018, Liaskos et al. studied the exact controllability of the stochastic singular linear system (51) by using the C_0-semigroup method in the sense of strong solution in Hilbert spaces in [72].

Suppose that (A_1)–(A_6) hold true, and

$$E[\int_0^{\tau} \int_0^t \|M_0(L^{\perp})^{-1}S_2(s-t)(L^{\perp})^{-1}(Cu(s) + f(s))\|_H dsdt] < \infty.$$

Then, the controlled stochastic singular linear system (51) has a unique strong solution $x_u(t), t \in [0, \tau]$, which admits the form:

$$x_u(t) = \overline{(P_1^{\perp}|_D)^{-1}}(L^{\perp})^{-1}S_2(t)L\xi$$

$$+ \int_0^t \overline{(P_1^{\perp}|_D)^{-1}}(L^{\perp})^{-1}S_2(t-s)[Cu(s) + f(s)]ds$$

$$+ \int_0^t \overline{(P_1^{\perp}|_D)^{-1}}(L^{\perp})^{-1}S_2(t-s)Bdw(s), t \in [0, \tau], \tag{53}$$

where $S_2(t)$ is the C_0-semigroup generated by the operator $M_0(L^{\perp})^{-1}$.
The following result was obtained in [72]:

Theorem 35 ([72]). *Suppose that $S_2(t)v(t) - f(t) \in \mathrm{ran}(C), P - a.s., a.e.$ in $[0, \tau]$. Then, there exists at least one $u \in L^2([0, \tau], \Omega, K)$, such that the corresponding strong solution $x_u(t)$, which* *admits the form of (53), satisfies the initial condition $x_u(0) = \xi$ and the terminal condition $x_u(\tau) = \xi_\tau$ and hence stochastic singular linear system (51) is exactly controllable.*

5.2. GE-Semigroup Method for a Class of Time Invariant Systems

In this subsection, we discuss the controllability of the following time invariant stochastic singular linear system by using GE-semigroup in the sense of mild solution in Banach and Hilbert spaces, respectively,

$$Adx(t) = Bx(t)dt + Cv(t)dt + Ddw(t), x(0) = x_0, t \geq 0, \tag{54}$$

where $x(t)$ is the state process valued in H, $v(t)$ is the control process valued in U, $w(t)$ is the standard Wiener process on Z, $x_0 \in L^2(\Omega, F_0, P, H)$ is a given random variable, H, U, Z are Banach or Hilbert spaces; $A \in B(H), C \in B(U, H), D \in B(Z, H), B : \mathrm{dom}(B) \subseteq H \to H$ is a linear operator. This subsection is organized as follows. Firstly, the GE-semigroup is introduced and the mild solution of (54) is obtained; Secondly, the controllability of (54) is discussed in Banach spaces; Thirdly, the controllability of (54) is discussed in Hilbert spaces.

5.2.1. GE-Semigroup and Mild Solution of System (54)

In this part, the existence and uniqueness of the mild solution to system (54) are considered by GE-semigroup theory.

Definition 21 ([73–77]). *Suppose $\{U(t) : t \geq 0\}$ is one parameter family of bounded linear operators in Banach space H, and A is a bounded linear operator. If*

$$U(t+s) = U(t)AU(s), t, s \geq 0,$$

then $\{U(t) : t \geq 0\}$ is called a GE-semigroup induced by A.
If the GE-semigroup $U(t)$ satisfies

$$\lim_{t \to 0^+} \|U(t)x - U(0)x\|_H = 0,$$

for arbitrary $x \in H$, then it is called strongly continuous on H.

Lemma 1 ([73,74,76,77]). *If GE-semigroup $U(t)$ is strongly continuous on H, then there exist $M \geq 1$ and $\omega > 0$, such that*

$$\|U(t)\|_{L(H,H)} \leq Me^{\omega t}, t \geq 0,$$

i.e., $U(t)$ is exponentially bounded.

Definition 22 ([75–77]). *Suppose $U(t)$ is strongly continuous GE-semigroup induced by A. If*

$$Bx = \lim_{h \to 0^+} \frac{AU(h)A - AU(0)A}{h} x,$$

for every $x \in D_1$, where

$$D_1 = \{x : x \in \mathrm{dom}(B) \subseteq H, U(0)Ax = x, \exists \lim_{h \to 0^+} \frac{AU(h)A - AU(0)A}{h} x\},$$

then B is called a generator of GE-semigroup $U(t)$ induced by A.

Now, we consider the initial value problem (54).

Definition 23. *If B is a generator of GE-semigroup $U(t)$ induced by A, $x_0 \in L^2(\Omega, F_0, P, \overline{D_1})$, and $v(t) \in L^2([0,b], \Omega, U)$; $Cv(t), Ddw(t) \in A(L^2([0,b], \Omega, \overline{D_1}))$, the mild solution $x(t, x_0)$ to (54) is defined by*

$$x(t, x_0) = U(t)Ax_0 + \int_0^t U(t-\tau)Cv(\tau)d\tau + \int_0^t U(t-\tau)Ddw(\tau). \tag{55}$$

From the above knowledge, we have the following proposition.

Proposition 1 ([76,77]). *If B is the generator of GE-semigroup $U(t)$ induced by A, $v(t) \in L^2([0,b], \Omega, U)$, $x_0 \in L^2(\Omega, F_0, P, \overline{D_1})$; $Cv(t), Ddw(t) \in A(L^2([0,b], \Omega, \overline{D_1}))$, and $U(0)$ is a definite operator, then there exists unique mild solution $x(t, x_0)$ to (54), which is given by (55).*

In the following, we suppose that Proposition 1 holds true.

5.2.2. Controllability of System (54) in Banach Spaces

In this following, we discuss the exact (approximate) controllability of system (54) in Banach spaces. Some necessary and sufficient conditions are given.

Definition 24. *(a) Stochastic singular system (54) is said to be exactly controllable on $[0, b]$, if for all $x_0 \in L^2(\Omega, F_0, P, \overline{D_1})$, $x_b \in L^2(\Omega, F_b, P, \overline{D_1})$, there exists $v(t) \in L^2([0,b], \Omega, U)$, such that the mild solution $x(t, x_0)$ to (54) satisfies $x(T, x_0) = x_b$;*
(b) Stochastic singular system (54) is said to be approximately controllable on $[0, b]$, if for any state $x_b \in L^2(\Omega, F_b, P, \overline{D_1})$, any initial state $x_0 \in L^2(\Omega, F_0, P, \overline{D_1})$, and any $\epsilon > 0$, there exists a $v \in L^2([0,b], \Omega, U)$, such that the mild solution $x(t, x_0)$ satisfies

$$\|x(b, x_0) - x_b\|_{L^2(\Omega, F_{T_1}, P, \overline{D_1})} < \epsilon.$$

In order to discuss the controllability, we introduce the following concepts. Banach space $\{v(t) \in U : Cv(t) \in A(\overline{D_1})\}$ is still denoted by U. Controllability operator

$$C_0^b : L^2([0,b], \Omega, U) \to L^2(\Omega, F_b, P, \overline{D_1})$$

associated with system (54) is defined as

$$C_0^b v = \int_0^b U(b-\tau)Cv(\tau)d\tau.$$

It is obvious that operator C_0^b is a bounded linear operator, and its dual

$$C_0^{b*} : L^2(\Omega, F_b, P, (\overline{D_1})^*) \to L^2([0,b], \Omega, U^*)$$

is defined by

$$C_0^{b*} z^* = C^* U^*(b-\tau)E(z^*|F_\tau).$$

where $z^* \in L^2(\Omega, F_b, P, (\overline{D_1})^*)$.

The following results were obtained in [76].

Theorem 36 ([76]). *Stochastic singular system (54) is exactly controllable on $[0, b]$ if, and only if, $\mathrm{ran}(C_0^b) = L^2(\Omega, F_b, P, \overline{D_1})$.*

Theorem 37 ([76]). *Assume that H and U are reflexive Banach spaces. Stochastic singular system (54) is exactly controllable on $[0, b]$ if, and only if, one of the following conditions hold:*
(a) $\|C_0^{b*} z^*\|_{L^2([0,b], \Omega, U^*)} \geq \gamma \|z^*\|_{L^2(\Omega, F_b, P, (\overline{D_1})^*)}$ for some $\gamma > 0$ and all

$$z^* \in L^2(\Omega, F_T, P, (\overline{D_1})^*);$$

(b) $\ker(C_0^{b*}) = \{0\}$ *and* $\operatorname{ran}(C_0^{b*})$ *is closed.*

Theorem 38 ([76]). *Stochastic singular system (54) is approximately controllable on* $[0, b]$ *if, and only if,* $\overline{\operatorname{ran}(C_0^b)} = L^2(\Omega, F_b, P, \overline{D_1})$.

Theorem 39 ([76]). *Stochastic singular system (54) is approximate controllable on* $[0, b]$ *if, and only if,*
$$\ker(C_0^{b*}) = \{0\}.$$

See [76] (p. 908) for the illustrative example.

5.2.3. Controllability of System (54) in Hilbert Spaces

In this following, we discuss the exact (approximate) controllability of system (54) in Hilbert spaces. Some necessary and sufficient conditions are given. In order to discuss the controllability, we introduce the following operator.

Hilbert space $\{v(t) \in U : Cv(t) \in A(\overline{D_1})\}$ is still denoted by U.

Controllability Gramian operator $G_c^b : L^2(\Omega, F_b, P, \overline{D_1}) \to L^2(\Omega, F_b, P, \overline{D_1})$ in connection with stochastic descriptor linear system (54) is defined as

$$G_c^b z = \int_0^b S(b - t)CC^*S^*(b - t)E(z|F_t)dt.$$

The following results were obtained in [77].

Theorem 40 ([77]). *The necessary and sufficient condition for the stochastic singular linear system (54) to be exactly controllable on* $[0, b]$ *is that one of the following conditions is true:*
(a) $< G_c^b z, z >_{L^2(\Omega, F_b, P, \overline{D_1})} \geq \gamma \|z\|^2_{L^2(\Omega, F_b, P, \overline{D_1})}$ *for some* $\gamma > 0$ *and all* $z \in L^2(\Omega, F_b, P, \overline{D_1})$;
(b) $\lim_{\lambda \to 0^+} \|(\lambda I + G_c^b)^{-1} - (G_c^b)^{-1}\|_{B(L^2(\Omega, F_b, P, \overline{D_1})), L^2(\Omega, F_b, P, \overline{D_1}))} = 0$;
(c) $\lim_{\lambda \to 0^+} \|\lambda(\lambda I + G_c^b)^{-1}\|_{B(L^2(\Omega, F_b, P, \overline{D_1}), L^2(\Omega, F_b, P, \overline{D_1}))} = 0$;
(d) $\ker(C_0^{b*}) = \{0\}$ *and* $\operatorname{ran}(C_0^{b*})$ *is closed.*

Theorem 41 ([77]). *The necessary and sufficient condition for the stochastic singular linear system (54) to be approximately controllable on* $[0, b]$ *is that one of the following conditions is true:*
(a) $< G_c^b z, z >_{L^2(\Omega, F_b, P, \overline{D_1})} > 0$ *for all* $z \in L^2(\Omega, F_b, P, \overline{D_1}), z \neq 0$;
(b) $\lim_{\lambda \to 0^+} < \lambda(\lambda I + G_c^b)^{-1}x, z >_{L^2(\Omega, F_b, P, \overline{D_1})} = 0$ *for all* $x, z \in L^2(\Omega, F_b, P, \overline{D_1})$;
(c) $\lim_{\lambda \to 0^+} \|\lambda(\lambda I + G_c^b)^{-1}z\|_{L^2(\Omega, F_b, P, \overline{D_1})} = 0$ *for all* $z \in L^2(\Omega, F_b, P, \overline{D_1})$.

5.3. GE-Evolution Operator Method for a Class of Time-Varying Systems

In this subsection, we discuss the controllability of the following time varying stochastic singular linear system by using GE-evolution operator in Hilbert spaces,

$$Adx(t) = B(t)x(t)dt + C(t)v(t)dt + D(t)dw(t), x(0) = x_0, t \geq 0, \tag{56}$$

where $A \in B(H)$ is a deterministic and constant operator, $B(t) : \operatorname{dom}(B(t)) \subseteq H \to H$ is a linear operator (possibly unbounded), $B(t), C(t), D(t)$ are deterministic and time varying operators; $C(t) \in P([0, b], B(U, H)), D(t) \in P([0, b], B(Z, H))$; $x(t)$ is the state process valued in H, $v(t)$ is the control process in U, $w(t)$ is the stand Wiener process valued in Z, $x_0 \in L^2(\Omega, F_0, P, H)$ is a given random variable, H, U, Z are Hilbert spaces. This subsection is organized as follows. Firstly, the GE-evolution operator is introduced and the mild solution of (56) is obtained; Secondly, the controllability of (56) is discussed by GE-evolution operator in the sense of mild solution in Hilbert spaces.

5.3.1. GE-Evolution Operator and Mild Solution of System (56)

In the following, we discuss mild solution of time varying stochastic singular system (56) according to GE-evolution operator. First of all, we recall the GE-evolution operator, and then the mild solution of (56) is given.

Definition 25 ([78–80])**.** *Let* $\Delta(b) = \{(t,s) : 0 \le s \le t \le b\}$. $U(t,s) : \Delta(b) \to B(H)$ *is said to be a GE-evolution operator induced by A on $[0,b]$ if it has the following properties:*
(a) $U(t,s) = U(t,r)AU(r,s), 0 \le s \le r \le t \le b$;
(b) $U(s,s) = U_0, 0 \le s \le b$, where U_0 is a definite operator independent of s;
GE-evolution operator $U(t,s)$ is said to be strongly continuous on $[0,b]$ if it has the following property:
(c) $U(\cdot,s)$ is strongly continuous on $[s,b]$ and $U(t,\cdot)$ is strongly continuous on $[0,t]$;
GE-evolution operator $U(t,s)$ is said to be exponential bounded on $[0,b]$ if it has the following property:
(d) There exist $M \ge 1$ and $\omega > 0$, such that

$$\|U(t,s)\|_{B(H)} \le Me^{\omega(t-s)}, 0 \le s \le t \le b.$$

Definition 26 ([78–80])**.** *Assume that $U(t,s)$ is a strongly continuous and exponential bounded GE-evolution operator induced by A. If*

$$B(t)x = \lim_{h \to 0^+} \frac{AU(t+h,t)A - AU(t,t)A}{h} x, t \in [0,b],$$

for every $x \in D_0(t)$, where

$$D_0(t) = \{x : x \in \mathrm{dom}(B(t)) \subseteq H, U_0 Ax = x,$$

$$\exists \lim_{h \to 0^+} \frac{AU(t+h,t)A - AU(t,t)A}{h} x, t \in [0,b]\},$$

then $B(t)$ is called a generator of GE-evolution operator $U(t,s)$.

In the following, we always assume that $B(t)$ is the generator of GE-evolution operator $U(t,s)$ induced by A and $D_0(t) = D_0$ is independent of t.
Now, we consider the initial value problem (56).

Definition 27. *If $x_0 \in L^2(\Omega, F_0, P, \overline{D_0})$, $v(t) \in L^2([0,T], \Omega, U)$; $C(t)v(t), D(t)dw(t) \in A(L^2([0,b], \Omega, \overline{D_0}))$, the mild solution $x(t, x_0)$ to (56) is defined by*

$$x(t, x_0) = U(t,0)Ax_0 + \int_0^t U(t,\tau)C(\tau)v(\tau)d\tau + \int_0^t U(t,\tau)D(\tau)dw(\tau). \tag{57}$$

Proposition 2 ([80])**.** *There exists unique mild solution $x(t, x_0)$ to (56), which is given by (57), if $v(t) \in L^2([0,b], \Omega, U)$, $x_0 \in L^2(\Omega, F_0, P, \overline{D_0})$; $C(t)v(t), D(t)dw(t) \in A(L^2([0,b], \Omega, \overline{D_0}))$, and $(U_0 B(t))|_{D_0}$ satisfies the following assumptions:*
(P_1) For $t \in [0,b]$, $(\lambda I + (U_0 B(t))|_{D_0})^{-1}$ exists for all λ with $\mathrm{Re}\lambda \le 0$ and there is a constant $M > 0$, such that

$$\|(\lambda I + (U_0 B(t))|_{D_0})^{-1}\|_{B(H)} \le \frac{M}{|\lambda| + 1},$$

for all $\mathrm{Re}\lambda \le 0, t \in [0,b]$.
(P_2) There exist constants $L > 0$ and $0 < \alpha \le 1$, such that

$$\|((U_0 B(t))|_{D_0} - (U_0 B(s))|_{D_0})((U_0 B(\tau))|_{D_0})^{-1}\|_{B(H)} \le L|t-s|^\alpha,$$

for $t, s, \tau \in [0,b]$.

In the following, we suppose that Proposition 2 holds true.

5.3.2. Controllability of System (56)

In this part, the exact controllability and approximate controllability of system (56) are discussed by using GE-evolution operator in the sense of mild solution in Hilbert spaces. In order to discuss the controllability, we introduce the following concepts.

Hilbert space $\{v(t) \in U : C(t)v(t) \in A(\overline{D_0})\}$ is still denoted by U.

Controllability operator $C_0^T : L^2([0,b], \Omega, U) \to L^2(\Omega, F_b, P, \overline{D_0})$ and Controllability Gramian $G_c^b : L^2(\Omega, F_b, P, \overline{D_0}) \to L^2(\Omega, F_b, P, \overline{D_0})$ associated with system (56) are defined as

$$C_0^b v = \int_0^b U(T, \tau) C(\tau) v(\tau) d\tau,$$

$$G_c^b z = \int_0^b U(b, \tau) C(\tau) C^*(\tau) U^*(b, \tau) E(z|F_\tau) d\tau,$$

respectively. It is obvious that operators C_0^b and G_c^b are bounded linear operators, and the dual

$$C_0^{b*} : L^2(\Omega, F_b, P, \overline{D_0}) \to L^2([0,b], \Omega, U)$$

of C_0^b is defined by $C_0^{b*} z = C^*(\tau) U^*(b, \tau) E(z|F_\tau)$, where $z \in L^2(\Omega, F_b, P, \overline{D_0})$ and

$$G_c^b = C_0^b C_0^{b*}.$$

Definition 28. *(a) Time varying stochastic singular system (56) is said to be exactly controllable on* $[0,b]$, *if for all* $x_0 \in L^2(\Omega, F_0, P, \overline{D_0})$, $x_b \in L^2(\Omega, F_b, P, \overline{D_0})$, *there exists* $v(t) \in L^2([0,b], \Omega, U)$, *such that the mild solution* $x(t, x_0)$ *to (56) satisfies* $x(T, x_0) = x_b$;

(b) Time varying stochastic singular system (56) is said to be approximately controllable on $[0,b]$, *if for any state* $x_b \in L^2(\Omega, F_b, P, \overline{D_0})$, *any initial state* $x_0 \in L^2(\Omega, F_0, P, \overline{D_0})$, *and any* $\epsilon > 0$, *there exists a* $v \in L^2([0,b], \Omega, U)$, *such that the mild solution* $x(t, x_0)$ *to (56) satisfies*

$$\|x(b, x_0) - x_b\|_{L^2(\Omega, F_b, P, \overline{D_0})} < \epsilon.$$

The following results were obtained in [80].

Theorem 42 ([80]). *The necessary and sufficient conditions for time-varying stochastic singular system (56) to be exactly controllable on* $[0, b]$ *are* $\mathrm{ran} C_0^b = L^2(\Omega, F_b, P, \overline{D_0})$.

Theorem 43 ([80]). *Time varying stochastic singular system (56) is exactly controllable on* $[0, b]$ *if, and only if, one of the following conditions is true:*
(a) $< G_c^b z, z >_{L^2(\Omega, F_b, P, \overline{D_0})} \geq \gamma \|z\|^2_{L^2(\Omega, F_b, P, \overline{D_0})}$ *for some* $\gamma > 0$ *and all*

$$z \in L^2(\Omega, F_b, P, \overline{D_0});$$

(b) $\lim_{\lambda \to 0+} \|(\lambda I + G_c^T)^{-1} - (G_c^T)^{-1}\|_{L(L^2(\Omega, F_b, P, \overline{D_0}), L^2(\Omega, F_b, P, \overline{D_0}))} = 0$;
(c) $\lim_{\lambda \to 0+} \|\lambda(\lambda I + G_c^T)^{-1}\|_{L(L^2(\Omega, F_b, P, \overline{D_0}), L^2(\Omega, F_b, P, \overline{D_0}))} = 0$;
(d) $\|C_0^{b*} z\|_{L^2([0,b], \Omega, U)} \geq \gamma \|z\|_{L^2(\Omega, F_b, P, \overline{D_0})}$ *for some* $\gamma > 0$ *and all* $z \in L^2(\Omega, F_b, P, \overline{D_0})$;
(e) $\ker(C_0^{b*}) = \{0\}$ *and* $\mathrm{ran}(C_0^{b*})$ *is closed.*

Theorem 44 ([80]). *The necessary and sufficient conditions for time varying stochastic singular system (56) to be approximately controllable on* $[0, T]$ *are that one of the following conditions is true:*
(a) $< G_c^b z, z >_{L^2(\Omega, F_b, P, \overline{D_0})} > 0$ *for all* $z \in L^2(\Omega, F_b, P, \overline{D_0}), z \neq 0$;
(b) $\lim_{\lambda \to 0+} < \lambda(\lambda I + G_c^T)^{-1} x, z >_{L^2(\Omega, F_b, P, \overline{D_0})} = 0$ *for all* $x, z \in L^2(\Omega, F_b, P, \overline{D_0})$;
(c) $\lim_{\lambda \to 0+} \|\lambda(\lambda I + G_c^T)^{-1} z\|_{L^2(\Omega, F_b, P, \overline{D_0})} = 0$ *for all* $z \in L^2(\Omega, F_b, P, \overline{D_0})$;
(d) $\ker(C_0^{b*}) = \{0\}$.

The details of applicable example can be found in [80].

5.4. Stochastic GE-Evolution Operator Method for a Class of Time Invariant Systems

In this subsection, we discuss the controllability of the following time varying stochastic singular linear system by using stochastic GE-evolution operator in Banach spaces,

$$Adx(t) = Bx(t)dt + Cv(t)dt + Dx(t)dw(t), t \geq 0, x(0) = x_0, \tag{58}$$

where $x(t)$ is the state process valued in H, $v(t)$ is the control process valued in U, $w(t)$ is the one-dimensional standard Wiener process, $x_0 \in L^2(\Omega, F_0, P, H)$ is a given random variable, H, U are Banach spaces; $A, D \in B(H), C \in B(U, H), B : \text{dom}(B) \subseteq H \to H$ is a linear operator. The organization of this subsection is as follows. Firstly, the concept of stochastic GE-evolution operator is introduced, and the mild solution to system (58) is given by stochastic GE-evolution operator. Secondly, The exact controllability and approximate controllability of (58) are discussed by stochastic GE-evolution operator in the sense of mild solution in Banach spaces, respectively.

5.4.1. Stochastic GE-Evolution Operator and Mild Solution of System (58)

In the following, the stochastic GE-evolution operator is introduced, and the mild solution of system (58) is give by stochastic GE-evolution operator.

Definition 29 ([81])**.** *Let $\Delta_b = \{(t,s) : 0 \leq s \leq t \leq b\}$. A family of stochastic operators $\{S(t,s) : (t,s) \in \Delta_b\}$ on H is said to be a stochastic GE-evolution operator induced by A on $[0,b]$ if it has the following properties:*
(i) $S : \Delta_b \times \Omega \to B(H)$ is strongly measurable;
(ii) $S(t,s)$ is strongly F_t−measurable for $t \geq s$;
(iii) $S(s,s) = S_0, 0 \leq s \leq b$, and $S(t,r)AS(r,s) = S(t,s)$ for any $0 \leq s \leq r \leq t \leq b$, where $S_0 \in B(H)$ is a steady operator independent of s;
(iv) For any $\xi \in H, (t,s) \to S(t,s)\xi$ is mean square continuous from Δ_T into H.

In the following, we always suppose that B is a generator of GE-semigroup $U(t)$ induced by A.

Now, we consider the mild solution of stochastic singular linear system (58).

Definition 30. *If $v(t) \in L^2([0,b], \Omega, U), x_0 \in L^2(\Omega, F_0, P, \overline{D_1})$, then the mild solution $x(t, x_0) \in L^2([0,b], \{F_t\}, \overline{D_1})$ to (58) is defined by*

$$x(t, x_0) = U(t)Ax_0 + \int_0^t U(t - \tau)Cv(\tau)d\tau + \int_0^t U(t - \tau)Dx(\tau, x_0)dw(\tau), \tag{59}$$

where $L^2([0,b], \{F_t\}, \overline{D_1})$ denotes the Banach space of all $\overline{D_1}$−valued processes x with norm

$$\|x\|_{L^2([0,b], \{F_t\}, \overline{D_1})} = \sup_{t \in [0,b]} (E\|x(t)\|_{\overline{D_1}}^2)^{1/2} < +\infty.$$

Lemma 2 ([81])**.** *If $v(t) \in L^2([0,b], \Omega, U), x_0 \in L^2(\Omega, F_0, P, \overline{D_1})$;*

$$Cv(t) \in A(L^2([0,b], \Omega, \overline{D_1})),$$

then system (58) has a unique mild solution $x(t, x_0) \in L^2([0,b], \{F_t\}, \overline{D_1})$, which is given by (59).

Definition 31. *We say that stochastic GE-evolution operator $S(t,s)$ induced by A is related to the linear homogeneous equation*

$$Adx(t) = Bx(t)dt + Dx(t)dw(t), x(s) = x_0, 0 \leq s \leq t \leq b, \tag{60}$$

if $x(t) = S(t,s)Ax_0$ is the mild solution to (60) with $x(s) = S(s,s)Ax_0 = x_0$ for arbitrary $x_0 \in L^2(\Omega, F_0, P, \overline{D_1})$.

In the following, we suppose that there exists a stochastic GE-evolution operator $S(t,s)$ induced by A related to (60) and Lemma 2 holds true. Furthermore, we suppose that the following estimates hold for any $0 \le s \le t \le b$ and $\xi \in L^2(\Omega, F_s, P, \overline{D_1})$:

$$E \int_s^t \|S(r,s)\xi\|_{\overline{D_1}}^2 dr \le c\|\xi\|_{L^2(\Omega, F_s, P, \overline{D_1})}^2;$$

$$\sup_{r \in [s,t]} E\|S(r,s)\xi\|_{\overline{D_1}}^2 \le c\|\xi\|_{L^2(\Omega, F_s, P, \overline{D_1})}^2.$$

We can obtain the following theorem.

Theorem 45 ([81]). *The mild solution $x(t, x_0)$ to (58) can be written in the form*

$$x(t, x_0) = S(t,0)Ax_0 + \int_0^t S(t,s)Cv(s)ds. \tag{61}$$

5.4.2. Controllability of System (58)

In the following, we discuss the exact and approximate controllability of stochastic singular linear system (58) by using stochastic GE-evolution operator theory, some criteria are obtained. In order to discuss the controllability, we introduce the following concepts.

Banach space $\{v(t) \in U : Cv(t) \in A(\overline{D_1})\}$ is still denoted by U.

Controllability operator $C_0^b : L^2([0,b], \Omega, U) \to L^2(\Omega, F_b, P, \overline{D_1})$ associated with system (58) is defined as

$$C_0^b v = \int_0^b S(T,\tau)Cv(\tau)d\tau.$$

It is obvious that operator C_0^b is a bounded linear operator, and the dual

$$C_0^{b*} : L^2(\Omega, F_b, P, \overline{D_0}) \to L^2([0,b], \Omega, U)$$

of C_0^b is defined by $C_0^{b*}z = C^*S^*(b,\tau)E(z|F_\tau)$, where $z \in L^2(\Omega, F_b, P, \overline{D_1})$.

Definition 32. *(a) Stochastic singular linear system (58) is called to be exactly controllable on $[0,b]$, if for all $x_0 \in L^2(\Omega, F_0, P, \overline{D_1})$, $x_b \in L^2(\Omega, F_b, P, \overline{D_1})$, there exists $v(t) \in L^2([0,b], \Omega, U)$, such that the mild solution $x(t, x_0)$ to stochastic singular linear system (58) which is given by (61) satisfies $x(T, x_0) = x_b$;*

(b) Stochastic singular linear system (58) is called to be approximately controllable on $[0,b]$, if for any state $x_b \in L^2(\Omega, F_b, P, \overline{D_1})$, any initial state $x_0 \in L^2(\Omega, F_0, P, \overline{D_1})$, and any $\epsilon > 0$, existence $v \in L^2([0,b], \Omega, U)$ makes that the mild solution $x(t, x_0)$ which is given by (61) satisfies

$$\|x(b, x_0) - x_b\|_{L^2(\Omega, F_b, P, \overline{D_1})} < \epsilon.$$

The following results were obtained in [81].

Theorem 46 ([81]). *Stochastic singular system (58) is exactly controllable on $[0,b]$ if, and only if, $\mathrm{ran}(C_0^b) = L^2(\Omega, F_b, P, \overline{D_1})$.*

Theorem 47 ([81]). *Assume that H and U are reflexive Banach spaces. Stochastic singular system (58) is exactly controllable on $[0,b]$ if and only if one of the following conditions holds:*
(a) $\|C_0^{b*}z^*\|_{L^2([0,b],\Omega,U^*)} \ge \gamma\|z^*\|_{L^2(\Omega,F_b,P,(\overline{D_1})^*)}$ for some $\gamma > 0$ and all

$$z^* \in L^2(\Omega, F_b, P, (\overline{D_1})^*);$$

(b) $\ker(C_0^{b*}) = \{0\}$ and $\mathrm{ran}(C_0^{b*})$ is closed.

Theorem 48 ([81]). *The necessary and sufficient condition for the stochastic singular linear system (58) to be approximately controllable on* $[0, b]$ *is* $\overline{\mathrm{ran}(C_0^b)} = L^2(\Omega, F_b, P, \overline{D_1})$.

Theorem 49 ([81]). *Stochastic singular systems (58) is approximate controllable on* $[0, b]$ *if, and only if, one of the following conditions holds:*
(a) $\|C_0^{b*} z^*\|_{L^2([0,b],\Omega,U^*)} > 0$ *for all* $z^* \in L^2(\Omega, F_b, P, (\overline{D_1})^*), z^* \neq 0$;
(b) $\ker(C_0^{b*}) = \{0\}$.

The practical example can be found in [81] if there is a need.

5.5. Stochastic GE-Evolution Operator Method for a Class of Time-Varying Systems

In this subsection, we study the controllability and observability of the following time varying stochastic singular linear system by using stochastic GE-evolution operator in Banach spaces,

$$O_1 dv(t) = O_2(t)v(t)dt + O_3(t)u(t)dt + O_4(t)v(t)dw(t), t \geq 0, v(0) = v_0,$$

$$x(t) = O_5(t)v(t), \tag{62}$$

where $v(t)$ is the state process valued in Y_1, $u(t)$ is the control process valued in Y_2, $w(t)$ is the one-dimensional standard Wiener process, $v_0 \in L^2(\Omega, F_0, P, Y_1)$ is a given random variable, $x(t)$ is the output process valued in Y_3, Y_1, Y_2, Y_3 are Banach spaces;

$$O_1 \in B(Y_1), O_3(t) \in P([0, T], B(Y_2, Y_1)), O_4(t) \in P([0, b], B(Y_1)),$$

$O_5(t) \in P([0, b], B(Y_1, Y_3)), O_2(t)$ is a linear operator from $\mathrm{dom}(O_2(t)) \subseteq Y_1$ to Y_1; $O_1, O_2(t)$, $O_3(t), O_4(t), O_5(t)$ are deterministic and constant operators; This subsection is organized as follows. Firstly, the mild solution of (62) is obtained by stochastic GE-evolution operator; Secondly, the exact controllability of (62) is discussed by using stochastic GE-evolution operator in the sense of mild solution in Banach spaces; Thirdly, the approximate controllability of (62) is discussed by using stochastic GE-evolution operator in the sense of mild solution in Banach spaces; Fourthly, the observability of (62) is studied, and the dual principle is given; At last, we give an example to illustrate the validity of the theoretical results obtained in this subsection.

5.5.1. Mild Solution of System (62)

In this part, we always suppose that $O_2(t)$ is a generator of GE-evolution operator $V(t, s)$ induced by O_1 and

$$D = \{v \in \mathrm{dom}O_2(t) \subseteq Y_1, V_0 O_1 v = v,$$

$$\exists \lim_{h \to 0^+} \frac{O_1 V(t + h, t)O_1 - O_1 V(t, t)O_1}{h} v, 0 \leq t \leq b\}$$

is independent of $t, 0 \leq t \leq b$.

Now, we consider the mild solution of time varying stochastic singular linear Equation (62).

Definition 33. *If* $u(t) \in L^2([0, b], \Omega, Y_2), v_0 \in L^2(\Omega, F_0, P, \overline{D})$, *then the mild solution* $v(t, v_0) \in L^2([0, b], \{F_t\}, \overline{D})$ *to time varying stochastic singular Equation (62) is defined by*

$$v(t, v_0) = V(t, 0)O_1 v_0 + \int_0^t V(t, \tau)O_3(\tau)u(\tau)d\tau + \int_0^t V(t, \tau)O_4(\tau)v(\tau, v_0)dw(\tau). \tag{63}$$

Lemma 3. *Time varying stochastic singular Equation (62) has a unique mild solution, which is given by (63), if* $u(t) \in L^2([0,b], \Omega, Y_2), v_0 \in L^2(\Omega, F_0, P, \overline{D})$;

$$O_3(t)u(t) \in O_1(L^2([0,b], \Omega, \overline{D})),$$

and $(V_0O_2(t))|_D$ *satisfies following assumptions:*

(P_1) For $t \in [0,b], (\lambda I + (V_0O_2(t))|_D)^{-1}$ *exists for all* λ *with* $\mathrm{Re}\lambda \leq 0$ *and there is a constant M, such that*

$$\|(\lambda I + (V_0O_2(t))|_D)^{-1}\|_{B(Y_1)} \leq \frac{M}{|\lambda| + 1},$$

for all $\mathrm{Re}\lambda \leq 0, t \in [0,b]$, *where I denotes the identical operator on D,* $(V_0O_2(t))|_D$ *denotes the restriction of* $V_0O_2(t)$ *on D.*

(P_2) There exist constants L and $0 < \alpha \leq 1$, *such that*

$$\|((V_0O_2(t))|_D - (V_0O_2(s))|_D)((V_0O_2(\tau))|_D)^{-1}\|_{B(Y_1)} \leq L|t-s|^\alpha,$$

for $s, t, \tau \in [0,b]$.

Proof. First of all, according to Theorem 6.1 of [82] (see P.150 of [82]), we have that $V(t,s)|_{O_1(\overline{D})}$ is a unique evolution operator induced by O_1 with generator $O_2(t)$ on $O_1(\overline{D})$. Let Y_{11} denote the space of all $\overline{D}$ valued processes ξ, such that

$$|\xi|_{Y_{11}} = \sup_{t \in [0,b]} (E\|\xi(t)\|_{\overline{D}}^2)^{1/2} < +\infty.$$

For any $\xi(t) \in Y_{11}$ define

$$P_1(\xi)(t) = V(t,0)O_1v_0 + \int_0^t V(t,s)O_3(s)u(s)ds$$

$$+ \int_0^t V(t,s)O_4(s)\xi(s)dw(s), t \in [0,b],$$

and

$$P_2(\xi)(t) = \int_0^t V(t,s)O_4(s)\xi(s)dw(s), t \in [0,b].$$

Assume, see (d) of Definition 25, that $\|V(t,s)\|_{B(Y_1)} \leq M_1, 0 \leq s \leq t \leq b$, we have

$$|P_2(\xi)|_{Y_{11}} \leq \sup_{t \in [0,b]} (E \int_0^t \|V(t,s)O_4(s)\xi(s)\|_{\overline{D}}^2 ds)^{1/2}$$

$$\leq M_1\|O_4(s)\|_{P([0,b],B(Y_1))} b^{1/2} |\xi|_{Y_{11}}, t \in [0,b].$$

Therefore, if b is sufficient small, P_1 is a contraction and it is easy to see that its unique fixed point can be identified as the mild solution to time varying stochastic singular Equation (62). The case of general b can be handled in a standard way. $\square$

Theorem 50. *Suppose that stochastic GE-evolution operator* $G(t,s)$ *induced by* O_1 *is related to the linear homogeneous time varying stochastic singular equation*

$$O_1 dv(t) = O_2(t)v(t)dt + O_4(t)v(t)dw(t), v(s) = v_0, 0 \leq s \leq t \leq b, \tag{64}$$

Lemma 3 holds true, and the following estimates hold for any $0 \leq s \leq t \leq b$ *and* $\xi \in L^2(\Omega, F_s, P, \overline{D})$:

$$E \int_s^t \|G(r,s)\xi\|_{\overline{D}}^2 dr \leq c\|\xi\|_{L^2(\Omega, F_s, P, \overline{D})}^2;$$

$$\sup_{r \in [s,t]} E\|G(r,s)\xi\|_{\overline{D_1}}^2 \leq c\|\xi\|_{L^2(\Omega, F_s, P, \overline{D})}^2.$$

Then, the mild solution $v(t, v_0)$ to time varying stochastic singular Equation (62) can be written in the form

$$v(t, v_0) = G(t, 0)O_1 v_0 + \int_0^t G(t, s)O_3(s)u(s)ds. \tag{65}$$

Proof. Since $G(t, 0)O_1 v_0$ and $G(t, s)O_3(s)u(s)$ are mild solutions of time varying stochastic singular Equation (64) with $v(0) = v_0$ and $v(s) = G(s, s)O_3(s)u(s)$, respectively, we have that

$$G(t, 0)O_1 v_0 = V(t, 0)O_1 v_0 + \int_0^t V(t, \tau)O_4(\tau)G(\tau, 0)O_1 v_0 dw(\tau),$$

$$G(t, s)O_3(s)u(s) = V(t, s)O_1 G(s, s)O_3(s)u(s) + \int_s^t V(t, \tau)O_4(\tau)G(\tau, s)O_3(s)u(s)dw(\tau)$$

$$= V(t, s)O_3(s)u(s) + \int_s^t V(t, \tau)O_4(\tau)G(\tau, s)O_3(s)u(s)dw(\tau).$$

We have to prove that the process $v(t, v_0)$ in (65) is a solution to the integral Equation (63). By the representation of $v(\tau, v_0)$, we have

$$\int_0^t V(t, \tau)O_4(\tau)v(\tau, v_0)dw(\tau) = \int_0^t V(t, \tau)O_4(\tau)G(\tau, 0)O_1 v_0 dw(\tau)$$

$$+ \int_0^t V(t, \tau)O_4 D(\tau)(\int_0^\tau G(\tau, s)O_3(s)u(s)ds)dw(\tau)$$

$$= G(t, 0)O_1 v_0 - V(t, 0)O_1 v_0 + \int_0^t ds \int_s^t V(t, \tau)O_4(\tau)G(\tau, s)O_3(s)u(s)dw(\tau)$$

$$= G(t, 0)O_1 v_0 - V(t, 0)O_1 v_0 + \int_0^t [G(t, s)O_3(s)u(s) - V(t, s)O_1 G(s, s)O_3(s)u(s)]ds$$

$$= G(t, 0)O_1 v_0 - V(t, 0)O_1 v_0 + \int_0^t G(t, s)O_3(s)u(s)ds - \int_0^t V(t, s)O_3(s)u(s)ds,$$

where the stochastic Fubini theorem is given in Theorem 4.33 of [83]. Therefore,

$$v(t, v_0) = G(t, 0)O_1 v_0 + \int_0^t G(t, s)O_3(s)u(s)ds$$

$$= V(t, 0)O_1 v_0 + \int_0^t V(t, \tau)O_3(\tau)u(\tau)d\tau + \int_0^t V(t, \tau)O_4(\tau)v(\tau, v_0)dw(\tau),$$

which proves (63). $\square$

In the following, we always assume that time varying stochastic singular Equation (62) has a unique mild solution in the form of (65).

In order to obtain the criteria of controllability, the following concepts are introduced. Banach space $\{u(t) \in Y_2 : O_3(t)u(t) \in O_1(\overline{D})\}$ is still denoted by Y_2. Controllability operator

$$Q_C^b : L^2([0, b], \Omega, Y_2) \to L^2(\Omega, F_b, P, \overline{D})$$

associated with time varying stochastic singular Equation (62) is defined as

$$Q_C^b u = \int_0^T G(T, \tau)O_3(\tau)u(\tau)d\tau.$$

It is obvious that operator Q_C^b is a bounded linear operator, and its dual

$$Q_C^{b*} : L^2(\Omega, F_b, P, (\overline{D})^*) \to L^2([0, b], \Omega, Y_2^*)$$

is defined by

$$Q_C^{b*} y^* = O_3^*(\tau) G^*(b, \tau) E(y^* | F_\tau).$$

where $y^* \in L^2(\Omega, F_b, P, (\overline{D})^*)$.

5.5.2. Exact Controllability of System (62)

In this part, we discuss the exact controllability of time varying stochastic singular Equation (62) by stochastic GE-evolution operator theory, some criteria are obtained.

Definition 34. *Time varying stochastic singular Equation (62) is called to be exactly controllable on* $[0, b]$, *if for all* $v_0 \in L^2(\Omega, F_0, P, \overline{D})$, $v_b \in L^2(\Omega, F_b, P, \overline{D})$, *there exists* $u(t) \in L^2([0, b], \Omega, Y_2)$, *such that the mild solution* $v(t, v_0)$ *to time varying stochastic singular Equation (62) satisfies* $v(b, v_0) = v_b$.

From the Definition 34, we can obtain the following theorem immediately.

Theorem 51. *Time varying stochastic singular Equation (62) is exactly controllable on* $[0, b]$ *if, and only if,* $\mathrm{ran}(Q_C^b) = L^2(\Omega, F_b, P, \overline{D})$.

Theorem 52. *Assume that* Y_1 *and* Y_2 *are reflexive Banach spaces. Time varying stochastic singular Equation (62) is exactly controllable on* $[0, b]$ *if, and only if, one of the following conditions holds:*
(a) $\|Q_C^{b*} y^*\|_{L^2([0,b],\Omega,Y_2^*)} \geq \gamma \|y^*\|_{L^2(\Omega,F_b,P,(\overline{D})^*)}$ *for some* $\gamma > 0$ *and all*

$$y^* \in L^2(\Omega, F_b, P, (\overline{D})^*);$$

(b) $\ker(Q_C^{b*}) = \{0\}$ *and* $\mathrm{ran}(Q_C^{b*})$ *is closed.*

Proof. (a) $\Rightarrow$ (b) Notice that (a) implies that Q_C^{b*} is injective. To prove that Q_C^{b*} has closed range, assume that $Q_C^{b*} y_n^*$ is a Cauchy sequence in $L^2([0, b], \Omega, Y_2^*)$, then (a) implies that y_n^* is a Cauchy sequence in $L^2(\Omega, F_b, P, (\overline{D})^*)$. Since Q_C^{b*} is a bounded linear operator, if $\lim_{n \to +\infty} y_n^* = y^*$, then $\lim_{n \to +\infty} Q_C^{b*} y_n^* = Q_C^{b*} y^*$ and so Q_C^{b*} has closed range.
(b)$\Rightarrow$(a). (b) shows that Q_C^{b*} has an algebraic inverse with domain equal to $\mathrm{ran}(Q_C^{b*})$. Since $\mathrm{ran}(Q_C^{b*})$ is closed, it is a Banach space under the norm of $L^2([0, b], \Omega, Y_2^*)$, i.e.,

$$\|u^*\|_{\mathrm{ran}(Q_C^{b*})} = \|u^*\|_{L^2([0,b],\Omega,Y_2^*)}, u^* \in \mathrm{ran}(Q_C^{b*}).$$

By Corollary A.3.50 of [84], we have that $(Q_C^{b*})^{-1}$ is bounded on this range, i.e., there exists a $\gamma > 0$, such that

$$\|(Q_C^{b*})^{-1} u^*\|_{L^2(\Omega,F_b,P,(\overline{D})^*)} \leq \frac{1}{\gamma} \|u^*\|_{L^2([0,b],\Omega,Y_2^*)},$$

for every $u^* \in \mathrm{ran}(Q_C^{b*})$. Substituting $u^* = C_0^{T*} y^*$ proves (a).
It remains to show that (a) is equivalent to exact controllability of time varying stochastic singular Equation (62).
Necessity. Assume that time varying stochastic singular Equation (62) is exactly controllable. By Theorem 51, we have $\mathrm{ran}(Q_C^b) = L^2(\Omega, F_b, P, \overline{D})$.
If Q_C^b is a one to one operator, then $(Q_C^b)^{-1}$ exists on $L^2(\Omega, F_b, P, \overline{D})$. According to the continuity of operator Q_C^b we have that $(Q_C^b)^{-1}$ is a closed operator. From the closed graph theorem, we obtain that $(Q_C^b)^{-1}$ is a bounded linear operator on $L^2(\Omega, F_b, P, \overline{D})$, i.e.,

$$(Q_C^b)^{-1} \in B(L^2(\Omega, F_b, P, \overline{D}), L^2([0, b], \Omega, Y_2)).$$

Therefore

$$((Q_C^b)^{-1})^* \in B(L^2([0,b],\Omega,Y_2^*), L^2(\Omega,F_b,P,(\overline{D})^*)).$$

This implies that there exists $\gamma_b > 0$, such that

$$\|((Q_C^b)^{-1})^* v^*\|_{L^2(\Omega,F_b,P,(\overline{D})^*)} \le \gamma_b \|v^*\|_{L^2([0,b],\Omega,Y_2^*)}. \tag{66}$$

Assume $y^* \in L^2(\Omega,F_b,P,(\overline{D})^*)$, then

$$u^* = Q_C^{b*} y^* \in L^2([0,b],\Omega,Y_2^*).$$

Therefore, for all $y_0 \in L^2(\Omega,F_b,P,\overline{D})$, we find that

$$< y_0, ((Q_C^b)^{-1})^* u^* >=< y_0, ((Q_C^b)^{-1})^* Q_C^{b*} y^* >$$

$$=< (Q_C^T)^{-1} y_0, Q_C^{T*} y^* >=< y_0, y^* >,$$

where $< y_0, y^* >= y^*(y_0)$. From (66), we obtain that

$$\|y^*\|_{L^2(\Omega,F_b,P,(\overline{D})^*)} = \sup_{\|y_0\|_{L^2(\Omega,F_b,P,\overline{D})}=1} | < y_0, y^* > |$$

$$\le \|((Q_C^b)^{-1})^* u^*\|_{L^2(\Omega,F_b,P,(\overline{D})^*)}$$

$$\le \gamma_b \|u^*\|_{L^2([0,b],\Omega,Y_2^*)} = \gamma_b \|Q_C^{b*} y^*\|_{L^2([0,b],\Omega,Y_2^*)},$$

i.e.,

$$\|Q_C^{b*} y^*\|_{L^2([0,b],\Omega,Y_2^*)} \ge \frac{1}{\gamma_b} \|y^*\|^2_{L^2(\Omega,F_b,P,(\overline{D})^*)}$$

$$= \gamma \|y^*\|_{L^2(\Omega,F_b,P,(\overline{D})^*)},$$

where $\gamma = \frac{1}{\gamma_b}$. This implies that (a) holds.

If Q_C^b is not a one to one operator, then

$$\ker(Q_C^b) = \{u : u \in L^2([0,b],\Omega,Y_2), Q_C^b u = 0\} \ne \{0\}.$$

A factor space is defined as follows

$$Y_{21} = L^2([0,b],\Omega,Y_2)/\ker(Q_C^b) = \{u_1 : u_1 = \{u + u_2 : u_2 \in \ker(Q_C^b)\}\}.$$

For $u_1 \in Y_{21}$,

$$\|u_1\|_{Y_{21}} = \inf_{u_2 \in \ker(Q_C^b)} \|u + u_2\|_{L^2([0,b],\Omega,Y_2)}.$$

If we define operator

$$Q_1^b : Y_{21} \to L^2(\Omega,F_b,P,\overline{D}), Q_1^b u_1 = Q_C^b u,$$

then

$$Q_1^b \in B(Y_{21}, L^2(\Omega,F_b,P,\overline{D})),$$

and Q_1^b is a bijective operator. It can be seen from the above proof that

$$\|Q_1^{b*} y^*\|_{Y_{21}^*} \ge \gamma \|y^*\|^2_{L^2(\Omega,F_b,P,(\overline{D})^*)}.$$

According to the definition of Y_{21} and Q_1^b, we obtain

$$\|Q_1^{b*} y^*\|_{Y_{21}^*} = \|Q_C^{b*} y^*\|_{L^2([0,b],\Omega,Y_2^*)}.$$

This implies that (a) holds.

Sufficiency. Assume (a). It is need to prove that if $y \in L^2(\Omega, F_b, P, \overline{D})$, then $y \in \mathrm{ran}Q_C^b$.

From

$$Q_C^b \in B(L^2([0,b], \Omega, Y_2), L^2(\Omega, F_b, P, \overline{D})),$$

we find that

$$Q_C^{b*} \in B(L^2(\Omega, F_b, P, (\overline{D})^*), L^2([0,b], \Omega, Y_2^*)).$$

For $y \in L^2(\Omega, F_b, P, \overline{D})$, we can define a functional f on $\mathrm{ran}Q_C^{b*}$ satisfying

$$f(Q_C^{b*}g^*) = <y, g^*>, g^* \in L^2(\Omega, F_b, P, (\overline{D})^*). \tag{67}$$

This implies that f is linear for $Q_C^{b*}g^*$. According to (a), if

$$\lim_{n \to \infty} Q_C^{b*} g_n^* = 0,$$

then

$$\lim_{n \to \infty} g_n^* = 0,$$

and

$$\lim_{n \to \infty} f(Q_C^{b*} g_n^*) = \lim_{n \to \infty} <y, g_n^*> = 0.$$

Therefore, f is continuous linear functional on

$$\mathrm{ran}(Q_C^{b*}) \subset L^2([0,b], \Omega, Y_2^*).$$

By Hahn–Banach theorem, we have that f can be extended as a continuous linear functional on $L^2([0,b], \Omega, Y_2^*)$. According to $Y_2^{**} = Y_2$, the existence of

$$u \in L^2([0,b], \Omega, Y_2) = L^2([0,b], \Omega, Y_2^{**})$$

makes

$$f(Q_C^{b*}g^*) = <u, Q_C^{b*}g^*>, g^* \in L^2(\Omega, F_b, P, (\overline{D})^*). \tag{68}$$

According to (67) and (68), we obtain that for every $g^* \in L^2(\Omega, F_b, P, (\overline{D})^*)$,

$$<y, g^*> = <Q_C^b u, g^*> .$$

Hence $y = Q_C^b u$, i.e.,

$$\mathrm{ran}(Q_C^b) = L^2(\Omega, F_b, P, \overline{D}).$$

From Theorem 51, time varying stochastic singular Equation (62) is exactly controllable. $\square$

5.5.3. Approximate Controllability of System (62)

In this section, we discuss the approximate controllability of time varying stochastic singular Equation (62). Some necessary and sufficient conditions are obtained.

Definition 35. *Time varying stochastic singular Equation (62) is called to be approximately controllable on $[0,b]$, if for any state $v_b \in L^2(\Omega, F_b, P, \overline{D})$, any initial state $v_0 \in L^2(\Omega, F_0, P, \overline{D})$, and any $\epsilon > 0$, existence $u \in L^2([0,b], \Omega, Y_2)$ makes that the mild solution $v(t, v_0)$ to time varying stochastic singular Equation (62) satisfies*

$$\|v(b, v_0) - v_b\|_{L^2(\Omega, F_b, P, \overline{D})} < \epsilon.$$

It is obvious that the necessary and sufficient conditions for the time varying stochastic singular Equation (62) to be approximately controllable on $[0, b]$ are

$$\overline{\mathrm{ran}(Q_C^b)} = L^2(\Omega, F_b, P, \overline{D}). \tag{69}$$

Theorem 53. *Time varying stochastic singular Equation (62) is approximate controllable on $[0, b]$ if, and only if, one of the following conditions holds:*
(a) $\|Q_C^{b*}y^*\|_{L^2([0,b],\Omega,Y_2^*)} > 0$ for all $y^* \in L^2(\Omega, F_b, P, (\overline{D})^*), y^* \neq 0$;
(b) $\ker(Q_C^{b*}) = \{0\}$.

Proof. It is obvious that (a) is equivalent to (b). We only need to prove that (b) is equivalent to approximate controllability of time varying stochastic singular linear Equation (62).
If
$$\overline{\mathrm{ran}(Q_C^b)} = L^2(\Omega, F_b, P, \overline{D}), y^* \in \ker(Q_C^{b*}),$$

i.e., $Q_C^{b*}y^* = 0$, then

$$< u, Q_C^{b*}y^* >=< Q_C^b u, y^* >, u \in L^2([0, b], \Omega, Y_2).$$

Since $\overline{\mathrm{ran}(Q_C^b)} = L^2(\Omega, F_b, P, \overline{D})$, we have

$$< y, y^* >= 0, y \in L^2(\Omega, F_b, P, \overline{D}).$$

Therefore, $y^* = 0$, i.e., $\ker(Q_C^{b*}) = \{0\}$.
Conversely, if $\ker(Q_C^{b*}) = \{0\}$ but

$$\overline{\mathrm{ran}(Q_C^b)} \neq L^2(\Omega, F_b, P, \overline{D}),$$

then $\overline{\mathrm{ran}(Q_C^b)}$ is the proper subspace of $L^2(\Omega, F_b, P, \overline{D})$. According to Hahn–Banach theorem, there exists
$$y^* \in L^2(\Omega, F_b, P, (\overline{D})^*), y^* \neq 0,$$

such that
$$< Q_C^b u, y^* >= 0, u \in L^2([0, b], \Omega, Y_2).$$

Thus $< u, Q_C^{b*}y^* >= 0$, i.e., $Q_C^{b*}y^* = 0$. By $\ker(Q_C^{b*}) = \{0\}$, we find that $y^* = 0$. This contradicts $y^* \neq 0$. Therefore,

$$\overline{\mathrm{ran}(Q_C^b)} = L^2(\Omega, F_b, P, \overline{D}).$$

Hence (69) is true if, and only if, (b) holds, i.e., time varying stochastic singular Equation (62) is approximately controllable on $[0, b]$ if, and only if, (b) holds. $\square$

5.5.4. Observability

Consider the following time varying stochastic singular equation

$$O_1 dv(t) = O_2(t)v(t)dt + O_4(t)v(t)dw(t), t \geq 0, v(0) = v_0, x(t) = O_5(t)v(t), \tag{70}$$

and its dual time varying stochastic singular equation

$$O_1^* dv^*(t) = O_2^*(t)v^*(t)dt + O_5^*(t)u^*(t)dt + O_4^*(t)v^*(t)dw(t), t \geq 0, v^*(0) = v_0^*. \tag{71}$$

For the time varying stochastic singular Equation (70), the following concepts are defined.
The observability operator of time varying stochastic singular Equation (70) on $[0, b]$ is the continuous linear operator

$$Q_O^T : L^2(\Omega, F_b, P, \overline{D}) \to L^2([0, b], \Omega, Y_3)$$

defined by $Q_O^b y = O_5(t)G(b,t)E(y|F_t)$, its dual operator

$$Q_O^{b*} : L^2([0,b], \Omega, Y_3^*) \to L^2(\Omega, F_b, P, (\overline{D})^*)$$

is defined by

$$Q_O^{b*} x^* = \int_0^b G^*(b,t)O_5^*(t)x^*(t)dt.$$

Definition 36. *Time varying stochastic singular Equation (70) is said to be exactly observable on* $[0,b]$ *if* Q_O^b *is injective and its inverse is bounded on* $\mathrm{ran}(Q_O^b)$.

In the case of Definition 36, the state v_0 can be uniquely and continuously constructed from the knowledge of the output $x(t)$ in $L^2([0,b], \Omega, Y_3)$.

Definition 37. *Time varying stochastic singular Equation (70) is said to be approximately observable on* $[0,b]$ *if* Q_O^b *is injective.*

In the case of Definition 37, the state v_0 can be uniquely constructed from the knowledge of the output $x(t)$ in $L^2([0,b], \Omega, Y_3)$.
We can obtain the following dual principle.

Theorem 54. *Assume that* Y_1 *and* Y_3 *are reflexive. Time varying stochastic singular Equation (70) is exactly (approximately) observable on* $[0,b]$ *if, and only if, its dual time varying stochastic singular Equation (71) is exactly (approximately) controllable on* $[0,b]$.

Proof. Here, we only prove the case of exact observability. Since

$$Q_O^{b*} x^* = \int_0^b G^*(b,t)O_5^*(t)x^*(t)dt$$

happens to be the controllability operator Q_C^b of time varying stochastic singular Equation (71), so $Q_C^{b*} = Q_O^b$.
If the time varying stochastic singular Equation (70) is exactly observable, then there exists $1/\gamma > 0$, such that

$$\|(Q_O^b)^{-1}x\|_{L^2(\Omega,F_b,P,\overline{D})} \leq \frac{1}{\gamma}\|x\|_{L^2([0,b],\Omega,Y_3)},$$

for all $x \in \mathrm{ran}(Q_O^b)$. This implies that

$$\gamma\|y\|_{L^2(\Omega,F_b,P,\overline{D})} = \gamma\|(Q_O^b)^{-1}Q_O^b y\|_{L^2(\Omega,F_b,P,\overline{D})}$$

$$\leq \|Q_O^b y\|_{L^2([0,b],\Omega,Y_3)} = \|Q_C^{b*} y\|_{L^2([0,b],\Omega,Y_3)},$$

where

$$y = (Q_O^b)^{-1}x, y \in L^2(\Omega, F_b, P, \overline{D}).$$

According to Theorem 52 (a), we have that (71) is exactly controllable.
Assume next that the time varying stochastic singular Equation (71) is exactly controllable. From Theorem 52 (b), we have that Q_O^b is injective and has closed range. According to closed graph theorem $(Q_O^b)^{-1}$ is bounded on $\mathrm{ran} Q_O^T$. $\square$

Theorems 52 and Definitions 36 and 37 yield the following conditions for observability of time varying stochastic singular Equation (70).

Corollary 2. *Time varying stochastic singular Equation (70) is exactly observable on* $[0,b]$ *if, and only if, one of the following conditions holds for some* $\gamma > 0$ *and for all* $y \in L^2(\Omega, F_b, P, \overline{D})$:

(a) $\|Q_O^b y\|_{L^2([0,b],\Omega,Y_3)} \geq \gamma \|y\|_{L^2(\Omega,F_b,P,\overline{D})};$

(b) $\ker(Q_O^b) = \{0\}$ *and* $\mathrm{ran}(Q_O^b)$ *is closed.*

Corollary 3. *Time varying stochastic singular Equation (70) is approximately observable on* $[0,b]$ *if, and only if,* $\ker(Q_O^b) = \{0\}$.

5.5.5. An Illustrative Example

In this part, we give an example to illustrate the effectiveness of the obtained results.

According to [72], in input–output economics, many models were established to describe the real economics. The economics Leontief dynamic input–output model can be extended as an ordinary differential equation of the form:

$$O_1 \frac{dv(t)}{dt} = O_2(t)v(t) + O_3(t)u(t), x(t) = O_5(t)v(t) \tag{72}$$

in Banach space Y_1, where $O_1 \in B(Y_1)$ and $O_2(t) : \mathrm{dom}(O_2(t)) \subseteq Y_1 \rightarrow Y_1$ is a linear and possibly unbounded operator, $O_3(t), O_5(t) \in P([0,b], B(Y_1))$, while $v(t)$ and $u(t)$ are state process and control process valued in Y_1, respectively, for $t \geq 0$. However, in reality, there are many unpredicted parameters and different types of uncertainty that have not been implemented in the mathematical modelling process of this equation. Nonetheless, according to [85,86], we can consider a stochastic version of the singular Equation (72) with the one-dimensional standard Wiener process $w(t)$ used to model the uncertainties of the form:

$$O_1 dv(t) = O_2(t)v(t)dt + O_3(t)u(t)dt + O_4(t)v(t)dw(t), x(t) = O_5(t)v(t), \tag{73}$$

where $O_4(t) \in P([0,b], B(Y_1))$. This stochastic version of the input-output model is a time varying stochastic singular equation in Banach space Y_1 of the form (62).

We consider the following unforced time varying stochastic singular equation, i.e., $u(t) = 0$ in time varying stochastic singular Equation (73):

$$O_1 dv(t) = O_2(t)v(t)dt + O_4(t)v(t)dw(t), x(t) = O_5(t)v(t). \tag{74}$$

Time varying stochastic singular Equation (74) is the form of time varying stochastic singular linear Equation (70). In what follows, we will verify the effectiveness of Corollary 3.

If for some concrete engineering practice, the following data are taken in time varying stochastic singular Equation (74):

$$O_1 = \begin{bmatrix} U_1 & 0 \\ 0 & 0 \end{bmatrix}, O_2(t) = \begin{bmatrix} -(2t+1)U_1 & 0 \\ 0 & 5(t^2+1)U_2 \end{bmatrix},$$

$$O_4(t) = \begin{bmatrix} (2t)^{1/2}U_1 & 0 \\ 0 & 3t^2 U_2 \end{bmatrix}, O_5(t) = \begin{bmatrix} 7(t+1)^2 U_1 & 0 \\ 0 & 0 \end{bmatrix},$$

where U_1, U_2 are identical operators in Banach spaces Y_{11}, Y_{12}, respectively. Time varying stochastic singular Equation (74) can be written as

$$\begin{bmatrix} U_1 & 0 \\ 0 & 0 \end{bmatrix} \begin{bmatrix} dv_1(t) \\ dv_2(t) \end{bmatrix} = \begin{bmatrix} -(2t+1)U_1 & 0 \\ 0 & 5(t^2+1)U_2 \end{bmatrix} \begin{bmatrix} v_1(t)dt \\ v_2(t)dt \end{bmatrix}$$

$$+ \begin{bmatrix} (2t)^{1/2}U_1 & 0 \\ 0 & 3t^2 U_2 \end{bmatrix} \begin{bmatrix} v_1(t) \\ v_2(t) \end{bmatrix} dw(t),$$

$$x(t) = \begin{bmatrix} 7(t+1)^2 U_1 & 0 \\ 0 & 0 \end{bmatrix} \begin{bmatrix} v_1(t) \\ v_2(t) \end{bmatrix}, \tag{75}$$

where $\begin{bmatrix} v_1(t) \\ v_2(t) \end{bmatrix} \in Y_{11} \oplus Y_{12} = Y_1$. We can find that $\overline{D} = Y_{11}$. According to [87], we can obtain

$$G(t,s) = \begin{bmatrix} \exp[-\frac{3}{2}t^2 - t + \frac{3}{2}s^2 + s + \int_s^t (2r)^{1/2} w(r) ds] U_1 & 0 \\ 0 & 0 \end{bmatrix}.$$

It is obvious that time varying stochastic singular Equation (75) satisfies the conditions of Lemma 3. If $\begin{bmatrix} y \\ 0 \end{bmatrix} \in L^2(\Omega, F_b, P, \overline{D})$, and

$$Q_O^b \begin{bmatrix} y \\ 0 \end{bmatrix} = O_5(t) G(b,t) E(\begin{bmatrix} y \\ 0 \end{bmatrix} | F_t) = 0, t \in [0,b],$$

then

$$O_5(b) G(b,b) E(\begin{bmatrix} y \\ 0 \end{bmatrix} | F_b) = 7(b+1)^2 \begin{bmatrix} y \\ 0 \end{bmatrix} = 0,$$

i.e., $y = 0$. This implies that $\ker(Q_O^b) = \{0\}$. Therefore time varying stochastic singular Equation (75) is approximately observable by Corollary 3.

In this section, we have discussed the controllability of some types of stochastic singular linear systems. However, the following problems still need to be studied.

Problem 9. *How about the controllability of the following system?*

$$Ldx(t) = [A(t)x(t) + B(t)u(t)]dt + \sum_{k=1}^{\infty} C_k(t)x(t)dw_{1,k}(t)$$

$$+ \sum_{j=1}^{\infty} D_j(t)u(t)dw_{2,j}(t), x(0) = x_0,$$

where $L \in B(H)$ *and* $\ker(L) \neq \{0\}$, $A(t) : \mathrm{dom}(A(t)) \subseteq H \to H$ *is the generator of a GE-evolution operator induced by L in the Hilbert (or Banach) space H,* $B(t) : \mathrm{dom}(B(t)) \subset U \to H$ *is a linear operator, U is a Hilbert (or Banach) space;* $C_k(t) \in P([0,b], B(H))$, $D_k(t) \in P([0,b], B(U,H))$, *for each* $i \in \mathbb{N}$; *and in Hilbert spaces,*

$$\sum_{k=1}^{\infty} \sup_{0 \le t \le b} \|C_k(t)\|^2_{B(H)} < +\infty, \sum_{k=1}^{\infty} \sup_{0 \le t \le b} \|D_k(t)\|^2_{B(U,H)} < +\infty;$$

in Banach spaces,

$$\sum_{k=1}^{\infty} \sup_{0 \le t \le b} \|C_k(t)\|_{B(H)} < +\infty, \sum_{k=1}^{\infty} \sup_{0 \le t \le b} \|D_k(t)\|_{B(U,H)} < +\infty;$$

the countable set $\{w_{1,k}, w_{2,j}, k, j \in \mathbb{N}\}$ *consists of independent standard Wiener processes defined on the stochastic basis* $(\Omega, F, \{F_t\}, P)$.

6. Conclusions

We have introduced the latest progress in controllability of stochastic linear systems and put forward some problems that need to be further studied, which includes stochastic linear systems in finite dimensional spaces, stochastic linear systems in infinite dimensional spaces, stochastic singular linear systems in finite dimensional spaces, and stochastic singular linear systems in infinite dimensional spaces. The controllability and observability for a type of time-varying stochastic singular linear systems have been studied by using stochastic GE-evolution operator in the sense of mild solution in Banach spaces, some necessary and sufficient conditions have been obtained, the dual principle has been proved to be true, an example has been given to illustrate the validity of the theoretical results obtained in this part. Readers can easily and comprehensively understand the latest progress concerning the controllability of stochastic linear systems and further problems to be solved. The next research direction is how to solve these problems.

Funding: This research was funded by National Natural Science Foundation of China grant numbers 12126401 and 11926402.

Institutional Review Board Statement: Not applicable.

Informed Consent Statement: Not applicable.

Data Availability Statement: Not applicable.

Acknowledgments: The author would like to thank the anonymous reviewers and the Editor for their helpful comments.

Conflicts of Interest: The author declares no conflict of interest.

References

1. Kalman, R.E. Contributions to the theory of optimal control. *Bol. Soc. Mat. Mex.* **1960**, *5*, 102–119.
2. Connors, M.M. Controllability of discrete, linear, random dynamics systems. *SIAM Control Optim.* **1967**, *5*, 183–210. [CrossRef]
3. Aoki, M. On observability of stochastic discrete-time dynamic systems. *J. Frankl. Inst.* **1968**, *286*, 36–38. [CrossRef]
4. Fitts, J.M. On the global observability of nonlinear systems. In Proceedings of the 1st Sympsium on Nonlinear Estimation Theory and Applications, San Diego, CA, USA, 10–12 September 1970; p. 128.
5. Gershwin, S.B. A Controllability Theory for Nonlinear Dynamics Systems. Ph.D. Thesis, Harvard University, Cambridge, MA, USA, 1970.
6. Sunahara, Y.; Kishino, K.; Aihara, S. On stochastic observability of nonlinear discrete-time dynamical systems. *Int. J. Control* **1974**, *19*, 719–732. [CrossRef]
7. Sunahara, Y.; Kabluchi, T.; Asada, Y.; Aihara, S.; Kishino, K. On stochastic controllability for nonlinear systems. *IEEE Trans. Autom. Control* **1974**, *19*, 49–54. [CrossRef]
8. Sunahara, Y.; Aihara, S.; Kishino, K. On the stochastic observability and controllability for nonlinear systems. *Int. J. Control* **1975**, *22*, 65–82. [CrossRef]
9. Chen, H.F. On stochastic observability. *Sci. Sin.* **1977**, *20*, 305–324.
10. Sunahara, Y.; Aihara, S. On stochastic observability and controllability for nonlinear distributed parameter systems. *Inf. Control* **1977**, *34*, 348–371. [CrossRef]
11. Klamka, J.; Socha, L. Some remarks about stochastic controllability. *IEEE Trans. Autom. Control* **1977**, *22*, 880–881. [CrossRef]
12. Harris, S.E. Stochastic controllability of linear discrete systems with multicative noise. *Int. J. Control* **1978**, *27*, 213–227. [CrossRef]
13. Dubov, M.A.; Mordukhovich, B.S. Theory of controllability of linear stochastic systems. *Differ. Equ.* **1978**, *14*, 1609–1612.
14. Zabcjyk, J. *On Stochastic Controllability*; FDS Report, No 34; Universitat Bremen: Bremen, Germany, 1980.
15. Chen, H.F. On stochastic observability and controllability. *Automatica* **1980**, *16*, 179–190. [CrossRef]
16. Zabcjyk, J. Controllability of stochastic linear systems. *Syst. Control Lett.* **1981**, *1*, 25–31. [CrossRef]
17. Ehrhard, M.; Kliemann, W. Controllability of linear stochastic systems. *Syst. Control Lett.* **1982**, *2*, 145–153. [CrossRef]
18. Dubov, M.A.; Morduchovich, B.S. On controllability of infinite dimensional linear stochastic systems. In *Stochastic Control: Proceedings of the 2nd IFAC Symposium, Vilnius, Lithuanian SSR, USSR, 19–23 May 1986 (IFAC Symposia Series)*; Pergamon Press: Oxford, UK; New York, NY, USA, 1987; Volume 2, pp. 307–310.
19. Bensoussan, A. *Stochastic Control of Partially Observable Systems*; Cambridge University Press: London, UK, 1992.
20. Peng, S.G. Backward stochastic differential equation and exact controllability of stochastic control systems. *Prog. Nat. Sci.* **1994**, *4*, 274–283.
21. Bashirov, A.E.; Kerimov, K.R. On controllability conception for stochastic systems. *SIAM J. Control Optim.* **1997**, *35*, 384–398. [CrossRef]
22. Bashirov, A.E.; Mahmudov, N.I. On concepts of controllability for deterministic and stochastic systems. *SIAM J. Control Optim.* **1999**, *37*, 1808–1821. [CrossRef]
23. Bashirov, A.E.; Mahmudov, N.I. Controllability of linear deterministic and stochastic systems. In Proceedings of the 38th IEEE Conference on Decision and Control, Phoenix, AZ, USA, 7–10 December 1999; Volume 4, pp. 3196–3202.
24. Mahmudov, N.I.; Denker, A. On controllability of linear stochastic systems. *Int. J. Control* **2000**, *73*, 144–151. [CrossRef]
25. Mahmudov, N.I. Controllability of linear stochastic systems. *IEEE Trans. Autom. Control* **2001**, *46*, 724–731. [CrossRef]
26. Mahmudov, N.I. Controllability of linear stochastic systems in Hilbert spaces. *J. Math. Anal. Appl.* **2001**, *259*, 64–82. [CrossRef]
27. Mahmudov, N.I. On controllability of semilinear stochastic systems in Hilbert spaces. *IMA J. Math. Control Inf.* **2002**, *19*, 363–376. [CrossRef]

28. Liu, Y.Z.; Peng, S.G. Infinite horizon backward stochastic differential equation and exponential convergence index assignment of stochastic control systems. *Automatica* **2002**, *38*, 1417–1423. [CrossRef]
29. Mahmudov, N.I. Controllability and observability of linear stochastic systems in Hilbert spaces. *Prog. Probab.* **2003**, *53*, 151–167.
30. Mahmudov, N.I. Controllability of semilinear stochastic systems in Hilbert spaces. *J. Math. Anal. Appl.* **2003**, *288*, 197–211. [CrossRef]
31. Mahmudov, N.I. Approximate controllability of semilinear deterministic and stochastic evolution equation in abstract spaces. *SIAM J. Control Optim.* **2003**, *42*, 1604–1622. [CrossRef]
32. Mahmudov, N.I.; Zorlu, S. Controllability of non-linear stochastic systems. *Int. J. Control* **2003**, *76*, 95–104. [CrossRef]
33. Ugrinovskii, V.A. Observability of linear stochastic uncertain systems. *IEEE Trans. Autom. Control* **2003**, *48*, 2246–2269. [CrossRef]
34. Mahmudov, N.I.; Zorlu, S. Controllability of semilinear stochastic systems. *Int. J. Control* **2005**, *78*, 997–1004. [CrossRef]
35. Dauer, J.P.; Mahmudov, N.I.; Matar, M.M. Approximate controllability of backward stochastic evolution equations in Hilbert spaces. *J. Math. Anal. Appl.* **2006**, *323*, 42–56. [CrossRef]
36. Mahmudov, N.I.; Mckibben, M.A. Approximate controllability of second order neutral stochastic evolution equation. *Dyn. Contin. Discrete Impuls. Syst. Ser. B Appl. Algorithm* **2006**, *13*, 619–634.
37. Sakthivel, R.; Kim, J.H. On controllability of nonlinear stochastic systems. *Rep. Math. Phys.* **2006**, *58*, 433–443. [CrossRef]
38. Klamka, J. Stochastic controllability of linear stochastic systems with delay in control. *Bull. Pol. Acad. Sci. Tech. Sci.* **2007**, *55*, 23–29.
39. Gorac, D. Approximate controllability for linear stochastic differential equations in infinite dimensions. *Appl. Math. Optim.* **2009**, *60*, 105–132. [CrossRef]
40. Tang, S.J.; Zhang, X. Null controllability for forward and backward stochastic parabolic equations. *SIAM J. Control Optim.* **2009**, *48*, 2191–2216. [CrossRef]
41. Sakthivel, R.; Mahmudov, N.I.; Lee, S.G. Controllability of nonlinear impulsive stochastic systems. *Int. J. Control* **2009**, *82*, 801–807. [CrossRef]
42. Klamska, J. Stochastic controllability of systems with multiple delays in control. *Int. J. Appl. Math. Comput. Sci.* **2009**, *19*, 39–47. [CrossRef]
43. Bashirov, A.E.; Etikan, H.; Semi, N. Partial controllability of stochastic linear systems. *Int. J. Control* **2010**, *83*, 2564–2572. [CrossRef]
44. Sakthivel, R.; Nieto, J.J.; Mahmudov, N.I. Approximate controllability of nonlinear deterministic and stochastic systems with unbounded delay. *Taiwan J. Math.* **2010**, *14*, 1777–1797. [CrossRef]
45. Liu, F.; Peng, S.G. On controllability for stochastic control systems when the cofficient is time-varying. *J. Syst. Sci. Complex.* **2010**, *23*, 270–278. [CrossRef]
46. Liu, Q. Some results on the controllability of forward stochastic heat equations with control on the drift. *J. Funct. Anal.* **2011**, *260*, 832–851. [CrossRef]
47. Sathya, R.; Balachandram, K. Controllability of neutral impulsive Ito type stochastic integrodifferential systems. *Vietnam J. Math.* **2013**, *41*, 59–80. [CrossRef]
48. Liu, Q. Exact controllability for stochastic Schrodinger equations. *J. Differ. Equ.* **2013**, *255*, 2484–2504. [CrossRef]
49. Liu, X. Controllability of some coupled stochastic parabolic systems with fractional order spatial differential operators by one control in the drift. *SIAM J. Control Optim.* **2014**, *52*, 836–860. [CrossRef]
50. Liu, Q. Exact controllability for stochastic transport equations. *SIAM J. Control Optim.* **2014**, *255*, 397–419. [CrossRef]
51. Ning, H.; Qing, G. Approximate controllability of nonlinear stochastic partial differential systems with infinite delay. *Adv. Differ. Equ.* **2015**, *85*, 1–25. [CrossRef]
52. Gao, P.; Chen, M.; Li, Y. Observability estimates and null controllability for forward and backward linear stochastic Kuramoto-Sivashinsky equations. *SIAM J. Control Optim.* **2015**, *53*, 475–500. [CrossRef]
53. Das, S.; Pandey, D.; Sukavanam, N. Existence of solution and approximate controllability of a second order neutral stochastic differential equation with state dependent delay. *Acta Math. Sci.* **2016**, *36B*, 1509–1523. [CrossRef]
54. Fu, X.; Liu, X. Controllability and observability of some complex Ginzburg-Landau equations. *SIAM J. Control Optim.* **2017**, *55*, 1102–1127. [CrossRef]
55. Mokkedem, F.Z.; Fu, X. Approximate controllability for a semilinear stochastic evolution systems with infinite delay in L_p space. *Appl. Math. Optim.* **2017**, *75*, 253–283. [CrossRef]
56. Klamka, J.; Wyzwal, J.; Zawiski, R. On controllability of second order dynamical systems-a survey. *Bull. Pol. Acad. Sci. Tech. Sci.* **2017**, *65*, 279–295. [CrossRef]
57. Shukla, A.; Sukavanam, N.; Pandey, D.N. Controllability of semilinear stochastic control system with finite delay. *IMA J. Math. Control Inf.* **2018**, *35*, 427–449. [CrossRef]
58. Liu, L.Y.; Liu, X. Controllability and observability of some coupled stochastic parabolic system. *Math. Control Relat. Fields* **2018**, *8*, 829–854. [CrossRef]
59. Wang, Y.Q.; Yang, D.H.; Yong, J.M.; Yu, Z. Exact controllability of linear stochastic differential equations and related problems. *Math. Control Relat. Fields* **2017**, *7*, 305–345. [CrossRef]
60. Barbu, V.; Tubaro, L. Exact controllability of stochastic equations with multiplicative noise. *Syst. Control Lett.* **2018**, *122*, 19–23. [CrossRef]

61. Wang, Y.Q.; Zhou, X.X. Exact controllability of stochastic differential equations with memory. *Syst. Control Lett.* **2020**, *142*, 1–10. [CrossRef]
62. Sirbu, M.; Tessitore, G. Null controllability of an infinite dimensional SDE with stateand control-dependent noise. *Syst. Control Lett.* **2001**, *44*, 385–394. [CrossRef]
63. Shen, L.J.; Li, C.X.; Wang, L. Some remarks on the controllability of linear stochastic systems. In Proceedings of the 34th Chinese Control Conference, Hangzhou, China, 28–30 July 2015; pp. 598–601.
64. Dou, F.F.; Lu, Q. Partial approximate controllability for linear stochastic control systems. *SIAM J. Control Optim.* **2019**, *57*, 1209–1229. [CrossRef]
65. Gashi, B.; Pantelous, A.A. Linear backward stochastic differential equations of descriptor type: Regular systems. *Stoch. Anal. Appl.* **2013**, *31*, 142–166. [CrossRef]
66. Gashi, B.; Pantelous, A.A. Linear stochastic systems of descriptype: Theory and applications, safety, reliability, risk and life-cycle performance of structure and infrastructures. In Proceedings of the 11th International Conference on Structure Safety and Reliability, ICOSSAR 2013, New York, NY, USA, 16–20 June 2013; pp. 1047–1054.
67. Gashi, B.; Pantelous, A.A. Linear backward stochastic differential systems of descriptor type with structure and applications to engineering. *Probab. Eng. Mech.* **2015**, *40*, 1–11. [CrossRef]
68. Ge, Z.Q.; Ge, X.C. An exact null controllability of stochastic singular systems. *Sci. China Inf. Sci.* **2021**, *64*, 179202:1–179202:3. [CrossRef]
69. Ge, Z.Q. Impulse controllability and impulse observability of stochastic singular systems. *J. Syst. Sci. Complex.* **2021**, *34*, 899–911. [CrossRef]
70. Ge, Z.Q. Exact observability and stability of stochastic implicit systems. *Syst. Control Lett.* **2021**, *157*, 1–7. [CrossRef]
71. Liaskos, K.B.; Pantelous, A.A.; Stratis, I.G. Linear stochastic degenerate Sobolev equations and applications. *Int. J. Control* **2015**, *88*, 2538–2553. [CrossRef]
72. Liaskos, K.B.; Stratis, I.G.; Pantelous, A.A. Stochastic degenerate Sobolev equations: Well posedness and exact controllability. *Math. Meth. Appl. Sci.* **2018**, *41*, 1025–1032. [CrossRef]
73. Ge, Z.Q.; Zhu, G.T.; Feng, D.X. Exact controllability for singular distributed parameter system in Hilbert space. *Sci. China Ser. F Inf. Sci.* **2009**, *52*, 2045–2052. [CrossRef]
74. Ge, Z.Q.; Zhu, G.T.; Feng, D.X. Generalized operator semigroup and well-posedness of singular distributed parameter systems. *Sci. Sin. Math.* **2010**, *40*, 477–495.
75. Ge, Z.Q.; Feng, D.X. Well-posed problem of nonlinear singular distributed parameter systems and nonlinear GE-semigroup. *Sci. China Ser. F Inf. Sci.* **2013**, *56*, 128201:1–128201:14. [CrossRef]
76. Ge, Z.Q. Controllability and observability of stochastic singular systems in Banach spaces. *J. Syst. Sci. Complex.* **2021**. [CrossRef]
77. Ge, Z.Q. GE-semigroup method for controllability of stochastic descriptor linear systems. *Sci. China Inf. Sci.* **2021**. [CrossRef]
78. Ge, Z.Q.; Feng, D.X. Solvability of a time-varying singular distributed parameter system in Banach space. *Sci. Sin. Inf.* **2013**, *43*, 386–406. [CrossRef]
79. Ge, Z.Q.; Feng, D.X. Well-posed problem of nonlinear time varying singular distributed parameter systems. *Sci. Sin. Math.* **2014**, *44*, 1277–1298. [CrossRef]
80. Ge, Z.Q. GE-evolution operator method for controllability of time varying stochastic descriptor linear systems in Hilbert spaces. *IMA J. Math. Control. Inf.* **2021**. [CrossRef]
81. Ge, Z.Q. Controllability and observability of stochastic implicit systems and stochastic GE-evolution operator. *Numer. Algebra Control Optim.* **2021**. [CrossRef]
82. Pazy, A. *Semigroups of Linear Operators and Applications to Partial Differential Equations*; Springer: New York, NY, USA, 1983; pp. 149–150.
83. Prato, G.D.; Zabczyk, J. *Stochastic Equation in Infinite Dimensions*; Cambridge University Press: Cambridge, UK, 2014; pp. 119–216.
84. Curtain, R.; Zwart, H.J. *An Introduction to Infinite Dimensional Linear Systems Theory*; Springer: New York, NY, USA, 1995; pp. 581–608.
85. Oksendal, B. *Stochastic Differential Equation: An Introduction with Application*; Springer: New York, NY, USA, 1998; pp. 101–217.
86. Mao, X. *Stochastic Differential Equation and Their Applications*; Horwood Publishing: Chichester, UK, 1997; pp. 114–217.
87. Hu, S.G.; Huang, C.M.; Wu, F.K. *Stochastic Differential Equation*; Science Press: Beijing, China, 2008; pp. 55–62.

Article

Sparse Grid Adaptive Interpolation in Problems of Modeling Dynamic Systems with Interval Parameters

Alexander Yu Morozov *, Andrey A. Zhuravlev and Dmitry L. Reviznikov

Federal Research Center "Computer Science and Control" of Russian Academy of Sciences (FRC CSC RAS), 119333 Moscow, Russia; zhuravlyow.andrei@yandex.ru (A.A.Z.); reviznikov@mai.ru (D.L.R.)
* Correspondence: morozov@infway.ru

Abstract: The paper is concerned with the issues of modeling dynamic systems with interval parameters. In previous works, the authors proposed an adaptive interpolation algorithm for solving interval problems; the essence of the algorithm is the dynamic construction of a piecewise polynomial function that interpolates the solution of the problem with a given accuracy. The main problem of applying the algorithm is related to the curse of dimension, i.e., exponential complexity relative to the number of interval uncertainties in parameters. The main objective of this work is to apply the previously proposed adaptive interpolation algorithm to dynamic systems with a large number of interval parameters. In order to reduce the computational complexity of the algorithm, the authors propose using adaptive sparse grids. This article introduces a novelty approach of applying sparse grids to problems with interval uncertainties. The efficiency of the proposed approach has been demonstrated on representative interval problems of nonlinear dynamics and computational materials science.

Keywords: adaptive interpolation algorithm; interval ordinary differential equations (ODEs); sparse grids; hierarchical basis; multidimensional interpolation; high dimensions; molecular dynamics modeling

Citation: Morozov, A.Y.; Zhuravlev, A.A.; Reviznikov, D.L. Sparse Grid Adaptive Interpolation in Problems of Modeling Dynamic Systems with Interval Parameters. *Mathematics* **2021**, *9*, 298. https://doi.org/10.3390/math9040298

Academic Editor: Mikhail Posypkin
Received: 18 December 2020
Accepted: 28 January 2021
Published: 3 February 2021

Publisher's Note: MDPI stays neutral with regard to jurisdictional claims in published maps and institutional affiliations.

1. Introduction

Problems related to inaccurately specified data arise in many modern fields of science and technology. When applied to non-stationary processes, they are often formulated as dynamic systems with interval parameters. The result of solving such problems is an interval estimate of the set of possible system states depending on the uncertainties in the parameters. Basic methods of interval analysis are presented in books [1–5]. There are known methods based on the representation of a set of solutions through geometric primitives: parallelepipeds and ellipses [6,7], methods based on symbolic computation [8,9], as well as stochastic methods [10], such as Monte-Carlo methods. Methods based on classical interval arithmetic are subject to the so-called wrap effect [1], which manifests itself in an unlimited increase in the width of the obtained interval estimates of solutions. This effect arises due to the replacement of the exact form of the set of solutions by a simpler form, and for iterative methods, the divergence of intervals' boundaries is often exponential. Existing methods that are not subject to this effect, or weakly susceptible to it, often have exponential complexity with respect to the number of interval parameters. It concerns symbolic methods operating in series, Monte-Carlo methods, and the adaptive interpolation algorithm [11]. Therefore, there is a need for efficient approaches to reduce the computational complexity of methods that are not affected by the wrapping effect.

While solving a considered class of problems, the main idea is to construct an explicit dependence of the solution to the corresponding non-interval problem on the point values of the interval parameters. If such dependence is available, finding an interval estimate would be reduced to solving a certain number of constrained optimization problems for explicitly given functions.

Papers [11–14] describe the adaptive interpolation algorithm in detail. The essence of the algorithm is the dynamic construction of a piecewise polynomial function that interpolates the solution of the problem with a given accuracy. The theoretical basis of the algorithm is given in References [11,12]. The algorithm has a number of essential features: it is not subject to the wrapping effect [11]; efficiently parallelizes on GPUs; able to simulate rigid systems [13]; determines the presence of bifurcations and chaos in the system [14]. It has been tested on applied problems of chemical kinetics [13], gas dynamics and celestial mechanics, and complex dynamics with bifurcations and chaos [14]. Nevertheless, there is some drawback. The algorithm uses multidimensional interpolation on a regular grid, which requires $(p + 1)^d$ nodes, where p—a polynomial degree for each dimension and d—the number of dimensions. With a large number of interval parameters, the application of the algorithm becomes difficult. However, a typical situation is when the degree of influence of different parameters and their combinations on a solution can differ significantly; therefore, it naturally follows to use approaches that take into account these features and, as a consequence, reduce the computational complexity.

Within the framework of modeling methods for dynamical systems with interval parameters, it is worth noting the work [15], which describes a method based on the polynomial approximation of the solution, which requires points in the sample less than $(p + 1)^d$. This method has been successfully applied to the problem of modeling a rotating system with both random and interval variables [16]. This class of problems is significant from an applied point of view.

The curse of dimension, that is, the exponential growth of the number of calculations, is a critical problem. Typically, this situation arises when studying multidimensional functions presented in the form of a black box. The general tactic for reducing computational complexity is to determine and take into account the features of the function under consideration.

Sparse grids [17] are numerical methods for representing, integrating, or interpolating multidimensional functions based on a hierarchical basis [18,19] and reducing the curse of dimension. This approach was first presented by the Russian mathematician Smolyak in 1963. Classic sparse grids result from computational cost optimization for approximating functions with bounded mixed derivatives [20]. This fact is important since it imposes certain restrictions on the solution's dependence on interval parameters. Interpolation using sparse grids requires significantly fewer nodes than standard full grid interpolation.

There are many works devoted to sparse grids [21–24]. Reference [21] gives an initial introduction to sparse grids and the technique of combining them. It provides a program code in the Python programming language. In Reference [22], some parallelization issues are considered; Reference [23] provides an overview of the foundations and applications of sparse grids, with particular attention to the solution of partial differential equations.

The behavior of the solution to the ordinary differential equations (ODE) system can differ significantly depending on the parameters and initial conditions. Adaptive grids can drastically reduce computational costs by condensing nodes in regions with strong solution dependence on parameters and rarefaction in areas with weak dependence. Besides such adaptation, additional properties of the solution can be taken into account using sparse grids. This approach is effective when the interpolated function has a weak dependence on subsets of variables. For example, if the solution to an ODE system can be represented as a linear combination of functions from certain subsets of parameters and initial conditions, then it is sufficient to consider only the corresponding subsets and construct a grid only from them. Sparse grids are especially effective in multidimensional problems and can significantly reduce computational costs.

The main problem is the high computational costs when solving problems with uncertainties. The main goal of this work is to apply the previously proposed adaptive interpolation algorithm to the case of dynamical systems with a large number of interval parameters. The novelty lies in the application of sparse grids to problems with interval uncertainties, including problems of molecular dynamics.

The research methodology is based on methods of mathematical modeling, computational mathematics, and differential calculus. The statement of the problem is formulated in the form of the Cauchy problem for a system of ordinary differential equations with interval parameters. The method is tested on a representative set of problems.

The following sections give a description of the adaptive interpolation algorithm on sparse grids, present the results of testing the algorithm on a number of model problems of nonlinear dynamics, and solve an important problem of computational materials science, namely the determination of an interval stress tensor based on molecular dynamics modeling.

2. Algorithm for Adaptive Interpolation Using Sparse Grids

Dynamic systems with uncertainties in parameters arise in many practical areas. Traditionally, interval problems for dynamic systems are formulated in the form of the Cauchy problem for a system of ordinary differential equations (ODE) with interval initial conditions or parameters. It is necessary to obtain an interval estimate of the solution based on interval values of the parameters.

Consider the Cauchy problem with m interval initial conditions:

$$\begin{cases} \frac{dy_i(t)}{dt} = f_i(y_1(t), y_2(t), ..., y_n(t)), \ 1 \leq i \leq n, \\ y_i(t_0) \in \left[\underline{y_i^0}, \overline{y_i^0} \right], \ 1 \leq i \leq m, \\ y_i(t_0) = y_i^0, \ m+1 \leq i \leq n, \\ t \in [t_0, t_N]. \end{cases} \tag{1}$$

Hereinafter, the underline denotes the lower bound of the interval, and the overline—the upper bound of the interval.

If the ODE system is not autonomous or contains interval parameters, then fictitious equations are added to the system so that it would take the form of system Equation (1). A vector function $\mathbf{f} = (f_1, f_2, ..., f_n)^T$ meets all conditions ensuring the uniqueness and existence of a solution for all $y_i(t_0) \in \left[\underline{y_i^0}, \overline{y_i^0} \right], 1 \leq i \leq m$.

The goal is, for each moment of time t_k, to construct a piecewise polynomial vector function $\mathbf{P}^k (y_1^0, y_2^0, ..., y_m^0)$, where $y_i(t_0) \in \left[\underline{y_i^0}, \overline{y_i^0} \right], 1 \leq i \leq m$, which interpolates the dependence of the solution on the interval parameters with controlled accuracy. If the function $\mathbf{P}^k$ is available, finding the interval estimate of the solution (finding the left and right boundaries of the intervals) should be reduced to solving constrained optimization problems for an explicitly given function.

Suppose that the solution to $\mathbf{y}^k (y_1^0, y_2^0, ..., y_m^0)$ is known at the moment of time t_k, where $y_i^0 \in \left[\underline{y_i^0}, \overline{y_i^0} \right], 1 \leq i \leq m$. An adaptive sparse grid is constructed for the set formed by the interval initial conditions. Each grid point has a corresponding solution to the noninterval system (1) at pointwise values of interval parameters that correspond to the position of a node. To obtain an interval solution at the moment of time t_{k+1}, the transfer of all non-interval solutions contained in the grid nodes to the time layer $(k+1)$ is performed, followed by the adaptation of the grid and the construction of an interpolation polynomial $\mathbf{P}^{k+1}$.

A short description of sparse grid interpolation according to the works [20,21] is given below.

Consider the interpolation of a smooth function $f(x)$ of one variable on the unit interval $[0, 1]$. For the sake of simplicity, it is assumed that the function is equal to zero at the boundary points: $f(0) = f(1) = 0$.

The interpolation is performed on a piecewise linear hierarchical basis using the hat function:

$$\varphi(x) = \begin{cases} 1 - |x|, \ x \in [-1, 1] \\ 0, \ \text{otherwise} \end{cases}. \tag{2}$$

Define a set of grids G_l on a unit interval $[0, 1]$, where l is the level that determines the grid width $h_l = 2^{-l}$. The grid points $x_{l,i}$ are given as:

$$x_{l,i} = i \cdot h_l, \, 0 \leq i \leq 2^l.$$

Families of basis functions $\varphi_{l,i}(x)$ are generated based on the obtained sets of points, using the stretching and transfer of the hat Equation (2):

$$\varphi_{l,i}(x) = \varphi\left(\frac{x - i \cdot h_l}{h_l}\right). \tag{3}$$

A nodal basis is formed for each given l of Equation (3). Here, the common piecewise linear interpolation (Figure 1) is applied, and the corresponding polynomial is written as follows:

$$P(x) = \sum_{i=1}^{2^l-1} a_{l,i}\varphi_{l,i}(x), \, a_{l,i} = f(x_{l,i}). \tag{4}$$

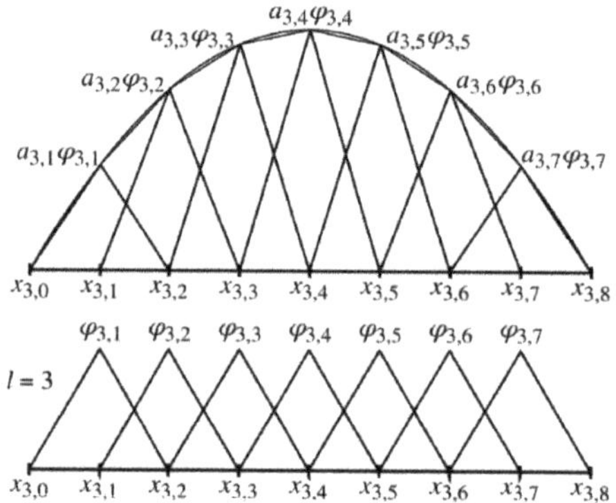

Figure 1. Interpolation on a nodal basis.

Let us make the transition to a hierarchical basis (Figure 2). The basis functions given by Equation (3) is expressed with even level indices k in terms of the basis level functions $(k-1)$:

$$\varphi_{k,2i}(x) = \varphi_{k-1,i}(x) - \frac{1}{2}(\varphi_{k,2i-1}(x) + \varphi_{k,2i+1}(x)), \, 1 \leq i \leq 2^{k-1} - 1.$$

In this case, the interpolation polynomial given by Equation (4) takes the following form:

$$P(x) = \sum_{k=1}^{l} \sum_{\substack{i=1, \\ i\,\text{odd}}}^{2^k-1} a_{k,i}\varphi_{k,i}(x), \, a_{k,i} = f(x_{k,i}) - \frac{1}{2}(f(x_{k,i-1}) + f(x_{k,i+1})) \tag{5}$$

Next, consider the multidimensional interpolation of a smooth function $f(x_1, x_2, ..., x_d)$ using d—dimensional unit cube $\Omega = [0, 1]^d$, provided that $f|_{\partial\Omega} = 0$. A multidimensional basis is constructed by the direct product of hierarchical one-dimensional bases:

$$\varphi_{\mathbf{l,i}}(\mathbf{x}) = \prod_{j=1}^{d} \varphi_{l_j,i_j}(x_j), \, 1 \leq i_j \leq 2^{l_j} - 1, \, i_j\,\text{odd},$$

where $\mathbf{l} = (l_1, l_2, ..., l_d)$ are the levels of the corresponding one-dimensional grids, $\mathbf{i} = (i_1, i_2, ..., i_d)$ is the basis function multi-index, $\mathbf{x} = (x_1, x_2, ..., x_d)$. If $\sum_{j=1}^{d} l_j \leq n + d - 1$, there is a sparse grid of n level; if $\max_{j=\overline{1,d}}(l_j) \leq n$, there exists a complete grid (Figure 3). The number of nodes in a sparse grid is estimated as $O\left(p(\log_2 p)^{d-1}\right)$, and the interpolation error is estimated as $O\left(h_n^2(\log_2 p)^{d-1}\right)$; for a full grid the respective number of nodes is $O\left(p^d\right)$, and the error is $O\left(h_n^2\right)$, where $p = 2^n - 1$ is the number of nodes in each dimension [20].

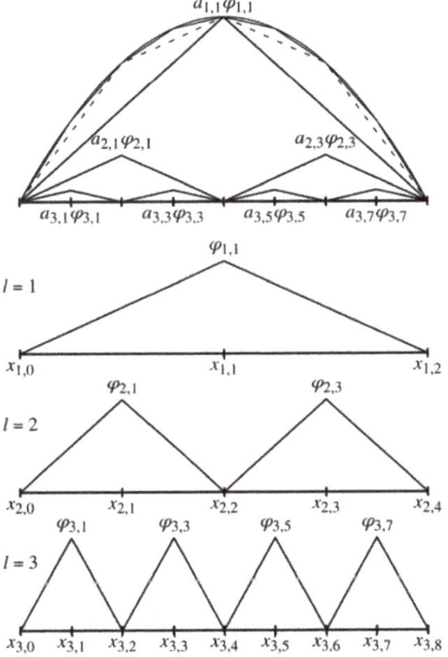

Figure 2. Interpolation on a hierarchical basis.

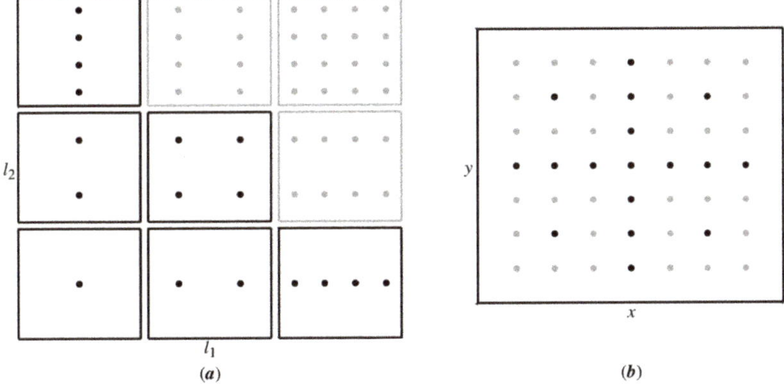

Figure 3. Sparse grid of the third level: black dots—sparse grid; black and grey dots—full grid: (**a**) sets of points corresponding to basis functions of the same level; (**b**) combining all points into one grid.

The interpolation polynomial is written as follows:

$$P(\mathbf{x}) = \sum_{\mathbf{l},\mathbf{i}} a_{\mathbf{l},\mathbf{i}}\,\varphi_{\mathbf{l},\mathbf{i}}(\mathbf{x}), \ \|\mathbf{l}\|_1 \le n + d - 1, \ 1 \le i_j \le 2^{l_j} - 1, \ i_j \text{ odd} \tag{6}$$

where

$$a_{\mathbf{l},\mathbf{i}} = \sum_{\Delta_1,\dots,\Delta_d} \left(-\frac{1}{2}\right)^{\sum\limits_{j=1}^{d} |\Delta_j|} f\left(x_{l_1,i_1+\Delta_1}, x_{l_2,i_2+\Delta_2}, \dots, x_{l_d,i_d+\Delta_d}\right), \ -1 \le \Delta_j \le 1, \ 1 \le j \le d. \tag{7}$$

In the case when the interpolated function has a nonzero value at the boundary, the one-dimensional basis is supplemented by two additional functions: $\varphi_{0,0}(x)$ and $\varphi_{0,1}(x)$ (Figure 4). Two values are added to the polynomial given by Equation (5): $a_{0,0}\varphi_{0,0}(x)$ and $a_{0,1}\varphi_{0,1}(x)$, where $a_{0,0} = f(0)$, $a_{0,1} = f(1)$. By analogy, for multidimensional interpolation, it follows that if $l_j = 0$, then $i_j = 0, 1$ in Equation (6) and $\Delta_j = 0$ in Equation (7). Allowance for boundary values in the multidimensional case can be considered as the construction of sparse grids for all faces of lower dimensions. Figure 5 shows a sparse grid, which takes into account the boundary values.

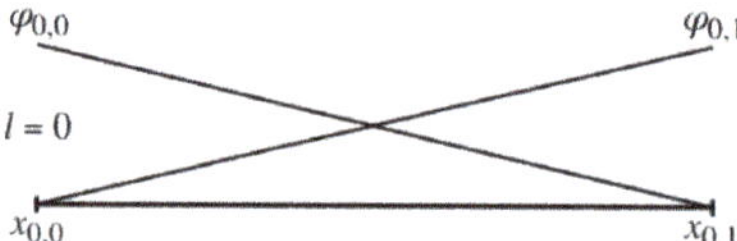

Figure 4. Additional basis functions taking into account boundary values.

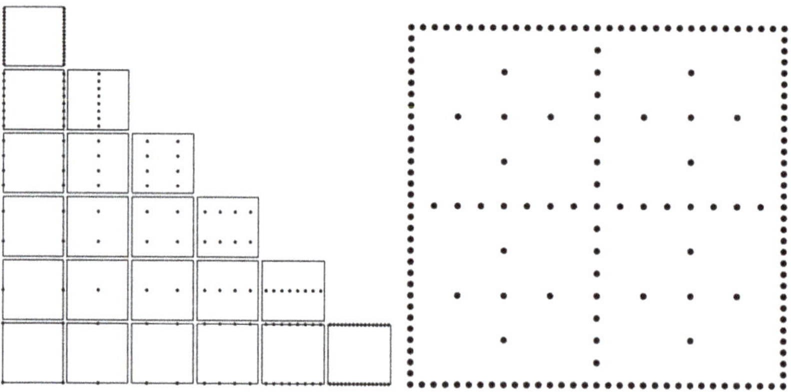

Figure 5. Sparse grid of the level $n = 4$, which takes into account boundary values.

In addition, there are adaptive sparse grids for which a general tree can be used to perform structuring. Each vertex of the tree corresponds to a certain basis function $\varphi_{\mathbf{l},\mathbf{i}}$. If the value of the corresponding coefficient $a_{\mathbf{l},\mathbf{i}}/\max(f(x_{\mathbf{l},\mathbf{i}}), 1) > \varepsilon$, where ε is some predetermined value, then each vertex creates $2d$ descendants, which correspond to the basis functions of the next level. This process continues recursively until the values $a_{\mathbf{l},\mathbf{i}}$ at all leaf vertices become less than ε. With this approach, it is important to make sure that there is no duplication of vertices.

Consider some examples. Figure 6 shows several functions $\mathbb{R}^2 \to \mathbb{R}$ and the resulting adaptive grid, Figure 7 shows grids for functions $\mathbb{R}^3 \to \mathbb{R}$.

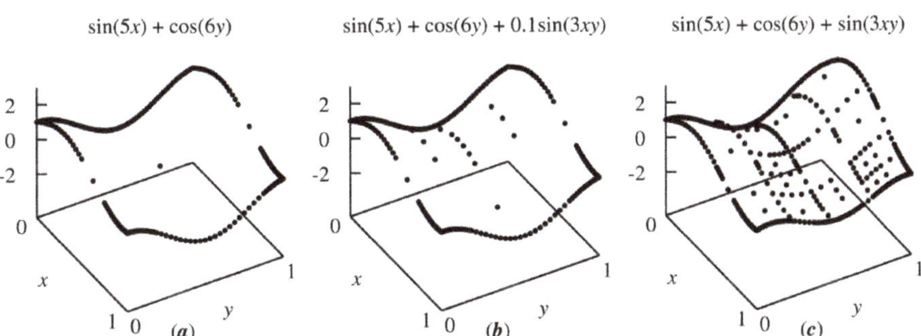

Figure 6. Examples showing interpolation using functions of two variables. (**a**) Linear combination of univariate functions. (**b**) Linear combination of univariate functions and a function of two variables x and y with a small coefficient. (**c**) Linear combination of univariate and a function of two variables x and y.

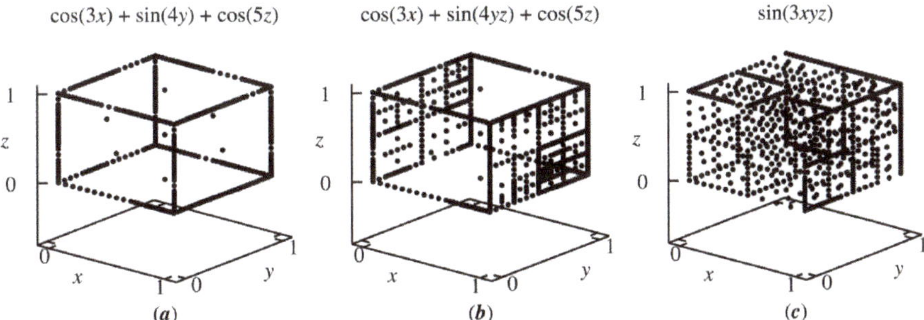

Figure 7. Examples of grids for functions of three variables. (**a**) Linear combination of univariate functions. (**b**) Linear combination of univariate functions and a function of two variables y and z. (**c**) Nonlinear function of three variables.

It can be seen from the figures that if the initial dependence is a linear combination of functions determined by certain subgroups of variables, then the adaptive sparse grid will become more dense not in the entire set (Figures 6c and 7c), but only in subsets of lower dimension that correspond to these subgroups (Figures 6a and 7a,b). The subsets for grid construction are determined by those subgroups of parameters, for which the mixed derivatives are nonzero, and the grid density directly depends on the values of these derivatives (Figure 6b,c).

To build a solution for the system given by Equation (1), the uncertainty area $y_i^0 \in \left[\underline{y_i^0}, \overline{y_i^0}\right], 1 \le i \le m$ is transformed with the help of displacement and stretching into a m-dimensional unit cube. Taking into account that solving the problem requires interpolating n functions at once (n is the number of phase variables of the system), Equations (6) and (7) will take the following form:

$$\mathbf{P}^k\left(\mathbf{y}^0\right) = \sum_{l,i} \mathbf{a}_{l,i}^k \varphi_{l,i}\left(\mathbf{y}^0\right),$$

where

$$\mathbf{a}_{l,i}^k = \sum_{\Delta_1,\dots,\Delta_m} \left(-\frac{1}{2}\right)^{\sum\limits_{j=1}^{m}|\Delta_j|} \mathbf{y}^k\left(y_{1,l_1,i_1+\Delta_1}^0, y_{2,l_2,i_2+\Delta_2}^0, \dots, y_{m,l_m,i_m+\Delta_m}^0\right), \quad -1 \le \Delta_j \le 1, 1 \le j \le m \tag{8}$$

The vector norm $\mathbf{a}_{l,i}^k$ (for example, the maximum one) can be used as a criterion for adapting the grid.

Construct an interpolation polynomial $\mathbf{P}^{k+1}\left(\mathbf{y}^0\right)$. All the solutions that participated in the calculation of the coefficients given by Equation (8) are transferred to the $(k+1)$-th time layer using some numerical integration method, after which a new set of $\mathbf{a}_{\mathbf{l},\mathbf{i}}^{k+1}$ coefficients is calculated and the adaptation of the grid is performed. When compacting the grid, the addition of new basis functions occurs at the k-th time layer and the solutions involved in computing the corresponding weight coefficients are transferred to the next layer.

The efficiency of the considered approach will be noticeable when many mixed derivatives of the solution with respect to the parameters $\dfrac{\partial^{\Sigma\alpha_i}y^k\left(y_1^0,y_2^0,...,y_m^0\right)}{\left(\partial y_1^0\right)^{\alpha_1}\left(\partial y_2^0\right)^{\alpha_2}...\left(\partial y_m^0\right)^{\alpha_m}}$, $\max\limits_{1\le i\le m}\alpha_i\le 2$, $y_i^0\in\left[\underline{y_i^0},\overline{y_i^0}\right]$, $1\le i\le m$ are negligible or equal to zero. Particularly, this takes place, if the solution to the ODE system can be represented as a linear combination of functions determined by a certain subset of interval parameters.

Thus, the scope of application of the proposed approach is rather wide and includes various dynamic systems. In the next section, it is demonstrated how the method is applied to some representative problems.

3. Approbation of the Algorithm for Nonlinear Dynamics Problems

To characterize computational costs, a criterion is determined, which is equal to the average number of integrated non-interval ODE systems at a time step in the computational process:

$$I=\frac{1}{N}\sum_{k=1}^{N}C_k,$$

where C_k is the number of nodes at the k step. A similar criterion exists for the classical adaptive interpolation algorithm [11]. The I value is equivalent to the number of sampling points from the original region of uncertainty.

To estimate the posterior interpolation error at the initial moment of time, n_{check} points are randomly generated:

$$y_i^j(t_0)=rand\left[\underline{y_i^0},\overline{y_i^0}\right],\ 1\le i\le m,\ 1\le j\le n_{check}.$$

For the initial conditions obtained, with the help of a numerical integration method, solutions are constructed at the final moment of time t_N. The relative posterior global estimate of the error is written as follows:

$$error=\max_{\substack{1\le j\le n_{check},\\ 1\le i\le n}}\frac{\left|P_i^N\left(y_1^j(t_0),y_2^j(t_0),...,y_m^j(t_0)\right)-y_i^j(t_N)\right|}{\max\left(\left|y_i^j(t_N)\right|,1\right)}.$$

Let us integrate several ODE interval systems using the described approach. The calculation is performed for two values of $\varepsilon=10^{-3}$ and $\varepsilon=10^{-5}$ (ε imposes a restriction on the values of the weight coefficients of the basic functions when constructing an adaptive sparse grid). First, let us take into account an ordinary differential system with two interval initial conditions, which describes a conservative oscillator:

$$\begin{cases} x\prime=y,\ y\prime=-\sin(x),\\ x(0)=x_0\in[-1,1],\ y(0)=y_0\in[0,1],\ t\in[0,25]. \end{cases}\tag{9}$$

Figure 8 shows a set of solutions for the system given by Equation (9) at different moments of time; it twists into a spiral structure during the integration. Figure 9 shows the grid resulting from applying the algorithm. The points in these two figures correspond to each other.

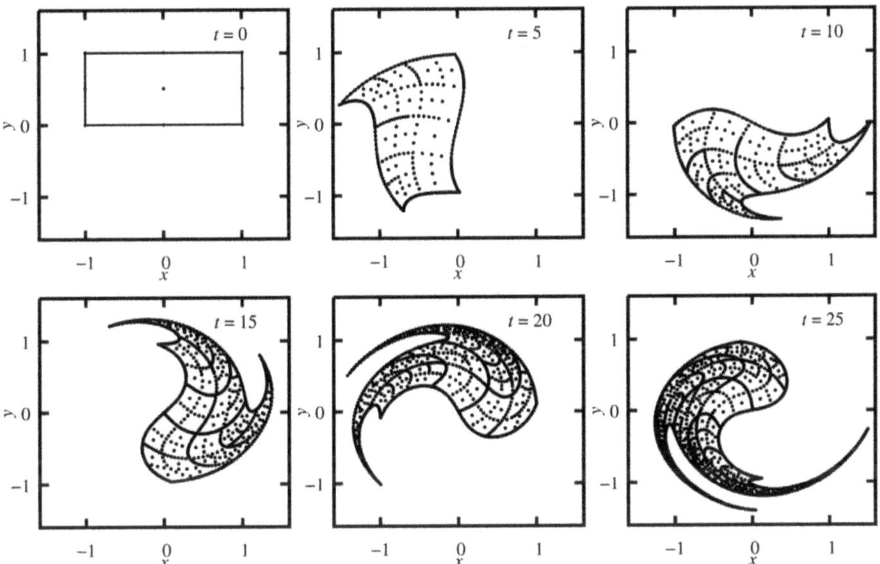

Figure 8. The interval solution of system given by Equation (9) at different moments of time.

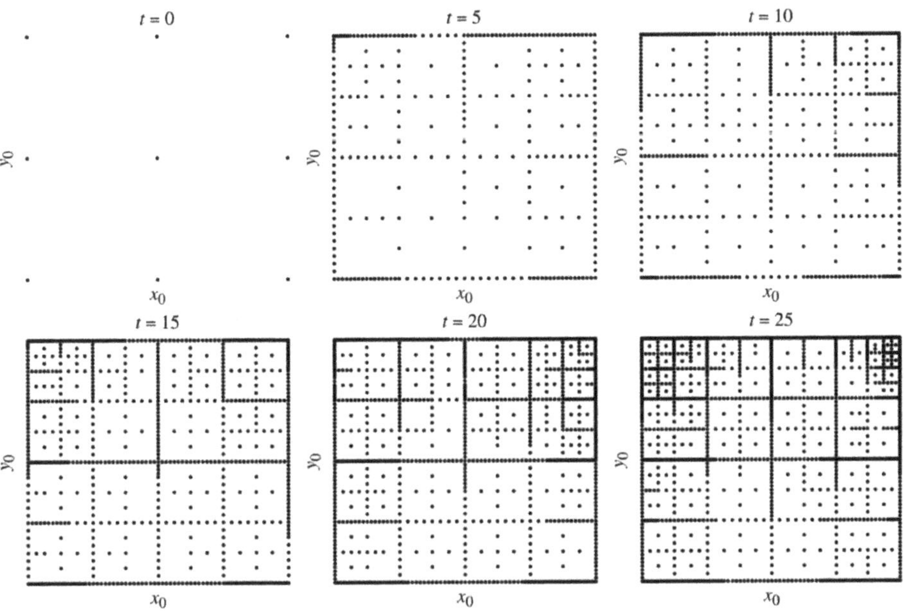

Figure 9. The grids obtained in the process of solving system given by Equation (9).

Table 1 shows a comparison of computational costs and error estimates for different approaches. When set to a low precision ($\varepsilon = 10^{-3}$), adaptive sparse grids work a little faster than the classical adaptive interpolation algorithm, and twice as fast as conventional sparse grids. However, for $\varepsilon = 10^{-5}$, the classical algorithm wins due to the application of an interpolation polynomial of a high degree. The levels of the grids were adjusted to obtain approximately the same error as in other approaches.

Table 1. Comparison of approaches for system given by Equation (9).

Methods	$\varepsilon=10^{-3}$		$\varepsilon=10^{-5}$	
	I	*error*	*I*	*error*
full grid (level 6 and level 8)	4225	3.6×10^{-3}	66,049	2.2×10^{-4}
sparse grid (level 7 and level 10)	1793	7.7×10^{-3}	36,865	6.9×10^{-5}
adaptive sparse grid	689	6.6×10^{-3}	9455	1.1×10^{-4}
adaptive interpolation algorithm, $p = 2$	3877	6.3×10^{-3}	52,195	1.8×10^{-4}
adaptive interpolation algorithm, $p = 4$	990	6.8×10^{-3}	4752	1.5×10^{-4}

Next, the Volterra-Lotka model with interval initial conditions and one interval coefficient is considered. The Cauchy problem in the case has the form:

$$\begin{cases} x' = 4x - \frac{5}{4}xy - \alpha x^2, \ y\prime = -2y + \frac{1}{2}xy - \frac{1}{20}y^2, \\ x(0) = x_0 \in [4, 5], \ y(0) = y_0 \in [2.8, 3.2], \ t \in [0, 25], \end{cases} \tag{10}$$

where $\alpha \in [-0.05, 0.05]$.

This model describes predator–prey interactions. A feature of the system is the fact that at $\alpha < 0$ there is an unstable focus and the amplitude of fluctuations in the population of species grows, and at $\alpha > 0$ the focus is stable and the state of the system tends to be stationary over time.

Figure 10 shows the set of solutions for the system at different points in time. The following picture is clearly observed here: some part of the set converges to a point, which corresponds to a stable focus, and another part of the set increases in its size, which corresponds to an unstable focus. Figure 11 shows the resulting grid. Due to the fact that uncertainty is present in the parameters, the set of solutions on the phase plane is only a projection of the three-dimensional set onto the two-dimensional phase space. The additional dimension corresponds to the interval parameter α.

Table 2 shows a comparison of the different approaches. Similar to the previous task, adaptive sparse grids are effective with lower accuracy ε.

Table 2. Comparison of approaches on system given by Equation (10).

Methods	$\varepsilon=10^{-3}$		$\varepsilon=10^{-5}$	
	I	*error*	*I*	*error*
full grid (level 4 and level 6)	4913	3.3×10^{-3}	274,625	2.0×10^{-4}
sparse grid (level 3 and level 7)	705	2.4×10^{-3}	19,713	4.3×10^{-5}
adaptive sparse grid	193	3.1×10^{-3}	3170	4.8×10^{-5}
adaptive interpolation algorithm, $p = 2$	544	4.6×10^{-3}	48,013	6.8×10^{-5}
adaptive interpolation algorithm, $p = 4$	369	1.6×10^{-3}	3978	5.2×10^{-5}

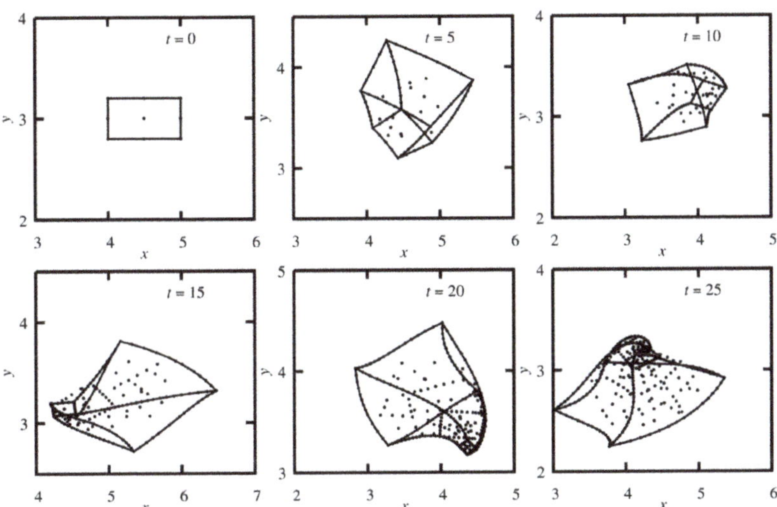

Figure 10. The interval solution of system given by Equation (10) at different times.

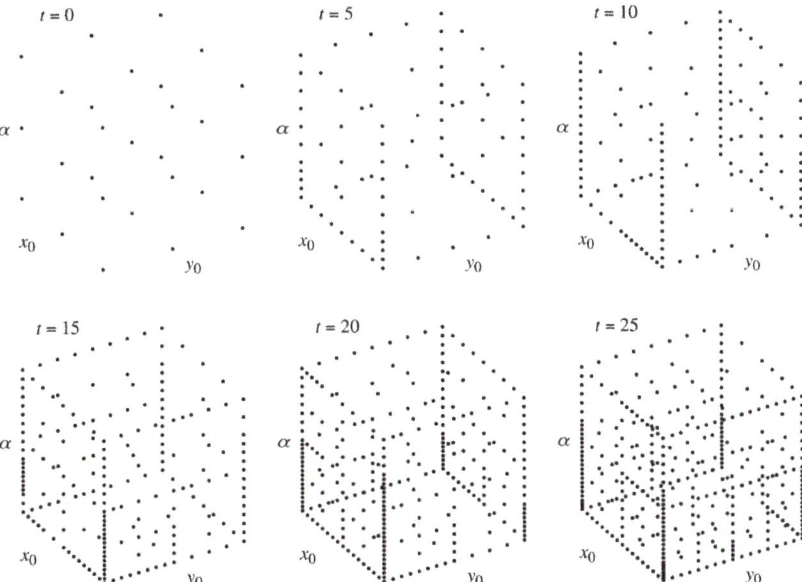

Figure 11. The grid obtained in the process of solving the system given by Equation (10).

Consider an ordinary differential system presenting the expanded Volterra-Lotka model with three interval initial conditions and seven interval parameters:

$$
\begin{cases}
x' = x(\delta_1 - y - \varepsilon x), \\
y\prime = -\gamma_1 y(\delta_2 - x + z) - \varphi y^2, \\
z\prime = -\gamma_2 z(\alpha - y),
\end{cases}
\quad
\begin{aligned}
& x(0),\, y(0),\, z(0),\, \delta_1,\, \delta_2,\, \gamma_1,\, \gamma_2 \in [1.0,\, 1.01], \\
& \varepsilon,\, \varphi \in [-0.0005,\, 0.0005], \\
& \alpha \in [0.9,\, 0.91].
\end{aligned}
\tag{11}
$$

Figure 12 shows the dependences of the interval estimates of solutions on time.

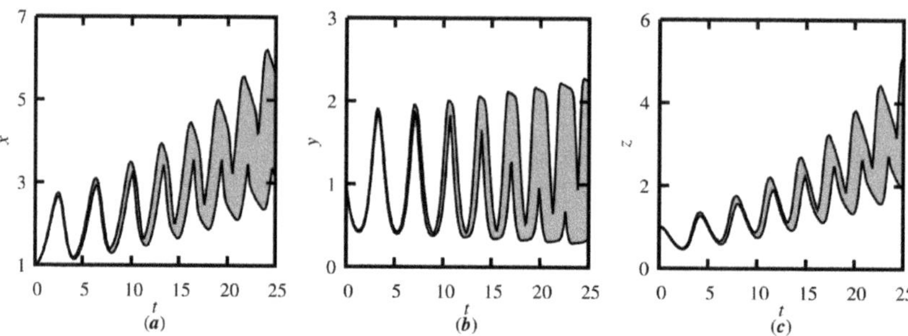

Figure 12. Time dependence of the upper and lower bounds for the solution of system given by Equation (11): (**a**) $x(t)$; (**b**) $y(t)$; (**c**) $z(t)$.

For a reasonable time, the solution was obtained using only adaptive sparse grids. For $\varepsilon = 10^{-3}$, the obtained result was $I = 81,566.1$ and $error = 1.2 \times 10^{-2}$.

Consider a model describing the motion of interacting bodies. The problem can be formulated as a dynamic system with interval initial velocities. The system of ordinary differential equations in dimensionless variables is as follows:

$$
\begin{cases}
(v_i^x)' = \sum\limits_{j=1, j \neq i}^{4} m_j(x_j - x_i)r_{i,j}^{-3}, \; (v_i^y)' = \sum\limits_{j=1, j \neq i}^{4} m_j(y_j - y_i)r_{i,j}^{-3}, \; (v_i^z)' = \sum\limits_{j=1, j \neq i}^{4} m_j(z_j - z_i)r_{i,j}^{-3}, \\
x'_i = v_i^x, \, y'_i = v_i^y, \, z'_i = v_i^z, \, 2 \leq i \leq 4, \\
x_1(0) = y_1(0) = z_1(0) = v_1^x(0) = v_1^y(0) = v_1^z(0) = 0, \\
x_{2,3}(0) = \pm 1, \, y_{2,3}(0) = z_{2,3}(0) = 0, \, v_{2,3}(0) = \begin{pmatrix} 0 & \pm v & 0 \end{pmatrix}^T + \Delta v_{2,3}^T, \\
y_4(0) = 1, \, x_4(0) = z_4(0) = 0, \, v_4(0) = \begin{pmatrix} 0 & 0 & v \end{pmatrix}^T + \Delta v_4^T, \\
t \in [0.0, 0.02]
\end{cases}
\tag{12}
$$

where $r_{i,j} = \sqrt{(x_j - x_i)^2 + (y_j - y_i)^2 + (z_j - z_i)^2}$ is the distance between two bodies, $v = 316.23$ is the initial velocity of bodies, $m_1 = 10^5$, $m_{2,3,4} = 10^{-5}$ are body masses, $\Delta v_{2,3,4} = ([-2, 2], [-2, 2], [-2, 2])$ are the interval uncertainties in body velocities.

Figure 13 shows graphs for the dependence of the interval estimates of the 2nd body coordinates and velocities on time. Similar to the previous problem, the solution was calculated only using adaptive sparse grids. For $\varepsilon = 10^{-3}$, the obtained result was $I = 133830.9$ and $error = 2.6 \times 10^{-2}$.

This system is demonstrative because the uncertainty in the speed of a particular body mainly affects the position and speed of that particular body and has little effect on other bodies. In this regard, the solution of the system will have a specific form, as most of the mixed derivatives will be close to zero.

Note that the classical adaptive interpolation algorithm for systems given by Equations (6) and (7) constructs sets of solutions with fewer integrations of the corresponding non-interval ordinary differential systems since it uses nonlinear interpolation. However, when the number of interval parameters increases (systems given by Equations (8) and (9)), the use of adaptive sparse grids becomes more efficient. When increasing the dimension of the problem, it is practically impossible to increase the degree of the interpolation polynomial in the adaptive interpolation algorithm to obtain higher accuracy due to the exponential growth of the number of nodes in the grid. Therefore, for high dimensional-problems, it is suitable to use methods that have lower accuracy, but at the same time allow reasonable computational costs; in particular, adaptive sparse grids.

The examples above demonstrate that by using sparse grids it is possible to simulate dynamic systems with ten interval uncertainties in a reasonable time. When solving system given by Equation (11), the equivalent number of sampling points was about 80 thousand, and in the case of using classical interpolation with the degree of polynomial equal to 4, the value would be of order 10^7. A lower estimate of the computational cost can be obtained. It follows from Equation (8) that the number of solved non-interval ODE systems cannot be less than 3^m. The upper estimate of the computational costs, in the general case, essentially depends on the features of the ODE system being solved, in particular on the values of the mixed derivatives of the solution with respect to the point values of the interval parameters. For comparison, the classical adaptive interpolation algorithm requires at least $(p+1)^m$ points, and the method proposed in Reference [15] requires $\frac{(m+p)!}{m!p!}$ points, where p is the degree of the interpolation polynomial.

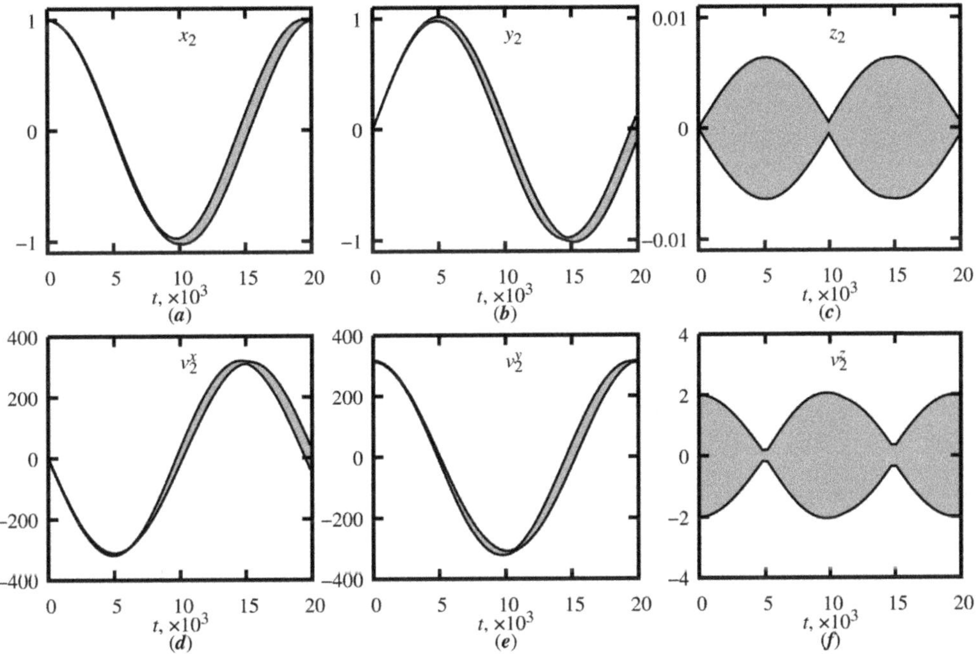

Figure 13. Time dependencies of upper and lower estimates of the 2nd body coordinates and velocities: (**a**) $x_2(t)$; (**b**) $y_2(t)$; (**c**) $z_2(t)$; (**d**) $v_2^x(t)$; (**e**) $v_2^y(t)$; (**f**) $v_2^z(t)$.

4. Computation of an Interval Stress Tensor for Materials with a Covalent Chemical Bond

Let us consider an applied problem of computational materials science, within the framework of which the stresses arising during the deformation of an ideal crystal are calculated [12]. Different angles are possible between the orientation of the crystal lattice and the direction of stretching with a fixed stretch value. The stress tensor thus becomes interval. This problem is solved using molecular dynamics simulation. The motion of atoms is described by the classical equations of dynamics:

$$\begin{cases} \mathbf{r}_i' = \mathbf{v}_i, \\ \mathbf{v}_i' = \dfrac{1}{m_i}\mathbf{F}_i, \end{cases}$$

where $\mathbf{r}_i$ is the radius vector of the atom with the number i, $\mathbf{v}_i$ is its velocity, m_i is its mass, and $\mathbf{F}_i$ is the force acting on the atom, in this case $\mathbf{F}_i = -\nabla_i E$, where E is the total energy of the system, and ∇_i is the gradient along the position of the atom with the number i.

In this problem, materials with a covalent interatomic bond are considered. The total energy of interaction between atoms of such materials is well described using the Tersoff potential [25]:

$$
\begin{cases}
E = \frac{1}{2}\sum_i \sum_{j\neq i} V_{ij}, \quad V_{ij} = f_C(r_{ij})\left(f_R(r_{ij}) + b_{ij}f_A(r_{ij})\right), \\[2mm]
f_C(r) = \begin{cases}
1, \, r < R - D, \\
\frac{1}{2}\left(1 - \sin\left(\frac{\pi}{2}\frac{r-R}{D}\right)\right), \, R - D \leq r < R + D, \\
0, \, R + D \leq r,
\end{cases} \\[2mm]
f_R(r) = A\exp(-\lambda_1 r), \, f_A(r) = -B\exp(-\lambda_2 r), \\[2mm]
b_{ij} = \left(1 + \beta^n \varsigma_{ij}^n\right)^{-\frac{1}{2n}}, \\[2mm]
\varsigma_{ij} = \sum_{k\neq i,j} f_C(r_{ik})g\left(\theta_{ijk}\right)\exp\left(\lambda_3^m (r_{ij} - r_{ik})^m\right), \\[2mm]
g(\theta) = \gamma\left(1 + \frac{c^2}{d^2} - \frac{c^2}{d^2 + (\cos(\theta) - \cos(\theta_0))^2}\right),
\end{cases}
$$

where E is total system energy, V_{ij} is the contribution to the interaction energy of atoms with numbers i and j, r_{ij} is the distance between atoms with numbers i and j, $f_C(r)$ is a cut-off function, $f_R(r)$ and $f_A(r)$ are the repulsion and attraction potentials, respectively, and R, D, A, B, n, m, λ_1, λ_2, λ_3, β, γ, c, d and $\cos(\theta_0)$ are potential parameters that are selected in order to reproduce the properties of the simulated material. Methods of parametric identification of the Tersoff potential parameters are considered in papers [26,27].

The initial positions of atoms and their number are determined by the structure of the crystal lattice and the restriction on the minimum size of the simulated space is specified by the structure of the potential.

Consider crystalline silicon as a typical material. The simulated sample is represented by eight unit cells of a diamond crystal lattice making up a cube of $2 \times 2 \times 2$ in size, with periodic boundary conditions; each unit cell contains eight unique atoms (Figure 14), so a total of 64 atoms are involved in the simulation. Initial speeds are considered to be zero. The initial conditions for a dynamical system can be represented as follows:

$$
\begin{cases}
\mathbf{r}_i(0) = \left((x,y,z)^T + (dx,dy,dz)^T\right)a, \, (x,y,z) \in \text{Base}, \, dx,dy,dz \in \{0,1\}, \, \mathbf{v}_i(0) = (0,0,0)^T, \\[2mm]
\text{Base} = \left\{\begin{array}{l}
(0,0,0), \, (0,0.5,0.5), \, (0.5,0,0.5), \, (0.5,0.5,0), \, (0.75,0.75,0.75), \\
(0.75,0.25,0.25), \, (0.25,0.75,0.25), \, (0.25,0.25,0.75)
\end{array}\right\},
\end{cases}
$$

where $a = 5.429 \times 10^{-10}$ m is the linear size of a unit cell of a silicon crystal.

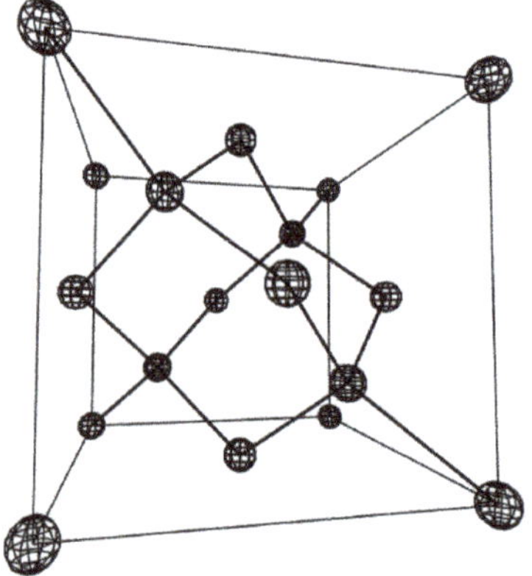

Figure 14. Unit cell of a silicon crystal.

To take into account deformation, 4 additional variables are introduced: one of them reflects the elongation value, and three more are responsible for the angle between the orientation of the lattice and the direction of stretching. In this case, the elongation is set to be fixed, and the variables responsible for the rotation are taken as interval. Rotation is generated evenly using quaternions [28].

The final system looks like this:

$$
\begin{cases}
\mathbf{r}_i' = \mathbf{v}_i, \ \mathbf{v}_i' = -\frac{1}{2m_i}\sum_i\sum_{j\neq i}\nabla_i\big(f_C(r_{ij})\big(f_R(r_{ij})+b_{ij}f_A(r_{ij})\big)\big), \\
r_{ij}(s,\mu_1,\mu_2,\mu_3) = \|\mathbf{S}(s)\mathbf{R}(\mu_1,\mu_2,\mu_3)\mathbf{r}_{ij}\|, \\
\mathbf{S}(s) = \mathrm{diag}(1+s,1,1), \\
\mathbf{R}(\mu_1,\mu_2,\mu_3) = \begin{pmatrix} 1-2(q_2^2+q_3^2) & 2(q_1q_2-q_3q_0) & 2(q_1q_3+q_2q_0) \\ 2(q_1q_2+q_3q_0) & 1-2(q_1^2+q_3^2) & 2(q_2q_3-q_1q_0) \\ 2(q_1q_3-q_2q_0) & 2(q_2q_3+q_1q_0) & 1-2(q_1^2+q_2^2) \end{pmatrix}, \\
(q_0,q_1,q_2,q_3) = \big(\sqrt{1-\mu_1}\sin(2\pi\mu_2),\sqrt{1-\mu_1}\cos(2\pi\mu_2),\sqrt{\mu_1}\sin(2\pi\mu_3),\sqrt{\mu_1}\sin(2\pi\mu_3)\big), \\
t \in \big[0,10^{-12}\big],
\end{cases} \tag{13}
$$

where $m = 4.65 \times 10^{-26}$ kg is the mass of atoms, $s = 0.1$ is the relative elongation of the sample, $\mu_1 \in [0.1,0.9]$, $\mu_2 \in [0.1,0.9]$, and $\mu_3 \in [0.1,0.9]$ are stretching direction parameters, $R = 2.85 \times 10^{-10}$ m, $D = 0.15 \times 10^{-10}$ m, $A = 6.12 \times 10^{-16}$ J, $B = 1.81 \times 10^{-17}$ J, $c = 9.69$, $d = 2.35$, $n = 4.16$, $\beta = 0.132$, $\lambda_1 = 3.36 \times 10^{10}$ m^{-1}, $\lambda_2 = 1.27 \times 10^{10}$ m^{-1}, $\lambda_3 = 1.19 \times 10^{10}$ m^{-1}, $\gamma = 5.71$, and $\cos(\theta_0) = -0.408$ are the parameters of the potential.

Integration of the resulting ordinary differential system (13) was carried out using the Verlet velocity method with a constant integration step of 10^{-15} s. As a result, the interval stress tensor was obtained (values are given in Pascals):

$$
\begin{pmatrix}
[-1.58 \times 10^{10}, -1.43 \times 10^{10}] & [-1.35 \times 10^{9}, 1.35 \times 10^{9}] & [-1.35 \times 10^{9}, 1.35 \times 10^{9}] \\
[-1.35 \times 10^{9}, 1.35 \times 10^{9}] & [-4.79 \times 10^{9}, -1.46 \times 10^{9}] & [-1.42 \times 10^{9}, 1.42 \times 10^{9}] \\
[-1.35 \times 10^{9}, 1.35 \times 10^{9}] & [-1.42 \times 10^{9}, 1.42 \times 10^{9}] & [-4.79 \times 10^{9}, -1.46 \times 10^{9}]
\end{pmatrix}
$$

For $\varepsilon = 10^{-2}$, the obtained result was $I = 1079132.3$ and $error = 2 \times 10^{-1}$.

Note that the possibilities of the proposed approach are not limited to a specific type of interatomic interaction potential in a material. The method can be applied to the simulation of the stress–strain state of materials with various types of chemical bonds, including the modeling of composite materials.

5. Discussion

In the previous sections, the proposed approach was tested on representative interval problems of nonlinear dynamics and computational materials science. It is found that, thanks to sparse grids, it is possible to integrate ODE systems with a large number of interval uncertainties in a reasonable time. To estimate the computational costs, a criterion was used that is equal to the equivalent number of sampling points from the original uncertainty region.

Table 1 shows estimates of the computational costs for the ODE system given by Equation (9) describing a conservative oscillator with two interval initial conditions for two values ε. For $\varepsilon = 10^{-3}$, the approach proposed in the paper works 1.5 to 5 times faster than the classical adaptive interpolation algorithm.

Table 2 shows the computational costs when integrating the ODE system given by Equation (10), describing the Lotka-Volterra model with two interval initial conditions and one interval parameter. Here, for $\varepsilon = 10^{-3}$, the use of adaptive sparse grids gives an acceleration of $1.9 - 2.8$ times compared to the classical algorithm, and for $\varepsilon = 10^{-5}$, the acceleration is from 1.25 time to 15 time.

For ODE systems given by Equations (11) and (12), it was possible to obtain a solution in a reasonable time only using the approach proposed in the paper since the number of interval uncertainties is quite large. To solve system given by Equation (11), the equivalent number of sampling points was about 80 thousand, and in the case of using the classical algorithm with a degree of polynomial 4, the value would be about 10 million. Thus, using sparse grids in this problem gives an acceleration of at least 125 times.

The tables show that adaptive sparse grids work faster than regular sparse grids, and even faster than full grids. This fact is in line with the theoretical foundations. The classical adaptive interpolation algorithm in example (9) with two interval uncertainties showed itself slightly better only when $\varepsilon = 10^{-5}$ and $p = 4$. This is primarily due to the chosen value of p. It is known that the greater the degree of the interpolation polynomial, the faster the error decreases with increasing mesh density. Therefore, it seems promising to use sparse grids on a nonlinear basis. We should also note the possibilities of applying adaptive grids to ODE systems not only with interval uncertainties but also with stochastic uncertainties, including applied nonlinear systems.

6. Conclusions

The adaptive interpolation algorithm allows simulating dynamic systems with interval parameters. In the course of the algorithm operation, a regular grid is constructed in the parameter space. The number of grid nodes depends exponentially on the number of interval parameters, which limits the scope of the algorithm. A typical situation is when the degree of influence of different parameters and their combinations on the solution can differ significantly. This can be used in adaptive interpolation. The paper presents an adaptive interpolation algorithm on sparse grids, which allows for reducing the exponential complexity when solving multidimensional problems in parameter space. The efficiency of the proposed approach has been demonstrated on representative interval problems of nonlinear dynamics and computational materials science. It is shown that, for most variants, adaptive sparse grids are more efficient than the classical adaptive interpolation algorithm in terms of computational costs. With the suggested method, it was possible to solve problems with up to 10 interval parameters in a reasonable amount of time. At the same time, the classical algorithm of adaptive interpolation failed to do so. Taking into account that an increase in the degree of the interpolation polynomial in the classical adaptive interpolation algorithm leads to higher accuracy and lower computational costs, we can outline the use of sparse grids with a nonlinear basis as a direction for further research.

Author Contributions: Methodology, software, investigation, A.Y.M.; investigation, software, validation, A.A.Z.; conceptualization, methodology, supervision, D.L.R. All authors have read and agreed to the published version of the manuscript.

Funding: This research was supported by the Ministry of Science and Higher Education of the Russian Federation, project No 075-15-2020-799.

Institutional Review Board Statement: Not applicable.

Informed Consent Statement: Not applicable.

Data Availability Statement: Data sharing not applicable.

Conflicts of Interest: The authors declare no conflict of interest.

References

1. Richtmyer, R.D.; Moore, R.E. Interval Analysis. *Math. Comput.* **1968**, *22*, 219. [CrossRef]
2. Moore, R.E.; Kearfott, R.B.; Cloud, M.J. *Introduction to Interval Analysis*; SIAM: Philadelphia, PA, USA, 2009.
3. Eijgenraam, P. The Solution of Initial Value Problems Using Interval Arithmetic Formulation and Analysis of an Algorithm. *Math. Comput.* **1984**, *42*, 343. [CrossRef]
4. Dobronets, B.S. *Interval Mathematics*; Krasnoyarsk State University: Krasnoyarsk, Russia, 2007. (In Russian)
5. Shary, S.P. *Finite Dimensional Interval Analysis*; Institute of Computational Technologies SB RAS. XYZ Publisher: Novosibirsk, Russia, 2019; p. 634. (In Russian)
6. Chernousko, F.L. *Evaluation of Phase States of Dynamic Systems. The Method of Ellipsoids*; Science: Moscow, Russia, 1988; p. 319. (In Russian)
7. Lohner, R.J. Enclosing the Solutions of Ordinary Initial and Boundary Value Problems. In *Computer Arithmetic: Scientific Computation and Programing Languages*; Wiley-Teubner Series in Computer Science; Wiley-Teubner: Stuttgard, Germany, 1987; pp. 255–286.

8. Makino, K.; Berz, M. Models and Their Applications. Numerical Software Verification Computations. In *Proceedings of the Numerical Software Verification 2017 Conference; Heidelberg, Germany, 22–23 July 2017*; Springer International Publishing: Berlin/Heidelberg, Germany, 2017; pp. 3–13.
9. Rogalev, A.N. Guaranteed Methods of Ordinary Differential Equations Solution on the Basis of Transformation of Analytical Formulas. *Vychisl. Tekhnol.* **2003**, *8*, 102–116. (In Russian)
10. Ermakov, S.M.; Mikhailov, G.A. *Statistical Modeling*; Science: Moscow, Russia, 1982. (In Russian)
11. Morozov, A.; Reviznikov, D.L. Adaptive Interpolation Algorithm Based on a kd-Tree for Numerical Integration of Systems of Ordinary Differential Equations with Interval Initial Conditions. *Differ. Equ.* **2018**, *54*, 945–956. [CrossRef]
12. Morozov, A.; Zhuravlev, A.A.; Reviznikov, D.L. Analysis and Optimization of an Adaptive Interpolation Algorithm for the Numerical Solution of a System of Ordinary Differential Equations with Interval Parameters. *Differ. Equ.* **2020**, *56*, 935–949. [CrossRef]
13. Morozov, A.; Reviznikov, D.L.; Gidaspov, V.Y. Adaptive Interpolation Algorithm Based on a kd-Tree for the Problems of Chemical Kinetics with Interval Parameters. *Math. Model. Comput. Simul.* **2019**, *11*, 622–633. [CrossRef]
14. Morozov, A.; Federal Research Center Computer Science and Control of the Russian Academy of Sciences; Reviznikov, D.L. Moscow aviation Institute (national research University) Modeling of Dynamic Systems with Interval Parameters in the Presence of Singularities. *Nelineinaya Din.* **2020**, *16*, 479–490. [CrossRef]
15. Fu, C.; Ren, X.; Yang, Y.-F.; Lu, K.; Qin, W. Steady-state response analysis of cracked rotors with uncertain-but-bounded parameters using a polynomial surrogate method. *Commun. Nonlinear Sci. Numer. Simul.* **2019**, *68*, 240–256. [CrossRef]
16. Fu, C.; Xu, Y.; Yang, Y.; Lu, K.; Gu, F.; Ball, A. Response analysis of an accelerating unbalanced rotating system with both random and interval variables. *J. Sound Vib.* **2020**, *466*, 115047. [CrossRef]
17. Smoljak, S.A. Quadrature and Interpolation Formulae on Tensor Products of Certain Classes of Functions. *Dokl. Akad. Nauk. Sssr* **1963**, *148*, 1042. (In Russian)
18. Faber, G. Über stetige Funktionen. (Mit 2 Figuren im Text). *Math. Ann.* **1909**, *66*, 81–94. [CrossRef]
19. Yserentant, H. Hierarchical bases. In *ICIAM 91: Proceedings of the Second International Conference on Industrial and Applied Mathematics, Washington, DC, 8–12 July 1991*; SIAM: Philadelphia, PA, USA, 1992; pp. 256–276.
20. Gerstner, T.; Griebel, M. Sparse Grids. In *Encyclopedia of Quantitative Finance*; Wiley: Hoboken, NJ, USA, 2010.
21. Garcke, J. *Sparse Grids in a Nutshell*; Sparse Grids and Applications; Lecture Notes in Computational Science and Engi-neering; Springer: Berlin/Heidelberg, Germany, 2013; Volume 88, pp. 57–80.
22. Brumm, J.; Scheidegger, S. Using Adaptive Sparse Grids to Solve High-Dimensional Dynamic Models. *Econometrica* **2017**, *85*, 1575–1612. [CrossRef]
23. Bungatrz, H.-J.; Griebel, M. Sparse grids. *Acta Numerica.* **2004**, *13*, 147–269.
24. Zhang, Z.; Tretyakov, M.V.; Rozovskii, B.; Karniadakis, G.E. A recursive sparse grid collocation method for differential equations with white noise. *SIAM J. Sci. Comput.* **2014**, *36*, A1652–A1677. [CrossRef]
25. Tersoff, J. New empirical approach for the structure and energy of covalent systems. *Phys. Rev. B* **1988**, *37*, 6991–7000. [CrossRef] [PubMed]
26. Abgaryan, K.K.; Posypkin, M. Optimization methods as applied to parametric identification of interatomic potentials. *Comput. Math. Math. Phys.* **2014**, *54*, 1929–1935. [CrossRef]
27. Abgaryan, K.K.; Grevtsev, A.V. Parametric Identification of Tersoff Potential for Two-Component Materials. *Agent Multi-Agent Syst. Technol. Appl.* **2020**, *173*, 257–268. [CrossRef]
28. Shoemake, K. Uniform random rotations. *Graph. Gems Iii (Ibm Version)* **1992**, 124–132. [CrossRef]

Article

High-Performance Tracking for Proton Exchange Membrane Fuel Cell System PEMFC Using Model Predictive Control

Mohamed Derbeli [1], Asma Charaabi [2], Oscar Barambones [1,*] and Cristian Napole [1]

[1] System Engineering and Automation Department, Faculty of Engineering of Vitoria-Gasteiz, Basque Country University (UPV/EHU), 01006 Vitoria-Gasteiz, Spain; derbelimohamed1@gmail.com (M.D.); cristianmario.napole@ehu.eus (C.N.)

[2] LR11ES20 Laboratory of Analysis, Conception and Control of Systems, National Engineering School of Tunis, University of Tunis El Manar, Tunis 1002, Tunisia; asmacharaabi@gmail.com

* Correspondence: oscar.barambones@ehu.eus

Abstract: Proton exchange membrane (PEM) fuel cell has recently attracted broad attention from many researchers due to its cleanliness, high efficiency and soundless operation. The obtention of high-performance output characteristics is required to overcome the market restrictions of the PEMFC technologies. Therefore, the main aim of this work is to maintain the system operating point at an adequate and efficient power stage with high-performance tracking. To this end, a model predictive control (MPC) based on a global minimum cost function for a two-step horizon was designed and implemented in a boost converter integrated with a fuel cell system. An experimental comparative study has been investigated between the MPC and a PI controller to reveal the merits of the proposed technique. Comparative results have indicated that a reduction of 15.65% and 86.9%, respectively, in the overshoot and response time could be achieved using the suggested control structure.

Keywords: proton exchange membrane; proton electrolyte membrane; PEM; fuel cell; PEMFC; power electronic converter; DC–DC boost converter; model predictive control; MPC

Citation: Derbeli, M.; Charaabi, A.; Barambones, O.; Napole, C. High-Performance Tracking for Proton Exchange Membrane Fuel Cell System PEMFC Using Model Predictive Control. *Mathematics* **2021**, *9*, 1158. https://doi.org/10.3390/math9111158

Academic Editors: Mikhail Posypkin, Andrey Gorshenin and Vladimir Titarev

Received: 19 April 2021
Accepted: 18 May 2021
Published: 21 May 2021

Publisher's Note: MDPI stays neutral with regard to jurisdictional claims in published maps and institutional affiliations.

1. Introduction

Due to its abundance in the universe, hydrogen has become one of the most important fuels for energy production. Hydrogen represents up to more than 75% of all normal matter mass, and it accounts for over 90% of all atoms on earth [1]; it could be produced by either simple methods, such as the electrolysis of water, or industrial methods using steam reforming. The production cost of hydrogen is expected to fall by 50% by the middle of this century, and that could pave the way for more sustainable sources of energy [2]. The latter has encouraged thousands of scientists and researchers to pursue research in hydrogen cells.

A proton exchange membrane fuel cell (PEMFC), which uses hydrogen as the main fuel, has recently attracted great attention due to its cleanliness, high efficiency, high power density and quiet operation [3]. It can be used for a wide range of applications, including automotive, stationary and portable power supplies [4–7]. For most of those applications, the PEMFC is usually used in conjunction with a DC–DC power converter that generates highly regulated DC voltage for end-use. Therefore, the control design plays the main role in a PEMFC power system, not only for performance improvement reasons but also for safety operation.

During the last few years, many control algorithms have been designed for PEMFC power systems; the pros and cons of the recently reported ones are listed in Table 1. Hence, linear proportional integral (PI), proportional derivative (PD) and proportional integral derivative (PID) have been, respectively, used by various research groups/researchers [8–10], to keep the PEMFC operating at an appropriate power point. Although these controllers are especially sensitive when they face a large load variation, results showed a gradual and smooth rise to the desired operating power point with an acceptable tracking performance. To increase the robustness of the PID and obtain a better dynamic performance, various research groups/researchers [11] have applied a fractional order proportional integral derivative (FOPID) controller to a DC–DC four-switch buck-boost (FSBB) converter used in a PEMFC power system. The obtained results have shown that the proposed method achieved better performance in comparison with the integer-order and Two-Zero/Three-Pole (TZTP) controller. Hence, an overall efficiency of 92%, more than the one obtained with TZTP, can be retained using the FOPID. The performances of the PID have also been improved by various research groups/researchers [12] via the application of the slap swarm algorithm (PID-SSA). Comparative results with other methods, such as incremental resistance algorithm (IRA), mine-blast algorithm (MBA), and grey wolf optimizer (GWM), have indicated better performance of the proposed PID-SSA in terms of efficiency and reliability. However, despite the massive work done on improving the performance of the PID, it is still sensitive to cope with the non-linearity of the power converter, which leads many researchers to focus on the non-linear algorithms.

Various research groups/researchers [13] have proposed fuzzy logic control (FLC) to overcome the drawbacks of the conventional P&O, where the results have indicated a chattering reduction of 78.6% and an improvement of 63% in the settling time. To improve the performance of the FLC, various research groups/researchers [14] have proposed particle swarm optimization (FLC-PSO). Comparative results with the FLC have demonstrated the effectiveness of the FLC-PSO in reducing the overshoot from 65.833% to 63.115% while ensuring high tracking efficiency (99.39%). However, despite the reduction of 2%, an overshoot up to more than 63% is still undesirable. Reddy and Sudhakar [15] optimized the FLC via an adaptive neuro-fuzzy inference system (ANFIS). Simulation and experimental results have indicated that an increase of 1.95% in the average DC link and a reduction of 17.74% in the average time taken to reach the operating power point can be achieved using the proposed ANFIS algorithm.

The artificial neural networks and meta-heuristic algorithms have also been used by various research groups/researchers [16–19]. Hence, in comparison with FLC, efficiency improvements and a faster response of 45% are obtained by various research groups/researchers [16] via the application of the neural network algorithm (NNA). The latter was also proposed by [17] to overcome the drawbacks of the P&O. The obtained results showed that a reduction of 86% and 74%, respectively, in power oscillations and settling time can be achieved. In [18], a genetic algorithm (GA) was used to improve the power quality of the PV generator. Results have demonstrated that in comparison with the conventional P&O and the incremental conductance (IC), the proposed GA can achieve a reduction of 97% in the oscillations of output power. Khanam et al. [19] made a comparative study among ant colony optimization (ACO), particle swarm optimization (PSO), differential evolution (DE) and P&O. Results have demonstrated the effectiveness of the ACO in terms of convergence time over the other proposed methods. Hence, in comparison with P&O, a reduction of 90.61% and 5.13% are, respectively, obtained via the application of ACO and PSO.

The application of the sliding mode control (SMC) for the PEMFC system was proposed by various research groups/researchers [3,20,21]. To counteract the chattering phenomenon of the SMC, integral fast terminal sliding mode control (IFTSMC), backstepping sliding mode control (BSMC), high-order sliding mode based on twisting (TA), super-twisting (STA), prescribed convergence law (PCL) and quasi continue (QC) have been, respectively, proposed by [21–26]. Results have demonstrated that high chattering reductions such as 84% and 91% via the application of the QC and STA can be achieved using the proposed algorithms.

Table 1. Summary of the recently reported approaches used for the PEMFC power system.

Reference	Year	Controller	Converter	Features	Drawbacks
Ref. [8] Ref. [9] Ref. [10]	2017 2014 2020	PI PD PID	Boost converter - Buck-boost converter	- Less energy consumption. - Simplicity of implementation - Frequently used in the industry. - Low computational requirements.	- Sensitive against large load variation. - Inappropriate control parameters leads to the system instability. - Not proper for non-linear systems. - Parameters setting is difficult.
Ref. [11]	2020	FOPID	FSBB	- High robustness in comparison with PID. - Less energy consumption.	- Complex implementation. - Abundant parameters are required to be adjusted.
Ref. [12]	2021	SSA-PID	Boost converter	- Reasonable execution time. - Good convergence acceleration. - Few parameters tuning.	- Suffers from premature convergence. - Unsuccessful to achieve the near-global solution.
Ref. [13]	2017	FLC	Boost converter	- Uses simple mathematics. - Simplicity of rules modifications. - Simplicity of implementation.	- Stability is not guaranteed. - The accuracy is not guaranteed since the outputs are perceived as a guess. - Necessity of human expertise.
Ref. [14]	2019	FLC-PSO	Boost converter	- Easy to implement. - Few parameters to adjust.	- High implementation cost. - complex calculation. - Needs memory to update velocity.
Ref. [15]	2019	ANFIS	Boost converter	- Capability of adaptation. - Expert knowledge is not required. - High convergence speed and tracking accuracy in comparison with FLC.	- Requires large data for training and learning. - Abundant parameters are required to be adjusted. - High computational cost.
Ref. [16] Ref. [17]	2018 2018	NNA	Interleaved boost Boost converter	- Similar to human reasoning. - No exact model is required - Possibility application for feed forward control.	- Needs an expert for a good initialization. - Stability is not guaranteed. - Abundant parameters are required to be adjusted.
Ref. [18]	2018	GA	Boost converter	- Easy to understand. - Effective for noisy environments. - Works well for mixed discrete/continuous problem. - Supports multi-objective optimization.	- Sometimes inappropriate for real-time applications. - Needs an expert for the implementation. - The objective function is hard to design. - Computationally expensive.
Ref. [19]	2019	ACO PSO DE	Boost converter	- High convergence speed. - High tracking accuracy. - High efficiency.	- Complex calculation. - High implementation cost. - Optimization process is lengthy.
Ref. [3] Ref. [20] Ref. [21]	2017 2019 2019	SMC	Boost converter	- High robustness. - Simple structure. - Easy parameter tuning. - Wide operation range.	- Excessive chattering effect. - Considerable energy consumption. - Lack of robustness during the reaching phase.
Ref. [22]	2021	IFTSMC	Boost converter	- Robust to parameter uncertainties and disturbances. - Finite time convergence. - Capable of reducing the chattering. - High convergence speed.	- Requires the knowledge of the system boundary uncertainties. - Problem of intrinsic singularity. - Convergence problem may occur when the states are away from the equilibrium.
Ref. [23]	2018	BSMC	Boost converter	- Stability is guaranteed. - Popular technique for high-order systems. - Uncertainties could be handled.	- Complex design. - Requires an exact mathematical model. - Sensitive to parameter variation. - Requires the measures of all the states.
Ref. [24] Ref. [21] Ref. [25] Ref. [26]	2020 2019 2020 2020	TA STA PCL QC	Boost converter	- Capability of chattering reduction. - Robust to uncertainties and disturbances. - Finite time convergence.	- Complex design. - Complex stability demonstration. - Accuracy is not guaranteed. - Unable to use for first-order systems.
Ref. [27] Ref. [28,29] Ref. [30] Ref. [31] Ref. [32]	2019 2019 2020 2020 2020	MPC	Buck converter 3-phase inverter Two-level inverter Boost converter High-gain converter	- Offers multiple variables control. - Prediction on upcoming disturbance. -Upcoming control actions prediction. - Peak load shifting capability. - Enhanced energy saving. - Enhanced transient response: peak, rise and settling time reduction.	- Plant model is required. - Requires specific background knowledge of the method.

Due to their significant benefits, predictive control methods have attracted the intention of many researches and they have been implemented in a wide range of applications, including power converters, actuator faults, pharmaceuticals industry, chemical processes, and induction motors [27–38]. Hence, in comparison with the conventional P&O algorithm, an improvement of 10.52% in the overall PV system efficiency was achieved by various research groups/researchers [27] via the application of the MPC technique.

In [28], an overall efficiency of 90% for a grid connected system was achieved by applying the MPC for a three-phase inverter, where the efficiency was approximately 98% for the maximum power point tracking (MPPT) control method and 92% for the inverter. A Lyapunov-function-based MPC was proposed by authors of [29], where the results showed that the proposed control strategy maintains the active and reactive powers close to the desired values with an error of less than 3%. Various research groups/researchers [30] have proposed a combination of MPC with an extended Kalman filter (EKF) for a two-level inverter. High performances in terms of robustness and potential noise rejection were obtained. Successful MPP tracking with an efficiency of up to 98% was obtained by various research groups/researchers [31]. In the latter, the MPC is proposed for a boost converter used in a renewable energy system. Various research groups/researchers [32] have compared the MPC with different algorithms, such as IncCond, hill climbing, PSO, and FLC. Except for the design complexity, results have demonstrated that the proposed MPC has succeeded over the other methods in terms of efficiency, steady-state oscillation, tracking speed and accuracy.

In this work, an MPC based on a global minimum cost function for a two-step horizon was designed and implemented in a boost converter integrated with a Heliocentric hy-Expert^{TM} fuel cell FC-50W. The aim is to maintain the system operating point at an adequate and efficient power stage with high-performance tracking. First, the experimental system, including the fuel cell, the dSPACE, the converter and the programmable load, is explained. Then, the proposed method is designed for a two-step horizon, wherein the cost function is adopted based on the stack current. For investigation, the effectiveness of the proposed method is revealed through a comparison study with a PI controller, which is tuned through the Ziegler–Nichols technique. Finally, some conclusions and perspectives are pointed out.

2. Materials and Methods

2.1. Hardware Description

A general overview of the different components used on the experimental test bench is provided in Figure 1, and the main components are described as follows:

- **PEM FC50**: The technical data of the PEM FC50 are described in Table 2. The fuel stack is supplied by hydrogen through a metal hydride storage cylinder 60 SL, which is connected to the manometer that decreases the pressure. The stack contains 10 cells stacked in series and generates a rated power of 40 W.
- **DC–DC boost converter**: The power converter used in the test bench is constructed by the TEP-192-Research Group of Huelva University. Unlike the commercial converters, this boost converter offers a PWM control input where the controller could be designed via the user. It is characterized by an IGBT transistor with an input switching frequency equal to 20 kHz; the maximum input voltage and current are, respectively, equal to 60 V and 30 A with an accuracy of 0.5%; while, the maximum output voltage and current are around 250 V and 30 A.
- **MicroLabBox dSPACE DS1202**: The dSPACE-DS1202 is an effective device for fast control systems due to its high performance when turning the theoretical design into a real-time experiment. The device includes more than 100 various type of input/output channels with a dual core processor and independent co-processor that manages host PC communication. By adding the library of real-time implementation (RTI) in a Simulink–Matlab interface, it allows the use of the basic toolboxes in order to configure all the I/O sensors as well as the PWM signal required for controlling the system. Then, a generated C code will be sent to the MicroLabBox by the RTI when compiling

the Simulink model. Hence, a PWM pulse is produced using the converted code given by the MicroLabBox. The control desk software is used for creating an interface with the graphical user interface (GUI), which allows to visualize and observe the online evolution of the obtained signals with clear figures that make the online evaluation of the different parameter changes easier and faster.

- **Electronic programmable load**: The characteristics of the electronic programmable load used in this work are described in Table 3. The experimental tests were carried out under an abrupt change of the load resistance through an electronic programmable load BK 8500B. The latter is used instead of the classical manual sliding resistive load since the programmable device cloud provides considerable advantages such as generating a list of resistance waveform sequence with speed, accurate values and high resolution in real-time.

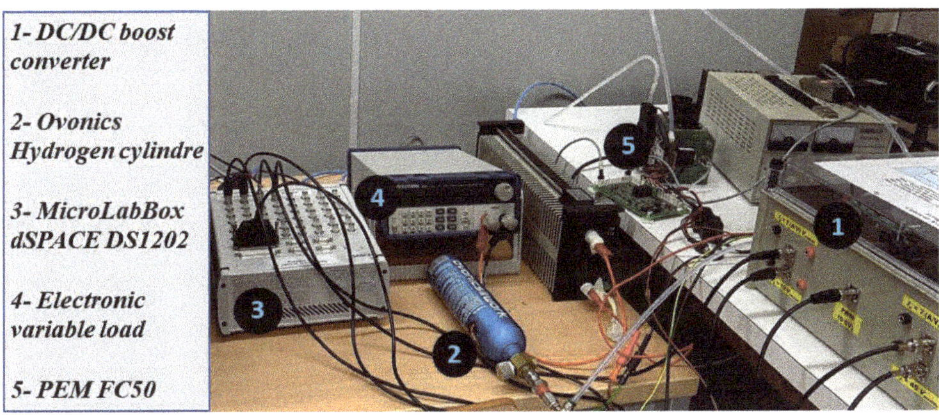

Figure 1. Overview of the experimental test bench.

Table 2. PEMFC technical data.

PEMFC Features		Electrical Features	
Type	Heliocentris FC50	Operating Voltage	2.5–10 V
Cooling	fans	Operating Current	0–10 A
Fuel	H_2	Rated power	40 W
Dimensions	$12 \times 10.3 \times 13.5$ cm	Maximum power	50 W
Weight	1150 g	Open-circuit voltage	9 V
Hydrogen Flowmeter		**Hydrogen 15 bar Kit**	
Precision	0.8% of the the quantified value	Inlet pressure	1–15 bar
Measuring range	10–1000 sml/min	Outlet pressure	0.6 ∓ 0.2 bar
Thermal		**Hydrogen 200 bar kit**	
Operating temperature	15–50 °C	H_2 inlet pressure	200 bar
Max. start temperature	45 °C	H_2 outlet pressure	1–15 bar
Fuel characteristics		**Hydrogen Detector**	
Recommended purity	5.0 (99.999%)	Type of sensor	H_2 4%
Hydrogen input pressure	0.4–8 bar (5.8–11.6 psig)	Measuring principle	3 electrode sensor
Hydrogen consumption	Max. 700 sml/min (at 0 °C, 1013 bar)	Range	0–4%

Table 3. Characteristics the electronic programmable load BK 8500B.

Parameter	Range	Accuracy	Resolution
CR Mode Regulation	0.1–10 Ω	∓ (1% + 0.3% FS)	0.001 Ω
Input current ≥ FS 10%	10–99 Ω	∓ (1% + 0.3% FS)	0.01 Ω
Input Voltage ≥ FS 10%	100–999 Ω	∓ (1% + 0.3% FS)	0.1 Ω
	1 k–4 kΩ	∓ (1% + 0.8% FS)	1 Ω
CV Mode Regulation	0.1–18 V	∓ (0.05% + 0.02% FS)	1 mV
	0.1–120 V	∓ (0.05% + 0.025% FS)	10 mV
CC Mode Regulation	0–3 A	∓ (0.1% + 0.1% FS)	0.1 mA
	0–30 A	∓ (0.2% + 0.15% FS)	1 mA
Current Measurement	0–3 A	∓ (0.1% + 0.1% FS)	0.1 mA
	0–30 A	∓ (0.2% + 0.15% FS)	1 mA
Voltage Measurement	0–18 V	∓ (0.02% + 0.02% FS)	1 mV
	0–120 V	∓ (0.05% + 0.025% FS)	10 mV

2.2. Control Design

The main feature of the model predictive control (MPC) is its capability to predict the future behavior of the desired control variables [39]. In other words, it is an optimization technique that computes the next control action by minimizing the cost function, which is the difference between the predicted variable and the specified reference. The MPC is also characterized by a straight-forward implementation, it has no issue with the stability, and the quality of the response depends on the control design. In MPC, the future predicted state path is called the prediction horizon. The latter is the number of samples T_s over which a prediction of the plant states/outputs is evaluated. According to Figure 2, the future values of output variables at the samples $k + 1, k + 2$, etc., are predicted using the dynamic model of the process $(X(k))$ and current measurements. Furthermore, according to this figure, it is noticed that the control actions are based on both future predictions and current measurements. The manipulated control variables $u(k)$ at the k-th sampling time are computed such that the objective function J is minimized. These control variables will be implemented as a control signal to the process.

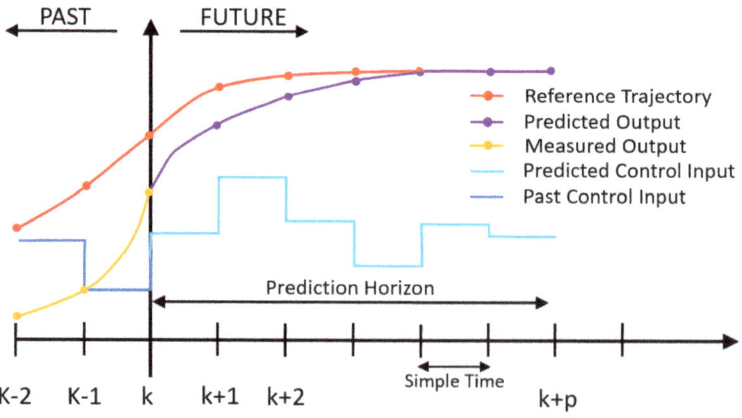

Figure 2. Basic concept for model predictive control (MPC).

Figure 3 illustrates the scheme of the proposed MPC approach for power electronic converters, where $i_L(k)$, $V_{stack}(k)$ and $V_{out}(k)$ are the measured variables used in the model to compute the predictions $i_L(k+1)$ of the controlled variables. The model used for the prediction is a discrete time state-space model, which can provide predictive capability for the MPC controller [40]. The design of the MPC control for a high step-up power electronic converter (boost converter) can be done using the following steps [39]:

- Modeling the power converter and determining its state-space model.
- Obtaining the discrete time state-space model that allows the prediction of the future behavior.
- Defining the cost function *J* that represents the desired behavior of the system.
- Determining the MPC control law that minimizes the cost function *J*.

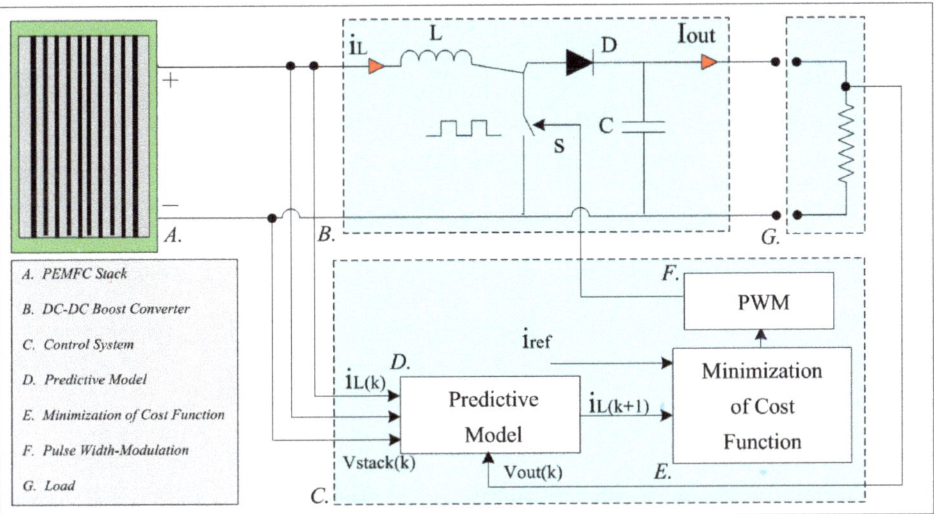

Figure 3. MPC scheme for power electronic converters.

According to [3], the equations of the boost converter for the open and close switch case are, respectively, given in Equations (1)–(5), where the state-space model is presented in Equation (5).

$$\frac{dI_L}{dt}(t) = \frac{1}{L}(V_{stack}(t) - V_{out}(t)) \tag{1}$$

$$\frac{dV_{out}}{dt}(t) = \frac{1}{C}(I_L(t) - V_{out}(t)) \tag{2}$$

$$\frac{dI_L}{dt}(t) = \frac{1}{L}(V_{stack}(t)) \tag{3}$$

$$\frac{dV_{out}(t)}{dt} = \frac{1}{RC}(-V_{out}(t)) \tag{4}$$

$$\begin{bmatrix} \frac{dI_L(t)}{dt} \\ \frac{dV_{out}(t)}{dt} \end{bmatrix} = \begin{bmatrix} 0 & \frac{-(1-D(t))}{L} \\ \frac{(1-D(t))}{C} & -\frac{1}{RC} \end{bmatrix} \cdot \begin{bmatrix} I_L(t) \\ V_{out}(t) \end{bmatrix} + \begin{bmatrix} \frac{1}{L} \\ 0 \end{bmatrix} V_{stack}(t) \tag{5}$$

According to [27,30,31], and by using the sampling time T_s, the discretized equations of the boost converter can be given as (6) and (7) for the open switch case, and (8) and (9) for the close switch case.

Open switch:

$$I_L(k+1) = I_L(k) - \frac{T_s}{L}V_{out}(k) + \frac{T_s}{L}V_{stack}(k) \tag{6}$$

$$V_{out}(k+1) = V_{out}(k) - \frac{T_s}{RC} V_{out}(k) + \frac{T_s}{C} I_L(k) \tag{7}$$

Close switch:

$$I_L(k+1) = I_L(k) + \frac{T_s}{L} V_{stack}(k) \tag{8}$$

$$V_{out}(k+1) = V_{out}(k) - \frac{T_s}{RC} V_{out}(k) \tag{9}$$

Using the descritized equations given in Equations (6)–(9), or by using the the forward Euler approximation [41] given in Equation (10), the discrete-time state-space model of the boost converter can be written as Equation (11):

$$x(k+1) = (I + T_s A)x(k) + T_s B d(k) \tag{10}$$

$$\begin{bmatrix} I_L(k+1) \\ V_{out}(k+1) \end{bmatrix} = \begin{bmatrix} 1 & -(1-D(k))\frac{T_s}{L} \\ (1-D(k))\frac{T_s}{C} & 1-\frac{T_s}{RC} \end{bmatrix} \begin{bmatrix} I_L(k) \\ V_{out}(k) \end{bmatrix} + \begin{bmatrix} \frac{T_s}{L} \\ 0 \end{bmatrix} V_{stack}(k) \tag{11}$$

The control objective is to make the stack current $I_L(k)$ as close as possible to the reference current $I_{ref}(k)$. This could be obtained by minimizing the cost function J, which is defined as the error between the predicted value and the desired reference value. The expression of the cost function can be written as Equation (12). Hence, if the used prediction horizon is equal to one $h = 1$, then once the values of the controlled variables are obtained at the next sample time and for both switching states, $s = 0$ and $s = 1$, the cost function J will be evaluated. The block scheme of the proposed MPC technique is shown in Figure 4.

$$J_{s=n}^{n=0,1} = |I_{L,s=n(k+1)} - I_{ref}| \tag{12}$$

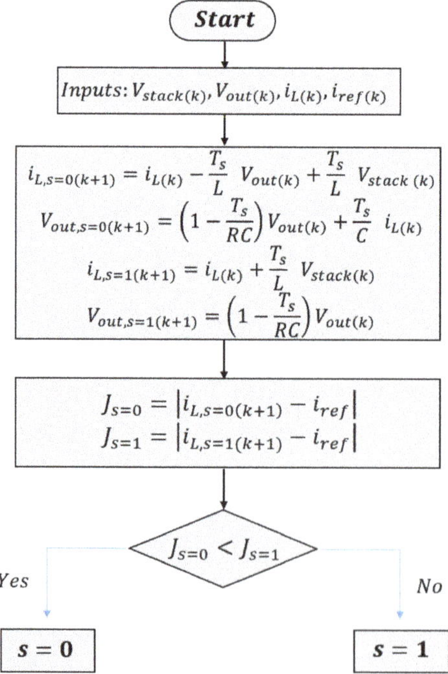

Figure 4. Block scheme of the proposed MPC technique.

By evaluating the cost function *J* for both states, it selects the one at which the next predicted value is closer to the value of the desired reference current i_{ref}. It should be noted that the MPC approach has the capability of predicting the next n-samples of the prediction horizon, which means that the cost function at the future n-step can be calculated. The discrete-time system that provides the n-samples of the future prediction horizon can be written as Equations (13) and (14).

$$I_L(k+n+1) = I_L(k+n) - (1 - D(k+n))\frac{T_s}{L}V_{out}(k+n) + \frac{T_s}{L}V_{stack}(k+n) \tag{13}$$

$$V_{out}(k+n+1) = (1 - D(k+n))\frac{T_s}{C}I_L(k+n) + (1 - \frac{T_s}{RC})V_{out}(k+n) \tag{14}$$

In this work, an MPC with a prediction horizon equal to two $h = 2$ is used. To this end, the calculation of the controlled variable I_L at time t_{k+2} is necessary. However, this could be an easy task by using Equations (13) and (14). The process of the proposed MPC technique with a prediction horizon $h = 2$ is depicted in Figure 5. According to this figure, to calculate the value of the predicted controlled variable $I_{L(k+2)}$, the calculation of the system variables at time t_{k+1} is required.

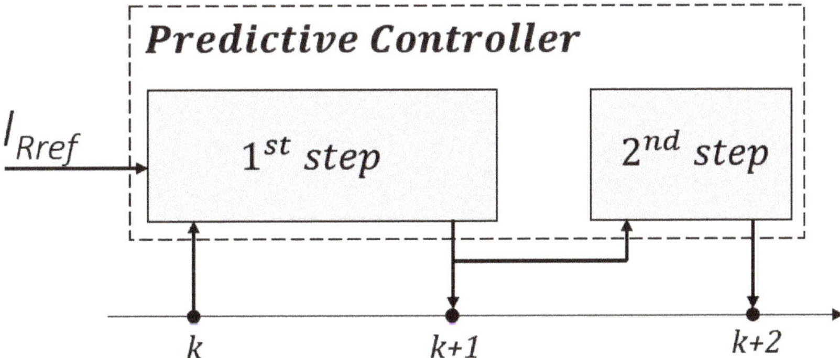

Figure 5. Schematic diagram of the proposed MPC process with a 2-step prediction horizon.

Figure 6 illustrates the operating principle of the proposed MPC technique. Hence, by observing the system behavior for the future two-step horizon and by evaluating the cost function at each step, it will be possible to select the best switching state at which the cost function has the lowest value. All the possible sets of switching states that could be evaluated for $h = 2$ are given in Equation (15).

$$\begin{cases} S_{(k+1)} = 0 \quad and \quad S_{(k+2)} = 0 \\ S_{(k+1)} = 0 \quad and \quad S_{(k+2)} = 1 \\ S_{(k+1)} = 1 \quad and \quad S_{(k+2)} = 0 \\ S_{(k+1)} = 1 \quad and \quad S_{(k+2)} = 1 \end{cases} \tag{15}$$

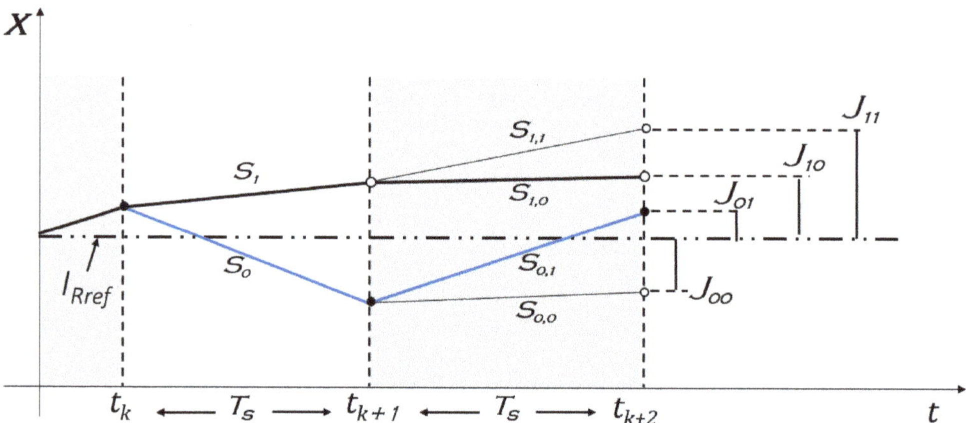

Figure 6. Schematic diagram of the proposed MPC operating principle.

It should be noted that there are two strategies that could be used to calculate the predicted state $X(k+2)$:

- The first one is to evaluate the cost function at each step (sampling time). For instance, by taking the example presented in Figure 6 where the performed switching actions are indicated with the bold black line; at first, when the sampling time is t_k, the controller has to choose between S_1 and S_0, where the choice is based on the most preferred switching condition that leads to minimizing the cost function J. Since S_1 is selected in this example, it means that the predicted controlled variable $I_{L,s=1(k+1)}$ that corresponds to S_1 is the closest to the desired reference I_{ref}. Following the same criterion for the two-step horizon at which the sampling time is t_{k+1}, the controller will decide between S_{11} and S_{10}. Since S_{10} is selected, then, the cost function J_{10} is performed and considered as the cost function of the previous step at the sampling time t_{k+1}. However, despite the simplicity of this strategy, it may fall in a local lower cost function since the cost functions J_{01} and J_{11} that, respectively, correspond to the switching states S_{01} and S_{11}, were not evaluated.
- The second strategy is to evaluate the cost functions of all the sets of switching states given in Equation (15), and finally, the lowest cost function is performed. The performed switching actions using this method are indicated with the bold blue line. The main feature of this method is its capability to calculate the global lower cost function for the two-step horizon. Therefore, a new cost function for the two-step prediction horizon is defined in Equation (16). The latter is composed of the error at the sampling time t_{k+1} plus the error at the sampling time t_{k+2}.

$$J_{s=m}^{n=0,1 \& m=0,1} = \left| I_{L,s=m(k+2)} - I_{ref} \right| + J_{s=n} \tag{16}$$

The evaluation of the four cost functions J_{00}, J_{01}, J_{10} and J_{11}, for the two-step horizon is presented in Figure 7. The combination with the lower cost function value for the two-step prediction horizon is represented by the black color, where faded colors were used for the combinations with higher cost function values. According to these combinations, if the first method of prediction is used, the preferred cost function belongs to Combination 3 since $S_1 < S_0$ and $S_{10} < S_{11}$. If we only consider the evaluation of the cost function for the one-step (Equation (12)), the preferred cost function belongs to Combination 3 or 4 since $S_1 < S_0$. If we only consider the evaluation of the cost function for the two-step ($J_{s=m}^{m=0,1}$), the preferred cost function belongs to Combination 2 since S_{01} is lower than S_{00}, S_{10} and S_{11}. However, although this evaluation gives the same result as the proposed method for the example presented in Figure 7, it may not be the most appropriate for other examples.

Therefore, a combined cost function involving the two steps, as defined in Equation (16), can provide the best switching condition for tracking the desired reference.

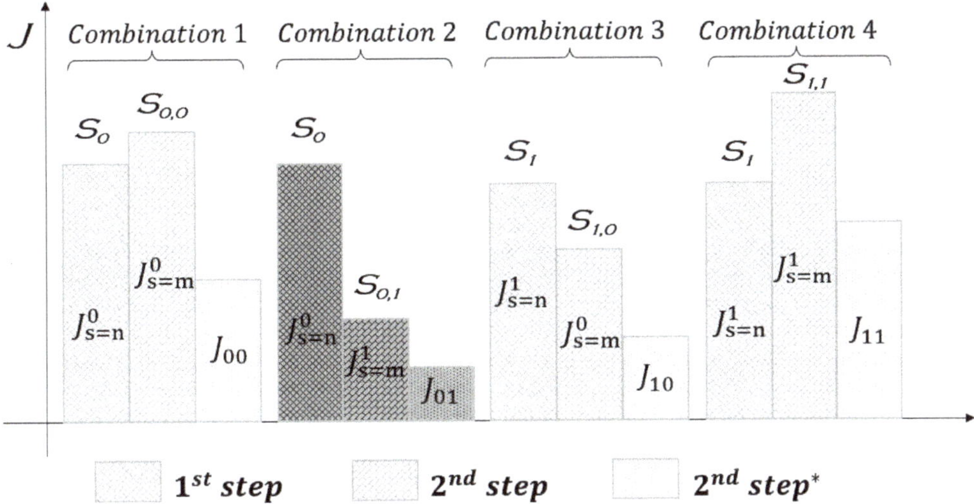

Figure 7. Schematic diagram of the switching condition combinations for the 2-step horizon and the evaluation of the respective cost functions.

2.3. Performance Metrics Used

To achieve the best performance, the gains of the controller were obtained through the minimization of the integral of the absolute error (*IAE*), which is given in Equation (17). This helps to adjust the controller parameters through a decrement in the tracking error in real-time.

$$IAE = \sum_{i=1}^{N} |e_i| \Delta t \tag{17}$$

where e_i is the tracking error and N is an observation data length time for the calculation.

Since the main objective of this research is the tracking performance enhancement, not only was the *IAE* calculated but other types of metrics were also used to gather accurate results. These were the root-mean-square-error (*RMSE*) and the relative root-mean-square (*RRMSE*), which are reflected in Equations (18) and (19), respectively, where r_i is the reference along the *i*-th *sample*.

$$RMSE = \sqrt{\frac{1}{N} \sum_{i=1}^{N} (e_i)^2} \tag{18}$$

$$RRMSE = \sqrt{\sum_{i=1}^{N} (e_i)^2 / \sum_{i=1}^{N} (r_i)} \times 100\% \tag{19}$$

3. Results

Figure 8 tackles the response behavior of the stack current signal under the application of the proposed MPC method and the classical PI control. To test the performance of the controllers and their capability of counteracting the disturbance, load resistance variation is applied at two times instances $t_1 = 25$ s and $t_2 = 45$ s. These times correspond, respectively, to resistance rising from 20 to 50 Ω and decreasing from 50 to 20 Ω. The coefficient parameters of the PI controller were tuned through the minimization of *IAE*, and they are equal to 0.02 and 10 for the proportional and integral terms, respectively.

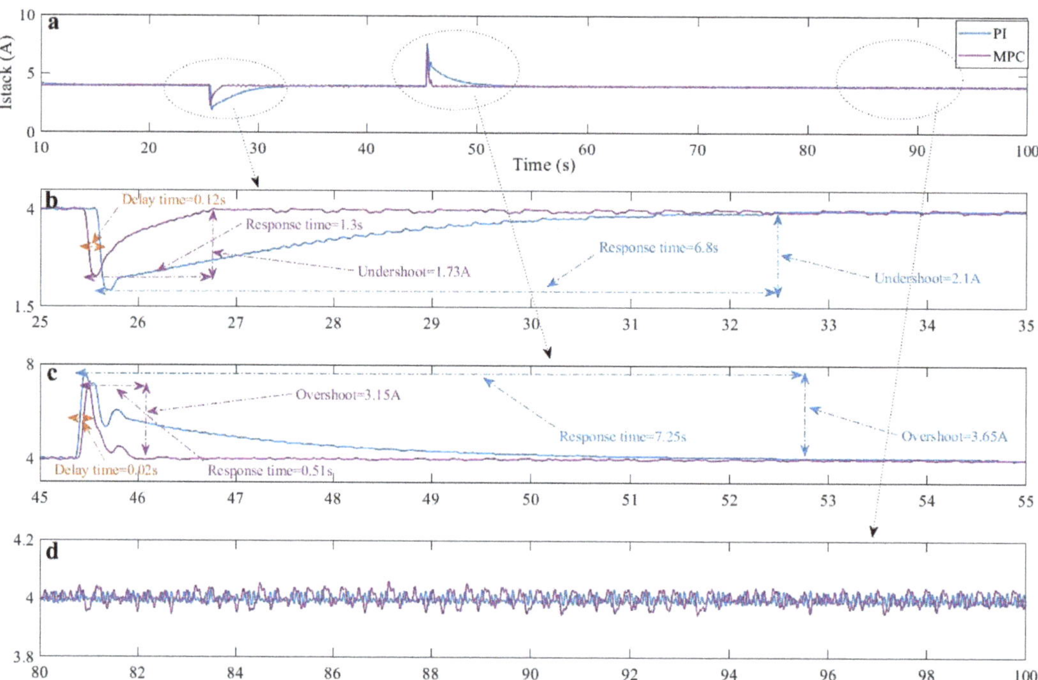

Figure 8. (**a**) Stack current signal; (**b**) stack current behavior when increasing the load resistance; (**c**) stack current behavior when decreasing the load resistance; (**d**) steady state.

It is clear from the first load variation, depicted in Figure 8b, that the MPC approach converges rapidly to the reference current with a response time equal to 1.3 s against an important response value for the classical PI controller, which is around 6.8 s. It should be noted that 0.12 s of the response time was caused by the delay time, which occurred at the moment in which the load variation was applied. Hence, the proposed MPC controller achieved a significant improvement in the convergence speed of almost 81%. On the other hand, the MPC presents a reduced undershoot equal to 1.73 A compared with the conventional PI method, which is around 2.1 A. Consequently, the proposed algorithm can effectively reduce the undershoot with an enhancement of 17.61% compared with the PI controller.

The impact of reducing the load resistance on the response of the stack current is illustrated through Figure 8c. It is obviously clear from this figure that the PI controller takes a significant time to reach the current reference with a response time equal to 7.25 s, while only 0.51 s is obtained via the proposed MPC, which effectively outperforms the convergence speed of the PI with 92.9%. According to this figure, it is noticed that the current signal controlled via the proposed MPC made a delay time of 0.02 s. However, this time is almost negligible, and it has no negative effect on the response time. Regarding the overshoots, a significant one of almost 3.65 A is shown on the response behavior of the conventional PI, while an improvement of around 13.69% on the overshoot is obtained using the proposed MPC method.

Figure 9a–c illustrates, respectively, the real-time response of the PEMFC voltage, power and duty cycle delivered by the classical PI and the proposed MPC approach. The slight variation between the experimental test of the PI and MPC that appeared in a,b and c occurred due to the effect of the operating temperature on the membrane since it is difficult to carry out two experiments at exactly the same temperature. It should be noted that this variation did not appear in the graphs of the stack current (Figure 8) since it is a controlled signal where both of the algorithms drive the stack current to operate at the same reference current I_{ref}.

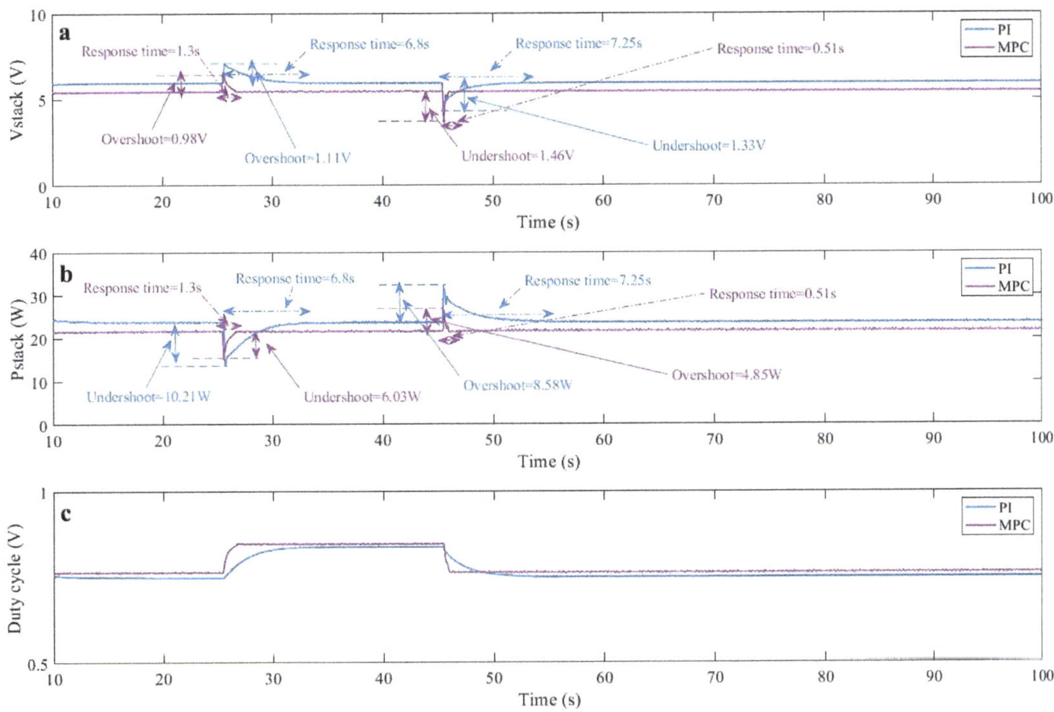

Figure 9. (**a**) PEMFC stack voltage signal; (**b**) PEMFC stack power; (**c**) duty cycle signal.

According to Figure 9a, the effectiveness of the proposed MPC algorithm over the conventional PI appears to reduce the overshoots and undershoots of the stack voltage. Thus, the PI controller presents a voltage value around 1.11 V and 1.33 V for the first and the second load variation, respectively. On the other hand, the proposed MPC shows values of 0.98 V and 1.46 V for the same load variations.

From Figure 9b, it can be seen that the proposed MPC method effectively tracks the desired output power of the PEMFC with an almost negligible ripple around the steady state. Moreover, in comparison with the conventional PI controller, the results show that a reduction of 4.18 W and 3.73 W in the undershoot and overshoot are obtained for the first and the second load variation, respectively.

The real-time responses of the output current, voltage and power for the DC–DC boost converter are depicted in Figure 10a–c. The latter clearly shows the impact of the variable load resistance on the response behavior of the output current and the output voltage for the two controllers. Furthermore, the slow converging and high overshoots of the PI controller in comparison with the proposed MPC are clearly presented in this figure.

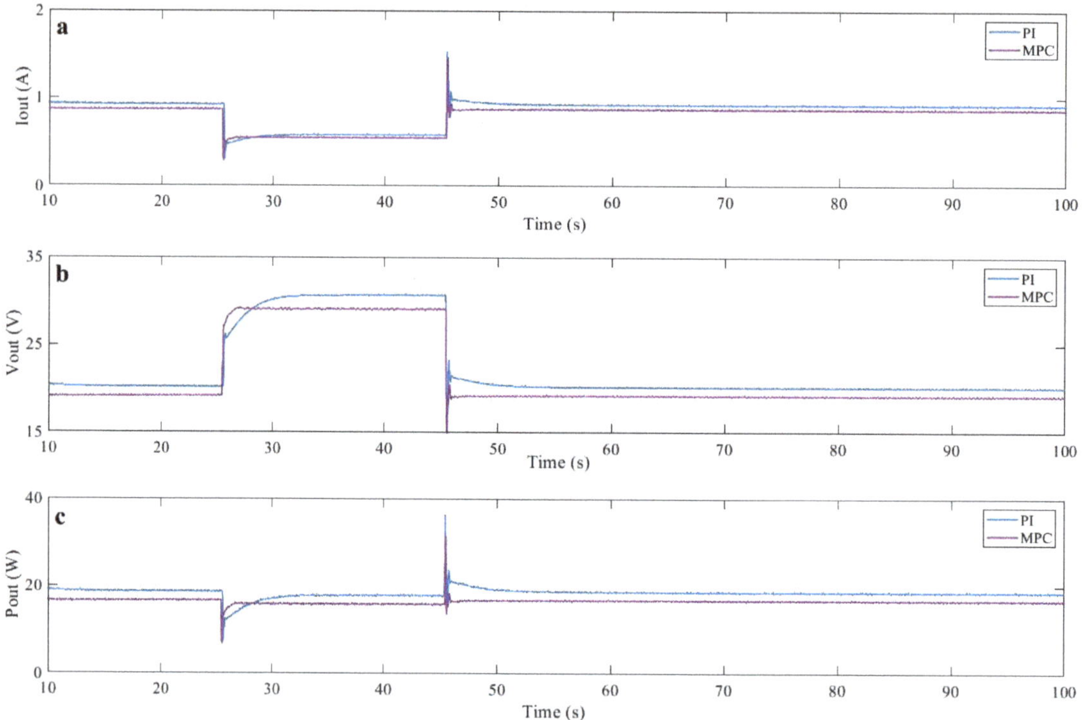

Figure 10. (**a**) DC–DC output current signal; (**b**) DC–DC output voltage signal; (**c**) DC–DC output power signal.

Finally, it is clearly demonstrated in the above results that the proposed MPC has succeeded in overcoming the drawbacks of the conventional PI controller. Hence, a robust and fast response, as well as better dynamic behavior when facing large load variation, are obtained via the application of the proposed MPC method.

Performance Metrics Comparison

To obtain high control performance, the error signal should be reduced so as to improve the tracking accuracy. Consequently, the *IAE* was minimized by tuning the corresponding gains, and therefore, the metrics in terms of error were determined during a period of two load variations. Table 4 enlists the obtained values of the IAE, *RMSE* and *RRMSE* for both controllers.

According to this table, the *IAE* revealed an expected improvement for the proposed MPC where the conventional PI showed a value of 4.48 times higher than the proposed controller. Regarding the *RMSE*, the reflection is similar for the same period. The MPC yields an *RMSE* of 0.2068, whereas the PI downgraded the performance to 0.5085, which implies a difference of 2.46 times. Finally, the *RRMSE* endures the previous trend where the proposed MPC overcame the comparisons. Hence, the PI showed a value of 12.7%, whereas the MPC diminished up to 5.17%, resembled by a 2.45-times difference.

Table 4. Comparison of the different metrics.

IAE		*RMSE*		*RRMSE* (%)	
MPC	PI	MPC	PI	MPC	PI
2.0607	9.2310	0.2068	0.5085	5.1705	12.7115

4. Conclusions

The purpose of this paper was to improve the performance of the PEM fuel cell system via the application of a predictive module controller (MPC). The proposed controller scheme was designed based on a global minimum cost function for a two-step horizon in order to enhance the efficiency and the convergence tracking speed of the power delivered by the PEM fuel cell system.

A real-time implementation of the MPC method compared with a PI controller was realized to reveal the advantages of this proposed approach, where the robustness was tested via the application of large load variation through an advanced electronic variable resistance device.

Experimental results have clearly demonstrated the effectiveness of the proposed MPC method over the conventional PI controller. The latter showed an undershoot of 2.1 A, an overshoot of 3.65 A, and a response time of 6.8 and 7.25 s, respectively, for the first and second load variation. On the other hand, results of the proposed MPC showed an undershoot of 1.73 A, an overshoot of 3.15 A, and a response time of 1.3 and 0.51 s, respectively, for the same first and second load variation applied to the PI controller. Hence, the controlled stack current signal has achieved significant improvement in the convergence speed with an average value of 86.9% and a reduced overshoot around 15.65%. Therefore, high tracking accuracy with a fast and robust response as well as global stability of the closed-loop system are obtained via the application of the proposed MPC method.

Finally, the experimental results obtained in this work are quite encouraging, and they pave the way for further advanced research in the performance improvement of PEM fuel cell systems.

Author Contributions: Conceptualization, M.D.; methodology, M.D.; software, M.D.; validation, M.D. and O.B.; formal analysis, M.D. and A.C.; investigation, M.D., A.C. and C.N.; resources, O.B.; data curation, M.D.; writing—original draft preparation, M.D. and A.C.; writing—review and editing, M.D., A.C., O.B. and C.N.; visualization, M.D.; supervision, O.B.; project administration, O.B.; funding acquisition, O.B. All authors have read and agreed to the published version of the manuscript.

Funding: The authors wish to express their gratitude to the Basque Government, through the project EKOHEGAZ (ELKARTEK KK-2021/00092), to the Diputación Foral de Álava (DFA), through the project CONAVANTER, and to the UPV/EHU, through the project GIU20/063, for supporting this work.

Institutional Review Board Statement: Not applicable.

Informed Consent Statement: Not applicable.

Acknowledgments: The authors want to acknowledge the UPV/EHU for supporting this work.

Conflicts of Interest: The authors declare no conflict of interest.

Abbreviations

The following abbreviations are used in this manuscript:

PEM	polymer electrolyte membrane
PEMFC	polymer electrolyte membrane fuel cell
MPC	model predictive control
PI	proportional-integral
PD	proportional derivative
PID	proportional integral derivative
FOPID	fractional order PID
FSBB	four-switch buck-boost
TZTP	two-zero/three-pole
PID-SSA	PID based slap swarm algorithm
IRA	incremental resistance algorithm
MBA	mine-blast algorithm
GWM	grey wolf optimizer

P&O	perturb and observe
FLC	fuzzy logic control
FLC-PSO	FLC based on particle swarm optimization
ANFIS	adaptive neuro-fuzzy inference system
NNA	neural network algorithm
GA	genetic algorithm
IC	incremental conductance
PSO	particle swarm optimization
ACO	ant colony optimization
DE	differential evolution
SMC	sliding mode control
IFTSMC	integral fast terminal sliding mode control
BSMC	back-stepping sliding mode control
TA	twisting algorithm
STA	super-twisting algorithm
PCL	prescribed convergence law
QC	quasi-continuous algorithm
MPPT	maximum power point tracking
EKF	extended Kalman filter
PWM	pulse width modulation
IAE	integral of the absolute error
RMSE	root mean square error
RRMSE	relative root mean square error

References

1. Magoon, C.R., Jr. *Creation and the Big Bang: How God Created Matter from Nothing*; WestBow Press: Edinburgh, UK, 2018.
2. Choudhury, D.; Kraft, D.W. Big Bang Nucleosynthesis and the Missing Hydrogen Mass in the Universe. *AIP Conf. Proc.* **2004**, *698*, 345–348.
3. Derbeli, M.; Farhat, M.; Barambones, O.; Sbita, L. Control of PEM fuel cell power system using sliding mode and super-twisting algorithms. *Int. J. Hydrogen Energy* **2017**, *42*, 8833–8844. [CrossRef]
4. Thounthong, P.; Mungporn, P.; Pierfederici, S.; Guilbert, D.; Bizon, N. Adaptive Control of Fuel Cell Converter Based on a New Hamiltonian Energy Function for Stabilizing the DC Bus in DC Microgrid Applications. *Mathematics* **2020**, *8*, 2035. [CrossRef]
5. Bizon, N.; Thounthong, P. A Simple and Safe Strategy for Improving the Fuel Economy of a Fuel Cell Vehicle. *Mathematics* **2021**, *9*, 604. [CrossRef]
6. Bizon, N.; Thounthong, P. Energy efficiency and fuel economy of a fuel cell/renewable energy sources hybrid power system with the load-following control of the fueling regulators. *Mathematics* **2020**, *8*, 151. [CrossRef]
7. Bahrami, M.; Martin, J.P.; Maranzana, G.; Pierfederici, S.; Weber, M.; Meibody-Tabar, F.; Zandi, M. Multi-stack lifetime improvement through adapted power electronic architecture in a fuel cell hybrid system. *Mathematics* **2020**, *8*, 739. [CrossRef]
8. Derbeli, M.; Farhat, M.; Barambones, O.; Sbita, L. Control of proton exchange membrane fuel cell (pemfc) power system using pi controller. In Proceedings of the IEEE 2017 International Conference on Green Energy Conversion Systems (GECS), Hammamet, Tunisia, 23–25 March 2017; pp. 1–5.
9. Rubio, J.D.J.; Bravo, A.G. Optimal control of a PEM fuel cell for the inputs minimization. *Math. Probl. Eng.* **2014**, *2014*. [CrossRef]
10. Belhaj, F.Z.; El Fadil, H.; Idrissi, Z.E.; Koundi, M.; Gaouzi, K. Modeling, Analysis and Experimental Validation of the Fuel Cell Association with DC-DC Power Converters with Robust and Anti-Windup PID Controller Design. *Electronics* **2020**, *9*, 1889. [CrossRef]
11. Qi, Z.; Tang, J.; Pei, J.; Shan, L. Fractional controller design of a DC-DC converter for PEMFC. *IEEE Access* **2020**, *8*, 120134–120144. [CrossRef]
12. Fathy, A.; Abdelkareem, M.A.; Olabi, A.; Rezk, H. A novel strategy based on salp swarm algorithm for extracting the maximum power of proton exchange membrane fuel cell. *Int. J. Hydrogen Energy* **2021**, *46*, 6087–6099. [CrossRef]
13. Derbeli, M.; Sbita, L.; Farhat, M.; Barambones, O. Proton exchange membrane fuel cell—A smart drive algorithm. In Proceedings of the IEEE 2017 International Conference on Green Energy Conversion Systems (GECS), Hammamet, Tunisia, 23–25 March 2017; pp. 1–5.
14. Luta, D.N.; Raji, A.K. Fuzzy rule-based and particle swarm optimisation MPPT techniques for a fuel cell stack. *Energies* **2019**, *12*, 936. [CrossRef]
15. Reddy, K.J.; Sudhakar, N. ANFIS-MPPT control algorithm for a PEMFC system used in electric vehicle applications. *Int. J. Hydrogen Energy* **2019**, *44*, 15355–15369. [CrossRef]
16. Reddy, K.J.; Sudhakar, N. High voltage gain interleaved boost converter with neural network based MPPT controller for fuel cell based electric vehicle applications. *IEEE Access* **2018**, *6*, 3899–3908. [CrossRef]
17. Chorfi, J.; Zazi, M.; Mansori, M. A new intelligent MPPT based on ANN algorithm for photovoltaic system. In Proceedings of the IEEE 2018 6th International Renewable and Sustainable Energy Conference (IRSEC), Rabat, Morocco, 5–8 December 2018; pp. 1–6.

18. Hadji, S.; Gaubert, J.P.; Krim, F. Real-time genetic algorithms-based MPPT: study and comparison (theoretical an experimental) with conventional methods. *Energies* **2018**, *11*, 459. [CrossRef]

19. Khanam, N.; Khan, B.H.; Imtiaz, T. Maximum Power Extraction of Solar PV System using Meta-Heuristic MPPT techniques: A Comparative Study. In Proceedings of the IEEE 2019 International Conference on Electrical, Electronics and Computer Engineering (UPCON), Aligarh, India, 8–10 November 2019; pp. 1–6.

20. Derbeli, M.; Barambones, O.; Farhat, M.; Sbita, L. Efficiency Boosting for Proton Exchange Membrane Fuel Cell Power System Using New MPPT Method. In Proceedings of the IEEE 2019 10th International Renewable Energy Congress (IREC), Sousse, Tunisia, 26–28 March 2019; pp. 1–4.

21. Derbeli, M.; Barambones, O.; Ramos-Hernanz, J.A.; Sbita, L. Real-time implementation of a super twisting algorithm for PEM fuel cell power system. *Energies* **2019**, *12*, 1594. [CrossRef]

22. Silaa, M.Y.; Derbeli, M.; Barambones, O.; Napole, C.; Cheknane, A.; Gonzalez De Durana, J.M. An Efficient and Robust Current Control for Polymer Electrolyte Membrane Fuel Cell Power System. *Sustainability* **2021**, *13*, 2360. [CrossRef]

23. Derbeli, M.; Barambones, O.; Sbita, L. A robust maximum power point tracking control method for a PEM fuel cell power system. *Appl. Sci.* **2018**, *8*, 2449. [CrossRef]

24. Derbeli, M.; Barambones, O.; Farhat, M.; Ramos-Hernanz, J.A.; Sbita, L. Robust high order sliding mode control for performance improvement of PEM fuel cell power systems. *Int. J. Hydrogen Energy* **2020**, *45*, 29222–29234. [CrossRef]

25. Derbeli, M.; Barambones, O.; Silaa, M.Y.; Napole, C. Real-Time Implementation of a New MPPT Control Method for a DC-DC Boost Converter Used in a PEM Fuel Cell Power System. *Actuators* **2020**, *9*, 105. [CrossRef]

26. Silaa, M.Y.; Derbeli, M.; Barambones, O.; Cheknane, A. Design and Implementation of High Order Sliding Mode Control for PEMFC Power System. *Energies* **2020**, *13*, 4317. [CrossRef]

27. Lashab, A.; Sera, D.; Guerrero, J.M. A dual-discrete model predictive control-based MPPT for PV systems. *IEEE Trans. Power Electr.* **2019**, *34*, 9686–9697. [CrossRef]

28. Güler, N.; Irmak, E. MPPT Based Model Predictive Control of Grid Connected Inverter for PV Systems. In Proceedings of the 2019 8th International Conference on Renewable Energy Research and Applications (ICRERA), Brasov, Romania, 3–6 November 2019; pp. 982–986.

29. Golzari, S.; Rashidi, F.; Farahani, H.F. A Lyapunov function based model predictive control for three phase grid connected photovoltaic converters. *Solar Energy* **2019**, *181*, 222–233. [CrossRef]

30. Ahmed, M.; Abdelrahem, M.; Kennel, R. Highly Efficient and Robust Grid Connected Photovoltaic System Based Model Predictive Control with Kalman Filtering Capability. *Sustainability* **2020**, *12*, 4542. [CrossRef]

31. Irmak, E.; Güler, N. A model predictive control-based hybrid MPPT method for boost converters. *Int. J. Electr.* **2020**, *107*, 1–16. [CrossRef]

32. Abdel-Rahim, O.; Wang, H. A new high gain DC-DC converter with model-predictive-control based MPPT technique for photovoltaic systems. *CPSS Trans. Power Electr. Appl.* **2020**, *5*, 191–200. [CrossRef]

33. Xue, D.; El-Farra, N.H. Forecast-triggered model predictive control of constrained nonlinear processes with control actuator faults. *Mathematics* **2018**, *6*, 104. [CrossRef]

34. Wong, W.C.; Chee, E.; Li, J.; Wang, X. Recurrent neural network-based model predictive control for continuous pharmaceutical manufacturing. *Mathematics* **2018**, *6*, 242. [CrossRef]

35. Zhang, Z.; Wu, Z.; Rincon, D.; Christofides, P.D. Real-time optimization and control of nonlinear processes using machine learning. *Mathematics* **2019**, *7*, 890. [CrossRef]

36. Durand, H. Responsive economic model predictive control for next-generation manufacturing. *Mathematics* **2020**, *8*, 259. [CrossRef]

37. Banholzer, S.; Fabrini, G.; Grüne, L.; Volkwein, S. Multiobjective model predictive control of a parabolic advection-diffusion-reaction equation. *Mathematics* **2020**, *8*, 777. [CrossRef]

38. Aziz, A.G.M.A.; Rez, H.; Diab, A.A.Z. Robust Sensorless Model-Predictive Torque Flux Control for High-Performance Induction Motor Drives. *Mathematics* **2021**, *9*, 403. [CrossRef]

39. Rodriguez, J.; Kazmierkowski, M.P.; Espinoza, J.R.; Zanchetta, P.; Abu-Rub, H.; Young, H.A.; Rojas, C.A. State of the Art of Finite Control Set Model Predictive Control in Power Electronics. *IEEE Trans. Ind. Inform.* **2013**, *9*, 1003–1016. [CrossRef]

40. Rodriguez, J.; Cortes, P. *Predictive Control of Power Converters and Electrical Drives*; John Wiley & Sons: Hoboken, NJ, USA, 2012; Volume 40.

41. Bououden, S.; Hazil, O.; Filali, S.; Chadli, M. Modelling and model predictive control of a DC-DC Boost converter. In Proceedings of the IEEE 2014 15th International Conference on Sciences and Techniques of Automatic Control and Computer Engineering (STA), Hammamet, Tunisia, 21–23 December 2014; pp. 643–648.

MDPI

St. Alban-Anlage 66

4052 Basel

Switzerland

Tel. +41 61 683 77 34

Fax +41 61 302 89 18

www.mdpi.com

Mathematics Editorial Office

E-mail: mathematics@mdpi.com

www.mdpi.com/journal/mathematics